THE LAW OF
PARTNERSHIPS AND
CORPORATIONS

Second Edition

Other books in the *Essentials of Canadian Law* Series

ESSENTIALS OF CANADIAN LAW

THE LAW OF PARTNERSHIPS AND CORPORATIONS

Second Edition

J. ANTHONY VanDUZER

Faculty of Law

The University of Ottawa

THE LAW OF PARTNERSHIPS AND CORPORATIONS, Second Edition
© Irwin Law, 2003

Published in 2003 by

Irwin Law Inc.
Suite 501
347 Bay Street
Toronto, Ontario
M5H 2R7
www.irwinlaw.com

ISBN: 1-55221-058-8

National Library of Canada Cataloguing in Publication Data

VanDuzer, J. Anthony (John Anthony), 1958-
    The law of partnerships and corporations / J. Anthony
VanDuzer. — 2nd ed.

(Essentials of Canadian law)
Includes bibliographical references and index.
ISBN 1-55221-058-8
    1. Partnership—Canada. 2. Corporation law—Canada. 3. Sole proprietorship—Canada. I. Title. II. Series.

KE1345.V36 2003   346.71'066   C2003-902560-8
KF1355.V36 2003

The publisher acknowledges the financial support of the Government of Canada through the Book Publishing Industry Development Program (BPIDP) for our publishing activities. The publisher also acknowledges the Government of Ontario through the Ontario Media Development Corporation's Ontario Book Initiative.

Printed and bound in Canada.

1 2 3 4 5   07 06 05 04 03

SUMMARY
TABLE OF CONTENTS

DETAILED
TABLE OF CONTENTS

FOREWORD

Canadian corporate law is messy. The federal government has its own corporate law statute, as does each of the ten provinces. Although there are similarities among these statutes, there are also substantial differences. Not only that, but provincial securities regulation also regulates corporate governance, and needs to be accounted for in any treatment of the Canadian corporate law regime. Further complicating matters are the many liabilities and duties, based on a range of statutes and common law doctrines, that regulate corporate behaviour.

Tony VanDuzer has written an indispensable book on the structure and operation of Canadian partnership and corporate law. Ever mindful of the complexities of the legal regime, he skilfully navigates his treatise through a number of doctrinal areas and gives the reader an appreciation of how the system works. He does so in a way that is sensitive to the distinct market and regulatory environment in which Canadian corporations operate.

All in all, this book is a distinguished piece of scholarship, and I commend it to both practitioners and students of corporate law.

Ronald J. Daniels
Dean, Faculty of Law
University of Toronto

ACKNOWLEDGMENTS

I would like to thank the following people for their assistance in reviewing drafts of chapters for the second edition of this book: Anita Anand, David Debenham, and Derek Smith. I remain indebted to Jeremy Farr, Marc LeBlanc, Jeffrey MacIntosh, Douglas Scott, Sean Wise, and Jacob Ziegel, who were kind enough to review chapters for the first edition. I also wish to thank my research assistants Goldie Bassi, Jaqueline Yost, Arend Wakeford, and Michael McGraw, who helped out with various aspects of this edition. Any errors, of course, remain my sole responsibility.

I gratefully acknowledge the support of the Common Law Section at the University of Ottawa; the University of Toronto, Faculty of Law, (where most of the first edition of this book was written); and Macleod Dixon. I was assisted substantially by financial support from the Law Foundation of Ontario and, for the second edition, from the Foundation for Legal Research.

Finally, I am very grateful to my wife, Jodie Karpf, without whose constant indulgence and support this book would not have been possible, and my children, Taylor and Eli, who put up with their father's too frequent absences to work on this book, mostly without complaint.

J. Anthony VanDuzer

LIST OF STATUTES, REGULATIONS, AND ABBREVIATIONS

Statutes*

ABCA	*Business Corporations Act*, R.S.A. 2000, c. 13-9
APA	*Partnership Act*, R.S.A. 2000, c. P-3
BCCA	*Company Act*, R.S.B.C. 1996, c. 62
BCPA	*Partnership Act*, R.S.B.C. 1996, c. 348
CBCA	*Canada Business Corporations Act*, R.S.C. 1985, c. C-44, as amended, including the substantial amendments given effect by S.C. 2001, c. 14 (the *2001 Amendments*)
CIA	*Corporations Information Act*, R.S.O. 1990, c. 39
MCA	*The Corporations Act*, R.S.M. 1987, c. C-225
MPA	*The Partnership Act*, R.S.M. 1987, c. P-30
NBBCA	*Business Corporations Act*, S.N.B. 1981, c. B-9.1 as amended by *An Act to Amend the Business Corporations Act*, S.N.B. 1984, c. 17
NBPA	*Partnership Act*, R.S.N.B. 1973, c. P-4
NCA	*Corporations Act*, R.S.N. 1990, c. C-36
NPA	*Partnership Act*, R.S.N. 1990, c. P-3
NSCA	*Companies Act*, R.S.N.S. 1989, c. 81, as amended by *Investors Protection Act*, S.N.S. 1990, c. 15
NSPA	*Partnership Act*, R.S.N.S. 1989, c. 334
NSPBNA	*Partnerships and Business Names Registration Act*, R.S.N.S. 1989, c. 335
NwtBCA	*Business Corporations Act*, S.N.W.T. 1996, c. 19
OBCA	*Business Corporations Act*, R.S.O. 1990, c. B.16
OBNA	*Business Names Act*, R.S.O. 1990, c. B.17
OEPCA	*Extra-Provincial Corporations Act*, R.S.O. 1990, c. E.27
OLPA	*Limited Partnerships Act*, R.S.O. 1990, c. L.16
OPA	*Partnerships Act*, R.S.O. 1990, c. P.5
OSA	*Securities Act*, R.S.O. 1990, c. S.5
PEICA	*Companies Act*, R.S.P.E.I. 1988, c. C-14
PEIPA	*Partnerships Act*, R.S.P.E.I. 1988, c. P-1
CCQ	*Civil Code of Québec*, S.Q. 1991, c. 64, ss. 2186 -2266.
QCA	*Companies Act*, R.S.Q. 1977, c. C-38
SBCA	*The Business Corporations Act*, R.S.S. 1978, c. B-10
TA	*Trade-marks Act*, R.S.C. 1985, c. T-13
UKCA	*Companies Act* (U.K.), 1989, c. 40
YBCA	*Business Corporations Act*, R.S.Y. 1986, c. 15

Regulations*

CBCA Regulations	SOR/2001-512
OBCA Regulation	R.R.O. 1990, Reg. 62
OSA Regulation	R.R.O. 1990, Reg. 1015

* All statutes and regulations referred to include all amendments up to August 31, 2002. Only certain major amendments are specifically indicated in the list above.

CHAPTER 1

INTRODUCTION

A. INTRODUCTION TO THIS BOOK

This book provides an overview of the essential features of the law governing the most common forms of business organization in Canada: the sole proprietorship, the partnership, and the corporation. It is intended to be an accessible and practical reference for law and business students, lawyers, accountants, and others concerned with understanding business organizations.

The law governing business organizations touches all of us, in a variety of diverse and overlapping ways — as employees, managers, customers, creditors, and, most significantly, investors. Although only some of us invest our money directly in businesses, almost all of us have some stake as investors. The money we deposit in our bank accounts, the premiums we pay to our insurance companies, and our contributions to our pension funds are all reinvested by these financial intermediaries in businesses.[1]

As investors and in our other relationships with business enterprises, the main way business organizations law affects us is by allocating the risks associated with carrying on the business. Every business carries on a commercial activity that involves certain risks. Although the specific sources of risk will vary from one business to the next, in every business

---

1   Some money deposited in bank accounts is not invested in business, but loaned to consumers.

the fundamental nature of the risk is the same: Will the business prosper or fail? In general, business organizations law strikes a balance between the interests of investors and the other stakeholders, including employees, managers, customers, creditors, and the public, by establishing rules that determine who benefits from the success of the business and who is responsible for its losses. In this regard, business organizations law determines when individual investors are personally liable for the debts and other obligations of the business. By affecting the allocation of the risks of doing business in this way, the law governing business organizations affects the incentives for entrepreneurs to engage in business. It also affects the risks incurred by other stakeholders in their dealings with businesses. A second function of business organizations law is to provide an organizational structure for the operation of businesses.

This book examines the balance struck between the interests of investors and other stakeholders in the sole proprietorship, the partnership, and the corporation, and the particular kind of organizational structure the law provides for each form of business organization. Emphasis is placed on the practical application of legal rules in an everyday context and the role that lawyers play in advising their business clients about these rules.

This chapter continues with an examination of the basic nature of a business and the interests of its stakeholders, and then looks at the essential elements of the law governing business organizations. Next, the basic characteristics of the sole proprietorship, the partnership, and the corporation, as well as some other methods of carrying on business, such as joint ventures and franchises, are described. Some of the advantages and disadvantages of each are identified based on both legal and practical considerations.

In the remainder of the book, partnerships and corporations, respectively, are addressed in detail. In relation to each, the following areas are covered:

- **Creation** — How is the business organization formed?
- **Internal Organization** — What are the relationships among the people who own and those who manage the business and how are they governed?
- **External Relationships** — What are the relationships between the business organization and those it deals with, such as its creditors, customers, and tort[2] victims, and how are they governed?

---

2   A tort is an act or omission giving rise to civil liability. The most common tort is negligence. If a person can prove that the act or omission of another meets the

In addition to these basic questions, the discussion of partnerships in Chapter 2 also covers three special kinds of relationships: limited partnerships, limited liability partnerships, and joint ventures.

Chapters 3 through 12 on corporations make up the largest section of the book, reflecting the pervasive use of the corporation to carry on business. Although the content of these chapters follows the model outlined above, the discussion is much more detailed. Most of the discussion focuses on the most common type of corporation in the marketplace — corporations with few shareholders and carrying on a small business. Nevertheless, some of the distinctive issues relevant to large public corporations, such as corporate governance, insider trading, and takeover bids, will be addressed in passing throughout the book and are the focus of Chapter 11.

Unlike the other forms of business organization, the corporation is an entity separate in law from the people who own it, the shareholders, and those who are responsible for managing it, the directors and officers. Chapter 3 introduces the corporation, tracing the historical development of corporate law in Canada and examining the constitutional competence of the federal and provincial governments to incorporate and regulate corporations. This chapter also looks at the nature of the corporation's separate legal personality. Chapter 4 outlines the process of and considerations relating to incorporation. Chapter 5 discusses some of the operational issues that are created by the corporation's separate legal existence, such as how a corporation becomes liable in contract and for torts and crimes.

The rest of the book is devoted largely to the internal relationships in the corporation. The legal scheme set out in Canadian corporate statutes is explained and some of the current issues of corporate governance in practice are discussed. Chapter 6 deals with the nature of shares, the ownership interests in the corporation. Chapter 7 deals with the division of the power to manage and control the corporation among the shareholders; the directors, who are elected by the shareholders to manage the corporation; and the officers, who are appointed by the directors and to whom the directors delegate management authority. Chapter 8 deals with the duties of directors and officers. The focus is on corporate law duties designed to ensure that directors and officers manage competently in the corporation's best interests. The burgeoning statutory duties of directors and officers, imposed to

---

legal standard for negligence, that person will be entitled to compensation from the other person for losses suffered as a result.

ensure the attainment of other public policy objectives such as compliance with environmental legislation, are considered, as is the expanding scope of tort liability faced by directors and officers. Chapter 9 looks at the remedies available to shareholders when directors and officers fail to meet their legal obligations. In Chapter 10 the technical and practical aspects of fundamental corporate changes, such as the amalgamation of two corporations and the dissolution of a corporation, are considered. Chapter 11 addresses some of the issues of specific relevance to larger public corporations, such as takeover bids and insider trading. A brief introduction to securities law is included as well.

The final chapter of the book, Chapter 12, introduces an important current issue in business organizations law: corporate social responsibility. It looks at the responsibilities of corporations to be accountable for their actions to non-shareholder stakeholders, including employees and the public.

B. WHAT IS A BUSINESS AND HOW DOES LAW GOVERN BUSINESS ORGANIZATIONS?

All businesses carry on some commercial activity and, in doing so, become the focus of a variety of relationships (see figure 1.1).[3] Businesses need money, which is provided by the owners of the business or third-party investors or lenders, like banks. They use the money for the purposes of the business, including buying inputs for their products from suppliers, and paying their employees. Businesses sell their products, whether they are goods or services, to customers. All these activities are carried out through employees to some extent. Businesses pay taxes and their success or failure affects the health of the economy. Businesses need someone to manage all these relationships with investors, suppliers, customers, and government.

One of the major concerns of business organizations law is the relationship of owners and managers to the business and to each other. We look at what rights the sole proprietor, the partner, and the shareholder have to manage the business themselves and to monitor and control others who manage. We also look at what remedies are available to owners where management is acting in a manner inconsistent with the best interests of the business.

---

3   The idea for presenting stakeholder interests in this way came from E.E. Palmer & B. L. Welling, *Canadian Company Law: Cases, Notes and Materials*, 3d ed. (Toronto: Butterworths, 1986), at 2–5.

Figure 1.1   Stakeholders in Business Organizations

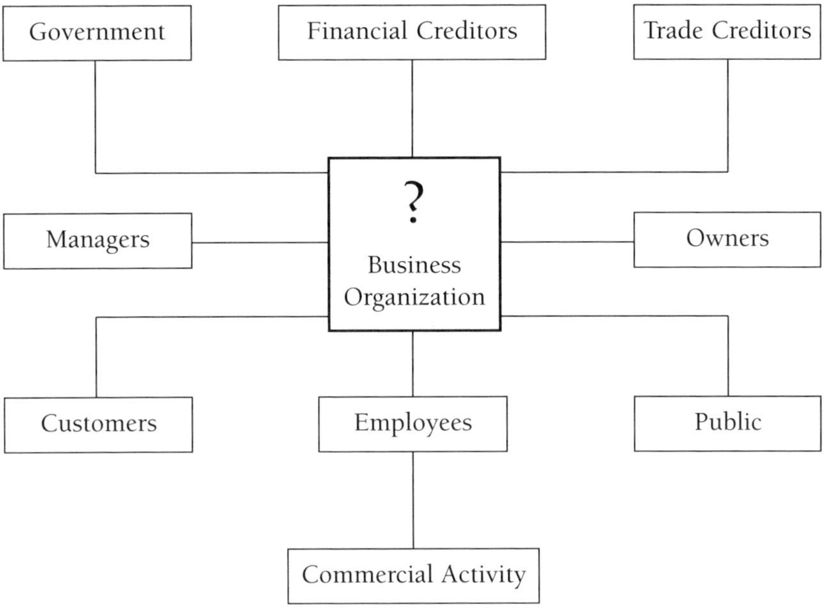

The second major concern of business organizations law is the responsibility of the business, the owners, and the managers to other stakeholder groups. The focus of business organizations law in this regard, however, is narrow. For the most part, relations between non-shareholder stakeholders and business organizations, their owners, and their managers are governed by other types of laws.

The rights and obligations of employees in relation to the business are governed by their contracts of employment, subject to a range of regulatory laws including employment standards and occupational health and safety legislation. There are a small number of limited kinds of protection for employees in business organizations law, but its main impact on employees is to determine who bears responsibility for obligations to employees: Is it the owners, the managers, or the organization itself that is responsible for paying employees' wages, for example? In Chapter 12 we discuss briefly the extent to which business organizations law permits or requires managers to take employees' interests into account in making business decisions.

The relationships between a business and its trade creditors (e.g., suppliers of goods and services to the business), financial creditors (e.g., banks), and customers are not the subject of business organizations law either but are dealt with under various other categories of law, such as contract, tort, property, commercial, and criminal law. Business organizations law is concerned with the narrower issue of when the business organization is liable for the obligations created under these other categories of law. In other words, we will not look at the substantive basis of a claim that a crime or a tort, for example, has been committed, but rather at the circumstances in which a business organization can be said to have committed the crime or the tort. As with employees, business organizations law does provide certain limited protection for creditors and customers, and addresses the extent to which management is permitted or required to take their interests into account in its decision making.

Business organizations have a complex and multifaceted relationship with the public. Decision making by business organizations has an enormous impact on the public interest in relation to such areas as employment, the environment, and tax revenues. The consequence, of course, is that businesses are subject to a variety of forms of direct regulation in these areas. Such regulation is not the subject of business organizations law. We are concerned in this book with the limited ways in which business organizations law permits or requires management to take public interests into account in its day-to-day decision making. We discuss as well the implications of imposing personal liability on directors and officers when the corporation fails to comply with its obligations, a common feature of many regulatory schemes.

Businesses operate, then, within a web of relationships involving a number of stakeholders which are regulated by a wide variety of laws designed to achieve a range of public policy objectives. Business organizations law focuses primarily on a subset of these relationships — those between owners, managers, and the business. It is important to remember, however, that the other relationships and the rules that govern them not only constitute the context in which business organizations law operates but also have a significant impact on the behaviour of management and owners.

C. BASIC FORMS OF BUSINESS ORGANIZATIONS

1) Sole Proprietorships

The sole proprietorship is the simplest form of business organization. It comes into existence whenever an individual starts to carry on business for her own account without taking the steps necessary to adopt some other form of organization, such as a corporation. If you started painting houses in your neighborhood for money, you would be carrying on business as a sole proprietor. Although the sole proprietor may enter into contracts of employment with others and, in this way, allocate certain functions in the business to them, the sole proprietor is the sole owner of the business and the only person entitled to manage it. Indeed, both legally and practically, there is no separation between the sole proprietorship business organization and the person who is the sole proprietor. One consequence is that the sole proprietor may not be an employee of the business. A sole proprietor cannot contract with herself.

Because there is no distinction between the sole proprietorship and the person who is the sole proprietor, all benefits from the business accrue to the sole proprietor and all obligations of the business are his responsibility. In terms of the relationships between the business and the other stakeholders in the business, the sole proprietor's complete responsibility has several important implications:

- the sole proprietor is exclusively responsible for performing all contracts entered into in the course of the business, including, for example, sales contracts with customers, financial commitments, contracts with suppliers, and employment contracts;
- the sole proprietor is exclusively responsible for all torts committed by her personally in connection with the business, and she is vicariously liable for all torts committed by employees in the course of their employment;
- all the sole proprietor's personal assets, as well as those contributed to the business, may be seized in fulfilment of the obligations of the sole proprietor's business; and
- for income tax purposes, the income or loss from the business is included with the income or loss from other sources in calculating the sole proprietor's personal tax liability.

The chief attraction of the sole proprietorship is its simplicity and ease of creation — a person simply starts to carry on business. It is equally easy to dissolve; the sole proprietor simply ceases to carry on business. Ceasing to carry on business, however, has no effect on liabilities incurred in connection with the business while it was being carried on.

The chief disadvantage of the sole proprietorship is unlimited personal liability. All the sole proprietor's personal assets, not just those of the business, may be taken by third parties in satisfaction of obligations of the business. As the scale of the business and the related liabilities increase, this exposure to personal liability becomes an increasingly important disincentive to using this form of business organization. It is hard to imagine a person being willing to carry on a large manufacturing business if he was liable personally for all payments to suppliers and employees and for all product liability claims. The magnitude of the liability risk and the difficulty of managing it in such a large operation would discourage carrying on the business as a sole proprietorship. By comparison, the corporation, but not the partnership, provides protection against personal liability. While it is true that a sole proprietor could try to manage liablity risk through insurance or provisions in contracts with customers and suppliers, incorporation is cheaper and, in most respects, more effective.

Another problem with the sole proprietorship is raising money. Every business needs additional investment to grow. It is not possible to divide up ownership of the sole proprietorship, so the only method of financing is for the sole proprietor to borrow money directly. As will be discussed below, an advantage of both the partnership and especially the corporation is that they permit a wider range of investment possibilities. In practice, unlimited personal liability and limited financing options mean that the sole proprietorship is used only for relatively small businesses.

One of the few legal requirements in connection with the use of a sole proprietorship is that the name of the sole proprietorship may have to be registered under the business names legislation in each province in which the proprietorship is carrying on business. In Ontario, registration is governed by section 2(2) of the *Business Names Act* (*OBNA*).[4] Registration is required if a sole proprietor is using a name other than simply her own. So, for example, Anne Kumar would not have to register if she were carrying on a convenience store business using only her own name, but would if she chose instead to use the name World's Best Milk and Nuts or Kumar's Milk and Nuts. A sole proprietor may also register voluntarily (*OBNA*, s. 4).

The *OBNA* and other provincial names legislation contain certain incentives to register. In Ontario, if you do not register when required to, without reasonable cause, you are committing an offence and are liable for a fine of up to $2000 (*OBNA*, s. 10(2)). Also, you may not sue in Ontario for an obligation incurred in connection with the business

---

4   Each province has its own legislation which follows the Ontario scheme in most respects. E.g., Alberta, *Partnerships Act*, R.S.A. 2000, c. P-3 [*APA*], ss. 110 to 115; British Columbia *Partnerships Act*, R.S.B.C., c. 348 [*BCPA*], ss. 81-90.1; Nova Scotia *Partnerships and Business Names Registration Act*, R.S.N.S. 1989, c. 335 [*NSPBNA*].

except with leave of the court (*OBNA*, s. 7).[5] The court must grant you leave to sue if your failure to register was inadvertent, there is no evidence that the public has been deceived or misled, and, at the time of application to the court, you have filed a registration (*OBNA*, s. 7(2)).

The main reason for these incentives is to ensure that there is a public record that creditors and others can search to find out the identity of the person behind the business name who will bear responsibility for any obligation of the business. The registration of the name of your sole proprietorship also has the effect of discouraging anyone who searches the register from using your registered name and so reduces the likelihood of confusion in the marketplace. This is one reason to register even if you are not obliged to.

Another advantage to registration is the right to statutory damages up to $500 against any person who registers a name that is deceptively similar to your registered name and that causes injury to you (*OBNA*, s. 6). It is important to note that this right is in addition to any other legal right you may have in connection with someone using a confusingly similar name. For example, you may have a claim against such a person under the common law tort of passing-off.[6]

Where a plaintiff in an action brought under the *OBNA* is successful, the court must also order the cancellation of the offending registration. The availability of statutory damages and cancellation encourages sole proprietors to police the names register themselves and so protects the integrity of the register. Registration does not mean, however, that no one else can use the name. This kind of proprietary right is protected only in specific circumstances under provincial passing-off laws and federal trade-marks law. These laws are discussed in relation to corporate names in Chapter 4.

The only other category of requirement for sole proprietorships, one that applies equally to all forms of business organization, is licensing. In order to commence certain types of businesses, a sole proprietor must obtain a licence from the appropriate level of government. For example, most municipalities in Ontario require the proprietors of taxi-driving businesses and restaurants to obtain a licence. Provincial governments have enacted licensing requirements for many types of businesses, such as real estate agents, car dealers, and securities dealers. In areas of federal legislative competence, licensing requirements may also be imposed. Anyone starting up a business must comply with the relevant licensing requirements.

---

5   The inability to sue is not imposed under the *BCPA*, *ibid.*
6   Passing off and other rights in names are discussed in Chapter 4.

2) Partnerships

a) Introduction

The law of partnerships developed as part of the common law in England. Eventually the law was codified in the English *Partnership Act* of 1890. All provinces, other than Quebec, have partnership legislation based on this English statute.[7] The Ontario *Partnerships Act*[8] (*OPA*) is typical. Quebec also has partnership law that has many similarities to the legislation in the common law provinces.

b) Characteristics

In a manner similar to sole proprietorships, partnerships come into being as a matter of law when two or more persons carry on business together with a view to a profit (*OPA*, s. 2). Sometimes it is easy to tell if you have created a partnership. For example, if you agree with your friend to carry on a house-painting business during the summer in which you are both responsible for finding customers, doing the painting, and paying the expenses, and in which each of you will receive one-half of the profits, you have created a partnership. There are, however, a wide variety of ways in which people may pool their knowledge, skills, and resources to create a partnership. We will examine the specific criteria for determining whether a partnership relationship exists in Chapter 2. In this introductory discussion, we will simply describe the general characteristics of partnerships.

By definition, partnerships involve more than one person, so there is a need for rules to govern the relationships among partners. Issues such as who will do what in managing the partnership business and how responsibility is allocated if things go wrong need to be addressed. The Ontario *Partnerships Act* sets out a framework of such rules in sections 20–31. These rules are not mandatory (*OPA*, s. 20). The *Partnerships Act* provides a kind of standard-form agreement or set of default rules that apply unless the partners agree to something else. These default rules may be and typically are modified, supplemented, and replaced by rules agreed on by the partners in a contract between them called a partnership agreement. The default nature of the statutory rules gives partners great flexibility to put in place an internal structure customized to their particular needs.

---

7   See Chapter 2.
8   R.S.O. 1990, c. P.5 [*OPA*]. The specific provisions of provincial statutes in other provinces are discussed in Chapter 2.

Like sole proprietorships, partners carry on business themselves directly. The partnership is not a legal entity separate from the partners. One consequence is that a partner cannot enter into a contract of employment with the partnership. Such an arrangement would require him to contract with himself. Another consequence with greater significance is that all benefits of the partnership business accrue directly to the partners, and all partners are personally liable for the obligations of the business. Each partner is liable to perform all contractual obligations agreed to by other partners in connection with the partnership business, even if the partner did not consent to the obligation. All partners are liable for all torts committed by partners in connection with the business and are vicariously liable for the torts of employees of the partnership committed in the course of their employment.

We will discuss the rules governing how partnerships incur obligations to third parties later in this section, but, once liability for an obligation has been established, each partner is liable to the full extent of the obligation. All her personal assets, not just assets the partner has committed to the business, may be seized to satisfy it. As among the partners, the partnership statutes provide that each is liable to contribute equally to any obligation owed by the partnership to a third party (e.g., *OPA*, s. 24) unless they agree to some other allocation. The allocation among the partners has no effect on third parties. A creditor or a tort victim may proceed against and recover the full amount of her claim from any partner or all partners. Once a partner pays a partnership obligation in excess of his allocation, he may seek to recover a contribution from the others in accordance with the partnership statute or their agreement.

For the purpose of determining the liability of partners for income tax in connection with the partnership business, the income (or loss) of the business is calculated for the partnership by adding up all revenues of the partnership business and deducting expenses. Each partner's share is allocated to her in accordance with the partner's entitlement under the partnership statute or the partnership agreement and is included in her personal income tax calculation.

Partnership statutes create a code governing when a partnership is liable to third parties (e.g., *OPA*, ss. 6–19). Unlike the provisions just discussed governing the internal relationships among partners, these rules are mandatory. They will be discussed in detail in Chapter 2. The basic principle is that each partner is the agent of the partnership, meaning that each of the partners may bind the partnership when acting in the usual course of the partnership business (e.g., *OPA*, s. 6). A third party will be unable to rely on the ability of a partner, acting in the usual course of the partnership business, to bind the partnership only if the partner in fact does not have authority, perhaps because of a restriction in the partnership agreement, and the third party is aware of the limit on the partner's authority.

This principle of "mutual agency" effectively allocates to the partners the risk of unauthorized behaviour by an individual partner. It creates an organizational concern: How can the partners ensure that individual partners do not enter into obligations that, collectively, the partnership does not want? Given the unlimited personal liability of each partner, this concern is significant. Both legal and practical protections are available to partners, as discussed in Chapter 2.

All partnerships in Ontario must register their names under provincial business names legislation (e.g., *OBNA*, s. 2(3)).[9] The other provisions of names legislation described above in relation to sole proprietorships apply equally to partnerships, as does the discussion of business licences.

3) Corporations

a) Formation

Unlike the sole proprietorship and the partnership, a corporation does not come into existence simply by virtue of one or several people starting a business. Creation, called incorporation in most Canadian jurisdictions, occurs upon making a filing with the appropriate government authority and paying the requisite fee. Incorporation may be under the federal *Canada Business Corporations Act* (*CBCA*)[10] or under the corporate statute in a province or territory. In Chapter 4, we will talk about how incorporation is accomplished in some detail. It is sufficient to note here that the corporation is entirely a statutory creature.

As with partnerships, it is possible for shareholders in a corporation to customize their relationship to the corporation and each other. Subject to some limits, they may augment or replace the statutory scheme through provisions in the various components of the corporate constitution (the articles and by-laws of the corporation, and resolutions of directors and shareholders) as well as through contracts among shareholders, called shareholders' agreements.

---

9 The rules in this regard vary somewhat from province to province. *NSPBNA*, s. 3(1); *BCPA*, above note 4, s. 81; and *APA*, above note 4, s. 106 are similar to the Ontario Act.

10 R.S.C. 1985, c. C-44 [*CBCA*].

Upon incorporation, the filing made by the corporation becomes a matter of public record. No registration under provincial business names legislation is required for corporations unless they use a name different from their corporate name. The discussion above concerning the business licences needed by sole proprietorships applies equally to corporations.

b) Characteristics

i) Separate Legal Existence

Unlike the sole proprietorship and the partnership, the corporation is an entity endowed with a separate legal existence. The corporation itself carries on business, owns property, possesses rights, and incurs liabilities. Shareholders have a bundle of rights in relation to the corporation through their ownership of shares, but they do not own the business carried on by the corporation or the property belonging to the corporation.[11] The rights and liabilities of the corporation are not the rights and liabilities of the shareholders. In contrast, sole proprietors and partners carry on the business, own its property, possess its rights, and are directly responsible for its liabilities.

Separate legal existence has three other important implications. First, a shareholder can be an employee and a creditor of the corporation because there is a legal entity, separate from the shareholder, to be the other party to the employment contract or the credit obligation. Second, because it is distinct from the people who are the shareholders, the corporation has perpetual existence; it is not dependent in any way on the continuation of its shareholders. The corporation is not affected if a shareholder dies or withdraws from the corporation by selling her shares. Third, for income tax purposes, the corporation is taxed separately. Income or loss from the business carried on through the corporation is determined and taxed at the corporate level. Shareholders pay tax only when they receive something from the corporation, such as a dividend or some other distribution of assets.

It is often said that shareholders have "limited liability" for the obligations of the corporation. This is misleading, however. Shareholders have no direct liability at all for obligations of the corporation. In order to obtain shares, shareholders provide the corporation with money, property, or services that then belong to the corporation. Shareholders are said to have limited liability because their maximum loss in connection with their investment in the corporation is limited to the

---

11   *Kosmopoulos v. Constitution Insurance Co. of Canada*, [1987] 1 S.C.R. 2.

value of the money, property, or services they have transferred to the corporation in return for their shares. Creditors, employees, and other claimants against the corporation can demand to be paid out of the assets of the corporation, but, once the corporation's assets are exhausted, the creditors cannot claim to be paid by the shareholders personally. In the worst case, if all the assets of the corporation are taken by creditors, the shareholder's shares will be worth nothing. They will have lost all their investment, but that is all they will lose. In short, shareholders are not directly liable for the obligations of the corporation, but their maximum potential loss is limited to the amount they have invested. As will be discussed in Chapter 3, this limitation on shareholder liability shifts some of the risk associated with the commercial activity in which the corporation is engaged from the shareholders to other stakeholders.

Finally, even though the corporation is a separate legal entity, it can act only through individuals, often referred to generically as "agents" of the corporation. In this sense, agents include directors, officers, and anyone else who may act on behalf of the corporation in relation to outsiders. In Chapter 5, we look at the law governing the circumstances in which a corporation will be bound by the acts of its agents. In general, like a partnership, a corporation will be bound by a contractual commitment to a third party when the agent who negotiated it is actually authorized by the corporation to enter into the commitment on the corporation's behalf or reasonably appeared to have such authority. The law imposes liability on the corporation for crimes and torts committed by its agents when the agent can be said to be acting on behalf of the corporation, unless some particular mental state must be shown as an element of the tort or crime, such as an intention to commit the tort or crime. In such a case, the courts have determined that the corporation is liable only if the agent who has this mental state can be considered to be acting as the corporation itself for the purposes of committing the tort or crime. The difference between an agent acting *on behalf of a corporation* and one acting *as the corporation* is discussed in Chapter 5.

ii) Separation of Ownership and Management

The rights and obligations of managers and those with interests represented by shares of the corporation are legally distinct. Under the organization imposed by statute federally and in each province and territory, corporations are managed by a board of directors, which is elected by shareholders by majority vote, and by officers, who are appointed and delegated responsibilities by the directors. Shareholders do not participate, as shareholders, in the management of the corporation.[12] In many corporations, especially small ones, however, these legally distinct roles are played by the same people — the shareholders are also the directors and officers. As the business gets larger, directors and officers are less likely to hold all the shares of a corporation, though often they do hold shares. Large corporations like Nortel Networks Inc. have thousands of shareholders, including their officers and directors.

The separation of ownership and management creates a number of issues regarding the internal relationship in the corporation between shareholders, on the one hand, and officers and directors (referred to in this section collectively as "management"), on the other. From the shareholders' point of view, the key issue in this relationship is how shareholders can control management and ensure that management acts in their interests.

One of the challenges faced by corporate law in addressing this issue is that the nature of the rules needed to ensure that management is accountable to shareholders will be different depending on a number of variables, including, in particular, the scale of the corporation. For example, in corporations involving only a few shareholders, where each is actively engaged in the business, the need for formal accountability mechanisms may be minimal. The situation may be similar to the small partnership discussed above. Not only will the shareholders likely be aware of what is going on in the corporation but they may be the directors and officers themselves.

By contrast, in a large corporation with thousands of geographically dispersed shareholders, each having only a small financial interest in the corporation, shareholders will not be able to monitor, much less control, management in these informal ways. At the same time, management is in a position where its interests may be thought to diverge from those of shareholders. As soon as a manager has less than 100 percent of the shares of a corporation, she can benefit by indulging in perquisites at the expense of the corporation. For example, she may be tempted to pay herself an excessive salary or shirk her duties, resulting in a diminution in the value of the shareholders' investment in the corporation.[13] Even if the manager has some shares in the corporation, the loss on her investment caused by her opportunistic behaviour is more than offset by the

---

12 Under the *CBCA* and provincial statutes modelled after it, shareholders may assume the powers of the directors when they use a unanimous shareholder agreement (*CBCA*, above note 10, s. 146(2)). This device is discussed in Chapter 7.

13 The costs of such opportunistic behaviour and expenditures by shareholders to guard against it are referred to as "agency costs" and are discussed in Chapter 7.

benefits. She receives the full amount of the benefit, whereas the loss is inflicted on the corporation. As a shareholder, the impact of the loss on her is limited by the size of her shareholding. For example, assume that the manager has 1 percent of the common shares of a corporation. If she pays herself a bonus of $1,000,000, she gets the full amount of the bonus. The corporation loses $1,000,000, but the reduction in the value of her shares is only 1 percent of $1,000,000 or $10,000.

There is a risk also that, because management receives most of its income from the corporation's activities, it will be reluctant to cause the corporation to take risks. Shareholders, by contrast, are more likely to want the corporation to take appropriate risks, since their exposure to loss from the corporation's activities typically is much less.[14]

Because of the sometimes conflicting interests of management and shareholders, corporate law contains a variety of legal mechanisms designed to ensure that management is accountable to shareholders without unduly constraining the freedom of action management needs to be able to do its job of running the business in the most effective way. As discussed in Chapter 7, these legal mechanisms are supplemented by some market-based mechanisms that drive management to act in shareholder interests. The four major kinds of legal accountability mechanisms are set out in figure 1.2.

Figure 1.2   Corporate Law Mechanisms Providing Management Accountability to Shareholders

---

- **Corporate democracy**: Shareholders have the collective power to determine who the directors are and so to influence the directors' choice of officers and what decisions the directors make. As well, certain fundamental changes cannot be made to the corporation without shareholder approval.

- **Directors' and officers' duties**: Management has a duty to act in the best interests of the corporation and to take reasonable care in performing its responsibilities, thereby protecting shareholders' interests.

---

14   The assertion that shareholders are likely to have a higher risk tolerance than managers is based on portfolio theory, which provides that by holding a large diversified portfolio of investments, much of the business-specific risk of poor returns on individual investments will be offset by higher returns on other investments in the portfolio. Shareholders, at least in public corporations, typically will have a variety of investments, of which their shareholding in a particular corporation will be only one. Managers, by contrast, will have a large investment in the corporation for which they work. It will be their major source of income. See, generally, P. Halpern, J.F. Weston, & E.F. Brigham, *Canadian Managerial Finance*, 4th ed. (Toronto: Dryden, 1994).

- **Shareholder rights to information:** Shareholders have certain rights of access to information which help them to know whether management is performing its duties.
- **Shareholder remedies:** Shareholders have certain remedies in the event that management's duties are not performed.

The primary power of shareholders is to elect directors in the first place, to refuse to re-elect them, and to remove them. In principle, this gives shareholders the power to ensure that directors and the officers they appoint will act in their best interests. As discussed in Chapter 7, the effectiveness of corporate democracy may be limited in some circumstances, such as where there are large numbers of shareholders who may find it difficult to exercise their will collectively or in corporations of any scale where there is a majority shareholder who can determine the outcome of any shareholder vote.

Given these sorts of problems with corporate democracy, the effectiveness of the other accountability mechanisms is very important to shareholders. The standards of behaviour to which management must conform and the ability of shareholders to monitor management performance — and, ultimately, to seek relief where those standards have not been complied with — are critical issues in corporate law, and they are addressed in Chapters 7 through 11. In some ways, shareholders' concerns are similar to those of partners in partnerships where management responsibilities have been delegated to one of the partners or to someone else. The degree of separation of ownership and management which typically exists in large corporations, however, makes shareholders' concerns more pressing. Also, because the corporation is almost universally the form chosen to carry on businesses of any size in Canada, how these concerns are resolved is a much more important matter of public policy. For both these reasons, the provisions of corporate law to address these concerns are much more developed than those in partnership law. To illustrate more specifically some of the concerns shareholders may have about managers and how the duties imposed on managers are responsive to these concerns, consider the following examples.

Shareholders do not want managers of the corporation to be negligent in managing the corporation's business. To address this concern, the common law, the *CBCA* (s. 122(1)(b)), and most provincial corporate statutes impose a duty of care on managers.

Shareholders do not want management to be engaged in activities that put its interests ahead of those of the corporation and the shareholders. For example, shareholders would be justifiably unhappy if managers were diverting business from the corporation to themselves or exercising their management powers to maintain themselves in office rather than for the benefit of the corporation. The latter concern might arise where a takeover bid is made for the corporation and the bidder has announced that he will replace management if the bid is successful. In such a situation, the managers' personal interest in maintaining their jobs may be in conflict with the interests of the corporation, which might benefit from the new management.

Similarly, shareholders would not want management to favour one group of shareholders over another. As a democratically elected body, directors may feel that they have a mandate to act in accordance with the wishes of the majority; after all, they hold their jobs because of the goodwill of the holders of a majority of shares. But this should not give them the right to ignore — or, worse, trample on — the interests of the minority.

To address these types of problems, the common law, the *CBCA*, and most provincial corporate statutes impose obligations on management to act in the best interests of the corporation and prohibit managers from favouring the interests of one group of shareholders over another (e.g., *CBCA*, s. 122(1)(a)). This fiduciary duty requires managers to act in the best interests of the corporation as a whole. Corporate statutes in most Canadian jurisdictions also provide that minority shareholders may obtain relief if the majority shareholder causes the corporation to act in a manner that is unfair or oppressive to the interests of the minority or if management acts in such a way (e.g., *CBCA*, s. 241).

4) Other Forms and Methods of Carrying on Business

Several other forms or methods of carrying on business[15] are commonly referred to and, although they are not the focus of this book, are mentioned here to clarify some terms used in relation to business organizations and to give a more complete picture of the options for carrying on business.

a) Special Forms of Corporations
In this book, we discuss the general law applicable to corporations carrying on business. There are some businesses, however, that can be carried on only through special kinds of corporations incorporated and

---

15   See, generally, D.J. Bourgeois, *The Law of Charitable and Non-Profit Organizations*, 3d ed. (Toronto: Butterworths, 2002).

governed under statutes which combine many of the features of the general corporate law with other provisions imposing a scheme of regulation on these businesses. Banks, for example, must be incorporated and operated under the federal *Bank Act*.[16] Insurance businesses must be incorporated and are governed by either federal or provincial legislation regulating the insurance business.[17] There are also corporations created under special acts of Parliament or a provincial legislature. All these special forms of corporations are outside the scope of this book. As well, this book deals only with business organizations. Special kinds of corporations and other forms of organization are used to carry on charitable activities.

b) Joint Venture

A joint venture is not a distinct form of business organization, nor a relationship that has any precise legal meaning. The term "joint venture" is used loosely to refer to a wide variety of legal arrangements in which two or more parties combine their resources for some limited purpose, for a limited time, or both. A joint venture may be established, for example, by a contract in which the joint venturers agree that they will do certain things to carry out their common purpose; by two people carrying on business together, in which case the joint venture is a partnership; or by two people forming a corporation to carry out their common purpose. Although the legal consequences of a joint venture that is a corporation or a partnership are clear, the legal consequences of a joint venture relationship that is neither a partnership nor a corporation are not. Joint ventures are discussed at the end of Chapter 2.

c) Strategic Alliance

Like joint venture, the term "strategic alliance" has no precise legal meaning and is used to refer to a wide variety of relationships between business organizations involving more or less legal formality and greater and lesser degrees of working together among the alliance participants. A joint venture or a partnership may be referred to as a strategic alliance. The terms may also be used to describe less involved relationships, such as, for example, an agreement to do research and development together, to market products jointly, or simply to share information.

---

16   S.C. 1991, c. 46

17   The federal statute is the *Insurance Companies Act*, S.C. 1991, c. 47. The Ontario *Insurance Act*, R.S.O. 1990, c. I.8, is an example of provincial legislation.

d) Licence

A licence is a purely contractual relationship under which one party, the licensor, agrees to permit another, the licensee, to use something, usually some form of intellectual property such as a patent, trade-mark, or copyright, in return for compensation, usually in the form of a royalty. One example of a licence would be an agreement by a trade-mark owner, such as McDonald's, to permit someone else, such as one of its franchisees operating a McDonald's restaurant in Calgary, to use its trade-mark in the franchisee's business. In this example, the licence was agreed to in the context of a franchise agreement, but licences may also be part of other business arrangements such as joint ventures or partnerships, as well as stand-alone contractual arrangements.

e) Franchise

A franchise is a purely contractual relationship under which the franchisor gives the franchisee the right to operate its business "system" in return for a set of fees. The parties typically provide in their agreement that their relationship does not constitute a partnership or a joint venture. The basic terms of the relationship consist of a licence in which the franchisor gives the franchisee the right to use its trade-marks and promises to provide certain assistance in running the franchised business, including training. In return, the franchisee agrees to operate the franchised business in accordance with the standards of the franchisor and to pay certain fees based, in part, on the sales of the business.

Franchisors know much more about their businesses than prospective franchisees, who are often inexperienced. As well, franchises are complex arrangements which tend to be offered on a take-it-or-leave-it basis by the franchisor. For both these reasons, prospective franchisees may not fully appreciate the nature of the risks associated with a franchise. Alberta and Ontario have enacted legislation that imposes obligations on franchisors for the protection of current and prospective franchisees.[18] The key elements of the legislation are set out in Figure 1.3.

---

18   *Franchises Act*, S.A. 1995, c. F-17.1 (Alta); *Arthur Wishart Act (Franchise Disclosure), 2000*, S.O. 2000, c. 3. The Ontario statute is named after Arthur Wishart, who first proposed a public inquiry into the franchising industry.

Figure 1.3   Key Elements of Franchise Legislation in Alberta and
Ontario

- **Duty of Fair Dealing:** Franchisors have a minimum obligation to deal fairly with franchisees and prospective franchisees. Franchisors must act in good faith and in accordance with reasonable commercial standards.

- **Disclosure:** Franchisors must provide extensive disclosure to prospective franchisees regarding the nature of the franchise business and the risks associated with it.

- **Withdrawal Right:** Any franchisee who signs a franchise agreement has a right to withdraw from the agreement within sixty days of signing if the disclosure document was not provided at least fourteen days before the earlier of the date that
  - the franchisee signed the agreement or
  - the franchisee was required to pay any money to the franchisor.
  The franchisee may withdraw within two years of signing the franchise agreement if the required disclosure documents were never provided.

- **Damages for Misrepresentation:** Franchisees have the right to damages for any misrepresentation in disclosure documents.

- **Right to Organize:** Franchisees have the right to organize themselves to deal collectively with the franchisor.

---

f) Distributorships

Distributorship does not have a precise legal meaning. Business people may say that a distributorship exists when one business agrees to sell another's product. Usually, the distributor buys the products for itself and then resells them on its own behalf.[19] In addition to selling the basic product, a distributor may also perform some of the responsibilities that would normally fall upon the supplier or manufacturer. The distributor may, for example, provide warranty service. A supplier or manufacturer would be interested in selling through a distributor where the distributor is able to get its products to more customers more efficiently than the supplier or manufacturer could do so itself.

---

19   Where the distributor does not buy the products itself but merely negotiates sales of the products on behalf of the supplier or manufacturer, the distributor is usually referred to as an agent. See, generally, M. McInnes, I. Kerr, J.A. VanDuzer & C. Carmody, *Managing the Law: The Legal Aspects of Doing Business* (Toronto: Pearson, 2003), c. 20.

D. CHAPTER SUMMARY

We began this chapter by describing the focus of this book: the sole proprietorship, the partnership, and the corporation. Next, we described the nature of a business as the nexus of a variety of stakeholder relationships and defined what aspects of these relationships are governed by business organizations law. Business organizations law is primarily concerned with the relationships between owners and managers of business organizations. The interests of other stakeholders are addressed primarily under other kinds of laws. The rest of the chapter was devoted to introductory discussions of the sole proprietorship, the partnership, and the corporation.

The sole proprietorship is the simplest form of business organization; it comes into existence whenever a person begins to carry on a business. A sole proprietor has unlimited personal liability for the obligations of the business and is solely entitled to its benefits. The only legal requirements are name registration under provincial business names legislation and a business licence in some cases.

A partnership comes into existence when two or more people start to carry on business together with a view to a profit. Partnerships are governed by special statutes in each province that provide default rules governing the relations of partners to each other. These rules apply in the absence of an agreement to the contrary. Mandatory rules govern the relationship of the partnership to persons dealing with the partnership. Like the sole proprietor, the partners in a partnership are personally responsible for the obligations of the business and are entitled to the benefits from it. Each partner is considered the agent of the partnership for the purpose of creating partnership obligations within the course of the partnership business. Unlimited personal liability combined with the ability of all partners to bind the partnership create significant risks for partners.

A corporation is formed upon making a prescribed filing with the appropriate government authority. Unlike the other forms of business organization, a corporation is a legally separate entity from its shareholders and managers. The corporation alone is responsible for the obligations of the business it carries on and is solely entitled to the benefits from the business. Although, in small corporations, shareholders and managers may be the same people, their roles are legally distinct. Shareholders have a financial interest in the corporation represented by their shares; they vote to elect directors who have responsibility for the management of the business and the affairs of the corporation. The directors may delegate some of their management responsibility to officers. Where management and shareholders are not the same people, the potential exists for managers to engage in opportunistic behaviour, favouring their own interests over those of the corporation by, for example, excessively indulging in perquisites and shirking work. Corporate law encourages management accountability through corporate democracy, management's fiduciary duty and duty of care, shareholder rights to information, and shareholder remedies.

There are other methods of carrying on business, such as joint ventures, strategic alliances, licences, franchises, and distributorships.

FURTHER READINGS

BOURGEOIS, D.J., *The Law of Charitable and Non-profit Organizations*, 3d ed. (Toronto: Butterworths, 2002)

BUCKLEY, F.H., M. GILLEN, & R. YALDEN, *Corporations: Principles and Policies*, 3d ed. (Toronto: Emond Montgomery, 1995)

CARY, W.L., & M.A. EISENBERG, *Cases and Materials on Corporations*, 6th ed. (Mineola, N.Y.: Foundation Press, 1994)

CLARK, R., *Corporate Law* (Toronto: Little Brown & Co., 1986)

DANIELS, R.J., & J.G. MACINTOSH, "Toward a Distinctive Canadian Corporate Law Regime" (1991) 29 Osgoode Hall L.J. 863

FLANNIGAN, R., "The Economic Structure of the Firm" (1995) 33 Osgoode Hall L.J. 105

GOWER, L.C.B., *Principles of Modern Company Law*, 5th ed. (London: Stevens, 1993)

HADDEN, T., R.E. FORBES, & R.L. SIMMONDS, *Canadian Business Organizations Law* (Toronto: Butterworths, 1984)

IACCOBUCCI, F., M.L. PILKINGTON, & J.R.S. PRICHARD, *Canadian Business Corporations* (Agincourt: Canada Law Book, 1977)

LAW SOCIETY OF UPPER CANADA, *Bar Admission Course Reference Materials: Business Law* (Toronto: Law Society of Upper Canada, 2003)

MANZER, A.R., *A Practical Guide to Canadian Partnership Law* (Aurora: Canada Law Book, 1995) (looseleaf)

MORSE, G., ed., *Palmer's Company Law*, 25th ed. (London: Sweet & Maxwell, 1992)

REITER, B.J. & M. A. SHISHLER, *Joint Ventures: Legal and Business Perspectives* (Toronto: Irwin Law, 1999)

SCAMMELL, E.H., & R.C. BANKS, eds., *Lindley and Banks on the Law of Partnership*, 18th ed. (London: Sweet & Maxwell, 2002)

SHISHLER, M.A., "The Graham Decision Revisited: The Fading Promise of the Joint Venture as a Distinct Legal Concept," (1998) 31 Can. Bus. L.J. 118

SIMMONDS, R.L., & P.P. MERCER, *An Introduction to Business Associations in Canada: Cases, Notes and Materials* (Toronto: Carswell, 1984)

SUTHERLAND, H., ed., *Fraser's Handbook on Canadian Company Law*, 8th ed. (Toronto: Carswell, 1994)

WELLING, B., *Corporate Law in Canada: The Governing Principles*, 2d ed. (Toronto: Butterworths, 1991)

ZIEGEL, J.S., ed., *Studies in Canadian Company Law*, vol. 2 (Toronto: Butterworths, 1973)

ZIEGEL, J.S., *et al.*, *Cases and Materials on Partnerships and Canadian Business Corporations*, 3d ed. (Toronto: Carswell, 1994)

CHAPTER 2

PARTNERSHIPS

A. WHAT IS A PARTNERSHIP?

1) Introduction

Originally, partnership law developed as part of the English common law. In a common law system, the law in areas not governed by statute consists of the accumulation of rules made in judicial decisions. Once a rule is applied in a particular case, it becomes a precedent: all courts are bound to decide all subsequent cases in a manner consistent with this rule.[1] The application of the rule from the precedent case to different facts in subsequent cases clarifies and refines the rule. As a result of this binding character of precedent cases, it is often said that common law is made by judges.

Prior to the enactment of partnership legislation, the English courts, in deciding individual cases, had developed rules of their own to determine when a partnership relationship existed and what its legal consequences were. In the late nineteenth century, the judge-made rules for partnerships were codified in the English *Partnerships Act* of 1890.

---

1   To be precise, only courts lower in the hierarchy of courts than the court rendering a decision are bound to follow the decision. So, for example, a decision of the Ontario Court of Appeal is binding on the Ontario Superior Court of Justice, but not on the Supreme Court of Canada.

In Canada, the provinces have constitutional jurisdiction to enact laws regulating partnerships under section 92(13) of the *Constitution Act, 1867*, which gives the provinces jurisdiction in relation to "Property and Civil Rights." All the provinces except Quebec are common law jurisdictions, like the United Kingdom, and all have enacted statutory regimes based on the English *Partnerships Act* of 1890.[2] Few changes have been made to these provincial statutes since their enactment, and there is an extensive body of judicial decisions interpreting them. These decisions are also precedents binding on courts in subsequent cases. The common law continues to apply to the extent not inconsistent with the applicable provincial legislation.[3]

In Quebec, Canada's only civil law jurisdiction, partnerships are governed by the *Civil Code*.[4] In civil law jurisdictions, judges do not make the law in the common law sense. All law has its source in the *Civil Code*. Although previous decisions are used to argue in favour of a particular interpretation of the *Civil Code*, they are not binding on courts in future cases.

Under the *Civil Code*, the nature of a partnership is different, in some respects, from partnerships under the laws in the other provinces. A partnership in Quebec takes on different characteristics depending on the manner in which the partnership is formed. Partnerships are either "declared" or "undeclared." Declared partnerships are those registered under the *Code*, while undeclared partnerships are similar to partnerships in the common law jurisdictions in that no registration is required for them to exist. An important difference between undeclared partnerships under the *Code* and partnerships in common law jurisdictions is that, in an undeclared partnership, only those partners who are known by a third-party creditor doing business with an undeclared partnership are liable to the third party. In a declared partnership, all partners are liable whether the third party knows about them or not. Declared partnerships may be limited partnerships, very like limited partnerships in the common law jurisdictions, or general partnerships, which have characteristics similar to common law partnerships as discussed below.[5] Limited partnerships are a special kind of partnership discussed near the end of this chapter.

---

2   See, for example, Ontario *Partnerships Act*, R.S.O. 1990, c. P.5 [*OPA*]; Alberta *Partnership Act*, R.S.A. 2000, c. P-3 [*APA*]; British Columbia *Partnership Act*, R.S.B.C. 1996, c. 348 [*BCPA*]; and Nova Scotia *Partnership Act*, R.S.N.S. 1989, c. 334 [*NSPA*].

3   *OPA, ibid.*, s. 45.

4   Civil Code of Quebec, Arts. 2186–2266.

5   Civil Code of Quebec, Arts. 2250–2257.

The statutory law in Quebec and the other provinces deals with the nature of the partnership, the relationship of the partners to each other and to outsiders dealing with the partnership, and the dissolution of the partnership. In no jurisdiction, however, do these provisions provide a complete code to regulate the affairs of partnerships, with the result that the substantial body of judicial decisions dealing with partnerships constitutes an important source of the law governing partnerships. As well, partners will frequently supplement or modify the rules governing their relationship in a contract commonly referred to as a partnership agreement. Some of the ways in which this is done are described below. In order to deal with any issue involving a partnership, one must have regard to the relevant partnership statute, the case law, and any partnership agreement.

This chapter focuses on the partnership law of the common law provinces, emphasizing the Ontario *Partnerships Act*, though some comparisons with Quebec law and the laws of other provinces are included. It also discusses some of the considerations relevant to drafting partnership agreements. Limited partnerships and joint ventures are considered at the end of this chapter.

2) The Legal Nature of Partnership

Provincial partnership laws[6] provide that a partnership exists any time there are

> … persons carrying on a business in common with a view to profit …[7]

As noted in Chapter 1, a partnership is like a sole proprietorship in that partners themselves carry on business directly; the partnership is not a legal entity separate from its partners. The chief consequence is that each partner is liable to the full extent of his personal assets for debts and other liabilities of the partnership business as provided in the partnership statutes.[8] A further consequence is that, in the absence of an

---

6   References to provincial partnership laws in this chapter mean those laws in the common law provinces.

7   *OPA*, above note 2, s. 2. The remainder of the definition reads as follows: "… but the relation between members of a company or association that is incorporated by or under the authority of any special or general Act in force in Ontario or elsewhere, or registered as a corporation under any such Act, is not a partnership within the meaning of this Act." See *BCPA*, above note 2, s. 2; and *NSPA*, above note 2, s. 4 to similar effect.

8   E.g., *OPA*, above note 2, ss. 10–13; *BCPA*, above note 2, ss. 11–15; and *NSPA*, above note 2, ss. 12–15.

agreement to the contrary, the continued existence of the partnership depends on the continuing participation of the partners who make it up.[9] Another is that a partner may not be an employee of the partnership business. Similarly, except in several discrete situations contemplated by statute, a partner cannot also be a creditor of the partnership. There is not a legal person, separate from the partner, with whom she may contract.[10] Nevertheless, there are several ways in which a partnership is treated as a collective entity.

- For the sake of convenience, a partnership is often called a "firm" and the name under which the partnership carries on business is called the firm name.[11]
- For income tax purposes, the income (or loss) from the partnership business is calculated at the firm level, adding up all the revenues of the partnership business and deducting all the related expenses. The partnership is not taxed as a separate entity on this income, however. It is allocated out to the partners in accordance with their entitlements under the partnership statute or the partnership agreement and must be included in their individual returns. The partner's share of the income or loss from the partnership business must be included even if all profits are reinvested in the business and no cash is actually paid to the partner.[12]
- Actions against a partnership may be commenced and must be defended using the firm name.[13] Any order made against a partner-

---

9   See the discussion of the dissolution of partnerships and partnership agreements in sections D and E of this chapter and *OPA*, *ibid.*, ss. 19, 26, 32, & 33. See *BCPA*, *ibid.*, ss. 20, 29, 35, 36 & 38; and *NSPA*, *ibid.*, ss. 21, 29, 35 & 36 to similar effect.

10   *Thorne* v. *New Brunswick (Workmen's Compensation Board)* (1962), 33 D.L.R. (2d) 167 (N.B.C.A.); *Craig Brothers* v. *Sisters of Charity*, [1940] 4 D.L.R. 561 (Sask. C.A.). Under the Quebec *Civil Code*, a partnership may be a separate legal person (Art. 2188 C.C.Q.). It is possible to structure the relationship of a partner to resemble that of an employee. A provision may be made for fixed periodic payments like wages to be paid to a partner, and the other partners may agree to indemnify this partner against any losses in the business. In such cases, it may be difficult to determine if the person is actually a partner or simply an employee being compensated out of profits. See section 3.3(b) of the *OPA*, *ibid.*, and Interpretation Bulletin No. IT-138R, "Computation and Flow-Through of Partnership Income" (29 January 1979), items 10 and 11, in which Revenue Canada indicates its acceptance, for tax purposes, of a partnership where one partner receives a fixed salary.

11   E.g., *OPA*, above note 2, s. 5; *BCPA*, above note 2, s. 1; and *NSPA*, above note 2, s. 7.

12   *Income Tax Act*, R.S.C. 1985 (5th supp.), c. 1, s. 96 [*ITA*].

13   In *Unical Properties* v. *784688 Ontario Ltd.* (1990), 75 O.R. (2d) 284 (Gen. Div.), an action in the name of a partnership against one of the partners was dismissed

ship may be enforced against the property of the partnership as well as against the property of any person who was served personally and either did not deny being a partner or was adjudged to be a partner.[14]

As will be discussed below, the possibility that partnership assets may be subject to creditors' claims means that a person who became a partner after an obligation of the partnership was incurred, but prior to enforcement of a judgment based on the obligation, could find that the value of his interest in the partnership is diminished as a result of the seizure of partnership property in satisfaction of the obligation. That a partner's interest may be affected as a consequence of an obligation incurred prior to his joining the partnership seems clearly inconsistent with the notion that the partnership is no more than the people who are the partners from time to time.[15]

It is important to recognize that this legal conception of the partnership as no more than the partners is typically quite different from the view that many business people have of the partnership. Often they will think of the business and its assets and liabilities as separate from their personal assets and liabilities.

The policy that the common law courts express for imposing unlimited liability on anyone found to be a partner is a fundamental principle of the law of agency: if a business is being carried on by someone (called the agent) on behalf of someone else (called the principal), the principal should be responsible for the obligations of the business. In accepting a commitment on behalf of the partnership, a third party should be able to rely on the personal creditworthiness of each person who is, or appears to be, carrying on the business and that is what the law provides.

The following example shows how the unlimited liability rule works and how it should affect a creditor's decision making. Assume that Jordan and Celine are the only partners in a law firm. The partnership has asked you to provide $100,000 worth of computer equipment on sixty days' credit, meaning that they will pay for it sixty days after you deliver it. You should base your decision to enter into that contract on the assets of the business *and* the personal assets of Jordan and Celine. To see why this is true, suppose that you provide the supplies but are not paid on time. If the business's assets are worth only $50,000, you could get a judgment against the partnership and seize

---

on the basis that the partnership was not a legal entity separate from the defendant partner.

14   E.g., Ontario Rules of Civil Procedure, O. Reg. 8.06.

15   See section C, "Liability of the Partnership to Third Parties" in this chapter.

those assets *and* seek the remaining money owed from Jordan and Celine personally. You could collect $25,000 from each, or $50,000 from either. If you choose the second option and collect $50,000 from Jordan, he is entitled to be indemnified to the extent of one-half ($25,000) from Celine, unless they had previously agreed to some other arrangement.

3) Definition of Partnership

a) General

One practical problem for business people and the lawyers who advise them is to know when a partnership relationship will be found to exist. Persons carrying on a business may be willing to accept the risk of unlimited liability associated with being a partner because of other benefits of the partnership form (such as the ability to deduct losses from the partnership business against income from other sources for tax purposes), or because they can manage the risk in some way (perhaps because they work in the business each day and can easily maintain control over what liabilities are created). Nevertheless, other persons involved with a business — lenders, for example — will want to avoid this risk and will not have arranged their affairs so they are either compensated for or protected against this risk. For such a person, being found to be a partner may have disastrous, unanticipated financial consequences. In the case law, the issue of whether a person is a partner usually arises where the partnership business has become insolvent and a creditor is looking for someone with assets to claim against. The creditor then argues that a particular person with assets should be liable for the obligations of the business because he is a partner. Lawyers need to be aware of the circumstances in which a partnership will be found to exist in order to ensure either that their clients do not inadvertently become involved in a relationship where they will be found to be a partner or that they take appropriate steps to manage the risk of being found a partner.[16]

The purpose of this section is to explain when a partnership relationship exists, by reference to the elements of the definition of partnership in provincial partnership statutes: two or more people carrying on business in common with a view to a profit.

"Carrying on a Business": Giving meaning to "carrying on a business" is the least difficult challenge in the definition. "[B]usiness" is

---

16   Risk-management strategies are discussed below in section A(3)(e) of this chapter ("Managing the Risk of Being Found a Partner").

defined as including "every trade, occupation and profession."[17] These broad, non-exhaustive words have been defined as encompassing any ongoing activity or even a single transaction.[18] In a recent English case, it was held that a restaurant business that never opened its doors was a partnership. Acquiring the real property for the restaurant premises, buying and taking delivery of the furniture, entering into a credit agreement to purchase a carpet, contracting for the laundry of table linen, and advertising the restaurant were found to consitute carrying on the restaurant business and the persons engaged in these activities were held to be partners.[19]

The idea of carrying on business together usually suggests the need for an enduring relationship, but even that factor may be inconclusive. There is probably no partnership if two competitors simply cooperate on an isolated transaction, as when a pair of software companies split the cost of a particular research project. The courts have said, however, that a partnership *may* arise even in relation to a single, time-limited activity.[20]

A business is less likely to be found a partnership if the people involved are merely passive investors, for example, if several people jointly own an apartment building and collect rent. The situation may be different, however, if co-ownership of real estate is combined with active participation in its management and sharing of profits.[21] In one case, the Supreme Court of Canada held that the receipt of rent under a number of equipment leases could constitute a business.[22] Although this case did not address the issue of whether a partnership existed, it was cited in a more recent Supreme Court decision as authority for the proposition that the passive receipt of rents could be a business satisfying the requirements for the existence of a partnership.[23]

"View to a Profit": The words "view to a profit" simply mean that the undertaking is not for the purpose of carrying out charitable, social, or cultural purposes. A partnership need have only a view to profit. There is no need actually to make profits. Two recent Supreme Court of

---

17 *OPA*, above note 2, s. 1. See *BCPA*, above note 2, s. 6; and *NSPA*, above note 2, s. 2 to similar effect.
18 *Thrush v. Read*, [1950] O.R. 276 (C.A.).
19 *Khan v. Miah*, [2001] 1 All E.R. 20 (H.L.).
20 *Spire Freezers Ltd. v. The Queen* (2001), 196 D.L.R. (4th) 210 (S.C.C.) [*Spire*].
21 *A.E. Lepage Ltd. v. Kamex Developments Ltd.* (1977), 16 O.R. 193 (C.A.), aff'd (*sub nom. A.E. LePage v. March*) [1979] 2 S.C.R. 155 [*A.E. Lepage*].
22 *Hickman Motors Ltd. v. The Queen* (1997), 148 D.L.R. (4th) 1 (S.C.C.).
23 *Spire*, above note 20.

Canada cases have clarified the requirement that investors must have a "view to a profit" for a partnership to come into existence.[24]

In *Spire Freezers Ltd.* v. *The Queen*, a partnership was established to develop a luxury condominium project and operate a low-rent apartment complex. Through a complex series of transactions, Spire Freezers Ltd. acquired a 50 percent interest in the partnership from Peninsula Cove Corporation, one of the original partners. In a subsequent transaction, the other original partner, BCE Developments Inc., sold its interest in the partnership to a number of other investors. It then bought the condominium development from the partnership for a price that created a $10,000,000 loss in the partnership.

Spire's main purpose in acquiring an interest in the partnership was to deduct its share of that loss against its other income and thereby reduce the income tax that it had to pay. Along with the other new investors, however, Spire continued to manage the apartment complex, which earned profits over a number of years, although not enough to offset the $10,000,000 loss. Revenue Canada refused to allow Spire to deduct the loss. It argued that Spire was not a partner because it was never carrying on a business "with a view to a profit."

The Supreme Court of Canada held that Spire was a partner and allowed the deduction. Even if Spire's main purpose was to deduct partnership losses, it also intended to carry on the business of the apartment complex. And even though the profits from that business were not sufficient to make up the $10,000,000 loss, that did not mean that the business was not being carried on with a view to a profit. The remaining business was not just "window dressing." Spire had an ownership interest in a substantial asset and performed significant management activity.

The Court reached the opposite conclusion in *Backman* v. *The Queen*. Again, a business invested in a partnership to take advantage of the deductibility of the partnership losses. In *Backman*, however, the remaining assets in the partnership were nominal and little management was required. The Supreme Court found that there was no partnership because there was no business being carried on with a view to a profit.

"In Common": These words mean that the putative partners are carrying on business together, based on some kind of agreement. The agreement may be written, oral, or implied. Whether an agreement exists is determined objectively, in the sense that persons may be characterized

---

24   *Spire, ibid.; Backman* v. *The Queen* (2001), 196 D.L.R. (4th) 193 (S.C.C.).

as partners without their knowledge[25] and even contrary to their express intention[26] so long as the court decides that the circumstances show the existence of an agreement. What the agreement must relate to is an intention to participate in a relationship that fits within the definition of partnership. As in other areas of law, whether the parties describe themselves as partners or not in their agreement is not conclusive. Nor is an express provision in a written agreement denying that the parties intended to be partners. Such provisions may help to clarify the intended effect of other clauses of the parties' agreement where such clauses are not clear, but, in every case, regard must be had to all the facts, including the rights and obligations created by the parties' agreement, their conduct, and any other relevant circumstances.[27]

Provincial partnership statutes set out some guidelines to assist in determining whether persons are carrying on a business together.[28] Common ownership of property does not make the co-owners partners (e.g., *OPA*, s. 3.1). Similarly, the sharing of gross returns, meaning business revenues without deduction of related expenses, does not create a partnership (e.g., *OPA*, s. 3.2). Since the old decision of *Waugh* v. *Carver*,[29] the principal indicia of carrying on a business in common has been whether profits were shared. This rule is set out in section 3.3 of the Ontario *Partnerships Act*:

> Receipt by a person of a share of the profits of a business is proof, in the absence of evidence to the contrary, that the person is a partner in the business, but the receipt of such a share or payment, contingent on or varying with the profits of a business, does not of itself make him or her a partner in the business[.]

Unsnarling the difficult construction of this provision does not yield a rebuttable presumption of partnership where sharing of profits is found. Section 3.3 does not say that sharing profits alone is conclusive that a person is a partner in the absence of evidence to the contrary, though it very nearly says so. Although something more is required, it is not clear what this is. In order to flesh out what is required, it is necessary to consider the case law.

---

25 *Robert Porter & Sons Ltd.* v. *Armstrong*, [1926] S.C.R. 328 [*Porter*].

26 *Weiner* v. *Harris* (1909), [1910] 1 K.B. 285 (C.A.).

27 *Adam* v. *Newbigging* (1888), 13 App. Cas. 308 (H.L.), at 315, Lord Halsbury; *Lansing Building Supply Ltd.* v. *Ierullo* (1990), 71 O.R. (2d) 173 (D.C.) [*Lansing*].

28 E.g., *OPA*, above note 2, s. 3; *BCPA*, above note 2, s. 4; and *NSPA*, above note 2, s. 5.

29 (1793), 2 Hy. Bl. 235, 126 E.R. 525 (C.P.).

In *Cox* v. *Hickman*[30] it was established that the fundamental characteristic of the relationship of partnership is mutual agency: a partnership exists where each person alleged to be in partnership carries on the business on behalf of the other alleged partners. The issue often arises in situations where there is a partnership, and the question is whether a particular person is a partner in the partnership. In such a case the test is whether the business is being conducted on behalf of that person. In this regard, one of the most important indicia of partnership is the sharing of profits (see figure 2.1).

Figure 2.1   Definition of Profits

Profits =	Revenues	less	expenses
	[all monies received in connection with the business]		[all monies paid to earn the revenue: e.g., for acquiring the goods or services sold; wages to employees, etc.]

The rationale for this focus on profits can be easily explained. If a person was to be compensated out of revenues, she would have a stake only in how much the business could sell. On the other hand, if a person is sharing profits, that person must also be concerned about how the business is managed, including, in particular, how expenses are managed. This stake in the effectiveness of management means that the sharing of profits is more suggestive of being in business together. Similarly, agreements to share losses as well as profits are strongly indicative of partnership, though partnership can exist even though the agreement between the parties contains a provision indemnifying one of them against losses from the business.

Prior to *Cox* v. *Hickman*, several cases, including the leading case of *Waugh* v. *Carver*, had held that sharing of profits was conclusive of partnership. The sharing of profits test was found to be too broad, however, because, in part, there are a variety of relationships in which profits may be shared but where it is not accurate to say that the parties are carrying on business together. An illustrative list of relationships that should not give rise to an inference of partnership even though there is sharing of profits is set out in section 3.3(a) to (e) of the Ontario *Partnerships Act*. A relationship is not that of partners carrying on business together but some other relationship in the following circumstances:

---

30   (1860), 8 H.L. Cas. 268.

- a lender receives repayment of a debt or some other fixed amount out of profits;
- an employee's remuneration varies with profits, such as under a profit-sharing plan;
- a lender's compensation is to be a share of profits or based on an interest rate varying with profits;
- a spouse or child of a deceased partner receives an annuity paid out of profits; and
- the purchaser of a business pays a share of profits of the business to the vendor as consideration for the sale of the business.[31]

This list identifies relationships that are not partnerships. It does not assist with the more difficult and fundamental question of whether any particular relationship is, in law, one of these relationships or a partnership. The following section deals only with what distinguishes partnerships from the first relationship in this list: that between a debtor and a creditor. Determining when a person is a partner as opposed to a creditor of a business has proven difficult, whereas distinguishing employment relationships, annuities paid to spouses or children of deceased partners, and vendor and purchaser relationships from partnerships has been relatively straightforward.

b) Debtor/Creditor Relationships

Both cases discussed in this section deal with claims by a creditor of an existing partnership against persons the creditor alleges are partners. In each case, the reason the creditor pursued the claim in this way is that the acknowledged partners were insolvent.

Cox v. Hickman provides an excellent example of a sharing of profits where a partnership relationship was not found to exist. It also illustrates the difficulty of drawing a clear distinction between creditors and partners in many situations. In this case, B. Smith & Sons, an ironworks business in financial difficulty, entered into an arrangement with its creditors under which the property of the business was transferred to certain trustees who were appointed by the creditors to operate the business. The debtors retained beneficial ownership in that, if and when all the debts were paid, they would receive anything left over. The creditors were given the right to make rules for the conduct of the business, and could choose to wind it up, that is, sell off all the assets and distribute the resulting proceeds. Profits earned were paid to the creditors. Several creditors, including Cox and Wheatcroft, were

---

31   See similarly *BCPA*, above note 2, s. 4; and *NSPA*, above note 2, s. 5.

appointed trustees. While the business was being operated by the trustees, it became indebted to Hickman. Hickman sued Cox and Wheatcroft alleging that they, along with the other creditors, were partners in a partnership carrying on the ironworks business.

The House of Lords held that Cox and Wheatcroft were not partners. The basis of the decision was that the sharing of profits, in this case, was not sufficient for a finding of partnership. To find a partnership involving Cox and Wheatcroft, the business had to be carried on for the benefit of Cox and Wheatcroft as principals. Here the true relationship was debtor and creditor. The trustees were held to be carrying on the business on behalf of the debtors. The debtors received the benefit of the profits but had agreed to have the profits applied for the exclusive purpose of paying off their creditors. Some of the judges in the Court of Appeal[32] had agreed that the true basis of partnership was not simply sharing of profits. But they nevertheless found Cox and Wheatcroft to be partners, because they characterized the facts differently. On the basis of the extensive involvement of the creditors in the business, including their access to the books and their ability to control who were the trustees and to make rules for the business, these judges determined that the business was being carried on for the benefit of the creditors, and so they should be considered partners.

This case shows that, even accepting the agency basis of partnership, it will often be difficult, on particular facts, to determine if a partnership exists or, given the existence of a partnership, if certain persons are partners in it. It also raises the question of the relevance of the involvement of an alleged partner in the partnership business to a determination of partnership. The discussion of *Pooley* v. *Driver*[33] illustrates how the rights belonging to a person alleged to be involved in and even to control the partnership business, as well as the behaviour of an alleged partner in connection with the business, are relevant to determining whether she is a partner.

In *Pooley* v. *Driver*, Borrett and Hagan were partners carrying on a grease, pitch, and manure business. They entered into a partnership agreement that provided, among other things, that the "capital"[34] of the partnership would be split between Borrett and Hagan and persons "advancing money by way of loan" (referred to here as the "Lenders");

---

32 In the English judicial hierarchy, the House of Lords hears appeals from decisions of the Court of Appeal.

33 (1876), 5 Ch. D. 458 [*Pooley*].

34 "Capital" is a slippery term whose meaning may vary depending on the context in which it is used. Often it refers to the total amount contributed to a business by owners and lenders. See the definition in the glossary.

and that profits from the partnership business were to be paid out to Borrett, Hagan, and the Lenders in accordance with their interests in the capital. In the partnership agreement, Borrett and Hagan promised to do the following:

- to carry on the business to the best of their ability;
- not to distribute the property of the business to the partners;
- to prepare annual accounts;
- to have a valuation of the business done every year;
- not to borrow or hire employees without the consent of the other partners; and
- not to permit assets of the business to be seized by creditors to satisfy the debts of the business.

Under the agreement, within six months of the termination of the partnership, the amounts owed to all the creditors of the business would be determined and the creditors paid. Then the partnership would repay the money advanced by the Lenders, less any amount needed to satisfy the creditors. The Lenders could be asked to repay profits paid out to them if this was necessary to pay off the creditors. In addition, the Lenders were supposed to enter into a loan or "contributorship" agreement that repeated many of the provisions of the partnership agreement and also provided as follows:

- The covenants in the partnership agreement were incorporated in the loan agreement and so were enforceable by the Lenders. These covenants included a right to compel Borrett and Hagan to use the invested capital in carrying on the business of the partnership.
- Each Lender's entitlement to profits would be determined annually, based not just on the profits made but also on the amount invested by all Lenders in aggregate. For example, if Lenders bought all twenty units available to them out of the sixty units of capital in the partnership, each unit would have an entitlement to one-sixtieth of the profits. If only ten were purchased, each unit would have an entitlement to one-fiftieth of profits.
- The bankruptcy of a Lender meant that the Lender's relationship with the partnership was terminated, subject only to an obligation of the partnership to repay the amount the Lender had invested.
- Repayment of Lenders' investments was to come out of the assets of the partnership.

The term of both the partnership agreement and the loan agreement was fourteen years.

This rather complex relationship was expressly designed to ensure that the Lenders were not found to be partners. The English law at the time contained a provision virtually identical to section 3.3(d) of the Ontario *Partnerships Act*. Section 3.3(d) provides as follows:

> [T]he advance of money by way of a loan to a person engaged or about to engage in a business on a contract with that person that the lender is to receive a rate of interest varying with the profits, or is to receive a share of the profits arising from carrying on the business, does not of itself make the lender a partner with the person or persons carrying on the business or liable as such, provided that the contract is in writing and signed by or on behalf of all parties thereto[.]

By identifying the Lenders as persons "advancing money by way of loan" and giving them a return that depended on the profits of the partnership, Borrett and Hagan sought to fit the Lenders within this provision. In looking at the whole relationship between the Lenders and the partnership as described in the partnership and loan agreements, however, the court concluded that the Lenders were partners.

In support of this conclusion, the court made the following points:

- The fact that the alleged partners had an interest in capital just like the interest of the acknowledged partners, Borrett and Hagan, is indicative of an ownership interest in the business rather than a creditor's claim against the business.
- The Lender's ability to enforce the covenants of the partnership agreement gives them a degree of participation and control that would be unusual for lenders, though not for partners.
- Having the return on the Lender's investment vary with the aggregate amount invested in the business is highly unusual for a lender, but not for a partner.
- The provision terminating the relationship of any Lender who goes bankrupt might not be unusual for a partnership in which the solvent partners would not want the trustee in bankruptcy of the bankrupt partner succeeding to the rights of a partner, but would be highly unusual for a lender.
- It would be highly unusual for a lender to be required to pay back all profits received as well as its original investment if there were insufficient partnership assets otherwise to pay off all other creditors. Such an obligation is more like partnership liability.
- Coincidence of the loan and partnership terms suggests that the Lenders were partners.

The court's analysis also demonstrates the very limited operational effect of paragraphs (a) to (e) of section 3.3 of the Ontario *Partnerships Act* and similar provisions under other provincial laws. The court made it clear that these provisions are examples only of relationships that are not partnerships. In every case, the court must decide if, based on all the circumstances, the most accurate characterization of the relationship is one of partnership or some other relationship. In this case, the court had to decide if the relationship was partnership or that of debtor and creditor. That the return to the alleged partner is dependent on profits, as described in section 3.3(d), does not, in any way, mean that the relationship is therefore deemed not to be a partnership. It simply means that the sharing of profits in these circumstances does not, by itself, give rise to a presumption of partnership. Indeed, the court went on to say that it was not sure that provisions like section 3.3(d) have any effect. For section 3.3(d) to apply, the court must determine that there has been "an advance by way of loan." But this requires that a determination be made that the relationship is one of debtor and creditor, and not partnership. Once such a determination has been made there is no need to rely on section 3.3(d).[35]

This discussion of the *Cox* and *Pooley* cases reveals that there are various factors that a court will take into account in determining whether any given relationship is a partnership or a debtor and creditor relationship. None is conclusive.[36] Some of these factors have been relied on in other contexts to determine if a partnership exists, such as where the parties own property together. The following section discusses cases dealing with co-ownership relationships.

c) Co-ownership
Section 3.1 of the Ontario *Partnerships Act* provides that holding property in some form of common ownership does not, of itself, create a partnership in relation to the property, even if the co-owners share profits made from the use of the property.[37] Co-ownership may arise in

---

35 In light of this conclusion, it is perhaps surprising that if one does have a relationship falling within section 3.3(d), section 4 of the *OPA*, above note 2, provides that repayment of such a lender is postponed until all other creditors have been paid in the event that the business becomes insolvent. See similar provisions in *BCPA*, above note 2, s. 5; and *NSPA*, above note 2, s. 6.

36 See other cases in which a loan repaid out of profits has been combined with some control over the business and no partnership found: *Mollwo, March & Co. v. Court of Wards* (1872), L.R. 4 P.C. 419 (no profits received); *Re Young, ex p. Jones*, [1896] 2 Q.B. 484; *Canada Deposit Insurance Corp. v. Canadian Commercial Bank*, [1992] 3 S.C.R. 558 (repayment out of profits held not equivalent to sharing profits).

37 See similar provisions in other provincial statures such as *BCPA*, above note 2, s. 4; and *NSPA*, above note 2, s. 5.

a variety of circumstances where the relationship would not be considered a partnership. For example, co-ownership may arise by operation of law, such as on the passing of title to a piece of real estate from one person to several on the owner's death. In such a case, the new co-owners may not even be aware that they had become co-owners. They would have no intention of carrying on business in common with a view to a profit and so would not be partners.

Being able to distinguish relationships that are partnerships from those involving only co-ownership is important because co-ownership relationships have different legal consequences. Unlike partners, co-owners are not agents of each other. One co-owner is at liberty to deal with his interest in the common property as his own without the consent of the others. As will be discussed below, the ability of a partner to transfer her interest in the partnership is limited. In the absence of the agreement of all partners, a partner cannot transfer her interest, though she can transfer her right to receive profits. Also, in a partnership, the firm's property is to be held jointly as an asset of the business. No partner has the right to deal with the property separately. The partner's right is to a division of profits, not to any particular property of the partnership business.[38]

Where, in addition to co-owning property, the co-owners share profits from the use of the property, the relationship approaches a partnership, but there must be something more than simply owning property and sharing the profits from it to create a partnership; some management or other business activity must exist. How much activity is required, however, is elusive. The mere fact that co-owners intend to acquire, hold, and sell property does not make them partners. One way of formulating the question to ask is, was "the intention of the co-owners . . . 'to carry on a business' or simply to provide by an agreement for the regulation of their rights and obligations as co-owners of a property"?[39]

Several cases have addressed the circumstances in which a partnership may be found to exist where there is co-ownership. In *A.E. LePage Ltd.* v. *Kamex Developments*,[40] for example, the co-owners of some real

---

38   Partners have no right in partnership property *in specie* (i.e., in its existing form), nor to compel the sale of partnership property while the partnership exists. Upon dissolution, however, a partner has the right to have the partnership property sold and the proceeds divided: *Porter*, above note 25, at 330. For a more complete review of the differences between co-ownership and partnership, see E.H. Scammell & R.C. Banks, eds., *Lindley and Banks on the Law of Partnership*, 18th ed. (London: Sweet & Maxwell, 2002), at 75–78.

39   *A.E. LePage*, above note 21, at 195 (C.A.).

40   *Ibid.*

property were held not to be partners, even though, in addition to co-ownership, the parties had put in place the following arrangements:

- profits were to be paid to each co-owner in proportion to her interest and each was liable to pay any deficiency in the same proportions;
- no co-owner could sell her interest without offering it first to the other co-owners (a "right of first refusal"); and
- any sale or other dealing with the property required approval by majority vote of the co-owners.

The court held that the ability of the co-owners to deal with their individual interests separately was incompatible with an intention that the property become part of a partnership, since partners have no right to do so. The right of first refusal was not considered to be inconsistent with the co-owners' basic right to deal with their respective interests. The co-owners' intention to keep their property separate was confirmed by their individual treatment of their respective interests for income tax purposes. They made individual decisions regarding whether to deduct the capital cost allowance (CCA)[41] relating to the property against their personal income. Because the court did not find the co-owners to be partners, the action by one of them who purported to enter an exclusive listing agreement for the sale of the property without the authorization of the others was not binding on the co-owners.

Where, in addition to co-ownership and sharing profits, there is substantial participation in the activities associated with the management of the co-owned property, a partnership will likely be found. While it is clear that a person need not have any control over management in order to be found a partner,[42] it is difficult to be precise regarding how much activity is required to be added to co-ownership in order to create a partnership. Use of a common bank account, an agreement to share the costs of developing the business, and common participation in financing the business and in dealing with tenants' concerns were all held to be indicative of a partnership between co-owners of a shopping centre in *Volzke Construction* v. *Westlock Foods Ltd.*[43] Practically speaking, determining when a partnership will be found in real estate co-ownership cases is challenging since, in almost all real estate holdings, some management will be required.

---

41 Capital-cost allowance is the equivalent of depreciation for income tax purposes. See the examples of capital-cost allowance deduction at the end of this chapter.
42 *Volzke Construction* v. *Westlock Foods Ltd.* (1986), 70 A.R. 300 (C.A.).
43 *Ibid.* In this case, a contributing factor to the finding of partnership was a finding in another proceeding that the parties were partners.

d) Agreeing to be a Partner

In the cases considered so far, the courts dealt with claims against persons who wanted to avoid the liabilities arising out of being found a partner. In *W. v. M.N.R.*,[44] the court considered a claim by some widows and daughters of deceased lawyers that they were partners in a law firm partnership. The widows and daughters of the deceased did not contribute or participate in the business of the firm in any way. Revenue Canada had challenged the status of the widows and daughters as partners because it objected to the taxation of the partnership profits in the hands of the widows and daughters. In its view, the partners working in the business, who were paying tax at a higher marginal rate, should have been liable for the tax. The court held that it was sufficient for a finding of partnership that the widows and daughters had entered into an agreement in which they were identified as partners and they acknowledged, albeit not in the operative part of the agreement but in a recital, that they were liable for losses as well as entitled to receive profits. The court also noted that they had acted in accordance with the agreement.[45] Accordingly, Revenue Canada's challenge was defeated.

In order for an agreement to be effective in creating a partnership, it must extend to all the essential elements of a partnership. In a dispute between two business people, one alleged that there was a partnership between them. The court found that there was no partnership because the alleged partners had not agreed on the date the partnership business was to be commenced, or the contribution of one of the putative partners. The court reached this conclusion even though there was evidence that the parties considered themselves partners and had acted as such.[46]

---

44   [1952] Ex.C.R. 416.

45   This case is also noteworthy because it shows that, in general, the court will apply the principles of partnership law to determine the appropriate tax treatment of a particular relationship (see Interpretation Bulletin IT-90), "What Is a Partnership?" (17 February 1973). The possibility of allocating partnership income to persons who do not participate in the partnership business has been expressly eliminated by amendment to the *ITA*, above note 12. Now, under section 103(1.1) of the *ITA*, where partners do not deal at arm's length, the allocation of income must be reasonable, having regard to the capital invested in or work performed for the partnership by the partners or other relevant factors. This has no effect on whether, as a matter of partnership law, there is a partnership. In *Schettler v. M.N.R.* ((1994), 7 C.C.E.L. (2d) 213 (T.C.C.)), it was held that the absence of any effective control means that a person is unlikely to be found a partner. See to similar effect A.R. Manzer, *A Practical Guide to Canadian Partnership Law* (Aurora: Canada Law Book, 1995) (looseleaf) [*Manzer*], at 2-23.

46   *Surerus Construction and Development Ltd. v. Rudiger* (2000), 11 B.L.R. (3d) 21 (B.C.S.C.).

Figure 2.2   Some Factors Suggesting a Partnership Relationship

- Sharing profits
- Sharing responsibility for losses, including guaranteeing partnership debts
- Jointly owning property
- Controlling the partnership business
- Participating in management
- Stating an intention to form partnership in contract
- Making government filings showing partnership (e.g., registration under business names legislation, tax returns)
- Having access to information regarding the business
- Having signing authority for contracts, bank accounts
- Holding oneself out as a partner
- Contributing money, services, or property as capital (especially if contribution is complementary to the contribution of others for the purpose of running a business)
- Full-time involvement in the business
- Use of a firm name, perhaps in advertising
- Firm having its own personnel and address

e) Managing the Risk of Being Found a Partner

The foregoing survey of partnership case law illustrates an important aspect of partnership law: the difficulty of defining precisely the circumstances in which a partnership may be found to exist. This has important implications for lawyers advising their clients. If a client wants to avoid being a partner, the lawyer will have to give careful consideration to the relationship her client intends to enter to see if there is a risk of a partnership being found based on the extent to which the factors discussed above are present, especially the sharing of profits. If there is a risk of partnership being found, a client must be advised to take whatever steps are available to avoid this consequence. These include contractual provisions stating the nature of the relationship[47] and structural changes to the relationship itself, taking into account the factors discussed. Steps may also be taken to minimize the consequences of being found a partner, such as holding the partnership interest in a corporation and creating indemnification provisions in the

---

47   Though, of course, stating that the parties are not partners will not be enough in itself (*I.R.C. v. Williamson* (1928), 14 T.C. 335 (Ct. Sess., Scot.) at 340); *Dickenson v. Gross (Inspector of Taxes)* (1927), 11 T.C. 614 (K.B.); *Lansing*, above note 27. Regard must be had to what is done under the agreement.

agreement establishing the relationship.[48] Finally, the client will need to consider if he is being appropriately compensated for any residual risk of partnership liability.

B. THE RELATIONSHIP OF PARTNERS TO EACH OTHER

1) General

In most cases, the relations of partners to each other will be specified in their partnership agreement. Like other provincial statutes, the Ontario *Partnerships Act* (ss. 20–31) provides a set of default rules to govern the parties' relations to the extent that they have not been addressed by agreement.[49] These provisions have been created by statute as a sort of standard-form contract to make it easier to set up a business as a partnership by reducing the need for the parties to create a set of rules from scratch. The rules operate only in default of agreement because different partnerships will need different rules. The flexibility in possible internal structures afforded by the use of default rules is one of the major advantages of partnerships. The value of the default rules will depend on how closely they approximate what prospective partners will want. Unfortunately, the partnership legislation in most provinces has never been amended significantly and does not respond to the needs of modern partnerships. This section describes the framework of default rules in provincial legislation. In section E ("Partnership Agreements") below, the kinds of changes often made to these rules will be discussed. Finally, the remainder of this section describes the fiduciary duty each partner owes to his fellow partners as well as the nature of a partner's interest in partnership property.

2) Default Rules

The default rules governing partners' relations are based on certain presumptions about the nature of partnership. The archetypal partnership contemplated by the Ontario *Partnerships Act* and other provincial statutes is one in which there are a small number of partners all of whom are equal, both in terms of their financial interest in the partner-

---

48   These strategies will be discussed in section E in this chapter ("Partnership Agreements").

49   See similar provisions in *BCPA*, above note 2, ss. 21-34; and *NSPA*, above note 2, ss. 22–34.

ship and in terms of their rights to participate in the business of the partnership. In practice, such equality rarely occurs. Typically, partners make unequal contributions of capital and services to the business. Each partner's interest in the partnership and the returns each partner expects on her contributions tend to vary accordingly. Also, in all but the smallest partnerships, the partners will delegate certain management functions to particular partners or committees of partners because the participation of all partners in all decisions will be unduly cumbersome. Because there are likely to be significant differences between what partnership legislation provides in its default rules and what the parties' expectations and intentions are, these provisions can be a trap for the unwary. It is essential to know what the default rules are and to ensure that they are changed by agreement where appropriate. The most important default rules are set out in figure 2.3.

Figure 2.3   Default Rules in the Ontario *Partnerships Act*

- Each partner shares equally, both in the capital of the partnership and in any profits distributed, and must contribute equally to any losses incurred (s. 24.1).
- Each partner is entitled to be indemnified in respect of payments made or liabilities incurred in the ordinary course of the partnership business, or to preserve the business or property of the firm (s. 24.2).
- A partner is not entitled to interest on capital contributed (s. 24.4).
- If a partner makes a contribution to the partnership in excess of the amount that he has agreed to contribute, he is entitled to interest at 5 percent per year on the excess contribution (s. 24.3).
- Each partner has a right to participate in the management of the partnership business (s. 24.5).
- Decisions regarding ordinary matters connected with the partnership business may be decided by a majority of the partners (s. 24.8).
- Each partner has equal access to the partnership books (s. 24.9).
- Admission of a new partner (s. 24.7) and any change in the nature of the partnership business (s. 24.8) require unanimous consent.
- No majority of partners may expel a partner (s. 25).
- Any person who takes an assignment of a partner's interest, whether as a purported transfer or for the purposes of taking security for the performance of some obligation of the partner, has no rights as a partner, except to receive the share of the partnership profits to which the assigning partner would otherwise be entitled (s. 31).
- Any partner may terminate the partnership by giving notice to the others (ss. 26 & 32).
- Any variation of the default rules requires unanimous consent (s. 20).

3) Fiduciary Duty

In addition to the default rules described in the previous section, partners owe each other a fiduciary duty: they must deal with the partnership and with their partners in the utmost good faith. Partners must never put their personal interests ahead of the interests of the partnership. Although there is no general expression of this duty in the Ontario *Partnerships Act*, it is well established in the common law that the fiduciary duty is a guiding principle of partnership law.[50] Such a duty is expressly provided for in other provincial partnership statutes.[51]

There are several provisions in the Ontario *Partnerships Act* which create specific obligations consistent with this general duty. Each partner is obliged to render to each other partner "true accounts and full information" regarding all matters affecting the partnership (*OPA*, s. 28). It has been held that each partner has a right to access documents prepared by and for the partnership.[52] Each partner must also account to the partnership for certain benefits obtained without the consent of the other partners. These benefits include those derived by the partner from "any transaction concerning the partnership or from any use by the partner of the partnership property, name or business connection" (*OPA*, s. 29(1)), and any profits made by competing with the partnership business (*OPA*, s. 30).[53]

The precise content of the fiduciary duty depends on the facts. Consequently, some examples may be of assistance. In *Rochwerg* v. *Truster*,[54] a partner in a firm of accountants became a director of one of the firm's clients. He also purchased 8000 common shares in the client for what was a fair price at the time and acquired options to purchase an additional 24,000 common shares for a nominal price. The partner disclosed the directorship to his partners and paid the director's fees he received to the partnership. He did not disclose his investment because he believed that it was a private transaction. Ultimately, the Ontario Court of Appeal decided that his duty under section 28 required him

---

50   For example, *Hitchcock* v. *Sykes* (1914), 49 S.C.R. 403 at 407.

51   Section 22(1) of the *BCPA*, above note 2, expresses a general duty in the following terms: "[A] partner must act with the utmost fairness and good faith towards the other members of the firm in the business of the firm."

52   *Dockrill* v. *Coopers & Lybrand Chartered Accountants* (1994), 129 N.S.R. (2d) 166 (C.A.).

53   These provisions in the Ontario Act also appear in other provincial partnership statutes, such as the *BCPA*, above note 2, ss. 31–33; and the *NSPA*, above note 2, ss. 31–33.

54   (2002), 58 O.R. (3d) 687 (C.A.).

to have disclosed the investment because it affected the partnership. He was required to account for the profits he made from the shares and options because they were a benefit derived from the partnership business connection for the purposes of section 29.

In *Mohammadamin* v. *Zameni*,[55] a partner's non-competition obligation was held to extend beyond the termination of the partnership. Zameni sold his interest in the partnership's auto parts business and then set up a competing business nearby. The court found that this was a breach of his fiduciary duty not to damage the goodwill of the partnership.[56]

In *Olson* v. *Gullo*,[57] it was held that the profits received by one partner who sold part of the real property owned by the partnership had to be paid over to the partnership based on section 29(1) as well as common law principles of fiduciary duty. One of the difficult features of cases like this is that the partner in breach of his duty receives a benefit from the breach because, as a partner, he shares in the profits when they are paid over to the partnership.

By agreement, partners may exclude certain activities from the full operation of the fiduciary duty. For example, partners may agree that one of them may carry on a business similar to that carried on by the partnership, but in another city, without having an obligation to account for the profits she makes from the business. Such an agreement would prevent arguments with respect to whether the individual partner's business was appropriating opportunities that should belong to the partnership or was competing with the partnership.

4) Partnership Property

Partnership property consists of all property contributed to the partnership as well as all property acquired on its behalf or for the purpose and in the course of the partnership business.[58] In particular, where property is bought with money belonging to the partnership, it is deemed, in the absence of evidence to the contrary, to have been

---

55 (2000), 3 B.L.R. (3d) 140 (Ont. Sup. Ct. J.) [*Mohammadamin*].

56 *Prothroe* v. *Adams* (1997), 33 B.L.R. (2d) 149 (Alta. Q.B.) sets out some of the limitations on the scope of the fiduciary duty.

57 (1994), 17 O.R. (3d) 790 (C.A.). *Lafrentz* v. *M & L Leasing Limited Partnership* (2000), 8 B.L.R. (3d) 219 (Alta. Q.B.) is another case on indemnification of partners.

58 This is expressly provided in some partnership statutes (e.g., *OPA*, above note 2, s. 21(1); and *NSPA*, above note 2, s. 23(1)) but not in others (e.g., *BCPA*, above note 2; and *APA*, above note 2).

bought on behalf of the partnership.[59] Where property is treated as partnership property, it becomes partnership property even if title is retained by an individual partner. Once property becomes partnership property, it must be held and used exclusively for the purposes of the partnership and in accordance with the terms of the partnership agreement.[60] A partner loses his individual beneficial interest in property contributed to a partnership. If, for example, a partner agreed to use a car he owned to carry on the partnership business, it would become partnership property. He could not sell the car without the consent of his partners, even though he remained the legal owner.

The rules with respect to what is partnership property and what can be done with it may be changed by agreement. Where partners intend to continue to have a personal interest in property used in the partnership or acquired with partnership money, it is important to ensure that there is a clear, written understanding as to the partner's individual interest.

C. LIABILITY OF THE PARTNERSHIP TO THIRD PARTIES

1) Basic Rules

Unlike the default rules governing the internal relations of partners, the rules governing the relationships between partnerships and third parties are mandatory in the interests of ensuring that persons dealing with partnerships are protected.[61] In general, all partners are liable for all liabilities of the partnership.[62] Who is a partner is an issue that has frequently been the subject of litigation. As evidenced by the cases discussed in section A ("What Is a Partnership?"), typically the litiga-

---

59   *OPA, ibid.,* s. 22; *BCPA, ibid.,* s. 24; and *NSPA, ibid.,* s. 24.

60   *OPA, ibid.,* s. 21(1); *BCPA, ibid.,* s. 23(1); and *NSPA, ibid.,* s. 23(1). Partnership property is treated as personal property (*OPA, ibid.,* s. 23; *BCPA, ibid.,* s. 25; and *NSPA, ibid.,* s. 25.).

61   Nevertheless, provisions that address the risks associated with liabilities to third parties may be included in the partnership agreement. These provisions include internal monitoring and control mechanisms to reduce the likelihood of unauthorized liabilities and arrangements to allocate risk among partners. See section E ("Partnership Agreements"), in this chapter.

62   Under the Quebec *Civil Code,* a partner in an undeclared partnership becomes liable only if the third party knows that the person is acting as a partner (Art. 2253 C.C.Q.).

tion is initiated by an unpaid creditor when the partnership, if there is one, or the business otherwise being carried on is insolvent. As a way of seeking to have its claim paid, the creditor will argue that a person with assets is a partner. The main subject of this section, however, is how persons who are partners in a partnership become liable to third parties.

Partnerships become liable in contract when, based on principles of agency, someone who is an agent of the firm enters into a contract on its behalf. Under the Ontario *Partnerships Act* and other provincial statutes,[63] each partner is constituted an agent of the firm. Section 6 provides that the acts of a partner for carrying on the business of the firm in the usual way bind the firm. The rule does not apply where the partner in fact has no authority and the person with whom the partner is dealing either knows that the partner has no authority or does not know or believe her to be a partner.[64] There is no partnership liability for acts outside the usual scope of the partnership business. What is the usual scope of the business will depend on the nature of the business activity in which the partnership is actually engaged.

A partnership is liable for the torts of its agents or employees, based on general principles of tort law. Liability arises where the partnership authorized the tort or ratified it after it was committed, or where the tort was committed by the agent or employee in the course of his duties. Where any tort liability is established, the firm is liable for all damages to the same extent as the partner herself.[65]

Partners may even be liable for fraudulent acts of their partners. In *Ernst & Young Inc. v. Falconi*,[66] the estate of a partner in a law firm was held liable for the acts of another partner in assisting clients who were bankrupt to make fraudulent dispositions of their property contrary to the *Bankruptcy Act*. The fraudulent activity was held to be in the ordinary course of the law firm's business. The court said that the test is "whether the unlawful acts are of the sort that would be within the

---

63 E.g., *BCPA*, above note 2, s. 7; and *NSPA*, above note 2, s. 8.

64 See *OPA*, above note 2, s. 9; *BCPA*, ibid., s. 10; and *NSPA*, ibid., s. 11.

65 *OPA*, ibid., s. 11; *BCPA*, ibid., s. 11; and *NSPA*, ibid., s. 12. Section 12 of the *OPA*, s. 13 of the *BCPA*, and s. 14 of the *NSPA*, specifically impose liability on the firm for certain misapplications of funds received from a third party by a partner or by the firm. In *General Electric Capital Canada Inc. v. Deloitte & Touche*, [2002] O.J. No. 4368 (QL) (Sup. Ct. J.), aff'd [2003] O.J. No. 370 (Div. Ct.), the court refused to strike out a claim against the partners and the partnership arising out of the same facts. It concluded that the issue of when a partner who was acting in the course of the firm's business was directly personally liable along with the firm for negligence was unsettled.

66 (1994), 17 O.R. (3d) 512 (Gen. Div.).

scope of the partnership if done for legitimate, as opposed to illegitimate, purposes as seen from the perspective of the overall business of the partnership."[67] It was sufficient that the partner used the assets and facilities of the law firm to perform services normally performed by a law firm in carrying out the transactions as a result of which the creditors of the firm's clients suffered loss.[68]

A similar conclusion was reached recently in *Dubai Aluminium Co. Ltd. v. Salaam.*[69] The English House of Lords held that a law firm partnership was liable for the dishonest acts of one of the partners. To assist some clients of the firm to accomplish a fraud, the partner gave them advice and prepared documents for them. The Court of Appeal determined that the partnership should not be held liable since the firm had not authorized the activities of the partner. The court stated that it was not part of the business of the firm to plan, draft, and sign sham agreements to give effect to a dishonest scheme. On appeal, the House of Lords determined that the question was not whether the dishonest conduct was specifically authorized by the firm, but rather whether the partner was authorized to engage in conduct of the same kind as the dishonest conduct. So long as the dishonest conduct was sufficiently closely connected to acts that the partner was authorized to engage in, the conduct may be regarded as done in the course of the business of the firm. On the facts in this case, the House of Lords found that this test was met.

The time at which the liability arises is critical for determining who is responsible for it. In general, partners are liable only for obligations incurred while they were partners in the firm. All obligations of the firm are obligations of every partner who was a member of the firm at the time the obligation arose.[70] It does not matter whether any partner sought to

---

67   *Ibid.*, at 516–17.

68   *Ernst & Young Inc. v. Falconi* was cited as a correct application of the law by the Ontario Court of Appeal in *McDonic v. Heatherington* (1997), 31 O.R. (3d) 577 (C.A.)(leave to appeal to Supreme Court of Canada dismissed).

69   [2003] 1 All E.R. 97 (H.L.), rev'g (2000), 3 W.L.R. 910 (C.A.).

70   Liability of individual partners for torts under *OPA*, above note 2, section 11 is joint and several pursuant to section 13, while liability for "debts and obligations of the firm" is only joint under section 10. The distinctions between these two kinds of liability have been all but eliminated under modern rules of civil procedure. The original common law rule was that, where liability was only joint, a creditor of a partnership who obtained a judgment against one partner would not be able to take action against any other partner, even if he was unable to recover the judgment amount from the partner he originally sued (*Kendall v. Hamilton* (1879), 4 App. Cas. 504 (H.L.)). If liability was joint and several, the creditor would not lose her rights against the other partners. This rule has been abolished in Ontario by section 139(1) of the *Courts of Justice Act* (R.S.O. 1990, c. C-43).

be held liable by a third party actually approved the obligation entered into.[71] A partner is liable even though she may have a right to be indemnified, in whole or in part, by the partner who incurred the obligation for the firm. Indemnification where a partner has paid a partnership obligation is provided for in the Ontario *Partnerships Act* and other partnerships laws,[72] and is often dealt with specifically in partnership agreements.[73] Liability for obligations of the firm continues after the partner leaves the firm (*OPA*, s. 18(2))[74] and binds her estate (*OPA*, s. 10).[75]

A partner is not responsible for liabilities of the firm which arose prior to his becoming a partner (*OPA*, s. 18).[76] An effective exception to this rule arises where partnership assets are seized by a creditor after a person becomes a partner in satisfaction of an obligation to the creditor which arose prior to that person joining the partnership. Figure 2.4 provides an example. As mentioned above, such proceedings are

Figure 2.4   Example of Effect of Pre-partnership Liability

In 1997 ABC partnership incurred a debt of $5,000 to a supplier which it did not pay. The supplier sued the partnership in 1997. X joined ABC partnership in 1998, paying $10,000 for a 10 percent interest in the partnership. The $10,000 was invested in acquiring assets for use in the partnership business.

In 1999 the supplier obtained judgment against the partnership and obtained an order of seizure and sale against the partnership. Certain assets were sold and the proceeds used to pay the supplier's judgment. Even though the obligation to the supplier was incurred prior to X joining the partnership, and X was not responsible for it, the value of X's interest in the partnership has been diminished as a result of satisfying the judgment resulting from the debt.

Also, as noted above, it is possible under the Ontario Rules of Civil Procedure to sue a firm using the firm name (R. 8.01). A creditor who obtains an order against a partnership in such an action may apply to the court for leave to enforce it against any partner who has not previously been an individual party to the suit.

71   For an example of the imposition of liability on a lawyer for breaches by his partner of his fiduciary duty and duty as a solicitor, where the lawyer did not participate in the wrongful activity, see *Korz v. St. Pierre* (1987), 61 O.R. (2d) 609 (C.A.). See also *Bet-Mur Investments Ltd. v. Spring* (1994), 20 O.R. (3d) 417 (Gen. Div.) [*Bet-Mur*].

72   *OPA*, above note 2, s. 24; *BCPA*, above note 2, s. 27; and *NSPA*, above note 2, s. 27.

73   See section E ("Partnership Agreements"), in this chapter.

74   *BCPA*, above note 2, s. 19(2); and *NSPA*, above note 2, s. 20(2).

75   *BCPA*, *ibid.*, s. 11; and *NSPA*, *ibid.*, s. 12.

76   *BCPA*, *ibid.*, s. 19(1); and *NSPA*, *ibid.*, s. 20(1).

expressly permitted by the Ontario Rules of Civil Procedure. Except as discussed below, a partner is not liable for obligations of the partnership incurred after she leaves (see figure 2.5).

2) Holding Out

A person may be held liable for obligations of a partnership even though he was never a partner or was not a partner at the time the partnership incurred the obligation, if he was held out as a partner. Section 15 of the Ontario *Partnerships Act* imposes liability on persons held out as partners:

> Every person, who by words spoken or written or by conduct represents himself or herself or who knowingly suffers himself or herself to be represented as a partner in a particular firm, is liable as a partner to any person who has on the faith of any such representation, given credit to the firm, whether the representation has or has not been made or communicated to the persons so giving credit by or with the knowledge of the apparent partner making the representation or suffering it to be made.[77]

Examples of representations that may give rise to liability under this provision include use of a person's name in the firm name, on a sign at the premises of the firm, or on the firm's invoices or letterhead. An essential element of the holding out is that the person held out must knowingly permit it. It is not sufficient, for example, if the person was negligent or careless by failing to ensure that she was not held out as a partner.[78] It should be noted also that the person held out does not have to know that the holding out was to the particular person who advanced credit to the firm. Knowledge of a general holding out, such as in advertising, is sufficient.

To establish liability based on holding out, the person who advanced credit to the firm must have relied on the holding out in doing so.[79] In *National Building Society* v. *Lewis*,[80] a client of a law firm relied on a title opinion in granting a mortgage. The title opinion turned out to be mistaken and the firm was held liable for negligence. The client argued that a lawyer employed by the firm should be personally liable

---

77   There are similar provisions in other provincial statutes (e.g., *BCPA ibid.*, s. 16; and *NSPA*, *ibid.*, s. 17).

78   *Tower Cabinet Co. Ltd.* v. *Ingram*, [1949] 2 K.B. 397 [*Tower*].

79   *Bet-Mur*, above note 71.

80   (1998), 2 W.L.R. 915 (C.A.).

on the basis that he was held out as a partner. The employee had no involvement in the transaction but was identified on the firm letterhead in a manner that suggested that he was a partner. The court held that in the absence of any proof that the client had relied on the employee being a partner, liability for holding out did not arise. The client had relied on the opinion — not on the employee being a partner.

One of the most common situations in which a holding out may occur is when a partner retires. In such a case, there may be various conflicting interests at stake. The retiring partner is generally interested in limiting her liability for obligations arising after retirement. Persons who dealt with the firm prior to the retirement and who innocently continue to rely on the creditworthiness of the retired partner in their dealings with the firm will expect to hold the retired partner liable even in the absence of some post-retirement holding out as contemplated in section 15. There would be no such expectation, however, if these old clients of the firm never knew that the retiring partner was a member of the firm. On the other hand, those who deal with the firm for the first time after the retirement could not reasonably expect to hold the retiring partner liable to them in the absence of some representation to them that she is a partner at that time. Finally, in many cases, the retiring partner's name will be part of the firm name and the continuing partners will have an interest in the continuity of the firm name to ensure that any goodwill associated with it is not lost after the retirement.[81] Use of the firm name is likely to be found to be a holding out, sufficient to render the retiring partner liable for obligations arising after retirement. The Ontario *Partnerships Act* and other provincial statutes have several provisions that strike a sort of balance between these various interests.

A retired partner is liable to every person who has dealt with the firm *prior* to his retirement for obligations of the firm incurred after retirement unless

- actual notice of the retirement is given to the person (*OPA*, s. 36(1));
- the person never knew that the retiring partner was a partner (*OPA*, s. 36(3)); or
- the partner left the firm because he became insolvent or died (*OPA*, s. 36(3).[82]

---

81   This was the case, for example, in *Dominion Sugar Co.* v. *Warrell* (1927), 60 O.L.R. 169 (C.A.).

82   A similar scheme is created under the laws of other provinces: e.g., *BCPA*, above note 2, ss. 19, 39; and *NSPA*, above note 2, ss. 20(3), 39.

Section 15(2) specifically, though seemingly unnecessarily, provides that a partner who dies is not liable for obligations of the firm arising after death even if the partner's name continues to be used in the firm name.

Persons who deal with the firm for the first time after a retirement are entitled to hold liable any person who is an apparent member of the firm (*OPA*, s. 36(1)). A person will be an "apparent member" if, for example, her name is used in the firm name or on letterhead, invoices, or signs at the business premises, or if an express representation is made that the person is a partner. A person may be an apparent partner if her name appears as a partner in a registration under provincial business names legislation, such as the Ontario *Business Names Act*, or if her membership in the partnership is notorious because, for example, she is extremely well known. "Apparent" means "apparent to the person dealing with the firm" so as to give that person the impression that the person is a partner.

Although it may seem reasonable that, as section 36(1) provides, someone dealing with the firm for the first time should be able to treat an apparent partner as a partner, several other provisions make it imprudent to do so. Section 36(2) provides that a retired partner is not liable to such persons if a notice that the partner has retired has been published in the *Ontario Gazette*.[83] In effect, new clients of a firm are deemed to have notice of any retirement so advertised. Also, this section provides that a retiring partner is not liable to any person who deals with a partnership after the retirement who did not know that the person was a partner. The net effect of these provisions is that the retired partner will be liable for any obligation incurred by the partnership after retirement only if the actions making her an apparent partner also constitute a holding out within the meaning of section 15. In other words, she must hold herself out or knowingly permit herself to be held out as a partner. This was the conclusion reached in *Tower* v. *Ingram*.[84] In *Tower*, Ingram was a partner in a firm whose name was used on firm letterhead after his retirement, but without his permission and contrary to his express instructions. The court held that a third party who dealt with the firm for the first time after Ingram's retirement and received the letterhead could not hold Ingram liable because there

---

83   The *Ontario Gazette* is the official publication of the Ontario legislature.

84   Above note 78; *Coatsworth & Cooper Ltd.* v. *Schotanus*, [1962] O.R. 1118 (H.C.J.). In *Bass Brewer Ltd.* v. *Appleby*, [1997] 2 Butterworths Company L. C. 700 (C.A.), a partnership that gave an individual the right to use its name to conduct business as a receiver was held liable for the individual's misappropriation of a client's funds.

had been no holding out for the purposes of section 15. In the absence of a holding out, section 36(3) had the effect of insulating Ingram from all liability for obligations of the partnership incurred after his retirement to all persons who did not know him to be a partner prior to the date of his retirement. In other words, the plaintiff could have succeeded only if, prior to Ingram's retirement, he had known that Ingram was a partner in the firm. Being an "apparent" partner is not enough. The rules relating to a partner's liability are summarized in figure 2.5.

Two practical questions must be addressed based on this thorny analysis. First, what should a retiring partner do to minimize her liability for obligations of the partnership after her retirement? Second, what should a person contemplating dealing with a partnership do to assess the creditworthiness of a partnership?

In answer to the first question, the retiring partner should ensure that all persons who had dealings with the firm prior to the date of her retirement have actually received notice of her departure. If this is impractical, a newspaper advertisement may give notice to a significant number of clients. She should also ensure that she documents her instructions to the remaining partners that notice is to be given to ensure that liability based on holding out cannot be claimed. As well, she should ensure that notice of her retirement is published in the *Ontario Gazette* and that the partnership's registration under the *OBNA* is amended. She should have her name removed from the firm name.[85] If she agrees to permit her name to continue being used, she should insist on a reliable indemnification from the remaining partners for any liability she incurs as a result.

For persons dealing with the partnership, if the creditworthiness of a particular person is to be relied on, it would be desirable to obtain some form of specific representation or acknowledgment of that person's membership in the partnership. If there is any uncertainty, checking the *Ontario Gazette* would also be prudent.

3) Risk Management in Partnerships

There are practical protections against unauthorized activity in partnerships which are likely to be even more effective than the legal protections, such as the fiduciary duty, mentioned above. Most partnerships involve only a small number of individuals, each being vitally involved in the business and affairs of the partnership on a daily basis. There is

---

85   For more discussion of partnerships names, see section E ("Partnership Agreements") in this chapter.

Figure 2.5 Liabilities of Partner D to Third Parties Dealing with Partnership under the Ontario *Partnerships Act*

D is a member of the partnership in 2000		
1999	**2000**	**2001**
No liability (s. 18(1))	Unlimited liability (ss. 6, 10–13) • continues after retires (s. 18 (2)) • binding on estate (s. 10)	No liability (implicit in ss. 10 & 36(3)) UNLESS 1. Creditor dealt with firm before retirement (**exceptions:** the creditor either (a) did not know **D** was a partner prior to retirement (s. 36(3)) or (b) is given actual notice of retirement) OR
Except • Obligation arises ▶ • Holding out that **D** a partner permitted by **D** s. 15(1)	Execution against partnership property: Ontario *Rule of Civil Procedure* 8.06 (1)	2. Creditor dealt with firm for the first time after **D**'s retirement, was no notice of retirement in *Ontario Gazette* (s. 36(2)) **and** was holding out by or on behalf of **D** (s. 15(1)) BUT NEVER LIABILITY after **D** dies, or becomes insolvent (ss. 15(2) & 36(3))

no separation of ownership and management. Also, typically, there is a relationship of trust and confidence among partners because they know each other well. In such circumstances, the likelihood of unauthorized activity is reduced at the same time as the opportunity to monitor the activities of one's fellow partners is increased.

As a partnership gets bigger, involving more and more people as partners and employees, these practical protections break down. In the large law and accounting firms, for example, few partners are actively involved in all aspects of the business of the partnership, and formal monitoring mechanisms must be established. The law of partnerships was developed to address small businesses and so has little in the way of specific provisions designed to address the needs of the large modern partnership. Consequently, as discussed below in this chapter, these mechanisms must be created in the partnership agreement. An alternative available in some cases is the limited liability partnership.

4) Limited Liability Partnerships for Professionals

The absence of practical protections against unauthorized liability in large modern partnerships, combined with an explosion in professional liability, has encouraged professionals to lobby for changes to the laws governing them to permit them to carry on business using a corporation, which, as will be discussed in the next chapter, has the effect of limiting the liability of the owners of the business. It is important to note that the use of a corporation would not reduce the risk associated with carrying on a business. Instead, it has the effect of shifting risk to non-owners dealing with the business.

While incorporation with full limited liability is not permitted for most professionals in most Canadian jurisdictions,[86] Alberta and Ontario have amended their partnership laws to allow some professional partnerships, such as lawyers and accountants, to limit their liability for negligence by agreeing to become "limited liability partnerships." Under this special form of general partnership individual partners are not personally liable for the professional negligence of their partners or of employees or other persons unless the partner directly supervised them.[87] The firm remains liable. Individual partners are liable for their own negligence. In Ontario, a partnership must meet the following requirements to become a limited liability partnership:

- the partners must sign an agreement designating the partnership as a limited liability partnership;
- the business of the partnership is the practice of a profession governed by a statute which permits a limited liability partnership to practise the profession;

---

86   Ontario recently passed a law allowing professional partnerships to incorporate for tax purposes. Full corporate limited liability is not granted under the statute: *Balanced Budgets for Brighter Futures Act, 2000*, S.O. 2000, c. 42. Alberta and British Columbia also permit such "professional corporations." This special form of corporation is discussed in Chapter 3.

87   *APA*, above note 2, as amended by S.A. 1999, c. 27; *Limited Liability Partnerships Act*, S.O. 1998, c. 2.

- the governing body of the profession requires the partnership to carry a minimum amount of liability insurance;
- the partnership is registered under the *Business Names Act*; and
- the partnership name contains the words "limited liability partnership," "LLP," "L.L.P.," or their French equivalents (*OPA*, s. 44.1–44.3).[88]

Several professions in Ontario and Alberta meet these requirements[89] and most large law and accounting firms in these jurisdictions have now become limited liability partnerships. All partners remain personally liable for obligations other than negligence, and the limited liability partnership is the same as a general partnership in all other respects.

D. DISSOLUTION OF THE PARTNERSHIP

Because the partnership is not a legal entity separate from its partners, it is inherently fragile. This is reflected in the many ways in which it may be dissolved, as provided in the Ontario *Partnerships Act* and the partnership laws of other provinces.[90] Many of these provisions may be varied by agreement and typically are changed to render the partnership more stable. These aspects will be discussed further in section E ("Partnership Agreements"), below.

Unless the partners have agreed otherwise, the partnership is terminated in the following circumstances:

- if formed for a fixed term, on the expiry of the term (*OPA*, s. 32(a));
- if not formed for a fixed term, on notice by one partner to all the others (*OPA*, ss. 26 & 32(c));[91]
- if formed for a single adventure or undertaking, on termination of the adventure or undertaking (*OPA*, s. 32(b)); and
- on the death or insolvency of any partner[92] (*OPA*, s. 33 (a)).

---

88   The *APA*, *ibid.*, has slightly different requirements (ss. 81-82), including giving notice to all existing clients where an existing partnership continues as a limited liability partnership (s. 85).

89   E.g., lawyers governed by the Ontario *Law Society Act*, R.S.O. 1990, c. L.8 (as amended by S.O. 1998 c. 21, s. 28), s. 61.1.

90   E.g., *BCPA*, above note 2, ss. 29, 35-8; and *NSPA*, above note 2, ss. 29, 35-8.

91   See, for example, *Blundon* v. *Storm*, [1972] S.C.R. 135. In *Keith* v. *Mathews Dinsdale and Clark*, [1999] O.J. No. 1202 (QL) (Gen. Div.) [*Keith*], the partnership agreement provided only that a partner could withdraw on six months' notice. The court held that this meant that the parties had agreed that the partnership could not be dissolved by notice from a partner.

92   PWA Corporation sought to have a limited partnership it had entered into with Air Canada for the operation of an airline reservation system terminated on the

The partners may also provide that other events will result in the termination of the partnership, such as the inability of a partner to continue to work in the partnership. Section 33(b) contemplates that partners may agree that dissolution should occur if any partner permits his share of the partnership property to be charged for his personal debts.

Termination occurs regardless of any agreement by the partners if it becomes illegal for the business of the partnership to be carried on at all or illegal to be carried on by the members of the partnership (*OPA*, s. 34). The disbarment of all the lawyers in a law firm partnership is an example of a situation that would trigger dissolution under this section. The Act also provides that a court may order dissolution on a wide variety of grounds, including mental incapacity of a partner, persistent breaches of the partnership agreement, and a catch-all ground: a court may order dissolution when, in the opinion of the court, it is just and equitable to do so.[93] Examples of situations in which the court might be disposed to order dissolution would be the refusal by a group of partners to permit a partner to exercise her rights to participate in the management of the partnership, as provided in section 24.5 of the Ontario Act, or irreconcilable differences among the partners.[94]

Section 44 of the Ontario Act provides a skeleton of a process to deal with the settlement of the many claims needing to be dealt with on dissolution. Debts and liabilities to persons who are not partners are paid first, then debts to partners (other than advances of capital), and then capital is returned. Anything left is distributed to partners in accordance with their entitlement to profits. The statutory scheme may be fleshed out in a partnership agreement.[95]

---

grounds of the insolvency of the general partner, Gemini Group Automated Distribution Systems Inc., although the claim was based on a reference to insolvency in the partnership agreement and not section 32, *OPA*, above note 2. PWA also sought dissolution on the ground set out in section 35(f) that it was just and equitable to do so. The action failed on both grounds. The court found that the limited partnership was not insolvent. *PWA Corp. v. Gemini Group Automated Distribution Systems Inc.* (1993), 101 D.L.R. (4th) 15 (Ont. Gen. Div.), aff'd (1993), 15 O.R. (3d) 730 (C.A.) [*PWA*].

93 See the discussion on dissolution in Chapter 10.

94 See also *PWA*, above note 92.

95 Similar provisions are found in the other partnership statutes (e.g., *BCPA*, above note 2, ss. 42-47; and *NSPA*, above note 2, ss. 42–47). In *Mohammadamin*, above note 55, one partner bought out the other for $30,000 plus 50 percent of the net assets of the business. The court held that this agreement replaced the scheme of distribution on dissolution provided for in the *OPA*, above note 2.

E. PARTNERSHIP AGREEMENTS

1) General

The foregoing discussion provides an outline of the law of partnership. But the law, as indicated in many places in this chapter, provides only the barest framework of rules for the regulation of the relations among partners and the conduct of the business of a partnership. Also, for particular partnerships, the rules may be inappropriate. For both these reasons, it is commonplace for partners to enter into a partnership agreement to flesh out their relationship, though in many cases no written agreement may be prepared. In this section, we will discuss some of the considerations that should go into drafting a partnership agreement, with emphasis on how the agreement interacts with the law of partnership. The purpose of this section is not, however, to provide a comprehensive guide to all the provisions needed in partnership agreements.[96]

The main purposes of partnership agreements are as follows.

- To modify the default provisions of the provincial partnershp legislation,[97] either to replace them or to supplement them by extending and tailoring them to the particular needs of the partners. The partners will need to provide a structure for operating the partnership where the legislation is silent or where the partners want something different from what it provides.
- To respond to the mandatory provisions of the provincial partnership legislation, especially those providing for liability to third parties, by structuring the relations among partners to address liability among partners, and to create reporting, monitoring, and control mechanisms to manage liability risk.
- To reproduce provisions of provincial partnership legislation for partners' information.

---

96   A useful discussion of the considerations for drafting a partnership agreement and a good precedent are set out in the Ontario *Bar Admission Course Reference Materials: Business Law* (Toronto: Law Society of Upper Canada, 2003), c. 2.

97   E.g., *OPA*, above note 2, ss. 20-33; *BCPA*, above note 2, ss. 21-34; and *NSPA*, above note 2, ss. 22-34.

2) Selected Elements of Partnership Agreements and Commentary

a) Name

A partnership may carry on business using any name it likes. Professional partnerships often use the names of individual partners in the firm name, though many large firms use the names of deceased partners in the interests of continuity. The name of the partnership raises a number of issues in addition to the practically important and often sensitive question of whose name appears in the firm name. Some of the more important issues are identified below. Names are a complex subject, and a comprehensive treatment of issues associated with them is far beyond the scope of this book.

Ownership Issues The name of the partnership forms part of the goodwill of the business and belongs to the partners. In the absence of some provision in the partnership agreement, each may be entitled to use the name on the dissolution of the firm. The partnership agreement should address who is entitled to use the firm name in the event that there is a change in membership or dissolution of the partnership. To avoid conflict, the partners may agree that, on the withdrawal of a partner, neither the withdrawing partner nor the remaining partners may use the firm name. Where a "name" partner is retiring from the business or profession or dies, the firm may want to continue to use the name, perhaps because of the prestige associated with it. In such a case, the partnership agreement may provide for the continued use of the name. If so, the agreement should address the risk of liability described below.

Liability Issues The use of a person's name as part of the firm name with his knowledge constitutes holding that person out as a partner within the meaning of provincial partnership statutes. Any person so held out after he leaves the partnership will be liable to persons dealing with the firm after his departure.[98] Accordingly, if a person's name is going to be used after she leaves, the remaining partners of the firm should agree to indemnify her against any such liabilities. This agreement will have no effect on her liability to third parties, but it gives her a right to recover any amount she has to pay from her former partners. Since a deceased partner's estate is not liable for obligations of the partnership after she leaves the partnership, there is no need for an indemnity in cases where a partner dies and the firm continues to use the deceased partner's name in the firm name.

---

98   See section C ("Liability of the Partnership to Third Parties") above in this chapter in which holding out is discussed.

Registration Issues Under some provincial laws such as the Ontario *Business Names Act*, partners must register their firm name. In choosing a name, it is advisable to search the register maintained in the province as well as trade directories and other sources of information to ensure that the name chosen or a similar name is not already being used by someone else. Use of a name that conflicts with someone else's name may expose the partnership to loss of goodwill if it subsequently has to change its name and to possible liability for passing-off, trade-mark infringement, and contravention of the Ontario *Business Names Act* (s. 6).[99]

b) Description of Business

As agents of the partnership, each partner's authority is limited by the nature of the business undertaken.[100] The scope of each partner's authority to bind the partnership to a third party will be determined by what the partnership does rather than by any limit in the partnership agreement, unless the third party has knowledge of the limit.[101] Nevertheless, there are several reasons to describe the business in the partnership agreement.

Describing the business makes clear what activities are to be considered to be carried on for the benefit of the partnership. This description will help to avoid disagreements in the future about what income earned by the partners must be paid to the firm. In a law firm partnership, for example, the partners may want to provide expressly that the business includes teaching a law school course or writing papers, so any fees or honoraria received are income of the partnership. Such a provision gives specific content to partners' obligation to account for all benefits derived from any use by a partner of the partnership property, name, or business connection[102] and helps to avoid conflicts over what is personal and what is partnership income. For the same reason, many partnership agreements provide that each partner will devote her full time and attention to the business of the partnership and will not engage in any other business without the consent of the other partners. If there are some specific business activities of partners outside the firm business, identifying them as permitted will help to avoid future disagreements.

---

99 In other provinces, name registration requirements may be different. E.g., *APA*, above note 2, ss. 106-109; *BCPA*, above note 2, ss. 81-90.1; and Nova Scotia *Partnerships and Business Names Registration Act*, R.S.N.S. 1989, c. 335, ss. 3-7.

100 *OPA*, above note 2, s. 6; *BCPA*, ibid., s. 7; and *NSPA*, ibid., s. 8.

101 *OPA*, ibid., ss. 6 & 9; *BCPA*, ibid., ss. 8 & 10; and *NSPA*, above note 2, ss. 8 & 11.

102 *OPA*, ibid., s. 29; *BCPA*, ibid., s. 32; and *NSPA*, ibid., s. 32.

Describing the business also gives substance to partners' non-competition obligations. Recall that a partner's fiduciary obligation obliges him not to compete with the partnership business and that he must account to the partnership for all profits made if he does.[103] Describing the business of the partnership helps to define what constitutes competition with the partnership business for all these purposes. Many partnership agreements also contain provisions prohibiting partners from competing with the business for a period of time and in a limited geographic area after they leave the partnership.[104]

Finally, describing the scope of the partnership business provides the basis for the firm to claim against a partner for liabilities imposed on the firm as a result of unauthorized actions by the partner that are outside the firm's defined business. Typically, an agreement would allow the partners to seek indemnification from any partner who saddles the partnership with a liability outside the defined business of the firm.

c) Membership of Partnership

The admission of a new partner is one of the most important decisions for a partnership and often one of the most difficult. Provincial partnership statutes provide that, in the absence of an agreement to the contrary, all partners must consent to the admission of a new partner.[105] Because the contributions of partners to the partnership are usually not equal, this requirement for unanimity is often changed to some lesser degree of agreement, perhaps weighted by each partner's economic interest in the partnership. It is also common to articulate some of the criteria for admission, such as years of experience.

Partnership statutes are silent on the arrangements for admission to partnership. Issues such as what capital contribution new partners

---

103 *OPA*, *ibid.*, s. 29; *BCPA*, *ibid.*, s. 33; and *NSPA*, *ibid.*, s. 30. There is some old authority for the proposition that simply using information acquired in the course of one's involvement as a partner for purposes outside the scope of the partnership business does not give rise to the obligation to account (*Aas* v. *Benham*, [1891] 2 Ch. 244 (C.A.)).

104 Non-competition provisions of this type must be reasonable in area and time, not contrary to the public interest, and no more restrictive than necessary to protect the business interests of the partnership in order to be enforceable (*Bassman* v. *Deloitte, Haskins and Sells of Canada* (1984), 4 D.L.R. (4th) 558 (Ont. H.C.J.); *Baker* v. *Lintott* (1983), 141 D.L.R. (3d) 571 (Alta. C.A.)). In *Mohammadamin*, above note 55, it was held that a partner's fiduciary duty prevented him from leaving the firm and starting up a directly competing business.

105 E.g., *OPA*, above note 2, s. 24.7; *BCPA*, above note 2, s. 27(g); and *NSPA*, above note 2, s. 27(g).

will be required to make and how to determine the new partner's interest in capital and share in profits should be addressed in the agreement.

The expulsion of a partner is prohibited under the default rules of the provincial partnership statutes,[106] so many agreements provide for expulsion on the vote of some specified majority. The partnership agreement may set out certain other rules governing the circumstances in which partners must leave the partnership. For example, withdrawal may be mandatory on reaching a stipulated retirement age or on a partner becoming incapable of working full time in the business. For each kind of withdrawal, it should be provided that the partnership is not dissolved and some formula should be established for determining how the departing partner is to be paid her share of capital and profits and how she is to be compensated for any work in progress to which she has contributed but which has not yet been billed.

d) Capitalization

The amount contributed by the partners to the firm is called its capital. Capital contributions and partners' entitlements to capital should be dealt with in the partnership agreement.

Every partnership needs money to pay the costs of setting up the partnership business and to cover ongoing operating expenses, such as salaries and rent, while work is being done and before it is billed and paid for.[107] Money may be needed at various other times in the life of a business, such as to buy new equipment or to expand the business. Money may be raised from the partners or from a third party, such as by borrowing it from a bank. The partners will need to agree on what will be the initial contributions of capital by the partners, including contributions by partners who join the firm in the future. They may also want to provide for the basis on which additional amounts of capital will be contributed by the partners in the future. For example, it may be provided that, when additional capital is required, each partner must contribute an amount calculated by reference to her percentage entitlement to profits of the firm. The circumstances in which capital may be withdrawn are often addressed as well. It is common in law firm partnerships for capital contributions of new partners to be used to return capital contributions of more senior partners. The agreement may also provide for some way to keep track of each partner's aggregate contributions over time. In the absence of a specific agreement as to

---

106 E.g., *OPA, ibid.,* s. 25; *BCPA, ibid.,* s. 28; and *NSPA, ibid.,* s. 28 .
107 This second type of capital is called "working capital."

what is each partner's share in capital, all partners share equally.[108] Each partner will be entitled to receive his share capital when he leaves the partnership, so the partners may want to agree on the process by which this will be done.[109]

Under the Ontario Act, no interest is paid on capital advanced, and partners who make loans to the partnership are entitled only to 5 percent interest unless the partners otherwise agree.[110]

e) Arrangements Regarding Profits and Their Distribution

Pursuant to provincial statutes, all profits are to be divided equally among the partners.[111] This provision is almost invariably changed to allocate to each partner a share commensurate with her contribution to the firm. There are many kinds of contributions to the business of a firm, both direct and indirect. Each partnership must decide what kinds of contributions to take into account and what weight to give to each for the purpose of allocating profits. These kinds of issues will be resolved differently from business to business, but the following are some kinds of contributions typically considered in law firm partnerships:

- capital contributions;
- billable hours worked;
- hours worked on matters that were not billable;
- fees billed and collected;
- total billings to new clients introduced to the firm by the partner;
- total billings to clients of which the partner is in charge; and
- business development.

As is evident from this list of factors, each partner's entitlement will change each time the factors are evaluated. Most firms make an evaluation on an annual basis.

It is also necessary to provide for how the profits are to be distributed. Typically, partners are permitted to draw against their anticipated

---

108 *OPA*, above note 2, s. 24.1; *BCPA*, above note 2, s. 27(a); and *NSPA*, above note 2, s. 27(a).

109 Section 42 of the *OPA*, *ibid.*, provides that if an outgoing partner is not paid her share of capital, she is entitled, in the absence of any agreement to the contrary, to receive either a share of profits attributable to the use of her capital from the date she left the firm or interest of 5 percent per year on the capital. The Nova Scotia Act has a similar provision (*NSPA*, *ibid.*, s. 45). The British Columbia Act requires that interest be paid at a fair rate (*BCPA*, *ibid.*, s. 45).

110 *OPA*, *ibid.*, ss. 24.3 & 24.4. The Nova Scotia Act has the same provisions (*NSPA*, *ibid.*, s. 27(c) & (d)). The British Columbia Act provides that there is no interest on capital but a fair interest rate is to be paid on loans (*BCPA*, *ibid.*, s. 27(c) & (d)).

111 E.g., *OPA*, *ibid.*, s. 24.1; *BCPA*, *ibid.*, s. 27(a); and *NSPA*, *ibid.*, s. 27(a).

share of the profits, based on forecast profits and their previous year's entitlement, subject to an adjustment at the annual review.

f)   Management

The default rules in provincial partnership legislation provide that all partners are entitled to participate in management and that decisions on ordinary matters are to be made by a majority of partners, but decisions relating to the nature of the partnership business require the consent of all partners.[112] Management relations vary tremendously in their nature and complexity depending on partnership size and other variables. As a result, while it is usual to change these default rules to some extent, it is hard to generalize about partnership management structures. Nevertheless, some comments may be made.

Usually the requirements for consent by a numerical majority and unanimous consent for certain decisions are replaced by a decision-making structure reflecting the typically unequal economic interests of the partners. Also, as the partnership becomes larger, more of the decision making, particularly of a routine nature, is delegated to a committee of partners, a single partner, or, in some very large firms, a professional manager who is not a partner.[113]

The provincial statutes contain no procedures for partnerships to act collectively. Rules about procedures, such as notice and quorum requirements for meetings of the partnership, will usually be included in a partnership agreement.

Management arrangements are an important way in which the risk created by mutual agency may be addressed. Restrictions on who may sign contracts and write cheques, as well as authorization and reporting requirements for particular activities (e.g., giving legal opinions), are examples of how the risk of unauthorized or otherwise undesirable activity with the potential for creating liability for the firm and for the partners may be reduced. As a result, there are often provisions for such internal monitoring and control mechanisms in partnership agreements. It is important to remember that these mechanisms will have no effect on avoiding liability to a third party where they are contravened, but, to the extent that they are implemented in practice, they will tend to prevent liability from arising. Also, where one partner fails to observe requirements imposed in the partnership agreement, the

---

112   *OPA, ibid.*, ss. 24.5 & 24.8; *BCPA, ibid.*, s. 27(e) & (h); and *NSPA, ibid.*, s. 27(e) & (h).

113   Delegation of powers in a partnership is expressly recognized in the Quebec *Civil Code* (Art. 2213 C.C.Q.).

other partners will have a claim for breach of contract and perhaps grounds for dissolution.[114]

g) Dissolution

As noted, the provincial laws permit partnerships to be dissolved easily and in a variety of ways. Typically, in the interests of ensuring the continuity of the business, the partners will agree that the partnership shall not be dissolved in many of the circumstances contemplated in the provincial statutes. Dissolution on the death or insolvency of a partner and on notice from one of the partners are usually excluded and replaced by a provision requiring unanimous or some degree of majority consent for dissolution. In some partnership agreements, dissolution may be precluded altogether, replaced by a provision dealing with withdrawal of partners.[115] Partners may agree on certain other specified events that will result in dissolution.

The statutory scheme under section 44 of the Ontario *Partnerships Act* dealing with the settlement of the many claims needing to be dealt with on dissolution may be fleshed out in an agreement.[116]

F. JOINT VENTURES

Joint ventures are not a distinct form of business organization, nor a relationship that has any precise legal meaning. Functionally, the term "joint venture" is used to describe a relationship among persons who agree to combine their money, property, knowledge, skills, experience, time, or other resources for some common purpose. Usually the joint venturers agree to share the profits and losses from the venture, and each has some degree of control over it. The distinguishing feature of a joint venture is that it is an arrangement set up for a limited time, for a limited purpose, or both. "Joint venture" is used loosely to refer to all sorts of legal arrangements given effect in corporations and partnerships and in relationships based exclusively on contract.

---

114 *OPA*, above note 2, s. 35(d); *BCPA*, above note 2, s. 38(d); and *NSPA*, above note 2, s. 38(d).

115 In *Keith*, above note 91, the partnership agreement provided only that a partner could withdraw on six months' notice. The court held that this meant that the parties had agreed that the partnership could not be dissolved by notice from a partner.

116 See, similarly, *BCPA*, above note 2, ss. 42 & 47; and *NSPA*, above note 2, ss. 42 & 47. See also *Mohammadamin*, above note 55, for an example of the partners agreeing to vary the scheme of distribution on dissolution.

For example, a small mineral-exploration business that has rights in certain claims might combine its resources with those of a larger business with the financial strength and experience to develop the claims. This activity could be described as a joint venture and could be carried on through a corporation in which each business was a shareholder; a partnership, in which each was a partner; or by the parties together, with the parties' respective rights and obligations governed only by a contract between them.

While the legal consequences of a joint venture that is a corporation or a partnership are clear, the legal consequences of a joint venture relationship that is not a partnership or a corporation are not. The main question is to what extent are there legal consequences associated with the joint venture outside those specifically provided for in the agreement creating the relationship?

Central Mortgage & Housing Corp. v. *Graham*[117] suggests that in a joint venture with the following characteristics, each of the joint venturers is responsible for all obligations of the joint venture, just as each partner is responsible for all obligations of a partnership:

- contribution by both parties of money, property, skill, or knowledge to a common undertaking;
- joint interest in the subject matter of the joint venture;
- mutual control and management;
- arrangement limited to one project;
- expectation of profit; and
- mutual sharing of profit.

In this case, Central Mortgage and Housing Corporation (CMHC) initiated a relationship with a builder, Bras D'Or, under which it provided the financing for Bras D'Or to build some houses to specifications provided by CMHC on property owned by Bras D'Or. The financing was secured by a mortgage on the property in favour of CMHC. CMHC was consulted during construction and had the right to approve the purchasers. With each sale by Bras D'Or, the purchaser would assume a portion of the debt owed by Bras D'Or to CMHC as well as a portion of the mortgage relating to the property sold. Bras D'Or would be released to the same extent. Graham bought one of the houses from Bras D'Or and, after taking possession, stopped making payments on the mortgage because of some defects in the house. CMHC commenced foreclosure proceedings, and Graham counterclaimed for damages based on the defects, alleging that CMHC was liable for the defects because it was in a joint venture

---

117 (1973), 13 N.S.R. (2d) 183 (S.C.T.D.).

with the seller, Bras D'Or. The court, relying exclusively on American authority, held that the relationship in this case satisfied the factors identified above sufficiently that there was a joint venture. Consequently, CMHC was liable for the obligations of its fellow venturer Bras D'Or.

CMHC v. *Graham* has never been overruled and was cited as an accurate statement of the law in *Bow Valley Husky (Bermuda) Ltd.* v. *Saint John Shipbuilding Ltd.*[118] Nevertheless, neither in that case nor in other subsequent Canadian cases outside Nova Scotia has a joint venture been found to have the partnership-like legal characteristics attributed to it in *CMHC* v. *Graham.*[119] This may be because, if all the incidents of a joint venture listed above are present, a partnership will be found in most cases. It is important to remember that what is often cited as the key identifying feature of a joint venture, limitation to a specific project, can also occur in partnerships. It is expressly contemplated in provincial partnership statutes,[120] and such a limit has been present in other cases in which a partnership was found.[121]

Even if their legal position is not appropriately analogized to partnership, joint ventures may have more limited legal consequences. Some courts have held that parties to a joint venture owe a fiduciary to each other in relation to the activities of the joint venture.[122] As with partners,[123] this duty means that joint venturers cannot put their individual interests ahead of the interests of the joint venture. Another aspect of the fiduciary duty is the obligation not to disclose confidential information provided by one joint venturer to the other for the purposes of the joint venture.[124]

A striking example of one joint venturer attempting to enrich itself at the expense of the other in breach of a fiduciary duty occurred in *Won-*

---

118 (1995), 130 Nfld. & P.E.I.R. 92 at 103 (Nfld. C.A.), aff'd on other grounds [1997] 3 S.C.R. 1210.

119 See cases cited in J.S. Ziegel, *et al.*, *Cases and Materials on Partnerships and Business Corporations*, 3d ed. (Toronto: Carswell, 1994), at 81–83.

120 *OPA*, above note 2, s. 32(b); *BCPA*, above note 2, s. 35(b); and *NSPA*, above note 2, s. 35(b).

121 E.g., *Pooley* v. *Driver*, above note 33.

122 *Hogar Estates Ltd.* v. *Shebron Holdings Ltd.* (1979), 25 O.R. (2d) 543 (H.C.J.).

123 See section B(3) above ("Fiduciary Duty").

124 This duty of confidentiality may be imposed even in the absence of a fiduciary duty between parties who are negotiating only to establish a joint venture where the "circumstances of a relationship are such that one party is entitled to expect that the other will act in his interests in and for the purposes of the relationship" (P.D. Finn, "The Fiduciary Principle" in T.G. Youdan, ed., *Equity, Fiduciaries and Trusts* (Toronto: Carswell, 1988), at 46, cited in *LAC Minerals Ltd.* v. *International Corona Resources Ltd.*, [1989] 2 S.C.R. 574, at 644). See *Fines* v. *Vanderveen* ((1994), 55 C.P.R. (3d) 61 (Ont. Gen. Div.)) for an example of an unsuccessful attempt to invoke this protection.

sch Construction Co. v. *Danzig Enterprises Ltd.*[125] Wonsch had entered into a joint venture agreement with Danzig to build and operate an apartment and office complex. In constructing the building, Wonsch had incurred substantial indebtedness to the National Bank of Canada. Danzig took an assignment of the debt owed by Wonsch, paying the Bank significantly less than the full amount, and immediately sued Wonsch for the full amount. The court held that Danzig owed a fiduciary duty to Wonsch which precluded it from, in effect, trying to make a profit from dealing in Wonsch's debt incurred for the purposes of the joint venture.

In recent cases, the courts have made clear that a fiduciary duty will not be found in all joint ventures. Relying on the policy that fiduciary duties should not be imposed on commercial parties who have recorded their relationship in an agreement, the courts have said that a fiduciary duty will be found only where one party is vulnerable to the other in some way. In general, there must be some inequality of bargaining power resulting in an unfair agreement.[126]

G. LIMITED PARTNERSHIPS

1) General

A limited partnership is a specialized vehicle designed to fulfil the needs of particular investors who want to be able to share in partnership profits but limit their liability for partnership losses. In most cases, limited partners are not interested in participating in management. Their investment is passive in nature. In Ontario, limited partnerships are governed by the *Limited Partnerships Act* (*OLPA*) and, to the extent that the Act is silent, by the *Partnerships Act* and the common law.[127] Each province has legislation dealing with limited partnerships which is similar in basic design to the Ontario Act.[128]

Every limited partnership must consist of at least one general partner with unlimited liability and one limited partner with limited liability

---

125 (1990), 1 O.R. (3d) 382 (C.A.).

126 *Visagie* v. *TVX Gold Inc.* (2000), 49 O.R. (3d) 198 (C.A.) applying the decision of the Supreme Court of Canada in *Cadbury Schweppes Inc.* v. *FBI Foods Ltd.*, [1999] 1 S.C.R. 142. In this case, the court still found that there was a common law duty of confidence. See also, *Canada Southern Petroleum Ltd.* v. *Amoco Canada Petroleum Co.*, [2001] A.J. No. 1222 (QL) (Q.B.).

127 *OPA*, above note 2, ss. 45 & 46.

128 E.g., *APA*, above note 2, Part 2; *BCPA*, above note 2, Part 3; and Nova Scotia *Limited Partnerships Act*, R.S.N.S. 1989, c. 259.

Figure 2.6   Types of Partnerships

General Partnership	Limited Liability Partnership	Limited Partnership
(or simply partnership)	Same as General Partnership	At least one general partner (unlimited personal liability) and one limited partner (liability limited to amount contributed to partnership)
Each partner has unlimited personal liability	EXCEPT	
Ontario *Partnerships Act* ss. 6, 10–13	Each partner only liable for own negligence and that of persons under her direct supervision or control	Ontario *Limited Partnerships Act* ss. 8, 9
	Ontario *Partnerships Act* ss. 10, 44.1	

(*OLPA*, s. 2(2)). Unlike general partnerships, however, limited partnerships do not come into existence simply by virtue of persons carrying on business; a declaration must be filed with the registrar appointed under the *Business Names Act* (*OLPA*, s. 3). The declaration expires after five years unless renewed. Expiry does not terminate the limited partnership, but an additional fee must be paid for renewal (*OLPA*, s. 3(3)). The limited partnership does not have separate legal existence.[129]

The general partner has all the rights and powers and is subject to the same restrictions and unlimited personal liability as a partner in a general partnership, subject to certain additional constraints designed to protect the limited partners (*OLPA*, s. 8). By contrast, limited partners have certain fairly narrowly defined rights and their liability is limited to the extent of their contribution (*OLPA*, s. 9).

Limited partners have the right to share in profits and to have their contribution returned (*OLPA*, ss. 11 & 15). In addition, section 10 of the Ontario Act provides that a limited partner has the same rights as a general partner to

- inspect books and make copies;
- get full and true information regarding the limited partnership and to be given a complete and formal account of the partnership affairs; and
- obtain dissolution by court order.

Where the interests of the limited partnership, often called "units", are to be distributed to the public for the purposes of provincial secu-

---

129 *Kucor Construction and Developments & Associates v. The Canada Life Assurance Co.* (1998), 41 O.R. (3d) 577 (C.A.).

rities laws, the requirements of such laws must be met. This may mean that a disclosure document (called a prospectus) must be prepared and distributed to investors who have a civil claim for any misrepresentation in it. The regulation of the distribution of securities to the public is discussed in Chapter 11.

A limited partner may transact business with the limited partnership but cannot hold a security interest in its assets and cannot receive anything from the limited partnership if it is insolvent. Unlike a general partner, a limited partner may be an employee of the partnership (*OLPA*, s. 12).

Participation by limited partners in management is subject to significant restrictions. A limited partner may "enquire into the state and progress of the limited partnership business and may advise as to its management" (*OLPA*, s. 12(2)(a)), but if the limited partner "takes part in the control of the business" (*OLPA*, s. 13(1)) or allows her name to be used in the firm name (*OLPA*, s. 6(2)), she loses her limited liability. In practice, drawing a distinction between advising as to management and taking part in control has been difficult.[130]

One of the more difficult issues in this regard arises in the common situation where the general partner is a corporation and individual limited partners are involved as directors, officers, employees, and/or shareholders in the corporation. In these circumstances, a person who acts in his capacity as an employee, officer, or director of the general partner very often may be taking part in the control of the limited partnership. When does doing so result in the loss of the limited partner's limited liability? In *Haughton Graphic Ltd.* v. *Zivot*,[131] Zivot was a limited partner in a limited partnership as well as the controlling shareholder and president of the corporation that was the general partner. In his capacity as president of the corporate general partner, he acted as the manager of the limited partnership. The court held that he was personally liable as a general partner on the basis that he took part in the control of the limited partnership business. In interpreting the *Partnerships Act* of Alberta,[132] the court expressed the view that any time a limited partner was an employ-

---

130 In *Stillwater Forest Inc.* v. *Clearwater Forest Products Inc.*, [2000] S.J. No. 789 (QL) (Q.B.), a case decided under s. 64 of the Saskatchewan *Partnership Act*, R.S.S. 1978, c. P-3, a shareholder who participated in the refinancing of the limited partnership business was found not to have taken part in the control of the business. The court determined that financing was important to the business but not its essential function.

131 (1986), 33 B.L.R. 125 (Ont. H.C.J.), aff'd 38 B.L.R. xxxiii (C.A.), leave to appeal denied 38 B.L.R. xxxiii (S.C.C.).

132 *APA*, above note 2.

ee, officer, or director of a corporate general partner and, in that capacity, took part in the control of the business, he would be liable personally as a general partner for the obligations of the partnership.[133] This position seems unduly broad, since it systematically disregards the separate existence of the corporation[134] and has not been followed in subsequent cases. In *Nordile Holdings Ltd.* v. *Breckenridge*,[135] the court specifically held that where individual limited partners act only in their capacities as directors and officers of a corporate general partner, they are not liable as general partners. Since Zivot was also the controlling shareholder in *Haughton*, it may be possible to argue that the right approach is that limited partners may act as employees, officers, and directors of corporate general partners and take part in control without losing their limited liability, unless they also control the corporate general partner.

A limited partner's interest is transferable, but the transferee has the full rights of the transferor (i.e., becomes a substituted limited partner) only if all partners consent, or the transfer is in accordance with the partnership agreement (*OLPA*, s. 18). It is common in most limited partnerships, especially those in which the limited partnership units are publicly traded, to provide that transfers may occur in some simpler fashion, such as with the consent of the general partner.

A limited partner has a right to receive repayment of her investment in these circumstances:

- on dissolution of the limited partnership;
- at the time specified in the partnership agreement;
- on six months notice, if no time is specified in the partnership agreement; and
- on the unanimous consent of all partners (*OLPA*, s. 15(1)).

No return of a limited partner's investment may occur if there are not enough assets to pay the claims of all creditors (*OLPA*, s. 15(2)).[136]

---

133 Above note 131 at 134.
134 See section G ("Disregard of Separate Corporate Personality") in Chapter 3.
135 (1992), 66 B.C.L.R. (2d) 183 (C.A.), aff'g (21 February 1991), (B.C.S.C.) [unreported] [case summarized at [1991] B.C.W.L.D. 860]. In this case, the court also held that liability of the limited partners could be excluded by a contractual provision stating that the obligations were solely those of the limited partnership and not the limited partners, thus appearing to permit the alteration of the rules set out in the *BCPA*, above note 2. See, generally, L. Philipps, "The Amazing Three-Headed Limited Partner: Reflections on Old Loopholes and New Jurisprudence," (1993) 21 Can. Bus. L.J. 410.
136 There is a similar provision restricting distributions to shareholders of corporations in many Canadian corporate statutes (e.g., *Canada Business Corporations Act*, R.S.C. 1985, c. C–44, s. 42). See Chapter 6.

Dissolution of a limited partnership occurs in the same circumstances as for a general partnership — death, incompetence, and retirement of a general partner — unless at least one general partner remains and the partnership agreement provides for continuation or all the partners agree (*OLPA*, s. 21). Dissolution also occurs on the withdrawal of all limited partners (*OLPA*, s. 23) or if (a) a limited partner's contribution is not returned when it is required to be or (b) the liabilities of the limited partnership are not paid or the assets of the limited partnership are not enough to pay the liabilities (*OLPA*, s. 15(4)). Finally, just as in any general partnership, dissolution may occur by court order under section 35 of the *Partnerships Act*.

Two final points may be made. A person can be both a general and a limited partner (*OLPA*, s. 5(1)). A general partner's liability can only be unlimited, and becoming a limited partner has no effect on this liability. A general partner may nevertheless want to be a limited partner in order to participate in distributions of losses and profits, and any distribution of assets on dissolution to the same extent as limited partners with respect to the limited partnership units that it owns. Finally, limited partnerships formed under the laws of one province must register if they carry on business in another (e.g., *OLPA*, s. 25), and they are subject to penalties if they do not (e.g., *OLPA*, s. 35). Limited partners do not, however, lose their limited liability if the limited partnership fails to register (e.g., *OLPA*, s. 27).[137]

2) Tax Effects

One of the most common reasons for investing in limited partnerships is to receive a share of tax losses generated by the limited partnership business. Sharing losses may be very attractive to individuals with high incomes from other sources. The losses will be deductible against that income, with the effect of reducing the individual's overall tax liability.

Figures 2.7A and 2.7B are examples of how the federal government may use the tax treatment of limited partners to encourage investment in an identified industry by adjusting the rate at which a business may deduct capital cost allowance on certain equipment used in the industry. CCA is an amount that may be deducted from income under the *Income Tax Act*. Notionally, CCA deductions are permitted to reflect the reduction in the remaining useful life of the equipment. By increasing the rate

---

137 In general, the effectiveness of limited liability will be governed by the law of the jurisdiction in which the limited partnership was created (Manzer, above note 45, at 9-45 & 9-46).

Figure 2.7A Taxation of Limited Partnerships: Case 1

Assume (a) A business acquires film equipment for $1,000,000 in 2000, its first year of operation.
(b) The business has revenue of $100,000 in 2000.
(c) The tax rate for the business is 50 percent.
(d) The only expense deductible from revenue for tax purposes is CCA.
(e) Under the *Income Tax Act*, CCA may be deducted in each year at the rate of 5 percent of the acquisition cost of the film equipment (reflecting an expected useful life of twenty years).

If a Corporation Owned the Business

Tax paid by corporation for 2000 would be

Revenue	$100,000	
less CCA	50,000	(5% of $1,000,000)
Taxable income	50,000	
less tax of 50%	25,000	
After tax income	$ 25,000	

There would be no tax consequences for shareholders unless the corporation pays a dividend to shareholders.

If a Limited Partnership Owned the Business

The taxable income of $50,000 would be allocated to the limited partners in accordance with their respective interests in the limited partnership and added to their other income for the purposes of calculating their personal taxes owing for 2000.

---

at which CCA may be taken on assets acquired for use in identified industries, such as the film, mineral exploration, and manufacturing industries, the federal government can make investments in those industries through limited partnerships attractive to investors with high taxable incomes. Businesses in these industries will be able to create tax losses in their first years of operation by taking large deductions for CCA. By investing in limited partnerships that are engaged in these businesses, investors will be able to deduct the losses resulting from CCA deductions against their other income to reduce their overall tax liability. Figure 2.7B provides an example of the effect of such "accelerated" CCA.

Figure 2.7B Taxation of Limited Partnerships: Case 2

Assume the same facts as in Case 1, except that the permitted CCA deduction is not 5 percent but 100 percent in the year of acquisition. The calculation of taxable income for the business for 2000 would change as follows:

Revenue	$ 100,000	
less CCA	1,000,000	(100% of 1,000,000)
Loss	(900,000)	

For the Corporation: This loss will mean that no taxes are payable for 2000. The loss will be deductible, subject to certain limitations, against income in future years. There are no tax consequences for shareholders. Much of the benefit to the corporation is deferred to future tax years.

For the Limited Partners: Subject to certain limitations in the *Income Tax Act*, this loss may be deducted by limited partners against their other income to reduce their overall tax liability for 2000.

H. CHAPTER SUMMARY

This chapter provides a brief overview of the law of partnership and a practical discussion of the considerations for structuring partnerships in light of the legal framework.

A partnership has no existence separate from the partners who make it up. A number of significant consequences flow from this fact, the most important of which are that partners have unlimited personal liability for the obligations of the partnership business and, in the absence of an agreement to the contrary, partnerships may be dissolved by any of the partners. Partnerships come into existence without any formality; it is sufficient if two or more persons begin to carry on business together with a view to a profit. In each case, the existence of a partnership will be determined by whether the parties intended to enter into such a relationship. The fundamental test for such an intention is whether the business is being carried on for the benefit of the alleged partners. The most significant indicia of such an intention is sharing profits from the business activity, though one must be careful to distinguish other relationships in which profits are shared, such as some creditor/debtor and co-ownership relationships. Other important indicia include participation in the management and control of the partnership and common ownership of property. No single factor is conclusive. Whether a partnership exists depends on the circumstances of each case.

The relationship of partners to each other is governed by default rules in partnership legislation which operate unless the parties agree on some other arrangement. The relationship between partners and third parties dealing with the partnership is governed by a set of mandatory rules. In general, all partners are liable for all obligations incurred in the course of the partnership business while they are partners. After a person dies or becomes bankrupt, he will not be liable for obligations incurred afterwards. If he leaves the partnership in other circumstances, he may continue to be liable for new obligations of the partnership unless he was never known to be a partner or notice is given that he has ceased to be a partner. Persons who are not partners will nevertheless be liable as partners if they knowingly allow themselves to be held out as partners.

Partnership agreements are a critical supplement and complement to the law of partnerships. The default provisions of partnership legislation governing the relations among partners provide an inadequate and out-of-date skeleton of a structure not suitable for most partnerships. Often the default rules governing the relations among partners, including those dealing with management, interests in profits and capital, membership in the partnership, and dissolution will need to be changed. It will also be desirable, in most circumstances, to create monitoring and control arrangements for the purpose of reducing the likelihood of unauthorized behaviour, procedures to govern how the partnership is to act collectively, and provisions to deal with how liability imposed under partnership law will be allocated among the partners.

Finally, we looked at contractual joint ventures and limited partnerships. Joint ventures, although they are not partnerships, may have some lesser partnership-like legal consequences. In some circumstances, joint venturers owe each other a fiduciary duty not to put their personal interests ahead of the interests of the venture and have liability for obligations incurred in connection with the venture. Limited partnerships are like general partnerships except that the liability of at least one partner is limited to the amount she invested in the partnership. Such limited partners also have restrictions on their ability to participate in management. If a limited partner violates the restrictions, he loses his limited liability and becomes a general partner.

FURTHER READINGS

DEARDS, E., "Partnership Law in the Twenty-first Century" (2001) J. Bus. L. 357

BOWES, R.H., "Limited Liability Professional Partnerships," (2000) 34 Can. Bus. L. J. 3

BROMBERG, A.R., *Crane and Bromberg on Partnership* (St. Paul: West, 1968)

ELLIS, M.V., *Fiduciary Duties in Canada* (Don Mills: De Boo, 1988)

FLANNIGAN, R.D., "The Control Test of Investor Liability in Limited Partnerships" (1983) 21 Alta. L. Rev. 303

FLETCHER, K.L., *The Law of Partnership in Australia and New Zealand*, 6th ed. (Sydney: Law Book Co., 1991)

GOWER, L.C.B., ed., *Pollock on the Law of Partnership*, 15th ed. (London: Stevens, 1952)

HEPBURN, L.R., & W.J. STRAIN, *Limited Partnerships* (Toronto: Carswell, 1983) (looseleaf)

KELLOUGH, H.J., "The Business of Defining a Partnership under the Income Tax Act" (1974) 22 Can. Tax. J. 189

LAW SOCIETY OF UPPER CANADA, *Bar Admission Course Reference Materials: Business Law* (Toronto: Law Society of Upper Canada, 2002) c. 2

LOKE, A.F. H., "Fiduciary Duties and Implied Duties of Good Faith in Contractual Joint Ventures," [1999] J. Bus. Law 538

MANZER, A.R., *A Practical Guide to Canadian Partnership Law* (Aurora: Canada Law Book, 1995) (looseleaf)

PHILIPPS, L., "The Amazing Three-Headed Limited Partner: Reflections on Old Loopholes and New Jurisprudence" (1993) 21 Can. Bus. L.J. 410

SCAMMELL, E.H., & R.C. BANKS, eds., *Lindley and Banks on the Law of Partnership*, 18th ed. (London: Sweet & Maxwell, 2002)

WATEROUS, R.N., "Some Problems in the Formation and Function of the Small Professional Partnership" [1977] Spec. Lect. L.S.U.C. 19

ZIEGEL, J.S., et al., Cases and Materials on Partnerships and Canadian Business Corporations, 3d ed. (Toronto: Carswell, 1994)

CHAPTER 3

INTRODUCTION TO CORPORATE LAW

A. INTRODUCTION

In this chapter, we introduce the corporation from a variety of perspectives. After a historical overview of the development of corporate law in Canada, we will briefly describe the current form of corporate law in terms of the following questions:

- What is the constitutional competence of the federal government and the provinces in relation to corporations?
- What is the current process of incorporation and organization of corporations in Canada?
- What is the function of corporate law and what policies underpin it?
- What are the implications of the separate legal existence of the corporation?
- To what extent is the *Charter of Rights and Freedoms* applicable to corporations?

B. A BRIEF HISTORICAL NOTE ON CANADIAN CORPORATE LAW

Before the nineteenth century, only two types of incorporation were provided for in English and Canadian law. First, a corporation could be created by exercise of the royal prerogative. This was done by the

Crown issuing letters patent sometimes referred to as a "Royal Charter." Second, incorporation could be effected by a special or general Act of the legislature. Incorporation by an enactment of the legislature rarely occurred, though Canadian legislatures sometimes passed special acts to permit incorporation for a particular purpose. A small number of royal charters were granted, such as the charter of the Hudson's Bay Company granted by England in 1670.

In 1849 statutes were passed in Upper and Lower Canada allowing for the incorporation of companies for the purpose of building roads and bridges.[1] Incorporation did not require the exercise of the royal prerogative but was obtained by the registration of certain documents in the county in which the work was to be done. These companies did not resemble modern business corporations. They were organizations set up for a limited purpose, and did not provide limited liability.

In 1850 the United Provinces of Canada enacted a general statute for incorporation.[2] Following the American approach, the new Act permitted incorporation for mining, shipbuilding, manufacturing, and chemical businesses through an expeditious process that did not depend on the exercise of the royal prerogative. Like the 1849 Acts, incorporation was obtained simply by the registration of certain documents. Unlike those incorporated under the 1849 Acts, corporations under this Act had two of the defining characteristics we associate with the modern corporation: separate legal personality and limited liability. In contrast to modern corporations, however, their life was limited to fifty years.

In 1862 the English *Companies Act*[3] was passed. It, too, was based on a registration approach; the Act provided for incorporation on the filing of the documents required by statute: a memorandum of association and articles of association. Unlike earlier legislation, however, this Act permitted incorporation for any commercial purpose.

For some reason, the United Provinces of Canada reverted to a model based on the exercise of royal prerogative in a new general incorporation statute passed in 1864.[4] Under this Act, letters patent

1   *An Act to Authorize the Formation of Joint Stock Companies for the Construction of Roads and Other Works in Upper Canada*, S.C. 1849, c. 84; and *An Act to Authorize the Formation of Joint Stock Companies in Lower Canada for the Construction of Macadamized Roads, and of Bridges and Other Works of Like Nature*, S.C. 1849, c. 56.

2   *An Act to Provide for the Formation of Incorporated Joint Stock Companies, for Manufacturing, Mining, Mechanical or Chemical Purposes*, S.C. 1850, c. 28.

3   *Companies Act* (U.K.), 1862, c. 89.

4   *An Act to Authorize the Granting of Charters of Incorporation to Manufacturing, Mining, and Other Companies*, S.C. 1864, c. 23.

were issued on application to the Governor in Council. The letters patent approach was followed in the federal incorporation statute enacted in 1869[5] and in provincial legislation in Prince Edward Island, New Brunswick, Quebec, Ontario, and Manitoba. In contrast, by 1900, Nova Scotia, Newfoundland, Saskatchewan, Alberta, and British Columbia had enacted corporate legislation providing for incorporation through filing a memorandum and articles of association following the English registration approach.

There are certain conceptual differences between the registration and letters patent approaches. As mentioned above, the creation of a corporation under letters patent statutes is a discretionary act of the Crown. Under a registration approach, incorporation must be granted by the state so long as the documents filed satisfy the statutory requirements. Also, a letters patent corporation is deemed to have the rights and powers of a natural person, whereas a corporation under the English registration system (referred to here as a "memorandum corporation") has only the powers provided for expressly or by implication in its articles. In effect, this meant that actions of memorandum corporations frequently were attacked as outside their corporate powers or *ultra vires*. Under English registration model statutes, the incorporators have to provide a set of rules in the memorandum and articles of association governing how the corporation is to function internally: who is authorized to act for the corporation; how the shareholders and directors exercise power; and so on. With letters patent corporations, these rules are set out in the corporation's by-laws or in the statute. The significance of this distinction is that letters patent corporations do not have to file their by-laws with the state, so much less information concerning the internal working of such corporations becomes a matter of public record. As well, prior to the enactment of modern corporate statutes, persons dealing with a corporation were deemed to have notice of what was on the public record, with the result that, if the requirements of the memorandum or articles were not satisfied in connection with the creation of an obligation to such a person, the obligation could not be enforced. This doctrine of *constructive notice* meant, therefore, that the greater public disclosure required in relation to the internal operation memorandum corporations increased the risk for third parties that their contracts would not be enforced where corporate porcedures were not followed.[6]

---

5   *Canadian Joint Stock Companies Letters Patent Act*, S.C. 1869, c. 13.
6   See section D ("Liability of Corporations in Contract") in Chapter 5.

Perhaps most important, the memorandum and articles of association of memorandum corporations constitute a contract between the members and between the corporation and the members.[7] This contract has two major consequences. First, the memorandum and articles of association are the primary source of the allocation of powers between the directors and the shareholders. Second, the directors act as delegates of the shareholders, and any power not granted to the directors in the memorandum and articles or the statute remains in the shareholders. Under letters patent statutes, by contrast, directors derive their powers from the statute, though some derogation in favour of shareholders is permitted. It is at best unclear whether shareholders in letters patent corporations have a residual authority.[8] This distinction may become relevant where a dispute has arisen between a shareholder and the corporation. The members of a registration corporation can sue civilly for a breach of the memorandum or articles, though their entitlement to damages is limited,[9] whereas shareholders of letters patent corporations must rely, primarily, on statutory remedies.

Throughout most of the twentieth century, Canadian registration and letters patent statutes changed very little. Then, in 1970, Ontario engaged in a wholesale amendment of its corporate law.[10] Based on the Lawrence Committee Report[11] in 1967, the Ontario legislature finally abandoned the letters patent system in favour of a registration system. Unlike the English-style memorandum and articles of association statutes, however, under the new Ontario Act incorporation was effected by filing a simple document called "articles of incorporation." This approach followed the Model Business Corporations Act drafted by the Committee on Corporate Laws of the American Bar Association.

In 1975, based on the recommendations of the Dickerson Committee,[12] the federal government implemented its own new corporate law

---

7   See British Columbia *Companies Act*, R.S.B.C. 1996, c. 62, s. 13 [*BCCA*]; *Companies Act* (U.K.), 1989, c. 40 s. 14; *Hickman v. Kent or Romney Marsh Sheep-Breeders' Association*, [1915] 1 Ch. 881.

8   See, generally, B. Welling, *Corporate Law in Canada: The Governing Principles*, 2d ed. (Toronto: Butterworths, 1991) [Welling], at 38–40 & 48–73, for a discussion of the confused state of the law on the nature of this "statutory contract."

9   J. Ziegel *et al.*, *Cases and Materials on Partnerships and Canadian Business Corporations*, 3d ed. (Toronto: Carswell, 1994) [Ziegel], at 263–268.

10   *The Business Corporations Act*, R.S.O. 1970, c. 53.

11   Ontario, *Interim Report of the Select Committee on Company Law* (Toronto: Queen's Printer, 1967).

12   R.V.W. Dickerson, J.L. Howard, & L. Getz, *Proposals for a New Business Corporations Law for Canada*, 2 vols. (Ottawa: Information Canada, 1971).

statute: the *Canada Business Corporations Act* (*CBCA*). The *CBCA* adopted an articles of incorporation approach along the same general lines as the new Ontario Act but went much further in the protection of minority shareholders.

Most corporate statutes in Canada now follow the *CBCA* model. In 1982 Ontario enacted legislation which, for the most part, mirrored the federal legislation (S.O. 1982, c. 4, now R.S.O. 1990, c. B.16). The *CBCA* model was also adopted in

- Alberta (*Business Corporations Act*, R.S.A 2000, c. B-9 (*ABCA*));
- Saskatchewan (*The Business Corporations Act*, R.S.S. 1978, c. B-10 (*SBCA*));
- Manitoba (*The Corporations Act*, R.S.M. 1987, c. C225 (*MCA*));
- Northwest Territories and Nunavut (*Business Corporations Act*, S.N.W.T. 1996, c. 19); and
- Yukon (*Business Corporations Act*, R.S.Y. 1986, c. 15).

To a lesser extent, the *CBCA* model formed the basis for corporate law reforms in

- Newfoundland (*Corporations Act*, R.S.N. 1990, c. C-36 (*NCA*)); and
- New Brunswick (*Business Corporations Act*, S.N.B. 1981, c. B-9.1 (*NBBCA*)).

The *CBCA* has also influenced major reforms of corporate law in Quebec[13] and Nova Scotia (R.S.N.S. 1989, c. 81; S.N.S. 1990, c. 15 (*NSCA*)). British Columbia reformed its corporate law in 1973 (now the *Company Act*, R.S.B.C. 1996, c. 62 (*BCCA*)) and, although many of the same changes brought about by the *CBCA* were introduced, the B.C. legislation remains distinct, still following the memorandum and articles of association model in the English *Companies Act*. Prince Edward Island retains its letters patent model statute (*Companies Act*, R.S.P.E.I. 1988, c. C-14 (*PEICA*)).

Both the memorandum and articles of association model for corporate statutes, like British Columbia's, and the articles of incorporation model now dominant elsewhere in Canada provide for incorporation on the registration of certain documents. No exercise of government discretion is required. Nevertheless, there are several differences between them. Essentially, the articles of incorporation model, like the letters patent model, creates a statutory allocation of powers, rights, and responsibilities among shareholders, directors, and officers. Much

---

13   Quebec now has two corporate laws: *Companies Act*, R.S.Q. 1977, c. C-38 (*QCA*), and part 1A of that Act as enacted by S.Q. 1980, c. C-38.

of the structure of the corporation is provided by the corporate statute, though, to some extent, this structure may be changed by the parties in the articles or by other means, such as a unanimous shareholders' agreement (USA).[14] The directors are directed to "manage, or supervise the management of, the business and affairs of a corporation" (*CBCA*, s. 102(1)). The Act provides that these powers may be delegated subject to certain limitations (*CBCA*, s. 115(1) & (3)), and it grants certain limited rights for shareholders to have a say in how the corporation is managed.[15] By contrast, under the memorandum and articles of association model, many of the basic rights and obligations of the shareholders are provided for in the memorandum and articles of association, and the memorandum and articles are considered to be a contract between the corporation and the shareholders as discussed above.[16] One must be careful to keep these differences in mind when considering the applicability of judicial decisions rendered in relation to a corporation created under one model to a situation involving a corporation created under the other. Perhaps the most important practical implication of these differences is that, in most cases, shareholders of corporations incorporated under articles of incorporation statutes may not commence a civil suit for breach of the articles but must rely on the statutory remedies provided.[17] In practice, the remedies introduced in the *CBCA* provide much better protection of shareholders' interests than contractual remedies in memorandum corporation jurisdictions.[18] This difference between the two approaches has diminished in importance over time as many of the shareholder-protection features of the *CBCA* have been adopted in the *NSCA* and the *BCCA*. Improved share-

---

14 See Chapter 4.

15 See Chapter 7.

16 See, for example, section 13 of the *BCCA*, above note 7:

> [T]he memorandum and articles, when registered, bind the company and its members to the same extent as if each had been signed and sealed by the company and every member and contained convenants on the part of every member, his heirs, executors and administrators to observe the mememorandum and the articles.

17 The *Canada Business Corporations Act*, R.S.C. 1985, c. C-44 [*CBCA*], does provide that a shareholder, or a creditor, may seek to enforce compliance with the Act, the articles, the by-laws, or any unanimous shareholders' agreement (s. 247). See similar provisions in Ontario *Business Corporations Act*, R.S.O. 1990, c. B.16 [*OBCA*], s. 253, and Alberta *Business Corporations Act*, R.S.A. 2000, c. B-9 [*ABCA*], s. 248.

18 *Ibid*. See also J.G. MacIntosh, "Minority Shareholders Rights in Canada and England: 1860–1987," (1989) 27 Osgoode Hall L.J. 561.

holder remedies continue to distinguish *CBCA* model statutes from letters patent statutes, such as the current *PEICA*.

The *CBCA* made other significant changes to corporate law in Canada: the new Act provided significantly greater flexibility in structuring the corporation by changing mandatory rules into rules that applied except to the extent that the incorporators agreed to change them (called "default rules"); constructive notice and the doctrine of *ultra vires* were abolished; and shareholders were permitted, by unanimous agreement, to assume some or all of the powers of the directors, thus altering the statutory division of powers. Because of the pre-eminence of the *CBCA* as a model for corporate law in Canada, this book focuses on the federal statute, noting the differences between it and the provincial regimes where relevant.

In the discussion of Canadian corporate law that follows, extensive references will be made to both English and American authorities. Notwithstanding the differences between the articles of incorporation and memorandum and articles of association models, there continues to be a strong English influence present in the Canadian cases dealing with the basic concepts and doctrines we share with the United Kingdom arising out of our common legal traditions. As noted, however, the predominant model for corporate law statutes in Canada is American. For this reason and because of the wealth of U.S. case law and scholarship on corporate law issues, as well as the extremely close business ties between the two countries, the influence of American precedents is strong and increasing. Yet, that said, there remain significant differences between the form and content of the regulation of corporate behaviour and the business contexts in the two countries in which corporations operate.[19]

C. CONSTITUTIONAL MATTERS: DIVISION OF POWERS

1) Introduction

As discussed in the foregoing historical overview, both the federal and the provincial governments have enacted corporate law statutes from

---

19   For an excellent discussion of these issues, see R.J. Daniels & J.G. MacIntosh, "Toward a Distinctive Canadian Corporate Law Regime," (1991) 29 Osgoode Hall L. J. 863.

time to time. In this section, we will discuss their respective jurisdictions to incorporate and to regulate corporations.

2) Jurisdiction to Incorporate

a) Provincial Incorporation
Under section 92(11) of the *Constitution Act, 1867*, the provinces have jurisdiction over the "Incorporation of Companies with Provincial Objects." The limitation imposed by the reference to provincial objects has been interpreted narrowly. It has nothing to do with the nature of the corporation's business operations, nor does it impose an effective limitation on the territory within which the corporation operates. All it means is that a province can create corporations with powers exercisable within the province. A province is not capable of endowing a corporation with the right to carry on business in any other jurisdiction, including any other province. One province can grant a corporation the capacity to carry on business in other jurisdictions, but it will become able to do so only if it obtains the permission of the other jurisdiction.[20]

Practically speaking, within Canada, such permission is routinely granted under extra-provincial licensing regimes set up by each province.[21] Under these regimes, corporations incorporated under the laws of another province or territory, or a foreign jurisdiction, may obtain a licence to carry on business on the filing of certain basic information and a fee. Although the decision to grant such a licence is discretionary, licences are rarely refused, except where the name of the corporation seeking to do business in a province is likely to be confused with the name of a business already being carried on in the province.[22] As a result, the mobility of a provincial corporation, at least within Canada, is almost unrestricted.

---

20 *Bonanza Creek Gold Mining Co. Ltd.* v. *R.*, [1916] 1 A.C. 566 (P.C.). The nature of provincial jurisdiction is reflected in section 16 of the *OBCA*, above note 17: "A corporation has the capacity to carry on its business, conduct its affairs and exercise its powers in any jurisdiction outside Ontario to the extent that the laws of such jurisdiction permit." See, similarly, *BCCA*, above note 7, s. 34, and Nova Scotia *Companies Act*, R.S.N.S. 1989 [*NSCA*], c. 81, s. 26(13) .

21 E.g., *BCCA*, *ibid.*, Part 10; and Manitoba *The Corporations Act*, R.S.M. 1987 [*MCA*], c. C225, Part XVI.

22 The Ontario *Extra-Provincial Corporations Act*, R.S.O. 1990, c. E.27, automatically grants a licence to all corporations incorporated in any Canadian jurisdiction (s. 4). See Chapter 4.

b) Federal Incorporation

The *Constitution Act* grants the federal government limited powers to incorporate in certain areas, such as the incorporation of banks, but contains no express general power of incorporation. In *Citizens Insurance Co. of Canada v. Parsons*,[23] however, it was held that such a power was implicit in the federal government's residual jurisdiction to "make Laws for the Peace, Order and good Government of Canada, in relation to all Matters not coming within the Classes of Subjects by this Act assigned exclusively to the Legislatures of the Provinces."[24] The Privy Council reasoned that, since the provinces had been given the jurisdiction to incorporate corporations with provincial objects, the federal government must have jurisdiction to legislate in relation to the incorporation of corporations with objects to be carried out in more than one province. The validity of federal incorporation, however, is not dependent on the corporation, in fact, carrying on business in more than one province.

Unlike provincially incorporated corporations, federally incorporated corporations have a right to carry on business in each province. A federally incorporated corporation cannot be barred from carrying on business in a province as a result of its name being confusing with one already in use in the province or for any other reason.[25] Upon commencing business in a province, however, federal corporations are required to file information similar to that required of a provincial corporation in an application for an extra-provincial licence. So, in practice, there is often little difference in the treatment of federal and provincial corporations.

3) Jurisdiction to Regulate

a) Provincial Regulation of Federal Corporations

To what extent can a provincial government regulate a federally incorporated corporation? This is an important question in light of the extensive provincial regulation of various business activities. The

---

23   (1881), 7 App. Cas. 96 (P.C.).

24   The preamble to section 91 of the *Constitution Act, 1867* (U.K.), 30 & 31 Vict., c. 3 [*CA 1867*].

25   This is one reason that the federal government conducts a much more careful review of names proposed for corporations to be incorporated than the provinces. See "Names" in section B ("The Process of Incorporation and Organization"), in Chapter 4.

answer is based on traditional division of powers jurisprudence.[26] The following outline is a brief overview.

Provinces cannot legislate solely in relation to the status or powers of a federal corporation. In other words, provinces cannot legislate restrictions on the powers of federal corporations, such as, for example, removing limited liability.[27] Provinces cannot directly regulate intra-corporate relations, such as those between directors and shareholders,[28] or require a federal corporation to use a name other than its corporate name for business purposes in the province because of the risk of confusion in the provincial marketplace between the corporation's name and the name used by a business already being carried on in the province.[29]

Provinces can legislate to affect directly the way in which federal corporations exercise their powers if two requirements are met:

- the legislation can be justified as primarily in relation to a provincial head of jurisdiction in section 92 of the *Constitution Act, 1867*; and
- the legislation is not inconsistent with federal law.

If the second requirement is not met, the provincial law will be ineffective to the extent of the inconsistency based on the doctrine of paramountcy.[30] So, for example, provincial securities legislation designed to protect Ontario investors may be validly enacted under the province's jurisdiction to legislate in relation to property and civil rights under section 92(13) of the *Constitution Act* so long as it is not inconsistent with federal corporate law. Provincial securities legislation that regulates the way in which securities of a federal corporation are sold in the province by requiring sales through provincially registered dealers has

---

26   This subject is reviewed effectively by Professor Peter Hogg in *Constitutional Law of Canada*, 4th ed. (Toronto: Carswell, 1997) [Hogg], Chapter 23.

27   Ontario legislation preventing unlicensed corporations, including federal corporations, from holding freehold property was upheld as not being in relation to the status or powers of a federal corporation (*Great West Saddlery Co. v. R.*, [1921] 2 A.C. 91 (P.C.)).

28   Though, as will be discussed in Chapter 11, provincial securities law has a significant impact in this area.

29   *Reference Re Constitution Act, 1867*, ss. 91 & 92 (1991), 80 D.L.R. (4th) 431 (Man. C.A.) [*Reference Re Constitution Act*].

30   *Multiple Access Ltd. v. McCutcheon*, [1982] 2 S.C.R. 161. In that case, separate insider trading legislation enacted by Ontario which was largely duplicative of insider trading rules imposed by the federal government on corporations incorporated federally was upheld on the basis that there was no actual conflict between the two schemes. Paramountcy does not restrict the regulation of foreign extra-provincial corporations.

been upheld as validly enacted and not inconsistent with federal law.[31] By contrast, legislation giving provincial regulators the power to prohibit the sale of securities — in the interests of protecting investors if a corporation refuses to make requested changes to its articles — has been held to be inconsistent with federal corporate law, which gives corporations the right to issue securities.[32]

Name registration statutes are another example of valid provincial legislation. Such legislation, which exists in every province, requires registration of business names used by corporations carrying on business in the province which are different from their corporate names. Its purpose is to provide the public with a means of ascertaining the legal identity of the person legally responsible for a business that is conducted under a name other than the corporate name. This is a matter of civil rights in the province, and such registration requirements can be imposed on federal corporations.[33]

Provinces can also enact laws that are solely within one of the enumerated heads of section 92 of the *Constitution Act, 1867*, such as labour law, contract law, and much industry specific-legislation, even if the effect is, indirectly, to affect the way the federal corporation carries on business or even to sterilize the federal corporation by prohibiting it from carrying on business. An example of this sort of provincial legislation was the British Columbia legislation setting up a provincially operated automobile insurance scheme that precluded private insurance companies from offering automobile insurance in the province. The Supreme Court of Canada upheld this legislation as validly enacted in relation to property and civil rights in the province even though one of its effects was to preclude federal insurance companies from carrying on business in British Columbia.[34]

To summarize, a province cannot enact legislation that operates directly to affect some essential aspect of a federal corporation, but provinces have jurisdiction to regulate most businesses and their activities, including their ability to sell securities, their relations with their employees, and the contracts they enter into. A federal corporation is subject to provincial regulation to the extent that it is involved in these businesses or activities.[35]

---

31 *Lymburn v. Mayland*, [1932] A.C. 318 (P.C.).
32 *Manitoba (A.G.) v. Canada (A.G.)*, [1929] A.C. 260 (P.C.).
33 *Reference Re Constitution Act*, above note 29.
34 *Canadian Indemnity Co. v. British Columbia (A.G.)* (1976), [1977] 2 S.C.R. 504.
35 Welling, above note 8, at 20.

b) Federal Regulation of Provincial Corporations

Since most business areas are within the jurisdiction of the provinces, federal regulation of provincial corporations may be thought of as somewhat less important than the provincial regulation of federal corporations and it has generated little jurisprudence. There are, however, several critically important areas within federal regulatory competence, such as telecommunications and interprovincial transportation.[36]

Professor Hogg's view is that the federal government may not regulate provincial corporations directly in relation to their corporate status or characteristics. It may, however, directly affect the way in which provincial corporations exercise their powers if the legislation can be justified as primarily in relation to an area of jurisdiction assigned to the federal government.[37]

c) Regulation of Extra-provincial Corporations

Both provincial and federal governments have broad jurisdiction to regulate corporations operating outside the Canadian province or foreign jurisdiction in which they were incorporated. Each provincial government is competent to legislate in ways that affect the status and characteristics of such an extra-provincial corporation for the purposes of its operations within the province. Similarly, the federal government may legislate so as to affect the status and characteristics a foreign or provincial corporation operating outside its jurisdiction of incorporation.[38] In each case, of course, the legislation would have to be otherwise within the constitutional power of the legislating government. Apart from extra-provincial licensing schemes enacted in each province, neither level of government has enacted legislation that imposes a heavier regulatory burden on extra-provincial corporations incorporated in Canada, though some statutes discriminate against foreign incorporated corporations.[39]

---

36   Such matters fall within federal jurisdiction under the residual jurisdiction created by the Peace, Order and Good Government clause or the jurisdiction under section 91(29) and section 92(10) over interprovincial undertakings (*CA 1867*, above note 24).

37   Hogg, above note 26, at Chapter 23, ¶23-18 to 23-19.

38   *Ibid.*, at 23-16 to 23-19.

39   E.g., the *Income Tax Act*, R.S.C. 1985 (5th Supp.), c. 1 [*ITA*].

D. INCORPORATION AND ORGANIZATION

1) What Is a Business Corporation?

The corporate statutes we will be looking at govern business corporations. Charitable and other not-for-profit entities are governed under separate statutory regimes.[40] Similarly, the corporate statutes do not apply to certain entities carrying on businesses subject to their own separate scheme of regulation. The *CBCA* does not apply to banks, which are governed by the *Bank Act*; insurance companies, which are governed by the *Insurance Companies Act*; or trust and loan companies, which are governed by the *Trust and Loan Companies Act* (*CBCA*, s. 3(4)).[41]

2) The Incorporation Process

The process of incorporation will be discussed in more detail in Chapter 4, but it is useful here to outline the basic elements as a way of introducing the sources of the rules governing the relationships among directors, shareholders, and officers as well as some basic vocabulary.

When one or more people or corporations decide that they want to carry on business using a corporation, they must file certain prescribed material with the branch of the federal government or one of the provincial or territorial governments having responsibility for incorporations.[42] Under the *CBCA*, it is necessary to file the following with the Corporations Directorate of Industry Canada:

- articles of incorporation (s. 6, Form 1);
- notice of registered office (s. 19(2), Form 3);
- notice of directors (s. 106, Form 6);
- a name-search report on the proposed name of the corporation; and
- the fee of $250.[43]

---

40 Federally non-profit and charitable corporations may be incorporated under the *Canada Corporations Act*, R.S.C. 1970, c. C-32. In Ontario, incorporation is under the *Corporations Act*, R.S.O. 1990, c. C.38. Incorporation under these Acts is by letters patent.

41 See *OBCA*, above note 17, s. 2; *BCCA*, above note 7, ss. 2–4, for exclusions from the scope of the corporate statute.

42 See Chapter 4 for a discussion of considerations relevant to choosing the jurisdiction under which to incorporate.

43 Currently, the fee is reduced to $200 if incorporation is done on-line. The fee for incorporation under the *OBCA*, above note 17, is $330. Other documents may be required in other jurisdictions as discussed in Chapter 4.

The articles are by far the most important of these documents because they set out the fundamental characteristics of the corporation: the name of the corporation, the class and number of shares authorized to be issued, the number of directors, any restrictions on transferring shares, and any restrictions on the business the corporation may carry on.

Once these documents are properly filed along with the fee, the Director appointed to administer the CBCA issues a certificate, to which the articles are attached (Form 2), certifying that the corporation was incorporated on the date of the certificate (CBCA, ss. 8 & 9). The corporation comes into existence on the date of this certificate (CBCA, s. 9). The directors named in the notice of directors hold office until the first meeting of shareholders at which an election of directors is held (CBCA, s. 106(2)). The provisions in the articles may be changed only by articles of amendment filed with the Director after approval by a special resolution of shareholders.[44]

On incorporation, the corporation may commence carrying on a business. The business may be a new one, or an existing business may be transferred to the corporation. Unlike a partnership, there is no need for a corporation to carry on business; its existence derives exclusively from issuance of the certificate under the statute. Several more steps are required, however, before the corporation is fully organized.

First, the directors should have a meeting and pass a resolution to issue shares to the shareholders. Typically, at the first meeting, the directors will adopt arrangements for carrying on the formal legal business of the corporation, including how notice is given of meetings of directors and shareholders, what constitutes a quorum, who may sign contracts on behalf of the corporation, and what the offices of the corporation (e.g., president and secretary) will be. These arrangements are usually set out in a by-law. To take effect, a by-law must be passed by the directors, but it continues in effect only if it is passed by the shareholders at their next meeting following the approval by the directors (CBCA, s. 103). Because making, amending, and repealing by-laws ultimately requires shareholder approval, including these arrangements in a by-law serves to entrench them as part of the corporation's constitution.[45]

At the first meeting, directors will pass resolutions dealing with other organizational matters, such as appointing officers, and making

---

44   A special resolution is a resolution signed by all shareholders or passed at a meeting of shareholders by a majority of not less than two-thirds of the votes cast by shareholders present and voting at the meeting (CBCA, above note 17, s. 2(1) (definition of special resolution), see below. See, similarly, OBCA, ibid., ss. 1(1) (definition of special resolution), 9, 11, 12 & 110.

45   See Chapter 4.

banking arrangements, such as authorizing certain people to sign cheques on behalf of the corporation. Once the shares are issued, it is common, though not necessary, to have a shareholders' meeting at which any by-laws approved by the directors are voted on and an auditor appointed.

A final organizational step that often occurs in corporations with few shareholders is that the shareholders enter into an agreement to govern their relationship with each other. Shareholders may wish to customize the way in which the corporation is governed by agreeing to alter the rights and obligations provided for in the *CBCA*.[46]

In order to determine what rules govern a corporation, its shareholders, directors, and officers, it is necessary to take into account not just the governing corporate statute and the case law but also the elements of the corporate constitution identified above: the articles of incorporation, the by-laws, directors' resolutions, shareholders' resolutions, and any shareholders' agreement. These documents are agreed to by the directors or shareholders, or both, and represent, in that sense, private arrangements between them. They are private arrangements which are bounded by various mandatory provisions of the corporate statutes and are, to a greater or lesser extent, enforceable through statutory mechanisms, as discussed in Chapter 9.

All these documents (other than directors' resolutions and minutes of directors' meetings) must be maintained by the corporation at its registered office (*CBCA*, s. 20), usually in something called a "minute book," and shareholders and creditors must be given access to them (*CBCA*, s. 21). Articles and any other document filed with the Director appointed under the *CBCA*, such as the notice of directors and notice of registered office, are placed in a publicly accessible record.

E. FUNCTION OF CORPORATE LAW

1) Introduction

A business organization is used to run a business, and various classes of people have an interest in that business. In Chapter 1, we described the business organization as a nexus of relationships among such stakeholders. In the corporation, these stakeholders are the shareholder/owners, the managers (consisting of the officers and directors),

---

46   Shareholders' agreements are discussed in section G ("Shareholders' Agreements") of Chapter 7.

employees, creditors (both trade and financial), customers, the public, and government. In this section, we deal with what function corporations and corporate law fulfil in relation to these stakeholders.

In general, corporate law operates to encourage people to invest money in starting, maintaining, and expanding businesses. To understand how it does so, it is necessary first to consider how people make decisions about investing. The basic corporate finance model for investment decision making holds that people make decisions to invest based on an evaluation of the returns expected from the investment and the risk associated with those returns. Returns may take the form of interest on a loan, dividends on shares, an increase in the price of shares, or something else. Risk may be thought of as the likelihood that the expected returns will be received in light of the range of possible returns the investor could receive. The rational investor will invest only if the expected returns are sufficient, given the risks associated with those returns. The riskier the investment, the higher must be the expected returns because the investor will require compensation for bearing the additional risk that the expected returns will not be received. In choosing between two investments promising the same expected returns, the rational investor should invest in the one promising returns that are less risky. Figure 3.1 illustrates the implications of the relationship of risk and return for investment decision making.

Figure 3.1   Example of How Risk and Expected Returns Affect Investment Decision Making

Canada Savings Bonds (CSBs) are a low-risk investment because the payment obligation is undertaken by the federal government. Indeed, since there is virtually no other possible return than the stated interest rate, the range of possible returns and the risk is 0.

Because CSBs are a "no risk" investment, you might be prepared to buy them when they promise a return in the form of interest of, say, 5 percent.

By contrast, investing in the shares of a diamond-exploration business is much riskier. If the business finds diamonds, your shares may skyrocket in value such that the best possible return may be, say, 500 percent. On the other hand, it is certainly possible that no diamonds will ever be found, in which case not only will you receive no positive return but your shares may be worthless. This worst case represents a negative return, or a loss, of 100 percent. So the range of possible outcomes is from a 500 percent gain to a 100 percent loss. Given the risk that this range of possible outcomes represents, an investor would not invest in the diamond-exploration business unless she expected returns substantially higher than the returns on the no-risk CSBs.

Other things being equal, a business opportunity will become more attractive for investors as the returns increase or as the risk associated with those returns diminishes, or both. Corporate law does both and so operates to encourage investment. As will be discussed below, corporate law also contains certain provisions that provide protection for other stakeholders,[47] though this is very much a secondary purpose of corporate law. The main legal ways in which the interests of other stakeholders are protected are through regulation in other areas (such as commercial law, labour law, products liability law, and so on).

2) Corporate Law Increases Returns by Decreasing Costs

Like partnership law, corporate law provides certain presumptive or default rules that apply to govern the relationship between the corporation and its shareholders in the absence of some other rule being agreed on by the corporation and its shareholders and expressed in the articles, by-laws, or a shareholders' agreement. In this way, corporate law provides a sort of standard-form contract that parties setting up a corporation may adopt, in whole or in part, or may replace with their own arrangements. To the extent that this standard-form contract is a good approximation of what most parties would have worked out for themselves if they had the time and money to do so, the availability of the standard form will save the parties money. In economists' jargon, it reduces the transaction costs of setting up a corporation. Some examples of these default rules are the rules regarding the calling and conduct of shareholders' and directors' meetings (*CBCA*, ss. 94–114 & 117–19). These kinds of default rules are called "enabling rules" and increase returns to shareholders by reducing the costs of setting up a corporation.

As discussed in more detail in the next section, corporate law also reduces costs by providing limited liability. Although there are alternative ways of reducing liability, such as contractual provisions and insurance, they are not usually as inexpensive or comprehensive as incorporation.

3) Corporate Law Decreases Shareholder Risk

a) Limited Liability
Though shareholders are often said to have limited liability for the obligations of the corporations, this is really only a somewhat inaccurate

---

47   See "Corporate Law Decreases Shareholder Risk" and "Balancing Mandatory Rules Protecting Non-shareholder Stakeholders" in section E ("The Function of Corporate Law") in this chapter.

way of saying that the most a shareholder can lose in connection with the business of the corporation is the amount of her investment. Corporate law provides that a shareholder is not directly liable for the debts and obligations of the corporation at all.

By providing a simple cost-effective mechanism to limit shareholders' potential loss, corporate law reduces the risk associated with investing. It caps the worst possible return at a loss of 100 percent of a shareholder's investment. This may be contrasted with a partnership in which the maximum loss is all of a partner's business and personal assets. Capping the risk encourages investment. The size of the incentive created by corporate law will depend on the cost effectiveness of corporate limited liability as compared with other ways of limiting risk, such as through insurance or contractual provisions, as well as how effectively it protects shareholders. We will discuss some of the limits of limited liability below. Notwithstanding these limits, limited liability does protect shareholders effectively and cheaply. Contracts have to be negotiated and will not protect shareholders against those not in a contractual relationship with the corporation, such as tort victims. Insurance policies always have their own exclusions, do not apply to liabilities arising from ordinary commercial obligations, and require relatively substantial premiums on an ongoing basis.

It is important to note that limited liability for shareholders does not eliminate risk but shifts it to other stakeholders, such as employees and creditors. Limiting the pool of assets that creditors and employees may claim against to those belonging to the corporation increases the likelihood that there will be insufficient assets to pay the creditors, employees, and others with financial claims against the corporation. By providing limited liability, corporate law represents an intervention in the marketplace that strikes a particular balance between the interests of shareholders and those of claimants against the corporation, a balance that favours shareholders.

b) Mandatory Rules Protecting All Shareholders

Corporate law reduces the risk of investing in a corporation by imposing certain mandatory rules designed to protect shareholders from abuse by management. We will discuss the problem of management misbehaviour in more detail below.[48] For the purposes of this introduction, it is sufficient simply to note that where management is not carried out by the shareholders themselves, there is a risk that managers

---

48   See Chapters 7 and 8.

will act to benefit their own interests instead of those of the corpora-tion and the shareholders. As is discussed in Chapter 1, corporate law seeks to ensure that management is accountable through various mandatory rules. In addition to giving shareholders the power to deter-mine collectively who becomes a director, corporate law

- imposes standards of behaviour on managers, such as their fiduciary duty to act in the best interests of the corporation (*CBCA*, s. 122(1)(a));
- facilitates shareholder monitoring of managers, such as by requiring disclosure of financial information (*CBCA*, s. 155(1)); and
- provides a variety of remedial procedures for shareholders to obtain relief in the event that management misbehaves (e.g., providing for an application to obtain compliance with the corporate statute, *CBCA*, s. 247).

In all these ways, corporate law decreases risk. These rules also increase expected returns for shareholders to the extent that they prevent man-agers from enriching themselves at the expense of the corporation.

c) Mandatory Rules Protecting Minority Shareholders

Finally, corporate law contains a variety of mandatory rules to protect the interests of minority shareholders from exploitation by the majori-ty. Since corporations operate based on majority rule, any person or group of persons who has control of a majority of the votes attached to the corporation's shares has control of the corporation. Such a person can control who are elected as directors and the outcome of any vote by shareholders. Because directors are elected by majority vote, there is a risk that they will favour the interests of majority shareholders over those of the minority in exercising their power to manage the corpora-tion. A majority shareholder may exert its power in ways beneficial to itself at the expense of the corporation and minority shareholders, such as by causing the corporation to enter into a favourable contract with itself. To guard against this risk, mandatory rules require a two-thirds majority for shareholder approval of certain fundamental changes to the corporation, such as the sale of "all or substantially all the property of a corporation" (*CBCA*, s. 189(3)), and give minority shareholders a right to be bought out if they disagree with the outcome of a vote approving such changes (*CBCA*, s. 190). All these shareholder-protection devices decrease the risks associated with minority shareholder investment and are likely to increase expected returns. Because they impose limits on control by majority shareholders, they increase the risks and decrease the returns for majority shareholder investors correspondingly.

d) Balancing Mandatory Rules Protecting Non-shareholder Stakeholders

As mentioned above, protection of the interests of stakeholders other than shareholders typically is provided by legislation outside the corporate law area. Nevertheless, corporate law does contain certain mandatory rules in favour of such stakeholders. For example, a corporation may not pay dividends to shareholders if it is insolvent, or if it would be insolvent after making the payment (*CBCA*, s. 42). This indirectly benefits creditors and others with financial claims against the corporation, like employees, by ensuring that assets needed to pay those obligations are not transferred to shareholders. The courts have also developed certain rules that permit them to disregard corporate law's limited liability rule and to impose personal liability on shareholders in some circumstances.[49] These mandatory rules represent a further intervention in the marketplace to shift the risk associated with business activities carried on by a corporation back to the corporation and the shareholders.

Throughout this book, we will be looking at how corporate law operates to encourage investment through the combination of mandatory and enabling rules described above, as well as the extent to which it balances these incentive measures with rules protecting the interests of other stakeholders.

F. THE NATURE OF THE CORPORATION

1) Separate Legal Existence and Limited Liability

Incorporation brings into existence a new legal person whose rights and obligations may be thought of as analogous to those of a human person.[50] Section 15(1) of the *CBCA* provides that a "corporation has the capacity and, subject to this Act, the rights, powers and privileges of a natural person." Other corporate statutes have similar provisions.[51] In this section, we discuss what this definition means in legal and practical terms.

---

49   See section G ("Disregard of Separate Corporate Personality") in this chapter.

50   The current corporate law as described in this section is based on the notion that the corporation is solely a creation of the statute. There are, however, other theoretical constructions of the nature of corporate personality. For a brief discussion of these alternate constructions, see Ziegel, above note 9, at 138–39.

51   For example, *OBCA*, above note 17, s. 15; *ABCA*, above note 17, s. 16(1); *BCCA*, above note 7, ss. 21–25.

The separate legal existence of the corporation was authoritatively confirmed by the House of Lords in *Salomon* v. *Salomon & Co.*[52] In that case, Aron Salomon transferred a leather-boot business carried on by him as a sole proprietor to a corporation in which he and six of his family members were shareholders. As part of the consideration paid for transfer of the business, the corporation issued debentures to him which represented a claim against the corporation for £10,000, secured against the assets of the business now owned by the corporation. It also issued shares to him. As a result, after the transfer, he held the vast majority of the shares and was in effective control of the corporation as well as being a secured creditor. Shortly after the business was transferred to the corporation, it ran into serious financial difficulty, despite Salomon's best efforts. Ultimately, a liquidator was appointed to gather in the assets of the corporation, pay off the debts, and transfer any remaining assets to the shareholders. If the secured claim of Salomon were paid first, as it normally would be, there would have been no assets left out of which to pay the unsecured creditors.

The liquidator claimed that the corporation was a sham in that it was merely Salomon carrying on business in another name. It was argued that Salomon was still personally carrying on the business; the corporation was merely his agent for doing so. Since the corporation was only an agent, Salomon's claim under the debentures was really a claim against himself and so unenforceable.

The House of Lords rejected the liquidator's claim. It held that what Salomon had done was exactly what was contemplated in the *Companies Act* of 1862 and that all the requirements of the Act had been complied with. In these circumstances, there was no reason not to give effect to the separate legal existence of the corporation and to permit Aron Salomon's claim to be paid ahead of the unsecured creditors. It did not matter that Aron Salomon was in effective control of the corporation, the other six shareholders being family members under his control and, in the words of Lord MacNaughton, "mere nominees of Mr. Salomon — mere dummies." The House of Lords said there was no requirement in the Act that the shareholders each have a mind of his own.[53] The fact

---

52 [1897] A.C. 22 (H.L.) [*Salomon*].

53 Apparently this was not the intention of the English Parliament. The purpose for requiring seven shareholders was to avoid incorporation of small partnerships (P. Ireland, "The Triumph of the Company Legal Form, 1856–1914" in J. Adams, ed., *Essays for Clive Schmitthoff* (London: Professional Books, 1983) at 29, cited in Ziegel, above note 9, at 122). Incorporation by a small number or even a single person is expressly permitted under Canadian corporate statutes.

that the business was precisely the same after it was transferred to the corporation as it was before, that the same persons were the managers, and that the same hands ultimately received the financial rewards associated with the business, did not make the corporation the agent of the shareholder.

This case is almost universally cited for the proposition that the corporation is a separate legal entity. Yet, notwithstanding the strong position taken in the case and the substantial influence it has had on the development of Canadian corporate law, we discuss below the various ways in which the courts have eroded the separateness of legal personality.[54] In the remainder of this section, we flesh out the consequences of the separate legal personality of the corporation.

As indicated in *Salomon*, the separate legal existence of the corporation means that a shareholder may also be a creditor, even a secured creditor of the corporation. This is permitted under Canadian corporate law. The only restriction is that the granting of a security interest in favour of a shareholder may not be given effect if the purpose of doing so is to defeat the claims of existing creditors.[55]

Another consequence of the separate existence of the corporation is that a corporation owns its own property. The shareholders have certain property-like rights in the corporation but no property interest in the assets of the corporation.[56]

The specific bundle of rights that shareholders have will depend on the provisions set out in the articles and the corporate statute, as will be discussed in Chapter 6. In general, shares represent a claim on the residual value of the corporation after the claims of all creditors have been paid.[57] The value of this residual claim will be a function of the value of the corporation's business. Unfortunately, valuing a business is a complex and inevitably imprecise exercise because the value will

---

54   See section G ("Disregard of Separate Corporate Personality") in this chapter.

55   See, for example, the Ontario *Fraudulent Conveyances Act*, R.S.O. 1990, c. F-29 [*Fraudulent Conveyances Act*], and the federal *Bankruptcy and Insolvency Act*, R.S.C. 1985, c. B-3.

56   *Army & Navy Department Store* v. *M.N.R.*, [1953] 2 S.C.R. 496, approved in *Bow Valley Husky (Bermuda) Ltd.* v. *Saint John Shipbuilding Ltd.* (1995), 130 Nfld. & P.E.I.R. 92, at 105 (Nfld C.A.), aff'd on other grounds, [1997] 3 S.C.R. 1210 [*Bow Valley*].

57   Where there is only one class of shares, it must have this residual claim (*CBCA*, above note 17, s. 24(3)). Where there is more than one class of shares, at least one must have this claim (*CBCA*, s. 24(4)). Typically, the other classes will have some other limited claim on assets, such as a claim to the return of the amount invested for those shares. See Chapter 6.

depend on a variety of factors that will change over time. For example, the value of a business will rest, in part, on the value of the tangible assets owned by the business, which themselves may be difficult to assess. How much is a piece of commercial real estate in downtown Toronto worth? Increasingly, it will also depend on intangible assets that are even harder to value. How much is Coca-Cola's "Coke" trademark worth? The value of corporate assets will also depend on what you intend to do with them. Most businesses are worth more as an operating unit or as a "going concern" than if the assets were sold piecemeal. The value of an ongoing business in excess of the value of the assets sold piecemeal is called "goodwill." The expected future growth of the business will also be a significant factor in determining value.[58]

The courts considered this residual nature of the claim represented by shares of a corporation in *Kosmopoulos* v. *Constitution Insurance Co. of Canada*.[59] Kosmopoulos was the sole shareholder in and the only director of a corporation carrying on a leather-goods business. He was not careful to distinguish his personal rights and obligations from those of the corporation and, as a result, the insurance on the assets of the corporation's business was taken out in his name rather than in the name of the corporation. When a fire damaged assets of the business, the insurance company refused to pay on the ground that Kosmopoulos did not have an "insurable interest" in the assets. The Supreme Court ultimately determined that, even though Kosmopoulos had no ownership interest in the assets, his interest as the sole shareholder in the residual value of the corporation's assets gave him such a substantial stake in those assets that it could amount to an insurable interest.

Recall that, with partnerships, a partner cannot be an employee of the partnership because the partnership is not a legal entity separate from the partners. Since a corporation is a separate entity, a shareholder may be an employee of the corporation in which he holds shares just as he may be a secured creditor. In *Lee* v. *Lee's Air Farming Ltd.*,[60] a person was held to be capable of entering a contract of employment with a corporation of which he held all but one of the shares and was appointed "governing director ... for life." The Judicial Committee of the Privy Council expressly held that it did not matter that this would

---

58 For a discussion of business valuation from a lawyer's point of view, see V. Krishna, "Determining the 'Fair Value' of Corporate Shares" (1988) 13 Can. Bus. L.J. 132, and F.M. Buckley, M. Gillen, & R. Yalden, *Corporations: Principles and Policies*, 3d ed. (Toronto: Emond Montgomery, 1995) [*Buckley*] at 1–13.

59 (1983), 42 O.R. (2d) 428 (C.A.), aff'd [1987] 1 S.C.R. 2 [*Kosmopoulos*].

60 (1960), [1961] A.C. 12 (P.C.).

mean that he would negotiate his employment contract with himself acting on behalf of the corporation.[61]

One important implication for lawyers of the separation between the legal personality of the corporation and its shareholders is that a corporation may need to be provided with legal advice separately from the shareholders. The interests of a majority shareholder, a minority shareholder, and the corporation itself may come into conflict in some circumstances. Where this occurs, a lawyer must be careful to ascertain who her client is.[62]

2) Balancing Rules Protecting Other Stakeholders

a) Limits on Limited Liability

Limited liability is a creation of the law designed to encourage entrepreneurship by shifting the risk of business activity from shareholders to other stakeholders. Although it is often said that the courts strictly adhere to limited liability as a feature of separate corporate personality, there are a variety of circumstances in which they do not, with the result that personal liability is imposed on shareholders. In other words, despite the express statutory grant of limited liability (*CBCA*, s. 45),[63] the courts have arrogated to themselves the power to disregard the separateness of corporate legal personality. Unfortunately, the many cases in which this approach has been taken "illustrate no consistent

---

61   A final issue relating to the nature of the corporate personality arises in the context of criminal proceedings against the corporation when a director, officer, or senior employee is called to testify: Does a corporation have a right against self-incrimination and, if so, when is it violated? See the discussion of the right against self-incrimination guaranteed by section 11(d) of the *Charter of Rights and Freedoms*, Part I of the *Constitution Act, 1982*, being Schedule B to the *Canada Act 1982* (U.K.), 1982, c. 11, in section I ("Application of the *Charter of Rights and Freedoms* to Corporations") of this chapter. See also S.A. Trainor, "A Comparative Analysis of a Corporation's Right against Self-Incrimination" (1995) 18 Fordham Int'l L.J. 2139.

62   See Law Society of Upper Canada, *Rules of Professional Conduct*, Rule 2.04, which addresses how lawyers in Ontario must deal with such conflicts (www.lsuc.on.ca/services/RulesProfCondpage_en.jsp (visited August 27, 2002)).

63   See, similarly, *OBCA*, above note 17, ss. 40, 92(1); *BCCA*, above note 7, ss. 55–57. The *CBCA*, above note 17, itself imposes liability on shareholders in certain limited circumstances: section 38 (distributions to shareholders contrary to the Act), section 146(5) (liabilities of directors when directors' powers assumed in unanimous shareholders' agreement), and section 226(5) (court may permit action against shareholders to recover distributions on dissolution of the corporation). *CBCA*-model statutes have similar provisions.

principle."[64] Section H of this chapter ("Disregard of Separate Corporate Personality"), below, deals with these cases.

Another source of personal liability is torts. Directors and officers of corporations may be held liable for torts committed in connection with the corporation's business where they have some involvement in the activity constituting the tort. It is important to keep in mind the conceptual distinction between imposing liability on corporate managers — the directors and officers — and imposing it on those putting their money at risk — the shareholders. In the former case, it is at least not precise to say that the corporation's existence is being completely disregarded and limited liability destroyed. Liability is imposed based on the policy that individuals should be responsible for their torts. Nevertheless, imposing liability in cases where a director or an officer is acting in the course of her responsibilities clearly circumscribes the separateness of the legal person. Corporations can act only through individuals so it would be more consistent with the separateness of legal personality of the corporation to hold only the corporation liable when directors and officers are acting on the corporation's behalf. As well, the practical effect of imposing liability on officers and directors may be much the same as disregarding separate legal existence since, at least in small corporations, the managers and the shareholders are likely to be the same people. Imposing liability on managers who are also shareholders is as likely to discourage them from engaging in business activity as if liability had been imposed on them in their capacity as shareholders. Tort liability is discussed in Chapter 8, section D ("Liability of Corporate Managers for Torts").

A variety of other sources of management liability may be identified. Directors are liable, for example, under corporate statutes for unpaid wages in certain limited circumstances (e.g., *CBCA*, s. 119). Directors may also incur liability under other federal and provincial statutes for corporate obligations, such as liability for amounts withheld from employee wages which the corporation has failed to remit to the Canada Customs and Revenue Agency.[65] Most other statutes imposing liability on management do not permit other stakeholders to recover against directors and officers directly. Instead, a finding of liability means that the manager is guilty of an offence and subject to a fine or even imprisonment,[66] thus discouraging actions which would undermine the public policy which such statutes are intended to protect.

64   *Clarkson Co. v. Zhelka*, [1967] 2 O.R. 565 (H.C.J.) [*Clarkson*].
65   *ITA*, above note 39, s. 227.1.
66   For example, *Occupational Health and Safety Act*, R.S.O. 1990, c. O.1.

In practice, all these sources of liability for managers reduce the benefit of limited liability in the small corporation where the same person is both a shareholder and a manager. In this introductory chapter, we will deal only with the case law on disregarding separate corporate personality and, with it, limited liability.

b) Other Rules Protecting Non-shareholder Stakeholders

Before we proceed to examine the disregard of corporate personality, we should note several other ways in which corporate law seeks to balance the shifting of risk to non-shareholder stakeholders caused by limited liability.

First, the *CBCA* and other corporate statutes[67] require all corporations to have as part of their name a word or abbreviation which indicates that the business is being carried on by an entity with limited liability. Under the *CBCA*, every corporation's name must include one of the following: Corporation (or Corp.), Limited (or Ltd.), Incorporated (or Inc.), or the French equivalents of these terms (*CBCA*, s. 10(1)). Usually, this "legal" part of the name follows the rest of the name. Each corporation must set out its full legal name on all "contracts, invoices, negotiable instruments and orders for goods or services made by or on behalf of the corporation" (*CBCA*, s. 10(5)). A corporation may use another name, but the other name must not include one of the listed legal elements, so people dealing with it do not believe they are dealing with two corporations. The full corporate name must appear as well. So, for example, a corporation's letterhead might say "123456 Canada Inc. doing business as Landco Real Estate Development." Failing to comply with the requirement to set out the full corporate name on the listed documents is an offence (*CBCA*, ss. 10(5) & 251).[68]

Second, the corporate statutes have certain rules protecting the assets of the corporation for the benefit of creditors and others with claims against a corporation. Unlike some other jurisdictions, most corporate statutes in Canada no longer require any minimum investment by shareholders (called "capitalization"); a corporation may issue one share for $1 and then start to carry on business. Although the absence of a requirement for some meaningful financial commitment on the part of shareholders is sometimes said to encourage frivolous incorporations, it is important to note that minimum initial capitalization requirements do little to protect non-shareholder stakeholders

---

67   *OBCA*, above note 17, s. 10; *BCCA*, above note 7, ss. 16, 106 & 107; *NSCA*, s. 10(a)(i).

68   It may also be an offence under provincial names legislation (e.g., *Business Names Act* (Ontario), R.S.O. 1990, c. B.17, ss. 2(6) & 10).

after incorporation. Money invested by shareholders does not create a pool against which creditors and others may claim. It will be used for the purposes of the business, such as to purchase assets or to pay expenses. There is no guarantee that a shareholder's investment will not be squandered or lost. For this reason, the approach taken in Canadian corporate statutes is to impose rules designed to prevent certain uses of a corporation's assets which will render it unable to pay its obligations. For example, shares can be issued only for money or property that has a value not less than the fair equivalent of what the corporation could have got if it had issued shares for money. Shares cannot be issued on credit (*CBCA*, s. 25(3)).[69] The *CBCA* also contains restrictions on distributions to shareholders. The corporation cannot

- pay dividends,
- redeem or repurchase shares, or
- make payments on the exercise of certain shareholder remedies

if the corporation is insolvent or would be made insolvent by the transactions (*CBCA*, ss. 34, 35, 36, 190(26) & 241(6)). The *CBCA* restricts certain other payments by the corporation, such as commissions paid in connection with the purchase of shares (s. 41) and indemnities paid to directors and officers to reimburse them for liabilities they incur in connection with fulfilling their responsbilities (s. 124). Directors are personally responsible for any payment made in contravention of these rules (*CBCA*, s. 118).[70]

Third, the corporation or its directors may be liable if they act in a manner that is "oppressive to or is unfairly prejudicial to or that unfairly disregards the interests of any security holder, creditor, director or officer" (e.g., *CBCA*, s. 241(2)). This provision was intended primarily to protect shareholders in small corporations and has been used extensively for this purpose. The class of persons who may seek relief, however, includes "any other person who, in the discretion of the court, is a proper person to make an application" (*CBCA*, s. 238). In an increasing number of cases, creditors and other types of claimants have been permitted to seek relief under this provision. The range of relief the court may grant is virtually unlimited, and personal liability has been imposed on directors and shareholders. As a result, liability for oppression is another way in which the protection of limited liability may be lost. The oppression remedy will be discussed in Chapter 9.

---

69 See Chapter 6. The similar provisions in other corporate statutes are discussed in that chapter.

70 Similar provisions in other corporate statutes are discussed in Chapter 8.

There are also sources of liability for which the beneficiary is the corporation. Each director and officer has a fiduciary duty to act in the best interests of the corporation and a duty to exercise reasonable care, diligence, and skill in discharging her obligations (e.g., *CBCA*, s. 122(1)). As noted, directors have a specific liability to the corporation for issuing shares for inadequate consideration and authorizing certain payments contrary to the Act (e.g., *CBCA*, s. 118). These restrictions provide an indirect benefit for other stakeholders in the sense that they protect the interests of the legal entity against which they have a claim. Managers' liability for breach of fiduciary duty and duty of care and their statutory liabilities will be addressed in Chapter 8.

Finally, as noted above, the corporate statutes provide for certain public filings so that people dealing with a corporation will be able to find out something about it. The articles, notice of registered office, and notice of directors become matters of public record once filed. Whenever any of the information in any of these documents changes, a new filing must be made. As well, certain annual filings must be made under the laws of the jurisdiction in which incorporation took place. For example, an annual return with certain basic information must be filed under the *CBCA* (s. 263, Form 22). Corporations doing business in a province, wherever they were incorporated, must also make certain information filings.[71] Corporations that have distributed their shares to the public must file their financial statements under the *CBCA* (s. 160). Additional filings for public corporations are typically required under provincial securities laws.[72]

G. DISREGARD OF SEPARATE CORPORATE PERSONALITY

1) Introduction

Separate corporate personality is the principal way in which the risk of business activity is shifted from shareholders to other stakeholders.[73]

---

71   A corporation doing business in Ontario must file an initial return and an annual return (*Corporations Information Act*, R.S.O. 1990, c. C.39, ss. 3, 3.1).

72   Information filings are discussed in Chapter 4. Securities law requirements for public disclosure are discussed in Chapter 11.

73   See *CBCA*, above note 17, ss. 15 & 45, and Salomon, above note 52. Other corporate statutes have similar provisions (e.g., *OBCA*, above note 17, ss 15, 40, 92(1); *BCCA*, above note 7, ss. 55–57).

Although courts "rigidly adhere"[74] to the separateness of corporate personality, they have refused to accept it in the three situations described below. In these cases, the courts disregard the separate existence of the corporation in relation to some specific claim, usually the claim of a creditor of the corporation whose claim would not be paid because the corporation has insufficient assets to satisfy it. Disregarding the corporation in this way does not destroy its separate existence for all purposes, but only for the limited purpose of granting relief to the creditor directly against the shareholder. Unfortunately, the cases in this area "illustrate no consistent principle."[75] The courts typically refer to disregarding the separate personality of the corporation using the picturesque if somewhat antiquated and ultimately obscuring expression of piercing the "corporate veil."[76]

2) It Is Just Not Fair

Courts have held that they have the power to ignore the separate existence of the corporation where to fail to do so would yield a result which is "flagrantly opposed to justice."[77] It is not clear what this means and there is no easy way to predict when a court will be provoked to act on this basis. In *Transamerica Life Insurance Company of Canada* v. *Canada Life Assurance Company*,[78] the court made it plain that any uncertainty in this standard does not give the court *carte blanche* to disregard the corporation's separate personality:

> There are undoubtedly situations where justice requires that the corporate veil will be lifted. The cases and authorities already cited indicate that it will be difficult to define precisely when the corporate veil is to be lifted, but that lack of a precise test does not mean that a court is free to act as it pleases on some loosely defined 'just and equitable standard.'[79]

One can say that the courts are likely to be more sympathetic to claims by third parties, such as creditors and tort victims, than to those

---

74   *Big Bend Hotel* v. *Security Mutual Casualty Co.* (1980), 19 B.C.L.R. 102, at 108 (S.C.) [*Big Bend Hotel*].

75   *Clarkson*, above note 64.

76   *Littlewoods Mail Order Stores Ltd.* v. *McGregor (Inspector of Taxes)*, [1969] 3 All E.R. 855 (C.A.).

77   *Kosmopoulos*, above note 59, at 10 (S.C.C.).

78   (1996), 28 O.R. (3d) 423 (Gen. Div.), aff'd [1997] O.J. No. 3754 (QL)(C.A.).

79   *Ibid.*, at 433. See also, *Toronto Board of Education* v. *Brunel Construction 2000 Ltd.*, [1997] O.J. No. 3783 (QL) (Gen. Div.).

by shareholders who benefit from separate corporate personality. In *Kosmopolous*, discussed above, the court declined to disregard the separate existence of a corporation at the request of the sole shareholder in order to give him an ownership interest in the assets of the corporation which would have allowed him to recover insurance proceeds for loss of the corporation's assets.[80] There are, however, cases in which the courts have disregarded the separate existence of the corporation for the benefit of shareholders.[81] Also, the courts are more likely to disregard separate personality if doing so results in liability being imposed on another corporation as the shareholder rather than on an individual.[82] In many cases where separate corporate personality is disregarded, there is some element of unfairness in the way the corporation is being used, combined with one or more of the other bases described below.

3) Objectionable Purpose

Where a corporation has been incorporated in order to do something or to facilitate the doing of something that would be illegal or improper for the individual shareholders to do personally, or in order to reduce taxes paid to the Canada Customs and Revenue Agency, the courts have been willing to disregard separate legal personality in some circumstances.

The most common ground relied on by the courts is fraud. One set of circumstances in which fraud has been held to be a basis for disregarding separate corporate existence involves using the corporation to effect a purpose or commit an act that the shareholder could not effect or commit on her own. *Big Bend Hotel Ltd.*[83] is an example. Kumar had had fire-loss insurance cancelled as a result of a previous fire-loss claim. He incorporated a corporation to own a hotel and had the corporation apply for fire insurance instead of applying himself. In the application, he failed to disclose his previous fire-loss. When the hotel burned

---

80   *Kosmopoulos*, above note 59; *Rich v. Enns*, [1995] 6 W.W.R. 257 (Man. C.A.).

81   E.g., *DHN Food Distributors Ltd. v. London Borough of Tower Hamlets*, [1976] 3 All E.R. 462 (C.A.) [*DHN*]. In *Manley Inc. v. Fallis* (1977), 2 B.L.R. 277 (Ont. C.A.), the court allowed a subidiary to enforce an obligation owed to its parent corporation. In *Meditrust Healthcare Inc. v. Shoppers Drug Mart* (2002), 165 O.A.C. 147, a parent corporation was allowed to claim damages for loss of goodwill in connection with actions injuring the business it carried on through subsidiaries and licencees.

82   *De Salaberry Realties Ltd. v. M.N.R.* (1974), 46 D.L.R. (3d) 100 (Fed. T.D.) [*De Salaberry*]; *DHN*, ibid.

83   Above note 74.

down, the insurance company refused to pay and the corporation sued. The court held that Kumar's failure to disclose his personal fire-loss history was fraudulent. The corporation's sole purpose was to disguise the fraud and so the court refused to permit the corporation's claim, in effect treating the claim as if it had been made by Kumar personally.

Gilford Motor Co. Ltd. v. *Horne*[84] is another example. The defendant had entered into an agreement not to solicit the customers of his former employer. He incorporated a corporation to carry on a competing business and sought to attract the employer's customers. The court held that the corporation could not be used to permit the defendant to avoid his contractual obligations and ordered that the corporation cease soliciting the employer's customers.[85]

Fraud also arises where assets are transferred from a corporation that has an obligation to a third party to a shareholder for the purpose of rendering the corporation incapable of performing the obligation. Although such a transaction may be attacked under provincial fraudulent conveyances legislation[86] or, as discussed in Chapter 8, by using the tort of inducing breach of contract, it has also been held to be an appropriate case for disregarding the separate existence of the corporation and imposing liability on the shareholders.[87]

Sometimes the fraud will consist of a representation to a third party that the person the third party is dealing with is not the corporation but an individual or, perhaps, another corporation that has substantial assets.[88] In order for a court to disregard the separate existence of the corporation to impose liability on a shareholder, however, the fraud

---

84 [1933] 1 Ch. 935 (C.A.).

85 Buckley calls this case an example of gap-filling (Buckley, above note 58). The employer failed to provide specifically that competition through a corporation was included in the defendant's non-competition promise. In refusing to recognize the corporation, the court was simply filling this gap in the contract (at 100–1).

86 For example, *Fraudulent Conveyances Act*, above note 55.

87 For example, *Fidelity Electronics of Canada Ltd.* v. *Fuss* (1995), 77 O.A.C. 34 (Div. Ct.). See J.S. Ziegel, "Creditors as Corporate Stakeholders: The Quiet Revolution — an Anglo-Canadian Perspective" (1993) 43 U.T.L.J. 511, regarding the trend towards imposing obligations to creditors on the directors of corporations that are insolvent or on the verge of insolvency. Ziegel notes that this trend is evidenced both legislatively and in the courts in other Commonwealth jurisdictions, but, with the exception of increasing access to the oppression remedy, is largely absent in Canada. See, however, *Re Trizec Corp.* (1994), 21 Alta L.R. (3d) 435 (QB), in which the court suggested that such a duty existed.

88 For example, *Pacific Rim Installations Ltd.* v. *Tilt-Up Construction Ltd.* (1978), 5 B.C.L.R. 231 (Co. Ct.).

must be such as to misrepresent the identity of the corporation, not merely some attribute of the corporation, such as its assets. In *B.G. Preeco I (Pacific Coast) Ltd. v. Bon Street Holdings Ltd.*,[89] the court refused to disregard the separate existence of the corporation in an obvious case of fraud. Two individual defendants acted on behalf of a corporation named "Bon Street Developments Ltd." in negotiating the purchase of some property. The vendors knew that the corporation had substantial assets. Just prior to the closing of the transaction, the two individuals changed the name of the corporation to "Bon Street Holdings Inc." and the name of a corporation without assets to "Bon Street Developments Ltd." The contract was signed on behalf of the new Bon Street Developments Ltd. While the court found the individual defendants liable for fraud, it was not prepared to disregard the separate existence of the insolvent corporation to hold them or the original Bon Street Developments Ltd. liable under the contract because the fraud did not relate to the identity of the corporation, but only to its assets.

This case provides an interesting example of a practical difference between liability in tort for fraud and liability for breach of contract in terms of the damages available. The plaintiffs had pursued their claim that the separate existence of the corporation should be disregarded, and liability for breach of contract should be imposed on the original Bon Street Developments Ltd. or on the individuals involved, on the basis that the breach of contract claim against the new Bon Street Developments Ltd. was worthless and the measure of damages for the fraud judgment against the individuals was much less (about $500,000) than the damages that might have been obtained for breach of contract (about $1,400,000). Tort damages are intended to put the tort victim in the same position he would have been in if the tort had not been committed, whereas contract damages are intended to put the innocent party in the same position as if the contract had been fulfilled. Here the property rapidly declined in value after the sale was negotiated. As a result, only contract damages would have given the vendor the high price agreed to in the contract.

---

89   (1989), 37 B.C.L.R. (2d) 258 (C.A.). In *Phillips v. 707739 Alberta Ltd.* [2000] 6 W.W.R. 280 (Alta. Q.B.), aff'd [2001] A.J. No. 1161 (QL), leave to appeal denied [2002] S.C.C.A. No. 64 (QL), an individual tried to substitute a numbered corporation he controlled for himself at the closing of his purchase of an interest in a restaurant business. The court found that the vendors could hold the individual personally liable for the unpaid purchase price based on a variety of grounds, including the fact that the vendor did not intend to contract with the numbered corporation and piercing the corporate veil. See similarly, *3253791 Canada Inc. v. Armstrong* (2002), 27 B.L.R. (3d) 230 (Ont. Sup. Ct. J.).

As illustrated in *B.G. Preeco I (Pacific Coast)* v. *Bon Street Holdings Ltd.* and discussed in Chapter 8, fraudulent representations by a director, officer, or shareholder that a corporation has sufficient assets to meet its obligations will result in personal liability for fraud for the director, officer, or shareholder.[90] In several cases liability has been attached where the misrepresentation was not fraudulent and even in the absence of the usual contract law requirement that the representation be relied on.[91] In *Wolfe* v. *Moir*,[92] an officer of a corporation that operated a roller skating rink was held personally liable for negligence in connection with an injury to a skater. The basis of the court's decision was that the business was advertised using the officer's name, and not the corporation's name, in contravention of the *ABCA*.[93]

Historically, courts have been sympathetic to arguments that the use of a corporation to reduce taxes is an improper purpose and a basis for disregarding separate corporate personality. The "interests of the Revenue" have been considered to be a special case.[94] In *De Salaberry*,[95] a case decided in the early 1970s, the court disregarded the separate existence of one corporation in a large corporate group. It had been argued that a sale of land by the corporation was an isolated transaction such that the proceeds should be characterized as a capital gain. At the time of the transaction, capital gains were not subject to tax. The court held that, when one disregarded the separate existence of the corporation, it became clear that the sale was part of a business of buying and selling land being carried on by the whole group of corporations under common control, so the proceeds from the sale were income from a business and fully taxed.

With its decision in *Stubart Investments Ltd.* v. *M.N.R.*,[96] in 1984, the Supreme Court of Canada signalled that the courts should be less willing to disregard the separateness of corporate personality in the interests of imposing tax liability on the use of corporations even where no business purpose for the corporation is shown, other than minimizing tax liability. In 1988 the *Income Tax Act* was amended to introduce what has been called the "General Anti-avoidance Rule" (s.

---

90   E.g., *Baltimore Aircoil of Canada Inc.* v. *Process Cooling Systems Inc.* (1993), 16 O.R. (3d) 324 (Gen. Div.).

91   G.H.L. Fridman, *The Law of Contracts in Canada*, 4th. ed. (Toronto: Carswell, 1999), at 308.

92   (1969), 69 W.W.R. 70 (Alta. S.C.T.D.) [*Wolfe*].

93   See also *Tato Enterprises Ltd.* v. *Rode* (1979), 17 A.R. 432 (Dist. Ct.) [*Tato*].

94   *Kosmopoulos*, above note 59, at 10 (S.C.C.).

95   Above note 82.

96   [1984] 1 S.C.R. 536.

245(2)). This provision allows the Canada Customs and Revenue Agency to disregard transactions if they are abusive tax-avoidance transactions. A transaction is a tax-avoidance transaction if it is entered into without any real purpose other than obtaining a tax benefit. Such an avoidance transaction is abusive if it results in a misuse of some specific provision in the *Income Tax Act* or the provisions of the Act read as a whole. It remains to be seen to what extent the courts will disregard separate corporate personality now that power to address tax avoidance is expressly provided for in the General Anti-avoidance Rule. In practical terms, the application of this provision is an important issue for tax planning.

The courts have also disregarded separate corporate existence in certain other circumstances where a corporation is being used to avoid other statutory requirements. Judicial intervention of this kind has been relatively rare.[97]

4) Agency

The third basis on which courts have purported to disregard separate corporate personality is by finding that the corporation is merely acting as the agent of someone else, usually the controlling shareholder that is, itself, a corporation. Conceptually, the corporate form is not disregarded by a holding that it is an agent. Rather, the business of the corporation or whatever activity gives rise to the claim by a third party is determined to be carried on not by the corporation directly but only as an agent of the controlling shareholder. The courts often use evocative but ultimately unhelpful language to describe the corporation in these circumstances — for example, "sham," "cloak," "conduit," or "alter ego."

---

97   For example, *Nedco Ltd.* v. *Clark* (1973), 43 D.L.R. (3d) 714 (Sask. C.A.)(labour law — employees of parent corporation allowed to picket subsidiary). There are also some cases in which statutes expressly provide that the separate existence of corporations shall be disregarded (e.g., *Employment Standards Act*, R.S.O. 1990, c. E.14, ss. 1(d) & 12), interpreted in *550551 Ontario Ltd.* v. *Framingham* (1991), 4 O.R. (3d) 571 (Div. Ct.)). In *Northeast Marine Services Limited* v. *Atlantic Pilotage Authority*, [1995] 2 F.C. 132 (C.A.), a pilotage authority awarded a contract for pilotage services to someone other than the applicant, even though the applicant had submitted the lowest bid. The authority was concerned about the financial stability of the applicant based on the financial difficulties of a corporation under common ownership with the applicant. The court held that the authority was entitled to look behind the separate legal existence of the applicant for this purpose.

The main test for the existence of this peculiar form of agency is whether there is extensive control by the shareholder over the corporation. The factors referred to in *Smith, Stone and Knight Ltd.* v. *Birmingham Corp.*[98] are almost universally cited as those relevant to a determination whether agency exists:

- Were the profits treated as profits of the shareholder?
- Was the person conducting the business appointed by the shareholder?
- Was the shareholder the head and brain of the trading venture?
- Did the shareholder govern the adventure and decide what should be done and what capital should be committed to the venture?
- Did the shareholder make the profits by its skill and direction?
- Was the shareholder in effectual and constant control?[99]

Extensive and even complete control by a single person, however, is contemplated in the *CBCA*, so the existence of control satisfying the test in *Smith* cannot in any way be conclusive. Earlier in this chapter, we noted that there may be various reasons a person might decide to carry on business through a corporation, including limited liability and tax planning. Similarly, there are legitimate reasons that corporations may carry on business through a subsidiary corporation in which they hold all the shares. It may be, for example, that the parent corporation will carry on several businesses through separate subsidiary corporations in order to ensure that claims arising out of a particular business cannot be satisfied out of the assets of the others. Where subsidiaries are used, the degree of control by the parent corporation may range from absolute, such as where the same person owns 100 percent of the parent corporation and is the sole director and officer of the parent and the subsidiary, to minimal, such as where a subsidiary operates as if it were independent.

There is nothing in any corporate statute which suggests that any particular degree of control is inappropriate or prohibited. In *Alberta Gas Ethylene Co.* v. *M.N.R.*,[100] Madame Justice Reed observed that *Smith* does not stand for the proposition that one must ignore the separate

---

98 [1939] 4 All E.R. 116 (K.B.) [*Smith*].

99 These factors were treated as an independent basis for disregarding the separate existence of the subsidiary in *Tridont Leasing (Canada) Ltd.* v. *Saskatoon Market Mall Ltd.*, [1995] 6 W.W.R. 641 (Sask. C.A.) [*Tridont*]. The court held that the test was not met in that case. As discussed below, meeting these factors alone should not be sufficient to disregard the separate existence of the corporation.

100 [1989] 41 B.L.R. 117 (Fed. T.D.), aff'd [1990] 2 C.T.C. 171 (Fed. C.A.).

existence of a subsidiary corporation when the six criteria are met. One must ask for what purpose the corporation was incorporated and used, and consider the overall context in which the obligation to the third party arose. This test was applied in *Sun Sudan Oil Co.* v. *Methanex Corp.*[101] In *Gregorio* v. *Intrans-Corp.*,[102] it was held that the policy behind holding a parent corporation liable is "to prevent conduct akin to fraud that would otherwise unjustly deprive claimants of their rights."[103] Where the court is able to find that a subsidiary had been set up for a legitimate business purpose, disregarding the separate existence of the subsidiary is inappropriate.[104]

5) Other Factors

Often courts are not very clear about whether they are talking about fairness, objectionable purpose, or agency as the basis on which they are disregarding the separate legal existence of the corporation, even though they are conceptually distinct.[105] Some or all of these factors are frequently relied on. Several other factors have been referred to by the courts as supporting decisions to disregard the corporation's existence, regardless of the basis for doing so. Lack of respect for the corporate form is cited in some cases as supporting the disregard of corporate personality.[106] In others, however, lack of respect, in the form of lack of proper corporate authorization for transactions and the use of shareholder funds to pay corporate obligations, has been found insufficient.[107] Inadequate or "thin" capitalization is also sometimes referred to as supporting the disregard of corporate personality.[108] This situation occurs when the shareholders' investment in a corporation is inadequate to meet its anticipated obligations.

---

101 (1992), 134 A.R. 1, at 15 (Q.B.); see, similarly, *Harris* v. *Nugent* (1995), 172 A.R. 309 (Q.B.) [*Harris*].

102 (1994), 18 O.R. (3d) 527 (C.A.). The same approach was applied in *Woodbine Truck Centre Ltd.* v. *Jantar Building Systems Inc.*, [1997] O.J. No. 1555 (QL)(Gen. Div.).

103 *Ibid.*, at 536.

104 *Harris*, above note 101; *Bow Valley*, above note 56; *Tridont*, above note 99.

105 E.g., *Walkovszky* v. *Carlton*, 223 N.E.2d 6 (N.Y.C.A. 1966) [*Walkovszky*]; *De Salaberry*, above note 82.

106 E.g., *Shibamoto & Co.* v. *Western Fish Producers Inc. (Trustee of)* (1991), 48 F.T.R. 176 (T.D.) [*Shibamoto*]; *Tato*, above note 93; *Wolfe*, above note 92.

107 E.g., *Rockwell Developments Ltd.* v. *Newtonbrook Plaza Ltd.*, [1972] 3 O.R. (2d) 199 (C.A.).

108 E.g., *De Salaberry*, above note 82, but rejected in *Walkovszky*, above note 105.

H. SPECIAL CORPORATIONS WITHOUT LIMITED LIABILITY

Under the Nova Scotia *Companies Act*,[109] a corporation can be incorporated with a form of unlimited liability. Shareholders are not liable for the obligations of the business carried on by the corporation on an ongoing basis, but, where the creditors of the company obtain an order to wind it up or the corporation becomes bankrupt, shareholders become liable to contribute to the company's debts and the cost of winding up. Liability extends to former shareholders who held their shares within one year of the commencement of the winding up. In most other respects an unlimited liability company is governed by the same rules as apply to other companies incorporated in Nova Scotia.[110]

Nova Scotia is the only Canadian jurisdiction to permit unlimited liability companies to be created for any purpose. Recently, Ontario began to permit lawyers, accountants, and certain other professionals to incorporate their professional practices. Shareholders of such corporations are not liable for the obligations of the corporation, but they remain personally liable for professional negligence in the course of the corporation's business. To incorporate as a professional corporation in Ontario, the following requirements must be met:[111]

- all of the issued shares of the corporation are owned by one or more members of the same profession;
- all officers and directors of the corporation are shareholders of the corporation;
- the name of the corporation includes the words "professional corporation;" and
- the articles of incorporation provide that the corporation may not carry on a business other than the practice of the profession.

The legislation provides that all shareholders are liable for all professional liability claims against the corporation, including acts by employ-

---

109 *NSCA*, above note 20, s. 9.
110 On some of the tax advantages associated with using unlimited liability companies, see G.T.W. Bowden, "The Benefits of Using a Nova Scotia Unlimited Liability Company," presented to the Taxation Subsection of the British Columbia Branch of the Canadian Bar Association on 20 March 2002.
111 *Balanced Budgets for Brighter Futures Act, 2000*, S.O. 2001, c. 42, Sched. amending the *OBCA*, above note 17, and certain other statutes regulating specific professions including the *Law Society Act*, R.S.O. 1990, c. L.8. This change permitted lawyers to practise through professional corporations beginning 1 November 2001.

ees or agents on behalf of the corporation. In all other respects, the rules governing the professional corporation are the same as those governing all other corporations under the Ontario *Business Corporations Act*.[112]

Professional corporations may also be incorporated in Alberta under the *ABCA*, provided many of the same requirements are met. The liability of the shareholders in such corporations, however, is the same as if they were partners in a partnership. Liability and other rules relating to professional corporations are set out in the statutes governing each profession that is permitted to incorporate.[113]

I. APPLICATION OF THE *CHARTER OF RIGHTS AND FREEDOMS* TO CORPORATIONS

As discussed above, incorporation brings into existence a new legal person whose rights and obligations may be thought of as analogous to those of a human person. Does a corporate person have rights under the *Charter*? Though it is still too early to be able to describe how each provision of the *Charter* applies to a corporation, a number of cases have considered the application of the *Charter* in different contexts, and it is possible to sketch the outlines of this aspect of a corporation's separate legal personality.

The *Charter* defines the classes of person who benefit from *Charter* rights in different ways. The defining language used in relation to some rights excludes corporations. The right to vote (s. 3), certain mobility rights (s. 6(1)), and minority language rights (s. 23) are conferred only on "[e]very citizen." Since corporations cannot obtain Canadian citizenship, they cannot benefit from these rights. "Every individual" is entitled to equality rights under section 15. Although it might seem obvious that a corporation is not an individual, several arguments have been made to the contrary and there has not yet been a definitive judicial statement on this issue.[114]

---

112 *OBCA, ibid.*, s. 3.2. British Columbia permits lawyers to incorporate provided that similar requirements are met. The special rules regarding such professional corporations are set out in the *Legal Profession Act*, S.B.C. 1999, c. 9, Part 9.

113 E.g., *Legal Profession Act*, R.S.A. 2000, c. L-8, Part 8.

114 See G.D. Chipeur, "Section 15 of the Charter Protects People and Corporations — Equally" (1986), 11 Can. Bus. L. J. 304. In *Little Sisters Book and Art Emporium* v. *Canada* (1996), 131 D.L.R. (4th) 486 (B.C.S.C.); aff'd (1998), 160 D.L.R. (4th) 385 (B.C.C.A.), varied (2000), 193 D.L.R (4th) 193 (S.C.C.), the court

Other language used in the *Charter* is broad enough to include corporations. The rights granted on being charged with an offence (s. 11) and certain mobility rights under section 6(2) are granted to "[e]very person" and may extend to corporations, since corporations have the capacity, rights, powers, and privileges of a natural person under most corporate legislation (e.g., *CBCA*, s. 15(1)). In *Parkdale Hotel Ltd.* v. *Canada (A.G.)*,[115] however, the court held that a person did not include a corporation for the purpose of enjoying the mobility right under section 6(2), on the basis that the purpose of the provision was not the protection of corporations.[116] Such a purposive approach to interpretation has been applied generally in relation to the *Charter*.

Section 11(b), the right to be tried within a reasonable time, has been held to apply to corporations but only to a limited extent.[117] In relation to a corporation, the right is infringed only if the delay in getting to trial was such as to deny the corporate accused the ability to make full answer and defence to the charges. This right is already guaranteed under section 11(d), the right to be presumed innocent and to be tried before an impartial tribunal, which does apply to corporations, and section 7, the right to life, liberty, and security of the person. As a result, the protection under 11(b) may not represent a significant additional benefit to a corporate accused.[118]

In a pre-*Charter* case, *R.* v. *N.M. Paterson & Sons Ltd.*,[119] it was held that the right against self-incrimination, now protected under section 11(c) of the *Charter*, did not prevent a manager of a corporation from being compelled to testify at a trial of the corporation. There has been no definitive ruling on the applicability of section 11(c) to corporations. The key question is whether a person who, in effect, is the corporation for the purposes of the offence, in the sense that she was in

---

dealt with an argument by a bookstore that seizure of certain materials constituted an infringement of freedom of speech (s. 2(b)) and equality rights (s. 15). The court decided that the bookstore could argue the violation of s. 15 because it had standing to argue a violation of s. 2(b). This aspect of the judgment was not addressed on appeal.

115 [1986] 2 F.C. 514 (T.D.).

116 This view was confirmed in *Canadian Egg Marketing Agency* v. *Richardson*, [1998] 3 S.C.R. 157 [*Canadian Egg*].

117 *R.* v. *CIP Inc.*, [1992] 1 S.C.R. 843. In *R.* v. *741290 Ontario Inc.* (1991), 2 O.R. (3d) 336 (Prov. Div.), it was held that a corporation has a right to be tried within a reasonable time in accordance with s. 11(b), but the presumption of prejudice associated with a delay is weaker for a corporation than for a natural person.

118 Hogg, above note 26, at ¶34-2.

119 [1980] 2 S.C.R. 679.

control of the corporation, can be compelled to testify against the corporation or whether this would violate the right against self-incrimination. In *R. v. Amway Corp.*, Mr. Justice Sopinka suggested that even in this situation, employees are compellable to testify against the corporations they work for.[120]

With regard to another provision of section 11, in *Re PPG Industries*, it was held that that a corporate accused charged with an offence under the *Combines Investigation Act* did not have the right to a trial by jury as guaranteed by section 11(f).[121]

"Everyone" defines those who have the protection of the most important provisions of the *Charter*: the fundamental freedoms of expression, conscience, religion, peaceful assembly, and association guaranteed under section 2; the right to life, liberty, and security of the person guaranteed under section 7; the rights against arbitrary search and seizure guaranteed under section 8; and the legal rights guaranteed under sections 10 and 12. "Everyone" does not inherently exclude corporations, and the extension of any specific protection to corporations will depend on whether the substance of the protection is one that a corporation may enjoy.

Although it has been held that a corporation cannot enjoy freedom of religion,[122] corporations do enjoy freedom of expression, at least to some extent, even though such expression may be of an entirely commercial nature, such as advertising.[123] In *Canadian Egg Marketing Agency v. Richardson*, the Supreme Court considered a claim by a corporation that its freedom to associate was being infringed by territorial restrictions on where it could market its eggs. The right to associate was treated as a right which could be exercised by the corporation, though the issue was not specifically addressed by the Court. However, the egg marketing by the defendants was not found to be protected by that

---

120 [1989] 1 S.C.R. 21, at 37.

121 (1983), 146 D.L.R. (3d) 261 (B.C.C.A.).

122 *R. v. Big M Drug Mart Ltd.*, [1985] 1 S.C.R. 295 [*Big M*]. See also, *R. v. Church of Scientology* (1997), 33 O.R. (3d) 65 (C.A.), leave to appeal dismissed [1997] S.C.C.A. No. 683 (QL) [*Church of Scientology*]. In this case, for the purposes of its decision, the court assumed, without deciding, that the criminal prosecution of a non-profit corporation with religious objects for the conduct of individuals acting on its behalf could violate the freedom of religion of the individuals. Ultimately, the court found that there was no violation of the *Charter* because any infringement of s. 2 was justified under s. 1. The circumstances in which corporations can be criminally responsible for acts of individuals is discussed in Chapter 5.

123 *Irwin Toy Ltd. v. Quebec (A.G.)*, [1989] 1 S.C.R. 927 [*Irwin Toy*]; *RJR-MacDonald Inc. v. Canada (A.G.)*, [1995] 3 S.C.R. 199 [*RJR*].

right, even though the Court recognized that it was impossible for the corporation to market eggs by itself.[124] The Court held that protecting a right to associate to market eggs would be tantamount to protecting the activity itself, which went beyond what was intended by the creation of the right. There has been no case law on the applicability of the other fundamental freedoms to corporations.

In *Irwin Toy*[125] it was held that, because a corporation cannot be imprisoned or lose its life, it cannot enjoy the right to life, liberty, and security of the person guaranteed under section 7. This decision was confirmed by the Supreme Court of Canada in *R. v. Wholesale Travel Group Inc.*[126] In *R. v. Agat Laboratories Ltd.*, however, it was held that a corporate accused does have a right to make full answer and defence to the charges against it, a right that, as noted above, is protected under section 7.[127]

Corporations are entitled to protection against unreasonable search and seizure under section 8.[128] However, it is not clear whether the rights arising under sections 9 and 10 on being detained or arrested can sensibly be applied to corporations.

As with the protection of individuals under the *Charter*, the protection available to corporations is subject to the balancing requirement contained in section 1: a provision infringing a *Charter* right will nevertheless be upheld if it is a "reasonable ... [limit] prescribed by law as can be demonstrably justified in a free and democratic society." Several judicial statements have suggested that the balancing required by section 1 should be different if the person whose rights have been infringed is a corporation. In *Reference Re S. 94(2) of the Motor Vehicle Act (British Columbia)*,[129] Mr. Justice Lamer suggested, in *obiter*, that an exception under section 1 could more easily be justified in such a case:

> Even if it be decided that s. 7 does extend to corporations, I think the balancing under s. 1 of the public interest against the financial interests of a corporation would give very different results from that of

---

124 *Canadian Egg*, above note 116, at 163.

125 *Irwin Toy*, above note 123.

126 [1991] 3 S.C.R. 154 [*Wholesale Travel*]. But see *Southam Inc. v. Canada (Combines Investigation Branch, Director of Investigation & Research)* (1982), 42 A.R. 109 (Q.B.), aff'd on other grounds (*sub nom. Canada (Director of Investigation & Research, Combines Investigation Branch) v. Southam Inc.*), [1984] 2 S.C.R. 145 [*Southam*] which suggests that a corporation should be granted status but denied protection intended for human persons.

127 [1998] A.J. No. 304 (QL) (Prov. Ct. Crim. Div.).

128 *Southam*, above note 126; *Church of Scientology*, above note 122.

129 [1985] 2 S.C.R. 486, at 518.

balancing the public interest and the liberty or security of the person of a human being.

He repeated this view in *Wholesale Travel.*

This relative hostility to corporations claiming *Charter* rights was also expressed in strong terms by the dissenting justices in *RJR-Mac-Donald Inc.* v. *Canada (A.G.)*, in which the federal government's ban on tobacco advertising and promotions was struck down. Mr. Justice La Forest, in this respect writing for Justices L'Heureux-Dubé, Gonthier, and Cory, confirmed the position taken by the Court in *Rocket* v. *Royal College of Dental Surgeons*[130] that, though no "special tests" apply to commercial expression, a sensitive, case-oriented approach should be taken to the determination of its constitutionality. Courts must consider the expression in its factual and social context. Because of the harm engendered by tobacco and the profit motive underlying its promotion, cigarette advertising was described as being "as far from the 'core' of freedom of expression values as prostitution, hate mongering, or pornography"[131] and thus entitled to a very low degree of protection under section 1. The dissenting justices found that the federal legislation could be justified under section 1. Mr. Justice Iacobucci, joined in this respect by Chief Justice Lamer, did not find that the legislation could be justified under section 1, but he agreed that expression, solely for the purpose of financial gain from selling a product with known deleterious effects on public health, was deserving of only narrow protection.[132] Madame Justice McLachlin, with Justices Sopinka and Major, also found that the legislation could not be justified under section 1, but she acknowledged that restrictions on commercial speech may be easier to justify than other infringements. She determined, however, that "motivation to profit is irrelevant to the determination of whether the government has established that the law is reasonable or justified as an infringement of freedom of expression."[133]

Finally, a line of cases has held that, even where a particular *Charter* provisions has no application to corporations, a corporation may argue that the provision is unconstitutional because it would violate the rights of an individual in certain circumstances. Where a corporation has been charged with a penal offence and an individual charged with the same offence could successfully argue that the provision creating the offence violated her rights under the *Charter* in some way, the

---

130 [1990] 2 S.C.R. 232, at 246.
131 *RJR*, above note 123, at 282–83.
132 *Ibid.*, at 354.
133 *Ibid.*, at 348.

provision will be struck down as it applies to the corporation on the basis that no one may be convicted under an unconstitutional law.[134] In *Canadian Egg Marketing Agency*, it was held that this doctrine applies equally where the corporation is the subject of a civil suit.[135] This defence will not be available to a corporation if the provision is expressed to apply only to corporations.[136]

Figure 3.2   When can a corporation rely on the *Charter*?

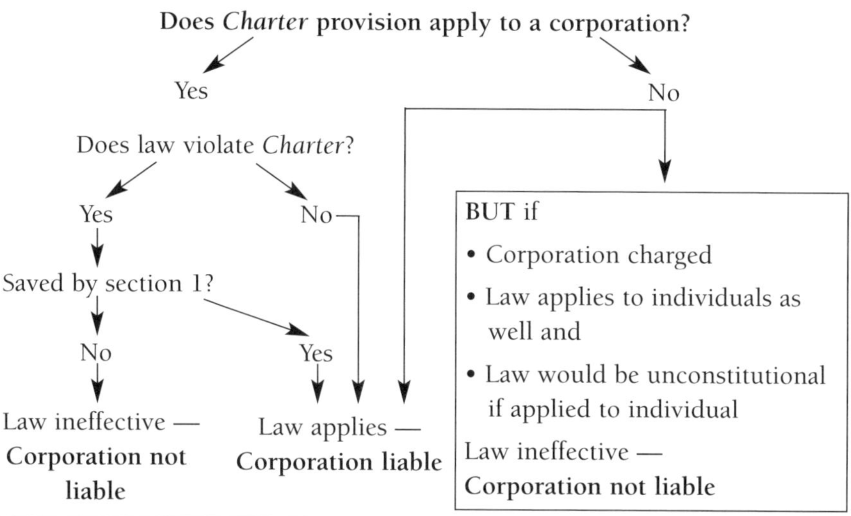

J. CHAPTER SUMMARY

This chapter builds on the introduction to the corporation begun in Chapter 1 in several ways. It provides background information on the

---

134 *Big M*, above note 122, at 313–14, applied in *R. v. Metro News Ltd.* (1987), 56 O.R. (2d) 321 (C.A.) and *Wholesale Travel*, above note 126. In *Church of Scientology*, above note 122, the church was not permitted to argue in its defence that the rights of non-citizens to participate in a jury had been infringed.

135 *Canadian Egg*, above note 116 (application for injunction to stop egg producer from selling product outside territory of production). See Hogg, above note 26, at ¶56.2(e).

136 *Wholesale Travel*, above note 126. Corporations have, however, sought public interest standing to assert rights that they could not exercise. Such standing is available if (i) the challenged action raises a serious legal question; (ii) the plaintiff has a genuine interest in the resolution of the question; and (iii) no other reasonable and effective means exist to bring the matter before a court (Hogg, *ibid.*, ¶56.2(d)).

history of Canadian corporate law, the constitutional responsibilities of the federal and provincial governments, and the incorporation process. In addition, it develops the discussion begun in Chapter 1 of the context in which corporate law operates through an examination of the economic function of corporate law and the application of the *Charter* to corporations. Finally, this chapter describes the legal nature of the corporation and the circumstances in which the courts will disregard it.

Canadian corporate law developed from both English and American antecedents. The current federal corporate law, the *CBCA*, was enacted in 1975 and has formed the model that subsequent corporate law reform in most, but not all, provinces has followed. The *CBCA* model is the focus of this book.

Both the federal and provincial governments have constitutional authority to create corporations, the primary difference being that provincial corporations have the capacity but not the right to carry on business outside their province of incorporation, whereas federal corporations have both the capacity and the right to carry on business anywhere in Canada. Both federal and provincial jurisdictions have a limited power to regulate corporations incorporated in other jurisdictions, so long as such regulation is otherwise within their legislative competence.

Corporate law in all Canadian jurisdictions is designed to encourage investment in business. It does so by increasing the returns to shareholder investors and decreasing the risk associated with those returns. Corporate law accomplishes the former largely by reducing the transaction costs associated with setting up and operating a corporation. It accomplishes the latter primarily by limiting the loss exposure of shareholders to the amount of their investment and by imposing mandatory rules designed to protect shareholders. Corporate law contains various sorts of protection for non-shareholder stakeholders as well, but this is very much a secondary role.

Under corporate law the corporation has a separate legal existence, a status that has various important implications. It means that a shareholder may contract with the corporation, including being an employee or a creditor of the corporation. More important, it means that shareholders have limited liability. There are, however, various statutory exceptions to limited liability. Also, the courts have determined that they have the power to disregard the separate existence of the corporation, although it is far from clear in what circumstances such a power will be exercised. In some cases, courts have permitted the separate legal existence of the corporation to be disregarded simply because they have concluded that it would not be fair to refuse to do so. In others, they have concluded that the corporation is not truly carrying on business on its own behalf but rather is acting on behalf of its share-holder as an agent or is being used for an objectionable purpose.

With regard to the *Charter*, the courts have permitted corporations to claim *Charter* rights where the language of the *Charter* may be interpreted to extend to corporations and there is some sensible way in which the substance of the rights may be exercised by a corporation. The Supreme Court of Canada, however, has suggested that the courts should be less vigilant in protecting rights of corporations as compared with those of individuals.

FURTHER READINGS

BERLE, A.A., & G.C. MEANS, *The Modern Corporation and Private Property*, rev. ed. (New York: Harcourt, Brace & World, 1968)

BOURGEOIS, D.J., *The Law of Charitable and Non-Profit Organizations*, 3d ed. (Toronto: Butterworths, 2002)

BOWDEN, G.T.W., "The Benefits of Using a Nova Scotia Unlimited Liability Company," presented to the Taxation Subsection of the British Columbia Branch of the Canadian Bar Association on March 20, 2002

BUCKLEY, F.H., M. GILLEN, & R. YALDEN, *Corporations: Principles and Policies*, 3d ed. (Toronto: Emond Montgomery, 1995)

CARY, W.L., & M.A. EISENBERG, *Cases and Materials on Corporations*, 8th ed. (Mineola, N.Y.: Foundation Press, 2000)

CHAPMAN, B., "Trust, Economic Rationality, and the Corporate Fiduciary Obligation" (1993) 43 U.T.L.J. 547

CHAPMAN, B., "Corporate Law in the 80s" [1982] Spec. Lect. L.S.U.C.

DANIELS, R.J., & B. LANGILLE, eds., "Special Issue on the Corporate Stakeholder Debate: The Classical Theory and Its Critics" (1993) 43 U.T.L.J. 297–796

DANIELS, R.J., & J.G. MACINTOSH, "Toward a Distinctive Canadian Corporate Law Regime" (1991) 29 Osgoode Hall L.J. 863

DAVIES, WARD, & BECK, *Canadian Corporate Law Precedents* (Toronto: Carswell, 1989)

DICKERSON, R.V.W., J.L. HOWARD, & L. GETZ, *Proposals for a New Business Corporations Law for Canada*, 2 vols. (Ottawa: Information Canada, 1971)

EASTERBROOK, F.H., & D.R. FISCHEL, *The Economic Structure of Corporate Law* (Boston: Harvard University Press, 1991)

GOWER, L.C.B., *Principles of Modern Company Law*, 5th ed. (London: Stevens, 1993)

HALPERN, P., M.J. TREBILCOCK, & S. TURNBULL, "An Economic Analysis of Limited Liability in Corporation Law" (1980) 30 U.T.L.J. 117

ISH, D., *The Law of Canadian Co-operatives* (Toronto: Carswell, 1981)

LABRIE, F.E., & E.E. PALMER, "The Pre-Confederation History of Corporations in Canada" in J.S. Ziegel, ed., *Studies in Canadian Company Law*, vol. 1 (Toronto: Butterworths, 1967) 33

NEYERS, J. W., "Canadian Corporate Law, Veil-Piercing, and the Private Law Model Corporation" (2000), 50 U. of T. L. J. 173

ONTARIO, *Interim Report of the Select Committee on Company Law* (Toronto: Queen's Printer, 1967)

RISK, R.C.B., "The Nineteenth Century Foundations of Business Corporations in Ontario" (1973) 23 U.T.L.J. 270

SARGENT, N.C., "Corporate Groups and the Corporate Veil in Canada: A Penetrating Look at Parent-Subsidiary Relations in the Modern Corporate Enterprise" (1988) 17 Man. L.J. 156

SARNA, L., ed., *Corporate Structure, Finance and Operations: Essays on the Law and Business Practice*, 7 vols. (Toronto: Carswell, 1986)

TOLLEFSON, C., "Corporate Constitutional Rights and the Supreme Court of Canada" (1993) 19 Queen's L.J. 309

WALDRON, M.A., "The Process of Law Reform: the New B.C. Companies Act" (1976) 10 U.B.C. L. Rev. 179

WEGENAST, F.W., *The Law of Canadian Companies* (Toronto: Burroughs, 1931)

ZIEGEL, J.S., et al., *Cases and Materials on Partnerships and Canadian Business Corporations*, 3d ed. (Toronto: Carswell, 1994)

CHAPTER 4

INCORPORATION: CONSIDERATIONS AND PROCESS

A. INTRODUCTION

The process of incorporation was briefly described in Chapter 3. In this chapter we will examine the process in detail. We will look at both the legal requirements and some of the practical aspects of incorporation, as well as some of the considerations related to which jurisdiction an incorporator should choose.

B. THE PROCESS OF INCORPORATION AND ORGANIZATION

1) Incorporation

Under most Canadian corporate statutes, a corporation may be incorporated by one or more corporations or individuals, or a combination of both. Although there are no qualifications that must be met by corporate incorporators, under the *CBCA* individual incorporators cannot be any of the following:

- less than eighteen years of age;
- of unsound mind as found by a court in Canada or elsewhere; or

- have the status of bankrupt (*CBCA*, s. 5).[1]

The incorporators must file certain prescribed material with the Corporations Directorate of Industry Canada if incorporation is under the *CBCA*. If incorporation under the laws of a province is chosen, then the prescribed documents must be filed with the branch of the provincial government having responsibility for incorporations.[2] Under the *CBCA* it is necessary to file the following:

- articles of incorporation (s. 6, Form 1);[3]
- notice of registered office (s. 19(2), Form 3);
- notice of directors (s. 106, Form 6);
- a name-search report on the proposed name of the corporation; and
- the fee of $250.[4]

a) Articles

As noted in Chapter 3, the articles are by far the most important of the documents filed on incorporation because they set out the fundamental characteristics of the corporation: its name, the province within Canada where its registered office is to be situated, the class, number, and characteristics of shares authorized to be issued, the number of directors, any restrictions on transferring shares, and any restrictions on the business the corporation may carry on. Each of these items is discussed below in turn.

---

1   Similar provisions are in other corporate statutes modelled on the *Canada Business Corporations Act*, R.S.C. 1985, c. C-44 [*CBCA*]. E.g., Ontario *Business Corporations Act*, R.S.O. 1990, c. B-16 [*OBCA*], s. 4(2); and Alberta *Business Corporations Act*, R.S.A. 2000, c. B-9 [*ABCA*], s. 5. Under the British Columbia *Companies Act*, only individuals may incorporate a company (*Companies Act*, R.S.B.C. 1996, c. 62 [*BCCA*], s. 5(1)).

2   See section C ("Jurisdiction of Incorporation") in this chapter for a discussion of considerations relevant to choosing a jurisdiction for incorporation.

3   Under the *BCCA*, *ibid.*, it is necessary to file articles and a memorandum of association (s. 8).

4   The fee is reduced to $200 if incorporation is done online. The *CBCA* forms are available from and may be filed through the Electronic Filing Centre on the Corporations Directorate website, <http://strategis.ic.gc.ca/sc_mrksv/corpdir/corpFiling/engdoc/index.html>. In Ontario, incorporation forms may be obtained from the government of Ontario website and then filed through two primary service providers under contract from the Ministry of Consumer and Business Services. In British Columbia, the necessary forms are contained in the schedules to the *BCCA*, above note 1, and can be downloaded from the website of the Ministry of Finance — Corporate and Personal Property Registries and filed electronically.

i) Names

The problems associated with corporate names are both legally complex and practically important. On a practical level, it is difficult to find a name that is not already in use. Once an enterprise chooses a name and starts to use it, the name begins to have value associated with it. Apart from any personal attachment to a corporate name, its financial value based on its use may be substantial. It may be recognized by consumers or business customers as indicative of prestige, product quality, or service. This sort of value is commonly referred to as goodwill. The use of the name by someone else may be severely damaging to the goodwill associated with the name. One policy behind name regulation is the protection of the legitimately created goodwill of a particular business against appropriation by others. There is also a general public interest in the regulation of names. The courts have stated that "the danger to be guarded against is that the person seeing or hearing one name will think it to be the same as another which he has seen or heard before."[5] In other words, name regulation seeks to prevent confusion in the marketplace.

Legally, name regulation is a tangle of provincial and federal jurisdictions. The *CBCA* and the provincial corporate statutes have provisions regulating the use of names by corporations incorporated under them. In addition, the federal *Trade-marks Act*[6] grants rights in names based on their use in association with goods and services. Each province regulates the use of names in its jurisdiction by corporations (other than the names they are incorporated with), wherever they are incorporated, and the provincial common law protects certain interests in names through the tort of passing-off. The following subsections outline briefly the legal framework for corporate names.

aa) Corporate Law Rules Regarding Names

The *CBCA*, like other corporate statutes in Canada, regulates the use of names of corporations to ensure that they are neither confusingly similar to other names used by businesses nor deceptively misdescriptive. The starting point is section 12(1)(a), which provides that a *CBCA* corporation may not be incorporated with or carry on business using a name that is "prescribed, prohibited or deceptively misdescriptive." If a name is contrary to this provision, the Director who administers the

---

5   *John Palmer Co. v. Palmer-McLellan Shoepack Co.* (1917), 45 N.B.R. 8, at 56 (C.A.).
6   R.S.C. 1985, c. T-13 [*TA*].

CBCA may refuse to incorporate a corporation that proposes to use it or, if the name is already being used by a corporation, order that the name be changed (*CBCA*, s. 12(2)).[7] Under the *OBCA*, a hearing must be held before any name change is ordered (*OBCA*, s. 12(1)).[8]

The *CBCA Regulations* set out both absolute and qualified prohibitions for the purposes of section 12. Names that may never be used are those that are obscene (*CBCA Regulations*, s. 23) or those that contain phrases like "United Nations" and "Air Canada" which others are exclusively entitled to (*CBCA Regulations*, s. 21). Sections 22 and 26 of the *CBCA Regulations* prohibit the use of certain names without consent. For example, without consent, one cannot use a name which suggests that a business is sponsored by or affiliated with the government of Canada, a university, or a professional association; nor can one use another person's family name without that person's consent.

Of greater practical significance are the provisions that deal with names which are not distinctive enough or are confusing. Section 24 sets out the criteria by which the inherent distinctiveness of a name must be judged. A name is not distinctive and cannot be used if it is

- only descriptive, in any language, of the quality, function, or other characteristic of the goods or services in which the corporation deals or intends to deal (e.g., Apples Inc. for a seller of apples);
- primarily or only the name or surname used alone of an individual who is living or has died within thirty years preceding the request for the name (e.g., Pierre Trudeau Inc.); and
- primarily or only a geographic name used alone (e.g., Japan Inc.).

An exception to this prohibition permits the use of names that are not inherently distinctive but that, through use, have acquired a secondary meaning (e.g., General Motors Inc.). In other words, if a name has been used in Canada for so long that it has obtained a level of recognition which distinguishes it from its competitors, it is not prohibited. Usually, in order to ensure that a name is found to be distinctive, it must combine a distinctive element with a descriptive element.

---

7   As noted above, it is necessary for each corporation to have a legal element in its name, such as "Inc." or "Limited." The Director may exempt a corporation continued under the *CBCA*, above note 1, from the requirement to have a legal element in its name (s. 10(2)). It is not clear why the Director would do so.

8   Some provincial statutes follow the federal statute (e.g., *ABCA*, above note 1, s. 12). Under the *BCCA*, above note 1, the rules are similar to those under the *Canada Business Corporations Regulations* SOR/2001-512 [*CBCA Regulations*] (ss. 17 & 18).

Distinctive elements may be a coined word (e.g., "Xerox" in Xerox Corporation), an arbitrarily chosen real word (e.g., "Dome" in Dome Mines Ltd.), a family or geographic name, or some other word. A descriptive element describes the business in which the corporation is engaged (e.g., "Mines" in Dome Mines Ltd.).

It is the whole name that must be distinctive (*CBCA Regulations*, s. 19). So, if the distinctive element is a highly original coined word, like Xerox, no descriptive element may be required. If the distinctive element is weaker, a descriptive element will be necessary.

This question of distinctiveness is not simply a technical legal issue. It is very important to business. There are already many similar and general names in the marketplace. A highly distinctive name is most likely to be noticed and remembered and is, therefore, more valuable.

In addition to inherent distinctiveness, the *CBCA Regulations* address confusion with other names and trade-marks. Other names include all names under which a business is carried on, whether it is being carried on through a corporation, partnership, or individual (collectively referred to as "trade-names"). A corporate name is confusingly similar to a trade-name or trade-mark if its use would likely lead to the inference that the business carried on under the corporate name and the business carried on under the trade-name or trade-mark are the same (*CBCA Regulations*, s. 18). Section 25 of the *Regulations* sets out a list of factors to be considered in assessing whether a corporate name is confusingly similar to a trade-mark or trade-name:

- the inherent distinctiveness of the whole or any element of the corporate name and the trade-mark or trade-name, and the extent to which either has become known;
- the length of time the corporate name and the trade-mark or trade-name have been in use and which was used first;
- the nature of the goods, services, or business associated with the corporate name and with the trade-mark or trade-name, including the likelihood of any competition between the corporation using or proposing to use the name and other businesses using the trade-mark or trade-name;
- the nature of the trade with which the corporate name and the trade-mark or trade-name is associated, including the nature of the products or services and the means by which they are offered or distributed (e.g., wholesale or retail);
- the degree of resemblance between the corporate name and the trade-mark or trade-name in appearance or sound, or in the ideas suggested by them; and

- the territorial area in Canada in which the corporate name or the trade-name is likely to be used.[9]

In *I. Browns Packaging Inc.* v. *Canada (Consumer and Corporate Affairs)*,[10] the court considered an appeal from a decision by the Director appointed under the *CBCA* that the name I. Browns Packaging Inc. was not confusingly similar to Brown's Bottle (Canada) Ltd. I. Browns Packaging Inc. was incorporated by Irwin Browns, a former shareholder in Browns Bottle (Canada) Limited. The court found that I. Browns Packaging Inc. designed packaging products for a small number of industrial customers, whereas Browns Bottle (Canada) Limited acted as a distributor for various packaging products. Although these businesses were not found to be identical, the court determined that there was some overlap, in the sense that the two businesses bought from some of the same suppliers and sold to some of the same customers. They might find themselves in competition in the future, although, since the market was a specialized one with few purchasers, there was little likelihood of confusion — and no actual confusion was established. The court also noted that the descriptive elements of the names, "Packaging" and "Bottle," were different. This difference, along with the use of the initial "I," rendered the names distinguishable. The court also noted that, at common law, a person has a right to use his own name and that the assessment of confusion should take Irwin Browns's right to use his name into account. The court concluded that the Director's decision should not be changed.

Sections 27 through 31 of the *CBCA Regulations* contain further rules about the possible confusion of names. These provisions deal with a variety of particular circumstances, including what a corporation must do to use a name that is confusingly similar to the name of another corporation where that corporation has not carried on business for two years (s. 28), or where a corporation is taking over the business of another corporation and intends to use the name that the other corporation used (s. 30). In general, the corporation that wants

---

9   This provision was interpreted in *Unitel International Inc.* v. *Unitel Communications Inc.*, (1992), 101 Sask. R. 48 (Q.B.). This case was an appeal of a decision of the Director under the *CBCA*, above note 1, s. 246(b), refusing to grant Unitel International Inc.'s application for an order requiring Unitel Communications Inc. to change its name. Based on a review of the application of the factors set out above, the court refused to overturn the Director's decision. The court indicated that great deference should be shown to the Director's decisions regarding names.

10   (1982), 24 B.L.R. 44 (Que. S.C.). See also *Merchant Commercial Real Estate Services Inc.* v. *Alberta (Registrar of Corporations)* (1997), 48 Alta. L.R. (3d) 119 (Q.B.) for another example of the application of these provisions.

the name must get the other corporation to consent to the use of the name and to undertake to dissolve or to change its name.

Names are also prohibited if they are "deceptively misdescriptive." Section 32 of the *CBCA Regulations* defines what is meant by this term. A corporate name is deceptively misdescriptive if it misdescribes, in any language,

- the business, goods, or services with which it is proposed to be used;
- the conditions under which the goods or services will be produced or supplied, or the persons to be employed in the production or supply of those goods or services; or
- the place of origin of those goods or services.

An example of a deceptively misdescriptive name might be "Made in Canada Mugs Inc." if the corporation's mugs were not made in Canada.

Subject to the rules described above, the *CBCA* specifically provides that the articles may set out the corporate name in an English form, a French form, an English and a French form, or a combined English and French form. A corporation may also have a form of its name in a third language for use outside Canada. A corporation may use and be legally designated by any of these forms (*CBCA*, s. 10(3) & (4)).[11]

bb) Provincial Registration and Licensing Rules Regarding Names
Each province regulates names used to carry on business within its borders. For example, in Chapter 1 we saw that most sole proprietorships and all partnerships carrying on business in Ontario must register their names under the Ontario *Business Names Act*. Corporations carrying on business in Ontario using a name other than their full corporate name must also register their other name. Failure to do so means that the defaulting party cannot maintain an action in the courts of Ontario in connection with an obligation of the business. With the consent of the court, however, an action may be permitted to proceed if the failure to register was inadvertent and there is no evidence that the public has been deceived or misled and, at the time of the application to court, the name has been registered (*OBNA*, s. 7). Failure to register is also an offence under section 10, but enforcement is rare.

Section 6 of the *OBNA* provides an incentive to private enforcement of the Act. A person who has registered a name may claim compensation of up to $500 for damages suffered as a result of another person registering a name that is the same as or deceptively similar to his own. If the claim is successful, the court must order the Registrar

---

11   The scheme is similar under the *OBCA* Regulation (R.R.O. 1990, Reg. 62, ss. 1–22).

appointed under the Act to cancel the offending registration. Claims for compensation under the *OBNA* are legally independent of any question of confusion under corporate statutes, trade-mark infringement, or common law passing-off, though liability under these various heads will often overlap in practice.

Provinces also regulate the use of corporate names by corporations incorporated outside the province. In general, corporations incorporated in other provinces or outside Canada must obtain permission in the form of a licence to carry on business.[12] These licences are routinely granted, except where the name of the extra-provincial corporation is confusingly similar to the name of a business already being carried on in the province. Federally incorporated corporations, however, have a right to carry on business in any province. It has been held by the Manitoba Court of Appeal that a province has no jurisdiction to refuse to permit a federal corporation to use its corporate name, since use of its name relates to the status of the corporation.[13]

In the same case, the court had to consider to what extent a province is competent to regulate a federal corporation's use of names other than its corporate name and any trade-mark it owns. It held that the provincial power to regulate the use of a business name depends on whether the corporation conducts business interprovincially or wholly within the province. Only in the latter case may the province regulate the use of the name.[14] The power granted to the Registrar under the Manitoba *Business Names Registration Act* to order the change of a name could not be applied to a federal corporation carrying on an interprovincial business.[15] The court held, however, that the provisions of the Act equivalent to those of section 2 of the Ontario Act, which require registration of a business name used by a corporation, were within the constitutional competence of the province regardless of the

---

12   E.g., in British Columbia, licences must be obtained under Part 10 of the *BCCA*, above note 1. In Ontario, corporations incorporated in other Canadian jurisdictions are permitted to carry on business in Ontario without individually applying for a licence (*Extra-Provincial Corporations Act*, R.S.O. 1990, c. E.27, s. 2). See section C ("Jurisdiction of Incorporation") in this chapter.

13   *Reference Re Constitution Act, 1867, ss. 91 & 92* (1991), 80 D.L.R. (4th) 431 (Man. C.A.). See, "Jurisdiction to Regulate" in Chapter 3.

14   The court acknowledged that, in practice, this will be a very difficult test to apply since it is conceivable that a corporation may be carrying on business in more than one province and still not be carrying on an interprovincial business (*ibid.*, at 445).

15   *Ibid.*, at 449. Provincial laws dealing with passing-off, discussed below in this section, would still apply.

nature of the corporation's business. They were validly enacted to permit the public in Manitoba to find out who is responsible for a business being carried on by a corporation under a name other than the corporation's legal name, a matter of civil rights within the province. The registration requirement was held not to impede the ability of interprovincial businesses to carry on their businesses.

The Manitoba Court of Appeal also held that a province has no jurisdiction to restrict the use of a trade-mark by a corporation out of concern that the trade-mark is similar to a business name in use in the province. Trade-marks are a matter within federal jurisdiction. A province is not prevented, however, from restricting the use of the trade-mark in a business name used by a corporation other than its corporate name in accordance with the rules described above. Any challenge to the use of the trade-mark itself would have to be under federal law, not provincial name registration legislation.

cc) *Trade-marks Act* Rules Regarding Names
A trade-mark is a word, phrase, or symbol used in association with goods or services. Use of a mark in association with goods or services in the marketplace gives the owner certain rights to use the mark exclusively in association with those goods or services, including a right to claim damages against anyone who infringes the mark. Registration of trade-marks is not required but is provided for under the *Trade-marks Act*.[16] Registration gives the registrant certain benefits, such as a presumption that the trade-mark is valid. Under section 20 of the *Trade-marks Act*, a trade-mark is infringed by the use of a confusing trade-mark or trade-name.[17] Confusion is defined in section 6 of the Act in essentially the same terms as in section 25 of the *CBCA Regulations*.

A trade-name for the purposes of the *Trade-marks Act* is simply a name used by a business. It may be a corporate name or another name used by the business. A trade-name is not a trade-mark unless it is used also to identify the goods or services of the business. It may be simple enough to distinguish a trade-mark from a trade-name where a business produces goods and the goods are sold with a mark attached to them which is different from the corporate name (e.g., Honda uses the trade-mark "Accord" on some of its cars), but in other cases it will be hard to tell what is the trade-mark and what is the trade-name. For example, many businesses use a trade-mark as part of their corporate

---

16   *TA*, above note 6.
17   Registration of a trade-mark that is confusing with a registered trade-mark is prohibited under *TA*, *ibid.*, s. 12.

name (e.g., Coca Cola uses the trade-mark "Coca-Cola" on its cola products as well as in its corporate name).

The relationship between rights under the *Trade-marks Act* and corporate legislation dealing with names is complex, and a full discussion is beyond the scope of this book. Nevertheless, a few general points should be made.

First, a corporate name or other trade-name is not necessarily a trade-mark, and the use of words claimed to be a trade-mark in a corporate name will be only one factor the court will consider in deciding whether a trade-mark is valid. The words must be used as a trade-mark to identify goods or services to be valid.[18]

Second, there are no cases that address the extent to which confusion for the purposes of trade-mark infringement and for the purposes of the corporate statutes are the same. So, for example, it is not clear whether a finding that one corporate name is confusingly similar to another under corporate law means that a trade-mark contained in the second name is also being infringed. Use of words constituting a trade-mark in a name, in some circumstances, may not be an infringing use of the mark. Thus, a corporation may be able to obtain an order under the relevant corporate law directing someone to change its corporate name because its use is confusing, but it may not be able to obtain damages for infringement of a trade-mark contained in the name under the *Trade-marks Act*.

Imagine that Apple Retail Sales Inc. (Apple Retail) uses the trade-mark "Apple" in association with the women's clothing that it has manufactured and sold at its retail store premises since 1990. A newly incorporated business with the name Apple Sales Inc. (Apple Sales) begins to carry on a business of selling sports equipment at a retail store. Apple Retail may be able to obtain an order directing Apple Sales to change its corporate name because it would be confusingly similar to Apple Retail Sales Inc. The court would have to make a separate assessment, however, of whether the use of the corporate name Apple Sales Inc. would be confusing with Apple Retail's use of the trade-mark "Apple." If Apple Sales does not sell clothes, and its sells its sports equipment only under the brands of well-known manufacturers, such as Brooks, it may be that Apple Sales has not infringed Apple Retail's trade-mark.

Third, the remedies are very different. A successful trade-mark infringement action may entitle the plaintiff to damages and an injunc-

18   *TA, ibid.*, s. 4.

tion directing the defendant to cease using the trade-mark and to deliver up any goods bearing the mark. A successful complaint under the corporate statutes results only in a direction to the corporation to change its name. Any use of a trade-mark would be unaffected.

Fourth, the Federal Court has jurisdiction over trade-mark matters, whereas corporate names disputes under the *CBCA* must be resolved, first, before the Director appointed under the *CBCA* and, then, on appeal, in provincial superior courts.[19]

dd) Passing-Off

A person carrying on business under a name has a common law right to seek an injunction to prevent someone else from selling products in a manner that is likely to deceive purchasers of the products into thinking they are purchasing the first person's products, thereby depriving her of profit.[20] Damages may also be claimed. Such "passing-off" actions may now also be brought under section 7(b) of the *Trade-marks Act*.

The Supreme Court of Canada has held that to succeed in a passing-off action the plaintiff must show the following:

- The plaintiff's business has a reputation or goodwill at the relevant time.
- The defendant has made a misrepresentation in the course of trade to prospective customers to the effect that there is a connection between the business of the plaintiff and that of the defendant. There is no requirement that the misrepresentation be deliberate and proof of intent to injure is not required, so long as injury to the plaintiff's business was a reasonably foreseeable consequence of the misrepresentation.
- The misrepresentation must cause actual damage to a business or the goodwill of the plaintiff, or be likely to do so.[21]

Greystone Capital Management v. *Greystone Properties*[22] provides an example of a successful passsing-off action. In that case, the plaintiff, Greystone Capital Management (Capital), had started carrying on a

---

19   The appeal right with respect to the Director's decisions is provided for in the *CBCA*, above note 1, s. 246.
20   *Fastening House Ltd.* v. *Fastway Supply House Ltd.* (1974), 3 O.R. (2d) 385 (H.C.J.).
21   *Ciba-Geigy Canada Ltd.* v. *Apotex Inc.* (1992), 44 C.P.R. (3d) 289 (S.C.C.). See also, *Erven Warnink BV* v. *J. Townend & Sons (Hull) Ltd.*, [1979] A.C. 731, at 742 (H.L.). See generally, D. Vaver, *Intellectual Property Law: Copyright, Patents and Trade-marks* (Concord: Irwin Law, 1997).
22   (1999), 87 C.P.R. (3d) 43 (B.C.S.C.).

business of soliciting investments under its corporate name in British Columbia in 1994. Several companies related to each other began carrying on similar and competing businesses, each using the word "Greystone" in their corporate names, in 1995. The court found that, before the defendants had begun to use the Greystone name, Capital had established a reputation in the investment community in British Columbia, even though it had no office or even a telephone listing in the province. The court also found that the adoption of corporate names incorporating the word "Greystone" constituted a misrepresentation by the defendants that their businesses were connected with Capital's and that some people had confused the defendant's business with Capital's. The court ordered that the defendant corporations change their corporate names to names that did not include the word Greystone within four months.

Claims for damages for passing-off are legally independent of any question of confusion under corporate statutes, trade-mark infringement, or liability under business names legislation. There are several important limitations on a passing-off action which do not apply to trade-mark infringement. Most important, to establish passing-off, the plaintiff must prove that it has a reputation associated with the mark and some likelihood that the public will be deceived. While use of a trade-mark will be required for a successful infringement action, it is not necessary to prove that this use has resulted in a market reputation. Passing-off can be used only to protect a business against others operating in the region in which the plaintiff carries on its business. Once a trade-mark is registered, however, a court must recognize the plaintiff's right to use the mark across Canada regardless of the extent to which it has been used in any particular area for the purposes of trade-mark infringement actions. An infringement action can be successful against a confusingly similar mark without any proof of damage.

An example of the complexity of the relationship between all these rules about names was provided by the legal proceedings related to a dispute between the national furniture retailer Brick Warehouse Corp. (Brick Warehouse) and a furniture business in Winnipeg called Brick's Fine Furniture Ltd. (Brick's Fine Furniture). Brick's Fine Furniture challenged the Brick Warehouse's right to use its corporate name before the Director appointed under the *CBCA*. At about the same time, Brick Warehouse sued Brick's Fine Furniture in the Federal Court for infringing its trade-mark "Brick," which it had registered in association with furniture. Brick's Fine Furniture counterclaimed against Brick Warehouse alleging passing-off contrary to section 7 of the *Trade-marks Act*. Brick's Fine Furniture also sued Brick Warehouse in Manitoba for common law passing-off. In *Brick Warehouse Corp.* v. *Brick's Fine Furniture Ltd.*,[23] the Federal Court refused to order a stay of the proceedings before the *CBCA* Director while the trade-mark dispute on the same facts was being dealt with in the Federal Court. The passing-off action filed in Manitoba, however, was stayed on the basis that the the passing-off claim had been raised by counter claim in the Federal Court proceeding.[24] Ultimately, the dispute was settled out of court.

ee) Names and the Incorporation Process

As part of the incorporation process, a name search from a commercial name-search house, including an opinion that the name may be used, must be obtained and submitted with the other documents required for incorporation. The name search is done to ensure that the name chosen for incorporation is not confusingly similar to names already in use. Incorporation under the laws of a particular jurisdiction does not mean that the jurisdiction is conferring any absolute proprietary right to the name. The incorporator takes the risk that he may be required to change the corporation's name if it is deceptively similar to a tradename, trade-mark, or corporate name already in use (*CBCA*, s. 12)[25] or be sued for trade-mark infringement or passing-off. Most provincial jurisdictions no longer even review the required name search. The obligation to get one is imposed simply to ensure that the incorporator has done the search. By contrast, the federal Corporations Directorate of Industry Canada carefully reviews name searches and will not permit an incorporation to go ahead if it has concerns about the name. Sometimes this concern can result in extended discussions between the incorporator (or more likely her lawyer) and the Corporations Directorate and can cause frustrating delays in the incorporation process. Accordingly, where an incorporation must take place on a certain date, it is advisable to "pre-clear" the name by taking advantage of the possibility of reserving the name for up to ninety days in advance of incorporation (*CBCA*, s. 11).[26] By doing so, if the Corporations Directorate has any concerns about the name, there is an opportunity to address them in advance of the proposed incorporation date.

---

23 (1992), 42 C.P.R. (3d) 158 (Fed. T.D.).

24 *Brick's Fine Furniture Ltd.* v. *Brick Warehouse Corp.* (1988), decision of Hanssen, J. of the Manitoba Court of Queen's Bench (unreported), aff'd (1989), 25 C.P.R. (3d) 89 (Man. C.A).

25 Provincial schemes are similar. E.g., *OBCA*, above note 1, ss. 9 & 12; and *BCCA*, above note 1, ss. 17 & 18.

26 Some provincial schemes do not provide for such a right (e.g., Ontario), while others do (e.g., *BCCA*, *ibid.*, s. 15)

The name search may be obtained from various commercial search firms for a fee. The search is conducted in a database owned by the Corporations Directorate of Industry Canada called NUANS (Newly Upgraded Automated Name Search System). The NUANS database includes corporate names, trade-marks, and business names from across Canada. It is necessary to request a search which is "biased," meaning weighted, in favour of the jurisdiction chosen for incorporation. The NUANS database contains an enormous number of names, and the bias request is to ensure that the search picks up those names that are being used in the jurisdiction in which incorporation is sought. In addition to the required NUANS search, it is advisable to search local telephone and trade directories for similar names to ensure that the name chosen is not confusingly similar to other names and trade-marks.

A name search is not required if the incorporators are content simply to have a number assigned by the corporate regulator as the name for the corporation (e.g., 123456 Ontario Inc.). This may be attractive if the corporation will be carrying on no business in which public recognition would be an asset, such as simply holding a portfolio of private investments, or where a suitable name cannot be found.[27] A corporation with a number name may use another name so long as it complies with the provincial registration requirements described above and corporate law rules requiring for the use of the full corporate name on contracts, invoices, and other documents.[28]

ii) Registered Office

Under the *CBCA*, it is necessary to identify in its articles the province in Canada where the registered office of the corporation is to be situated. The street address of the registered office is set out in the Notice of Registered Office (Form 3). The "registered office" concept was introduced with the *CBCA*. It need not be the head office but only a place within the jurisdiction at which the records of the corporation are kept (*CBCA*, s. 20(1)) and which may serve as the address for correspondence with the *CBCA* Director and for service of documents (*CBCA*, s. 254). The province specified for the registered office may be changed only by amending the articles (*CBCA*, s. 173(1)(b)), which requires

---

27   Where a corporation is incorporated with a number name, the directors may amend the articles to adopt another name without the approval of shareholders, a requirement for any other amendment (*CBCA*, above note 1, s. 173(3)). Number names are not permitted under the laws of Nova Scotia or British Columbia. Amendment of articles is discussed in Chapter 10.

28   See Chapter 3, "Other Rules Protecting Non-shareholder Stakeholders."

approval by a special resolution of shareholders.[29] A change in the address or place within the province specified in the articles may be made with the approval of the directors. Where the directors approve such a change, a Notice of Change of Registered Office must be filed with the Director (*CBCA*, s. 19(3), Form 3).

The registered office of a provincial corporation must be located inside the incorporating province (e.g., *OBCA*, s. 14 & *NBBCA*, s. 4(1)). The municipality or township in which the registered office is located may be changed by special resolution of the shareholders (e.g., *OBCA*, s. 14(3)).[30] The address of the registered office within the municipality or township may be changed by the directors without shareholder approval.[31]

iii) Class and Number of Shares

The articles define the classes of shares the corporation is authorized to issue. They set out the name by which each class of shares is to be identified (e.g., "common shares") as well as the "rights, privileges, restrictions and conditions" of each class, such as whether they vote, receive dividends, or share in the distribution of the assets of the corporation on its dissolution after the creditors are paid. We discuss some of the many possibilities for creating shares with different characteristics and some of the rules regarding share provisions in Chapter 6.

In many small corporations, there is only one class of shares, typically named common shares, which vote and are entitled to receive dividends declared by the board of directors from time to time and the remaining property of the corporation on dissolution. Corporations may have other classes of shares with different characteristics. In general, the bundle of characteristics belonging to each class of shares will determine their price and their attractiveness to investors with different sorts of preferences. For example, investors who want to receive a fixed annual return, but do not want to participate in the management of the corporation, would be interested in a class of shares that (i)

---

29   A special resolution is a resolution signed by all shareholders or passed at a meeting of shareholders by a majority of not less than two-thirds of the votes cast by shareholders present and voting at the meeting (*CBCA*, above note 1, s. 2(1)). Amendment of articles and by-laws is discussed in Chapter 10.

30   In British Columbia (*BCCA*, above note 1, ss. 39 & 40), and the Yukon (*Business Corporations Act*, R.S.Y. 1986, c. 15, s. 22), the place of the registered office may also be changed by directors' resolution.

31   Upon changing the address, an information filing must be made as well (e.g., Ontario *Corporations Information Act*, R.S.O. 1990, c. C.39 [*CIA*], s. 4).

offers a fixed annual dividend, paid before any dividend on any other class, and (ii) is entitled to receive back the amount invested before any payment to the holders of common shares or any other class of shares on dissolution of the corporation — even if the class had no voting right. Such shares are commonly referred to as "preferred shares."

It is also necessary to specify the number of shares the corporation may issue. Shares are issued by the directors, but they can issue shares only up to any maximum amount provided for in the articles. Additional shares may be issued only after amending the articles to raise or to remove the limit. This amendment requires shareholder approval by a special resolution. In some circumstances, limits may be desired. If, for example, shareholders want to avoid having additional shares issued by the directors to dilute their proportionate interest in the corporation, they may want the maximum number of shares authorized to be issued set at the total number of shares to be held by them. If no limit is specified, the corporation may issue an unlimited number of shares. In the interests of ensuring the maximum flexibility, it is common practice not to impose a limit.

iv) Number of Directors

Under the *CBCA*, it is necessary to specify in the articles the number of directors or a minimum and a maximum number of directors (*CBCA*, s. 6(1)(e)).[32] The choice of the appropriate number of directors will depend on a variety of factors specific to each corporation, including the scale of the corporation's business, the desire of shareholders to be members of or to be represented on the board, and the desirability of involving people with no relation to the corporation as directors on the board — perhaps because they have some needed expertise or experience. In addition, corporate statutes impose certain requirements: under the *CBCA*, corporations that have distributed their shares to the public[33] must have three directors, at least two of whom are not officers or

---

32   Provincial statutes based on the *CBCA*, above note 1, are similar. E.g., *OBCA*, above note 1, s. 224. Where cumulative voting is provided for in the articles, a fixed number of directors must be specified (*CBCA*, above note 1, s. 107(a)). Cumulative voting is discussed in Chapter 6.

33   The *CBCA Regulations*, above note 8, define "distributing corporation" as a corporation that is a reporting issuer under provincial securities laws, has issued a prospectus, or has shares being listed on a stock exchange (ss. 2(1) & (6)). The *CBCA*, *ibid.*, permits a corporation to apply to the Director to be deemed not to be distributing its securities to the public. See section B(1)(e) ("Considerations Relating to the Scale of the Corporation") below in this chapter.

employees of the corporation or affiliated corporations;[34] all other corporations need to have only one director (*CBCA*, s. 102(2)). The number
of directors or the minimum and maximum number of directors stated
in the articles may be changed only by amendment of the articles.[35]

v) Restrictions on Issuing, Transferring, or Owning Shares
In the absence of a restriction in the articles on share transfer, shares are
presumed to be freely transferable, unlike partnership interests. It is commonplace, however, for corporations with few shareholders to have some
kind of transfer restriction in the articles. In such corporations, each
shareholder has a strong interest in having some control over who the
other shareholders are. The shareholders typically work in the business
and will not want their fellow shareholders selling out, nor will they want
to have another person involved as a shareholder without their consent.
Against these considerations, each shareholder is likely to want as much
flexibility as possible to sell his own shares. In a corporation with few
shareholders, this flexibility is especially important because it is often difficult for a shareholder in such a corporation to find a buyer. There is no
ready marketplace in which the shares of such a corporation may be
priced and sold. As a result, when drafting share-transfer restrictions,
shareholders typically try to strike some form of balance between their
interest in controlling who the other shareholders are and their interest in
having the fewest restrictions on their right to sell their own shares. As
will be discussed in Chapter 6, this conflict often leads to the creation of
complex mechanisms in shareholders' agreements, such as provisions giving shareholders a right to buy the shares of any shareholder who wants
to sell her shares before they may be sold to a third party (called a "right
of first refusal"). In the articles, the usual restriction is simply a short provision requiring the directors or some specified majority of shareholders
to consent to the transfer. People to whom shares are transferred are not
subject to any restriction on transfer unless they are actually aware of the
restriction or the restriction or a reference to it is noted conspicuously on
the face of the share certificates they receive (*CBCA*, s. 49(8)).[36]

---

34 There are similar requirements in statutes modelled on the *CBCA*, *ibid.*, (e.g.,
    OBCA, above note 1, s. 115; *ABCA*, above note 1, s. 97). There is no require-
    ment for outside directors in the corporate statutes of Prince Edward Island,
    Quebec, or British Columbia.
35 Under the New Brunswick *Business Corporations Act*, S.N.B. 1981, c. B-9.1, the
    number of directors is specified in the by-laws (s. 60(2)).
36 Provincial statutes modelled on the *CBCA*, above note 1, have similar provisions
    (e.g., *OBCA*, above note 1, s. 56(3); and *ABCA*, above note 1, s. 48). See also
    BCCA, above note 1, s. 51(1)(e), requiring notice of restrictions on transfer.

Restrictions may be imposed on the issuance of shares as well. The *CBCA* model corporate statutes permit the inclusion in the articles of a right for each existing shareholder of a corporation to purchase any new shares to be issued in proportion to his holdings of shares prior to the issuance of shares to anyone else (*CBCA*, s. 28). Such a right is referred to as a "pre-emptive right." Variations on the form of pre-emptive right are permitted under some of the provincial statutes[37] but, in practice, most pre-emptive rights are set up as contemplated in the *CBCA* provision. Sometimes pre-emptive rights are found in shareholders' agreements.

Another kind of restriction on transfer or issuance defines the class of acceptable shareholders. For example, a corporation may want to prohibit transfers outside the existing group of shareholders. The most common restriction, however, is to prohibit transfers to non-Canadians, perhaps to ensure that the corporation continues to qualify under a government program requiring Canadian ownership. A corporation's articles may provide for restrictions on ownership of shares for the same purpose. Restrictions to ensure a minimum level of Canadian ownership and for certain other purposes are expressly contemplated in the *CBCA* and in some provincial statutes modelled after it (*CBCA*, ss. 32, 49(8) & (9) & 174; and *OBCA*, ss. 29, 42).[38] Such constraints must be conspicuously noted on a corporation's share certificates (e.g., *CBCA*, s. 49(10)). However, the restiction is nevertheless effective against the transferee, even if it is not noted (*CBCA*, s. 49(11)).[39] Where such restrictions have been included in the articles, some corporate statutes provide a procedure for the corporation to force the sale of any shares owned in a manner contrary to the restrictions (e.g., *CBCA*, ss. 46–47; *OBCA*, s. 45).[40]

vi) *Restrictions on the Business the Corporation May Carry On*
As discussed in Chapter 3, under earlier corporate statutes a corporation had to specify its "objects" in the corporate constitution. This obligation inevitably led to problems caused by corporations engaging in activities that were not contemplated in their objects. Such activities

---

37   E.g., *OBCA*, *ibid.*, s. 26; and *ABCA*, *ibid.*, s. 30. The *BCCA*, *ibid.*, imposes a a pre-emptive right on companies that are not reporting companies under the act (s. 41).

38   E.g., *ABCA*, *ibid.*, ss. 48, 174. The *BCCA*, *ibid.*, does not expressly address restrictions on the issuance of shares. Under the *CBCA* the only transfer or ownership restriction permitted for distributing corporations is one requiring ownership by resident Canadians (*CBCA*, above note 1, s. 49(9)).

39   Provincial statutes modelled on the *CBCA*, above note 1, have similar provisions. E.g., *ABCA*, *ibid.*, ss. 48(10) & (11); and *OBCA*, *ibid.*, ss. 56(8) & (10).

40   No such provision is found in the *ABCA*, *ibid.*

were considered *ultra vires* the corporation, and any obligations to third parties that were entered into by the corporation in connection with these activities were of no effect.

Under the *CBCA* model statutes, it is not necessary for the corporation to describe the activities in which it will engage. The corporation has all the capacity and, subject to certain limitations in the corporate statute, the rights, powers, and privileges of a natural person (*CBCA*, s. 15).[41] In order to avoid the risk of *ultra vires* activities, it is common practice not to include in the articles any restriction on the business the corporation may carry on.

The rule that *ultra vires* obligations are unenforceable against the corporation has been largely mitigated under the *CBCA*. If a restriction is included in the articles, the *CBCA* provides that the corporation is forbidden to act in a manner contrary to the restriction (*CBCA*, s. 16(2)). Nevertheless, if the corporation does something contrary to the restriction, the act is not invalid by reason only that it is contrary to the articles (*CBCA*, s. 16(3)). As a result, no third party should be prejudiced because the corporation, for example, enters into an obligation with the third party which is contrary to its articles.[42] The third party should still be able to enforce the obligation.

This provision does not mean, however, that the restrictions in the articles are of no effect. Shareholders may seek relief from any contravention of such a provision if its effect on the shareholders is "oppressive, unfairly prejudicial to or unfairly disregards [their] interests" (*CBCA*, s. 241(2)).[43] Also, both shareholders and creditors may apply to a court for an order restraining the corporation, or anyone acting on its behalf, from acting in a manner contrary to the articles or directing compliance with the articles (*CBCA*, s. 247).[44] It remains to be seen if a court would make such an order where the effect would be to deprive a third party of the benefit of a contract it had with the corporation.

---

41 E.g., *OBCA*, *ibid.*, s. 15; and *ABCA*, *ibid.*, s. 16. The *BCCA*, *ibid.*, provides that a corporation has the power and capacity of a person of full capacity subject to any restrictions in its memorandum (ss. 21 & 22). The Nova Scotia *Companies Act*, R.S.N.S. 1989, c. 81 [*NSCA*], above note 8, has a similar provision as well as a listing of specific powers and restrictions (s. 26).

42 Provincial statutes have similar provisions. E.g., *OBCA*, *ibid.*, s. 17; *ABCA*, *ibid.*, s. 17; and *BCCA*, *ibid.*, ss. 22 & 24. See Chapter 5, section D ("Liability of Corporations in Contract"), regarding qualifications to this protection.

43 Provincial schemes are similar. E.g., *OBCA*, *ibid.*, s. 248; *ABCA*, *ibid.*, s. 242; and *BCCA*, *ibid.*, s. 200.

44 Provincial schemes are similar. E.g., *OBCA*, *ibid.*, s. 253; *ABCA*, *ibid.*, s. 248; and *BCCA*, *ibid.*, s. 25.

vii) Other Provisions

A variety of other provisions are sometimes put in the articles. The *CBCA* contemplates that the articles may deal with the following types of matters: requirements for super majorities of directors or shareholders to approve certain decisions (s. 6(3) & (4)), limitations on the right to purchase shares (ss. 34 & 35), liens on the shares of shareholders who are indebted to the corporation (s. 45(2)), and the quorum for directors' meetings (s. 114(2)).[45] In addition, any provision permitted by the *CBCA* to be included in a by-law may be included in the articles (s. 6(2)).[46] The content of by-laws will be discussed below, but, in general, what may be included in a by-law is virtually unrestricted (*CBCA*, s. 103(1)).[47] The main difference between including a provision in the articles and in the by-laws is that the articles can be amended only by a special resolution of shareholders requiring approval by two-thirds of shareholders voting. In contrast, by-laws require approval by a simple majority only.[48] Also, the articles are a matter of public record, whereas the by-laws are not. Many lawyers suggest that the content of the articles should be minimized in order to simplify the process of incorporation and to avoid the need to amend the articles later if changes are desired.

Finally, if a corporation will be doing business in Quebec, it is the practice of some lawyers to include in the articles the borrowing powers and the powers to mortgage property contemplated by the *Special Corporate Powers Act* of Quebec.[49] The Act permits a corporation to mortgage property in Quebec when authorized by its constitution. Without the special provision, there is a risk that a corporation might be found not to have the powers dealt with in the Act.

---

45   Provincial statutes modelled on the *CBCA*, above note 1, have similar provisions. E.g., *OBCA*, *ibid.*, ss. 5(4) & (5), 30, 31, 40(2), 126(3); and *ABCA*, *ibid.*, ss. 6(3) & (4), 32, 33, 114(2). There are some variations. For example, under the *OBCA*, delegation by directors to a committee is subject to any by-law provisions (s. 127) and the by-laws may change the requirements regarding the location for directors' meetings.

46   Provincial statutes modelled on the *CBCA*, *ibid.*, have similar provisions. E.g., *OBCA*, *ibid.*, s. 5(3); and *ABCA*, *ibid.*, s. 6(2).

47   Provincial statutes modelled on the *CBCA*, *ibid.*, have similar provisions. E.g., *OBCA*, *ibid.*, s. 116, *ABCA*, *ibid.*, s. 102. Issues dealt with in the by-laws would be addressed in the articles of companies incorporated under the *BCCA*, above note 1, and the *NSCA*, above note 41.

48   A special resolution is a resolution signed by all shareholders or passed at a meeting of shareholders by a majority of not less than two-thirds of the votes cast by shareholders present and voting at the meeting (*CBCA*, *ibid.*, s. 2(1)). Amendment of articles and by-laws is discussed in Chapter 10.

49   R.S.Q. 1977, c. P-16, ss. 27 & 34.

b) Other Documents Required to Be Filed on Incorporation

As noted above, in addition to the articles, in order to incorporate under the *CBCA*, the incorporators must file a Notice of Directors and a Notice of Registered Office. The Notice of Directors lists the directors and their addresses and indicates whether they are resident Canadians. The *CBCA* requires that at least 25 percent of the directors be resident Canadians (s. 105(3)).[50] The Notice of Registered Office indicates the street address at which the registered office is located. The only reason for separate documents containing this information is to permit updated notices to be filed each time the information on directors or the address of the registered office changes (*CBCA*, ss. 19(3) & 113), without amending the articles. Under the *OBCA*, the address of the registered office and the identity, address, and Canadian residency status of the directors are contained in the articles (*OBCA Regulation*, s. 46). There is, however, no need to amend the articles when the directors change. It is sufficient to file an information document called a Notice of Change under the *Corporations Information Act*.[51] Under the *OBCA*, it is necessary for each director named in the articles to have consented to act as a director. The corporation must keep a copy of the signed consent at its registered office (*OBCA*, s. 5(2)).[52]

All jurisdictions charge a fee on incorporation. The fee for incorporation under the *CBCA* is $250 (*CBCA Regulations*, Schedule 5 (or $200 if incorporation documents are filed electronically)), while the fee under most provincial statutes is somewhat more. Under the *OBCA* it is $330 (*Minister's Fee Order* — Schedule 1 (or $300 if incorporation documents are filed electronically)).[53]

---

50   If there are less than four directors, at least one must be a resident Canadian. A majority of resident Canadian directors is required for corporations engaged in certain activities. "Resident Canadian" is defined in the *CBCA*, above note 1, s. 2, and *CBCA Regulations*, above note 8, s. 13. Other qualifications for directors are described in Chapter 7. Under many provincial statutes, a majority of directors must be resident Canadians (e.g., *OBCA*, above note 1, 118(3); and *ABCA*, above note 1, s. 105(3)).

51   *CIA*, above note 31, s. 4.

52   The *OBCA*, above note 1, requires that directors named in the articles (or elected or appointed in any other manner) consent in writing within ten days. Without such a consent, their election or appointment is not effective (S.O. 1994, c. 27, s. 71, amending *OBCA*, s. 119(9)).

53   The fee in British Columbia is $300 (*BCCA*, above note 1, Third Schedule). Name searches must also be filed with the articles, as discussed above under "Names and the Incorporation Process," above this chapter.

c) Completion of Incorporation

Once these documents required by the *CBCA* are properly filed along with the fee, the Director appointed to administer the *CBCA* issues a certificate (Form 2) certifying that the corporation, the articles of which are attached, was incorporated on the date of the certificate (*CBCA*, ss. 8 & 9). The corporation comes into existence on the date of the certificate (*CBCA*, s. 9). The directors named in the Notice of Directors hold office until the first meeting of shareholders (*CBCA*, s. 106(2)).[54] The provisions in the articles may be changed only by articles of amendment filed with the Director after approval by a special resolution of shareholders. This procedure is discussed in Chapter 10.

The actual process of filing the requisite documents with the fee and receiving a certificate of incorporation is expeditious, may be engaged in by anyone, and can be done online in many jurisdictions. Lawyers routinely incorporate corporations for their clients but now there are also a variety of commercial services offering to do incorporations more quickly and cheaply. Individuals may obtain incorporation kits to permit do-it-yourself incorporations.[55] As will be discussed below, there are many issues and potential pitfalls associated with incorporation which, in any case, is only the first step in organizing a business, so consideration must be given to the desirability of professional advice in connection with incorporations.

d) Post-Incorporation Organization

On incorporation, the corporation may commence carrying on a business. It may be a new business, or an existing business may be transferred to it. Unlike a partnership, there is no need for a corporation to carry on business; its existence derives exclusively from the issuance of the certificate under the statute.[56] Several more steps are required, however, before the corporation is fully organized.[57]

---

54   Provincial schemes based on the *CBCA*, above note 1, are similar. E.g., *OBCA*, above note 1, ss. 6, 7 & 119; and *ABCA*, note 1, ss. 8, 9 & 106. See also *BCCA*, *ibid.*, ss. 8, 9, 11, 12 & 110.

55   Several incorporation kits are available, including the "Incorporator and Business Guide" published by the Ontario Ministry of Consumer and Business Services. The main purpose of this kit is to assist incorporators in choosing an effective corporate name. Software designed to enable computer users to incorporate quickly and easily is also available commercially.

56   *Campbell v. Taxicabs Verrals Ltd.* (1912), 27 O.L.R. 141 (H.C.J.). Section 212 of the *CBCA*, above note 1, provides that the Director appointed to administer the Act may dissolve a corporation that has not commenced business within three years of incorporation or has not carried on business for three consecutive years. This discretion is rarely exercised. See Chapter 10.

57   The *CBCA*, *ibid.*, suggests an agenda for the first meeting of directors (s. 104).

First, the directors should have a meeting and pass a resolution to issue shares to the shareholders. Under some provincial statutes modelled on the *CBCA*, such as the *ABCA*, the issuance of shares is essential since, until the shares are issued, the only persons who may act for the corporation are the directors named in the Notice of Directors. Should anything happen to them, the corporation would be unable to act. The *2001 Amendments* cured this problem in the *CBCA* itself by providing that, in instances where a director resigns or is "removed," any person who manages or supervises the management of the business and the affairs of the corporation is deemed to be a director for the purposes of the Act (*CBCA*, s. 109(4) & (5) (lists exceptions)). This reform follows a similar provision in the *OBCA* (s. 115(4)). There is no requirement for any minimum amount to be paid into the corporation for shares. Some foreign jurisdictions impose minimum capitalization requirements to discourage frivolous incorporation.[58]

Also at the first meeting, the directors will typically adopt arrangements for carrying on the formal legal business of the corporation, including the following:

- requirements for directors;
- procedure for meetings of directors (e.g., how notice of meetings is given, what constitutes a quorum);
- remuneration and indemnification of directors;
- designation and specification of duties of officers;
- procedure for meetings of shareholders;
- procedure for payment of dividends;
- financial year of the corporation; and
- designation of those persons who may sign documents on behalf of the corporation.

These arrangements are usually set out in a by-law. The *CBCA* provides that certain elements of its default rules may be changed only by a by-law (e.g., the location, notice of, and quorum for directors' meetings (s. 114),[59] location of shareholder meetings (s. 132),[60] quorum (s.

---

58   Minimum capitalization requirements are discussed in Chapter 3, section F(2)(b) ("Other Rules Protecting Non-shareholder Stakeholders") and Chapter 6, section C ("Issuing and Paying for Shares").

59   Provincial statutes modelled on the *CBCA*, above note 1, have similar provisions, though not identical ones. E.g., *OBCA*, above note 1, s. 126; and *ABCA*, above note 1, s. 114. The *BCCA*, above note 1, s. 6, contemplates that many of these issues are to be addressed in the corporation's articles.

60   Some provincial statutes modelled on the *CBCA*, *ibid.*, have similar provisions. E.g., *ABCA*, *ibid.*, s. 131.

139),[61] and voting procedures (s. 141)).[62] All other matters may be dealt with in a resolution passed by the directors. It is common practice, however, to deal with all these matters in a general by-law. A general by-law is also useful as a handbook on corporate procedures, and by-laws are sometimes drafted to recite rules provided for in the corporate statute in the interests of providing a more complete compendium of applicable rules.

To take effect, a by-law must be passed by the directors, but it continues in effect only if it is passed by the shareholders at their next meeting following the approval of the by-law by the directors (*CBCA*, s. 103).[63] Because making, amending, and repealing by-laws ultimately requires shareholder approval, including arrangements in a by-law serves to entrench them more than dealing with them by resolution of the directors.[64]

Typically at the first meeting, directors will pass resolutions dealing with other organizational matters as well, such as appointing officers and making banking arrangements, including authorizing the opening of a bank account for the corporation and designating certain people to sign cheques on behalf of the corporation. Banks have standard-form resolutions that they require to be passed for this purpose. A corporate seal for the corporation may be approved at such an organizational meeting, though a seal is no longer required (*CBCA*, s. 23).[65] It is also usual to designate a form of share certificate. As will be discussed in Chapter 6, there is no need for a corporation to issue share certificates, though shareholders have a right to receive one on request (*CBCA*, s. 49(1)).[66]

Once the shares are issued, a shareholders' meeting is usually held at which any by-laws approved by the directors are voted on (*CBCA*, s. 104(1)).[67] By-laws must be approved by a simple majority of sharehold-

---

61   Most provincial schemes are similar. E.g., *OBCA*, *ibid.*, s. 101; *ABCA*, *ibid.*, s. 138; and *BCCA*, *ibid.*, ss. 144 & 148.

62   Most provincial schemes are similar. E.g., *OBCA*, *ibid.*, s. 103; *ABCA*, *ibid.*, s. 140; and *BCCA*, *ibid.*, s. 158.

63   Provincial statutes modelled on the *CBCA*, above note 1, are similar. E.g., *OBCA*, *ibid.*, s. 116; and *ABCA*, *ibid.*, s. 102.

64   See Chapter 10 for the process of making, amending, and repealing by-laws.

65   Provincial rules are similar. E.g., *OBCA*, above note 1, s. 13; *ABCA*, above note 1, s. 25; and *BCCA*, above note 1, ss. 35, 101.

66   Most provincial rules are similar. E.g., *OBCA*, *ibid.*, s. 54; *ABCA*, *ibid.*, s. 48; and *BCCA*, *ibid.*, s. 48.

67   Provincial statutes modelled on the *CBCA*, above note 1, are similar. E.g., *OBCA*, *ibid.*, s. 116(3); and *ABCA*, *ibid.*, s. 104.

er votes represented at the meeting. For small corporations with few shareholders, this meeting typically takes place immediately after the directors' meeting.

A final step in the organization of a corporation which often occurs in corporations with few shareholders is that the shareholders enter into an agreement. Shareholders may wish to customize the way in which the corporation is governed by agreeing to alter the rights and obligations provided for in the corporate statute. For example, all shareholders may agree to vote their shares for certain people as directors. Shareholders' agreements also often deal with the circumstances in which shares may be transferred such as by giving each shareholder a right to be offered first any shares that another shareholder proposes to sell to a third party. Shareholders' agreements are discussed in Chapter 7.

As mentioned in Chapter 3, in order to determine the rules that govern a corporation, along with its shareholders, directors, and officers, it is necessary to take into account not just the governing corporate statute and the case law but also the elements of the corporate constitution identified above: the articles of incorporation, the by-laws, directors' resolutions, shareholders' resolutions, and any shareholders' agreement. These documents are agreed to by the directors or shareholders, or both, and represent, in that sense, private arrangements between them. They are private arrangements which are bounded by various mandatory provisions of the corporate statutes and which are, to a greater or lesser extent, enforceable through statutory mechanisms that will be described in Chapter 9. As indicated, these arrangements may derogate from or otherwise respond to the provisions of the governing corporate statute.

All these documents, along with a register showing who owns the shares and other securities of the corporation, must be maintained by the corporation at its registered office or at any other place in Canada designated by the directors (*CBCA*, s. 20).[68] Records may be kept outside Canada if the corporation provides access to them in Canada by computer or otherwise (*CBCA*, s. 20(5.1)). Shareholders and creditors must be given access to them, except for minutes of meetings and resolutions of directors (*CBCA*, s. 21).[69] Access includes a limited right to make copies. These documents are usually bound in hard-copy form in something called a "minute book," though the *CBCA* permits them to

---

68 Most provincial schemes are similar. E.g., *OBCA*, *ibid.*, s. 140 (location must be in Ontario); *ABCA*, *ibid.*, s. 21 (location must be in Alberta); and *BCCA*, above note 1, s. 163 (location must be in British Columbia).

69 Most provincial schemes are similar. E.g., *OBCA*, *ibid.*, s. 145; *ABCA*, *ibid.*, s. 23; and *BCCA*, *ibid.*, ss. 164-167.

be retained in "any system of mechanical or electronic data processing or any other information storage device that is capable of reproducing any required information in intelligible written form within a reasonable time" (s. 22(1)).[70] Articles and any other document filed with the *CBCA* Director, such as the Notice of Directors and the Notice of Registered Office, are filed in a publicly accessible record maintained by the Corporations Directorate of Industry Canada.

e)   Considerations Relating to the Scale of the Corporation

Corporations are used by businesses ranging from small operations involving a single person as shareholder, director, and employee to huge multinational concerns with thousands of shareholders and employees. The terms "public corporation" and "private corporation," or "widely held corporation" and "closely held corporation," are sometimes used to distinguish corporations having a large number of shareholders from those having only a few. Although the vast majority of corporations fall into this second category, those that fall into the first are nevertheless extremely important owing to their enormous role in the economy.

To be effective, corporate law rules must be responsive to the often very different requirements of business enterprises of different scales. Certain procedures and other provisions of corporate law may be appropriate for one form and not for another. Consider, for example, the fundamental issue of how management will be made accountable to shareholders. Many public corporations have a large number of shareholders, most of whom have a relatively small stake in the corporation relative to its total value. Such corporations are managed by professional managers, with little direct participation from shareholders, and require rules of governance which impose formal legal mechanisms to ensure that management is held accountable to shareholders. For a small corporation with few shareholders, all of whom are involved in the business actively, the same formal measures will not only be unnecessary but will create a burden. The question of appropriate rules becomes even more complex when one takes into account some of the common characteristics of public corporations in Canada: the presence of a majority shareholder, with the power to determine the outcome of most shareholder votes, and of large institutional shareholders, such as pension funds and insurance companies, who have the financial incentive as well as the skills and expertise necessary to participate effectively as shareholders.

---

70   Most provincial schemes are similar. E.g., *OBCA ibid.*, s. 139; *ABCA, ibid.*, s. 24; and *BCCA, ibid.*, s. 170.

Both the federal and the provincial Acts address this problem of differences in scale in a modest way by imposing different requirements on certain defined types of corporations. The *OBCA*, for example, distinguishes between "offering" and "non-offering" corporations. Essentially, offering corporations are those that have offered their shares to the public. Non-offering corporations are all the rest.

Figure 4.1   Definition of Offering Corporation under the *OBCA*

An "offering corporation" is defined as "a corporation that is offering its securities to the public ..."

Offering securities to the public means, among other things, that the corporation has

a) filed a prospectus or statement of material facts with respect to any of its securities and some of the securities remain outstanding; or
b) has securities listed on the Toronto Stock Exchange (ss. 1(1) & (6)).

Non-offering corporations are all corporations not caught by this definition.

A corporation may obtain an order from the Ontario Securities Commission (OSC) that it is deemed not to be an offering corporation if the OSC determines such an order would not be prejudicial to the public interest. Certain provisions of the *OBCA* apply only to offering corporations, such as management's obligation to facilitate the exercise of shareholders' right to vote by sending all shareholders information about the corporation and the items on the agenda for shareholders' meetings, as well as a form allowing them to send in their vote without attending in person (s. 111). The form is called a "form of proxy" and the sending of information is called "mandatory proxy solicitation."[71] Other provisions of the *OBCA* apply differently. For example, the following requirements apply to offering corporations:

• the minimum number of directors of an offering corporation is three, while for a non-offering corporation it is one (s. 115(2));
• at least one-third of the directors must not be officers or employees of the corporation or any of its affililates (ss. 115(3); 2.2 (definition of affiliate));
• offering corporations must have their financial statements audited and file them with the OSC (ss. 149, 153, 154, & 156); and

---

71   Proxies and proxy solicitation are discussed in Chapter 7.

- offering corporations must appoint an audit committee of the board of directors, a majority of whom are not officers or employees of the corporation or any affiliated corporation, responsible for reviewing the financial statements of the corporation and reporting to the full board (ss. 158(1), & (2)).

With the exception of the requirement to have an audit, none of these requirements applies to non-offering corporations. The shareholders of non-offering corporations may dispense with the requirement to have an audit if they unanimously agree (*OBCA*, ss. 148, 149). This possibility does not exist for offering corporations.

Under the *CBCA*, if a corporation has distributed securities to the public and they remain outstanding and held by more than one person, it becomes subject to a more onerous set of obligations which mirror many of those imposed on offering corporations under the *OBCA*. The *CBCA* defines distributing securities to the public in essentially the same way as the *OBCA* defines offering securities to the public.[72] Like the *OBCA*, the *CBCA* permits a corporation to apply to the Director to be deemed not to be distributing its securities to the public when there are few shareholders. The Director may grant such an order provided it does not prejudice the public interest (s. 1(6) & (7)).

All distributing corporations must

- have three directors, at least two of whom are not officers or employees of the corporation or an affiliate of the corporation (non-distributing corporations need only one) (s. 102(2), s. 2(2)(definition of affiliate));
- appoint an auditor[73] and an audit committee of at least three directors, a majority of whom are not officers or employees of the corporation or an affiliate of the corporation (ss. 162 & 171); and
- file its financial statements with the Corporations Directorate of Industry Canada (ss. 155, 160, & 171(8)).

As well, insiders of such corporations must comply with the insider trading rules (ss. 126, 130, & 131). Provincially, insider trading is governed by securities laws in most provinces and is discussed in Chapter 11.

---

72   *CBCA Regulations*, above note 8, s. 2(1). The definition is not limited to corporations which have filed a prospectus in Ontario or the securities of which are listed on a stock exchange in Ontario and includes any corporation that is a reporting issuer for the purposes of provincial securities laws.

73   All corporations governed by the *CBCA*, above note 1, must appoint an auditor, but the shareholders of corporations that are not distributing corporations, or of corporations where the securities distributed to the public are no longer outstanding or are held by one person only, may agree not to appoint an auditor (s. 163).

The *CBCA* also makes a further distinction among corporations to determine the applicability of particular provisions. The most important is that all corporations with more than fifty shareholders, whether distributing corporations or not, and all distributing corporations must comply with mandatory proxy-solicitation requirements (s. 149(1) & (2)).[74]

The chief advantage of the *OBCA* and *CBCA* schemes is that it is easy to know whether or not a particular corporation is subject to a higher level of obligation; the criteria are specific. Relying on rigid, technical criteria to distinguish corporations of different scales, means, however, that these definitions tend to be both under- and over-inclusive. For this reason, and because the circumstances in which different rules apply are fairly limited, the schemes in Canadian corporate statutes cannot be said to approximate distinct, comprehensive codes for small and large corporations.

If it is contemplated at the time of incorporation that a corporation will be a public corporation, there are certain implications for the incorporation and organization of the corporation:

- the articles will not contain a restriction on share transfer because the shares will be widely held and freely transferable;
- no shareholders' agreement involving all shareholders will be necessary, since there will be too many shareholders for such an agreement to be feasible; and
- the by-laws will have to contain more elaborate provisions regarding shareholder meetings, since there will be more shareholders.

In the vast majority of cases, however, at the time of incorporation and for some period thereafter, the corporation will not be issuing its shares to the public. After the corporation has carried on business successfully for a time and a public issue of its securities is feasible, the articles and by-laws can be changed and any shareholders' agreement terminated in anticipation of the issue.

---

74   Provincial statutes modelled on the *CBCA*, above note 1, have similar provisions except that in some of them the threshold for the application of the proxy-solicitation requirements is fifteen shareholders. E.g., *ABCA*, above note 1, s. 149(2)(a). The trust indenture provisions in Part VIII of the *CBCA* and statues based on it apply only if the debt obligations issued under the indenture were issued as part of a distribution to the public (*CBCA*, *ibid.*, s. 88(2); and *ABCA*, *ibid.*, s. 81(2)).

C. JURISDICTION OF INCORPORATION

1) Introduction

In section B, we discussed the process of incorporation under the *CBCA*. In this section, we discuss the factors that someone would consider in choosing whether to incorporate under the federal statute or one of the provincial statutes. It is, of course, possible that incorporation in a jurisdiction outside Canada may be preferable in particular circumstances. Foreign incorporation will be discussed here only with respect to the requirements for such corporations to carry on business in Canada.

2) Factors Affecting Choice of Jurisdiction

a) Disclosure Obligations

Each jurisdiction under which a corporation may incorporate imposes certain obligations to disclose information regarding the corporation and the people involved in it. Disclosure may be a concern for competitive, personal, or other reasons. In Canada, disclosure does not play a significant role in the selection of an incorporation jurisdiction because information filings are similar in all jurisdictions of incorporation and, in most cases, will not be considered onerous. The basic federal and Ontario disclosure requirements are set out in figure 4.2 below.

Figure 4.2   Examples of Disclosure Obligations Imposed by Jurisdiction of Incorporation in Addition to Disclosure Required in Articles

CBCA

Filing: Annual return, s. 263, Form 22

- Financial year end
- Main types of business
- Whether there has been a change in directors or the registered office
- Date of last annual meeting
- Whether the corporation is a distributing corporation
- Whether there are more than fifty shareholders
- Whether a unanimous shareholders' agreement[75] is in place
- Jurisdictions in which the corporation carries on business

---

75   Unanimous shareholders' agreements are discussed in Chapter 7.

OBCA

Filing: Initial return and annual return *Corporations Information Act* (ss. 2(1) & 3.1)

- Name and address for service of documents for the directors and the five most senior officers of the corporation
- Date of election or appointment of directors and officers and Canadian residency status of directors
- Name of anyone ceasing to be a director or officer and date of departure
- Any change in any of this information since the last return filed (Regulation made under the *Corporations Information Act* (R.R.O. 1990, Reg. 182, s. 1(a)).

A corporation must also make filings in every province where it begins to carry on business outside its jurisdiction of incorporation. For example, upon commencing business in Ontario, a corporation incorporated federally, in another province or territory, or in a foreign jurisdiction must file an initial return under the *Corporations Information Act* (s. 3(1)), which requires disclosure of information similar to that required for corporations incorporated in Ontario. In addition to the information listed in figure 4.2, all such extra-provincial corporations must disclose the following:

- name of the jurisdiction in which the corporation was incorporated, continued, or amalgamated, whichever is the most recent;
- address of the corporation's head or registered office;
- date on which the corporation commenced or ceased activities in Ontario;
- name and office address of the corporation's chief officer or manager in Ontario and the date the person assumed or ceased to hold this position;
- address of the corporation's principal office in Ontario;
- any immediate former names of the corporation; and
- the code under the province's activities classification code applicable to the corporation.[76]

In many provinces, extra-provincial corporations must file an annual return confirming the same information (e.g., Ontario *Corporations*

---

76   Regulation made under the *CIA*, above note 31, R.R.O. 1990, Reg. 182, s. 2.

Information Act, s. 3.1).[77] Whenever any information in an initial or annual filing changes, a new filing is required to indicate the change (e.g., Ontario *Corporations Information Act*, s. 4).

Failure to make required filings and filing untrue or misleading information are offences under the *CBCA* and under provincial law (*CBCA*, ss. 250 & 251, Ontario *Corporations Information Act*, ss. 13 & 14). Under some provincial statutes, the failure to file also deprives a corporation of the right to sue in the province in connection with the business being carried on by the corporation except with leave of the court (e.g., Ontario *Corporations Information Act*, s. 18).[78]

b) Where the Corporation Will Carry on Business

As discussed above,[79] *CBCA* incorporation gives a corporation the right to carry on business in all provinces, whereas provincial incorporation gives the right to carry on business only in the province of incorporation. Provincial incorporation means that a corporation may carry on business in another province if it obtains a licence under provincial extra-provincial licensing legislation in place in the province. As noted above, although the granting of an extra-provincial licence is discretionary, it is rarely refused unless there is a problem with the corporation's name. Under the Ontario *Extra-Provincial Corporations Act*[80] (*OEPCA*), corporations incorporated under the laws of other Canadian provinces are exempt from the requirement to obtain a licence. Certain other provinces have reciprocal arrangements under which a corporation incorporated under the laws of one need not obtain a licence to carry on business in the other.[81] All corporations incorporated in foreign jurisdictions must obtain a licence.

Where a corporation is required to obtain an extra-provincial licence, it must submit an application, a name-search report, a certifi-

---

77   Under the Ontario rules, this requirement applies only to a foreign extra-provincial corporation licensed to carry on business in Ontario (Regulation under the *CIA*, *ibid.*, s. 6(2)).

78   Under the *BCCA*, above note 1, an annual report must be filed containing much of the same information as is required in Ontario (s. 333, Form 16 of Second Schedule for companies incorporated in British Columbia, s. 335, Form 17 Second Schedule for companies incorporated outside the province). As discussed above in this chapter, if a corporation uses a business name in a province which is different from its corporate name, it must register the name under provincial legislation.

79   See Chapter 3.

80   R.S.O. 1990, c. E.27.

81   Under the *BCCA*, above note 1, all extra-provincial corporations must obtain a licence (s. 297).

cate setting out that the corporation is a valid and subsisting corporation under the laws of its governing jurisdiction, an appointment of an agent for service in the province in which it wants to do business, and the required fee.[82] An agent for service is a person in the province who is authorized to accept service of documents on behalf of the corporation in connection with any lawsuit in which the corporation is involved. This requirement is intended to ensure that persons dealing with the corporation in the province are able to commence civil proceedings to pursue any claim against the corporation.

The obligation to obtain an extra-provincial licence arises when a corporation begins to carry on business in a province. What constitutes "carrying on business" varies from province to province. In Ontario, a corporation carries on business if it has a place of business in Ontario, holds an interest in real property there, or otherwise engages in business in the province (*OEPCA*, s. 1(2)).[83] A corporation is deemed not to carry on business if it is only taking orders or buying or selling goods or services through travelling representatives, advertisements, or the mail (*OEPCA*, s. 1(3)). Some provinces have even broader definitions of carrying on business, which include, for example, soliciting business in the province (e.g., *ABCA*, s. 264).

Failure to obtain a licence when one is required to do so under a provincial extra-provincial licensing statute is an offence. Liability extends to "any person who contravenes this act" and includes the corporation and any person who carries on its business in the province as well as directors and officers who authorized, permitted, or acquiesced in the offence (e.g., *OEPCA*, s. 20). An unlicensed extra-provincial corporation cannot sue before any provincial tribunal in respect of any contract made by it (e.g., *OEPCA*, s. 21). In some provinces, like Ontario, an unlicensed extra-provincial corporation may not own land (*OEPCA*, s. 22).[84] Licences may also be cancelled by the provincial official responsible for administering the extra-provincial licensing regime (e.g., *OEPCA*, s. 7).

Because it is relatively easy to obtain a licence in most circumstances, where a corporation is going to carry on business does not dictate whether incorporation in a particular province or federal incorporation should be chosen. Where a business is intended to be

---

82   In Ontario the fee is $30. In British Columbia it is $300. See above, "Process of Incorporation and Organization."

83   This provision was interpreted in *Success International Inc.* v. *Environmental Export International of Canada Inc.* (1995), 23 O.R. (3d) 137 (Gen. Div.).

84   Under the *BCCA*, above note 1, similar penalties and disabilities apply (ss. 312–314).

carried on across the country or, at least, in several provinces, federal incorporation avoids provincial licensing requirements altogether and so may be desirable.

c) Liability for Provincial Tax

The tax liability of a corporation is not significantly affected by its jurisdiction of incorporation. Provincial income tax is based on income earned in the province regardless of its jurisdiction of incorporation. As a result, tax is not usually a significant consideration in choosing a jurisdiction in which to incorporate.

d) Provisions of Corporate Law

In Canada, there has never been competition among jurisdictions for incorporation business as there has been in the United States. Both the federal and some provincial governments have worked towards more uniform laws across the country. Indeed, uniformity is one of the express objectives of the *CBCA* (s. 4). As a result, the differences in the corporate law regimes federally and in the provinces and territories are not so significant as to permit major relative advantages and disadvantages to be easily identified. Since the *CBCA* was introduced in 1975, almost identical statutes have been introduced in Ontario, Alberta, Saskatchewan, and Manitoba. Corporate legislation in Newfoundland and New Brunswick is based on the *CBCA* model, though there are more variations from it than in the other jurisdictions. Quebec has its own scheme, but, in many respects, it is similar in effect to the *CBCA*. With the *2001 Amendments*, the *CBCA* is now different in several respects from the provincial legislation based on the Act as it existed prior to the amendments. The main changes are highlighted in figure 4.3. The British Columbia and Nova Scotia legislation still follow a registration model based on the English *Companies Act*, although both provinces have adapted the model in significant ways. Nova Scotia adopted a Part III to its corporate statute which gives *CBCA*-like remedies to shareholders. Prince Edward Island retains a letters patent statute. See Chapter 3 for a discussion of the differences between these three models of incorporation and their consequences.

To the extent that there are differences in substantive law, some may be overcome through private arrangements. For example, under section 126(2) of the *OBCA*, a majority of directors' meetings must be held in Canada, unless the articles or by-laws provide otherwise. There is no equivalent restriction in the *CBCA*. This difference may be mitigated, however, by simply including an exception in the by-laws or articles as permitted in the *OBCA*. Alternatively, the directors could

Figure 4.3   Highlights of *2001 Amendments* to *CBCA*

- Requirements for Canadian resident directors reduced from 50 percent to 25 percent for most corporations (see above in this chapter)
- Solvency and capital-impairment tests for giving financial assistance to directors removed (see Chapter 8)
- General "due diligence" defence created for certain statutory liabilities (see Chapter 8)
- Circumstances in which corporation may indemnify directors and officers for liabilities incurred or obtain insurance against such liabilities broadened (see Chapter 7)
- Provisions permitting electronic communication with shareholders, electronic voting, and electronic participation in meetings introduced (see Chapter 7)
- Circumstances in which shareholders may make a proposal to put matters on the agenda for shareholders' meetings substantially revised (see Chapter 7)
- Rules restricting the manner in which shareholders may communicate with each other relaxed (see Chapter 7)
- Rules regarding unanimous shareholders' agreements clarified and strengthened (see Chapter 7)[85]

take decisions by all of them signing a written resolution rather than having a meeting at all (*OBCA*, s. 129(1)).[86]

As a consequence of the similarity in corporate law regimes, the practice of most lawyers is often to incorporate under provincial law in the province where business is to be carried on and to incorporate federally if it is contemplated that business will be conducted in more than one province. Differences in fees charged by the different jurisdictions will also have a significant effect, given the lack of other bases of differentiation. Currently, at $250, the *CBCA* is relatively inexpensive. Corporate law in foreign jurisdictions may be significantly different, and there may be substantial benefits to certain stakeholders to incorporation under the laws of particular jurisdictions.

e)   Recognition
If a business is to be carried on outside Canada, it may be preferable to incorporate under the *CBCA*. Foreign persons doing business with

---

85   For an overview of the *2001 Amendments* see W.D. Gray & C.W. Halladay, *Guide to CBCA Reform: Analysis and Precedents* (Toronto: Thomson, 2002).

86   This process of acting by signed resolution is discussed in Chapter 7.

the corporation may be unfamiliar with the provincial or territorial jurisdictions.

3) Continuance

After a decision is made regarding the jurisdiction for incorporation, it is possible under the corporate laws of most jurisdictions to migrate from one to another (e.g., *CBCA*, ss. 187–88; *OBCA*, ss. 180–81; *BCCA*, ss. 36–38; *ABCA*, ss. 181–82). In Canada this migration is called continuance. The procedure for continuance is discussed in Chapter 10.

D. PRE-INCORPORATION CONTRACTS

1) Introduction

A final difficult area related to incorporation is the effect of contracts entered into on behalf of a corporation before the date of its incorporation. Sometimes a person, typically referred to as an agent or promoter, will purport to enter into a contract with a third party on behalf of a corporation that has not yet come into existence. Such a pre-incorporation contract may occur, for example, when there has not been time to set up the corporation. In these circumstances, several difficult issues arise:

- Is the agent liable to perform the contract personally?
- Is the corporation liable if it adopts the contract after it comes into existence?
- If the corporation becomes liable, does the agent cease to be liable?

2) Common Law

Under the common law, it was clear that the corporation was not liable for contracts purported to be entered into on its behalf before it came into existence and could not be made so by any unilateral act of adoption or acceptance afterwards. For the corporation to be liable, there had to be a new contract between the corporation and the third party.[87] Such a contract would require a post-incorporation exchange of promises between the corporation and the third party.

The circumstances in which the agent would be personally liable were much less clear. Liability of the agent depended on the intention

---

87   *Kelner v. Baxter* (1866), L.R. 2 C.P. 174.

of the parties as determined by the courts based on all the circumstances. Although it was possible for the parties to state clearly whether the agent was to be liable, they seldom did so. In many cases the intention of the parties was divined from very refined interpretations of the language the parties used in the contract. For example, some cases held that the agent was not liable if the contract was expressed as made "by" the corporation, but he was liable if the contract was made "for" the corporation. Nevertheless, some general statements may be made regarding the situation at common law.

If the parties both knew that the corporation was not in existence, a presumption arose that the parties intended that the agent would be personally liable. This was the conclusion reached in *Kelner* v. *Baxter*.[88] In that case, the conclusion was confirmed by a provision in the contract requiring immediate delivery. The court reasoned that the parties must have intended that someone was to be liable for payment for the goods delivered. It was not reasonable to think that the supplier had agreed that its entitlement to payment was to be contingent on the incorporation of a corporation.

If the parties both thought that the corporation was in existence, no such presumption arose and the parties' intention had to be determined from all the circumstances. In *Black* v. *Smallwood*,[89] Black entered into a contract with Smallwood who purported to act on behalf of Western Suburbs Holdings Pty. Ltd. Both believed that the corporation was incorporated. Smallwood signed the contract as director of the corporation. In fact, the corporation had not been incorporated. When Black sued Smallwood alleging that Smallwood was personally liable, the court held that he was not. Since the parties both believed that the corporation was in existence, the court determined that they had not intended Smallwood to be personally liable.

Where the agent knew that no corporation was in existence but the third party believed that she was dealing with an existing corporation through the agent, one might think that no contract could arise because there would be no consensus between the parties. Some courts have reached this conclusion.[90] Nevertheless, often the courts have held the agent liable in contract in these circumstances. Even if the contract cannot be enforced against the agent, the third party may be able to claim damages against the agent where she can show a misrep-

---

88 *Ibid.*
89 [1966] A.L.R. 744 (Austl. H.C.).
90 For example, *Wickberg* v. *Shatsky* (1969), 4 D.L.R. (3d) 540 (B.C.S.C.) [*Wickberg*].

resentation by the agent that she was acting for a corporation which induced her to enter the contract to her detriment.[91]

3) Statutory Reform

The common law rules were unsatisfactory for several reasons. In many cases, third parties were denied relief based on highly artificial conclusions regarding the parties' intention. More important, the inability of the corporation to adopt contracts made for its benefit was often manifestly inconsistent with what the parties, in fact, intended. As a result, statutory reform has been attempted in most jurisdictions.

Section 14 of the *CBCA* and similar provisions in *CBCA* model statutes[92] attempt to reform the law to make the individual agent liable in most circumstances and to permit the corporation to adopt contracts made on its behalf before it came into existence. The elements of the scheme are as follows:

- A person who purports to enter into a contract with a third party by or on behalf of a corporation before it comes into existence is personally bound to perform the contract and is entitled to its benefits.
- If a corporation comes into existence and adopts the contract, the corporation is bound by and is entitled to the benefits of the contract and the agent is no longer bound by or entitled to the benefits of the contract.
- The third party may apply to a court for an order fixing both the corporation and the agent with liability (joint, joint and several, or apportioned) regardless of whether the corporation has adopted the contract or not.
- The third party and the agent may agree in the contract that the agent is not bound by the contract in any event.

---

91   Damages for a misrepresentation by an agent were ordered against the principal in *Betker v. Williams*, [1992] 2 W.W.R. 534 (B.C.C.A.). This case did not involve a pre-incorporation contract. One other possible claim the third party could make in these circumstances would be breach of warranty of authority (see *A.E. Lepage Ltd. v. Kamex Developments Ltd.*, [1979] 2 S.C.R. 155, discussed in Chapter 2; *Wickberg*, ibid., and *General Motors Acceptance Corp. v. Weisman* (1979), 23 O.R. (2d) 479 (Co. Ct.)). A practical problem that often arises with such a claim is that the damages suffered by the plaintiff are not the result of the breach of warranty, because the corporation either never came into existence, as in *Wickberg*, or is insolvent.

92   E.g., *OBCA*, above note 1, s. 21; and *ABCA*, above note 1, s. 15. There is no corresponding provision in the *BCCA*, above note 1.

The statutory reforms have tried to eliminate the problems of the common law. Now agents bear the risk of all liability prior to adoption of a contract, unless the agent's liability is expressly excluded by the agent and the third party, in which case the risk of non-adoption is transferred to the third party. This arrangement reflects the view that the agent is usually in a position to ensure that the corporation is incorporated and adopts the contract, and so can manage the risk of non-adoption more effectively than the third party. There are, however, several problems with the statutory scheme.

First, the *CBCA* and the corporate laws of Alberta, Manitoba, and Saskatchewan apply only to written contracts, so the old common law rules still apply to oral contracts made by or on behalf of a corporation. By contrast, the *OBCA*, *NBBCA*, and *QCA* do not distinguish between oral and written contracts, while the corporate laws of British Columbia, Nova Scotia, and Prince Edward Island do not address pre-incorporation contracts at all. These differences may lead to anomalous results, depending on the jurisdiction in which the agent chooses to incorporate. For example, if an agent enters into an oral pre-incorporation contract and then incorporates an Ontario corporation for the purpose of fulfilling the contract, the corporation can adopt the oral contract made by him and he is relieved from liability. If he incorporates a federal corporation, it cannot adopt the contract and his liability is determined at common law.

Second, if a corporation is never incorporated, it is unclear what rules should apply to determine the respective liability of the agent and the corporation. It may be argued that the provisions of a corporate statute come into play only when there has been an incorporation under that statute, since they refer to contracts made "before [the corporation] comes into existence" and, moreover, the scope of corporate law in each jurisdiction is limited to corporations incorporated in the jurisdiction (see Chapter 3). Jacob Ziegel has suggested that any provincial court in which this question arises should decide what law applies based on the conflicts of laws rules of that province. Others, like Maureen Maloney, have suggested that the applicable law should be determined by the intention of the agent who was going to incorporate.[93] As yet the courts have not resolved this problem.

---

93   J.S. Ziegel, "Promoter's Liability and Preincorporation Contracts: *Westcom Radio Group Ltd.* v. *MacIsaac*" (1990) 16 Can. Bus. L.J. 341, at 346–47; M.A. Maloney, "Pre-Incorporation Transactions: A Statutory Solution?" (1985) 10 Can. Bus. L.J. 409, at 432–35.

Third, the language used in some of the corporate statutes is problematic. Section 21(1) of the *OBCA*, for example, says that the agent is liable if she "enters into an oral or written contract in the name of or on behalf of a corporation before it comes into existence... ." A close reading of this provision suggests that it is necessary to determine that a *contract* exists in order for the section to have any application. But if it is necessary to find an effective contract, then the provision simply restates the common law rule that an agent is liable only if the parties intended the agent to be bound under the contract. Similarly, section 21(2) permitting the corporation to adopt a contract made for its benefit applies only if there is a contract, suggesting that adoption is permitted only where the agent is bound personally at common law. Such an interpretation has been suggested by some commentators and was adopted in Ontario in *Westcom Radio Group Ltd.* v. *MacIsaac*,[94] but it seems clearly contrary to the overall intention of the provision and has been strongly criticized.[95] *Westcom* was effectively overruled in *Szecket* v. *Huang*.[96] The Ontario Court of Appeal held that the intention of section 21 was to replace the common law and that it was not appropriate first to ask if there was a contract at common law before applying the statutory scheme.

Finally, the courts have been reluctant to grant relief under the provision permitting a court to hold the agent wholly or partly liable after the contract has been adopted by a corporation. The provision was intended to provide a remedy in circumstances where the agent had arranged to have the contract adopted by a corporation with insufficient assets to satisfy the obligations under the contract. In *Bank of Nova Scotia* v. *Williams*,[97] the court refused to exercise its discretion, because the third party entering the contract was not misled as to whom it was really contracting with and who would be responsible for performing the obligations under the contract.

An interesting application of the pre-incorporation contract rules of special interest to lawyers occurred in *Sherwood Design Services Inc.* v. *872935 Ontario Ltd.*[98] A law firm's client signed an agreement to purchase

---

94 (1989), 70 O.R. (2d) 591 (Div. Ct.). The *Westcom Radio* decision was applied in *Vacation Brokers Inc.* v. *Joseph*, [1993] O.J. No. 3036 (QL) (Co. Ct.).

95 For example, Ziegel, above note 93. The problems with preincorporation contracts are discussed in Industry Canada, *Proposals for Technical Amendments* (*Canada Business Corporations Act* Discussion Paper) (Ottawa: Industry Canada, 1995) at 14–15.

96 (1998), 168 D.L.R. (4th) 402 (Ont. C.A.), applied in *1394918 Ontario Ltd.* v. *1310210 Ontario Inc.* (2002), 57 O.R. (3d) 607 (C.A.).

97 (1976), 12 O.R. (2d) 709 (H.C.J.).

98 (1998), 158 D.L.R. (4th) 440 (C.A.).

some real property "on behalf of a corporation to be incorporated." The client then instructed the law firm to prepare the necessary documents to complete the transaction. A lawyer in the firm decided to use as the buyer a corporation that had already been incorporated by a partner in the law firm (the shelf corporation). He drafted a transfer of the one issued share from the partner to the client, a shareholder's resolution appointing the client as the sole director, a director's resolution authorizing the transaction, a legal opinion that the contract was enforceable against the shelf corporation, and some other documents in the name of the shelf corporation. He then sent the package of draft documents to the vendor's lawyer for comments, together with a cover letter indicating that the shelf corporation would complete the purchase. When the date came to close the transaction, the client decided that the price was too high. He therefore refused to take a transfer of the share, sign the resolutions, or pay the vendor. Subsequently, the law firm transferred the partner's share in the shelf corporation to another client, who began to carry on a profitable business through the shelf corporation. Eventually, the unpaid vendor sued the shelf corporation. The vendor alleged that the agreement to buy the property was a pre-incorporation contract that had been adopted by the corporation based on the sending of the draft documents by the purchaser's lawyers to the vendor's lawyers.

The issue in the case was whether the letter by the purchaser's lawyer to the vendor's lawyer indicating that the shelf corporation would complete the transaction and containing drafts of the documents necessary to complete the purchase should be viewed as an adoption of the contract by the shelf corporation. The Ontario Court of Appeal held that the communication was sufficient evidence of the corporation's intention to be bound. The court found that it would be within the usual authority of the lawyer acting for a purchaser to advise the lawyer on the other side of the transaction as to the identity of the corporation that would close the transaction. The court also noted that, as a policy matter, it is important for people to be able to rely on a lawyer's communications.

In a strong dissenting judgment, Mr. Justice Borins determined that the corporation could not have adopted the contract since the draft documents indicated that the control of the corporation had not been transferred to the purchaser. If the corporation was not yet under the purchaser's control, the purchaser could not cause it to adopt the contract. The lawyer's communication, at most, would be a notice of an intention to transfer control and then to have the corporation adopt the contract at a future date. Since the adoption never, in fact, occurred, the corporation should not be liable.

E. CHAPTER SUMMARY

In this chapter, we discussed the process of incorporation in some detail. We reviewed the documents required to be filed, identifying the information that must be included and briefly analysing the legal and practical issues to be addressed in completing these documents. We concentrated on the articles and the decisions that must be made by incorporators about the corporate name, the classes and number of shares to be created, the number of directors, the registered office, restrictions on issuing, transferring, and owning shares, and restrictions on the business that the corporation may carry on. The corporate name is often one of the most difficult and frustrating decisions faced by incorporators for practical and legal reasons. It is difficult to find a distinctive name that is not already in use, and names are governed by a tangle of provincial and federal legislation.

We also discussed the steps that must be taken after incorporation to flesh out the characteristics of the corporation through by-laws and directors' and shareholders' resolutions. In incorporating and organizing a corporation, one must bear in mind that there are some differences in the rules which apply and the provisions which need to be included in the articles of incorporation, depending on whether the corporation distributes its shares to the public or not.

One important choice faced by incorporators is what jurisdiction they should choose for incorporation. In this regard we noted that there are few differences between the Canadian jurisdictions in the terms of requirements for public disclosure, liability for provincial tax, or the provisions of corporate law. In any event, whatever jurisdiction is chosen, it is possible subsequently to change to another jurisdiction through the continuance process.

Finally, we discussed the special situation that arises when an agent purports to enter into a contract on behalf of a corporation to be incorporated. In most Canadian jurisdictions, such contracts are now enforceable against the agent unless a corporation is incorporated and adopts the contract, in which case the corporation alone is liable, or the agent and the other party to the contract agree to exclude the agent's liability. The provisions regulating pre-incorporation contracts have some defects that have undermined their effectiveness in some circumstances.

FURTHER READINGS

BLACK, B., & R. KRAAKMAN, "A Self-enforcing Model of Corporate Law" (1996) 109 Harv. L. Rev. 1911

CANADIAN CORPORATE LAW REPORTER (Toronto: CCH Canadian, looseleaf)

DANIELS, R.J., & J.G. MACINTOSH, "Toward a Distinctive Canadian Corporate Law Regime" (1991) 29 Osgoode Hall L.J. 863

EASSON, A.J., & D.A. SOBERMAN, "Pre-Incorporation Contracts: Common Law Confusion and Statutory Complexity" (1992) 17 Queen's L.J. 414

ESTEY, W.M., "Pre-incorporation Contracts: The Fog is Finally Lifting," (2000) 33 Can. Bus. L. J. 3

GRAY, W.D. & C.W. HALLADAY, *Guide to CBCA Reform: Analysis and Precedents* (Toronto: Thomson, 2002)

KINGSTON, R.A., & W. GROVER, *Canada Corporations Manual* (Toronto: Carswell, 1996) (looseleaf)

KOKONIS, J.D., "The Scheme of the Canadian Trade-marks Act" in G.F. Henderson, ed., *Trade-Marks Law of Canada* (Toronto: Carswell, 1993) 75

LAW SOCIETY OF UPPER CANADA, *Bar Admission Course Reference Materials: Business Law* (Toronto: Law Society of Upper Canada, 2003) c. 5

MYHAL, P.J., "Compliance with business names registration and informational filing requirements" (1991) 8 Bus. & L. 48

PERELL, P.M., "Pre-incorporation Contracts and *1394918 Ontario Ltd. v. 13102010 Ontario Inc.*: Some Answers, Some Questions," (2002) 37 Can. Bus. L.J. 291

PURI, P., "The Promise of certainty in the law of pre-incorporation contracts (Case comment)" (2001) 80 Can. Bar Rev. 1051

VAVER, D., *Intellectual Property Law: Copyright, Patents and Trademarks* (Concord: Irwin Law, 1997), chapter 4.

WADLOW, C., *The Law of Passing-Off* (London: Sweet & Maxwell, 1990)

CHAPTER 5

THE CORPORATION IN ACTION

A. INTRODUCTION

As discussed in Chapter 3, it is often helpful to think of corporations as having legal characteristics similar to those of natural persons. The comparison may only be taken so far, of course, and in this chapter we look at one of the most important differences between corporate and natural persons: the necessity for corporate persons to act through human agents. In particular, we will look at how corporations acting through agents can be said to enter into contracts and to commit crimes and torts. The rules governing corporate liability are fundamentally important to all the stakeholders in the corporation because they determine the legal consequences of the corporation's behaviour in the marketplace and, as a result, influence that behaviour. For example, the rules that determine when a corporation is bound by contracts will affect how a corporation sets up its contract-approval process. The corporation will want to ensure that only those employees whom it has given authority to enter into contracts are in a position to bind the corporation.

The theories of liability developed by the courts over the years have varied depending on whether the liability sought to be imposed was, on the one hand, contractual or, on the other, criminal or tortious. In imposing contractual liability, the courts have focused on whether the individual whose actions are alleged to have given rise to corporate liability was an *agent* of the corporation with authority to incur liability on behalf of the corporation. By contrast, to impose liability on a corporation for a crime or a tort, the courts have asked whether the person could be considered to be the same as the corporation for the purpose of the activity alleged to constitute the crime or the tort. The significance of these distinctions will be explained in the following sections.

B. LIABILITY OF CORPORATIONS FOR CRIMES

1) Introduction

Because corporations have "no soul to be damned; no body to be kicked"[1] but fundamentally comprise a locus of claims by the various stakeholders, as discussed in Chapter 1, the reasons for and consequences of imposing criminal liability on corporations are somewhat different from those associated with imposing such liability on natural persons. It seems unlikely, for example, that conviction for a criminal offence would have the same deterrent effect on a soulless corporation as it would have on an individual. Certainly the managers of a corporation will be discouraged from causing the corporation to commit crimes to some extent by the prospect that the corporation for which they are responsible will be found criminally liable. The deterrent effect associated with the prospective damage to the corporation's reputation caused by a criminal conviction, however, will not be as great as the deterrence resulting from the threat of personal responsibility. This problem is mitigated to a significant extent by provisions in the criminal law and many regulatory statutes which impose liability on the individuals through whom corporations commit crimes.

The remedies used to sanction criminal behaviour are problematic as well when a corporation is the offender. Imprisonment of the corporation itself is not possible and, if a fine is imposed on a corporation, its shareholders, employees, and others with financial claims against the corporation will suffer.[2] At the same time, despite the conceptual

---

1   Lord Thurlow, quoted by Glanville Williams, in *Criminal Law: The General Part*, 2d ed. (London: Stevens, 1961), at 856.

2   An alternative sentence was imposed in *R. v. NorthWest Territories Power Corporation*, [1990] N.W.T.R. 115 (Terr. Ct.). The court ordered the directors and the chief executive officer of a corporation convicted of a criminal offence to publish a public apology.

challenges associated with corporate criminality, the prospect of this most pervasive form of business organization, which wields such enormous economic power, being immune to criminal sanction is impossible to imagine.

For a time, the courts held that corporations were immune from criminal liability. More recently, however, the courts have developed rules on the basis of which corporations may be convicted of criminal offences.

2) Absolute Liability Offences

The simplest types of offences to deal with are absolute liability offences. These offences require only that the accused engaged in certain proscribed behaviour. No state of mind or *mens rea* needs to be shown, and no defence is available once the behaviour has been proven. Corporate liability for such an offence arises when a person who engages in the behaviour does so on behalf of the corporation. All acts of employees in the course of their employment will give rise to corporate liability for such offences.

Absolute liability offences punishable by imprisonment have been held to be unconstitutional as violating section 7 of the *Charter* — the right to life, liberty, and security of the person — with respect to individual accused.[3] No case has held that such offences infringe the rights of a corporate accused. Indeed, since a corporation may not be imprisoned, it is probable that a corporation does not have a section 7 right in the circumstances. As noted in Chapter 3, however, a corporation charged with an offence may challenge the constitutionality of the offence if it would violate section 7 rights of an individual accused.[4] If such a challenge were successful, the corporation could not be held liable for committing the offence.

3) Strict Liability Offences

As in the previous category of offence, liability for a strict liability offence arises on the commission of some proscribed act. And, as with absolute liability offences too, it is sufficient to impose liability on a corporation if a person was acting on behalf of a corporation in committing the act.

Strict liability is subject to a defence that the accused acted reasonably in the circumstances, often referred to as a "due diligence defence."

3   R. v. *Nguyen* (*sub nom.* R. v. *Hess*), [1990] 2 S.C.R. 906.
4   R. v. *Wholesale Travel Group Inc.*, [1991] 3 S.C.R. 154, at 180–81.

In effect, the fault required to be shown is negligence. The burden is on the accused to show on the balance of probabilities that it was not negligent, once it is proven that the act was committed.

Recently, the British Columbia Court of Appeal considered what was required to establish due diligence in a case involving a fuel spill caused by pipe corrosion which contravened provincial environmental law.[5] The court held that the corporate accused could avoid liability either where the cause of the events constituting the offence, in this case, the corrosion, was not reasonably foreseeable or, if the accused knew or ought to have known of the hazard, the accused took all reasonable steps to avoid commiting the offence. The court found that the corporate accused in this case had been duly diligent in that it was not aware of the corrosion and could not have foreseen it.

In a case with similar facts, the Ontario Court of Appeal clarified that the accused need not prove the cause of the spill to take advantage of the defence. If the exact cause of the spill is unknown, however, the accused must show that it took all reasonable care to avoid any foreseeable cause.[6]

For a corporation to rely on this defence, the person who must exercise due diligence on behalf of the corporation is someone who can be considered to be the directing mind and will of the corporation such that she may be considered to be the corporation itself.[7] This will be the person or persons who have responsibility to manage the business of the corporation in the area in which the offence occurred. As we will see, this concept, the "directing mind and will" of the corporation, is also used to determine whether the corporation is liable for a *mens rea* offence, and it will be discussed in more detail in the next section.

4) Offences Requiring *Mens Rea*

Most criminal offences require that the accused have a degree of knowledge or intention, referred to as *mens rea*, before there can be a conviction. Early common law cases held that a corporation could not be convicted of an offence requiring *mens rea*. Now liability may be found on the basis of the "identification theory." Under this theory, criminal liability may attach if the person having the necessary mental state and committing the crime has the identity of the corporation; in other words, she is the corporation for the purposes of the behaviour

---

5   R. v. *MacMillan Bloedel*, [2002] B.C.J. No. 2083 (QL) (C.A.).
6   R. v. *Petro-Canada*, [2003] O.J. No. 216 (QL) (C.A.).
7   R. v. *Sault Ste. Marie (City)*, [1978] 2 S.C.R. 1299 [*Sault Ste. Marie*].

constituting the offence. Typically, the natural person will be criminally responsible herself as well.[8] While simple to state, this theory is fraught with various complexities in practice.

The general test for whether the identity of the corporation and that of the individual coincide is as follows: Is the human actor who committed the crime a vital organ or a directing mind and will of the corporation? Any person who has governing executive control over an area of the corporation's business or affairs is considered to be the corporation in relation to that area. One consequence of this conception of the directing mind is that, in a given corporation, there may be many directing minds. There is no need for the directing mind to have general decision-making power for all aspects of the corporation's business. Not just the president or the board of directors may be the directing mind; each person responsible for a discrete aspect of the corporation's business, whether defined functionally, geographically, or otherwise, may incur criminal liability for the corporation. So, for example, in *R. v. Waterloo Mercury Sales Ltd.*,[9] liability was imposed on a corporation operating a car dealership as a result of the used car sales manager fraudulently causing odometers on used cars to be turned back. The used car sales manager was found to be the directing mind of the corporation for the purposes of the criminal activity. In essence, the test is whether an employee has been delegated, expressly or by implication, the authority to design and supervise the implementation of corporate policy, as opposed to only the authority to carry out such policy.[10]

In *R. v. Safety-Kleen Canada Inc.*,[11] the Ontario Court of Appeal held that a truck driver employed by a waste disposal business was not the directing mind and will of the corporation and so the corporation was not liable for the driver's actions in transporting hazardous waste without the necessary authorization. The driver was the corporation's only representative in a large geographical area and was responsible for collecting waste, billing, completing documentation, maintenance, and responding to calls from customers and regulators. The Court of Appeal found that, notwithstanding these responsibilities, he did not have any managerial or supervisory function and did not have any influence over the corporation's policies.

---

8   Because the natural person is the corporation for the purposes of committing the offence, it is not possible for him, at the same time, to conspire with the corporation to commit the offence.

9   (1974), 49 D.L.R. (3d) 131 (Alta. Dist. Ct.).

10   *"Rhone" (The) v. "Peter A.B. Widner" (The)*, [1993] 1 S.C.R. 497.

11   (1997), 32 O.R. (3d) 493 (C.A.).

Actions by employees giving rise to corporate liability are not limited to those taken in the course of their employment — that is, in accordance with the terms of their contracts of employment. The corporation is responsible for any act by a directing mind in the general area of her responsibility, even if not specifically authorized by a corporate rule or policy. Indeed, even if there is a corporate rule or policy prohibiting the action, that is no defence to corporate liability. In *Waterloo Mercury Sales*, the car dealership had a policy against turning back odometers, but the court held that this did not absolve the dealership from responsibility. Similarly, although a person must have actual power to make decisions in the relevant area for her mind to constitute the corporate mind, it is not necessary to find that the responsibility over the area was created in accordance with the express provisions of the corporate constitution or was formally authorized in any other way. The courts have imposed liability on corporations where, by virtue of the practice of the corporation, the person with the guilty mind exercised corporate authority in the area in which the offence was committed.

The result of holding corporations liable for acts by people in the area of their responsibility is that the corporation bears the risk associated with unauthorized activity; no simple statement of policy that crimes should not be committed will save the corporation. Indeed, it is not clear whether there is anything a corporation may do to avoid liability. In the United Kingdom it has been held that a corporation will be able to avoid liability for an offence involving the actions of a manager if it has in place an adequate system for selecting managers, takes sufficient care to train managers, and has a system for supervising and controlling them.[12] Although the *Tesco* case has been cited in a number of Canadian cases, it has been interpreted as holding that, as a result of such a system of supervision and control, a manager could not be considered to be a directing mind and will of the corporation.[13] Canadian courts have criticized *Tesco* on the basis that it set too high a standard for finding that a person is the directing mind and will of the corporation.[14]

---

12 *Tesco Supermarkets Ltd. v. Nattrass*, [1972] A.C. 153 (H.L.).

13 *Sault Ste. Marie*, above note 7.

14 *R. v. Canadian Dredge & Dock Co.*, [1985] 1 S.C.R. 622. In more recent English decisions, the House of Lords has broadened the circumstances in which a corporation may be held directly responsible for offences. For example, in *Meridian Global Funds Management Asia Ltd. v. Securities Commission*, [1995] 2 All E.R. 918 (J.C.P.C.) (N.Z.), it held that it was not necessary to meet the directing mind and will test in all cases. It determined that what degree of responsiblity required to be possessed by the guilty employee to impose liability on the corporation depends on the circumstances.

One difficult question in connection with corporate criminality is whether there can be corporate liability where the person alleged to be the directing mind of the corporation was acting in his own interests and against the corporation's. This issue was considered in the leading case on corporate criminal liability, *R. v. Canadian Dredge and Dock Ltd.*[15] In that case, several corporations were charged with fraud. They agreed in advance on who would submit the lowest bid to do dredging work at an inflated price. The lowest bidder would make payoffs to the others and subcontract some of the work to them. This fraud was negotiated by senior officers of each of the corporations. Sometimes an officer would keep for himself a portion of the payoff that was supposed to go to his corporation. The corporations argued that the identification theory could not operate when the alleged directing mind is perpetrating a fraud on the corporation in this way.

The court accepted that, where a person ceases completely to act in the interests of the corporation and acts "totally in fraud of the corporate employer," appropriating to herself all the benefits that should have gone to the corporation, the identification theory should not operate. On the facts of this case, however, the requirements of this very narrow exclusion were not met. The directing minds were not engaged in a scheme to deprive their corporations of all benefits associated with the dredging contracts and so the corporations were liable.

C. LIABILITY OF CORPORATIONS IN TORT

1) Introduction

A corporation may be liable in tort both vicariously and directly, in the sense that the corporation itself is found to be committing the tort. Each is discussed in turn below.

---

15   *Ibid.* On June 12, 2003, the federal government introduced two bills to enhance the criminal law rules relating to corporate activities. One of them, Bill C-45 (*An Act to amend the Criminal Code (criminal liability of organizations)*), broadens the category of persons whose behaviour may result in criminal liability for the corporation. The Bill provides that a corporation may be deemed to be a "party" to a criminal offence committed by one of its representatives if a senior officer was knowingly involved in the offence or was aware of the offence and knowingly failed to take all reasonable measures to stop the representative's participation in the offence. Unlike the common law standard, the senior officer need not be a "directing mind" of the organization.

2) Vicarious Liability

The corporation may be vicariously liable where a tort has been committed by someone acting on behalf of the corporation. In such a case, the person is personally liable for the tort, but the corporation may be vicariously liable as well where two criteria are met.

- There is a relationship of master and servant between the person and the corporation. In other words, the person must have the legal status of an employee, not an independent contractor.[16]
- The person committing the tort was acting in the course of her employment, and not on a frolic of her own.[17]

Vicarious liability of corporations is broad and relatively easy to establish once an employee has been identified as the person committing the tort. The key question is whether the employee was acting within the course of her employment. Vicarious liability will catch most situations where direct liability could have been found because a person who is a "directing mind" will usually also be an employee. Perhaps because of the broad reach of vicarious liability in most cases of alleged corporate liability, the law discussed in the next section on the circumstances in which direct corporate liability for torts arises is not very clear or well developed.[18]

In this context, it is necessary to remember that a director or an officer of a corporation is not an employee simply by being a director or an officer. In many cases, especially in smaller corporations, the directors and officers will also be in employment relationships with the corporation, but these are distinct legal relationships.

---

16 In *671122 Ontario Ltd.* v. *Sagaz Industries Canada Inc.* (2001), 17 B.L.R. (3d) 1 (S.C.C.), the Supreme Court held that a corporation was not vicariously liable where the person who had committed the tort was not an employee, though the Supreme Court acknowledged that there could be other relationships that give rise to vicarious liability.

17 A principal may be liable for torts committed by an agent who is not an employee in limited circumstances. This is a form of direct liability, however. In general, a corporation will be liable for an agent's fraud or negligent misrepresentation where the agent is acting within its actual or apparent authority. These concepts of authority are discussed in the next section in this chapter. In *Betker* v. *Williams*, [1992] 2 W.W.R. 534 (B.C.C.A.), a purchaser of a house relied on a negligent misrepresentation by the vendor's agent regarding the property. The vendor knew nothing about the misrepresentation but was held liable for the difference between what the purchaser had paid and what he would have paid if he had known the true situation.

18 B. Welling, *Corporate Law in Canada: The Governing Principles*, 2d ed. (Toronto: Butterworths, 1991), at 152–73.

3) Direct Liability

The corporation may be directly liable for a tort if the person committing the tort is not merely an employee but can be considered the directing mind and will of the corporation in such a way that the acts done are the acts of the corporation itself. Direct liability has been imposed on essentially the same basis as described above for the imposition of criminal liability.

For example, direct liability was imposed on a corporation where the boilers of a ship owned by the corporation proved defective and the cargo was lost. The English House of Lords held that the person who was negligent in not knowing about the defective boilers was the responsible manager of the ship. Since this person was the directing mind and will of the corporation for the purposes of taking care of the ship, the corporation was held liable to the owner of the cargo for its loss.[19]

Direct liability for an intentional tort was found in *Nelitz v. Dyck*.[20] An insurer made an appointment for an insured person to visit a chiropractor in connection with the resolution of the person's claim against the insurer. The insurer directed the person to submit to an examination from the chiropractor, but neither the insurer nor the chiropractor sought or obtained her consent to the treatment or advised her that she had a right to refuse the treatment. She sued the chiropractor and the insurance company for battery. The Ontario Court of Appeal held that the insurance company was not vicariously liable for the actions of the chiropractor because he was an independent contractor. The court did find, however, that the insurer could be held directly liable on the basis that it had retained the chiropractor to commit the tort. In the end, the insurer avoided liability because the court found that the insured person had consented to the examination.

D. LIABILITY OF CORPORATIONS IN CONTRACT

1) Introduction

A corporation can act only through natural persons to conclude contracts and otherwise enter into transactions. This section explains when a corporation is liable to perform contracts as a result of commit-

---

19   *Lennard's Carrying Co. Ltd. v. Asiatic Petroleum Co. Ltd.*, [1915] A.C. 705 (H.L.).
20   (2001), 52 O.R. (3d) 458 (C.A.).

ments made by persons purporting to act on its behalf. As previously discussed, a person acting on behalf of someone else is referred to as an agent, and the law dealing with the ability of such a person to bind the corporation in contract is a branch of the law of agency. With respect to corporations, the law of agency is particularly hard to apply because of the size and complexity of many corporate organizations. There may be many people within a given corporation whom one could consider to be an agent in connection with particular types of corporate obligations. Agents will include officers and directors. Depending on the circumstances, however, sales people, purchasing clerks, and others may all be considered agents of the corporation for particular purposes. Moreover, the way agents get their authority to act on behalf of the corporate principal is not always easy to pinpoint. In many corporate organizations, the sources and lines of authority are not clearly drawn.

The law of agency must seek to balance the interests of the principal, for our purposes the corporation, with the interests of third parties seeking to enter into binding contracts with the corporation. The principal will not want to be bound by any actions of an agent purporting to act on its behalf which it has not authorized. On the other hand, a third party will want to be able to rely on an agent having the authority to bind the principal with whom it seeks to contract without spending more than a minimal amount of time and money investigating whether the principal has conferred such authority on the agent. Investigating to determine with certainty that authority exists is a transaction cost, and business transactions will be promoted if such transaction costs can be minimized. If, in a particular area of business, the third party reasonably has relied on commonly accepted indicators of authority, such as a letter of introduction from the president on the corporation's letterhead indicating a person's title, in entering into a contract with the corporation, transactions will be encouraged if the law respects that reliance and enforces the contract. As well, any rule about the authority of agents must take into account that it may be impossible for the third party to determine if actual authority has been given to an agent because authority may be conferred in a document to which the third party has no access, such as the agent's contract with the principal.

In large transactions, the parties will do a significant amount of investigation to satisfy themselves that the person executing the agreements making up the transaction has authority to do so. These investigations will be supplemented by documentation, such as certificates identifying the officers of a corporation, certified copies of board resolutions authorizing certain people to enter into the transaction on behalf of the corporation, and legal opinions regarding authority. The vast majority of transactions between third parties and corporations, however, are entered into without the third party enquiring, to any significant extent, into the authority that the person it is dealing with has to bind the corporation. The size of most transactions simply does not justify incurring the costs associated with attaining the degree of legal certainty typical of large transactions. Fortunately, most transactions proceed without issues of authority arising. The issue of authority comes up most often in circumstances in which the corporation has refused to perform its obligation to a third party on the basis that the agent had no authority to bind the corporation and the third party sues the corporation. It is in these situations that the rules described in the remainder of this chapter are most relevant. The sections below set out the common law rules regarding the liability of corporations in contract, followed by a review of efforts at statutory reform.

2) Common Law Rules

In the extreme case where an agent has no connection of any kind with the principal, the law is clear — the principal is not liable.[21] The agent who falsely represents that he has authority may be liable for breach of warranty of authority[22] or fraudulent misrepresentation, but the corporate principal is not. Where the agent has some connection with a corporate principal, some ability to act on the principal's behalf, the general rule is that an agent cannot bind the corporation unless she has some kind of authority from the corporation to do so. At common law, the following types of authority were recognized:

- *Actual authority*: In some manner, the agent was actually authorized by the corporation to enter into the obligation sought to be enforced against the corporation.
- *Apparent authority*: Also called "ostensible authority," this authority is created by a representation by someone on behalf of the corpora-

---

21   Where an agent does not disclose that he is acting for a corporation, the agent and not the corporation will be liable. In *3253791 Canada Inc.* v. *Armstrong* (2002), 37 B.L.R. (3d) 230 (Ont. Sup. Ct. J.), a defendant sought to avoid personal liablity by claiming that a contract had been entered into on behalf of a corporation. Notwithstanding that the other party to the contract had received cheques in partial payment of the obligations under the contract and shipping labels in the name of the corporation, the court did not find that the parties intended that the corporation was to be the party to the contract.

22   E.g., *Yonge* v. *Toynbee*, [1910] 1 K.B. 215 (C.A.).

tion to a third party that the person the third party was dealing with had authority to bind the corporation. It was the authority of the agent as it reasonably appeared to the third party.

Figure 5.1   Agent's Authority to Contract with Third Party on Behalf of Corporation

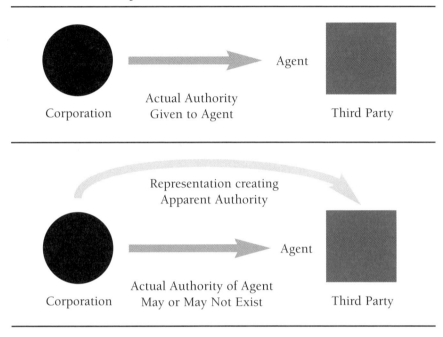

These two types of authority will often coincide in practice. For example, the office manager of a consulting business being carried on through a corporation may have actual authority to enter into a contract on behalf of the corporation for the purchase of photocopier paper because this power is given to the office manager in her contract of employment with the corporation. The office manager may also have apparent authority created by a letter from the president of the corporation to the paper supplier saying so. Nevertheless, one may exist without the other, and there are conceptual distinctions that must be kept in mind.

Actual authority is a legal relationship between the corporation and the agent which may arise as a result of powers being conferred on the agent by statute, the articles, the by-laws, a resolution of the board of directors, the terms of an employment contract, or some other permitted delegation within the organization of the business carried on by the corporation. Where the authority is conferred on a position or office, such as president, a person will have the authority of that position or office so long as he has been properly appointed. Actual authority includes not only authority expressly given but also authority that may be implied from the authority given. In *SMC Electronics Ltd.* v. *Akhter Computers Ltd.*,[23] the court held that a person with the job title "Director of Sales" had the implied authority to conclude a significant commission-splitting arrangement with another supplier on the basis that entering into such an agreement on behalf of the corporation was reasonably incidental to a job with this title. A third party dealing with an agent may be completely ignorant of the existence of the person's actual authority, but any agreement entered into by that person with the third party is binding on the corporation, if it fell within her actual authority.

A careful third party would want to know that the person she is dealing with has actual authority to contract on behalf of the corporation. In many cases, however, it will be difficult for third parties to satisfy themselves that actual authority is present because they will not have access to the internal corporate records or other private documents that create the authority. Only powers conferred in the articles and the statute are matters of public record.

As a result of the difficulty in establishing actual authority, third parties must often rely on apparent authority. Apparent authority is a legal relationship between the corporation and the third party created by a representation on behalf of the corporation that the agent has authority to contract with the third party. The representation may be express, or implied from the conduct of the corporation. Acquiescence to a person acting with certain authority may constitute a sufficient representation of authority. Perhaps the most common situation in which apparent authority arises is where a corporation appoints some person to hold a certain position. The courts have held that putting someone in a particular position constitutes a representation that the person has the authority usual for such a position. This kind of apparent authority is referred to as "usual authority." What is usual is determined by reference to the authority of agents in similar positions in similar corporations. This will be a question of fact in each case. Agents with titles like vice-president, treasurer, and secretary may have widely varying degrees of authority in different industries and even within an industry. Also, cases in which usual authority has been considered must be applied with caution because of the tendency for the responsibilities associated with particular positions in corporations to change over time.

---

23   [2001] B.C.L.C. 422 (C.A.).

In order for a third party to rely on apparent authority, the representation creating it must be made by someone with actual authority to make such a representation. Actual authority may consist in general authority to manage the business and affairs of the corporation, such as is held by the board of directors (*CBCA*, s. 102), or authority over the specific area of business within which the obligation arises. If a person has authority to manage a particular area of a business, typically that person will have authority to represent that another person has authority to enter into obligations in that area. A person who has authority to manage will not have authority to make a representation that someone else has authority, however, if there is a relevant restriction on his ability to delegate responsibility.[24]

The final requirement that must be satisfied before a third party may rely on apparent authority is that the representation must have induced the third party to have entered into the contract with the corporation. As a practical matter, this requirement is seldom hard to prove.

The leading case on these principles of corporate agency is *Freeman & Lockyer* v. *Buckhurst Park Properties (Mangal) Ltd.*[25] In that case, the defendant corporation had been formed by Kapoor and Hoon to purchase, develop, and resell a large estate. Kapoor and Hoon and a nominee of each of them made up the board of directors. The articles of the corporation permitted the appointment of a managing director, but this was never done. To the knowledge of the board, however, Kapoor acted in that capacity. Kapoor hired a firm of architects in connection with the development of the property for sale. The architects did their work but were not paid and they sued the corporation for their fee. The Court of Appeal held that, by permitting Kapoor to act as managing director, the board had represented that he had authority to enter into contracts of a kind that a managing director would, in the normal course, be authorized to enter into, including the contract with the architects. Since the articles of association conferred full management powers on the board, it had actual authority to make this representation. The court found that the architects had relied on Kapoor being authorized to contract on behalf of the corporation when they entered the agreement. As a result, the corporation was held liable to pay the architects' fee.

---

24 Section 115(3) of the *Canada Business Corporations Act*, R.S.C. 1985, c. C-44 [*CBCA*], sets out a list of powers that the board of directors may not delegate. These powers are discussed in Chapter 7. In general, these restrictions are not relevant to relations between the corporation and third parties, but rather relate to internal corporate matters such as declaring dividends.

25 [1964] 2 Q.B. 480 (C.A.).

At common law, a claim by a third party could not succeed if she knew of some restriction on the authority of the agent. This rule was fairly onerous because of another special rule applying to corporations. All persons dealing with a corporation were deemed to have knowledge of any restriction on the authority of an agent which was contained in any publicly filed document. So, for example, if the articles of a corporation stated that all leases must be signed by the president and the secretary, a third party could not enforce a lease signed by the president alone, even though a president would normally have the usual authority to enter into a lease on behalf of the corporation.[26]

In order to balance the risks that this rule of "constructive notice" created for third parties dealing with corporations, the courts developed a qualification that is referred to as the "indoor management rule" or the "rule in *Turquand's* case."[27] Under this rule, a person dealing with a corporation has no obligation to ensure that a corporation has gone through any procedures required by its articles, by-laws, resolutions, contracts, or policies to authorize a transaction or to give authority to a person purporting to act on behalf of the corporation. Compliance with such procedures is a matter of internal or "indoor" management with which outsiders do not have to concern themselves. For example, if a corporation's articles require a resolution of the board authorizing the president to borrow money, a third-party lender can assume that such a resolution has been passed. The lender does not have to investigate to be sure that it has been passed. This rule does not, however, relieve the third party from having to establish actual or apparent authority in order to enforce its claim against the corporation. So, in the example, if the necessary board resolution had not been passed, the lender would still have to be able to establish that the president had apparent authority to borrow money on behalf of the corporation in

---

26   Under the common law constructive notice rule, a third party dealing with the corporation was deemed to know also of any restriction on the business the corporation may engage in which is contained in the articles or any other public document. Any contract entered into outside the permitted business would be *ultra vires* and unenforceable. The third party could not rely on apparent authority if she had constructive notice of a restriction. As noted in Chapter 4, it is no longer necessary to include a statement of the permitted business of the corporation in the articles and, although it is possible to state restrictions on a corporation's business, this is not often done in practice. More important, even if restrictions are present, they have no effect on the enforceability of a claim by a third party (see Chapter 4).

27   *Royal British Bank v. Turquand* (1856), 6 E. & B. 327, 119 E.R. 886 (Ex. Ct.).

order to enforce its claim for repayment of the loan. What the rule does do is limit the effect of the constructive notice rule by making clear that it is only actual restrictions on authority of agents in public documents which will defeat a third party's claim. If a provision in a public document grants authority only on certain conditions or if certain procedures are followed, the third party does not need to enquire whether the conditions have been satisfied or the procedures complied with.

3) Statutory Reform

a) Introduction

When the *CBCA* was enacted in 1975, it abolished constructive notice and codified and supplemented the other common law rules described above. Similar statutory reforms have been undertaken in New Brunswick (*NBBCA*, s. 15), Newfoundland (*NCA*, s. 30), Nova Scotia (*NSCA*, s. 31), Ontario (*OBCA*, s. 18), Manitoba (*MBCA*, s. 17), Saskatchewan (*SBCA*, s. 17), and Alberta (*ABCA*, s. 17). In British Columbia, constructive notice has been abolished, but the rest of the *CBCA* scheme described below has not been adopted (*BCCA*, s. 26).

b) Constructive Notice Abolished

Section 17 of the *CBCA* provides that no person is deemed to have knowledge of any document relating to the corporation "by reason only" that the document has been filed with the Director and so is a matter of public record. The use of "by reason only" suggests that the drafters intended to leave open the possibility that knowledge may be deemed in some circumstances. As will be discussed below, this possibility is further addressed in section 18 of the *CBCA*.

c) Common Law Rules Codified and Expanded

Section 18 codifies some of the basic rules regarding apparent authority and enhances the ability of third parties to enforce contractual claims against corporations. Section 18 denies corporations the ability to rely on certain kinds of defects in the authority of a person purporting to act on behalf of a corporation in entering into a contract with a third party where a claim is made by the third party to enforce the contract:

> 18(1) No corporation and no guarantor of an obligation of the corporation may assert against a person dealing with the corporation or against a person who has acquired rights from the corporation that
>
> (a) the articles, by-laws and any unanimous shareholder agreement have not been complied with;

(b) the persons named in the most recent notice sent to the Director under section 106 [notice of directors] or 113 [notice of change of directors] are not the directors of the corporation;

(c) the place named in the most recent notice sent to the Director under section 19 [notice of registered office and notice of change of registered office] is not the registered office of the corporation;

(d) a person held out by a corporation as a director, an officer or an agent of the corporation has not been duly appointed or has no authority to exercise the powers and perform the duties that are customary in the business of the corporation or usual for a director, officer or agent;

(e) a document issued by any director, officer or agent of a corporation with actual or usual authority to issue the document is not valid or not genuine; or

(f) a sale, lease or exchange of property referred to in subsection 189(3) [of "all or substantially all the property of a corporation other than in the ordinary course of business"] was not authorized.

(2) Subsection (1) does not apply in respect of a person who has, or ought to have, knowledge of a situation described in that subsection by virtue of their relationship to the corporation.

Section 18(d) codifies an aspect of the common law rules. If a corporation makes a representation to a third party by holding someone out as a director, officer, or agent, the corporation cannot deny that the person is duly appointed or that she has the authority customary or usual for such a director, officer, or agent. Though the section does not expressly require that the holding out be by someone with actual authority to do so on behalf of the corporation, no case has interpreted the provision as ousting the pre-existing common law rule to that effect and there would seem to be nothing in the language which would suggest a legislative intention to make such a change.

The balance of section 18 deals with specific situations in which the corporation cannot rely on defects in actual authority to defeat claims by third parties that the corporation is bound by a contract entered into by an agent. The main purpose of these provisions is to ensure that corporations cannot escape their obligations to third parties because of internal corporate restrictions on authority or their failure to follow their own procedures.

Under section 18(a), any provision in a corporation's articles, by-laws, or a unanimous shareholders' agreement that restricts the authority of any person to bind the corporation, or requires some procedure to be followed before a transaction may be entered into, has no effect on a third party. As noted in Chapter 4, under the *CBCA* there is no need to state a corporation's objects, though it is possible to include in the corporation's articles restrictions on the business the corporation is permitted to carry on. Section 18(a) makes clear that no such restriction impairs the ability of a third party to enforce a contract inconsistent with the restriction.[28] Similarly, under section 18(b), if a person appears as a director in the most recently filed Notice of Directors or Notice of Change of Directors, the corporation cannot deny that such person is a director and, under section 18(c), a third party may rely on the registered office being that identified in the most recently filed Notice of Registered Office. The effect of section 18(b) is that, even if a person is no longer a director, he will have the usual authority of a director as long as his name appears on the public file. Section 18(c) is intended to ensure that a third party can rely on the address in the public file for the purposes of communicating with the corporation, including ultimately initiating legal proceedings to enforce its claim.

All these provisions are based on the same policy as the common law indoor management rule: third parties should not have to worry about whether internal corporate housekeeping is in order. The corporation is responsible for ensuring that its agents respect internal restrictions and procedures and that the public file is kept up to date and it bears the risk if it does not.

Section 18(f) protects third parties against claims by corporations that one specific kind of transactions was entered into by the corporation in a manner contrary to the *CBCA*.[29] A sale, lease, or exchange of "all or substantially all the property of a corporation other than in the ordinary course of business," as referred to in section 189(3), must be authorized by a special resolution of shareholders.[30] In accordance with

---

28   Section 16(3) provides that "no act of a corporation … is invalid by reason only that the act … is contrary to its articles or this Act."

29   Under the corresponding provision in the *ABCA*, R.S.A. 2000, c. B-9, s. 19, third parties are also protected against claims by a corporation that it is not liable to provide certain financial assistance, including assistance to any shareholder or director because the assistance was given in circumstances in which it was not authorized. Similarly, under the Ontario *Business Corporations Act*, R.S.O. 1990, c. B.16, a corporation cannot avoid an obligation to give financial assistance or to sell its assets on the basis that the obligation was not authorized, but no financial test is imposed for the giving of financial assistance (s. 19).

30   A special resolution is a resolution signed by all shareholders or passed at a meeting of shareholders by a majority of not less than two-thirds of the votes cast by shareholders present and voting at the meeting (*CBCA*, above note 24, s. 2).

section 18(f), the failure to obtain this shareholder approval has no effect on the ability of the person or persons who acquired the property to enforce their claim to it.

Finally, section 18(e) addresses the situation in which the person who is authorized to "issue" a signed document — that is, to deliver a signed copy to the other party indicating that the person on behalf of whom the document is delivered has agreed to the terms in the document — is not the person with authority to sign the document. Such a division of responsibility is common in organizations that must deal in large numbers of originally signed documents. For example, property management businesses may permit only the president to sign leases on behalf of the corporation. Usually, however, the signed lease is issued to the tenant by someone else, like the leasing manager or, perhaps, the superintendent of the building. The delivery of the lease is the act that indicates to the tenant that the property management company has agreed to the lease. The effect of section 18(e) is that a third party, like the tenant, can rely on a document issued to her by a person who has actual or usual authority to issue it. The corporation cannot later say that it was not signed by the proper person — in the example, the president.

Another common situation in which the authority to sign and the authority to issue are separated is the issuance of share certificates. Most share certificates are valid only if they are signed by the president and the secretary of the corporation. It is usual in most corporations to authorize someone else, often a third-party transfer agent, to deliver share certificates to the shareholder. Under section 18(e), as long as a shareholder receives his share certificate from a person with the actual or usual authority to issue share certificates, the corporation cannot claim that the share certificate is not valid.

Section 18(e) is a common-sense way of dealing with a common real-world problem. It was necessary also to reverse an old common law rule that a share certificate that had been fraudulently issued by the person responsible for issuing certificates was invalid. In *Ruben* v. *Great Fingall Consolidated*,[31] the secretary of a corporation who was responsible for issuing share certificates arranged to borrow money from a bank on the security of 5000 shares of the corporation he claimed to own. He created a share certificate for 5000 shares in the name of the bank, delivered it to the bank, and received the loan. The secretary did

---

31   [1906] A.C. 439 (H.L.).

not own the shares. He had forged the signatures of two directors of the corporation and affixed the corporate seal. The court held that the forgery rendered the issuance of the certificate a nullity; it was not simply a matter of internal management with no effect on third parties. The secretary's authority was only to issue the share certificates, not to create them, so the secretary could not have actual authority to create the certificate. Nor was there any representation by the corporation clothing him with apparent authority. Giving him the position of secretary could only be a representation that he had the authority usual for a secretary, which would include the authority to issue a certificate but not to create a certificate. Under section 18(e), the bank would have been able to rely on the certificate.

All the provisions of section 18 are subject to the significant qualification that the third party dealing with the corporation does not get the benefit of them if she knew of a defect in the authority of the person she was dealing with, or ought to have known of the defect by virtue of her "relationship to the corporation." This qualification essentially codifies the common law position regarding apparent authority: the third party must have relied on the authority of the person they were dealing with in entering the contract.[32] It is likely often to apply to arrangements with directors, officers, and shareholders who may be found to have reason to know of any defect in authority.

Finally, it is important to note that the *CBCA* and most other Canadian corporate statutes contain a provision to the effect that an act of a director or officer is valid notwithstanding any irregularity in his election or appointment or any defect in his qualifications (e.g., *CBCA*, s. 116; *OBCA*, s. 128; *BCCA*, s. 124; *ABCA*, s. 111(1)). Thus, a corporation cannot rely on such irregularities or defects to dispute the existence of actual authority. It has been held that the section does not apply where there was no appointment at all as opposed to an irregular one. In *Morris v. Kanssen*, a director who continued to act after his term expired, where the "office has been from the outset usurped without the colour of authority,"[33] was found not to have been appointed rather than irregularly appointed. Where a director's or officer's action is not saved under this provision, however, the director or officer may still be found to have apparent authority, applying the principles discussed above.

---

32 *Morris v. Kanssen*, [1946] A.C. 459 at 475 (H.L.).
33 *Ibid.*, at 471.

Figure 5.2   Corporate Liability in Contract — *Key Points*

Third party with contractual claim against corporation must allege that agent has **Actual Authority** (granted by the corporation) OR **Apparent Authority** (created by representation by person with actual authority to make representation)	Corporation **cannot deny authority** of agent based on defect in actual authority to enter contract or to make representation which is 1. In articles, by-laws, or USA 2. Based on person not being a director if public record says he is a director 3. A defect in appointment (s. 128) 4. Inconsistent with usual authority of office or position of agent	UNLESS third party knows or ought to have known of defect by virtue of relationship to corporation

E. CHAPTER SUMMARY

In this chapter, we discussed how the corporation acts through its human agents. In particular, we looked at the circumstances in which a corporation is liable in contract and when it is responsible for crimes and torts.

For absolute and strict liability offences where no particular mental state on the part of the wrongdoer need be shown, it is sufficient if a person acted on behalf of the corporation. Where the offence requires that the accused have some particular state of mind, the courts have developed a standard for attaching criminal responsibility for the acts of human agents: the agent who committed the criminal act must have acted in his capacity as the directing mind and will of the corporation in doing so, meaning that it is necessary to be able to identify the person who committed the crime as being the corporation for the purposes of the illegal act. In general, this identification requires that the wrongdoer have authority to make management decisions and corporate policy in relation to the area of the corporation's business in which the crime was committed. It is no defence to corporate liability to assert that the corporation sought to prevent the agent from engaging in the criminal activity.

Where a tort is committed by an employee acting within the scope of her employment, the corporation, as employer, will be vicariously liable. A corporation may also be directly liable in tort where the person committing the tort is a directing mind and will of the the corporation in relation to the area of the corporation's business in which tort was committed.

At common law, for a third party to be able to enforce a contract against a corporation, it was necessary to show that the person who acted on behalf of the corporation had actual or apparent authority to bind the corporation to the contract. To establish the latter, there must have been some representation on behalf of the corporation that the agent had the requisite authority. The representation must have been made by someone with actual authority to do so. The most common type of representation is putting an agent in an office or position that would usually have the authority to bind the corporation to the type of contract sought to be enforced. The third party must also have relied on the representation in order to enforce the contract. Third parties were deemed to have notice of defects in an agent's authority which were set out in any publicly filed document. This constructive notice of a defect in authority would defeat the third party's claim to have relied on a representation that the agent had authority.

The *CBCA* and the statutes modelled after it have codified and improved these common law rules. By abolishing the constructive notice rule and providing that a corporation will not be able to rely on its failure to act in accordance with the corporate legislation or its own internal procedures to escape liability in most circumstances, these statutes have also decreased the risk that a third party will be unable to successfully enforce a contract against a corporation.

FURTHER READINGS

ALEXANDER, C.R., "On the Nature of the Reputational Penalty for Corporate Crime: Evidence" (1999) 42 J. L. & Econ.489

COFFEE, J.C., " 'No Soul to Damn: No Body to Kick': An Unscandalized Inquiry into the Problem of Corporate Punishment" (1981) 79 Mich. L. Rev. 386

HANNA, D., "Corporate Criminal Liability" (1989) 31 Crim. L.Q. 452

HANSMANN, H., & R. KRAAKMAN, "A Procedural Focus on Unlimited Shareholder Liability" (1992) 106 Harvard L. Rev. 446

HANSMANN, H., & R. KRAAKMAN, "Toward Unlimited Shareholder Liability for Corporate Torts" (1991) 100 Yale L.J. 1879

LEEBRON, D.W., "Limited Liability, Tort Victims and Creditors" (1991) 91 Colum. L. Rev. 1565

PEARCE, F., & L. SNIDER, eds., *Corporate Crime: Contemporary Debates* (Toronto: University of Toronto Press, 1995)

QUAID, J.A., "The Assessment of Corporate Criminal Liability on the Basis of Corporate Identity: An Analysis" (1998) 43 McGill L.J. 67

RUBY, C., & K. JULL, "The Charter and Regulatory Offences: A Wholesale Revision" (1992) 14 C.R. (4th) 226

SAXE, D., "The Impact of prosecution of corporations and their officers and directors upon regulatory compliance by corporations" (1990) 1 J.E.L.P. 91

WELLS, C., *Corporations and Criminal Responsibility* (Oxford: Oxford University Press, 1993)

CHAPTER 6

SHARES

A. INTRODUCTION

A share is a bundle of rights against a corporation. Although a share is personal property, the claim it represents in the corporation is not a property right in the corporation's assets,[1] nor is it a proportionate ownership interest in the corporation itself.[2] The particular rights, privileges, restrictions, and conditions of each class of shares (referred to here collectively as "characteristics") are set out in the articles of the corporation, as discussed in Chapter 4. Subject to a few statutory and common law limitations, the characteristics that may be given to shares are restricted only by the imagination of the person drafting the articles. The characteristics of a share determine the risks associated with the holder's investment, the degree of control she has over the corporation, and her right to share in its profits and to receive the corporation's property when it dissolves. In this chapter, we will set out the statutory scheme relating to shares, as well as the most important common law rules. Some of the more common practices in drafting share provisions will also be described.

The basic rights associated with shares are as follows:

- to vote at any meeting of shareholders;

---

1 *Macaura v. Northern Assurance Co.*, [1925] A.C. 619 (H.L.).
2 *Bradbury v. English Sewing Cotton Co. Ltd.*, [1923] A.C. 744 (H.L.).

- to receive dividends declared by the board of directors; and,
- on dissolution of the corporation, to receive the property of the corporation remaining after creditors and any other persons with claims against the corporation are paid.

Where a corporation has only one class of shares, the rights of the holders of shares of that class are equal in all respects and must include each of the three basic rights listed above (*CBCA*, s. 24(3)).[3] If the articles provide for more than one class of shares, then each of the basic rights must be possessed by at least one class of shares, although all three rights are not required to be attached to the same class (*CBCA*, s. 24(4)). For example, if a corporation has three classes of shares, Class A, Class B, and Class C, each of the basic rights would have to be possessed by at least one of these classes. A single class, say Class A, might have all three rights and the other two none, or the rights might be distributed across the classes in some other way. If the articles are silent on the right to vote, then each share has one vote (*CBCA*, s. 140(1)).[4] Where a corporation has multiple classes of shares, all such shares are presumed to have equal rights, regardless of class, except to the extent specifically provided in the articles.

Each owner of a share is entitled to a share certificate and, if a corporation is authorized to issue more than one class of shares, or more than one series of shares of a class as discussed below, the characteristics of the class or series must appear on the certificate or a notice must appear stating that there are particular characteristics and that copies of the text of such characteristics may be obtained from the corporation (*CBCA*, ss. 49(1) & (13)).[5] Unless a shareholder requests one, however, there is no need for a corporation to issue a share certificate and, in order to minimize paper work, many smaller corporations do not bother. In any event, a record of ownership of shares, called a securities register, must be maintained as part of the corporate records at the registered office of the corporation or any other place in Canada

---

3   Most statutes based on the *Canada Business Corporations Act*, R.S.C. 1985, c. C-44 [*CBCA*], follow this approach. E.g., Alberta *Business Corporations Act*, R.S.A. 2000, c. B-9 [*ABCA*], s. 26. The Ontario *Business Corporations Act*, R.S.O. 1990, c. B.16 [*OBCA*], only requires that shares have the right to vote and to receive the remaining property of the corporation on dissolution (s. 22). This issue is not addressed in the *Companies Act*, R.S.B.C. 1996, c. 62 [*BCCA*].

4   Provincial rules based on the *CBCA*, *ibid.*, follow this model. E.g., *OBCA*, *ibid.*, s. 102(1); and *ABCA*, *ibid.*, s. 139. The *BCCA*, *ibid.*, has no such rule.

5   Provincial rules based on the *CBCA*, *ibid.*, follow this model. E.g., *OBCA*, *ibid.*, ss. 54(1), 56(2); and *ABCA*, *ibid.*, s. 48. The *BCCA*, *ibid.*, has a similar rule (s. 51).

designated by the directors (*CBCA*, ss. 20 & 50).[6] An entry in a securities register or a share certificate issued by a corporation is proof, in the absence of evidence to the contrary, that the person in whose name the share is registered is the owner of the shares described in the register or in the certificate (*CBCA*, s. 257(3)).[7]

B. COMMON CHARACTERISTICS OF SHARES

1) Classes

The *CBCA* refers only to "shares" (*CBCA*, s. 24).[8] There are no legal restrictions on what shares can be called or, with some qualifications, what characteristics they can be given in the articles. In practice, it is usual to designate one class of shares as "common shares" and give these shares the three basic rights identified in the previous section. Usually, no dividend may be paid on common shares until the dividend entitlements of all other classes of shares are paid. In addition, no payment to common shareholders on dissolution may occur before all other claimants, again including the holders of all other classes of shares, have been paid what is owed to them. The claims of others typically are limited to a fixed amount, but the common shares represent residual claims: they are entitled to whatever is left after everyone else is paid. Because of the residual nature of the claims of common shares, their value will vary with the success of the business. If the business generates a substantial surplus over what is needed to pay other claim holders, the value of the common shares will be large. If the assets of the corporation are insufficient to pay the other claimholders, the common shares may be worthless. Because common shares rank behind all others with claims against the corporation, they are considered the riskiest form of investment.

Consider the following simple example. Imagine that a corporation's assets are worth $100 and that its only liability is $50 that it owes to its bank. The value of the common shares is what is left after the

---

6   Provincial rules based on the *CBCA*, *ibid.*, follow this model. E.g., *OBCA*, *ibid.*, ss. 140 & 141; and *ABCA*, *ibid.*, ss. 21 & 49. The *BCCA*, *ibid.*, has a similar rule (s. 163). *CBCA* permits records to be kept outside Canada so long as they can be accessed at the registered office (*CBCA*, s. 5.1).

7   Provincial rules based on the *CBCA*, *ibid.*, follow this model. E.g., *OBCA*, *ibid.*, s. 266(3); and *ABCA*, *ibid.*, s. 260. The *BCCA*, *ibid.*, has a similar rule (s. 52).

8   The same approach is taken in provincial rules based on the *CBCA*, *ibid.* E.g., *OBCA*, *ibid.*, s. 22; and *ABCA*, *ibid.*, s. 26. The *BCCA*, *ibid.*, is similar (ss. 19, 20).

debt is paid — $50. This is because, if it were dissolved today, the corporation would sell all its assets, pay back the bank, and pay whatever was left to the holders of common shares. If the value of the corporation declines below $50, the residual value of the corporation's common shares will be $0.[9]

In small corporations, common shares may be the only class of shares, but multiple classes with a wide variety of characteristics are frequently found. Some public corporations have voting and "non-voting" or "subordinate voting" common shares. Non-voting common shares have the same characteristics as common shares except that they do not vote. Similarly, subordinate voting shares are the same as common shares except that they have fewer votes than the common shares. In practice, this difference is often accomplished by giving the regular common shares multiple votes, say ten, and the subordinate voting common shares only one vote. Usually, in such cases, most of the shares issued to the public are non-voting or subordinated voting common shares, while most of the regular voting shares are retained by a small group of shareholders, often the original shareholders in the corporation. In this way the corporation can raise capital by issuing shares without the original shareholders having to give up much control.

Many corporations also have one or more classes of "preferred" or "preference" shares which do not vote but which have a preference related to receiving some fixed dividend and on dissolution. A preference as to dividends means that dividends are paid on these shares first, before dividends are paid on common shares (or any other class over which the preferred shares have a priority as expressed in the share conditions set out in the articles). A preference on dissolution usually means that all the money paid into the corporation in return for the issuance of the preference shares must be paid back to the preferred shareholders before the remaining assets can be distributed to the holders of the common shares (or any other class of shares over which the preferred shares have priority).

Preferred shares will be attractive to an investor who does not want to have any say in how the business is managed but is interested in a fixed return. In promising a fixed return, preferred shares resemble debt, but there are some important differences between an investment in a corporation in the form of debt, such as a loan bearing interest, and one in the form of the purchase of preferred shares. An investment in

---

9   The residual nature of the claims of common shares on dissolution is discussed in Chapter 3.

preferred shares is riskier because, as will be discussed below, the directors may decide that it is in the corporation's best interests not to pay dividends, in which case a preferred shareholder will have no recourse in most circumstances. By contrast, if management decided not to pay interest on a debt, the creditor could then sue to recover the amount owed or even put the corporation into bankruptcy. Also, on dissolution, preferred shareholders get their investment back only after all loans and other prior claims have been paid. Because of the increased risks associated with an investment in preferred shares, investors typically require higher rates of return on preferred shares than they would require on debt.

2) Dividends

The profits of a corporation belong to the corporation and not to its shareholders. Profits may be distributed to shareholders by way of a dividend declared by the corporation's board of directors. Once declared, the dividend becomes a debt of the corporation owed to all shareholders entitled to share in the dividend.[10] Under the *CBCA*, dividends are paid to a person who is registered as a shareholder at a certain date referred to as a record date. If no record date is fixed by the directors, the record date is the close of business of the day on which the directors pass the resolution declaring the dividend (*CBCA*, s. 134).[11]

Each share has an equal right to receive any dividend declared by the corporation unless there are specific provisions in the articles granting different dividend entitlements to different classes of shares. The kinds of arrangements that may be made regarding dividends are highly variable, but there are two invariable rules:

- The declaration of dividends is a matter within the discretion of the directors. This rule has two corollaries:
  - the power to declare dividends cannot be delegated by the board of directors (*CBCA*, s. 115(3)(d)),[12] although, like any other power of the directors, it can be assumed by shareholders in a unanimous shareholders' agreement;[13] and

---

10   *Re Severn & Wye and Severn Bridge Railway Co.*, [1896] 1 Ch. 559.
11   Provincial rules based on the *CBCA*, above note 3, follow this model. E.g., *OBCA*, above note 3, s. 95; and *ABCA*, above note 3, s. 133. The *BCCA*, above note 3, has a similar rule (s. 73).
12   Provincial rules based on the *CBCA*, *ibid.*, follow this model. E.g. *OBCA*, *ibid.*, s. 127(3)(d); and *ABCA*, *ibid.*, s. 115(3)(d). The *BCCA*, *ibid.*, has no similar rule.
13   Shareholder agreements are discussed in Chapter 7.

- no provision of the articles or any shareholders' agreement can compel the directors to declare and pay dividends.[14]

• Dividends cannot be paid if there are reasonable grounds for believing that the corporation cannot meet either of the following financial tests:
   - the corporation is, or would after the payment be, unable to pay its liabilities as they become due (referred to as the "solvency test"); or
   - the realizable value of the corporation's assets would, after the payment, be less than the aggregate of its liabilities and stated capital of all classes (referred to as the "capital impairment test") (CBCA, s. 42).[15]

The meaning of stated capital is discussed in section C ("Issuing and Paying for Shares"), below, but essentially it consists of the historical total of all money or other assets paid into the corporation in return for shares. If dividends are paid in contravention of these requirements, the directors who consented to the declaration of the dividend are personally liable to pay the amount of the dividend back to the corporation (CBCA, s. 118(2)(c)).[16] This obligation is discussed further in Chapter 8.

Directors may be compelled to declare dividends if the failure to pay would be oppressive to shareholders (CBCA, s. 241)[17] or would breach the directors' fiduciary duty, though such circumstances are likely to be rare. The failure to pay dividends was held to be oppressive in *Ferguson v. Imax Systems Corp.*[18] when the failure occurred as part of a concerted effort by management to prevent one shareholder from receiving any benefit from the corporation. The shareholder was the estranged wife of the major shareholder. The other shareholders were not hurt by the failure to pay dividends because they or their spouses were compensated as employees.

Because the directors always have the discretion not to pay dividends, one of the most important characteristics of dividends is whether they are "cumulative" or not. If a dividend entitlement is

---

14   *Burland v. Earle*, [1902] A.C. 83 (P.C.).
15   Provincial rules based on the *CBCA*, above note 3, follow this model. E.g., *OBCA*, above note 3, s. 38(3); and *ABCA*, above note 3, s. 43. The *BCCA*, above note 3, has a similar rule (s. 127).
16   Provincial rules based on the *CBCA*, ibid., follow this model. E.g., *OBCA*, ibid., s. 130(2)(c); and *ABCA*, ibid., s. 118(3)(c). The *BCCA*, ibid., has a similar rule (s. 127).
17   Provincial rules based on the *CBCA* follow this model. E.g., *OBCA*, ibid., s. 248; and *ABCA*, ibid., s. 242. The *BCCA*, ibid., has a similar provision (s. 200).
18   (1983), 43 O.R. (2d) 128 (C.A.).

cumulative and the dividend is not paid when it is supposed to be, the entitlement continues until it is paid. Cumulative dividend provisions in corporate articles typically state that no dividends may be paid on other classes of shares until all cumulative dividends have been paid and that the amount of any unpaid cumulative dividends are added to the amount that the shareholder is entitled to be paid by the corporation if the share is repurchased or redeemed, or on dissolution. Redeeming and repurchasing shares are discussed in section D ("Redemption and Repurchase of Shares"), below.[19] If a dividend is not cumulative and is not paid when it is supposed to be, the shareholder has no claim to it. For a dividend to be cumulative, the amount of the dividend must be fixed — there must be some amount to cumulate.

If a share is entitled to a dividend in priority to dividends on shares of another class and the entitlement is not expressly described as non-cumulative, it is presumed to be cumulative.[20] It is not clear if a simple reference to a fixed dividend without a preference gives rise to this presumption. This discussion of cumulative dividends illustrates the importance of being as clear and explicit as possible when drafting share provisions.

Whether a class of shares participates in dividends in excess of those expressly provided for in the articles will depend on the interpretation of the specific language used to describe the dividend entitlements of that class. Where only a fixed dividend is specified for a particular class of shares, the courts have held that holders of shares of that class are not entitled to participate equally with the holders of shares of other classes in any other dividend declared.[21]

3) Rights on Dissolution

As noted, the *CBCA* requires that at least one class of shares be entitled to receive the remaining property of the corporation on dissolution and that this is a right usually given to the common shares. As a result of the principle of equality of shares, where there are multiple classes of shares, each share is entitled to participate on an equal basis in any remaining property of the corporation in the absence of any limitations on such entitlements which are expressly provided for in the articles.[22] Frequently, preferred shares are given the right to receive their "capi-

---

19   See section D ("Redemption and Repurchase of Shares") below.
20   *Ferguson & Forester Ltd.* v. *Buchanan*, [1920] Sess. Cas. 154 (Scot).
21   *Re Porto Rico Power Co.*, [1946] S.C.R. 178.
22   *Ibid.*

tal" back before any payment to the common shareholders but do not otherwise participate on dissolution. The share provisions must define what capital means for this purpose. Capital may be defined to mean the amount paid for the shares, plus all unpaid cumulative dividends. If shares of a class of preference shares were issued for different prices, the preference may attach to the average amount paid for the shares or, for each share, a portion of the stated capital for the class determined by dividing the stated capital for the class by the total number of issued shares of the class. The entitlement of each class of shares on dissolution must be addressed in drafting the share provisions.

4) Voting

a) Introduction

Voting is probably the most important shareholder right, though there may be practical impediments to exercising that right, particularly in large corporations, as discussed in Chapter 7. As noted above, all shares carry the right to one vote unless the articles provide otherwise. It is possible to provide that votes arise only in certain circumstances, such as the failure to pay dividends, or only on certain issues, or even that voting rights are different on different issues. Because of the principle of equality of shares, however, all shares within a class must have the same voting rights. In *Jacobsen* v. *United Canso Oil & Gas Ltd.*,[23] a by-law that purported to restrict each shareholder's votes to a maximum of 1000, regardless of the number of shares held, was struck down on this basis.[24]

Shareholders can agree to vote their shares in a particular way, and this is commonly done in shareholders' agreements (see Chapter 7). Otherwise, in general, shareholders can vote their shares however they like, subject to the limits imposed by the oppression remedy discussed in Chapter 9.

Since it is possible and, indeed, now commonplace for a corporation to have classes of shares that do not vote, there is a possibility that holders of shares that do vote may exercise their power to the detri-

---

23   (1980), 11 B.L.R. 313 (Alta. Q.B.).

24   At the time of this decision the corporation was governed by the *CBCA*, above note 3. It was subsequently continued under the Nova Scotia *Companies Act*, now R.S.N.S. 1989, c. 81, and a court stated, in *obiter*, that such a provision might not be prohibited under that statute (*Jacobsen* v. *United Canso Oil & Gas Ltd.* (1980), 40 N.S.R. (2d) 692 (S.C.T.D.)). As discussed below, the *CBCA* does permit holders of shares of one class to be treated differently if they hold different series of the class.

ment of the holders of those that do not. For significant changes to the corporation that will fundamentally alter the nature of shareholders' investments by affecting the returns to shareholders or the risks associated with those returns, even shareholders who do not otherwise have the right to vote may feel that they should have some say. It is open to shareholders to try to negotiate for protection in these circumstances, perhaps by requiring that a voting right arising only in these special circumstances be included in the share provisions. The policy of the *CBCA* and the statutes based on it, however, is to provide voting rights as mandatory protection for all shareholders in such circumstances, whether voting rights are provided for in the articles or not. The nature of this special voting protection is discussed below.

b) Special Vote

Under the *CBCA*, all shares vote on certain fundamental changes, even if they do not otherwise have the right to vote. These fundamental changes include the following:

- an amalgamation under which one corporation is combined with another corporation (*CBCA*, s. 183(3));
- the sale, lease, or exchange of all or substantially all the assets of the corporation, other than in the ordinary course of business (*CBCA*, s. 189(6));
- the continuance of a corporation incorporated under the *CBCA* under some other corporate law, with the result that it is governed by that law (*CBCA*, s. 188(4)); and
- the liquidation or dissolution of the corporation (*CBCA*, s. 211(3)).[25]

c) Class Vote

All shares of a class are entitled to vote separately as a class on certain fundamental changes, even if they are not otherwise entitled to vote, if shares of that class will be prejudicially affected in ways that are different from the ways that shares of other classes will be affected as specifically defined in the Act (*CBCA*, s. 176). These changes include

- an amalgamation (*CBCA*, s. 183(4));

---

25 Most provincial rules based on the *CBCA*, *ibid.*, follow this model. E.g., *ABCA*, above note 3. Under the *OBCA*, above note 3, shareholders not otherwise entitled to vote are entitled to vote on these fundamental changes only where they are entitled to vote separately as a class, as discussed in the next section of this chapter. Corporate changes are discussed in Chapter 10.

- a sale, lease, or exchange of all or substantially all the assets of the corporation, other than in the ordinary course of business (*CBCA*, s. 189(7)); and
- certain amendments to the articles (*CBCA*, s. 176).

Since these changes must all be approved by a special resolution,[26] the necessary two-thirds majority of shares must be obtained from all shares entitled to vote and from each class entitled to vote separately as a class. The *CBCA* also provides that any shareholder who disagrees with the outcome of any such vote may opt out of the corporation by requiring the corporation to buy her shares at their fair value (*CBCA*, s. 190(3)).[27] This remedy, referred to as the "dissent and appraisal remedy," is discussed in Chapter 9.

5) Cumulative Voting

In the usual situation where each share has one vote, a person who holds a majority of the shares can determine who the directors are — regardless of the views of the minority shareholders. Cumulative voting is a somewhat complex mechanism designed to ensure that minority shareholders can elect directors to represent them.[28]

Cumulative voting means that each shareholder has the number of votes equal to the number of shares she holds multiplied by the number of directors to be elected. Each shareholder can allocate her votes to one director or to any number of candidates as she chooses. The directors elected are determined by who gets the most votes. So, if there are five directors to be elected and eight candidates, the five candidates receiving the most votes will be elected. By allocating her votes to a single candidate, a minority shareholder may be able to ensure that the director is elected. Even with cumulative voting, whether a partic-

---

26   Recall that a special resolution is a resolution signed by all shareholders or passed at a meeting of shareholders by a majority of not less than two-thirds of the votes cast by shareholders present and voting at the meeting (*CBCA, ibid.*, s. 2).

27   Provincial rules based on the *CBCA, ibid.*, also provide dissent and appraisal rights. E.g., *OBCA*, above note 3, s. 185; and *ABCA*, above note 3, s. 190. The *BCCA*, above note 3, provides for dissent rights in a wider variety of circumstances (ss. 207 & 222). Voting entitlements are somewhat different in some provinces.

28   The requirements for cumulative voting discussed in this section are set out in the *CBCA, ibid.*, s. 107; *OBCA, ibid.*, s. 120; and *ABCA, ibid.*, s. 107. Cumulative voting is not addressed in the *BCCA, ibid.*

ular shareholder will have enough votes to elect a director will depend on the distribution of shares and the number of candidates for director. Consider the following examples.

Figure 6.1

Shareholder	Number of shares	Number of directors to be elected	Number of votes	Number of directors shareholder can elect
Malcolm	75	2	150	2
Avril	25	2	50	0

In the example in figure 6.1, even with the added voting strength provided by cumulative voting, Avril still does not have enough votes to elect a director. If Malcolm allocates seventy-five votes to each of two candidates, he can always out-vote Avril's fifty votes. If we increase Avril's percentage shareholding to 40 percent, as indicated in figure 6.2, cumulative voting allows Avril to elect one director, just like Malcolm.

Figure 6.2

Shareholder	Number of shares	Number of directors to be elected	Number of votes	Number of directors shareholder can elect
Malcolm	60	2	120	1
Avril	40	2	80	1

In order to set up a scheme of cumulative voting, it must be provided for in a corporation's articles. There must be a fixed number of directors and the terms of each director must end at the close of the first annual meeting held after their election. If directors had staggered terms, which is permissible in other circumstances, the purpose of the cumulative voting structure would be defeated. In the example above, if only one of the two directors was required to be elected each year, Malcolm could always out-vote Avril at each annual election and determine who the directors would be. The corporate statutes contain some provisions designed to prevent the cumulative voting system from being defeated. For example, any motion to remove a director is defeated if the number of votes against removal would have been sufficient to ensure that the director was elected under cumulative voting.[29]

There are alternatives to cumulative voting which would also ensure that a minority shareholder would be able to have board representation. Imagine, for example, that the articles provided for a special class of shares which was entitled to elect one or some number of directors. Issuing these shares to the minority shareholder would permit the minority shareholder to elect a director.

6) No Par Value

All shares used to have a nominal or "par" value, which was expressed in the articles. This value was to represent the intended issue price of the shares. In practice, however, while the issue price of a share was sometimes "at par," just as often it was not. Shares were often issued at prices above the par value (i.e., at a premium to par). The par value served no useful purpose because it did not disclose anything about the actual price at which a share was issued. In some cases, dividend and redemption entitlements were calculated by reference to par.

Par value has now been abolished under the *CBCA* and under corporate statutes in provinces other than Quebec (*QCA*, s. 123.39), Nova Scotia (*NSCA*, s. 10), New Brunswick (*NBBCA*, s. 22(1)), British Columbia (*BCCA*, s. 42), and Prince Edward Island (*PEICA*, s. 6). Section 24(1) of the *CBCA* provides that all shares issued under the *CBCA* are without nominal or par value. If a corporation incorporated under a regime that permits par value has shares with par value, and the corporation is continued under the *CBCA*, the shares are deemed to be without par value once the continuance occurs.[30]

7) Series of Shares

Because of the rule that rights of holders of shares of a class are equal in all respects, a corporation must have more than one class of shares if it wants to give different rights to different shareholders. The only circumstance in which shares within a class may be given different rights is when shares in that class are subdivided into different "series." Section 27 of the *CBCA* provides that the articles may authorize the issue of any class of shares in one or more series and fix or authorize

---

29   E.g., *CBCA*, *ibid.*, s. 107(g) and (h).

30   Provincial rules based on the *CBCA*, *ibid.*, follow this model. E.g., *OBCA*, above note 3, s. 22; and *ABCA*, above note 3, s. 26. Continuation is discussed in Chapter 10.

the directors to fix the following characteristics attaching to the shares of each series:

- number of shares in the series;
- designation of the series (i.e., a name such as "series F"); and
- other characteristics in the series (i.e., the "rights, privileges, restrictions, and conditions").[31]

In order to be able to issue shares in series, the articles must expressly permit it. If the characteristics of the series are not fixed in the articles, then a directors' resolution must be passed setting the characteristics of the series. The directors must send articles of amendment to the Director appointed under the *CBCA* setting out the number, designation, and characteristics of the shares in the series before any such shares may be issued (*CBCA*, s. 27(4)).

Why would a corporation want to be able to issue shares in series? Generally, issuing shares in series is of interest only to public corporations. It permits such corporations to create shares with particular characteristics faster and more cheaply than if the corporation had to amend its articles in the usual way to create a new class of shares by calling a meeting of shareholders to approve articles of amendment. Speed is usually important, so that a corporation can give the shares the exact characteristics that will make them attractive in the marketplace at a particular time, such as a certain dividend rate. An opportunity to issue shares at a low dividend rate may be lost if the corporation has to call a meeting of shareholders to amend articles to create a new class of shares; by the time the shareholder meeting has been held, the dividend rate in the market may have changed. Another saving is the cost of shareholder meetings. Public corporation shareholder meetings are expensive because they involve legal fees in connection with the preparation of materials to be sent to shareholders, the cost of mailing to large numbers of shareholders, renting rooms, and so on.

The only restriction on the use of series is that all shares of the same class must have the same priority in relation to receiving dividends and return of capital, even if they are in different series (*CBCA*, s. 27(3)). In other words, shares of one series cannot have a right to receive dividends or to receive what has been paid into the corporation on issuance of the shares which has priority over the same rights attaching to another series of shares of the class. If any cumulative div-

---

31   Provincial rules based on the *CBCA*, *ibid.*, follow this model. E.g., *OBCA*, *ibid.*, s. 25; and *ABCA*, *ibid.*, s. 29. The *BCCA*, *ibid.*, also provides for the issuance of shares in series (s. 229).

idends or amounts payable on return of capital to a series are not paid in full, the shares of all series of the same class participate rateably in respect of accumulated dividends and return of capital (*CBCA*, s. 27(2)). Participating "rateably" means that each share in the class receives the same amount of whatever is distributed.

8) Pre-emptive Rights

Both the *CBCA* and statutes modelled on it specifically provide that the articles or a unanimous shareholder agreement may contain a "pre-emptive right" (*CBCA*, s. 28).[32] If the articles contain such a right, then a corporation desiring to issue shares must offer them first to the existing shareholders as a condition of being able to issue shares. Once the existing shareholders have had a chance to buy the shares, any unsold shares may be offered for sale to others. Under the *CBCA*, it is contemplated that the pre-emptive right would permit shareholders to purchase shares only in proportion to their existing holdings. So, if a shareholder holds 10 percent of the currently issued shares, she would be entitled to purchase 10 percent of any new issue. Under the *OBCA*, there is no such restriction, and a corporation may set up the right however it likes in its articles. Most pre-emptive rights schemes work like the *CBCA* scheme in practice, however. In British Columbia, a pre-emptive right is mandatory for non-reporting corporations (*BCCA*, s. 41).[33]

A pre-emptive right may be attractive to shareholders for three reasons.

Avoiding dilution: A pre-emptive right allows existing shareholders to avoid the dilution of their proportionate interest in the corporation. For example, if a shareholder holds 10 out of 100 issued common shares, he has 10 percent of the shares and the same percentage of votes; if the corporation issues another 100 shares to someone else, however, his interest is diluted to 5 percent. With a pre-emptive right, he would be entitled to buy 10 percent of the new issue to keep his overall interest at 10 percent.

Constraining inappropriate issuance of shares: A pre-emptive right impairs the ability of directors to issue shares for improper purposes. For example, if an offer is made to acquire all the shares of a corporation (a "takeover bid"), the directors might be tempted to try to prevent the bid

---

32 E.g., *OBCA*, *ibid.*, s. 26; and *ABCA*, *ibid.*, s. 30.

33 A non-reporting company is similar to a non-offering corporation under the *OBCA*, *ibid.*, and a non-distributing corporation under the *CBCA*, above note 3. See *BCCA*, above note 3, s. 1(1)).

from being successful out of fear that they might lose their jobs if it were. One way they could try to defeat the bid would be to issue more shares to make the bid more expensive or, to issue shares to a person who will not sell to the takeover bidder (called a "White Knight").[34] A pre-emptive right will limit the ability of the directors to issue shares in this way. The issuance becomes more time-consuming, since the directors must comply with the pre-emptive right provision; such provisions usually specify some time period within which existing shareholders may decide whether they want to purchase shares. The pre-emptive right also prevents the issuance of shares directly to the White Knight.

Preventing issuance of shares at under value: The issuance of shares for less than they are worth would water down the price of all shares. Issuing shares at under value would likely be a breach of fiduciary duty by the directors in any event, but the pre-emptive right is a more direct way of ensuring that it does not happen and, if it does, that existing shareholders benefit. As discussed in Chapter 9, seeking relief for a breach of fiduciary duty is a procedurally cumbersome and time-consuming process.

An important limitation on the effectiveness of the pre-emptive right for any of these purposes is that it can be exercised only by those with the ability to pay. The courts have recognized that requiring shareholders to buy additional shares or face dilution of their proportionate interest will sometimes be unfair to shareholders who cannot afford to participate, and may give rise to a claim for relief under the oppression remedy.[35]

C. ISSUING AND PAYING FOR SHARES

1) Introduction

As discussed in Chapter 3, no minimum investment in shares of the corporation is required as a condition of incorporation. Also, there is

---

34   Issuing shares for the purpose of affecting control has been held to be a breach of fiduciary duty (*Bonisteel v. Collis Leather Co.* (1919), 45 O.L.R. 195 (Ont. H.C.J.)). More recent cases have permitted the issuance of shares to affect control if the directors acted honestly, in good faith, and in the reasonable belief that they were acting in the best interests of the corporation (*Teck Corp. v. Millar* (1972), 33 D.L.R. (3d) 288 (B.C.S.C.); *Olson v. Phoenix Industrial Supply Ltd.* (1984), 9 D.L.R. (4th) 451 (Man. C.A.)). See Chapter 8.

35   For example, *Re Sabex International Ltée.* (1979), 6 B.L.R. 65 (Que. S.C.); *Mazzotta v. Twin Gold Mines Ltd.* (1987), 37 B.L.R. 218 (Ont. H.C.J.). The oppression remedy is discussed in Chapter 9. Oppression provisions in provincial statutes are noted above (see note 17).

no requirement to set a maximum number of shares of a class that may be issued, though the articles may provide for one. If there is a maximum, shares can be issued only up to that maximum number. In order to issue additional shares, the articles would have to be amended to increase or remove the maximum number. The number of shares of a class authorized to be issued is called the "authorized capital."

The directors have the power to issue shares, and this power cannot be delegated to anyone else (CBCA, s. 115(3)(c)).[36] Under CBCA type statutes, the shareholders may, however, assume this power by means of a unanimous shareholders' agreement (USA). Under a USA, shareholders can assume any or all the powers of the directors. The use of USAs is discussed in Chapter 7.

Subject to the articles, by-laws, and any USA, shares can be issued to any person for whatever consideration the directors determine (CBCA, s. 25(i)).[37] Shares may be issued for money, property, or past services. If the consideration is other than money, directors are obliged to be sure that whatever is received is not less in value than the "fair equivalent of the money that the corporation would have received if the share had been issued for money" (CBCA, s. 25(4)). Pursuant to section 118(1) of the CBCA, if the directors fail to get the "fair equivalent," they are personally liable, jointly and severally, to make up the shortfall, unless they could not reasonably have known that the value of the property was not sufficient (CBCA, s. 118(6)) or they exercised the care, diligence, and skill that a reasonably prudent person would have exercised in comparable circumstances, including relying on a professional opinion regarding the value of the property (CBCA, s. 123(4)).[38]

Consideration for the issuance of shares must be paid in full, whatever it is, at the time the shares are issued under the corporate laws of all Canadian jurisdictions except Quebec (QCA, s. 66), Prince Edward Island (PEICA, s. 41), and Nova Scotia (NSCA, s. 48). It used to be that shares could be issued on the basis that payment of some part of the subscription price would be paid later. Such shares were referred to as "not fully paid." Under the CBCA, only "fully paid" shares can be

---

36   Provincial rules based on the CBCA, above note 3, follow this model. E.g., OBCA, above note 3, s. 127(3)(c); and ABCA, above note 3, s. 115(3)(c).

37   Provincial rules based on the CBCA, ibid., follow this model. E.g., OBCA, ibid., s. 23(1); and ABCA, ibid., s. 27(1). The BCCA, above note 3, has a similar rule (ss. 41, 42, 43, 55).

38   Similar liability is imposed under the OBCA, ibid., s. 130; and the ABCA, ibid., s. 118, though the defences are more limited. There is no defence to the similar liability imposed under the BCCA, ibid., s. 45.

issued (*CBCA*, s. 25(3)).[39] Consistent with this requirement for full payment, section 25(5) provides that a promissory note or a promise to pay is not property for which shares may be issued.[40] The *2001 Amendments* provide that certain debt obligations owed by a third party to the person who wants to buy shares can be transferred to the corporation by that person in return for shares (*CBCA*, s. 25(5)).

It used to be, as well, that shareholders could be asked by the directors to pay into the corporation more money from time to time as the corporation needed it. Such shares were called "assessable." Now all shares are "non-assessable" (*CBCA*, s. 25(2)).

2) Stated Capital Account

A corporation must maintain a separate account for each class and series of shares it issues, recording the "stated capital" for each class or series (*CBCA*, s. 26(1)).[41] Stated capital for a class or series is simply the historical total of the amount paid into the corporation in return for the issuance of shares of that class or series.[42] It is aggregated for each class or series of shares, rather than recorded on an individual share basis. The stated capital per share is simply the total for the class divided by the number of shares, even if shares of a class are issued for different prices at different times. The example of the calculation of stated capital at the end of section D ("Redemption and Repurchase of Shares"), below, shows how stated capital calculations are made.

Stated capital is not cash; it is simply a bookkeeping record. Once money, property, or past services are contributed to the corporation, they may be spent or otherwise used in the corporation's business. Stated cap-

---

39 See, similarly, *OBCA*, *ibid.*, s. 23; *ABCA*, *ibid.*, s. 27; and *BCCA*, *ibid.*, s. 43. It should be noted, however, that, if the corporation lends the shareholder the money to purchase the shares, the effect is the same as if the shares were not fully paid.

40 Most Canadian corporate statutes permit the corporation to pay a commission to a person in return for her agreement to purchase shares or to procure someone else to purchase shares (e.g., *CBCA*, above note 3, s. 41; *OBCA*, *ibid.*, s. 37; *ABCA*, *ibid.*, s. 42; and *BCCA*, *ibid.*, s. 47).

41 Provincial rules based on the *CBCA*, *ibid.*, follow this model. E.g., *OBCA*, *ibid.*, s. 24; and *ABCA*, *ibid.*, s. 26.

42 For certain transactions among related parties, including amalgamations, statutory arrangements, and continuance under the laws of another jurisdiction, and where the transferor, the corporation, and all holders of the class of shares to be issued to the transferor consent, the full amount of consideration received for the issuance of shares may not be added to the stated capital account (*CBCA*, *ibid.*, ss. 26(3)–(12)). These transactions are discussed in Chapter 10.

ital remains the same whether the money, property, or past services are wasted, saved, or used to increase the value of the corporation's assets.

Stated capital must be adjusted whenever shares are issued, including the payment of a dividend in the form of a share, or reacquired by the corporation. See the discussion in section D ("Redemption and Repurchase of Shares"), below. Stated capital is relevant for calculating whether the capital impairment test has been satisfied. As discussed above, the capital impairment test is required to be met before certain actions, such as declaring dividends, are permitted. See the discussion of dividends in section B, above.[43]

It is also possible to adjust stated capital with the approval of the shareholders by special resolution, subject to certain limits (*CBCA*, ss. 26(5) & 38).[44] This might be done where the stated capital exceeds the realizable value of the corporation's assets and the capital impairment test referred to above cannot be satisfied, or where the corporation wants to distribute capital to its shareholders. Except where the reduction is to match a shortfall in realizable assets, a corporation cannot reduce its stated capital if there are reasonable grounds for believing that

- the corporation is, or after the reduction would be, unable to pay its liabilities as they become due; or
- the realizable value of the corporation's assets would thereby be less than the aggregate of its liabilities.

The procedure for making adjustments to the stated capital account is discussed in Chapter 10.

D. REDEMPTION AND REPURCHASE OF SHARES

1) Introduction

In general, a corporation may not hold shares in itself or in a corporation that controls it (referred to in this section as a "parent corporation") (*CBCA*, s. 30).[45] There are two exceptions to this rule: the corporation may

---

43   Provincial rules based on the *CBCA*, *ibid.*, follow this model. E.g., *OBCA*, above note 3, s. 38(3); and *ABCA*, above note 3, s. 43.

44   Provincial rules based on the *CBCA*, *ibid.*, follow this model. E.g., *OBCA*, *ibid.*, s. 34; and *ABCA*, *ibid.*, s. 38. The *BCCA*, *ibid.*, has a similar rule (ss. 233–234).

45   This is known as the prohibition on corporate incest. Provincial rules based on the *CBCA*, *ibid.*, follow this model. E.g., *OBCA*, *ibid.*, s. 32; and *ABCA*, *ibid.*, s.

hold its own shares as security or as a trustee. A corporation may acquire its own shares by purchase or redemption, subject to certain limitations.

2) Holding Shares as Security or as a Trustee

A corporation may hold shares in itself or its parent corporation as trustee or as security for a transaction in the ordinary course of business (*CBCA*, s. 31).[46] To illustrate the second case, consider the following example. You own shares of Canadian Imperial Bank of Commerce (CIBC). You pledge your shares to the CIBC as security for a car loan. If you repay the loan, the CIBC returns the shares to you. If you fail to repay the loan, the CIBC can dispose of the shares and use the proceeds to pay itself back, giving any excess to you. The CIBC holds shares of itself as security for its loan to you, a transaction in the ordinary course of its business.

If a corporation does hold shares as security or as a trustee, it cannot vote them unless the corporation is holding as a trustee and then only in accordance with written instructions from the beneficiary (*CBCA*, s. 33).[47]

3) Purchase or Redemption of Shares

a) Purchase

A corporation can buy its own shares on any terms negotiated by the parties so long as doing so would not breach the financial tests in the *CBCA* (ss. 34 & 35). For most purposes, these are the same financial tests as for solvency and impairment of capital, which must be satisfied for the payment of dividends (*CBCA*, s. 34). If, however, the purchase

- is to settle or compromise a debt asserted by or against the corporation, to eliminate fractional shares;[48]
- to fulfil the terms of a contract between the corporation and a director, officer, or employee;

---

32. The rules in some other provinces (e.g., Nova Scotia and British Columbia) are more permissive.

46 Provincial rules based on the *CBCA*, *ibid.*, follow this model. E.g., *OBCA*, *ibid.*, s. 29; and *ABCA*, *ibid.*, s. 33.

47 Provincial rules based on the *CBCA*, *ibid.*, follow this model. E.g., *OBCA*, *ibid*, s. 29(8); and *ABCA*, *ibid.*, s. 33(3). Under the *2001 Amendments*, additional exceptions to the prohibition on corporate incest may be prescribed by regulation (*CBCA*, *ibid.*, s. 31(4)–(6)). Only one such exemption has been prescribed to date (*Canada Business Corporations Act Regulations*, SOR/2001-512, ss. 35–38).

48 Sometimes, usually as a result of a corporate reorganization, a shareholder may end up with less than a whole share.

- to satisfy the claim of a shareholder who has dissented from some action approved by the shareholders and who is entitled, as a result, to have his shares purchased under section 190 of the *CBCA*; or,
- where the court has found oppression under section 241, to comply with a court order to purchase shares (*CBCA*, ss. 35(2), 190(26), & 241(6)),[49] the capital impairment test is relaxed.

In such a case, the realizable value of the assets of the corporation after the payment need only exceed its liabilities plus the amount required to be paid on a liquidation or on a redemption of all the shares held by holders who have the right to be paid prior to the holders of shares to be purchased (*CBCA*, s. 35(1) & (3)). If a corporation does buy its own shares, it must either cancel them or, if its articles provide for a limited number of shares of that class, restore them to the status of authorized but unissued (*CBCA*, s. 39(6)).[50]

b) Redemption

A corporation may redeem its own shares, which simply means buying them in accordance with an express term permitting the purchase in the corporation's articles (*CBCA*, s. 36).[51] Such a term defines the circumstances in which redemption is permitted and specifies the price. Usually the price is the issue price plus all unpaid cumulative dividends.[52]

Redemption may be at the option of the corporation, in which case the shares are referred to as "redeemable" or "callable"; at the option of the shareholder, in which case they are referred to as "retractible" or "putable"; or on the occurrence of a specified event, such as the expiry of a time period or the failure to pay dividends for a certain number of years.

Before a corporation may redeem any of its shares, the directors must have reasonable grounds for believing that the basic financial tests for solvency and impairment of capital, discussed above in relation to dividends, are satisfied, subject to one modification. For the capital

---

49 Provincial rules based on the *CBCA*, above note 3, follow this model. E.g., *OBCA*, above note 3, ss. 30 & 31; and *ABCA*, above note 3, ss. 34 & 35. The *BCCA*, above note 3, has a similar rule but with a simple solvency test only (ss. 236–238).

50 Provincial rules based on the *CBCA*, ibid., follow this model. E.g., *OBCA*, ibid., s. 35; and *ABCA*, ibid., ss. 39 & 40. The rules under the *BCCA*, ibid., are set out in s. 238.

51 E.g., *OBCA*, ibid., s. 32; and *ABCA*, ibid., s. 36. The rules under the *BCCA*, ibid., are set out in s. 238.

52 Provincial rules based on the *CBCA*, ibid., follow this model. E.g., *OBCA*, ibid., ss. 33 & 35; and *ABCA*, ibid., ss. 37, 39 & 40. The *BCCA*, ibid., has different rules (s. 239).

impairment test to be met, the directors need only have reasonable grounds to believe that the realizable value of the corporation's assets exceeds its liabilities plus the stated capital for classes of shares ranking with or ahead of the shares to be redeemed. So, if a corporation had a class of redeemable preferred shares which ranked ahead of its common shares, and the directors wanted to redeem half of the outstanding preferred shares, they would have to be satisfied that there were reasonable grounds to believe that the realizable value of the corporation's assets was at least equal to the total of the corporation's liabilities plus the stated capital of the preferred shares which were not being redeemed. The directors would not have to be concerned about whether the realizable value of assets also exceeded the stated capital of the common shares.

4) Adjustments to Stated Capital

Whenever a corporation repurchases, redeems, or otherwise acquires its shares, it must deduct from its stated capital account the stated capital per share before the transaction, multiplied by the number of shares acquired (*CBCA*, ss. 37 & 39).[53] Figure 6.3 is an example of the way stated capital is adjusted for a repurchase and a stock dividend.

Figure 6.3   Example of Changes to Stated Capital Account

Corporate Action	Date	Price	Stated Capital Adjustment
Issues			
50 shares	1 January 2000	$5 per share	Add 5(50) = 250
50 shares	1 July 2000	$10 per share	Add 10(50) = 500
Stock dividend			
(1/10 of a share for each of 100 shares held)			
10 shares	1 September 2000	$15 per share*	Add 15(10) = 150
Repurchase			
10 shares	31 December 2000	$20 per share	Subtract 20(10) = 200

At 31 December 2000

Issued shares = [50 + 50 + 10] - 10 = 100
Stated capital = [250 + 500 + 150] - 200 = $700
Stated capital per share = 700/100 = $7.00

---

53   Provincial rules based on the *CBCA*, *ibid.*, follow this model. E.g., *OBCA*, *ibid.*, ss. 33 & 38; and *ABCA*, *ibid.*, ss. 35 & 37.

* When a stock dividend is declared, the declared amount of the dividend stated as an amount of money must be added to the stated capital account maintained for the shares of the class issued in payment of the dividend (*CBCA*, s. 43(2)).[54]

E. CHAPTER SUMMARY

In this chapter, we described the nature of shares as a bundle of rights against the corporation, the characteristics of which are largely determined by provisions in the corporation's articles. The shares of a corporation may be divided into one or more classes with different characteristics, though the rights of holders of shares of each class are equal in all respects. The right to vote, to receive dividends, and to receive the remaining property of the corporation on dissolution must each belong to at least one class of shares, but no class is required to have any particular right. Shares of a single class may be given some different characteristics if the articles of the corporation permit the corporation to issue shares in series. Where they do, the directors may set the characteristics of each series from time to time or the series of characteristics may be set in the articles.

In practice, most corporations have common shares, which have all the basic rights. Often a corporation will also have preferred shares, which are entitled to receive fixed dividends and the return of the capital invested on issuance before any such payment to the holders of the common shares.

There is almost no limit on the characteristics that may be given to shares, including dividend rights, voting rights, and pre-emptive rights. The payment of dividends is always a matter within the discretion of the directors. The *CBCA* prohibits the payment of dividends if the corporation is or would be rendered insolvent or its ability to repay its capital would be impaired. While basic voting rights are as provided in the articles, the *CBCA* requires that shareholders have a right to vote on certain fundamental changes to the corporation, even if they do not otherwise have a right to vote. In addition to this mandatory special voting right, the shareholders of a particular class have a right to vote separately as a class if such fundamental changes affect them differently from other classes. A pre-emptive right is a right of existing

---

54   Provincial rules based on the *CBCA*, *ibid.*, follow this model. E.g., *OBCA*, *ibid.*, s. 38(1), (2); and *ABCA*, *ibid.*, s. 44.

shareholders to have any new shares that the directors are proposing to issue offered to them first. Only to the extent that the shares are not purchased by the current shareholders may they be offered to others. The directors may issue shares for money, property, or past services that are equivalent to what the shares would have been issued for had they been issued for money. Whatever is paid must be paid in full at the time the shares are issued. The historical total of the amount paid to a corporation in return for shares of each class is recorded in the stated capital account.

Although a corporation may not hold its own shares, except in limited circumstances, it can acquire them in a negotiated purchase or in accordance with a redemption process set out in the corporation's articles, so long as doing so would not make the corporation insolvent or impair its ability to repay its capital. Whenever a corporation acquires its own shares, it must adjust its stated capital account accordingly.

FURTHER READINGS

BRYDEN, R.M., "The Law of Dividends" in J.S. Ziegel, ed., *Studies in Canadian Company Law*, vol. 1 (Toronto: Butterworths, 1967) 270

KRISHNA, V., & J. A. VANDUZER, "Corporate Share Capital Structures and Income Splitting: *McClurg* v. *Canada*" (1993) 21 Can. Bus. L.J. 335

WELLING, B., *Corporate Law in Canada: The Governing Principles*, 2d ed. (Toronto: Butterworths, 1991), c. 8

CHAPTER 7

MANAGEMENT AND CONTROL OF THE CORPORATION

A. INTRODUCTION: SHAREHOLDERS, DIRECTORS, AND OFFICERS — THE LEGAL SCHEME OF CORPORATE GOVERNANCE

In this chapter, we discuss how powers are allocated among shareholders, directors, and officers. The *CBCA* and most other modern corporate statutes in Canada provide for a clear division: shareholders choose directors who have the power and responsibility to manage or supervise the management of the corporation; directors appoint officers and delegate to them some of their powers and responsibilities relating to management. Shareholders' control over who the directors are is intended to render the directors accountable to shareholders. In many situations, however, this division of powers operates somewhat differently from what the corporate statutes appear to contemplate. The powers given to shareholders do not provide them with the practical ability to ensure that management is accountable to them. As well, boards of directors often do not play the pivotal role in managing the corporation contemplated by the legislation. In many large corporations, the officers dominate decision making in a manner not specifically addressed in the legislation in any significant way.

We will set out first the basic allocation of powers under Canadian corporate statutes and then discuss some of the problems with the operation of the statutory scheme in practice. The remainder of the chapter consists of a more detailed and technical exposition of how directors and shareholders exercise power under the *CBCA*, followed by a discussion of some qualifications to the legal model of corporate governance.

B. MANAGEMENT AND CONTROL UNDER THE *CBCA*

The traditional breakdown of power to manage and control the corporation is as follows:

- directors are responsible for managing, or supervising the management of, the business and the affairs of the corporation;
- officers exercise the power to manage delegated to them by the directors, and serve at the pleasure of the board; and
- shareholders are the residual claimants to the assets of the corporation, but their only power is to vote for the election of directors and to vote on proposals made to them.[1]

Under this breakdown, shareholders are essentially passive; they have no power to initiate action, to control management, or to act in relation to the ordinary business of the corporation except as specifically provided in the articles or by-laws.

In general, the *CBCA* and the statutes modelled after it adopt this traditional breakdown (*CBCA*, ss. 102, 115, & 121)[2] but enhance the shareholders' traditional passive role in several ways. Approval by shareholders is required before certain significant changes can occur to the corporation, and the *CBCA* gives shareholders a limited scope for actively initiating corporate action. To facilitate shareholder action, the *CBCA* gives shareholders certain rights of access to information. Finally, the *CBCA* improves shareholders' ability to seek relief from the behaviour of management by providing a broad range of remedial options.

---

1   *Automatic Self-Cleansing Filter Syndicate* v. *Cunninghame*, [1906] 2 Ch. 34 (C.A.) (shareholders cannot, by ordinary resolution, vary the mandate of the directors; amendment of the articles required); *Kelly* v. *Electrical Construction Co.* (1907), 16 O.L.R. 232 (H.C.J.) (shareholders cannot initiate the creation of a by-law).

2   E.g., Ontario *Business Corporations Act*, R.S.O. 1990, c. B-16 [*OBCA*]; Alberta *Business Corporations Act*, R.S.A. 2000, c. B-9 [*ABCA*]; Saskatchewan *The Business Corporations Act*, R.S.S. 1978, c. B-10; Manitoba *The Corporations Act*, R.S.M. 1987, c. C225; the Northwest Territories and Nunavut Business *Corporations Act*, S.N.W.T. 1996, c. 19; the Yukon *Business Corporations Act*, R.S.Y. 1986, c. 15; Newfoundland *Corporations Act*, R.S.N. 1990, c. C-36; and New Brunswick *Business Corporations Act*, S.N.B. 1981, c. B-9.1.

The situations in which the *CBCA* specifically provides for share-holder approval include the following fundamental changes to the corporation:

- amendment of articles (*CBCA*, s. 173);
- creation, amendment, and repeal of by-laws (*CBCA*, s. 103);
- sale, lease, or exchange of "all or substantially all the property of a corporation" other than in the ordinary course of business (*CBCA*, s. 189(3));
- amalgamation with another corporation (*CBCA*, s. 183); and
- dissolution of the corporation (*CBCA*, s. 211).[3]

The *CBCA* also provides for an active role for shareholders in two ways.

- Proposals: shareholders can have matters put on the agenda for dis-cussion at shareholders' meetings, including making, amending, or repealing by-laws (*CBCA*, ss. 137 & 103(5));
- Unanimous shareholders' agreements: shareholders can assume all powers of the board of directors, completely altering the allocation of powers as between directors and shareholders, if they unanimous-ly agree (*CBCA*, s. 146). Such an agreement may then allocate the assumed powers among the shareholders.

Both proposals and unanimous shareholders' agreements are discussed later in this chapter in detail.

The *CBCA* gives shareholders rights of access to information about the corporation, including information about past meetings of share-holders and financial records (*CBCA*, ss. 20, 21, 143, 160, & 243; Part XIX). These shareholder rights are discussed later in this chapter.

The *CBCA* provides remedies for abuse of directors' power to man-age such as the following:

- a right to apply to have the corporation's existence terminated (s. 214);
- a right to bring an action on behalf of the corporation, in some cir-cumstances, for breach by directors or officers of duties owed to the corporation (a "derivative action," s. 239);
- a right to seek relief from "oppression" of the interests of sharehold-ers or others by the corporation or the directors (s. 241);
- a right to seek an order directing directors and officers to comply with or to restrain them from breaching the *CBCA*, the articles, by-laws, or any unanimous shareholders' agreement (s. 247); and

---

3   All these corporate changes are discussed in Chapter 10.

- a right to seek rectification of corporate records (ss. 243).[4]

Notwithstanding these adjustments, under the scheme of the *CBCA*, directors retain the power to manage the corporation and the share-holders' power consists primarily of their ability to determine the composition of the board of directors and to vote on matters put to them. If a majority of shareholders are unhappy with the board of directors' management, they can replace the board at the next annual meeting, or can requisition a special meeting for this purpose (*CBCA*, s. 143 (requisition); s. 109 (removal by ordinary resolution)).

C. SHAREHOLDERS AND HOW THEY EXERCISE POWER

1) Shareholders' Meetings and Resolutions

To exercise their power to vote, shareholders must act collectively. Most commonly this is done by having a meeting at which a vote takes place on matters to be decided by shareholders. This section sets out the *CBCA* rules regarding shareholders' meetings.[5]

a) Types of Meetings
The first annual meeting of shareholders must be held within eighteen months of incorporation. Thereafter, each annual meeting must be held no later than fifteen months after the previous one or six months after the end of the corporation's preceding financial year (*CBCA*, s. 133). Annual meetings are identified and defined by the occurrence of three items of business:

- the election of directors;
- the receipt of financial statements and the auditor's report on the statements; and
- the re-appointment of an incumbent auditor (unless dispensed with by unanimous agreement of shareholders in certain circumstances) (*CBCA*, s. 135(5)).

Meetings to conduct any business other than these three items are called "special meetings" (*CBCA*, s. 135(5)). These may be called by

---

4   All these remedies are discussed in Chapter 9.
5   See the rules in *OBCA*, above note 2, ss. 92–107; *ABCA*, above note 2, ss. 131–144; and the British Columbia *Company Act*, R.S.B.C. 1996, c. 62 [*BCCA*], ss. 139–153, 161.

the directors any time (*CBCA*, s. 133(2)). To the extent that any special business is carried on at an annual meeting it is called an "annual and special meeting."

b) Calling Meetings

The directors are responsible for calling annual and special meetings of shareholders, but shareholders holding not less than 5 percent of shares that carry the right to vote at the meeting may require the directors to call a meeting (*CBCA*, s. 143). This kind of shareholder action is called a requisition. If the directors fail to call a meeting within twenty-one days of any such requisition by a shareholder, any shareholder may call a meeting and the corporation must reimburse the shareholder for the expenses of doing so (*CBCA*, s. 143(4)). Also, any director or shareholder entitled to vote may apply to a court to have a meeting called if it is impracticable to call a meeting within the time, or in the ways mentioned above, or to have a meeting conducted as prescribed in the by-laws or the *CBCA* (s. 144).

c) Place of Meetings

Shareholders' meetings must be at the place specified in the by-laws. In default of such specification, meetings must be in a Canadian location specified by the directors, or, with unanimous shareholder consent or, if permitted by the corporation's articles, at a place outside Canada (*CBCA*, s. 132). If permitted in the corporation's by-laws, whoever calls the meeting may decide that it will be held by any "telephonic, electronic or other communication facility" so long as it permits all participants to communicate adequately with each other during the meeting (*CBCA*, s. 132(5)).

d) Notice of Meetings

The *CBCA* provides minimum and maximum notice periods for meetings. The maximum is sixty days and the minimum is twenty-one days (*CBCA*, s. 135; *CBCA Regulation* s. 44).[6] Notice may be waived, and attendance by a shareholder is deemed to be a waiver of notice unless the shareholder attends for the purpose of claiming that the meeting is improperly called (*CBCA*, s. 136). Notice must go to

- each shareholder entitled to vote;
- each director; and
- the auditor of the corporation (*CBCA*, s. 135(1)).

---

6   For non-distributing corporations, the notice period may be shorter if provided in the corporation's articles or by-laws (*CBCA*, s. 135(1.1)). The differences between distributing and non-distributing corporations are discussed in Chapter 4.

Under section 135 of the *CBCA*, shareholders who are entitled to notice are those who appear in the shareholders' register on a certain date called the "record date." The record date is most significant for public corporations, the shares of which may change hands on a daily basis. The directors may fix a record date by resolution which is no more than sixty days or less than twenty-one days before the meeting (*CBCA*, s. 134; *CBCA Regulations*, s. 43). If, as is common, the directors do not do so, the *CBCA* provides that the record date is at the close of business on the day immediately preceding the day on which notice is given (s. 134(2)(a)). If a shareholder is not entitled to notice under this scheme, because he acquired his shares after the record date, he does not have the right to attend and vote at the meeting unless he has a validly executed proxy from the transferor as discussed in the next section (*CBCA*, s. 138(3) & (3.1)). Where the meeting is a special meeting, the notice must state the nature of the special business and the text of any special resolution to be put to the meeting for a vote (*CBCA*, s. 135(6)).

e) Proxies and Proxy Solicitation

Any shareholder not able to be personally present at a meeting may appoint another person, who need not be a shareholder, to represent her at the meeting and vote her shares (*CBCA*, s. 148(1)). The appointment, called a "proxy," must be in writing and signed by the shareholder. A proxy may be revoked at any time before the meeting with respect to which it was given. The person appointed to exercise the shareholder's vote (also referred to as a "proxy" or "proxy holder") has all the powers of a shareholder at the meeting, but the authority of the proxy is limited to that conferred by the terms of the proxy. The proxy holder must vote in accordance with any direction given by the shareholder. Failure to do so is an offence (*CBCA*, s. 152(4)). Voting by proxy is exclusively a statutory right. There is no common law right to vote by proxy.

For all corporations incorporated under the *CBCA* which have more than fifty shareholders or which are distributing corporations, management must send shareholders a "management proxy circular" and a form of proxy (*CBCA*, ss. 148, 149, & 150).[7] As the number of shareholders of a corporation grows, the proxy-solicitation process is an

---

7   Prior to the enactment of the 2001 amendments (S.C. 2001, c. 14) [*2001 Amendments*] to the *Canada Business Corporations Act*, R.S.C. 1985, c. 44 [*CBCA*], the threshold was fifteen shareholders. Fifteen shareholders remains the threshold under some provincial laws modelled on the *CBCA*. E.g., *ABCA*, above note 2, s. 149.

increasingly important way of enhancing shareholder participation by providing both general and specific information regarding management proposals, as well as directly facilitating the exercise by shareholders of their voting rights through the proxy.

Under the *CBCA*, management is required to send annual financial statements to shareholders in connection with annual meetings (*CBCA*, s. 155). Most public corporations include the financial statements in a glossy annual report that also contains material such as statements from management and descriptions of the corporation's operations. Provincial securities laws have similar requirements regarding management proxy circulars, financial statements, and other material to be sent to shareholders.[8]

The contents of the management proxy circular are prescribed by regulation (*CBCA Regulations*, ss. 57–59) and include the following categories of information:

- a description of shareholders' rights to appoint a proxy and the procedure for doing so;
- transactions with insiders of the corporation (e.g., affiliated corporations, significant shareholders, directors, and officers);
- disclosure of shareholders holding more than 5 percent of the issued shares of the corporation;
- details about the directors who are proposed for election; and
- details about any special business to be dealt with at the meeting.

Shareholders who disagree with management proposals may also solicit the votes of their fellow shareholders. Such so-called "dissident shareholders" are entitled to obtain a list of shareholders, the shares they hold, and their addresses from the corporation and to contact other shareholders for the purpose of influencing their voting (*CBCA*, s. 21(3) & (9)). If a shareholder does solicit proxies, however, she must send out a "dissident's proxy circular" in the form prescribed by the regulations (*CBCA*, s. 150(1)(b), *CBCA Regulations*, ss. 61–64). The *2001 Amendments* permit greater scope for shareholders to communicate with each other without triggering these proxy circular requirements. Now the *CBCA* allows targetted solicitations to less than sixteen shareholders and solicitations by public broadcast, speech, or publication in prescribed circumstances, such as a speech in a public forum or a press release (*CBCA Regulation*, s. 67). There are certain other exemptions from the requirement to send out a dissident proxy circular specified in

---

8   Disclosure requirements under provincial securities laws are discussed in Chapter 11.

the *CBCA Regulations*. Communications regarding the business or affairs of the corporation which do not contain a form of proxy, for example, do not trigger this obligation (*CBCA Regulations*, s. 68).

Dissident proxy circulars have been relatively rare in the Canadian marketplace. They sometimes occur in connection with hostile takeover bids. When they do occur, they are often accompanied by advertising campaigns conducted by management and dissidents in the financial press. Under the more relaxed new rules in the *CBCA*, proxy battles waged in the press may become more common.

The rules about proxies and proxy solicitation may be enforced in the same way as other shareholder rights. A shareholder may seek a court order directing the directors to comply with the rules (*CBCA*, s. 247). In addition, section 154 of the *CBCA* specifically provides that a shareholder may apply to a court to restrain the distribution of a proxy circular that contains "an untrue statement of a material fact or omits to state a material fact ... [that is] ... necessary to make a statement contained therein not misleading in the light of the circumstances in which it was made." The court can also restrain the implementation of any resolution that was passed at a meeting held after the distribution of such a circular, or make any other order it sees fit.

Some progress has been made in adapting the proxy system to permit the use of modern communications technologies. The *OBCA* was amended in 1999 to allow proxies and revocation of proxies to be signed electronically.[9] Similar amendments were made to the *CBCA* in the *2001 Amendments*. As well, under the amendments, any notice or document required to be created or provided to shareholders or anyone else is satisfied by the creation or provision of an electronic document, so long as the articles or by-laws of the corporation do not provide otherwise (*CBCA*, s. 252.4). Notices and documents, including proxies and other shareholder communications, can be sent electronically only if the addressee has consented and designated an information system (such as e-mail) to receive the notice or document which is used by the sender (*CBCA*, s. 252.3). Documents may be posted on a website so long as each shareholder is notified individually of the posting via the designated information system (*CBCA Regulations*, s. 7(2)). Electronic signatures are permitted so long as certain conditions are met (*CBCA*, s. 252.7).[10]

---

9   S.O. 1999, c. 12, Schedule F.

10   Requirements for electronic documents are set out in Part XX.1 of the *CBCA*, above note 7, and ss. 6–12 of the *Canada Business Corporations Regulations*, SOR/2001-512 [*CBCA Regulations*]. Prior to the amendments, in *Newbridge Networks Corp., (Re)* (2000), 48 O.R. (3d) 47 (Sup. Ct. J.), a court authorized an

f) Shareholder Proposals

Normally, the agenda for shareholder meetings is set by the directors. This is especially true in large corporations where shareholders are remote from management. The *CBCA* provides a limited right for shareholders to add items to the agenda (*CBCA*, s. 137), including the amendment of by-laws and articles (*CBCA*, ss. 103(5) & 175(1)). Any shareholder entitled to vote may submit to the corporation notice — called a proposal — of any matter she proposes to discuss. If the corporation is required to send out a management proxy circular under the rules described above (*CBCA*, s. 150), the proposal must be included, along with a supporting statement from the proposing shareholder. Together, the proposal and the supporting statement may not exceed 500 words. Essentially, the proposal mechanism is intended to facilitate communication among shareholders at the expense of the corporation.

There are certain limits on the content of a proposal, designed, in part, to prevent frivolous use of this process. The proposal may include nominations for the election of directors only if the proposal is signed by the holders of not less than 5 percent of the shares entitled to vote. To be eligible to submit any proposal, on any matter, a shareholder or group of shareholders must

- hold voting shares equal to at least 1 percent of the total of voting shares outstanding at the date the proposal is submitted and worth at least $2000 at the close of business on the day before it is submitted; and
- have held the shares for at least six months prior to the date of submitting the proposal (*CBCA*, s. 137(1.1), *CBCA Regulations*, s. 46).

The corporation may require proof that these requirements are met (*CBCA*, s. 137(1.4)). Prior to the amendments, a single shareholder with one share could make a proposal.

Under the *2001 Amendments*, a beneficial holder of shares, who is not the registered owner, may submit a proposal. Previously, it had been held that only a registered shareholder was entitled to do so.[11] The change is an important one because of the significant numbers of shareholders who have their shares registered in the name of investment dealers and other financial intermediaries.

---

electronic procedure for option holders to receive notice of a meeting and to vote under the arrangement provisions of the *CBCA*. Arrangements are discussed in Chapter 10.

11   *Verdun v. Toronto Dominion Bank*, [1996] 3 S.C.R. 550.

A corporation does not have to circulate a proposal in five circumstances:

- the proposal is not submitted to the corporation at least ninety days before the anniversary date of the notice of the last annual meeting;
- it clearly appears that the proposal is
  - primarily for the purpose of enforcing a personal claim or redressing a personal grievance against the corporation, the directors, officers, or security holders; or
  - does not relate in any significant way to the business or affairs of the corporation;
- the proposing shareholder made a proposal within the last two years, then failed to show up, in person or by proxy, to speak to it at the meeting;
- substantially the same proposal was submitted within the last five years to a meeting of shareholders and the prescribed level of support was not obtained (3 percent of total shares voted at the first annual meeting at which the proposal is presented); or
- the right to make a proposal is being abused to secure publicity (*CBCA*, s. 137(5) and *CBCA Regulations*, ss. 49–51).[12]

The limits on what may be subject to a proposal apply equally to what may be the subject of a shareholder-requisitioned meeting.

Prior to the *2001 Amendments*, the *CBCA* contained another limitation: a corporation could refuse to distribute a proposal if it was primarily for the purpose of promoting general economic, political, racial, religious, social, or similar causes. This exclusion remains in the ABCA and several other provincial statutes based on the *CBCA*, but the OBCA follows the *2001 Amendments*. Several cases considered the scope of this limit on the use of proposals. In *Varity Corp.* v. *Jesuit Fathers of Upper Canada*,[13] a shareholder sought to have a corporation circulate a proposal to have the corporation divest its investments in South Africa. It was held that the primary purpose of the proposal, based on the language used and the supporting statement, was the abolition of apartheid in South Africa. Since the proposal was primarily for the purpose of promoting a political or social cause, the corporation was not

---

12   These rules are similar to those under the *OBCA*, above note 2, s. 99; and *ABCA*, above note 2, s. 136. Under the *BCCA*, above note 5, shareholder proposals are also permitted. While the requirements for standing to make a proposal are more strict, the rules regarding what can be raised in a proposal are more permissive (s. 156).

13   (1987), 59 O.R. (2d) 459 (H.C.J.), aff'd (1987), 60 O.R. (2d) 640 (C.A.).

obliged to distribute it. The court acknowledged that there was also a more specific purpose relating to the business of the corporation — the divestment of its interests in South Africa — but held that this objective did not prevent the exception from operating. Similarly, in *Re Greenpeace Foundation of Canada & Inco Ltd.*,[14] a proposal to institute pollution-control measures to limit sulphur dioxide emissions was held to be for the purpose of advancing an environmental cause and so fell within the exception. In the same case, the court ruled that the corporation could also refuse to circulate the proposal because a resolution to impose restrictions on emissions, although at a different level, had been defeated at a previous meeting. The *2001 Amendments* replace the social-cause exclusion with the exclusion for matters not relating to the business or affairs of the corporation in a significant way. It remains to be seen if the new scheme of the *CBCA* will lead to increased use of the proposal mechanism.

Some recent cases suggest that the attitude of the courts may be shifting slightly in favour of shareholder participation through the proposal mechanism, at least in relation to corporate governance issues. In 1997 the Superior Court of Quebec upheld the right of a shareholder of one of the banks to make proposals raising a range of corporate governance issues which the bank had sought to exclude. Among other things, the proposals dealt with increasing managerial accountability and reducing levels of executive pay.[15]

In contrast to the United States, the proposal mechanism has been used rarely in Canada. A study of 480 public corporations in Canada found only one proposal submitted in 1990 and none in 1991 or 1992.[16] A more recent study found that in 1998 there were eight shareholder proposals made by shareholders in 264 of the 294 corporations comprising the Toronto Stock Exchange 300 which were the subject of the study.[17]

g) Conduct of Meetings

Meetings are conducted by the same rules regarding quorum and procedure as apply to Parliament, except where the *CBCA* or the by-laws

---

14 (23 February 1984), (Ont. H.C.J.) [unreported] [summarized at (1984), 24 A.C.W.S. (2d) 349], aff'd 21 March 1984, (Ont. C.A.) [unreported] [summarized at (1984), 25 A.C.W.S. (2d) 322].

15 *Michaud v. Banque Nationale du Canada*, [1997] R.J.Q. 547 (S.C.).

16 C. McCall & R. Wilson, "Shareholder Proposals: Why Not in Canada?" (1993) 5 Corp. Governance Rev. 12.

17 D.S. Gauris, "1998 Proxy Season Review" (1998) 10 Corp. Governance Rev. 6.

provide otherwise. A discussion right is expressly provided for in section 137(1)(b): a shareholder is entitled to discuss any matter with respect to which she could have submitted a proposal at an annual meeting. The corresponding provision in the *OBCA* gives a discussion right at both special and annual meetings (s. 99(1)(b)).[18]

In addition to this statutory right, shareholders have a right to speak to the matters on the agenda; the chair cannot arbitrarily terminate the meeting to prevent shareholders from discussing an agenda item and voting on it.[19] The right to discuss may be terminated by the chair if she determines, in good faith, that it is being abused, such as where a shareholder seeks to obstruct the meeting.[20]

Under the *2001 Amendments*, the directors or shareholders calling a meeting may determine that it shall be held electronically if the by-laws allow it and the communications facility to be provided permits all participants to communicate with each other adequately during the meeting (*CBCA*, s. 132(5)). Unless the by-laws provide otherwise, any person entitled to attend any meeting may participate by means of such a communications facility if the corporation makes one available (*CBCA*, s. 132(4)). Any such person is deemed to be in attendance at the meeting.

h) Quorum

A majority of shares entitled to vote, represented in person or by proxy at the meeting, constitute a quorum unless the by-laws provide otherwise (*CBCA*, s. 139).[21] Most by-laws provide that a certain number of shareholders, often only two, must be present in person or by proxy to constitute a quorum for holding a meeting.

i) Voting

Unless the articles provide otherwise, each share gets one vote and matters are decided by a majority of votes cast on any resolution at the meeting. Special resolutions, required for amendments to articles and certain other fundamental changes, must be passed by two-thirds of

---

18   The *ABCA*, above note 2, follows the *CBCA*, above note 8 (s. 136(1)(b)).
19   *National Dwellings Society* v. *Sykes*, [1894] 3 Ch. 159 (Ch.); *Bomac Batten Ltd.* v. *Pozhke* (1983), 43 O.R. (2d) 344 (H.C.J.); *Canadian Express Ltd.* v. *Blair* (1989), 46 B.L.R. 92 (Ont. H.C.J.) [*Blair*]. The chair is obliged to act in a quasi-judicial fashion.
20   *Wall* v. *London and Northern Assets Corp.*, [1898] 2 Ch. 469 (C.A.).
21   Provincial statutes modelled on the *CBCA*, above note 8, are similar. E.g., *OBCA*, above note 2, s. 101; and *ABCA*, above note 2, s. 138. The *BCCA*, above note 5, is also similar. Section 144 provides that two is the quorum unless the articles provide otherwise.

the votes cast at the meeting (*CBCA*, ss. 140, 173, 183, & 189).[22] Unless the by-laws provide otherwise, voting is by a show of hands, but any shareholder may require that a ballot be taken — meaning that each vote is recorded on a ballot, which is collected and counted (*CBCA*, s. 141).[23]

Under the *2001 Amendments*, unless the by-laws provide otherwise, any vote may be held entirely by means of a telephonic, electronic, or other comunication facility made available by the corporation in accordance with the regulations. Any person participating in a meeting electronically and entitled to vote may vote electronically, unless there is a contrary provision in the by-laws (*CBCA*, s. 141(3) & (4) and *CBCA Regulations*, s. 45). Under the *CBCA Regulations*, electronic voting is subject to two requirements: the gathering of votes must be verifiable; and the corporation must not be able to identify how shareholders voted.

2) Access to Information

a) Introduction
The *CBCA* requires a corporation to provide shareholders with access to certain information to enhance their ability to monitor management and to exercise their rights as shareholders. Specifically, a corporation must maintain certain records and allow access to them by shareholders as well as certain other people, such as directors, officers, and creditors.

b) Specific Requirements
The articles, by-laws, any unanimous shareholders' agreement, minutes of meetings of shareholders, all notices of directors and notices of registered office, and a share register showing the owners of all shares must be maintained by the corporation (*CBCA*, s. 20(1)). All these documents may be examined and copied by shareholders and creditors, and their legal representatives, during business hours (*CBCA*, s. 21(1)). If the corporation is a distributing corporation, the copies are free; otherwise a reasonable charge may be imposed. Every shareholder, however, is entitled to one copy of the articles, by-laws, and any unanimous shareholders' agreement free of charge (*CBCA*, ss. 21(1) & (2)).[24]

---

22 Fundamental changes are discussed in Chapter 10.

23 Provincial statutes modelled on the *CBCA*, above note 8, are similar. E.g., *OBCA*, above note 2, s. 103; and *ABCA*, above note 2, s. 140. The *BCCA*, above note 5, is also similar (s. 158).

24 Similar rules can be found in the *OBCA*, *ibid.*, ss. 140, 146 & 258, and the *ABCA*, *ibid.*, ss. 21 & 23. The *BCCA*, *ibid.*, ss. 164–169 also has rules regarding access to basic documents.

Any list of shareholders or information from a share register that has been obtained cannot be used except in an effort to influence the voting of shareholders, in connection with an offer to acquire shares of the corporation, or for any other purpose relating to the affairs of the corporation. A person wishing to examine the securities register or obtain a list of shareholders must make a request to the corporation accompanied by an affidavit stating, among other things, that this restriction on use will be respected (*CBCA*, s. 21(1.1), (3) & (7)). All other inspection rights may be used for any other purpose, including competition with the corporation.[25] There is no right to inspect the minutes of directors' meetings. This exclusion reflects the exclusive allocation of management power to directors. Other rights of access to information include the right to requisition meetings and to ask questions (*CBCA*, s. 143) and the right to have inspectors and auditors appointed (*CBCA*, Part XIX). The inspection right is discussed in Chapter 9.

A corporation is also required to make certain limited disclosures to the public which shareholders may take advantage of. These disclosures were discussed in Chapter 4. Under the *CBCA*, the following items must be filed:

- articles (including all amendments);
- notices of directors and change of directors;
- notices of registered office and change of registered office;
- annual information returns (*CBCA*, s. 263; Form 22); and
- annual financial statements for distributing corporations (*CBCA*, s. 160).

In Ontario, additional publicly available information filings are required under the Ontario *Corporations Information Act*[26] and, for public corporations, under the Ontario *Securities Act*.[27] Other provinces have similar rules.

In connection with meetings of shareholders where shares are registered in the name of an intermediary, such as an investment adviser, the intermediary has an obligation to send information that it receives relating to a meeting to the beneficial owner. The intermediary is not permitted to vote the shares of the beneficial owner except in accordance with instructions from the owner (*CBCA*, s. 153).[28]

---

25 *Johnston v. West Fraser Timber Co.* (1980), 22 B.C.L.R. 337 (S.C.).

26 R.S.O. 1990, c. C.39.

27 R.S.O. 1990, c. S.5.

28 There is no similar provision in the *OBCA*, above note 2.

3) Signed Resolutions and Single Shareholder Meetings

In general, any action taken by shareholders must be given effect by a resolution passed at a meeting. Under the *CBCA*, if a class or series of shares has but a single shareholder, he alone can constitute a meeting, notwithstanding the etymological impossibility (*CBCA*, s. 139(4)). The *CBCA* also provides an alternative to meetings. Where a single shareholder or each shareholder, if there is more than one, signs a written resolution, it will be just as effective as if it had been passed at a meeting (*CBCA*, s. 142).[29] Proceeding in this way eliminates the need for shareholders to get together to meet and to worry about notices and other formalities associated with meetings. It is a commonplace expedient in small corporations, especially if the shareholders are not in the same location. Such a signed resolution becomes effective once the last shareholder has signed it.

D. DIRECTORS AND HOW THEY EXERCISE POWER

1) Qualifications

A person is not qualified to be a director if she is

- less than eighteen years of age;
- of unsound mind as found by a court in Canada or elsewhere;
- an undischarged bankrupt; or
- not an individual (*CBCA*, s. 105).

With regard to the last qualification, even though a corporation cannot be a director, a corporation may be an incorporator (*CBCA*, s. 5)).[30] There is no statutory requirement for directors to hold shares in the corporation, though the articles may provide for such a requirement (*CBCA*, s. 105(2)).

In most cases, under the *CBCA*, at least 25 percent of the directors must be resident Canadians (*CBCA*, s. 105(3)). In certain sectors prescribed by regulation and subject to some exceptions, the requirement is for a majority of the directors to be resident Canadians: uranium

---

29   There are similar rules in the *OBCA*, *ibid.*, ss. 101 & 104; *ABCA*, above note 2, ss. 138 & 141; and the *BCCA*, above note 5, ss. 140, 141 & 148(3).

30   Provincial statutes modelled on the *CBCA*, above note 8, have the same rule. E.g., *OBCA*, *ibid.*, s. 4(1); and *ABCA*, *ibid.*, s. 5(1).

mining, book publishing and distribution, book sales, and film distribution (*CBCA*, s. 105(3.1)–(4), *CBCA Regulation* s. 16). In most jurisdictions where legislation is based on the *CBCA*, a majority of directors for all corporations must be resident Canadians, which was the *CBCA* rule before the *2001 Amendments* came into force.[31] The *CBCA* requirement that a majority of each board committee be resident Canadians was repealed with the *2001 Amendments*, as well. These changes provide significant new flexibility which may be useful for *CBCA* corporations with foreign shareholders.

"[R]esident Canadian" is defined in section 1(1) to include Canadian citizens ordinarily resident in Canada and a permanent resident within the meaning of the *Immigration Act*[32] who is ordinarily resident in Canada.[33] There are no residency requirements under the corporate laws of Quebec, the Maritime provinces, or the territories.

A director ceases to hold office on becoming disqualified (*CBCA*, s. 108(1)(c)). However, any act of a director after she becomes disqualified is valid, notwithstanding the defect in her qualification (*CBCA*, s. 116).[34] So, for example, if the board approved a contract with a thrid party and one of the directors was disqualified, the contract would, nevertheless, be enforceable against the corporation.

Individuals cannot be made directors of *CBCA* corporations without their consent. People who are elected or appointed are deemed not to be directors unless

- they were at the meeting at which the election or appointment took place and did not refuse;
- they consented in writing either before their election or appointment or within ten days afterwards; or
- they acted as directors pursuant to the election or appointment (*CBCA*, s. 106(9)).

---

31 E.g., *OBCA*, *ibid.*, s. 118(3); and *ABCA*, *ibid.*, s. 105(3). The *BCCA*, above note 5, has similar requirements and, as well, stipulates that at least one director must be a resident of British Columbia (s. 109). Note that the *CBCA*, *ibid.*, provides that where federal law requires a specified level of Canadian ownership or control or restricts the number of shares any one shareholder may own or control, then a majority of directors must be resident Canadians (s. 105(3.1)).

32 R.S.C. 1985, c. I-2.

33 An exception is provided for persons who have been permanent residents for more than one year after they became entitled to apply for Canadian citizenship. *CBCA Regulations*, above note 10, s. 13, lists other categories of "resident Canadians."

34 Similar rules are found in other provincial statutes. E.g., *OBCA*, above note 2, ss. 121(1)(c) & 128; *ABCA*, above note 2, ss. 108(6)(c) & 116; and *BCCA*, above note 5, ss. 130(1)(c) & 124.

2) Election and Appointment of Directors

a) General

The election and appointment of directors under the *CBCA* and statutes modelled after it follow certain technical rules. The first directors of a corporation are those listed in the Notice of Directors filed with the articles. They become directors at the time the certificate of incorporation is issued and incorporation occurs (*CBCA*, s. 106(2)).[35] These directors hold office until the first meeting of shareholders, which must be held not more than eighteen months after incorporation (*CBCA*, s. 133).[36] At that meeting, and at each subsequent annual meeting at which an election is required, shareholders must, by simple majority, elect directors. The term of directors cannot extend for longer than the date of the third annual meeting following their election. In most cases, directors must be elected annually. If no term is specified on their election, the directors stay in office only until the annual meeting following their election (*CBCA*, s. 106(3)). If, however, the shareholders fail to elect directors when they are supposed to, for whatever reason, the incumbents remain in place until their replacements are elected, so there is no problem with the authority of the board of directors to act in the interim (*CBCA*, s. 106(6)).[37]

Under the *2001 Amendments*, where a corporation has no directors, any person who actually manages or supervises the management of the business and affairs of the corporation is deemed to be a director (*CBCA*, s. 109(4)). Exceptions are an officer acting under the direction of a shareholder, lawyers and accountants providing professional services, and creditor representatives (*CBCA*, s. 109(5)).[38]

b) Filling Vacancies on the Board

A vacancy on the board may occur for a variety of reasons: a director may resign, be removed by shareholders, or become disqualified. If there is no quorum remaining in place or a vacancy has occurred because somehow the shareholders failed to elect the required number

---

35 The process under the *ABCA ibid.*, is the same (s. 106). Under the *OBCA*, *ibid.*, the first directors are named in the articles (s.119). The first directors of companies incorporated under the *BCCA*, *ibid.*, are the subscribers to the memorandum (s. 110).

36 Annual meeting requirements are discussed above under "Shareholders Meetings and Resolutions."

37 Provincial statutes modelled on the *CBCA*, above note 8, have similar rules. E.g., *OBCA*, above note 2, s. 119(8); and *ABCA*, above note 2, s. 106(6).

38 The amendment follows the *OBCA*, *ibid.*, s. 115(4) & (5).

of directors at the shareholders' meeting, the remaining directors must call a shareholders' meeting to fill the vacancy (*CBCA*, s. 111(2)). If a quorum remains in place, the remaining directors may fill the vacancy by appointing a new director for the unexpired term of the director whose departure created the vacancy (*CBCA*, s. 111(1)). The articles may provide that all vacancies must be filled by shareholders (*CBCA*, s. 111(4)).[39] As well, so long as a quorum remains, the board can still act as a board.

Significant changes, including the wholesale replacement of the board, may be effected without getting shareholder approval, if one can obtain the cooperation of both the departing and the incoming directors and follow a process of sequential resignations and appointments. For example, assume that it is desired to change all the members of a board of five directors and that the required quorum is four directors. One director may resign and the remaining four appoint her successor. Then a second director resigns, and the remaining four, including the newly appointed director, fill the vacancy. In this way, the whole board may be replaced without a shareholder vote. This might be desirable if several directors wanted to resign and the board wanted to continue to operate until the next annual meeting, avoiding the expense of calling a special meeting just to elect new directors.

3) Number of Directors

Apart from one restriction, the choice of the number of directors is a matter for the shareholders to decide. Under the *CBCA* and statutes modelled after it, if the corporation has made a distribution of its shares to the public and those shares remain outstanding and are held by more than one person, the corporation must have three directors, at least two of whom are not officers or employees of the corporation (*CBCA*, s. 102(2)).[40]

The number of directors or a maximum and minimum number of directors must be specified in the articles of the corporation (e.g., *CBCA*, s. 6(1)(e)). The corporation may change the number or the minimum and maximum number of directors by articles of amend-

---

39   Provincial statutes modelled on the *CBCA*, above note 8, have similar rules. E.g., *OBCA*, *ibid.*, s. 124; and *ABCA*, above note 2, s. 111. See also, *BCCA*, above note 5, s. 131. Under the *OBCA*, *ibid.*, there are some restrictions on filling vacancies caused by increases in the size of the board.

40   The same requirment is imposed in the *OBCA*, *ibid.*, s. 115(2), and *ABCA*, *ibid.*, s. 101(2). Under the *BCCA*, *ibid.*, there is no requirement for outside directors.

ment. The process of amending articles is described in Chapter 10. In general, amendments require the approval of shareholders by special resolution. There is no specific mechanism for fixing the number of directors within a minimum and maximum set in the articles.[41]

4) Directors' Meetings

Like shareholders, directors exercise their power collectively, primarily at meetings. Modern corporate statutes set out a code for directors' meetings (e.g., *CBCA*, s. 114).[42]

a) Place
Unless the articles or by-laws specify a particular place, meetings may be held at whatever place the directors decide. There is no statutory default requirement under the *CBCA* (s. 114(1)).

b) Notice
Notice of meetings must be as specified in the corporation's by-laws under the *CBCA*. There is no default provision (s. 114). Under the *OBCA*, in default of any provision in the by-laws, ten days' notice must be given (*OBCA*, s. 126(9)). Notice may be waived and is deemed waived by attendance at a meeting, except if a director attends the meeting for the purpose of objecting to the meeting on the basis that it is not lawfully called (*CBCA*, s. 114(6)).

c) Conducting Meetings
At directors' meetings, as at shareholders' meetings, certain procedures must be followed. Some minimum number of directors, called a quorum, must be present or no business may be carried on. A quorum may be set out in the articles or the by-laws. In default of such provision, a quorum consists of a majority of directors, if the articles specify a fixed number of directors, or a majority of the minimum number of directors permitted by the articles (*CBCA*, s. 114(2)).[43] Regardless of what quorum is, the directors may not carry on business unless 25 percent of the

---

41   Under the *OBCA*, *ibid.*, the number is fixed by a special resolution of shareholders. In the same way, the shareholders may give the directors the power to fix the number of directors (s. 124(3)).

42   Similar schemes are found in provincial statutes modelled on the *CBCA*, above note 8. E.g., *OBCA*, *ibid.*, s. 126; and *ABCA*, above note 2, s. 114.

43   Under the *OBCA*, *ibid.*, there is less flexibility. Quorum cannot be less than two-fifths of the number of directors or the minimum number of directors (s. 126(3)).

directors present are resident Canadians (*CBCA*, s. 114(3)). For corporations operating in particular sectors, where the *CBCA* requires a majority of the board to be resident Canadians, a majority of directors present must be resident Canadians.[44] These requirements may be satisfied, however, if, after a meeting, the requisite numbers of resident Canadians approve any business transacted at the meeting.

If all the directors consent, they may participate in meetings by telephone or another communication facility that permits all to commmunicate with each other adequately during the meeting (*CBCA*, s. 114(9)). It is common to obtain a general form of consent to such telephonic or electronic meetings from a person when he or she becomes a director.

When business is transacted at a meeting, it must be approved by the majority of directors' votes which is specified in the articles or by-laws. There is no statutory default in the *CBCA*.

Directors can transact whatever business they like, except that, at the first meeting following incorporation, the agenda is specified in section 104. This agenda is discussed in Chapter 4. Also, directors must call an annual meeting of shareholders at least every fifteen months, and directors must approve financial statements annually.[45]

d) Dissent by a Director

If a director is present at a meeting, including presence by telephone, he is deemed to consent to any resolution passed at the meeting unless he expresses his dissent in one of the following ways:

- requests that the dissent be recorded, and it is recorded in the minutes of the meeting;
- sends a written dissent to the secretary of the meeting before it is adjourned; or
- sends a dissent by registered mail or delivers it to the office of the corporation immediately after the meeting is adjourned (*CBCA*, s. 123).[46]

If a director votes for a resolution, she cannot dissent after the meeting. If a director is not present, she is deemed to consent if she does not,

---

44 See note 31 above and accompanying text. A majority of resident Canadians is required under some other statutes modelled on the *CBCA*, above note 8. E.g., *OBCA*, *ibid.*, s. 126; and *ABCA*, above note 2, s. 114.

45 Requirements for annual meetings are discussed above in this chapter under "Shareholders Meetings and Resolutions."

46 Similar provisions are found in other corporate statutes. E.g., *OBCA*, above note 2, s. 135; *ABCA*, above note 2, s. 123; and *BCCA*, above note 5, s. 127.

within seven days of becoming aware of a resolution, cause a dissent to be recorded in the minutes or send a written dissent to the corporation.

The purpose of these rules is to fix clearly the position that was taken by a director at a meeting in order to see if he was fulfilling his obligations to the corporation, including his duty of care and fiduciary duty. These duties are discussed in Chapter 8. Deemed consent makes it easier to prove that a director approved a particular action which is being challenged as a breach of duty. By making it impossible for directors to avoid responsibility by declining to take a position, these provisions help to encourage the active involvement of directors in decisions of the board.

e)   Signed Resolutions and Single Director Meetings

Where a corporation has only one director, that director may constitute a meeting. As an alternative to holding meetings, directors may act by resolution signed by all directors (*CBCA*, s. 117).[47] As when shareholders act by signed resolution, this alternative eliminates the need to deal with the requirements for notice of meetings as well as the need to have all the directors present at one place and time. The resolution becomes effective when it is signed by the last director.

E. OFFICERS

1) General

There is nothing in the *CBCA* which addresses what officers a corporation should have or what they are to do. Most corporations have officers called "president" and "secretary." Other common officers include "chief executive officer" (CEO), "chief financial officer," "vice-president," and "treasurer," though a variety of other offices are also in use. Although there are no fixed rules, a common corporate structure gives the CEO overall responsibility for running the corporation's business, while the day-to-day operations are delegated to other officers who report to the CEO.[48]

Directors have power to designate offices, like president and secretary, and to specify the duties of those offices, including delegating to them the power to manage the business and affairs of corporation.

---

47   This procedure is also permitted under most other corporate statutes. E.g., *OBCA*, *ibid.*, s. 129; *ABCA*, *ibid.*, s. 117; and *BCCA*, *ibid.*, 125(1).

48   Under the *BCCA*, *ibid.*, a president and a secretary are required (ss. 133–38)

Usually this delegation is done in a by-law passed at the time the corporation is organized just after incorporation. After setting up the offices in this way, the directors may appoint people, the officers, to fill them (*CBCA*, s. 121). The directors may subsequently delegate further matters to the officers they appoint. Limitations on the directors' ability to delegate are discussed below.

CBCA model legislation has few requirements for officers. The *2001 Amendments* introduced a definition of officer as follows:

> "officer" means an individual appointed as an officer under section 121, the chairperson of the board of directors, the president, the secretary, the treasurer, the comptroller, the general counsel, the general manager, a managing director of a corporation, or any other individual who performs functions for a corporation similar to those normally performed by an individual occupying any of those offices ... (*CBCA*, s. 2(1))

The introduction of this broad definition is significant. It clarifies that officers are not only individuals appointed by the board but all individuals holding certain titles or performing certain functions. All such people will be subject to the duties imposed on officers discussed in Chapter 8. The *OBCA* has a similar definition of officer (s. 1(1)).

Directors can be officers but need not be. Any person may hold two or more offices. No qualifications are required for officers except that they must be of "full capacity" (*CBCA*, s. 121(a)). This phrase is not defined in the Act but presumably means, at least, that officers must not be of unsound mind. There is no such requirement in the *OBCA*. If the board decides to appoint a managing director, he must be a resident Canadian (*CBCA*, s. 115(1)).[49] No act of an officer is invalid by reason only of a defect in her appointment or qualification (*CBCA*, s. 116).[50]

Because officers are typically given power to manage the business and affairs of the corporation, they are subject to the same duty of care and fiduciary duty as directors (*CBCA*, s. 122).[51] These duties are discussed in detail in Chapter 8.

The legal relationship created by appointing a person as an officer is distinct from any employment relationship that the person may have

---

49 The *BCCA*, *ibid.*, is different. The president must be a director and the officers must meet the same standards as the directors (ss. 133 & 134).

50 This saving provision exists under most other corporate statutes. E.g., *OBCA*, above note 2, s. 128; *ABCA*, above note 2, s. 116; and *BCCA*, *ibid.*, ss. 124 & 135.

51 Most other corporate statutes are similar. E.g., *OBCA*, *ibid.*, s. 134; *ABCA*, *ibid.*, s. 122; and *BCCA*, *ibid.*, ss. 118 & 135.

with the corporation, though, in practice, many or all of the duties associated with the employment contract may be coextensive with the duties of the office. The principal situation in which conflict between these relationships arises is termination of the person's involvement with the corporation. An officer can always be removed by the corporation. It is common for corporations to provide in their by-laws that officers hold office at the pleasure of the board of directors, so their appointment may be terminated at any time by a decision of the directors. An officer's employment contract, by contrast, may be terminated only for cause or on reasonable notice.[52] In the absence of cause or notice, the termination of a person as an officer will usually be a breach of his employment agreement, even where the right to remove officers from their offices has been stipulated in the articles or by-laws.[53]

2) Delegation

a) Delegation within the Corporation

Historically, directors had no power to delegate the management of the corporation to others. The power to delegate was necessary, however, for the development of large-scale organizations. Now sections 115 and 121 of the *CBCA* create a statutory code for delegation within the corporation. Directors can delegate their powers "to manage the business and affairs of the corporation" to a managing director (who must be a resident Canadian), to a committee of directors, or to one or more officers.[54] Under the *OBCA*, *ABCA*, and other statutes based on the *CBCA*, a majority of the members of the committee must be resident Canadians. There is no similar requirement in the *CBCA* itself or in the *BCCA*.

The language in section 121(a), permitting delegation to officers, is the same as that giving directors their general authority to manage the corporation in section 102(1). Both refer to the power "to manage the business and affairs of the corporation." Directors, then, can delegate all their power to officers. Such delegation is subject to two important limitations: they cannot delegate the power and responsibility to *supervise* the management of the business and affairs of the corporation; or

---

52   Provincial employment-tandards legislation may impose additional obligations, such as severance pay (e.g., Ontario *Employment Standards Act*, R.S.O. 1990, c. E.14).

53   *Southern Foundries (1926) Ltd. v. Shirlaw*, [1940] A.C. 701 (H.L.).

54   This procedure is also permitted under most other corporate statutes. E.g., *OBCA*, above note 2, s. 129; *ABCA*, above note 2, s. 117; and *BCCA*, above note 5, s. 125(1).

the specific powers listed in section 115(3). These powers relate mostly to decisions regarding shares, including the power to issue shares, to declare dividends on shares, and to purchase or redeem shares. They also include decisions to approve financial statements, management proxy circulars, takeover-bid circulars, and director's circulars.[55]

b) Delegation outside the Corporation

To what extent may power to manage be delegated to third parties outside the corporation? It may seem odd, at first glance, that a board of directors would be delegating power to a person outside the corporation at all, but, in fact, such delegation is common. For example, many corporations grant power to manage in relation to some specific area of their business to a management company that has special expertise in the area. Where the returns to the corporation can be improved by such delegation, management should not be precluded from adopting such a strategy.

External delegation is not dealt with in the *CBCA* or in other corporate statutes, but there is little doubt that it is now permitted. The main rule is that the board of directors may not delegate completely its control over the day-to-day management of the corporation's business; the board must retain the power to supervise the delegate in the performance of its duties. *Kennerson* v. *Burbank Amusement Co.*[56] is an example of a board exceeding this limit. In that case, the board delegated all control over the only asset it was responsible for managing — a theatre. It attempted to transfer control over "bookings, personnel, admission prices, salaries, contracts, expenses" and fiscal policies to Kennerson, the only condition being that he report to the board periodically. The court determined that this delegation conferred on Kennerson the practical control and management of the corporation subject only to a duty to report and account, and permitted no possibility of control being exercised by the board. The power of the directors to manage had been "completely sterilized," and so the delegation was held to be non-enforceable.[57] The length of delegation is also relevant to determining whether the board has retained sufficient control.[58]

---

55   Takeover bids are discussed in Chapter 11.
56   260 P. 2d 823 (Cal. C.A. 1953).
57   The court relied on *Long Park* v. *Trenton–New Brunswick Theatres Co.*, 77 N.E. 2d 633 (N.Y. C.A. 1948). In *Regional Steel Works (Ottawa-1987) Inc., Re* (1994), 25 C.B.R. (3d) 135 (Ont. Gen. Div.), it was held that an officer could have the power to assign a corporation into bankruptcy.
58   *Sherman & Ellis* v. *Indiana Mutual Casualty Co.*, 41 F. 2d. 588 (7th Cir. 1930).

What delegation is permissible is a question of degree. It is important to note that, in choosing a delegate and supervising the delegate, the directors are bound by their duty of care and their fiduciary duty.[59]

F. REMUNERATION AND INDEMNIFICATION OF DIRECTORS AND OFFICERS

1) Remuneration

Unless some arrangement is made in a corporation's articles or by-laws, or in a unanimous shareholders' agreement, the directors may set their own remuneration as well as that of all officers and employees (*CBCA*, s. 125).[60] Deciding on their own remuneration involves a conflict between directors' personal interests and the interests of the corporation which they have a fiduciary duty to put first (*CBCA*, s. 122).[61] Notwithstanding this conflict, the *CBCA* and other modern corporate statutes expressly permit directors to vote on the terms of their compensation (*CBCA*, s. 120(5)(b)).[62] This does not mean, however, that directors are not required to act in the best interests of the corporation in setting their remumeration. In *Radtke* v. *Machel*,[63] the court held that, where a director had decided upon his salary unilaterally, he had an obligation to ensure that the salary was fair.

The issues associated with this kind of conflict depend on the scale of the corporation. For closely held corporations, where managers, directors, and shareholders are the same individuals, inevitably there will be disagreements among the individuals involved about the amounts of compensation paid to each as well as, for example, the form of compensation. Because each individual will have differing needs for money from the corporation and will be in a different tax position, each will have her own preferences whether money is paid out as salary or as dividends or is retained in the corporation to increase the value of her share investment. The Canada Customs and Revenue Agency will

---

59   R. v. *Bata Industries Ltd.* (1992), 9 O.R. (3d) 329 (Prov. Div.) rev'd on other grounds [*Bata*]. See below note 72.

60   Statutes modelled on the *CBCA*, above note 8, are similar. E.g., *OBCA*, above note 2, s. 137; and *ABCA*, above note 2, s. 125. This issue is not addressed in the *BCCA*, above note 5.

61   Fiduciary duties are discussed in Chapter 8.

62   E.g., *OBCA*, above note 2, s. 132(5)(b); and *ABCA*, above note 2, s. 120(5)(b). The *BCCA*, above note 5, has a similar provision (s. 120(4)(d)).

63   [2000] O.J. No. 3019 (QL) (Sup. Ct. J.).

have a corresponding interest in these decisions. Ultimately, decisions about compensation in the closely held corporation will be made on whatever basis has been agreed among the parties. Where this results in the interests of one or more of the shareholders being prejudiced, a shareholder's only remedy is likely to be to sue for relief from oppression (*CBCA*, s. 241). In many oppression cases, the court has found excessive compensation to be oppressive.[64]

As the scale of the corporation increases and the identity of managers, directors, and shareholders diverges, different sorts of problems arise with the setting of compensation. In these circumstances directors and officers may be tempted to enrich themselves at the expense of the corporation by giving themselves excessive levels of compensation. The payment of excessive compensation diminishes the value of the residual claims to the corporation's assets represented by the shareholders' shares.[65] The nature of this problem is discussed in more detail under "Qualifications to the Legal Model of Corporate Governance" below.

2) Indemnification

As will be discussed in Chapter 8, directors and officers are subject to a wide range of potential liability in connection with fulfilling their responsibilities. Exposure to these liabilities creates a strong disincentive to becoming a director or an officer of a corporation. The disincentive is strongest for prospective directors since, in Canada, they are likely to receive relatively modest financial compensation for being a member of a corporation's board.

In response to liability concerns, a practice developed for corporations to indemnify directors and officers against liabilities they incurred. A scheme for indemnification is now set out in the *CBCA* (s. 124) and other corporate statutes.[66] The scheme seeks a balance: to permit indem-

---

64   See, for example, *Stech v. Davies*, (1987), 80 A.R. 298 (Q.B.). For a successful oppression application by a creditor based on excessive compensation, see *Prime Computer of Canada v. Jeffrey* (1991), 6 O.R. (3d) 733 (Gen. Div.), discussed in Chapter 9. Excessive compensation has been a significant concern of investors in the past few years. See the discussion below in the last section of this chapter.

65   The costs associated with the payment of excessive compensation and shareholder monitoring of compensation are specific examples of what are referred as "agency costs," the cost to the shareholder of having someone else manage the corporation on her behalf. Agency costs are discussed below ("Qualifications to the Legal Model of Corporate Governance").

66   E.g., *OBCA*, above note 2, s. 136; and *ABCA*, above note 2, s. 124. Under the *BCCA*, above note 5, indemnities are permitted but may be paid only with the permission of the court (s. 128).

nification in sufficiently broad circumstances to encourage responsible people to become directors or officers, and to deny indemnification in circumstances where directors are engaged in improper conduct. It has three parts. The corporation must indemnify directors and officers in certain circumstances, may indemnify in additional circumstances, and may obtain insurance for the benefit of directors and officers in a still broader range of circumstances. Most commentators have argued that the scheme is not exclusive of the circumstances in which indemnification may be granted,[67] though the issue has never been litigated.

Mandatory Indemnification: A corporation must indemnify a director or officer of the corporation, as well as anyone acting at the corporation's request as a director or officer or in a similar capacity, in a partnership, trust, or other entity, against any costs or expenses reasonably incurred by him in connection with the defence of any civil, criminal, administrative, investigative, or other proceeding in which he was involved because of his association with the corporation or other entity, if the individual

• was not judged by the court or other competent authority to have committed any fault or omitted to do anything that the individual ought to have done;
• complied with his fiduciary duty to act honestly and in good faith with a view to the best interests of the corporation or the other entity for which the individual acted as a director or officer or in a similar capacity; and,
• in the case of a criminal or administrative proceeding, had reasonable grounds for believing his conduct was lawful.

Discretionary Indemnity: Even where a director, or officer, or other person does not meet the first criterion because he was judged to have committed a fault, a corporation still has a discretion to indemnify the director or officer for the same costs and expenses, including any amount paid to settle an action or settle a judgment, so long as the other two criteria are met.

This provision was substantially modified by the *2001 Amendments* to broaden the circumstances in which indemnification could be paid and the categories of expenses that could be indemnified, such that now the *CBCA* provision is significantly more liberal than those in most provinces. The *CBCA* expressly permits the corporation to advance liti-

---

67   For example, J.I.S. Nicholl, "Directors' and Officers' Liability Insurance," in L. Sarna, ed., *Corporate Structure, Finance and Operations*, vol. 4 (Toronto: Carswell, 1986).

gation costs even, with court approval, in an action against the director or officer initiated by a shareholder on behalf of the corporation.[68] An indemnity in relation to costs and expenses incurred may also be paid in connection with such an action with court approval. As well, any individual who is a director or officer or fulfils a similar function in relation to a corporation, partnership, trust, or similar entity at the request of the corporation is eligible to be indemnified. Previously, only directors and officers of the corporation, and other corporations in particular kinds of relationships with the corporation, were eligible to be indemnified.[69]

The Supreme Court of Canada addressed the availability of an indemnity in *Consolidated Enfield Corp. v. Blair*.[70] Blair was the president and a director of Consolidated Enfield Corporation (Enfield). At the annual meeting of Enfield, a slate of nominees proposed by management, and including Blair, stood for election. Canadian Express Ltd., a major shareholder, nominated a candidate for director to replace Blair. On the basis of the votes cast by Canadian Express and its supporters, the Canadian Express candidate would have been elected. Before the meeting, however, Blair had been advised by legal counsel that Canadian Express could use its proxies to vote only for the management nominees. After the votes on the election of directors were cast, Blair was advised by legal counsel for the corporation that he, as chair, had to make a ruling about the results of the vote, notwithstanding that his own election was at stake. Legal counsel also advised that the votes cast by Canadian Express and its supporters against Blair were invalid. Blair took that advice and ruled that the management slate was elected. In subsequent legal proceedings, a court ruled that the votes cast in favour of the Canadian Express nominee were valid and so Blair had not been re-elected.[71]

Blair sought an order that he be indemnified by Enfield for his legal costs in connection with these proceedings. The trial court held that he could not be indemnified because he had not fulfilled his fiduciary duty in connection with the vote. Ultimately, the Supreme Court of

---

68 This is called a "derivative action" and is discussed in Chapter 9.

69 These kinds of requirements still exist in provincial statutes. In the *OBCA*, above note 2, for example, only current and former directors and officers of the corporation or corporations with respect to which the corporation was a shareholder or creditor who are so acting at the request of the corporation are eligible for indemnification (ss. 136(1) & (3)). Provincial indemnification provisions impose additional limitations on the availablity of indemnities.

70 [1995] 4 S.C.R. 5, aff'g (1993), 15 O.R. (3d) 783 (C.A.), rev'g [1992] O.J. No. 2291 (QL) (Gen. Div.).

71 *Blair*, above note 19, Holland, J.

Canada granted an indemnification order. Significantly, the Court held that the corporation had the obligation to establish that Blair had not acted in good faith with a view to the best interests of the corporation to avoid an obligation to indemnify. The Court also stated that, while reliance on legal advice is not a guarantee that indemnification will be available, where that reliance is reasonable and in good faith, the court will conclude that the director acted in compliance with his fiduciary duty. Here, where Blair was confronted with a novel and difficult legal question, it was reasonable to seek legal advice and to rely on it. Finally, the Court held that indemnification in these circumstances was consistent with the broad policy goals underlying the indemnification provisions. Limiting the availability of indemnification to encourage responsible behaviour should be balanced with sufficient flexibility in the granting of indemnification to attract strong candidates as officers and directors.

Under the *CBCA*, insurance may be obtained by the corporation for the benefit of a director or officer or any other individual eligible to be indemnified against any liability incurred by her in her capacity as a director or officer or similar capacity (*CBCA*, s. 124(3)). Prior to the *2001 Amendments*, the *CBCA* prohibited the corporation from obtaining insurance against liabilities involving a failure to comply with the person's fiduciary duty. Other *CBCA* model statutes retain such a requirement (e.g., *OBCA*, s. 136(4)). Under the amended *CBCA*, however, whether insurance will be so limited now depends on the insurance marketplace alone.

The availability of indemnities and insurance has become an increasingly complex issue as governments, seeking to improve compliance with environmental and other regulatory schemes, have turned to imposing personal liability on directors and officers. On the one hand, with the range and seriousness of potential liability increasing, indemnities and insurance become more and more important as a way of ensuring that competent people are willing to become officers and directors. On the other hand, indemnification and insurance will tend to reduce the effectiveness of the legislative scheme. The intended effect of imposing liability on directors and officers is to discourage businesses from acting illegally. If directors and officers are fully insulated from liability, this will not occur.

An interesting illustration of this problem arose in R. v. *Bata Industries Ltd.*[72] Several officers were convicted for offences under the

---

72   (1995), 101 C.C.C. (3d) 86 (Ont. C.A.), rev'g *Bata* above note 59, as varied by (1993), 14 O.R. (3d) 354 (Gen. Div.).

Ontario Water Resources Act[73] consisting of "failing to take all reasonable care to prevent … [the corporation] from causing or permitting an unlawful discharge [of wastes]." The judge ordered that the accused pay fines and that the corporation, Bata Industries, not indemnify them. The judge indicated that, if the corporation could indemnify officers against the consequences of their wrongdoing, the intended effect of the legislative scheme in imposing liability — discouraging illegal behaviour by businesses — would be undermined. On appeal, the court determined that the trial judge had no authority to make such an order because the statutory scheme expressly permitted indemnification in the circumstances of the case.

G. SHAREHOLDERS' AGREEMENTS

1) Introduction

Where a corporation has few shareholders, they will often want to customize their relationship to create an arrangement which is different from that contemplated in the relevant corporate legislation in several ways, including changing shareholder voting entitlements, imposing share-transfer requirements, and providing for a dispute-settlement mechanism. Under the *CBCA* and statutes modelled after it, the shareholders may even assume the powers of the directors in a unanimous shareholders' agreement.

2) Voting and Management

Shareholders in a corporation may want to exercise their power to vote on a basis different from the votes they have according to their share ownership. To do so, shareholders may, by contract, agree on how they will vote their shares. Imagine that three individuals, Sherry, Amman, and Yves, decide to set up a corporation to carry on a business of distributing computer software. Yves will contribute the $500,000 needed to set up the business and will be the sales manager. Amman, who recently completed his MBA but has little money, will be responsible for the financial side of the business. Sherry will contribute some software she has developed and will be in charge of supporting the software sold. The corporation's articles provided for only common shares.

---

73   R.S.O. 1990, c. O.40.

Because of his large financial contribution, Yves will get 90 percent of the shares, while Amman and Sherry will get 5 percent each. This division would entitle Yves to determine who will be on the board. He need not include Sherry or Amman. But what if Yves, Sherry, and Amman consider themselves to be in a relationship in which each should have an equal say and each wants to be on the board?

This problem could be addressed in a shareholder agreement in a variety of ways. All three could agree that they will vote their shares to elect all three as directors.[74] Amman, Sherry, and Yves may also agree that all decisions requiring shareholder approval must be made unanimously.

The potential scope for shareholders to agree on decision-making structures is subject to one important limitation. Shareholders may not by contract require directors to vote in a certain way. Directors have duties, the fiduciary duty and the duty of care which will be discussed in Chapter 8, and their decision-making discretion cannot be restricted so as to prevent them from being able to fulfil these duties.[75] This rule applies even when directors and shareholders are the same persons. Shareholders can bind themselves in how they vote their shares but not in how they exercise their discretion as directors.

As discussed in the section "Unanimous Shareholders' Agreements," below, since the *2001 Amendments* came into force, this constraint does not apply to unanimous shareholders' agreements (USA) involving *CBCA* corporations. Under a USA, all the shareholders agree that certain matters ordinarily falling to the directors will be decided only by the shareholders. The *2001 Amendments* expressly provide that, where shareholders have taken directors' powers under a USA, they can fetter their discretion as to how they exercise them. Unfortunately, in other statutes modelled after the *CBCA* prior to the *2001 Amendments*, there is no similar provision.

3) Share Transfer

In small corporations, share transfer is problematic for several reasons. Shares of closely held corporations are hard to sell because, typically, the business is tied up with the individuals who are the shareholders.

---

74   Section 146(1) of the *CBCA*, above note 8, as well as s. 108(1) of the *OBCA*, above note 2, and s. 145(1) of the *ABCA*, above note 2, expressly permit shareholders to contract how they will vote their shares. There is no corresponding provision in the *BCCA*, above note 5.

75   *Ringuet v. Bergeron*, [1960] S.C.R. 672; *820099 Ontario Inc. v. Harold E. Ballard Ltd.* (1991), 3 B.L.R. (2d) 113 (Ont. Gen. Div.), aff'd (1991), 3 B.L.R. (2d) 113 (Ont. Div. Ct.).

Unless the individuals who are running the business, perhaps even including the person who wants to sell, are agreeable to continuing to run the business, it may have little value. In the example above, it may be that the business could not continue without all three shareholders — Yves, Amman, and Sherry — being involved in the business. Although there is no legal impediment to a person selling his shares and continuing to be an employee or even a director and officer, in most real-world situations shareholders in closely held corporations seek to sell their shares only when they have decided to cease being active in the business. Usually, as long as they are working in the business, shareholders are reluctant to sell their shares because they do not want other people involved as shareholders. Once a shareholder decides to leave the business, she will be more interested in selling her shares because she loses her ability to monitor her fellow shareholder managers informally and, as a result, is not be able to ensure that they are doing their best to maximize the value of her investment.[76]

By contrast, the value of shares in a large publicly traded corporation is independent of who holds them. Most shareholders are not active in the business, so there will be no change in the business on the sale of their shares. As a result, shares of a public corporation are much more liquid than the shares in a closely held corporation.

Another problem with finding a buyer for an interest in a closely held corporation is that such interests are inherently hard to value. There is no market like the Toronto Stock Exchange to establish prices. Also, where there is a dominant controlling shareholder, the value of a minority interest may have to be discounted.

Share transfers are also difficult for non-financial reasons. Shareholders who are not selling their shares will want some say in who will be able to purchase the shares that are for sale. They may want to be able to control who becomes a shareholder, and to do so will want some restrictions on share transfer. At the same time, each shareholder has an interest in having a minimum of restrictions on his ability to sell his own shares, especially given the impediments to selling them described above.

To address these issues, it is common to set up some mechanism in a shareholders' agreement to restrict share transfers. In addition to the

---

76 The additional costs to her as a result of losing this ability to monitor the other shareholders and managers is an example of "agency costs," the costs for a shareholder associated with allowing someone else to manage the corporation. Agency costs are discussed below ("Qualifications to the Legal Model of Corporate Governance").

approval by directors or shareholders usually provided for in the articles and discussed in Chapter 4, a variety of other mechanisms are used. Typically, transfers are prohibited except as provided in the agreement. Perhaps the most common circumstance in which transfers are permitted is upon compliance with a "right of first refusal." In its simplest form, a right of first refusal is a requirement for a shareholder who wants to sell her shares to offer them first to the other shareholders at some price set by the shareholder. The other shareholders then have a limited time to purchase her shares at that price, usually in proportion to their existing share interests. If they do not purchase the shares, the shareholder may offer them for sale to third parties at the same price for a further limited time. The requirement to sell to third parties at the same price that she offered the shares to the other shareholders discourages the shareholder from stipulating an unreasonably high price for her shares.

Transfers may be permitted in certain circumstances without triggering transfer mechanisms such as the right of first refusal. These exceptions may include transfers to financial institutions as security for loans, and transfers to family members and to corporations controlled by the shareholder.

Shareholders' agreements also often provide that a shareholder must transfer his shares, either to the other shareholders or to the corporation, in some situations. For example, agreements commonly provide that, on the death of a shareholder, his estate must transfer his shares to the other shareholders. This is done so the surviving shareholders do not end up with the heirs of the deceased shareholder as shareholders. Shareholders' agreements with mandatory transfers on death often require the corporation or the shareholders to maintain some form of life insurance, the proceeds of which will be used to fund the purchase commitment. Other common situations in which transfers are mandatory include a shareholder retiring from active participation in the corporation's business, ceasing to be able to perform her duties in the business, and breaching the shareholders' agreement. In order to make these mandatory transfer provisions effective, it is necessary to have a value assigned to the corporation's shares, or to provide for a method to determine value, such as a formula based on annual income or valuation by the corporation's accountant.

Pre-emptive rights, which were discussed in Chapter 4, also may be included in shareholders' agreements. Under a pre-emptive right, a corporation cannot issue shares without offering them first to the existing shareholders. One reason to have such a right in a shareholders' agreement rather than the articles is that the articles are a matter of public record. Shareholders often do not want their private arrangements made public.

4) Dispute Settlement

A shareholders' agreement may govern the parties' relationships for a long time. Inevitably, as circumstances change, disputes among shareholders will arise sometimes. Some form of dispute-settlement mechanism, such as arbitration, is often included in shareholders' agreements to avoid the necessity of going to court to resolve such disputes. A full discussion of alternative dispute settlement is far beyond the scope of this book, but, in general, arbitration, mediation or some other alternative to going to court is desirable because it permits the resolution of disputes in a manner that is private, cheaper, and less adversarial. Resolving disputes through alternative dispute-resolution procedures is usually more conducive to the continuation of the relationship than court proceedings. If alternative dispute settlement is to be used by the shareholders, it is essential that it be agreed to at the time the shareholders' agreement is entered. Once a dispute has arisen, the likelihood of agreeing on a dispute-settlement process is substantially reduced. The parties must agree on what disputes will be subject to dispute settlement and what the process for the dispute settlement will be.[77]

5) Unanimous Shareholders' Agreements

When the CBCA was enacted in 1975, it sought to address the needs of closely held corporations by permitting all the shareholders of a corporation to agree to alter the allocation of power between directors and shareholders provided in the statute. In particular, decision-making power could be transferred from the directors to the shareholders (s. 146). This transfer permits great flexibility for the corporate organization to be shaped to reflect the bargaining among shareholders. Although such flexibility is a laudable objective, the provisions dealing with unanimous shareholders' agreements leave many issues unresolved in terms of how they are to work in practice.[78]

---

77   See *Seel* v. *Seel*, [1995] 7 W.W.R. 214 (B.C.S.C.), in which it was held that the arbitration provision should be enforced where there was a dispute over share valuation and the original valuation was not done in accordance with the agreement.

78   Provincial statutes based on the *CBCA*, above note 8, have similar provisions. E.g., *OBCA*, above note 2, s. 108; and *ABCA*, above note 2, s. 146. Non-*CBCA* statutes such as the *BCCA*, above note 5, do not.

A USA under the *CBCA* may restrict "in whole or in part, the powers of the directors to manage the business and affairs of the corporation." A shareholder who is party to such an agreement has "all the rights, powers, duties and liabilities of a director, whether they arise under this Act or otherwise" to the extent of the restriction and "the directors are thereby relieved of their duties and liabilities, … , to the same extent."[79] The effectiveness of the transfer of directors' liability is far from clear. For example, it is unclear whether the *CBCA* is capable of removing liabilities imposed on directors under legislation validly enacted in other jurisdictions. What is the constitutional basis for the federal government to enact a law that purports to remove the liability imposed on directors under a validly enacted provincial law? Prior to the *2001 Amendments*, a second and more serious problem was that it was not clear that the *CBCA* rules for USAs had corrected the problem associated with the inability of shareholders to fetter the discretion of directors because of the need to retain their freedom to fulfil their duties. Because the "duties" of the directors are transferred to the shareholders, it was possible to argue that the shareholders were similarly fettered, at least when exercising powers which would have been exercised by the directors in the absence of the shareholders' agreement. The *2001 Amendments*, however, specifically provide that shareholders may agree as to how they will exercise powers they have taken from the directors (*CBCA*, s. 146(6)). There is no equivalent provision in provincial statutes modelled on the *CBCA*, so the issue remains as to whether it is possible for shareholders of corporations incorporated under these laws who are exercising directors' powers under a USA to agree on how they will do so.[80]

There are a variety of other unresolved issues regarding how a corporation subject to a USA is to function.[81] Does it need a board of directors? How are shareholders to vote in exercising their acquired powers as directors: one vote per shareholder, or according to their share interests? Although shareholders can address the issues in their agreement, these uncertainties are bound to result in practitioners avoiding the

---

79   Prior to the *2001 Amendments*, above note 8, the statutory language did not state that the liabilities from which the directors are relieved are transferred to the shareholders. Some statutes based on the *CBCA*, *ibid.*, such as the *ABCA*, *ibid.*, have not been amended to correct this problem, so there is a question regarding the extent to which directors are protected against liabilities.

80   E.g., *OBCA*, above note 2, s. 108; and *ABCA*, *ibid.*, s. 146.

81   These issues are addressed in some detail in M. Disney, "The Shareholder Agreement: Some Basic Issues (Part 2)" (1995) 14 Nat'l Banking L. Rev. 51, at 54–62.

USA.[82] It is regrettable that the *2001 Amendments* did not address the deficiencies in the USA in a more thoroughgoing way.

6) Enforcing Shareholders' Agreements

In addition to any right a shareholder may have to go to court to enforce a shareholders' agreement as a contract, the *CBCA* and statutes modelled after it provide a range of other remedial options for enforcing shareholders' agreements. Breach of any shareholders' agreement may be held to constitute oppression under section 241 of the *CBCA*. However, the same provision may be used to defeat the enforcement of rights under a shareholders' agreement. In one case, the actions of a shareholder that were technically consistent with the provisions of the shareholders' agreement but that were engaged in for the purpose of improperly removing the other shareholder from the corporation were found to be oppressive.[83] Notwithstanding the apparent unfairness, it is not obvious that the court should have intervened in an agreement freely made between the parties. Nevertheless, this approach has been followed in other cases.[84]

Additional statutory rights benefit USAs.[85] Under section 247, a shareholder may make a summary application to have the provisions of any USA enforced.[86] Failure to comply with the terms of a USA may be grounds for dissolution of the corporation, and the *CBCA* expressly provides that a court may dissolve a corporation if some specified event has occurred which, under a USA, entitles a complaining shareholder to demand dissolution (*CBCA*, s. 214).[87]

Shareholders' agreements that are not USAs are binding on a transferee, or a person issued shares by the corporation, only if the transferee signs it. For this reason, it is common in shareholders' agreements to

---

82   Many of these issues were discussed and options for reform suggested in Industry Canada, *Unanimous Shareholder Agreements* (*Canada Business Corporations Act* Discussion Paper) (Ottawa: Industry Canada, 1996).

83   *Deluce Holdings Inc.* v. *Air Canada* (1992), 12 O.R. (3d) 131 (Gen. Div.).

84   E.g., *Re Bury and Bell Gouinlock Ltd.* (1984), 48 O.R. (2d) 57 (H.C.J.), aff'd (1985), 49 O.R. (2d) 91 (Div. Ct.) (exercise of right under agreement found oppressive).

85   Recently, the Supreme Court of Canada recognized that the USA was a quasi-constitutional document (*Duha Printers (Western) Ltd.* v. *Canada*, [1998] 1 S.C.R. 795, at 829 [*Duha Printers*]).

86   E.g., *OBCA*, above note 2, s. 253; and *ABCA*, above note 2, s. 248.

87   E.g., *OBCA*, *ibid.*, s. 207; and *ABCA*, *ibid.*, s. 215.

provide that the shareholders agree that all transfers and share issuances are conditional upon any new shareholder signing the agreement.

Under the *CBCA*, as amended by the *2001 Amendments*, any purchaser or transferee of shares in a corporation in respect of which the shareholders have entered into a USA is deemed to be a party to the agreement. But if the transferee has no notice of the agreement and is not aware of its existence, she is entitled to rescind the contract within thirty days of when she finds out about it (*CBCA*, ss. 49(8), 146(3) & (4)).[88]

The rules under the *OBCA* are somewhat different. There, a USA is enforceable against a person acquiring shares from an existing shareholder if the transferee is aware of it. If, however, there is a conspicuous reference to the agreement on the share certificate, any transferee is bound by the agreement even if she was not aware of it (*OBCA*, ss. 56(3) & 108(4)). In order to take advantage of this scheme, many shareholders' agreements provide that a notice of the agreement will be endorsed on all share certificates. This is also a prudent practice under the *CBCA* (s. 49(8)).

One of the unresolved issues associated with USAs under the *OBCA* is what happens when there is no notice and shares are transferred. Now that the agreement is no longer unanimous, does it lose all effect?

Similar uncertainty arises with respect to the effect on a USA of the issue of new shares to a person not already a party to the agreement. The deeming provisions in the *OBCA* only refer to transferees. It has been held that a shareholder who received shares issued on an amalgamation was not subject to these deeming provisions.[89] The *CBCA* refers to "purchasers" of shares though it remains to be seen whether this will be interpreted as including people who receive newly issued shares. The *ABCA* deeming provisions expressly include purchasers of shares from the corporation (*ABCA*, s. 146(2)).

Under the *ABCA*, all shareholder agreements signed by all shareholders are considered USAs and benefit from this statutory enforceability and access to the remedial provisions described above (s. 1(jj) (definition of USA)). By contrast, it seems that, under the *CBCA* and the *OBCA*, only shareholders' agreements that transfer directors' powers to the shareholders are USAs, and qualify for this enhanced statutory enforceability. Sometimes it may be hard to tell whether an agreement restricts the powers of the directors or not.[90]

---

88   This is the same approach as is followed in the *ABCA*, ibid., ss. 146(2)–(3).

89   *Sportscape Television Network Ltd. v. Shaw Communications Inc.* (1999), 46 B.L.R. (2d) 87 (Ont. Gen. Div.). Amalgamations are discussed in Chapter 10.

90   In *Duha Printers*, above note 85, the Supreme Court of Canada held that an agreement reserving the power to issue shares to the shareholders was a unanimous shareholders' agreement.

H. OBSERVATIONS ON MANAGEMENT AND CONTROL OF THE CORPORATION IN THEORY AND PRACTICE

1) Qualifications to the Legal Model of Corporate Governance

In order to understand how the allocation of power and responsibility under the *CBCA* and the provincial statutes modelled on the federal statute works, it is necessary to consider the various practical contexts to which it applies. These vary from the corporation with a single shareholder who is also the sole director and officer to the large public corporation with thousands of shareholders spread out around the world and many directors, a few of whom work as managers in the corporation. How the corporate law rules for management and control operate will vary significantly, depending on a corporation's position between these two extremes.

Consider first the corporation where one person is the sole shareholder, director, and officer. In these circumstances, the allocation of rights and responsibilities contemplated in the *CBCA* is formalistic and, for most practical purposes, irrelevant. As the sole participant in the corporation, this person has no incentive to favour her interests as a director or officer over her interests as a shareholder and no one, other than herself, to bear the consequences if she does so. If, for example, she pays herself an excessive salary in her capacity as an officer, she will suffer a corresponding diminution in the value of her interest as a shareholder. Equally, if she takes no salary or other compensation for her work for the corporation, she benefits to the same extent in terms of the increase in the value of her shares in the corporation.

This unity of interest breaks down as soon as our sole shareholder permits someone else to invest in shares of the corporation. Assume that she sells 75 percent of her shares to her father, who will not be active in the business. Now, if she pays herself an excessive salary, she receives 100 percent of the benefit of doing so, but her interest as a shareholder is diminished by only 25 percent — that is, to the extent of her remaining percentage share interest in the corporation. The potential for opportunistic behaviour of this kind to result in her personal enrichment gives our formerly sole shareholder an incentive to engage in such behaviour. This raises a concern for our new investor, her father. He is exposed to the risk of his daughter's opportunistic behaviour and will be interested in putting in place some mechanism to prevent it. Corporate law provides a variety of such mechanisms in the form of the shareholder voting and approval requirements and shareholder remedies. For example, the father could vote against the re-election of his daughter as director or seek relief under the oppression remedy. The costs to shareholders associated with losses due to opportunistic behaviour by corporate managers, and any expenditures by shareholders for the purpose of preventing these losses, are referred to as agency costs. They are the costs associated with an agent (i.e., someone other than the shareholder) managing the corporation in which the shareholder has his investment.

As the number of shareholders in a corporation increases and this separation between management and share ownership widens, the incentive for managers to engage in opportunistic behaviour also grows. If managers are shareholders at all, the size of their interest, typically, is very small relative to the aggregate of all shareholder interests, so the proportion of loss to them associated with acting in ways that further their own interests at the expense of the corporation's is correspondingly small. At the same time, the ability of shareholders to ensure that directors and, through them, management, are accountable to act in the corporation's interests, through the legal mechanisms described above, is reduced. In practice, at least in relation to larger corporations, the principal legal mechanisms referred to above — shareholder voting rights, information rights, and shareholder remedies — may be ineffective for a variety of reasons.

Notwithstanding their access to information rights, shareholders will often lack sufficient information to understand and evaluate management's performance. In addition, most shareholders will have a small financial stake relative to the cost of obtaining adequate information, especially considering that effective evaluation of what is going on in a business will often require paying for professional advice. As a result, shareholders will be discouraged from trying to acquire such information. Individual shareholders may hope and expect that others will do the information gathering and analysis.

Even if shareholders are able to gather sufficient information and to analyse it, mobilizing the large number of geographically and otherwise disparate shareholders that would be needed to defeat a management proposal or to elect a new board of directors will be difficult and costly. Since the benefits associated with an investment in information gathering and organizing collective action will accrue to all shareholders regardless of their individual contribution, it may seem to make sense to let others spend their money on doing it. The relatively small financial stake of individual shareholders discourages collective activity.

Also, under the *CBCA* and other statutes, the directors control the proxy-solicitation process (e.g., *CBCA*, s. 149).[91] For the most part, the directors determine what goes on the agenda for meetings and how it is described. The increasingly active participation in the securities markets of institutional investors, such as pension funds and mutual funds with large financial interests in individual firms and the resources and contacts to facilitate coordinated behaviour, may result in more effective monitoring of both opportunistic behaviour by management and collusion between management and controlling shareholders.[92] However while such problems may be reduced by the presence of institutional investors, they are unlikely to be eliminated entirely. As well, commentators have identified other impediments discouraging the exercise by institutional shareholders of their shareholder rights.[93]

Shareholder litigation to seek the enhanced remedies provided in the *CBCA* and other modern corporate statutes also faces certain challenges. Most important, litigation is an expensive, time-consuming, and uncertain exercise. Also, despite the improvements made recently in some jurisdictions, such as Ontario, in facilitating class actions by shareholders,[94] the impediments to shareholders acting collectively to exercise their voting rights effectively apply equally to shareholder litigation.[95]

91 E.g., *OBCA*, above note 2, s. 111; and *ABCA*, above note 2, s. 149. The *BCCA*, above note 5, s. 153 is similar.

92 R.J. Daniels & E.J. Waitzer, "Challenges to the Citadel: A Brief Overview of Recent Trends in Canadian Corporate Governance" (1994) 23 Can. Bus. L.J. 23; J. G. MacIntosh, "The Role of Institutional and Retail Investors in Canadian Capital Markets" (1993) 31 Osgoode Hall L.J. 371.

93 J.G. MacIntosh, "Institutional Investors and Corporate Governance" (1996) 26 Can. Bus. L. J. 145. MacIntosh refers to investment restrictions, limited monitoring capabilities, fiduciary conflicts of interest, a culture of passivity, and other factors as discouraging institutional investor activism. Impediments are also discussed in R. Crête & S. Rousseau, "De la passivité à l'activisme des investisseurs institutionnel au sein des corporations: le reflet de la diversité des facteurs d'influence" (1997) 42 McGill L. J. 3.

94 Notwithstanding such improvements, class-action cases on behalf of shareholders have proven complex. The ultimately successful efforts to certify a class on behalf of the shareholders of Bre-Ex in connection with one of the most notorious stock frauds ever perpetrated in Canada gave rise to substantial litigation: e.g., *Carom, v. Bre-Ex Minerals Ltd.*, [2000] O.J. No. 4014 (QL)(C.A.), varying (1999), 46 O.R. (3d) 315 (Div. Ct.), affirming (1998), 44 O.R. (3d) 173 (Sup. Ct. J.), leave to appeal to S.C.C. denied (2000), 157 O.A.C. 399.

95 These problems are somewhat mitigated in the Canadian marketplace where seven out of ten public companies have a controlling shareholder. In this situation, however, accountability concerns remain because minority shareholders face the risk that the controlling shareholder and the corporation will enter into transactions which are not in the best interests of all shareholders.

Another problem with the existing legal accountability mechanisms in the *CBCA* and other statutes is that they focus on the board of directors as the locus of management power and do not speak much of officers at all. Reading the *CBCA* and the older case law, one may get the impression that the board is engaged in high-level management activities such as setting business objectives and policy, choosing the senior management personnel, and closely supervising their activities. In fact, the board plays this role in very few corporations. To this extent, corporate law's treatment of the board as the locus of power is out of step with reality.

In small closely held corporations where all the shareholders are actively involved in the business, the formal separation of powers described in the preceding section of this chapter has little significance for how such a corporation operates. Although the shareholders must still elect a board and the board will still choose the officers, the effective decision makers will be the shareholder managers. Even if the board has a few directors from outside the shareholder group, in most cases they will act merely as advisers. As discussed above, the possibility of using a USA to transfer directors' powers to shareholders was introduced in the *CBCA* as a way of permitting these kinds of corporations to adopt a legal structure that more closely reflects their practice of direct management by shareholders.

In large public corporations, the board of directors seldom exercises the role traditionally ascribed to it either, but for different reasons. As noted above, in such corporations there are various impediments to the effective exercise of shareholder power over directors. Typically, however, this limitation does not result in the board becoming the locus of management power. Boards tend to be dominated by the full-time professional managers of the corporation. There are a variety of reasons for this result. It is management who is actively involved in the affairs of the corporation and has the necessary knowledge, experience, and expertise regarding its operations to deal with the complex issues that arise on a daily basis. Members of the board who are not part of the management team, on the other hand, are usually busy professionals or business people who do not have the time to engage in the continuous analysis that would be required to set policy and objectives and to make major decisions regarding the business. Even if they sought to do so, they would be largely dependent on the information and analysis provided by management and so would rarely be in a position to challenge management.

Research has shown that outside directors tend to defer to management because of what Mace has called a "culture of deference."[96] Out-

---

96   M.L. Mace, *Directors: Myth and Reality* (Boston: Harvard University Graduate School of Business Administration, Division of Research, 1971) at 184–206.

side directors are picked by management and may receive substantial compensation from the corporation. Sometimes an outside director of one corporation is also the chief executive of another and may have picked the chief executive of the first corporation to be on her board. In this situation, each has a reciprocal interest in not challenging each other's authority around the boardroom table. Similarly, it is common for professionals such as lawyers, accountants, and investment dealers to be represented on the boards of corporations that are their clients. For these directors, challenging management may put substantial fee revenue at risk. These reservations should not be taken as suggesting either that outside directors are incapable of meeting their obligations to the corporation or that substantial delegation to management is not permitted by the *CBCA*. As discussed above, such delegation is expressly allowed. Nevertheless, there are factors militating against boards of directors playing the kind of effective supervisory role that the *CBCA* seems to contemplate, and corporate law rules which assume that they do may be ineffective.[97] In the next section, recent reform proposals designed to improve the independence and effectiveness of boards are discussed.

Finally, an examination of corporate law rules, at least as they apply to public corporations with many shareholders, discloses only one set of accountability mechanisms. Where shares are traded in a marketplace, the dynamic of the marketplace itself will impose a certain discipline on management. Although it is beyond the scope of this book to describe the vast empirical and theoretical literature which has developed on this subject, it is important to point out some of the basic insights that a consideration of market forces yields.

In markets for corporate shares and other securities, as in other markets, prices are set as a result of supply and demand — the buying and selling activity of people trading in the market. Empirical evidence

---

97   The effectiveness of boards of public corporations in Canada was criticized in the *Report of the Toronto Stock Exchange Committee on Corporate Governance in Canada: Where Were the Directors?* (Toronto: Toronto Stock Exchange, 1994) [*Dey Report*]. A review published in 1999 on the effect of the Toronto Stock Exchange Rules adopted in response to this report, *Report on Governance: Five Years to the Dey* (Toronto: Institute of Corporate Directors and The Toronto Stock Exchange, 1999) suggested that some improvements in corporate governance had been achieved. A more recent study found that 35 percent of corporations were not in compliance with the disclosure requirements (J. McFarland, "Companies don't respect governance rules: study," *The Globe and Mail*, 20 January 2003, B1) [*TSE Compliance Study*]. For an example of outside directors playing an effective role, see *Brant Investments* v. *KeepRite Inc.* (1991), 3 O.R. (3d) 289 (C.A.).

has demonstrated that prices in markets for securities tend to reflect accurately all publicly available information.[98] This characteristic, called market efficiency, means that all public information about agency costs should be factored into the price. Expressed another way, a shareholder needs to worry less about the risk of management engaging in opportunistic behaviour because the price of the shares she bought was already reduced to reflect that risk at the time she bought them.

There are, however, still risks associated with opportunistic behaviour by management. For example, not all risks of such behaviour are foreseeable and so may not be factored into share price. Also, studies of stock markets suggest that prices do not reflect non-public or insider information known only to officers and directors of the corporation.[99] Agency costs known only to insiders will not be factored into share price. Nevertheless, to the extent that most agency costs are factored into share price, the corporate law mechanisms designed to monitor and control agency costs become less important.

The operation of securities markets can also enhance shareholders' ability to take advantage of corporate law mechanisms. Once a person has acquired shares, a drop in the price may reflect some new information or a change in circumstances that increases agency costs. In such a case, the shareholder may either sell, in which case he bears the full amount of this increase in agency costs, or he may try to exercise his vote to try to discipline management in some way. In choosing this second option, he would be faced with the problems described above in terms of collecting and analysing information and mobilizing his fellow shareholders. While neither of these options permit the shareholder to avoid agency costs, the general point is that prices in securities markets, in effect, provide information about agency costs and so facilitate the effective exercise of shareholder voting and other shareholder rights.

What is sometimes called the market for corporate control also reduces the impact of agency costs. A corporation that is being managed in the interests of enriching its management represents an opportunity. As a result of this self-enriching behaviour by its management, the corporation's share price will be lower than it would be if the corporation were being managed more effectively. By acquiring sufficient

---

98   This evidence is reviewed in R.J. Daniels & J.G. MacIntosh, "Toward a Distinctive Canadian Corporate Law Regime" (1991) 29 Osgoode Hall L.J. 863 at 872–74.

99   J.N. Gordon & L.A. Kornhauser, "Efficient Markets, Costly Information and Securities Research" (1985) 60 N.Y.U. L. Rev. 761.

shares to gain control of the corporation, a person could enhance the value of the firm and increase share price by improving management. Such a change in control is often accomplished by what is known as a takeover bid: a bidder offers to buy some or all of the shares held by existing shareholders, typically at a price in excess of the current market price, for the purpose of acquiring enough shares to replace the board of directors and have a new board put new management in place. The threat of such a hostile takeover bid, which, if successful, will result in the board and the officers losing their positions, should discourage management from engaging in the behaviour that created the opportunity for the bidder in the first place. They should be encouraged to manage so as to maximize the value of shareholders' investment. Some commentators have suggested that the discipline provided by the market for corporate control is so important that management's ability to defend against a hostile-takeover bid should be severely limited.[100] This point is discussed in more detail in Chapter 8.

The existence of these market mechanisms addressing agency problems has led some corporate law scholars to assert that legal rules can be justified only to the extent that the market can be shown not to operate effectively and that the significant role played by market forces leaves a narrow sphere of operation for corporate law.[101] Others have suggested that the capital and corporate-control markets do not work effectively, and so a substantial role must be played by mandatory corporate law rules.[102] Still others argue that it is not appropriate to use the market as the exclusive model for thinking about what corporate law rules should be.[103]

In thinking about the ways in which shareholders and directors exercise power under the existing corporate law regimes in Canada, one should keep in mind the issues raised in the foregoing discussion. The real-world context in which corporate law rules operate will have a significant impact on their effectiveness.

---

100 F.H. Easterbrook & D.R. Fischel, "The Proper Role of a Target's Management in Responding to a Tender Offer" (1982) 94 Harv. L. Rev. 1161.

101 E.g., F.H. Easterbrook & D.R. Fischel, "Corporate Control Transactions" (1982) 91 Yale L.J. 698, at 700–3.

102 E.g., V. Brudney, "Corporate Governance, Agency Costs, and the Rhetoric of Contract" (1985) 85 Colum. L. Rev. 1403, at 1410–11.

103 E.g., B. Chapman, "Trust, Economic Rationality, and the Corporate Fiduciary Obligation" (1993) 43 U.T.L.J. 547.

2) Rethinking the Legal Model of Corporate Governance for Public Corporations in Light of Enron and Other Corporate Scandals

How public corporations are governed is not just a function of the legal rules which are the subject of this book and the market forces discussed in the previous section. A variety of other factors may be identified, including the following.

A. *Business Practices*: How boards are organized and conduct themselves in practice has an impact on how well they function. Practices that have been identified as likely to improve the functioning of boards include

- practices designed to enhance the ability of the board to monitor and supervise management such as
  - having a chair of the board of directors who is not the chief executive officer (CEO);
  - having truly independent board members who have no other relationship with management or the corporation;
  - providing an enhanced role for independent board members by
    - giving them control of important committees, like the audit committee, and
    - giving them responsibility to choose the CEO, nominate new directors and hire and fire auditors; and
- adopting incentive schemes for directors and senior officers which appropriately align their financial interests with the interests of shareholders.

B. *Business Ethics*: The ethics and values of the officers and directors responsible for corporate decision making will have an impact on how diligently they seek to maximize the value of shareholders' investment as opposed to benefiting themselves, as well as determining the likelihood that they will engage in fraud, insider trading, and other illegal activities.

C. *Criminal Rules Dealing with Corporate Fraud*: Where ethics fail, the effectiveness of the criminal law and its enforcement to punish and deter fraud and other illegal activities will be an important determinant of corporate behaviour.

D. *Independence of Auditors from Management*: Auditors are responsible to shareholders for reviewing the financial statements prepared by management and reporting on whether they fairly present the financial condition of the corporation. Where the independence of auditors from management is compromised, the risk that management will be able to engage in fraud and manipulation in the presentation of financial information is increased. Independence of auditors from management may be compromised where management is in a position to determine if the auditing firm receives lucrative consulting work in addition to its audit responsibilities.

E. *CEO/CFO Certification of Financial Statements*: Imposing a requirement for the chief executive officer and/or the chief financial officer to certify the accuracy of financial statements and holding them personally liable for misrepresentations in the statements has been suggested as a useful way to give CEOs and CFOs stronger incentives to be vigilant regarding the accuracy of the financial disclosure made by the corporation.

F. *Effectiveness of Accounting Rules*: Whether accounting rules are effective to ensure that the financial condition of the corporation is fairly presented in its financial statements will have an impact on the ability of shareholders to monitor what management is doing.

In the wake of the recent corporate scandals in the United States, including the bankruptcy of Enron Corp. in December 2001, and the massive losses sustained by shareholders as a result, corporate governance in all its aspects has been subjected to intense scrutiny in Canada, the United States, and elsewhere. Changes have been initiated in many areas in an effort not only to avoid the kind of serious fraud alleged in the Enron case but also to strengthen corporate governance with a view to restoring investor confidence in the market. In this context, the adequacy of both the market-based disciplines on management behaviour discussed in the preceding section and the legal framework for corporate governance has been questioned.

Concerns have been expressed regarding the ability of market disciplines to keep management acting in the interests of shareholders. At the very least, the dramatic collapse of a number of major U.S. corporations suggests that, even if reliance on markets is the best approach to corporate governance, it can have great costs. Perhaps more fundamentally, many have asked why the markets did not do a better job of assessing the risk of collapse of a business like Enron? Why, for example, did the market price not reflect the risk that the auditors of Enron, Arthur Andersen, would be compromised in fulfiling their responsibilities to shareholders by their interest in retaining lucrative consulting business from Enron and that their audit of the financial information provided by the corporation was therefore not reliable?[104]

---

104 J. N. Gordon, "What Enron Means for the Management and Control of the Modern Business Corporation: Some Initial Reflections," (2002) 69 U. Chicago L. R. 1233, at 1235–1240.

One possible response to the perceived failure of the market would be to impose new rules for corporate governance, making mandatory some of the best corporate governance practices identified above. Proponents of the market disciplines argue, however, that, notwithstanding the pain caused by the dramatic fall in some share prices, it is the market which should be relied on to respond to the need for improvements in corporate governance. Changes to legal rules, they claim, will involve significant compliance costs and encourage only technical compliance and searching for loopholes.[105] By contrast, only true improvements in governance practices will be rewarded by the market.[106]

There is some evidence that major corporations have already engaged in significant reforms to their corporate governance systems beyond what is required by law in the interests of maintaining the confidence of their shareholders. Improvements have been made in accounting disclosure, for example, and more and more corporations are installing as the chair of the board of directors a person who is not also the chief executive officer, in order to enhance the effectiveness of board oversight of management.[107] As well, many large institutional shareholders are becoming more actively involved in ensuring that the corporations in which they are investing have strong corporate governance practices.[108]

---

105 M. Czarnecka, "Corporate Governance: Unbridled Ambition, Shameless Greed" *Lexpert* (February 2003) 58 [*Lexpert*], citing Douglas Hyndman, chair of the British Columbia Securities Commission; Letter from TSX President and CEO Barbara Stymiest to OSC Chair David Brown, dated 17 September 2002, available at <http://www.tsx.ca> [*TSE Letter*].

106 McKinsey & Company issued a report in July 2002 entitled *Global Investor Opinion Survey: Key Findings*, which found that 57 percent of institutional investors felt that corporate governance was as important or more important than financial issues as a criterion for investment. Investors would be prepared to pay a premium for shares of corporations with good governance (11 percent for Canadian corporations).

107 *Lexpert*, above note 105, citing securities lawyer Laura Sabia; TSE Letter, above note 105.

108 In February 2003 one of the largest institutional investors in Canada, the Canada Pension Plan Investment Board, released its new guidelines, *Proxy Voting Principles and Guidelines*. This document indicates that the board will take a much more aggressive approach in determining how to vote its shares on a range of corporate governance issues. See <http://www.cppib.ca/who/policy/Proxy_Voting_Guidelines.pdf>. Some U.S. institutional investors are adopting a similar approach (see C. H. Deutsch, "Revolt of the Shareholders: At Annual Meetings, Anger will Ratchet Up a Notch," *The New York Times*, 23 February 2003, Section 3, at 1).

Notwithstanding these improvements in governance practices, the United States Congress responded to Enron and other corporate scandals by substantially expanding the legal framework for corporate governance by enacting the so-called "Sarbanes-Oxley" Act in 2002.[109] Sarbanes-Oxley mandates an array of best-practices in corporate governance and creates a number of criminal offences relating to corporate fraud. Detailed rules to implement these changes are being developed by the U.S. Securities and Exchange Commission (SEC). New listing requirements approved by the New York Stock Exchange in August 2002 contain a variety of additional mandatory requirements relating to corporate governance. Key features of these new rules include the following:

- A majority of board members and all members of the corporate governance, audit, and compensation committees must be independent, meaning that they have no material relationship with the corporation, apart from their roles as directors.
- The corporate governance, audit, and compensation committees must each have a written charter with prescribed content.
- Audit committees must discharge certain prescribed responsibilities, including appointing, discharging, and supervising the corporation's auditors, and have a certain level of financial expertise.
- Corporations must adopt a code of business conduct.
- Corporations must adopt and disclose corporate governance guidelines.
- Loans to directors and officers are prohibited.
- Disclosure documents, including annual and quarterly financial statements, must be certified by senior officers.
- A lawyer who reasonably believes that a material violation of securities laws, breach of fiduciary duty or similar violation has occurred, is occurring, or is about to occur must report evidence of the material violation to the CEO, chief legal officer or other appropriate officer within the company (referred to as "up-the-ladder reporting")
- If an outside lawyer believes that the board or a board committee has not appropriately responded within a reasonable period of time to evidence of a material violation that is ongoing or about to occur and is likely to result in substantial injury to the company or investor, the lawyer must:
  – withdraw from representing the company, indicating that withdrawal is based on "professional considerations"; and

---

109 PUB L. No. 107-204, 116 Stat. 745 (2002).

– within one business day of withdrawing, notify the SEC in writing of this withdrawal for "professional considerations" (referred to as a "noisy withdrawal").

In Canada, there is an emerging consensus on the desirability of a strong rules-based response to perceived problems in corporate governance. This marks a departure from the approach followed in Canada since the mid-1990s which has relied on voluntary compliance. Based on a study for the Toronto Stock Exchange,[110] the TSX established a number of best-practices benchmarks for corporate governance in 1995. The TSX requires listed corporations to report each year on the consistency of their corporate governance practices with these benchmarks.[111] Such a voluntary "principles-based" approach to corporate governance is similar to the approach followed in Europe, the United Kingdom, and Australia. In many respects, the content of the TSX benchmarks anticipated the recent changes in the legal rules in the United States.

Following the enactment of Sarbanes-Oxley, some in Canada remain in favour of a voluntary principles-based approach. The head of the securities commission in British Columbia,[112] the CEO of the TSX,[113] and the Canadian Council of Chief Executives[114] have argued in favour of retaining the present system with some enhancements, including a few new mandatory requirements.[115] In rejecting the detailed rules-based approach being pursued in the United States, they emphasize the differences in the scale of public corporations in Canada as compared to the United States, arguing that the application of rigid rules of the Sarbanes-Oxley type would be too onerous in Canada. As well, given the small pool of potential independent directors and the inability of many Canadian businesses to pay significant directors' fees, it is argued that

---

110 Dey Report, above note 97.

111 TSX Company Manual, s. 473.

112 *Lexpert*, above note 105. Securities commissions or similar bodies in each province are specialized agencies of the government responsible for the administration and enforcement of provincial securities laws. The securities regime is described in Chapter 11.

113 TSE Letter, above note 105.

114 Canadian Council of Chief Executives, *Governance Values and Competitiveness: A Commitment to Leadership* (2002), available at <http://www.ceocouncil.ca>.

115 The TSX board of directors approved new, more rigorous disclosure requirements and amended corporate governance guidelines on March 26, 2002. Further revisions were issued in November, 2002. These changes which remain subject to OSC approval, address many of the same issues as Sarbanes-Oxley and the New York Stock Exchange Listing Requirements.

compliance with rules along the lines of Sarbanes-Oxley would be impossible. Supporters of this view claim that the relatively small number of large Canadian corporations that could comply with such rules have shares listed in the United States and so are obliged to comply with U.S. rules in any event. While some additional mandatory obligations may be acceptable, the core of the Canadian corporate governance rules should be voluntary compliance with principles accompanied by mandatory disclosure of the extent to which benchmarks for governance are met and reasons for any non-compliance.

Most other securities regulators, including the chair of the Ontario Securities Commission (OSC), have questioned the effectiveness of a voluntary principles-based approach.[116] Recently, this position found support from a study which showed that 35 percent of corporations listed on the TSX were not fully in compliance with even the relatively soft obligation to disclose the extent to which they met the suggested benchmarks.[117] The report concluded that this level of non-compliance was inviting the imposition of mandatory requirements.

In December 2002 Ontario passed Bill 198, which amended the Ontario *Securities Act*.[118] Among other things, the Act gives the OSC the power to make rules governing the composition and conduct of audit committees, requires corporations to adopt systems of internal controls as well as disclosure controls and procedures, and directs chief executive officers and chief financial officers to provide certifications related to internal controls and disclosure controls and procedures. In June 2003, the OSC, along with all the provincial securities regulators except the British Columbia Securities Commission agreed to adopt rules[119] or regulations requiring CEOs and Chief Financial Officers to

---

116 D. Brown, "The Need for Balance: Why Regulators Must Pursue a Fair Market for Both Investors and Issuers," (2002), 25 O.S.C.B. 6491. Even Peter Dey, the Chair of the Committee that produced the Dey Report, above note 97, which led to the current TSX voluntary principles-based regime has argued in favour of making the voluntary standards mandatory and more comprehensive (J. MacFarland, "Dey gives governance momentum," *The Globe and Mail*, 5 February 2003, at B2).

117 TSE Compliance Study, above note 96.

118 *Keeping the Promise for a Strong Economy Act (Budget Measures), 2002*, S.O. 2002, c. 22, Part XXVI.

119 Some securities regulators, such as the Ontario Securities Commission, have been given the power by statute to make legally binding rules. Other provinces must pass regulations. The new rules on certification, auditors and audit committees will be enacted by the OSC pursuant to *Keeping the Promise for a Strong Economy Act (Budget Measures), 2002*, S.O. 2002, c. 22, s. 187(3) [*2002 OSA Amendments*].

certify their corporation's financial statements, setting standards for auditor independence, and the operation of audit committees. Bill 198 also provides that new securities fraud offences are to be created and civil liablity is to attach for misrepresentations made by corporations in their disclosures to the public and where a required disclosure has not been made. As of June 2003, the securities fraud amendments had been proclaimed in force. The amendments to establish the civil liability regime were not in force.[120]

On June 12, 2003, the federal government introduced two bills to enhance the criminal law rules relating to securities market activities. Bill C-46 creates new criminal offences related to insider trading, which augment the offences created under the *CBCA* and provincial securities laws. A new offence is also created for corporations that retaliate against whistle blowers who provide information regarding an offence to law enforcement authorities.[121] As well, the Bill contemplates stiffer criminal penalties for capital market fraud. The penalty for defrauding the public or any person of property, money or valuable securities, or engaging in intentionally fraudulent acts that affect the public market price of shares will be increased to a maximum sentence of 14 years imprisonment from the current maximum of ten years. A companion bill, Bill C-46, broadens the category of persons whose behaviour may result in criminal liability for the corporation.[122] The Bill provides that a corporation may be deemed to be a party to a criminal offence committed by one of its representatives if a senior officer was knowingly involved in the offence or was aware of the offence and knowingly failed to take all reasonable measures to stop the representative's participation in the offence. Unlike the common law standard, the senior officer need not be a "directing mind" of the organization. The bill also enhances the investigatory powers of law enforcement officials and sets new and tougher sentencing guidelines for capital markets offences and offences committed by corporations.

Thinking on corporate governance in Canada has been dramatically affected by the major corporate scandals in the United States and the rules-based Amercian response. Some changes to aspects of corporate governance outside the legal framework have been introduced

---

120 The disclosure obligations of public corporations are discussed in Chapter 11.

121 Bill C-46, *An Act to amend the Criminal Code (capital markets fraud and evidence gathering)*. Insider trading is discussed in Chapter 11.

122 Bill C-45, *An Act to amend the Criminal Code (criminal liability of organizations)*. The common law rules regarding criminal responsibility are discussed in Chapter 5.

already.[123] The legal framework for corporate governance is likely to evolve significantly over the next few years.

I. CHAPTER SUMMARY

In this chapter, we discussed how powers are allocated among shareholders, directors, and officers. We began by noting the clear division of responsibilities and powers contained in the *CBCA*: directors have the power to manage, or supervise the management, of the business and affairs of the corporation. They may appoint officers and delegate to them most of their powers to manage. Shareholders are the claimants to the residual value of the corporation, but their only real power is to elect the directors and to vote on matters submitted to them.

We discussed the rules governing how shareholders exercise power through voting at meetings. We surveyed the various technical requirements for calling and holding meetings, including the use of proxies, someone the shareholder appoints to vote on his behalf, and management's responsibility to solicit proxies, by sending out a form of proxy as well as a variety of other information in a "management proxy circular." This document contains both general information regarding the corporation and specific information on matters to be voted on. We also discussed shareholder proposals, the mechanism by which shareholders can get matters put on the agenda for discussion at meetings. Finally, other access to information rights, which facilitate effective shareholder participation in the corporation, were identified.

Next we discussed directors and how they exercise power, beginning with the rules governing how people become directors and continuing with a survey of the technical rules governing the calling and holding of meetings. We noted that, for all but the smallest businesses, directors must delegate some of their powers to officers and, in some cases, to persons outside the corporate hierarchy. The *CBCA* requires that some powers relating to the internal corporate affairs of the corporation remain with the directors, but most may be delegated so long as the board remains able to exercise control over the delegate.

---

123 In July 2002, for example, the Canadian Securities Administrators, the Office of the Superintendent of Financial Insitutions and The Canadian Institute of Chartered Accountants (CICA) announced the creation of a new Canadian Public Accountability Board responsible for promoting auditor independence and overseeing the work of auditors of public companies. The CICA has also issued proposed new guidelines on auditor independence.

An important aspect of the law governing directors and officers is to what extent they may be indemnified for liabilities incurred in connection with fulfilling their responsibilities. With the expanding range of circumstances in which directors and officers may have personal liability, it will be difficult to attract competent people to assume these roles if they have to bear all the costs associated with such liability. On the other hand, if indemnification is too extensive, directors and officers will have no incentive to avoid conduct that is contrary to the interests of the corporation and prohibited by regulatory laws that impose personal liability. Under the *CBCA*, the primary way in which this balance is addressed is to require, as a condition of qualifying for indemnification, that a director or officer must have discharged her fiduciary duty to act in the best interests of the corporation. In *R. v. Bata Industries*, indemnification was upheld, even though the corporation was proposing to indemnify officers who were found guilty of offences under provincial environmental laws.

We also discussed shareholders' agreements. Such agreements serve two primary purposes: to create specific arrangements regarding the exercise of shareholders' powers which are different from what the governing corporate law would otherwise provide; and to create rules to govern share transfers. Where shareholder agreements are unanimous, they may further customize the structure of the corporation by transferring some or all of the directors' powers and responsibilities to the shareholders. Such unanimous shareholders' agreements are specifically sanctioned by the *CBCA* and statutes modelled after it, and benefit from certain enhanced enforcement rights in these statutes.

We examined, in general terms, how the division of power and responsibility in corporate law is unrealized in many public corporations, both in terms of the practical ability of shareholders to take advantage of the control mechanisms provided in the *CBCA* and in terms of the degree of control that directors really have over the management of the business and affairs of the corporation. We also discussed the ways in which the division of powers is often of little relevance for closely held corporations. Finally, we considered some of the new challenges to the legal model of corporate governance raised by the recent corporate failures in the United States and the imposition of detailed new rules for corporate governance in that country. There is an emerging consensus on expanding the existing legal framework to mandate particular corporate governance practices. This departs from the existing approach in Canada that relies on voluntary compliance with best-practices benchmarks accompanied by disclosure of the level of compliance and reasons for non-compliance.

FURTHER READINGS

BOWAL, P., "Expensive Day at the Office: Can Corporations Indemnify Their Agents Who Suffer Personal Liability for Regulatory Offenses?" (1995) 45 U.T.L.J. 247

CHEFFINS, B.R., *Company Law: Theory, Structure and Organization* (Oxford: Clarendon, 1997)

CLARK, R., *Corporate Law* (Boston: Little Brown & Co., 1986)

CRÊTE, R., *The Proxy System in Canadian Corporations: A Critical Analysis* (Montreal: Wilson & Lafleur, 1986)

DANIELS, R.J., & S.M. HUTTON, "The Capricious Cushion: The Implications of the Directors' and Officers' Liability Insurance Crisis on Canadian Corporate Governance" (1993) 22 Can. Bus. L.J. 182

DANIELS, R.J., & E.J. WAITZER, "Challenges to the Citadel: A Brief Overview of Recent Trends in Canadian Corporate Governance" (1994) 23 Can. Bus. L.J. 23

DAWSON, G.W., *Shareholders' agreements: an annotated guide* (Aurora, Ont.: Canada Law Book, 1996)

DIMMA, W.A., "Putting shareholders first" (1997) 62 Business Q. 33

DISNEY, M., "The Shareholder Agreement: Some Basic Issues" (Parts 1, 2, & 3) (1995) 14 Nat'l Banking L. Rev. 47, 51, & 67

EASTERBROOK, F.H., & D.R. FISCHEL, "Corporate Control Transactions" (1982) 91 Yale L.J. 698

EASTERBROOK, F.H., & D.R. FISCHEL, *The Economic Structure of Corporate Law* (Boston: Harvard University Press, 1991)

EWASIUK, R.W., *Drafting shareholders' agreements: a guide* (Scarborough, Ont.: Carswell, 1998)

FLANNIGAN, R., "Corporations controlled by shareholders: principals, agents or servants? (Parts 1–3)" (1990) 5 S.C.R.R. 6

HANSELL, C., *Directors and Officers in Canada: Law and Practice* (Toronto: Carswell, 1999)

HAY, R.J., & L.A. SMITH, "The Unanimous Shareholder Agreement: A New Device for Shareholder Control" (1985) 10 Can. Bus. L.J. 440

INDUSTRY CANADA, Unanimous Shareholder Agreements (*Canada Business Corporations Act* Discussion Paper) (Ottawa: Industry Canada, 1996)

JENSEN, M.C., & W.H. MECKLING, "Theory of the Firm: Managerial Behavior, Agency Costs and Ownership Structure" (1976) 3 J. Fin. Econ. 305

McCALL, C., & R. WILSON, "Shareholder Proposals: Why Not in Canada?" (1993) 5 Corp. Governance. Rev. 12

MacINTOSH, J.G., "The Role of Institutional and Retail Investors in Canadian Capital Markets" (1993) 31 Osgoode Hall L.J. 371

NATHAN, H.R., & M.E. VOORE, *Corporate Meetings: Law and Practice* (Toronto: Carswell, 1995)

NICHOLL, J.I.S., "Directors' and Officers' Liability Insurance" in L. Sarna, ed., *Corporate Structure, Finance, and Operations*, vol. 4, (Toronto: Carswell, 1986)

ROMANO, R., *The Genius of American Corporate Law* (New York: AEI Press, 1993)

ROMANO, R., ed., *Foundations of Corporate Law* (Oxford: Oxford University Press, 1993)

WAINBERG, J.G. & H. R. NATHAN, *Wainberg and Nathan's Company Meetings, Including Rules of Order*, 5th ed. (Don Mills: CCH Canadian Ltd., 2001)

CHAPTER 8

DUTIES AND LIABILITIES OF DIRECTORS AND OFFICERS

A. INTRODUCTION

In previous chapters, we discussed the problem of the agency costs faced by shareholders as a result of the incentives for directors and officers to act in their own interests rather than those of the corporation. In this chapter, we examine some of the ways the law addresses this problem by imposing duties on directors and officers which require them to meet certain standards of behaviour. Directors and officers are subject to a fiduciary duty to act "honestly and in good faith with a view to the best interests of the corporation," as well as a duty of care to "exercise the care, diligence and skill that a reasonably prudent person would exercise in comparable circumstances." These duties were developed by the common law courts and are now enshrined in statute in most Canadian jurisdictions (e.g., *CBCA*, s. 122(1)).[1]

The fiduciary duty and duty of care are owed to the corporation rather than to the shareholders directly. Because shareholders are not the direct beneficiaries of these duties, the common law courts did not allow shareholders to take action when these duties were not complied with. The *CBCA* and statutes modelled after it have greatly enhanced access to shareholder remedies by expanding the circumstances in

---

1   E.g., Ontario *Business Corporations Act*, R.S.O. 1990, c. B-16 [*OBCA*], s. 134(1); Alberta *Business Corporations Act*, R.S.A. 2000, c. B-9 [*ABCA*], s. 122(1)(a); and British Columbia *Company Act*, R.S.B.C. 1996 [*BCCA*], c. 62, ss. 118 & 135.

which shareholders can initiate actions for a breach of duty owed to the corporation if the directors refuse to do so. Also, the so-called oppression remedy creates not only a process for obtaining a remedy but a new substantive basis for shareholders to obtain relief where directors or the corporation have oppressed their interests. As a result, the oppression provisions create a new standard of behaviour for directors and officers which both complements and overlaps with the fiduciary duty and the duty of care. This standard will be discussed in detail in Chapter 9, as will a variety of remedial options available under the *CBCA* and other corporate statutes.

In addition to these obligations under corporate law, directors and officers face continually expanding sources of liability under a wide range of regulatory statutes that seek to promote enforcement of corporate obligations by imposing personal liability on directors, officers, and employees involved in the failure of the corporation to meet its obligations. We briefly discuss these statutory liabilities.

Finally, the courts have held directors and officers liable in tort in a variety of circumstances where they were acting in the course of their duties. The broad application of tort liablity in this way erodes the separate legal personality of the corporation. The last section of this chapter discusses the range of circumstances in which directors and officers may be found liable in tort.

B. FIDUCIARY DUTY

1) Introduction

The fiduciary duty is a general standard of behaviour imposed on directors and officers in relation to their dealings with and on behalf of the corporation. The *CBCA* provides the following pithy formulation of the duty:

> Every director and officer of a corporation in exercising their powers and discharging their duties shall ... act honestly and in good faith with a view to the best interests of the corporation ... (s. 122(1)(a)).

Even though countless cases have addressed the fiduciary duty, its content and even its rationale remain elusive. Some commentators from the law and economics school seek to justify and give content to the fiduciary duty based on the agency-cost analysis referred to in Chapter 7. They argue that the duty is necessary to counteract the incentive for directors and officers to benefit themselves personally at the expense of the corporation. The wide range of self-interested activity in which fiduciaries may engage renders it infeasible for shareholders to negotiate to be protected against such behaviour at the time of their investment. It would be simply too costly and too time-consuming to specify fully all the types of behaviour that fiduciaries are prohibited from engaging in. Because the negotiating costs preclude an agreement which addresses all possible situations, the imposition of a general statutory standard is justified. Based on this analysis, a court trying to determine what the fiduciary duty requires in any particular case must ask what the shareholders would have agreed to if they had been permitted to bargain and there were no costs associated with the bargaining process.[2] Another theory to explain the fiduciary duty is that it promotes the basic values of responsibility and integrity which are common to all members of society. A third is that the duty is imposed because directors and officers have the power to expose the corporation to risk of loss. Despite these analyses and others, there is no generally accepted theory that assists in deciding what the obligation requires in any particular case.

Nevertheless, the *CBCA* formulation does provide some guidance. The duty to act "honestly" seems straightforward enough: directors and officers are prohibited from acting fraudulently in relation to the corporation. They must not intend to deprive the corporation of some asset or benefit to which it is entitled for their personal gain. Beyond honesty, directors and officers must try to do what is best for the corporation.

As noted, the duty is owed to the corporation, not to the shareholders or to any other stakeholder or group of stakeholders. Thus, in each case, the content of the duty will be defined by reference to the interests of the corporation in the circumstances. Unfortunately, while it is fairly simple to determine the interests of particular stakeholders, it is often difficult, in the abstract, to think of what the interests of the corporation are, particularly if we think of the corporation as essentially the focus of stakeholder claims as discussed in Chapter 1. Also, the nature of stakeholder claims on the limited resources of the corporation is that, inevitably, they will be in conflict. To take a simple example, the interests of employees in high wages may conflict with creditors' interest in getting paid. While high wages may lead to happy, productive workers, it may reduce cash flow available to pay off creditors. To what extent do the "best interests" of the corporation require directors to accommodate the divergent interests of these groups, and on what basis should such accommodation be effected? In Canada, the courts have tended to disregard the interests of other stakeholders and

---

2   For example, F.H. Easterbrook & D.R. Fischel, "Corporate Control Transactions" (1982) 81 Yale L.J. 689.

to treat the interests of the corporation as coextensive with the interests of shareholders.[3] No corporation will maximize share value if it completely ignores the interests of its employees, customers, creditors, and other stakeholders, but management is not permitted to favour the interests of other stakeholders at the expense of share value. As discussed below, courts have been reluctant to review how management does this in the context of making business decisions.

The obligation to maximize shareholder value does not require that directors and officers do their best to promote the interests of any particular shareholder. It is an obligation to maximize the value of shareholders' investment in general. This is true even if the director is a nominee of a particular shareholder.[4] Where, however, some special relationship exists distinct from the director's or officer's position, such as a family relationship or another relationship of trust and dependency, a special obligation to that shareholder may arise which overlaps the fiduciary duty.[5]

Consistent with their conception of the fiduciary duty, the courts developed a rule that shareholders could agree to absolve a fiduciary of her breach of duty. Such absolution by shareholders, called ratification, is no longer effective to relieve a fiduciary of liability for a breach of fiduciary duty under statutes like the *CBCA*, but shareholder approval may be taken into account for certain purposes that are discussed at the end of this section.

The fiduciary duty to the corporation is similar to the obligation of a trustee to a beneficiary, at least to the extent that it requires directors

---

3   Some recent challenges to this view are discussed in Chapter 12. Some cases have suggested that, where a corporation is on the brink of insolvency, directors' fiduciary duty may require them not to take steps to prejudice creditors' interests (e.g., *369413 Alberta Ltd.* v. *Pocklington* (2000), 194 D.L.R. (4th) 109 (Alta. C.A.); *Canbook Distribution Corp.* v. *Borins* (1999), 41 O.R. (3d) 565 (Sup. Ct. J.)). In *Private Equity Management Co.* v. *Vianet Technologies Inc.* (2000), 48 O.R. (3d) 294 (Sup. Ct. J.), the court refused to strike out a statement of claim alleging such a duty, saying that the law is "fluid" (at 304–5). In *Peoples Department Stores (Trustee of)* v. *Wise*, [2003] Q.J. No. 505 (QL) (C.A.), application for leave to appeal to S.C.C. filed 28 March 2003 [*Peoples Department Stores*], the Quebec Court of Appeal held that, even where the corporation is on the brink of insolvency, management has no obligation to creditors. See, generally, D. Thomson, "Directors, Creditors and Insolvency: A Duty not to Oppress" (2000) 58 U of T Fac. L. Rev. 31.

4   *Deluce Holdings Inc.* v. *Air Canada* (1992), 98 D.L.R. (4th) 509 (Ont. Gen. Div.). The *ABCA*, above note 1, provides some scope from nominee directors to take special cognizance of the interests of the shareholders they represent. This provision is discussed below under "Other Breaches of Fiduciary Duty."

5   *Malcolm* v. *Transtec Holding Co.* (2001), 12 B.L.R. (3d) 66 (B.C.C.A.) [*Transtec*].

and officers not to put their personal interests ahead of the interests of the corporation. What this involves in practice can be discussed most meaningfully in the context of particular fact situations. We will deal with the following typical conflict-of-interest situations in some detail:

- the director or officer is involved in some transaction with the corporation in his personal capacity;
- the director of officer takes advantage of opportunities personally which it was her duty to try to obtain for the corporation;
- the director or officer competes with the corporation; and
- the director or officer stands to benefit personally by blocking a takeover bid for control of her corporation that would benefit the corporation.

Certain other situations in which conflicts of interest arise are discussed at the end of this section.

In almost all cases in which a breach of fiduciary duty occurs, the fiduciary has made some profit or received some advantage at the expense of the corporation. The principal remedy granted by the courts where a breach of fiduciary duty has occurred is to require the fiduciary to account for his profits to the corporation. The rationale behind this kind of relief is easy to see: if a fiduciary cannot profit from a breach of his fiduciary duty, he has no incentive to commit the breach.

2) Transacting with the Corporation

The conflict of interest arising when a director or officer contracts with the corporation may be illustrated by the following simple example. A person seeks to sell goods to the corporation of which she is a director. As the seller, she has an incentive to negotiate the highest possible price for her goods. The corporation's interest is precisely the opposite: it wants to get the goods for the lowest possible price. Her duty binds her to do whatever is in her power to get the lowest price for the corporation. If, as a director, she is charged with negotiating the contract on behalf of the corporation, she is in an acute conflict of interest. Even if she is not directly involved in the negotiations on behalf of the corporation as a director, she may be in a position to influence the corporation's decision making either directly, as a member of the board if the contract must be approved by the board, or indirectly, by virtue of her relationship with the corporation and its personnel.

Because of the inevitable conflict of interest for the directors in such situations, the courts developed a rule that these kinds of transactions were voidable — that is, they could be set aside — at the option of the corporation. There was no enquiry as to whether the transaction was a good or a bad deal for the corporation. This rigid standard was described in *Aberdeen Railway Co. v. Blaikie Bros.*,[6] a case involving the purchase of some chairs from a partnership in which a director was a partner:

> ... it is a rule of universal application that no one having such duties to discharge shall be allowed to enter into engagements in which he has or can have a personal interest conflicting or which possibly may conflict with the interests of those whom he is bound to protect. So strictly is this principle adhered to that no question is allowed to be raised as to the fairness or unfairness of a contract so entered into.

Under this strict rule, it did not matter if the fiduciary's interest was direct and beneficial, such as where she was dealing with the corporation herself, or indirect or as a trustee. An example of the latter case is *Transvaal Lands Co. v. New Belgium (Transvaal) Land and Development Co.*[7] In that case, a director of one corporation (Corporation A) held certain shares in a second corporation (Corporation B) as a trustee for the benefit of his wife under her father's will. In a transaction in which the director took no active part, all the shares held by Corporation B in a third corporation were sold to Corporation A. The court found that there was a breach of fiduciary duty. It did not matter that there was no direct conflict between the director's personal interest and his duty as director. As a trustee, the director was obliged to safeguard the interests of the beneficiary by ensuring that Corporation B got the highest price for the shares to be sold, just as he would if he were managing his own assets. As a director of Corporation A, he was obliged to seek the lowest possible price. In light of the conflict, the contract was voidable.

Part of the rationale for this strict rule was that the courts were reluctant to take responsibility for making difficult judgments about when a conflict is a problem. They did not want to have to assess when a personal interest in a transaction was significant enough to affect someone's judgment and behaviour. Such an assessment would depend significantly on the fiduciary himself and the situation in which he found himself. It would be hard for a court, many months later and removed from the situation, to make such an assessment with confidence. Also, the courts wanted to establish a clear rule which did not require the person in the conflict of interest to have to make a decision about whether the conflict was sufficiently serious that she should

---

6   (1854), [1843–1860] All E.R. Rep. 249 (H.L.) [*Aberdeen*].
7   [1914] 2 Ch. 488 (C.A.) [*Transvaal*].

refrain from entering the transaction or that she should take some other step to exclude herself from the transaction. As a result, even transactions in which the director's or officer's interest "possibly may conflict" with her duty were prohibited.

The *CBCA* and most other Canadian statutes have modified this rigid rule to permit certain transactions between a director or officer and her corporation which are beneficial to the corporation, provided certain procedural safeguards are observed. This change was motivated by the recognition that in some cases the best price or, perhaps, the only source of supply is a person related in some way to a director or officer. This situation will frequently occur in the case of transactions between affiliated corporations and transactions with closely held corporations. The scheme to be followed in relation to a transaction involving a director or officer of a corporation is set out in section 120 of the *CBCA*.[8]

Section 120 applies where a director or officer of a corporation

- is a party to a material contract or material transaction whether entered into or proposed with the corporation,
- is a director or officer or an individual acting in a similar capacity of a party to such a contract or transaction, or
- has a material interest in a party to such a contract or transaction.

No definition of material contract or transaction is found in the *CBCA*, and no cases have considered it.[9] It would appear that contracts which are not material, or in connection with which the director or officer does not have a material interest, cannot benefit from the scheme. Such a transaction will be a technical breach of fiduciary duty but likely will have no practical consequences. If a contract is not material, neither the corporation nor an interested director or officer will have much to gain or lose. For example, a director holding a few hundred shares in Bell Canada Enterprises Ltd., one of Canada's largest corporations, is not likely to be affected in performing his duty in connection with negotiating a telephone contract for the corporation. The materiality threshold may be intended simply to eliminate the need to comply with the requirements of the scheme for such trivial conflicts.

---

8   Other statutes modelled on the *CBCA*, R.S.C. 1985, c. C-44, as amended [*CBCA*], provide a similar scheme. E.g., *OBCA*, above note 1, s. 132; and *ABCA* above note 1, s. 120. The *BCCA*, above note 1, provides a different scheme (ss. 120–123, 35, 137).

9   The *Canada Business Corporations Act Regulations* (SOR/2001-512) [*CBCA Regulations*] provide some guidelines about the meaning of material for the purpose of what must be disclosed in a management proxy circular (s. 57(s)).

In this regard, one way of defining the materiality threshold for directors' or officers' interests is to ask whether the interest is such that there is any reasonable basis for a concern that it may affect his ability to perform his duty.

If section 120 applies to a transaction, an interested director or officer must give written notice to the corporation of the nature and extent of his interest or request to have this information entered in the minutes of a directors' meeting (*CBCA*, s. 120(1)). The Act sets out specific requirements regarding when notice must be given in section 120(2) and (3). There is no precise formula for how much detail must be provided in the notice. It will depend on the nature of the contract proposed and the context in which it arises. Nevertheless, in general, it must be sufficiently detailed to disclose the costs incurred and the possible profits to be received by the director or officer.[10] In other words, consistent with the language in the statute, it is not sufficient merely to mention that a fiduciary has an interest; it is necessary to state what the interest is and how far it goes.[11]

In some cases, such as where a director of a corporation is also the director of a corporation that is a customer of the corporation, disclosure would have to be made repeatedly. To address this kind of situation, the *CBCA* and other statutes permit a general notice to be made to the effect that a director or officer is interested in all contracts with a particular corporation (e.g., *CBCA*, s. 120(6)). There is no express requirement to disclose the nature and extent of one's interest in such a general notice, though it would be consistent with the scheme of section 120 to read such a requirement into the provision. As well, the *2001 Amendments* impose a requirement to disclose any material change in directors' and officers' interests from time to time.[12]

A contract in which a director or officer has an interest must be approved by the directors or shareholders to be enforceable (*CBCA*, s. 120(7) & (8)). Subject to certain limited exceptions, a director is prohibited from voting on any contract in which she has an interest

---

10   *Wedge* v. *McNeill* (1981), 33 Nfld. & P.E.I.R. 272 (P.E.I.S.C.), rev'd on other grounds (1982), 39 Nfld. & P.E.I.R. 205 (P.E.I.C.A.).

11   In *Neptune (Vehicle Washing Equipment) Ltd.* v. *Fitzgerald*, [1995] 3 All E.R. 811 (Ch.), a decision under the *English Companies Act*, (U.K.), 1985, c. 6, which contains a provision similar to section 120 of the *CBCA*, above note 8, it was held that a sole director must declare his interest at a meeting with himself. Though he need not say anything out loud, his interest must be entered in the minutes.

12   Under the amendments to the *CBCA*, *ibid.*, in 2001 (S.C. 2001, c. 14) [*2001 Amendments*], shareholders have a right to examine the minutes of directors' meetings relating to these disclosures (s. 120(6.1)).

(*CBCA*, s. 120(5)). Such a director or officer may, however, be present at a meeting of directors called to approve the contract and may be counted in the quorum. As noted in Chapter 7, the exceptional circumstances in which an interested director is permitted to vote include contracts relating to remuneration as a director, officer, employee, or agent and her indemnification, as well as contracts with affiliated corporations (*CBCA*, s. 120(5)).[13] Compliance with the technical requirements of the scheme does not mean that the director or officer is then free to act as she pleases. She is still obliged to act honestly, in good faith, and with a view to the best interests of the corporation.[14] She would be required, for example, to ensure that her remuneration was reasonable.

In addition to the proper notice and approval requirements being met, the contract must be fair and reasonable to the corporation. If all three requirements are met the contract is neither void nor voidable.[15] Since the *2001 Amendments*, the *CBCA* provides that the common law remedy of an accounting for profits is also excluded.[16] The director or officer cannot be required to pay over to the corporation any benefit received in connection with the transaction.

The *CBCA* provides an alternative scheme to save contracts where the requirements set out above have not been complied with. The contract may still be rendered enforceable and the director or officer may be free to keep any profits if three requirements are met:

- the director's or officer's interest was disclosed to shareholders in sufficient detail to indicate its nature;
- the contract or transaction was approved by a special resolution of the shareholders; and
- the contract or transaction was reasonable and fair to the corporation at the time it was approved (*CBCA*, s. 120(7.1)).

---

13   Affiliated corporations are defined in s. 1(2) of the *CBCA*, *ibid.*, as corporations under common control.

14   *Levy-Russell Ltd.* v. *Tecmotiv Ltd.* (1994), 13 B.L.R. (2d) 1 (Ont. Gen. Div.) [*Levy-Russell*].

15   A contract that is *void* cannot be enforced by either party. As noted, if a contract is *voidable* at the instance of one party, the contract may be enforced or not at the option of that party.

16   This change brings the *CBCA*, above note 8, into line with the *OBCA*, above note 1, s. 132(7), and the *ABCA*, above note 1, s. 120(8), which both relieve directors and officers of liability to account for profits. *Cook* v. *Deeks*, [1916] 1 A.C. 554 (P.C.) [*Cook*] suggests that an accounting is not available in these circumstances. Professor Welling, however, suggests that it is (B. Welling, *Corporate Law in Canada: The Governing Principles*, 2d ed. (Toronto: Butterworths, 1991) at 453–54) [*Welling*].

If any of these requirements have not been satisfied, the conflict of interest results in a breach of fiduciary duty and the contract is voidable at the option of the corporation. As will be discussed in Chapter 9, in some circumstances a shareholder, with the permission of the court, may initiate a derivative action on behalf of the corporation to seek relief for breach of fiduciary duty (*CBCA*, s. 239). Where requirements of section 120 are not met, however, the *CBCA* provides a more direct and expeditious way for shareholders to seek relief. A shareholder may apply directly to a court to set aside the contract. This provision expressly permits the court to make an order directing the director or officer to account for profits received by her as well (*CBCA*, s. 120(8)).[17]

It is important to note that compliance with the scheme set out in section 120 is the only way to avoid the consequences of a fiduciary breach under the *CBCA*. It used to be that corporations could insert in their constitution or by-laws their own mechanisms to render such contracts enforceable, such as a provision that rendered contracts enforceable if approved by shareholders.[18] This option is not available under the *CBCA* and the statutes modelled after it. The fiduciary duty, notwithstanding its common law roots, is now a statutory duty, as indicated above. The *CBCA* and statutes based on it[19] provide that "no provision in a contract, the articles, the by-laws or a resolution relieves a director or officer from the duty to act in accordance with this Act or the regulations or relieves him from liability for a breach thereof" (*CBCA*, s. 122(3)).

3) Taking Corporate Opportunities

A second situation in which a conflict between the personal interests of a fiduciary and her duty to the corporation arises in circumstances where the fiduciary considers investing or otherwise taking advantage of some project or opportunity in which the corporation may be said to have an interest. This situation arises frequently, since one of the principal tasks of management is to make choices about what projects the corporation should invest in, whether it be the acquisition of an

---

17   A court will not exercise its discretion to provide relief where it is satisfied that nothing would have turned out differently if the requirements of the act had been complied with (*Baranowski v. Binks Manufacturing Co.* (2000), 49 C.C.E.L. (2d) 170 (Ont. Sup. Ct. J.)).

18   For example, *Transvaal*, above note 7.

19   E.g., *OBCA*, above note 1, s. 134(3); and *ABCA*, above note 1, s. 122(3). The *BCCA*, above note 1, has a similar provision (s. 119).

asset, establishing a business, or entering a lucrative contract. If fiduciaries were permitted to invest personally in projects to the exclusion of the corporation, there is a risk that fiduciaries, in pursuit of their self-interest, would appropriate to themselves valuable investment opportunities that they should have sought for the corporation. The fiduciary duty applies to prohibit fiduciaries from allowing their personal interest to conflict with their duty to the corporation in this way.

A variety of difficult issues arise in determining what the fiduciary duty requires in relation to the appropriation of corporate opportunities. How does one determine if the opportunity belongs to the corporation, so that the fiduciary should be prohibited from taking it? Can it be said to belong to the corporation if the corporation, for some reason, could not have exploited the opportunity in any case, or had expressly rejected the opportunity? Is every opportunity in the area of the corporation's business a corporate opportunity? Does it make any difference if the fiduciary found out about the opportunity by virtue of his position as a director or officer? To what extent can a fiduciary take an opportunity after he has resigned as a director and officer? In the following section, we will seek to respond to these questions, though, as will become clear, it is very difficult and ultimately unhelpful to try to establish brightline distinctions in this area of the law.

Where a corporation is actively negotiating for an opportunity and has a reasonable prospect of getting it, there is no question that the corporation has an interest in the opportunity and a fiduciary is prohibited from exploiting it in her personal capacity. *Cook* v. *Deeks*[20] is a good example. In that case, three directors of a corporation were negotiating with a railway to obtain a construction contract for the corporation, as they had done on previous occasions. During the negotiations, they decided to obtain the contract for themselves, not the corporation. They informed the railway of their plan and, eventually, the contract was made between the directors and the railway. The court held that the directors had breached their fiduciary duty to the corporation because they had actively promoted their own interests at the expense of the corporation and used their positions with the corporation to do so. As a result, they were liable to pay the profits they had obtained from the contract over to the corporation.

Where there is some impediment to the corporation obtaining an opportunity, the courts have held that it nevertheless belongs to the corporation, with the result that the fiduciaries cannot exploit it themselves. An interesting example of this kind of situation occurred in *Regal*

---

20   *Cook*, above note 16.

(Hastings) Ltd. v. *Gulliver.*[21] The corporation, Regal (Hastings) Ltd. (Regal), owned one cinema and was seeking to obtain a lease of two others through a wholly owned subsidiary corporation. The landlord of the two cinemas refused to agree to the lease unless either the directors guaranteed the lease obligations personally or the amount invested in shares of the subsidiary was at least £5000. The directors were reluctant to provide the guarantees, and Regal had only £2000 to invest in shares of the subsidiary. At a meeting of the directors it was agreed that they would resolve the problem by personally investing the remaining £3000 in shares of the subsidiary. The shares were issued to the directors at a price of £1 per share. At the same meeting, the directors voted to approve the sale of Regal's interest in the three theatres to a purchaser. Ultimately, this sale was accomplished by selling the purchaser all the shares of Regal and the shares of the subsidiary held by the directors. The directors received £3.16 for their shares, giving them a profit of £2.16 per share. The new shareholders of Regal elected a new board of directors. The new board caused Regal to sue the former directors, alleging that they had breached their fiduciary duty and demanding that they hand over the profits they had made on the sale of the shares.

The court granted judgment for Regal. It held that the directors had used their positions as directors to make a personal profit, which the board was obliged to try to obtain for the corporation. The court stated that there was no requirement to find that the directors had not acted in what they thought was the best interests of the corporation, nor was it relevant whether the corporation could have otherwise obtained the leases. There does not have to be an actual conflict of interest for there to be a breach of fiduciary duty. This reasoning reflects the policy referred to above in *Aberdeen Railway* v. *Blaikie*[22] that fiduciary duty rules should be designed to remove any possible incentive for fiduciaries to put their interests first. Fiduciaries must not be permitted to decide whether to adopt a corporate strategy which benefits them personally over alternatives which do not. In addition to the obvious risk that directors might be tempted to characterize the opportunity as one the corporation could not obtain in any other way, permitting the directors to make this call would pose a problem for judicial oversight. Courts generally do not like to second-guess directors on issues such as whether there was any viable business alternative to the strategy benefiting the directors. They recognize that they do not have business expertise and that their conclusion on such ques-

21   [1942] 1 All E.R. 378 (H.L.).
22   Above note 6.

tions necessarily would be speculative. On the facts of *Regal*, it seems likely that some alternative could have been found which would not have involved the enrichment of the directors. Perhaps Regal could have borrowed the money on the strength of the offer to purchase the three cinemas. In any event, the rule is clear: the directors' fiduciary duty precluded them from profiting from any strategy they adopted. Given this basis for the rule, the fact that the new shareholders of Regal received an unexpected windfall was found to be irrelevant.[23]

In *Regal (Hastings)* v. *Gulliver*, the House of Lords articulated various tests for determining whether the directors had breached their duty. In essence, the Lords said that the directors had breached their duties if they received a profit through the acquisition and resale of their shares only by reason of the fact that they were directors and in the course of acting as directors. What does this mean as applied to the facts in *Regal*?

First, it means that the opportunity arose only because they were directors; otherwise, they would not have known of the opportunity,[24] nor would they have been able to obtain the shares in the subsidiary. Second, they acted as a board in conceiving and implementing the financing arrangement from which they benefited. Only the board could have caused the shares to be issued so as to provide the necessary financing.

The scope of the test in *Regal (Hastings)* v. *Gulliver* was narrowed in *Peso Silver Mines Ltd.* v. *Cropper*.[25] The board of directors of a mining corporation named Peso Silver Mines Ltd. (Peso) considered and, after receiving professional advice, rejected an opportunity to acquire certain mining claims because of constrained finances and for other business reasons. Cropper was a member of the board and an officer of the corporation. A few months after Peso had rejected the opportunity, Cropper, along with others, formed a corporation that acquired them. Ultimately, Peso sued Cropper, alleging breach of fiduciary duty and

---

23 See also *Hoffman Products Ltd.* v. *Karr* (1989), 70 O.R. (2d) 789 (H.C.J.), leave to appeal denied (1990), 72 O.R. (2d) 797 (Div.Ct.) for a decision on facts similar to *Regal* where the court reached an opposite result. Now, under the *CBCA* and similar statutes, former shareholders can seek relief under the oppression remedy (*CBCA*, above note 8, s. 241). If the same situation occurred today, the former shareholders of Regal could have claimed that their interests were oppressed, unfairly prejudiced, or unfairly disregarded.

24 In *Phipps* v. *Boardman*, [1965] Ch. 992 (C.A.), aff'd (*sub nom. Boardman* v. *Phipps*) (1966), [1967] 2 A.C. 46 (H.L.), the court held that knowledge gained by a trustee while acting as a trustee cannot be used by the trustee to gain personal profit.

25 (1965), 56 D.L.R. (2d) 117 (B.C.C.A.), aff'd [1966] S.C.R. 673.

claiming that Cropper's interest in the claims be turned over to it. The court denied relief on two bases. First, Peso ceased to have an interest in the claims when the board decided not to buy them. Second, the court rejected the notion that, merely because Cropper acquired knowledge of the opportunity by virtue of being a director and officer of Peso, he was thereafter prohibited from taking advantage of the opportunity personally. He must have had access to the opportunity only because of his position and, even then, the only thing he could not do was to take personal advantage of the opportunity through some action in his capacity as a director. Since here the claims were acquired independently of his position as a director, there could be no breach of his fiduciary duty.

This case has been criticized as making an express rejection of an opportunity a complete defence to a claim that a fiduciary breached his duty to the corporation. This simple expedient creates a risk that fiduciaries seeking to acquire an opportunity will simply contrive to have it rejected by the board.[26] The facile nature of this rule can be seen by noting how it led to opposite results on essentially similar facts in *Peso Silver Mines* v. *Cropper* and *Regal (Hastings)* v. *Gulliver*. In both cases, the directors decided that they could not proceed as planned because of the financial constraints on the corporation. Arguably the only difference was that in *Regal (Hastings)* v. *Gulliver* this decision was implicit in the directors' decision to implement an alternative strategy, while in *Peso Silver Mines* v. *Cropper* the board expressly rejected the opportunity.

Also, by requiring the fiduciary to have access to an opportunity and to have exploited the opportunity in the course of acting in his capacity as a fiduciary, the court in *Peso Silver Mines* v. *Cropper* severely constrained the classes of cases in which a breach of fiduciary duty could be found. This constraint was shattered in the decision of the Supreme Court of Canada in *Canadian Aero Service Ltd.* v. *O'Malley*.[27]

Canadian Aero Service Ltd. (Canaero) was in the business of mapping and geographic exploration. O'Malley, the president, and Zarzicki, the executive vice-president, were assigned to Guyana for the purpose of procuring a contract for mapping the country. After working on this project for some time, they resigned from Canaero and incorporated Terra Surveys (Terra) to perform work similar to what they had been doing for Canaero. Subsequently, the government of

---

26   This risk was cited by the court in *Irving Trust Co.* v. *Deutsch*, 73 F.2d 121 (2d Cir. 1934), in holding directors liable for breach of their fiduciary duty where they had acquired an opportunity after the board had decided that the corporation could not obtain sufficient financing to obtain the opportunity for itself.

27   (1973), [1974] S.C.R. 592 [*Canaero*].

Guyana asked for bids to map the country, and Terra's proposal was accepted over Canaero's. Canaero sued O'Malley and Zarzicki, alleging that they had breached their fiduciary duty to the corporation by taking the benefit of a corporate opportunity belonging to Canaero.

The Supreme Court of Canada ultimately held that O'Malley and Zarzicki did breach their duty. In reaching its conclusion, the Court determined that the test from *Regal (Hastings)* v. *Gulliver* was too restrictive to be used as a general test. In the view of the Supreme Court, the court in *Regal (Hastings)* v. *Gulliver* had characterized a breach of fiduciary duty as occurring where the fiduciary received "profits by reason only of being directors and in course of the execution of their office" simply because that reflected the facts in that case. It was not intended to define exhaustively the circumstances in which a fiduciary duty could be breached. The Court had to free itself from the limits imposed in *Regal (Hastings)* v. *Gulliver* because, in *Canadian Aero Service Ltd.* v. *O'Malley*, the Regal test clearly was not met: O'Malley and Zarzicki were not acting as fiduciaries when Terra acquired the project; and they did not obtain the project in the course of exercising their powers as officers of Canaero. Also, the project Terra acquired was somewhat different from the one they had been working on while with Canaero so, arguably, it was not even the same opportunity. Saying that the categories of breach of fiduciary duty are never closed, the Court developed an open-ended analysis based on a weighing of various factors that the court stated could not be listed exhaustively. In relation to a particular opportunity, the purpose of this analysis is to determine the answers to two questions:

- Does the opportunity belong to the corporation, considering how closely it is connected to the corporation?
- What is the relationship of the fiduciaries to the opportunity?

On the first question, the Court cited several factors as tending to show that the contract to map Guyana was a corporate opportunity of Canaero's. It was a specific opportunity that the corporation had been actively pursuing through the efforts of O'Malley and Zarzicki, rather than one that was simply in the same business area as the corporation's business. Though the ultimate contract was different in some respects from the one that O'Malley and Zarzicki had been working on while they were at Canaero, it was substantially the same opportunity. It was also a mature opportunity, in the sense that O'Malley and Zarzicki had done extensive work in preparing for it while they were with Canaero. The Court noted that the corporation's interest would have been even stronger if the contract had been awarded without a public bidding process but simply on the basis of the relationship that O'Malley and Zarzicki had developed while they were working for Canaero.

Regarding the relationship of the fiduciaries to the opportunity, the Court cited several factors as suggesting that they were directly involved in the opportunity they appropriated. They did preparatory work relating to the opportunity and negotiated for it on behalf of the corporation. They learned all about the opportunity through their positions. They quit for the purpose of taking advantage of it. Also, in the opinion of the Court, the fact that O'Malley and Zarzicki were high-ranking officers in the corporation imposed a higher duty on them. Based on the strength of the corporation's interest in the opportunity and the close relationship of the fiduciaries to the opportunity while they were acting in their fiduciary capacities, the Court concluded that O'Malley and Zarzicki had breached their fiduciary duty to Canaero.

In summary, a breach of fiduciary duty arises when a fiduciary takes something belonging to the corporation, putting her personal interests ahead of her duty to act in the best interests of the corporation. The policy of the common law is that such behaviour should be discouraged by requiring that any financial benefit from engaging in the behaviour be turned over to the corporation. With respect to the appropriation of corporate opportunities, the courts will not enquire into whether the corporation would have obtained the opportunity or whether the appropriation caused some loss to the corporation. If these exceptions were acknowledged, it would be like saying to the fiduciaries, "You decide if the corporation could have obtained the opportunity or would be hurt if you took it." That would put the person with the conflict of interest in the position of having to decide when it is permissible to take the opportunity, an inherently untenable situation. Moreover, courts do not want to second-guess fiduciaries' business judgment about these matters. Consequently, they have set up a rigid rule to ensure that corporations can seek relief every time an opportunity is appropriated. The problem then is how do you know when an opportunity belongs to the corporation and cannot be appropriated by a fiduciary?

In cases like *Cook* v. *Deeks*, it will be obvious that there is a breach. In other cases, it may be clear that a breach did not occur.[28] But in many

---

28   *Boucher* v. *Kennedy*, [1998] O.J. No. 1612 (QL) (Gen. Div.), aff'd [1999] O. J. No. 3407 (QL) (C.A.) is an example of a case in which an opportunity was found not to belong to the corporation. The court held that a senior employee did not have a duty to offer a finanical opportunity to the corporation where it was outside the business the corporation was formed to carry on and did not arise within the scope of the employee's employment.

situations, the answer will not be obvious. Whether a breach will be found depends on many factors relating to the nature or strength of the corporation's interest and the relationship to the opportunity of the person alleged to have breached his duty. What factors will be relevant will depend on the facts of each case. Some relevant factors are set out in figure 8.1.

Figure 8.1   Factors Relevant to Determining Whether Appropriation of Opportunity Is a Breach of Fiduciary Duty

Nature or Strength of the Corporation's Interest

Maturity: Had the corporation done anything to develop the opportunity? How close was the corporation to acquiring the opportunity?

Specificity: Was the opportunity identified by the corporation? How precisely? Was it only in the same general business area as the corporation's business? How closely did the opportunity appropriated resemble the opportunity the corporation was working on?

Significance of opportunity: Would the opportunity represent a major component of the corporation's business if acquired? Was it a unique opportunity or merely one of many?

Public or private opportunity: Was the opportunity publicly advertised or otherwise widely known? Was it one to which the fiduciaries had access only by virtue of their positions? Was it offered to the corporation?

Rejection: Had the opportunity been rejected in good faith by the corporation before the fiduciary acquired it?[29]

Relationship of the Fiduciary to the Opportunity

Position of fiduciary: The higher up the fiduciary is in the organization of the corporation, the higher the level of duty.

Relationship between the fiduciary and the opportunity: Was the opportunity in an area of the fiduciary's responsibility? Did the fiduciary negotiate for the opportunity on behalf of the corporation?

---

29   A rejection will not be determinative. The court will look into the circumstances in which the rejection was obtained. Unless the fiduciary did what was reasonably possible to get the board to accept it and was not in a position to determine the outcome of the board's vote, the rejection may not be sufficient on its own to allow the fiduciary to take the opportunity (K.P. McGuiness, *The Law and Practice of Canadian Business Corporations* (Toronto: Butterworths, 1999) at 752 [*McGuiness*]).

Knowledge as a fiduciary: How much knowledge did the fiduciary acquire about the opportunity through her position?

Involvement in competing business: Did the fiduciary acquire the opportunity through an existing business which was similar to or even competed with the business of the corporation and in which the fiduciary was involved?

Use of position: To what extent did the fiduciary accomplish the appropriation of the opportunity through his position?

Time after termination: If the fiduciary took the opportunity after she terminated her relationship with the corporation, how long was it after termination? What were the circumstances of her termination? Was she fired or did she leave voluntarily? Did she leave for the purpose of pursuing the opportunity she had been working on for the corporation?

The more factors in favour of a corporate interest in the opportunity and a close relationship between it and the fiduciary, the more likely it is that a court will find that there has been a breach of duty. In cases where the fiduciary has terminated her relationship with the corporation, as in *Canadian Aero Service* v. *O'Malley*, the fiduciary duty derives not from the statute but from the common law, since the statutory duty applies only while a person is a director or officer. In such cases, the court will seek to balance the interests of the corporation against the interests of the fiduciary seeking to terminate her connection with the corporation and to carry on business for her own account.

Various arguments may be cited in favour of this loose situation-based standard in appropriation of corporate opportunity cases. As an opportunity becomes more remote from the corporation, ultimately extending to any profitable business in which the corporation may engage, the likelihood of loss to the corporation is diminished. In these circumstances, the argument that it is inequitable to the corporation to permit the fiduciary to appropriate the opportunity becomes weak. Similarly, the agency-cost argument based on the potential cost to the corporation and shareholders of opportunistic behaviour by the fiduciary weakens. Two other factors may be cited in favour of a situation-based standard. It may be that different standards should be applied depending on whether the fiduciary is a person who is a full-time employee with the firm or an outside director receiving, perhaps, no compensation for her time. Also, the scale of the corporation, a factor not expressly cited by in *Canadian Aero Service* v. *O'Malley*, should be taken into account. As discussed in Chapter 7, the ability of shareholders in closely held corporations to choose their fiduciaries and to monitor them is much greater than that of shareholders in public corporations, so, arguably, a stricter standard should be applied in the latter case.[30]

As a practical matter, it is difficult to apply the Canaero test to the facts of hard cases — which is where a good test is really needed. One way to try to avoid problems of fiduciary duty is to disclose and obtain the consent of the corporation to activities that could be considered to involve opportunities belonging to the corporation. This will not be a reliable defence in all circumstances. Fiduciary duties are mandatory standards that cannot be avoided even by obtaining the consent of the corporation. Sometimes a fiduciary will have to resign before he will be free to pursue an opportunity.[31] Nevertheless, such a strategy will help to reduce the likelihood that conflicts will arise and may influence a court's assessment of whether an opportunity belongs to the corporation.

4) Competition by Directors and Officers

In general, as indicated above, it is not a breach of fiduciary duty to terminate one's relationship with a corporation and go into competition with it; otherwise, the fiduciary duty might become an unreasonable restraint of trade, preventing a person from earning a living, which is something the common law has tried to avoid.[32] What a fiduciary cannot do is to compete with the corporation while she remains in her capacity as a fiduciary. The conflict between the personal interests of the fiduciary and her duty to act in the best interests of the corporation is obvious in such situations and the courts, traditionally, have provided relief whenever any competition has been found.[33] Any competing fiduciary will be forced to pay over all her profits from the competing business to the corporation.

In addition, a fiduciary cannot use her fiduciary position and the opportunities afforded to her in that position to develop a competing business, then quit to begin competing.[34] In such cases, as we saw in

---

30   V. Brudney & R. C. Clark, "A New Look at Corporate Opportunities" (1981) 94 Harv. L. Rev. 997.

31   E.g., *Levy-Russell*, above note 14.

32   *Metropolitan Commercial Carpet Centre Ltd.* v. *Donovan* (1989), 42 B.L.R. 306 (N.S.T.D.).

33   In *Re Thomson*, [1930] 1 Ch. 203, the court granted relief against an executor who entered into competition with a business owned by the estate for which he was responsible.

34   *Bendix Home Systems Ltd.* v. *Clayton*, [1977] 5 W.W.R. 10 (B.C.S.C.). In *Coleman Taylor* v. *Oakes*, [2001] 2 B.C.L.C. 749 (Ch D.), the court held that extensive preparations to compete by a director before he quit breached his fiduciary duty.

Canadian Aero Service v. *O'Malley*, the courts will impose fiduciary obligations extending beyond the termination by the fiduciary.

Even where a fiduciary has not used his position to develop an opportunity in this way, he will have some obligations extending beyond the termination of his relationship with the corporation. A fiduciary cannot use confidential information belonging to the corporation, though it is not a breach to use skills, know-how, experience, and personal goodwill acquired by the fiduciary during his service to the corporation.[35] Similarly, if a departing fiduciary attracts customers or other employees by virtue of his qualifications or experience, this will not breach his fiduciary duty, but if he affirmatively solicits customers or employees relying on relationships developed during this time with the corporation he will be in breach.[36] Using a confidential customer list to solicit customers would be a clear breach. In other circumstances, it will be difficult to predict when a breach will be found. As a consequence, it is increasingly common for employers and fiduciaries who are employees to agree specifically on what is permitted post-employment in an employment contract.

Consistent with the strict approach of the common law, competition prohibited by the fiduciary duty includes not only competition by the fiduciary in his personal capacity but also competition by a corporation in which the fiduciary has an interest. One difficult area in this regard, which has been the subject of several cases, is persons with multiple directorships. Some old English cases held that being a director of two corporations, even if they are competitors, does not constitute a breach of fiduciary duty. The only restriction on a director in these circumstances was that she is prohibited from disclosing confidential information about one corporation to the other.[37] This relaxed approach is inconsistent with the strict approach expressed in such cases as *Aberdeen Railway* v. *Blaikie* and does not accurately state the law in Canada. Canadian cases have held that there is no absolute rule regarding multiple directorships. In each case, the question of breach of fiduciary duty will depend on the facts. The relevant question will be whether the fiduciary could act in the best interests of both corporations.[38] Where corporations are in active competition, it will be

---

35 *Pizza Pizza Ltd.* v. *Gillespie* (1990), 75 O.R. (2d) 225 (Gen. Div.).

36 These kinds of activities would be permissable for a non-fiduciary employee (McGuiness, above note 29, at 732–734).

37 *London and Mashonaland Exploration Co. Ltd.* v. *New Mashonaland Exploration Co. Ltd.*, [1891] W.N. 165 (Ch.).

38 *Abbey Glen Property Corp.* v. *Stumborg* (1978), 9 A.R. 234 (C.A.).

impossible to avoid the conclusion that a director of both corporations is in a conflict of interest and in breach of his fiduciary duty. For example, one cannot imagine that a person could be a member of the boards of Ford Motors Inc. and General Motors Inc. simultaneously and always be able to act in the best interests of both. On the other hand, it may be possible to be on the board of two corporations that carry on identical businesses, but in geographically distinct markets, without facing a conflict of interest.

5) Takeover Bids

No situation in which issues of fiduciary obligation arise has received more critical attention than the hostile takeover bid. When a bidder offers to purchase a controlling interest in a corporation, often one of the reasons is that the bidder believes the value of the corporation can be increased by some changes in management, typically including the replacement of existing directors and senior managers. In such circumstances, the self-interest of directors and senior managers may lead them to try to defeat the takeover bid. Often, this will be contrary to the interests of shareholders. Takeover bidders typically offer a substantial premium over the current market price, so shareholders who sell will receive a better price than they could otherwise get. Those who do not sell will reap the benefit of the improvements made by the bidder and the resulting increase in value of their shares. To the extent that directors and management may act to defeat the bid, not only will the shareholders lose the immediate benefits of the bid but incentives to engage in value-enhancing takeover bids generally will be reduced, because hostile takeover bids will be made more expensive and difficult to complete. The general disciplinary effect of the market for corporate control described in Chapter 7 will be impaired. Because fewer bids will be made directors and officers will not need to worry about them. If no defensive measures are available, the only way directors and management could prevent a takeover bid would be to manage the corporation so effectively that no bidder could improve value by making the bid. Following this argument, the courts should apply the fiduciary duty to prevent all defensive measures. Such a position is supported by the traditional common law policy that a fiduciary should not be permitted to be involved in situations where her personal interest possibly may conflict with her duty. To permit management to defend against takeover bids puts them in the kind of conflict of interest the common law has sought to avoid.

There are, however, motivations for takeovers other than changing management to increase value. Some of them are less threatening to management and may even encourage management to cooperate in the completion of the bid. There may be what is referred to as synergy between the bidder and the target. The combination of the two enterprises may lead to more efficient operations through more intensive use of available resources, such as plants. It may be that the combination will result in a diversified combined entity which will have more stable returns. For example, a bid might be launched to combine a heating business with an air-conditioning business to overcome the opposite seasonal downturns in each business. There are also other motivations that are less obviously positive. A bid might be made to eliminate a competitor. Finally, there are other non-economic reasons that may encourage takeovers, such as managerial self-aggrandizement.

The diversity of possible motivations for takeover bids means that a particular takeover bid may have a wide range of possible consequences. This range makes it difficult to formulate general rules to govern the behaviour of directors and managers when a bid is made or in anticipation of a bid. Some takeover transactions will be in the best interests of the corporation, its shareholders, and other stakeholders, while others will not be. While permitting management to defend against takeover bids puts them in the kind of conflict of interest the common law has long sought to avoid, prohibiting them from doing so means that takeovers which are not in shareholders' interests will be allowed to go ahead. The simplest example of the problem raised by a prohibition on defensive tactics is a bid at a price that the directors and officers correctly believe is less than the actual value of the corporation.[39] In such circumstances, some kinds of defensive measures by management will be in the best interests of the corporation and its shareholders.

Another factor complicating the regulation of defensive measures is the huge and constantly expanding range of measures in use. Historically, the most common method was for directors to issue shares to persons who would not tender into the bid.[40] More recently, some corporations have amended their articles to adopt what management call "shareholder rights plans" and their opponents call "poison pills."

---

39   In order for this to be the case, there would have to be some inefficiency in the way in which the market priced the shares of the corporation. The most likely situation in which this might occur is where the directors possess inside information that suggests a higher value.

40   For example, *Hogg v. Cramphorn Ltd.* (1966), [1967] Ch. 254 [*Hogg*].

These provisions work in various ways, but the archetypal model is that the shareholders receive rights to purchase additional shares of the corporation at some price much higher than the current market price of the shares. If a bidder purchases in excess of a specified percentage of the target's shares, the price at which the rights are exercisable drops to a level much below the market price. The bidder itself is precluded from exercising these rights. Management is given the power to waive the exercise of these rights. The result is that the bidder must either negotiate with management to exercise its waiver or face a dramatic increase in the cost of the bid as other shareholders exercise their rights. It is far beyond the scope of this book to describe these measures, much less analyse what the appropriate scope of management's use of them should be.[41] Doing so would necessitate dealing with the substantial theoretical and empirical literature on defensive measures.[42]

Figure 8.2   Fiduciary Duties and Takeover Bids

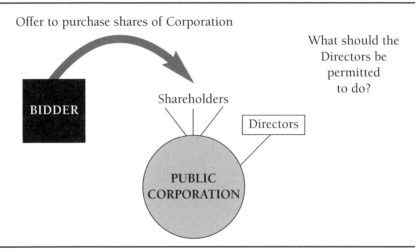

Nevertheless, it is possible to summarize the general position established in the few English and Canadian court cases on the actions of directors to defend against takeovers. A number of old cases had held that it was improper for directors to issue shares for the sole pur-

---

41   See J.S. Ziegel, *et al.*, *Cases and Materials on Partnerships and Canadian Business Corporations*, 3d ed. (Toronto: Carswell, 1994) at 645–59, for a selection of excerpts from the extensive literature on this subject.

42   Ziegel, *ibid.*, sets out a selected bibliography and useful excerpts from this literature at 643–83. See also F.H. Buckley, M. Gillen, & R. Yalden, *Corporations: Principles and Policies*, 3d ed. (Toronto: Emond Montgomery, 1995), at 1052–1167.

pose of defeating an attempt by someone to gain control of the corporation even if they *bona fide* believed such an action to be in the best interests of the corporation.[43] This approach was rejected in *Teck Corp.* v. *Millar*[44] on the basis that directors must be able to act in the best interests of the corporation in responding to a takeover bid. They should be able to consider the consequences of a takeover bid and exercise their powers to defeat it if they genuinely believe that the success of the bid would not be in the corporation's best interests. This, of course, raises a significant problem: How is the court to determine if the purpose of the directors' action is to protect the interests of the corporation? In *Teck Corp.* v. *Millar*, Justice Berger suggested that the courts should ask if there were reasonable grounds for the director's belief that they were acting in the corporation's best interests. This approach has been applied in some subsequent cases even where it has been acknowledged that one of the effects of the directors' actions has been incidentally to benefit the directors themselves by maintaining their positions.[45] Indeed, in *Olympia & York Enterprises Ltd.* v. *Hiram Walker Resources Ltd.*, the court seemed to suggest that the fiduciary duty to act in the best interests of the corporation imposed a positive duty to take defensive measures if the board believed the successful completion of the bid would not be in the interests of the corporation.[46]

Other cases have taken a more restrictive view. In *Exco Corp.* v. *Nova Scotia Savings & Loan Co.*,[47] the court held that the proper test was whether an action taken by the directors was not only in the best interests of the corporation but also inconsistent with any other interests, including the directors' personal interests.[48]

---

43 *Bonisteel* v. *Collis Leather Co.* (1919), 45 O.L.R. 195 (H.C.J.). This approach was also followed in the leading English case of *Hogg*, above note 40. Provincial securities regulators, especially the Ontario Securities Commission (OSC), play a leading role in the regulation of takeover bids. The OSC has a broad discretion to act in the public interest in recognition that each takeover bid is unique (Ontario *Securities Act*, R.S.O. 1990, c. S.5, ss. 104 & 127). The OSC and its public interest jurisdiction are discussed in chapter 11.

44 (1972), 33 D.L.R. (3d) 288 (B.C.S.C.). A similar approach had been followed in *Spooner* v. *Spooner Oils Ltd.*, [1936] 2 D.L.R. 634 (Alta. C.A.), and the Australian case *Ashburton Oil No Liability* v. *Alpha Minerals No Liability* (1971), 45 A.L.R.J. 162 (Austl. H.C.).

45 *Olympia & York Enterprises Ltd.* v. *Hiram Walker Resources Ltd.* (1986), 59 O.R. (2d) 254 (Div. Ct.).

46 *Ibid.*, at 271–72.

47 (1987), 78 N.S.R. (2d) 91 (S.C.T.D.).

48 *Ibid.*, at 271–72.

Accordingly, even the general criteria by which the actions of directors' and officers' conduct are to be judged are unclear. The cases also provide little guidance on the many second-level questions that must be addressed in order to assess whether the fiduciary duty has been satisfied in particular situations. For example, it is not clear how to determine if a particular defensive measure was reasonable. One guiding principle that has been endorsed by the courts is that shareholders rather than directors should have the right to determine to whom and on what terms they may sell their shares.[49]

Some guidance in this regard may be taken from a policy issued by the Canadian Securities Adminstrators, an organization of the provincial and territorial securities regulators.[50] National Policy 62-202,[51] sets out the regulators' views regarding defensive tactics in takeover bids. Although the policy statement does not purport to offer a code of behaviour for directors, it does express the policy basis for the regulation of takeover bids. It provides that the primary purpose of such regulation is to protect the *bona fide* interests of the shareholders of the target and to permit takeover bids to proceed in an open and even-handed environment. This policy suggests that defensive measures should not deny shareholders the ability to make a decision and that, whenever possible, prior shareholder approval should be obtained for proposed defensive measures. This policy was held to inform the content of directors' fiduciary duty in *347883 Alberta Ltd. v. Producers Pipelines Ltd.*[52]

In several recent cases the requirements of the fiduciary duty in the context of takeover bids have been clarified somewhat. The courts, instead of focusing on elucidating a single clear standard, have looked at whether the board of a corporation subject to a hostile takeover bid acted reasonably in the circumstances, not perfectly, including taking

---

49   This principle was most forthrightly set out by the English Privy Council in *Howard Smith Ltd. v. Ampol Petroleum Ltd.*, [1974] A.C. 821, at 837–38 (P.C.), per Lord Wilberforce. Courts in the United States have endorsed the view that defensive measures should be proportional to the problems with the bid (e.g., *Unocal Corp. v. Mesa Petroleum*, 493 A. 2d 946, at 955 (Del. 1985)).

50   The role of the Canadian Securities Administrators (CSA) and their policies are discussed in Chapter 11.

51   Issued by the CSA July 4, 1997 (formerly National Policy 38) adopted by Ontario Securities Commission (1997) 20 O.S.C.B. 3525.

52   (1991), 92 Sask. R. 81 (C.A.). In that case, the same standard was applied in holding that a shareholders' rights plan was oppressive of the interests of a minority shareholder. This policy was endorsed in *CW Shareholdings Inc. v. WIC Western International Communications Ltd.* (1998), 39 O.R. (3d) 755 (Gen.Div.) [WIC].

reasonable steps to minimize the conflict of interest and making an informed judgment as to the best available transaction for the shareholders. Often this is done by creating a committee of directors independent of management to make a recommendation to the board regarding how to respond to the bid. Since management has the most to lose, its conflict of interest is acute. Referring the question of how to respond to the bid to a committee independent of management reduces the risk that decision making will be affected by conflicts of interest. So long as the committee acts reasonably and its recommendations are accepted by the board, the directors will be found to have fulfilled their duty.[53] Where directors believe that a bid is too low, it may be reasonable for the directors to canvass the market to see whether other bidders may be encouraged to make a bid at a price higher than the existing bid. Unlike the the approach in the United States, Canadian courts have held that there is no general duty to set up an auction. In an auction, directors continually try to obtain higher and higher prices from competing bidders. Whether directors are required to try to set up an auction will depend on the circumstances.

Some cases have held that directors may give inducements to get other bidders to make an offer. One current issue is to what extent a board should be able to entice competing bids to be made by agreeing to pay a fee (called a "break fee") or otherwise compensate the bidder out of assets of the corporation if its bid is ultimately unsuccessful. The courts have approved the use of break fees so long as they are reasonably necessary to induce the new bid.[54]

Pente Investment Management Ltd. v. *Schneider Corp.*[55] provides a good example of the application of these principles. A controlling block of shares in the target of the bid, Schneider Corp., was held by a family group. The family had said that they would not sell to the bidder, Maple Leaf Foods Inc., a competitor of Schneider. The directors struck an independent committee to decide on how to respond to the bid. The committee retained its own financial and legal advisers. Determining that the price of the Maple Leaf bid was inadequate and recognizing that the family would not accept it in any case, the committee decided to canvass the market to see who else might make an offer. It

---

53 *Pente Investment Management Ltd.* v. *Schneider Corp.* (1998), 42 O. R. (3d) 177 (C. A.).

54 E.g., *WIC*, above note 52. The OSC was critical of a $100,000 payment authorized by the board of directors of a corporation to subsidize the expenses of a bidder in *In the matter of Cara Operations Limited and The Second Cup Limited*, (2002) 25 O.S.C.B. 7997, at para. 73.

55 Above note 53.

created a data room containing business information which could be accessed by potential bidders, if they agreed to keep the information confidential. Eventually, the committee elicited another bid from Smithfield. Smithfield said that it would withdraw its offer if it suspected that Schneider was just using its offer as leverage to extract higher offers from other bidders. The family decided to accept the Smithfield offer. The committee recommended to the board that the board endorse the Smithfield offer and the board did so. The court found that the board had fulfilled its duty. It was not obliged to go back to Maple Leaf to try to obtain a better offer in the circumstances.

6) Other Breaches of Fiduciary Duty

What has been described above are the most common situations in which a breach of fiduciary duty may occur. These categories are not immutable. Situations will arise in which more than one of them will be implicated. More important, as Mr. Justice Laskin said in *Canadian Aero Service* v. *O'Malley*, the categories of breach of fiduciary duty are not closed. There are an unlimited number of possible situations in which, if the fiduciary refers back to the broad statutory formulation in section 122(1)(a) of the *CBCA* and the principles developed in the case law, he may find himself in a situation where his personal interest and his duty conflict or is otherwise in breach of his duty to act honestly and in good faith with a view to the best interests of the corporation.

In Chapter 7, for example, we discussed the problem of directors deciding on their own compensation. The *CBCA* expressly permits directors to participate in such decisions notwithstanding the conflict (*CBCA*, s. 120(5)), though this does not relieve the directors from their duty to act in the best interests of the corporation. Another situation that often occurs is where a director of a corporation with a majority shareholder must make a decision in circumstances where the interests of the majority shareholder and those of the minority shareholders conflict. For example, the majority shareholder may want the corporation to enter into a transaction with it which is highly favourable to the majority shareholder but not good for the corporation or, as a result, the minority shareholders.[56] Because the majority shareholder has the statutory right to replace the directors, it will be tempting for a direc-

---

56   In this example, the majority shareholder will also suffer from any disadvantage or loss to the corporation in its capacity as a shareholder. The majority shareholder would enter the transaction only if the benefits it receives from the transaction in its personal capacity more than compensate for its loss as a shareholder.

tor to act in the way desired by the majority shareholder rather than in the interests of the corporation as a whole. If a director were to do so, she would be in breach of her fiduciary duty.[57]

Even if a director is elected to represent a particular constituency, it does not permit him to favour this constituency. In all his actions, such a director, like all directors, must act in the best interests of the corporation, even though this may disappoint the constituency that elected him. Under the *ABCA*, a director who is elected or appointed by the holders of a class or series of shares, or by employees or creditors, may give "special, but not exclusive, consideration to the interests of those who elected or appointed him" (*ABCA*, s. 117(4)). In a 1995 discussion paper, the Corporations Directorate of Industry Canada raised the question of whether a similar provision should be added to the *CBCA*.[58] No such provision was introduced in the *2001 Amendments*.

7) Reliance on Management and Others

In discharging their responsibility to manage in the best interests of the corporation, the directors in all but the smallest corporations must rely to some extent on management and other professionals. Under the *CBCA* and the statutes modelled after it, a limited defence to an alleged breach of fiduciary duty is available to directors who rely on others. Section 123(4) of the *CBCA* provides that a director is not liable for a breach of fiduciary duty if he relies, in good faith, on

- financial statements of the corporation represented to him by an officer or in a written report by the auditor of the corporation to reflect fairly the financial position of the corporation; or
- a report of a person whose profession lends credibility to a statement made by the person.[59]

---

57   See, for example, *Teck Corp.* v. *Millar* (1972), 33 D.L.R. (3d) 288 (B.C.S.C.). An example of another situation in which the fiduciary duty was held to be relevant is *Tongue* v. *Vencap Equities Alberta Ltd.* (1994), 148 A.R. 321 (Q.B.). In that case, it was held that the fiduciary duty of directors buying shares from minority shareholders required them to disclose information regarding resale possibilities known at the time of purchase.

58   Industry Canada, Directors' Liability (*Canada Business Corporations Act* Discussion Paper) (Ottawa: Industry Canada, 1995) at 22 [*Discussion Paper on Directors' Liability*].

59   Prior to the *2001 Amendments*, above note 12, reports of lawyers, accountants, engineers, and appraisers were specifically identified as meeting this requirement. This defence is also available in connection with a breach of the duty of care under s. 122(1)(b) (*CBCA*, above note 8).

This defence is limited to these specific circumstances in which reliance is permitted. It does not permit the directors to avoid liability by demonstrating that they acted reasonably in the circumstances. The strict fiduciary obligation continues to apply.

8) Shareholder Ratification of Breach of Fiduciary Duty

Before the enactment of the *CBCA*, it was possible in most jurisdictions for shareholders to absolve fiduciaries of the consequences of a breach of fiduciary duty by voting to approve or "ratify" it. The only circumstances in which a breach could not be ratified were where the transaction was oppressive to the interests of the minority. Ratification was not effective if it was obtained by some improper means.[60] The first exception was narrowly applied. It should not be confused with the much broader set of circumstances in which shareholders may seek relief from oppression under the *CBCA* and other Canadian statutes. To fit within the common law oppression exception, one usually had to show that there had been some give-away of corporate assets to the fiduciary, such as a sale of corporate assets at less than market value or an appropriation of a corporate asset, as in *Cook* v. *Deeks*.[61] Only such serious actions could not be ratified. The second exception was limited to circumstances in which the appropriate majority specified in a corporation's by-laws was not obtained, the notice of the meeting at which the ratification vote took place was improper, or some other procedural irregularity occurred.[62]

The rationale for permitting shareholder ratification was that it was needed to balance the strict application of the common law rules as expressed in *Aberdeen Railway* v. *Blaikie*. If, in any given case, the shareholders decided that a transaction involving a breach of duty was nevertheless acceptable to them, they could approve it. Conceptually this rationale is suspect, since fiduciary duties flow to the corporation, not the shareholders. The rule was also problematic in application because there was no prohibition against majority shareholders voting their shares to ratify breaches of fiduciary duty in which they were involved personally.[63] This shortcoming, combined with the narrow

---

60   The rules on shareholder ratification were first set out in *Foss* v. *Harbottle* (1843), 2 Hare 461, 67 E.R. 189 (Ch). This case is discussed in Chapter 9.

61   Above note 16.

62   *Bamford* v. *Bamford*, (1969), [1970] Ch. 212 (C.A.).

63   *North-West Transportation Co. Ltd. and Beatty* v. *Beatty* (1887), 12 App. Cas. 589 (P.C.).

interpretation given to what would be found to oppress the interests of the minority, gave wide scope for abuse of the ratification process.

For this reason, the *CBCA* greatly reduced the effect of shareholder approval of fiduciary breaches. Except in accordance with the scheme for rendering self-dealing contracts enforceable under section 120 of the *CBCA* and other provincial schemes, a shareholder resolution approving a breach of fiduciary duty does not cure a breach or relieve the fiduciary of liability for the breach (*CBCA*, s. 122(3)).[64] The only legal effect of such a resolution is that it must be considered by the court in deciding whether to grant a shareholder the right to bring a derivative action on behalf of the corporation for breach of fiduciary duty (*CBCA*, s. 242(1)),[65] and in determining whether any action of the corporation or the directors is oppressive under section 241 of the *CBCA*. Practically speaking, management may take some comfort from a shareholder resolution approving of their fiduciary breach, but it does not mean that shareholders are precluded from complaining about the breach at a later date. The effect of shareholder approval will be discussed further in Chapter 9.

C. DUTY OF CARE

1) Introduction

Section 122(1)(b) of the *CBCA* imposes a duty of care on directors and officers in the following terms:

> Every director and officer of a corporation in exercising their powers and discharging their duties shall ... exercise the care, diligence and skill that a reasonably prudent person would exercise in comparable circumstances.[66]

The content of this duty, like the fiduciary duty, is highly dependent on the facts, as evidenced by the reference to "comparable circumstances." It does appear to set a kind of objective standard by referring to the care, diligence, and skill of a reasonably prudent person, though the

---

64   E.g., *OBCA*, above note 1, s. 134(3); *ABCA*, above note 1, s. 123(3); and *BCCA*, above note 1, s. 119 (directors only).

65   E.g., *OBCA*, *ibid.*, s. 249(1); *ABCA*, *ibid.*, s. 243(1); and *BCCA*, *ibid.*, s. 201(4).

66   Other provinces also impose a duty of care: for example, *BCCA*, *ibid.*, s. 142(1)(b); Quebec *Companies Act*, R.S.Q. 1977, c. C-38, s. 123.83; and *OBCA*, *ibid.*, s. 134(1)(b).

case law on this issue is not conclusive. To the extent that it sets an objective minimum standard, the duty under the *CBCA* represents a significant departure from the common law, which required directors to exercise only the care that could be reasonably expected for a person of their knowledge and experience.[67] Under this subjective standard, the honest and diligent, but incompetent, director had nothing to fear. Under the statute, as will be discussed below, there appears to be a minimum threshold of competence. The precise standard to be met, however, depends upon the personal knowledge, experience, and position of each director and officer.[68]

2) The Standard of Care

As noted above, the standard of care is impossible to define exhaustively. Nevertheless, the case law provides some useful guidance to the application of the broadly worded statutory standard. Before examining some of the cases, however, we need to refer to several additional relevant provisions of the *CBCA* and other statutes.

First, traditionally the courts viewed directors' responsibilities as intermittent in nature, to be performed at periodic board meetings. Although a director should go to meetings, she was not bound to. As will be discussed below, the general standard of care in the *CBCA* likely demands a higher level of involvement. In addition, the Act contains a specific incentive to attend meetings and treat decisions responsibly. Under section 123, a director is deemed to consent to all resolutions passed at a meeting at which she was present unless she records her dissent. If the director misses a meeting, she is deemed to have consented to any resolutions passed unless, within seven days of finding out about what was done, she takes certain steps to record her dissent. The effect of this provision is that a director cannot escape responsibility by not attending meetings, as discussed in Chapter 7.[69]

Second, it is inevitable, especially in large corporations, that officers must rely on the advice of experts, including accountants, lawyers,

---

67 *Re City Equitable Fire Insurance Co. Ltd.* (1924), [1925] Ch. 407 (C.A.) [*City Equitable*].

68 *Soper v. Canada*, [1998] 1 F.C. 124 (C.A.) [*Soper*]. Recently, the Quebec Court of Appeal suggested that, so long as a director was acting honestly and exercising his business judgment, no breach of a duty of care would be found (*Peoples Department Stores*, above note 3).

69 There are similar provisions in the *OBCA*, above note 1, s. 135; and *ABCA*, above note 1, s. 123.

investment dealers, and engineers. This is even more true for directors. Before the enactment of the *CBCA*, directors and officers were entitled to trust employees and others to act honestly in performing their obligations and could rely on what they were told. Reliance by directors on others is now subject to an express statutory standard. As discussed above in relation to fiduciary duties, a director is not liable if she in good faith relies on financial statements and reports of lawyers and other professionals (*CBCA*, s. 123(4)).[70]

Third, it used to be commonplace for corporations to set their own standard of care at a level even lower than that imposed by the common law.[71] This practice is now precluded by statute. No provision in a contract, the articles, the by-laws, or a resolution relieves a director or officer from the statutory duty of care or from liability for breaching it (*CBCA*, s. 122(3)).

Apart from these statutory provisions, the substance of the duty of care must be gleaned from the case law. In contrast to the common law standard, the statutory formulation of the duty imposes a minimum standard of competence. Directors must have at least a rudimentary understanding of the business.[72] If a person who is a director does not have this minimal level of understanding, she should acquire it or resign. This requirement is often not appreciated in practice. It is still common for boards to have some number of passive "dummy" directors who take no interest in the affairs of the corporation and merely act as someone else's nominee. The statute is clear that being a nominee does not relieve a director from observing the standard of care.[73]

The reference in the statutory formulation to a person "in comparable circumstances" does, however, suggest that the duty retains a kind of subjective element. Even accepting this subjective dimension to the duty of care, however, directors and officers must diligently apply whatever skills and experience they possess. If a person has significant knowledge or experience, it will result in a higher standard of

---

70   A more detailed discussion is set out above in "Reliance on Management and Others."

71   For example, *City Equitable*, above note 67. The by-laws of the corporation provided that the directors were liable only for their "wilful neglect or default."

72   *Francis v. United Jersey Bank*, 432 A. 2d 814 (N.J.S.C. 1981) [*Francis*]. This case considered a statutory duty of care expressed in terms similar to section 122(1)(b) of the *CBCA*, above note 8.

73   The court in *Selangor United Rubber Estates Ltd. v. Cradock, (A Bankrupt) (No. 3)*, [1968] 2 All E.R. 1073 (Ch.), strongly criticized the failure of nominee directors to meet an appropriate standard of care.

care being required.[74] Also, the standard of care will vary, depending on a person's position in relation to whatever is the conduct alleged to constitute breach of duty. For example, serving on board committees, such as the audit committee, will constitute different comparable circumstances. All public corporations must have an audit committee charged with reviewing the financial statements and the financial-reporting process. Serving on the audit committee gives directors a greater opportunity to obtain knowledge about and to examine the financial affairs of the corporation than is available to directors who are not members. As a result, more would be expected of them in terms of overseeing the financial-reporting process and warning other directors about problems than would be required of directors who were not on the committee.[75]

In addition to some level of competence, some monitoring of the corporation is required by the duty of care. A director must keep himself informed about the business and affairs of the corporation. This requirement does not involve a detailed inspection of the day-to-day activities of the corporation, but it does include general monitoring of the corporation's policies and affairs as well as attending board meetings regularly.

Specifically with respect to the financial affairs of a corporation, it is not necessary for directors to audit the financial records of the corporation; the corporation pays its auditor to do that. What is required is that directors maintain some general familiarity with the financial status of the corporation through regular review of its financial statements. The nature and scope of the review will depend on the corporation and the business. As noted above, directors may rely on statements represented fairly to reflect the financial situation of the corporation; but if the financial statements show some problem, directors will have a duty to enquire about the problem and, in some cases, take further action.

In *Francis* v. *United Jersey Bank*,[76] for example, a director was found to have breached her duty of care where she paid no attention to a

---

74   *Soper*, above note 68 (recognizing that directors who are also managers must meet a higher standard of care); and *Re Standard Trustco Ltd.* (1992), 6 B.L.R. (2d) 241 (Ont. Sec. Com.) [*Standard*]. This case has been criticized as raising the standard for directors too much (J.G. MacIntosh, "Standard Trustco Case Signals Expansion of the 'Public Interest' Powers of Securities Regulators" (1993) 1 Corp. Financing 38).

75   *Standard, ibid.*

76   Above note 72.

problem appearing clearly on the face of the corporation's balance sheet. The financial statements disclosed ballooning loans to her sons which ultimately led to the insolvency of the corporation. The court held that she had a duty to review the financial statements and that, if she had done so, she would have seen the loans. On becoming aware of the loans, she would have had a duty to enquire about them and, if they were improper, as they were, to demand that the impropriety be addressed. The court went on to state that if no action was taken at that point by the wrongdoers, the director may have a duty to resign.

In *Francis* v. *United Jersey Bank*, the court also indicated that there are situations in which it is not enough simply to object and, if no adequate response is made, to resign. In some cases the director's duty will require her to take some further positive action, such as attempting to initiate legal action on the corporation's behalf to remedy some wrongdoing. This will be an unusual situation, perhaps like that in *Francis* v. *United Jersey Bank*, in which there is some activity that is both clearly identifiable and clearly wrongful. In such a situation, the action of a single director quite plausibly may stop the injury being caused to the corporation. Where the problem confronting the director is harder to pin down or remedy, such as general managerial incompetence, such extreme action likely would not be demanded of a director. Not only would it not be an appropriate response, but it would be unlikely to remedy the problem. To express this aspect of the duty more generally, what will be expected of a director will be determined, in part, by what strategy would have a reasonable likelihood of success in remedying the breach. In other words, there is a breach of duty only where the director's failure to act was a contributing cause of the injury to the corporation. In some cases, directors may have to seek advice of independent legal counsel to understand the nature of their obligations in particular situations.

Also, the duty cannot be delegated. In a small corporation, for example, the fact that one director is assigned responsibility for a certain area does not relieve the other directors from their duty of care in relation to that area. If one director, who was a chartered accountant, was responsible for dealing with the financial side of a corporation's business, the other directors would still be required to comply with a standard of care in relation to these matters. If one of these other directors became aware of a problem with the payment of debts, for example, he would be required to do everything reasonably possible to ensure that the corporation put in place procedures to prevent a recurrence. This might include requesting a board meeting to discuss the problem, inquiring into the problem, designing a solution, and monitoring to ensure that the solution is put into effect.[77] If, however, there was nothing to put the director on notice, no action would likely be required. If the director was not involved in the business of the corporation at all, she could rely on the directors who were involved to ensure that the debts were paid, but she would be required to take some action if she became aware of a problem.[78]

Where an alleged breach of the duty of care relates to business decisions rather than failing to detect and address wrongdoing, the courts have been reluctant to second-guess management. This reluctance has a variety of sources. The most commonly cited is the courts' lack of business expertise. As well, courts often say that they do not want to set the standard of care so high as to inhibit business people from doing their jobs or, as a result of the increased risk of personal liability, discourage people from becoming directors at all. In the United States, this reluctance has received recognition in what is referred to as the "business judgment rule." In Canada, the courts did not not adopt the standard of a business judgment rule until the late 1990s,[79] though the approach taken by the Canadian courts in practice was not easily distinguished from that in the United States. Under this rule, decisions are presumed not to be a breach of duty in the absence of fraud, illegality, or conflict of interest on the part of the decision maker.[80] In general terms, the rule requires that court defer to the business judgment of the directors where it has been exercised honestly, prudently, in good faith, and on reasonable grounds. The actions of directors are to be judged not against the perfect vision of hindsight but against the facts as they existed at the time the decision was made. They are not required to make a perfect decision but only a reasonable one in the circumstances.[81] Courts should not substitute their own judgment regarding the best business strategy for that of the directors. Some courts have also required that the process for making the decision be reasonable in the circumstances. For example, the decision maker must have made

---

77   *Fraser* v. *MNR* (1987), 87 D.T.C. 250 (T.C.C.); *Soper*, above note 68.
78   *Canada (Attorney General)* v. *McKinnon*, [2001] 2 F. C. 203 (C.A.), at 221; *Soper*, *ibid*. Both these cases considered s. 227.1 of the *Income Tax Act* (R.S.C. 1985, c. 1, 5th Supp.), which imposes a similar standard on directors with respect to remittance of income tax withholdings.
79   One of the first cases to clearly adopt the rule was *WIC*, above note 52.
80   *Shlensky* v. *Wrigley*, 237 N.E. 2d 776 (Ill. App. 1968).
81   There is no single reasonable decision. There will be a range of decisions which are reasonable: *WIC*, above note 52, at 192; *Paramount Communications, Inc.* v. *QVC Network Inc.*, 637 A. 2d 34 (Del. 1994), at 45.

reasonable efforts to ensure that she had the information and advice necessary to make the decision.[82]

Finally, it should be noted that, unlike breaches of the fiduciary duty, the corporation can indemnify the breaching officer or director for breaches of the duty of care.[83]

3) Other Duties Imposed On Directors And Officers

Directors and officers are subject to a wide range of additional duties under corporate statutes and an increasing array of regulatory laws. Indeed, the burden of these statutory duties is so great that many commentators have argued that they are substantially interfering with the governance of corporations. They argue that the risk of liability discourages people from becoming directors and encourage them to resign in situations where the risk is increased, such as impending insolvency. Unfortunately, it is in those situations in which the risk is greatest that the need for good, experienced directors is also greatest. Perhaps even more important, it is argued that the increased risks have two other pervasive negative effects. They represent strong disincentives for directors to agree that the corporation should embark on activities presenting increased liability risks, no matter how much doing so may be beneficial to its business. They also encourage directors to become overinvolved in the day-to-day operations of the business in order to try to manage their risk.[84] The magnitude of these effects is hotly debated.[85]

A discussion of the many regulatory statutes imposing personal liability on directors and officers is far beyond the scope of this book. In the remainder of the chapter, we will discuss the subset of duties imposed in corporate legislation.

Directors are liable to employees for up to six months' unpaid wages if the corporation is either bankrupt or in liquidation proceedings, or the corporation has been successfully sued for the debt and the judgment has been unpaid (*CBCA*, s. 119).[86] Directors are not liable

---

82   *Smith v. Van Gorkhom*, 488 A. 2d 858 (Del. S.C. 1985).

83   Indemnities are discussed in Chapter 7.

84   R.J. Daniels, "Must Boards Go Overboard? An Economic Analysis of the Effects of Burgeoning Statutory Liability on the Role of Directors in Corporate Governance" (1994) 24 Can. Bus. L.J. 229 [Overboard].

85   H.J. Glasbeek, "More Direct Director Responsibility: Much Ado About … What?" (1995) 25 Can. Bus. L.J. 416, responding to Overboard, *ibid.*

86   There are similar provisions in the *OBCA*, above note 1, s. 131, and *ABCA*, above note 1, s. 119, but not the *BCCA*, above note 1.

unless the lawsuit by the employee against the corporation was commenced not more than six months after the earliest of

- the date the payment was due,
- the commencement of liquidation and dissolution proceedings, or
- the bankruptcy of the corporation.

A director's responsibility ceases two years after he ceases to be a director (*CBCA*, s. 119(3)).[87] If a director pays, he becomes entitled to enforce the rights of the employee against the corporation to the extent of the payment and is entitled to contribution from the other directors (*CBCA*, ss. 119(5) & (6)). The Supreme Court of Canada has held that liability does not extend to an unsatisfied judgment for wrongful dismissal or other severance or termination payments.[88] In light of the overlap between this provision and provincial labour standards and other legislation, Industry Canada raised the question whether this provision should be repealed. No such change was made in the *2001 Amendments*.[89]

Directors are also personally liable under section 118 of the *CBCA* in various circumstances. They are liable if they vote for or consent to a resolution authorizing the following:

- a purchase or redemption or other acquisition of shares contrary to sections 34, 35, or 36;
- a payment of a dividend contrary to section 42; or
- a payment to a shareholder exercising its right under section 190[90] to require the corporation to purchase its shares for fair value when the shareholder dissents from certain fundamental changes approved by shareholders contratry to section 190(26) (*CBCA*, ss. 118(2)(a), (c) & (e)).

Each of these provisions prohibits the making of the payment referred to where there are reasonable grounds for believing that either the solvency or capital impairment tests would be breached.[91] As we saw in

---

87   The time period under the *OBCA*, above note 1, s. 131(2), and the *ABCA*, above note 1, s. 119, is six months. There is no similar provision in the *BCCA*, above note 1.

88   *Barrette v. Crabtree Estate*, [1993] 1 S.C.R. 1027. Liability for wrongful dismissal was found by the Saskatchewan Court of Appeal based on the different wording of Saskatchewan's *The Business Corporations Act*, R.S.S. 1978, c. B-10, (*Meyers v. Walters Cycle Co.* (1990), 85 Sask. R. 222 (C.A.)).

89   *Discussion Paper on Directors' Liability*, above note 58, at 10.

90   Section 190 is described in Chapter 9.

91   A corporation is also prohibited from making a payment ordered by a court to relieve the oppression of a shareholder where these tests are not met (*CBCA*, above note 8, s. 241(a)). It seems unlikely that a court would order a payment in such circumstances.

Chapter 6, the solvency test requires that the corporation must be able to pay its liabilities as they become due, and the capital impairment test requires that the realizable value of its assets must not be less than its liabilities plus its stated capital for all classes of shares. Directors are also liable for paying an unreasonable commission on the issuance of shares contrary to section 41, and for paying an indemnity where doing so is not permitted under section 124 (*CBCA*, ss. 118(2)(b) & (d)).

In each case, the directors are responsible for repaying the corporation any amounts paid out. Each director who has satisfied a judgment under any of these provisions is entitled to contribution from the other directors who were liable and has a right to seek a court order compelling the recipient to pay any money received to the director (*CBCA*, s. 118(4) & (5)).[92]

Directors are liable under the *CBCA* if they vote for or consent to a resolution authorizing the issuance of shares in return for property that is less than the fair equivalent of money the corporation could have received if the shares were issued for money. Where directors are liable, they must compensate the corporation to the extent of the shortfall (*CBCA*, s. 118(1)). Each director is entitled to contribution from the others. Directors are excused, however, if they did not know and could not reasonably have known that the share was issued in return for inadequate consideration (*CBCA*, s. 118(6)). This might occur, for example, if the directors relied on an expert valuation that turned out to be wrong.

The *2001 Amendments* added this sort of excuse, sometimes referred to as a "due diligence defence," in relation to all these bases of liablity under sections 118 and 119. The defence is also available in relation to alleged breaches of the duty to comply with the act, the regulations, the articles, the by-laws, and any unanimous shareholders' agreement under section 122(2). A director is not liable if she exercised the care, diligence, and skill that a reasonably prudent person would have exercised in comparable circumstances, including reliance in good faith on

- financial statements of the corporation represented to the director by an officer of the corporation or in a written report of the auditor of the corporation fairly to reflect the financial condition of the corporation; or

---

92   The same scheme is established under provincial corporate statutes modelled on the *CBCA*, above note 8. E.g., *OBCA*, above note 1, s. 130; and *ABCA*, above note 1, s. 118. The *BCCA*, above note 1, has a similar scheme in ss. 45 & 127.

- a report of a person whose profession lends credibility to a statement made by the professional person (*CBCA*, s. 123(4)).

Similarly worded due diligence defences are available under many regulatory statutes imposing liability on directors. In general, the due diligence defence requires directors to do what is reasonable in the circumstances to prevent the offence from occurring. The circumstances relevant to determining what is reasonable are similar to those relevant to determining the scope of the duty of care. Unlike the *CBCA*, other Canadian corporate statutes do not have such an all-encompassing due diligence defence.

D. LIABILITY OF CORPORATE MANAGERS FOR TORTS

In general, directors and officers (collectively in this section referred to as managers) are not liable for the corporation's torts simply by virtue of their positions with the corporation. At the same time, where managers commit torts in the course of their employment, they are personally responsible, just as they would be if they were not acting in the course of their employment. The manager who negligently drives a fork-lift truck into a customer's truck may be personally liable in negligence. Where people are acting outside the scope of their authority from the corporation, it does not do violence to the separateness of the corporation's existence to hold them liable. By contrast, imposing tort liability on individuals acting on behalf of the corporation can be argued to be inconsistent with separate corporate personality. Failing to distinguish when people are acting in their personal capacity from when they represent the corporation ignores the separateness of the corporation. Where the people acting in the business are also the shareholders, holding them liable threatens limited liability. In considering cases in which such liability has been sought, the courts have recognized the tension between the tort principle that each person should be responsible for her own wrongs and the principle of separate corporate personality.[93]

Unfortunately, the courts have not been consistent in defining the circumstances in which personal liability will attach or how the tort and corporate law principles should be reconciled resulting in a morass of inconsistent and irreconcilable decisions. In general, whether a

---

93   *Mentmore Manufacturing Co. v. National Merchandise Manufacturing Co. Inc.* (1978), 89 D.L.R. (3d) 195 at 202 (Fed. C.A.).

director or officer or employee is responsible for tortious acts depends on the degree and kind of his personal involvement. Where he has performed, ordered, procured, counselled, aided or abetted the action constituting the tort, he is likely to be found liable.[94] It is not a defence to argue that the tort was committed for the benefit of the corporation or within the course of his duties.[95] On the other hand, where a person has only general management responsibilities in the area of the corporation's operations in which the tort was committed, but no knowledge or involvement in the actions constituting the tort, he is unlikely to be found liable.[96]

In *Scotia Macleod Inc.* v. *Peoples Jewellers Inc.*,[97] the Ontario Court of Appeal suggested a test for liability that provides greater protection to directors and officers acting within the scope of their employment or authority and that gives greater deference to the separateness of the corporation. The court held that, for a claim against directors or officers to succeed, it is necessary to allege that they had committed tortious behaviour outside their formal decision making roles in the corporation. The court identified the usual categories of torts giving rise to personal liablity as fraud, deceit, dishonesty, or want of authority and added

> [a]bsent allegations which fit within the categories described above, officers or employees of limited companies are protected from personal liability unless it can be shown that their actions are themselves tortious or exhibit a separate identity or interest from that of the company so as to make the act or conduct complained of their own.[98]

In *ADGA Systems International Ltd.* v. *Valcom Ltd.*, the same court offered a clarification. The requirement that the actions of corporate managers have a "separate identity" from the corporation did not mean that corporate managers could not be held liable for torts when acting

---

94 For example, *Shibamoto & Co.* v. *Western Fish Producers Inc. (Trustee of)* (1991), 48 F.T.R. 176 (T.D.) (tort of conversion). "Aided" and "abetted" refer to engaging in some conduct which facilitates the tort. See D. Debenham, "Return to the Beaten Path: Directors' and Employees' Liability for Intellectual Property Torts after *Mentmore*" (2003) 16 I.P. J. 1, at 2.

95 In *Shibamoto, ibid.*, the conversion was for the benefit of the corporation.

96 *C. Evans & Sons Ltd.* v. *Spritebrand Ltd.*, [1985] 2 All E.R. 415 (C.A.).

97 (1995), 26 O.R. 3d 481 (C. A.).

98 *Ibid.*, at 491. This passage has been cited with approval in many subsequent cases including *Lana International Ltd.* v. *Monasco Aerospace Ltd.* (2000), 136 O.A.C. 71, at 79–80, *ADGA Systems International Ltd.* v. *Valcom Ltd.* (1999), 43 O.R. (3d) 101 (C.A.), at 112 [*ADGA*] and *Normart Management Ltd.* v. *West Hill Redevelopment Co.* (1998), 37 O.R. (3d) 97 (C.A.), at 103.

in the course of their duties. In *ADGA*, the court held that two senior employees and the sole director of Valcom were personally liable for inducing breach of contract on the grounds that they raided the staff of Valcom's competitor, ADGA. Both corporations were bidding for a contract with Corrections Canada to supply support and maintenance services for security systems. In order to tender, a bidder had to have at least twenty-five qualified technicians. ADGA, an experienced contractor, had forty-five such technicians. Valcom had none. The individual defendants induced forty-four of ADGA's technicians to leave their employment with ADGA and join Valcom. The court recognized that the defendants were acting in pursuit of the corporation's interests, but held that this did not shield them from liability.

The application of the approach of the Ontario Court of Appeal to intentional torts like fraud appears relatively straightforward. The policy of holding someone liable for serious intentional torts outweighs concerns about the sanctity of the separate corporate person. Moreover, the serious and wrongful nature of the intentional behaviour by the manager which constitutes the tort excludes it from being merely an act which can be said to be in the ordinary course of fulfilling one's duty to the corporation. Such a conclusion will be reinforced where the manager has engaged in the behaviour for personal gain. As will become evident from the review of the case law below, it is harder to characterize a manager's behaviour as exhibiting a "separate identity" from the corporation's in relation to negligence and some other torts. The result has been that the scope of personal liability for torts committed by corporate managers is an issue which has been repeatedly litigated since the late 1990s. The direction of the current case law appears to be towards a standard for liability based less on abstract and, ultimately, unsatisfactory concepts such as when the manager's behaviour demonstrates a separate identity from the corporation's, and more on the degree and kind of their personal involvement in the tort.[99]

With respect to negligence, Welling has suggested that the liability for negligence should be imposed only where the alleged tortfeasor has a duty towards the plaintiff arising out of a relationship to her, not simply by virtue of the corporation having a duty arising out of its relationship to the plaintiff and the tortious actions occurring in her general

---

99   This is the conclusion reached by Debenham in a very thorough analysis of the case law before and after the decision in *ADGA*, *ibid*. (D. Debenham, "The Scylla of Motions Court and the Charybdis of the Court of Appeal: The Scope of Directors' and Officers' Common Law Liabilities in the Post-*ADGA* Era" (2001) 25 Advocates Quarterly 21 [Debenham, "Scylla"].

area of responsibility. In the latter case, the tortfeasor should be considered merely the "human manifestation of the corporation" and, as such, not personally liable.[100]

In *Berger* v. *Willowdale A.M.C.*,[101] an employee slipped on the sidewalk while leaving work after a snowstorm. The *Workmen's Compensation Act*[102] barred her from suing the corporate employer in tort; she had to rely on the compensation scheme provided in the Act. Consequently, she sued the president personally, alleging that he was negligent. The court found that the sidewalk had not been cleared adequately. It also found that the president had a general responsibility to ensure that the workplace was safe, a task he had failed to discharge. He was in a position to know about the danger and to remove it, but failed to do so. As a result, he was liable in negligence. The court indicated that a personal duty would not arise in every case but would depend on a variety of factors, including[103] the size of the corporation, the number of employees, the nature of the business, and whether the danger should have been readily apparent to the manager. Here, the manager had the authority and the ability to control the situation and had ready access to the means to rectify the danger. Welling is critical of this case on the basis that the only relationship between the president and the employee arose by virtue of the president's position in the corporation. Other commentators have suggested that the case is an application of the basic common law principle of occupier's liability that a person in control of property has a duty of care to people who come onto the property to ensure that they are protected against hazards that are likely to harm them. The significance of the case is only that it holds that the person in control of property is not excused just because he is the president of a corporation that happens to own the property.[104]

Few subsequent cases have followed *Berger*,[105] though a number of cases have held that employees may be held liable for negligence for actions in the course of their employment. *London Drugs Ltd.* v. *Kuehne*

---

100   Welling, above note 16, at 117.
101   (1983), 41 O.R. (2d) 89 (C.A.), leave to appeal refused (1983), 41 O.R. (2d) 89 (S.C.C.) [*Berger*].
102   R.S.O. 1970, c. 505.
103   *Berger*, above note 101.
104   Debenham, "Scylla," above note 99, at 58.
105   This case was not followed in *Kavanagh* v. *Don Sloan Equipment Rentals Ltd.* (1988), 4 M.V.R. (2d) 34 (Ont. H.C.J.) or *Bradsil Ltd.* v. *602871 Ontario Ltd.*, [1996] O.J. No. 294 (QL) (Gen. Div.). One important result of this case was the imposition of tort liability on the president where a claim against the corporation would have failed.

& Nagel International Ltd.[106] is the leading case on employee liability for negligence. Two employees were found to have negligently damaged some property belonging to a customer of their corporate employer while moving the property in the course of their employment. The Supreme Court held that that they had a personal duty to the corporation's customer because damage to the customer's property was a foreseeable consequence of their failing to take the requisite care. Ultimately, the employees and their corporate employer escaped liability, however, on the basis of an exclusion of liability clause in the employer's contract with the plaintiff. The conclusion of the Court on the issue of negligence may be justified on the basis of the degree and nature of the employees' involvement in the activity giving rise to the damage.

Recently, there have been a number of decisions holding managers liable for negligent misstatement. In *NBD Bank, Canada* v. *Dofasco Inc.*[107] the vice-president (finance) of Algoma Steel made a number of oral and written misrepresentations to the NBD Bank regarding Algoma's financial health and the security for the bank's loan. The bank advanced additional funds on the basis of the misrepresentations. The court held the officer liable for the losses the bank sustained as a result. While the officer was acting only in his role as an officer, the direct relationship between the officer and the bank was sufficient to give rise to a personal duty for the officer.

In a recent English case, *Williams* v. *Natural Life Health Foods Ltd.*,[108] the House of Lords considered a claim that a franchisor had negligently given inaccurate advice regarding the likely financial returns on a franchise business inducing the plaintiffs to enter into a franchise agreement. The franchise never made any money and the plaintiffs sued. The House of Lords held that personal liability for negligence will attach only where there is reason to conclude that the victim reasonably relied on an individual undertaking that the individual would be personally liable. This standard is higher than the threshold for personal liability currently being applied in Ontario. The House of Lords found no such reliance in this case. Subsequently, in *Standard Chartered Bank* v. *Pakistan National Shipping Corp.*,[109] a case involving fraud by a director of a corporation, the House of Lords held the director personally liable. The House of Lords distinguished *Williams*, hold-

---

106 [1992] 3 S.C.R. 299
107 (1997), 34 B.L.R. (2d) 209 (Ont. Gen. Div.), aff'd (1999), 46 O.R. (3d) 54
      (C.A.), leave to appeal refused, [2000] S.C.C.A. No. 96 (QL).
108 [1998] 1 W.L.R. 830 (H.L.).
109 [2003] 1 All E.R. 173 (H.L.). See Debenham, "Scylla," above note 99, at 65–66.

ing that, unlike negligence, it was no defence in an action for fraud to characterize it as being committed on behalf of the corporation.

The tort of inducing breach of contract has presented special problems. The tort of inducing breach of contract is committed when a person, knowing that there is a contract between the plaintiff and a third party, induces the third party, without justification, to break the contract, with the intention of procuring the breach of contract.[110] Where the third party is the corporation that the managers work for, this principle has the potential virtually to eliminate the separate legal personality of the corporation. Every time the corporation breached a contract, the innocent party would have an action for breach of contract and a claim in tort against the corporate officer or employee who authorized the corporation to breach. This would be a windfall for the innocent party which it had not contracted for. However, an important exception to this general rule was described in *Said* v. *Butt*:

> ... if a servant acting *bona fide* within the scope of his authority procures or causes the breach of a contract between his employer and a third person, he does not thereby become liable to an action of tort at the suit of the person whose contract has thereby been broken.[111]

In *McFadden* v. *481782 Ontario Ltd.*,[112] it was held that the effect of this exception was to excuse directors and officers if they were acting "under the compulsion of a duty to the corporation." In that case, two directors authorized payments to themselves as shareholders that put the corporation in a position where it could not fulfil its contractual obligations to an employee. The employee successfully sued the directors on the basis that they induced the corporation to breach its contract with him. The court held that the directors could not fall within the *Said* v. *Butt* exception since they were acting with a view to their own interests and not those of the corporation, and so could not be said to be acting under the compulsion of a duty to the corporation.

Several other cases have held directors and officers of a corporation liable for inducing a breach of a contract to which the corporation was a party where they were acting outside the scope of their authority. For example in *Aiken* v. *Regency Homes Inc.*,[113] the court held two individu-

---

110 *Quinn* v. *Leathem*, [1901] A.C. 495 at 510 (H.L.).
111 [1920] 3 K.B. 497, at 506.
112 (1984), 47 O.R. (2d) 134 (H.C.J.).
113 [1991] O.J. No. 1201 (QL) (C.A.). See also *Einhorn* v. *Westmount Investments Ltd.* (1969), 6 D.L.R. (3d) 71 (Sask Q.B.), aff'd (1970), 11 D.L.R. (3d) 509 (Sask. C.A.). In *Lehndorff Canadian Pension Properties Ltd.* v. *Davis & Co.* (1987), 10 B.C.L.R. (2d) 342 (S.C.), directors who transferred assets out of the corpora-

als carrying on business through a corporation liable for inducing the corporation to fail to fulfil its contractual commitments to the plaintiff to build a house, in part by directing corporate funds to pay their personal expenses. The court found that their actions were "*mala fides* and outside the legitimate scope of their authority over the affairs of [the corporation]."

Recently a court did permit officers, directors, and employees of a parent corporation to rely on the compulsion of duty defence in connection with their participation in a breach of contract by the parent's subsidiary. The court held that they could rely on the defence so long as they were acting *bona fide* in the best interests of the subsidiary.[114]

The Ontario Court of Appeal in *ADGA*[115] made it clear that the compulsion of duty defence is available only where the contract that is breached is one to which the corporation for which the managers work is a party. It can never be available where the contract is between two third parties. In *ADGA* the officers of Valcom were alleged to have induced the breach of the contracts between ADGA and its employees, so the defence was not available.

Figure 8.3   Liability of Corporate Managers for Torts – Inducing Breach of Contract After *ADGA*

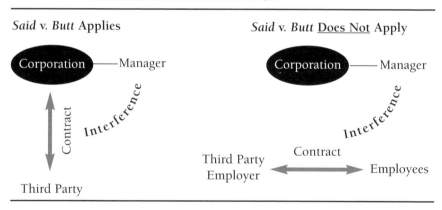

This compulsion of duty defence has been held not to be applicable in the context of other torts, including deceit and negligent misstate-

tion were held liable for inducing breach of contract by the corporation. An unsuccessful attempt was made to hold officers of the corporation liable for conspiring to induce a breach of contract. The extent to which the corporation is willing or obliged to indemnify the director or officer will have an impact on the effect of imposing liability. See Chapter 7.

114 *1175777 Ontario Ltd.* v. *Magda International Inc.* (2001), 145 O.A.C. 364.
115 Above note 88.

ment. In *Toronto Dominion Bank* v. *Leigh Instruments Ltd.* (*trustee of*),[116] the court refused to strike out a statement of claim against certain directors and officers of a corporation alleging that they had fraudulently given false information to the bank to encourage it to grant the corporation more credit. The court said that it is no excuse that the employee was obeying orders of the employer or that the act was expressly authorized or ratified by the corporation. With regard to the cases on inducing breach of contract, including *Said* v. *Butt*, the court simply said it was not dealing with such a case.[117] This approach is consistent with the trends in the case law discussed in the first part of this section.

E. CHAPTER SUMMARY

In this chapter, we considered the range of duties to which directors and officers are subject under Canadian corporate law. We mentioned the specific liabilities imposed on directors for certain discrete activities, such as paying dividends or issuing shares, in ways contrary to corporate law. Most of the chapter, however, was devoted to the general standards of behaviour created by the fiduciary duty and the duty of care now expressly provided for in most corporate statutes and to the scope of directors' and officers' liability in tort.

The fiduciary duty requires directors and officers to act honestly, in good faith, and with a view to the best interests of the corporation. It strictly prohibits them from allowing their personal interests to interfere with their duty to act in the best interests of the corporation. Acting in the best interests of the corporation also means not favouring the interests of one group of shareholders over those of another. Aside from these general principles, it is not possible to articulate what the fiduciary duty requires in the abstract; it will depend on the circumstances of each case. We looked at four kinds of situations in which the issue of fiduciary duty arises: a fiduciary having an interest in a contract with the corporation, appropriating an opportunity alleged to belong to the corporation, competing with the corporation, and taking defensive measures against a takeover bid for control of her corpora-

---

116   (1991), 4 B.L.R. (2d) 220 (Ont. Div. Ct.).

117   *Ibid.*, at 252. The compulsion of duty defence will not be available where, in addition to breaching a contractual obligation, the individual breaches a fiduciary or other equitable obligation to the innocent party to the contract (see D. Debenham, "Coming Armed with Spiers," (2003) 27 Adv. Q. 1, at 30).

tion. It is important to remember that the circumstances in which a breach of fiduciary duty may occur are not limited to these situations.

A contract in which a fiduciary has an interest is voidable but, if the fiduciary discloses her interest and the contract is approved by the directors or shareholders, and is fair and reasonable to the corporation, in accordance with corporate statutes, the contract will be enforceable. Where a fiduciary takes an opportunity belonging to the corporation, she will be required to account to the corporation for any profit she makes as a result. One difficult issue in this area is to determine when an opportunity belongs to the corporation and when a fiduciary is precluded from taking advantage of it. If the corporation's interest in the opportunity is strong and the relationship of the fiduciary to it is close, the fiduciary cannot take it. Determining whether this is the situation will depend heavily on the facts of each case. In almost all cases, competition by a fiduciary with the corporation will be a breach of fiduciary duty and the fiduciary will have to account for any profits earned by such competition.

When faced with a takeover bid, directors and officers are in a conflict of interest: the success of the bid may be in the best interests of shareholders but cost them their jobs. Notwithstanding the conflict, the courts have permitted directors to defend against a takeover bid in certain cases provided that they take steps to minimize the conflict of interest and act reasonably to advance the best interests of the corporation in developing a strategy to respond to the bid. Usually this is done by setting up a committee of directors independent of management to devise the corporation's response to the bid, because management's conflict of interest is most acute.

The duty of care under modern corporate statutes is objectively determined, though its specific content will depend on the facts of each case, including the knowledge and experience of the director or officer and the positions she occupies. In general, the duty requires a minimum standard of competence and regular attendance at meetings. As an incentive to attending meetings, directors are deemed to consent to decisions taken at meetings unless they record their dissent. In addition, the duty requires that directors stay generally informed about the business and affairs of the corporation and monitor what is going on. If directors are put on notice that there is a problem, the duty of care requires them to take steps to address it.

Directors and officers can be held liable for torts, even when acting in the course of carrying out their duties in good faith. While such liability arguably imperils the separate existence of the corporation, it is consistent with the tort principle that each person should be held liable for their own torts. In general, whether a person will be liable in tort will depend on the degree and nature of their personal involvement in the tort. With respect to the liability of an officer or director for inducing the breach of a contract to which the corporation is a party, however, acting *bona fide* in the interests of the corporation may provide an effective defence.

Finally, as noted in the introduction to this chapter, the oppression remedy contained in most Canadian corporate statutes establishes a new substantive standard of behaviour for directors and officers which complements and overlaps with their duties. This standard is described in detail in Chapter 9.

FURTHER READINGS

BECK, S.M., "The Quickening of Fiduciary Obligation: *Canadian Aero Services* v. *O'Malley*" (1975) 53 Can. Bar. Rev. 771

BRAITHWAITE, W.J., "Unjust Enrichment and Directors' Duties: *Abbey Glen Property Corp.* v. *Stumborg*" (1979) 3 Can. Bus. L.J. 210

BRUDNEY, V., Corporate Governance, Agency Costs, and the Rhetoric of Contract" (1985) 85 Colum. L. Rev. 1403

BRUDNEY, V., & R.C. CLARK, "A New Look at Corporate Opportunities" (1981) 94 Harv. L. Rev. 997

CHEFFINS, B.R., "Law, economics and morality: contracting out of corporate law fiduciary duties" (1991) 19 Can. Bus. L.J. 28–48

COHEN, Z., "Director's Negligence Liability to Creditors: A Comparative and Critical View" [2001] J. of Corp. L. 351

DANIELS, R.J., "Must Boards Go Overboard? An Economic Analysis of the Effects of Burgeoning Statutory Liability on the Role of Directors in Corporate Governance" (1994) 24 Can. Bus. L.J. 229

DEBENHAM, D., "The Scylla of Motions Court and the Charybdis of the Court of Appeal: The Scope of Directors' and Officers' Common Law Liabilities in the Post-*ADGA* Era" (2001), 25 Advocates Quarterly 21

DEMOTT, D.A., "Beyond Metaphor: An Analysis of Fiduciary Obligation" [1988] Duke L.J. 879

EASTERBROOK, F.H., & D.R. FISCHEL, "Corporate Control Transactions" (1982) 81 Yale L J. 689

EISENBERG, M.A., "Self-Interested Transactions in Corporate Law" (1988) 13 Journal of Corp. L. 997

FEASBY, C., "Corporate agents' liability in tort: a comment on *ADGA Systems International Ltd.* v. *Valcom Ltd.*" (1999) 32 Can. Bus. L.J. 291

FINN, P.D., *Fiduciary Obligations* (Sydney: Law Book Co., 1977)

FLANNIGAN, R., "The Fiduciary Obligation" (1989) 9 Oxford. J. Legal Stud. 285

GLASBEEK, H.J., "More Direct Director Responsibility: Much Ado About … What?" (1995) 25 Can. Bus. L.J. 416

HANSELL, C., *Directors and Officers in Canada: Law and Practice* (Toronto: Carswell, 1999)

INDUSTRY CANADA, *Directors' Liability* (*Canada Business Corporations Act* Discussion Paper) (Ottawa: Industry Canada, 1995)

JOHNSEN, K.C., "Golden Parachutes and the Business Judgement Rule: Toward a Proper Standard of Review" (1985) 94 Yale L.J. 909

KING, C.G.W., "Extending Fiduciary Principles to the Debtor-Creditor Relationship: A Canadian Perspective" (2002) 29 Man. L. J. 243

KLINCK, D., "Things of Confidence: Loyalty, Secrecy and Fiduciary Obligation" (1990) 54 Sask. L. Rev. 73

MACINTOSH, J.G., "Standard Trustco Case Signals Expansion of the 'Public Interest' Powers of Securities Regulators" (1993) 1 Corp. Financing 38

MACINTOSH, J.G., J. HOLMES, & S. THOMPSON, "The Puzzle of Shareholder Fiduciary Duties" (1991) 19 Can. Bus. L.J. 86

OSLER, HOSKIN, & HARCOURT, *Directors' Duties in Canada: A Guide to the Responsibilities of Corporate Directors in Canada*, 2d ed. (Toronto: Osler, Hoskin, & Harcourt, 1995)

Report of the Toronto Stock Exchange Committee on Corporate Governance in Canada: Where Were the Directors? (Toronto: Toronto Stock Exchange, 1994)

THOMPSON, D., "Directors, creditors and insolvency: a fiduciary duty or a duty not to oppress?" (2000) 58 U.T. Fac. L. Review 31

VOORHEIS, G.W., *Corporate Fiduciary Duties: Selected Difficulties* (Toronto, Ont.: Davies, Ward & Beck, 1990)

WAINBERG, J.M., & M.I. WAINBERG, *Duties and Responsibilities of Directors in Canada*, 6th ed. (Don Mills: CCH Canadian Ltd., 1987)

WELLING, B., "Individual liability for corporate acts: in defence of Hobson's choice" (2000) 12 S.C.L.R. (2d.)

WEINRIB, E.J., "The Fiduciary Obligation" (1975) 25 U.T.L.J. 1

CHAPTER 9

SHAREHOLDER REMEDIES

A. INTRODUCTION

Shareholder remedies are the means of ensuring that the interests of shareholders are protected and that the rights to which they are entitled under statute, at common law, or under the corporation's articles, by-laws, directors' and shareholders' resolutions, and any unanimous shareholders' agreements may be exercised. The initial focus of this chapter is procedural. We are concerned with the procedures available to shareholders to assert claims, rather than the substantive bases for those claims, which, in large part, are the subject of the previous chapters of this book. When we turn to deal with the oppression remedy, however, we are discussing both a substantive basis of protection and a procedure for making a claim. The oppression remedy, which we have referred to extensively throughout the book, represents an emerging standard of behaviour that not only complements the duties imposed on management described in Chapter 8 but is coming to rival the fiduciary duty as the operative measure against which all management activities must be judged. In large part, this is due to the procedural advantages of bringing an oppression claim.

The two main bases on which a shareholder may assert a claim for relief are the derivative action, and the oppression action. Before the enactment of the *CBCA* there was no oppression remedy available in most Canadian jurisdictions,[1] and the derivative action was subject to certain limitations. One of the major objectives of the *CBCA* was to provide greater access to more effective remedies for minority shareholders.[2]

Owning a share carries with it certain rights that are clearly personal to the holder of the shares, such as the right to vote, the right to timely and informative notice of meetings, and the right to inspect the books and records of the corporation. These personal rights may derive from the governing corporate statute, the articles and by-laws of the corporation, the common law,[3] or a shareholders' agreement. The major limitation on a personal action to enforce such rights is that the most important legal constraints on directors and officers, the fiduciary duty and the duty of care, are obligations owed to the corporation, rather than directly to the shareholder. As a result, breaches of these duties cannot be the basis of a personal action by a shareholder.

In some circumstances, a shareholder may commence a derivative action on behalf of the corporation for breach of these duties or for any other obligation to the corporation where the corporation is not taking action to pursue its own rights. This is not an uncommon situation since, in many cases, the same people who have allegedly breached their duties, the directors and senior officers, are the people who must decide whether to cause the corporation to sue. In such a case, the directors may well have a different view of whether their conduct constitutes a breach of duty. As will be discussed below, before the enactment of the *CBCA*, the circumstances in which shareholders could initiate such a derivative action were narrow.

In order to properly plead its claim, a shareholder had to characterize the claim correctly as either personal or derivative. The general test developed by the courts to ascertain whether misconduct was a breach of a personal obligation to shareholders or to the corporation was to ask if the injury to the shareholders was merely incidental to an injury to the corporation.[4] So long as the injury did not occur only because

---

1　The oppression remedy was first introduced in Canada in the British Columbia *Companies Act*, R.S.B.C. 1960, c. 67, in 1960. It was interpreted narrowly until it was amended to add, among other things, "unfair prejudice" as a ground for relief in 1973 (S.B.C. 1973, c. 18).

2　R.V.W. Dickerson, J.L. Howard, & L. Getz, *Proposals for a New Business Corporations Law for Canada*, vol. 1 (Ottawa: Information Canada, 1971) at 158–63 [Dickerson].

3　In *Liu v. Sung* (1991), 13 C.B.R. (3d) 285 (B.C.C.A.), for example, a shareholder was permitted to sue a director in tort and for breach of contract.

4　*Goldex Mines Ltd. v. Revill* (1974), 7 O.R. (2d) 216 (C.A.) (sending out misleading information circular and misleading annual report described as breach of

the corporation was injured, then the claim will be permitted to proceed. An example of an injury that is only incidental to an injury to the corporation would be the diminution in the value of a shareholder's shares caused by the appropriation of a corporate asset by the directors.

It is impossible, however, to draw a clear and satisfactory distinction between an injury to the shareholder and an injury to the corporation. As the holder of the residual claim to the assets of the corporation, the shareholders' interests will be substantially affected by any injury to the corporation, as will the interests of many other stakeholders. The coincidence of shareholder and corporate interests is most obvious where the shareholder holds all the shares of the corporation,[5] but it will occur in virtually every case. Nevertheless, in terms of the procedure followed prior to the enactment of the *CBCA*, it was essential to characterize a claim clearly as personal rather than merely incidental to an injury to the corporation if a shareholder was to be able to proceed without being forced to seek relief by a derivative action. This was often difficult to do, since most actions by directors and officers which are injurious to shareholders could be characterized as a breach of fiduciary duty. Even the example of a breach of a personal right given above may be characterized as a breach of the directors' fiduciary duty. Is it not always contrary to the corporation's best interests to send out an inadequate notice of a meeting? Historically, the courts gave broad scope to what was considered a breach of directors' duties to the corporation. This limited the ability of shareholders to use the personal action.

As discussed in more detail in the next section, the derivative action was not an effective remedial option for shareholders either. The primary problem was that the courts would not permit shareholders to sue on behalf of the corporation where the conduct alleged to constitute the breach had been or could be ratified by a majority of shareholder votes. If the majority shareholder did not want to pursue the matter, minority shareholders were precluded from taking action. This rule was not applied in cases of very serious injury to the corporation.

In short, neither the derivative action nor the personal action provided ready access to relief for shareholders. As noted, one of the primary purposes of the drafters of the *CBCA* was to enhance the ability of shareholders to obtain relief. This purpose was accomplished by

---

personal right; pleading struck down because inextricably linked with claims for injuries to the corporation).

5   The effect of a loss of corporate assets on a sole shareholder was recognized by the Supreme Court of Canada in *Kosmopoulos v. Constitution Insurance Co. of Canada*, [1987] 1 S.C.R. 2, discussed in Chapter 3.

improving access to derivative actions and by introducing the oppression remedy. Under the *CBCA* and the statutes modelled after it, the shareholders may commence a derivative action for any injury to the corporation with leave of a court (*CBCA*, s. 239). Ratification by shareholders is no longer a bar. With the enactment of the oppression remedy, the need to characterize a claim as personal as a condition of initiating an action on a shareholder's behalf was eliminated. Relief from oppression seems to be available whether or not the claim is essentially personal or derivative, so long as the prescribed standard of behaviour has been violated.

Following a discussion of these general remedies, we will discuss briefly the various other types of remedies found in the *CBCA* and statutes modelled after it, including the following:

- orders directing compliance with the Act, a corporation's articles or a unanimous shareholders' agreement, or orders to restrain a breach (*CBCA*, s. 247);
- orders requiring the rectification of corporate records (*CBCA*, s. 243);
- orders to investigate the affairs of the corporation (*CBCA*, ss. 229–37);
- the right of a shareholder to dissent from certain proposed fundamental changes to the corporation and to be bought out by the corporation (*CBCA*, s. 190); and
- termination of the corporation's existence (*CBCA*, s. 214).

B. DERIVATIVE ACTION

The general rule that only a corporation may sue for an injury to it was developed in an old case called *Foss* v. *Harbottle*.[6] That case based the rule on the notion that, since the shareholders could approve or ratify breaches of duty to the corporation, it would be an inappropriate interference with majority rule for courts to permit actions by minority shareholders where the action had been or could be ratified by the majority. There were only four situations in which a minority shareholder could sue for an injury to the corporation:

Fraud on the minority: This situation was sometimes referred to as oppression of the minority, but common law oppression included a much narrower range of activities than oppression under the *CBCA* and other modern corporate statutes. Essentially it was limited to situations in which the management of the corporation was giving corpo-

---

6   (1843), 2 Hare 467, 67 E.R. 189 (Ch.).

rate assets away, typically to the majority shareholder. In such cases, the courts recognized that permitting majority rule would work a hardship on the minority shareholder.

Ultra Vires Acts: In situations where the act complained of was outside the limited powers of the corporation or was illegal, the majority was not permitted to ratify it and minority shareholders could sue on behalf of the corporation.

Defect in majority approval: In situations where the relevant corporate legislation or the articles of the corporation required approval by a specified majority of shareholders, and approval at that level was not properly obtained, shareholders could sue on behalf of the corporation.

Personal right: In situations where the personal rights of a shareholder were infringed, he could sue for relief. Such a suit is not an action on behalf of the corporation at all, but rather a situation to which the bar on derivative actions does not apply, and so it is not really an exception to the general rule.[7]

Under the *CBCA* and other modern corporate statutes in Canada, the curative effect of ratification has been abolished (*CBCA*, s. 122(3)).[8] The courts may still take shareholder approval of actions by the directors into account, but its relevance will depend on the circumstances. Shareholder approval may be relevant, for example, where a significant majority of disinterested shareholders who have received appropriate disclosure regarding what the directors have done approve the directors' actions and the action itself is not manifestly harmful to the corporation. On the other hand, a court would likely disregard an approval by a majority shareholder of actions taken by the shareholder in her capacity as a director or where the approval was improperly obtained.[9]

The restrictive conditions developed following *Foss* v. *Harbottle* have been replaced by a scheme allowing shareholders to proceed with derivative actions with court approval. Under the scheme, approval will be given if three conditions are met:

---

7   *Edwards* v. *Halliwell*, [1950] 2 All E.R. 1064 (C.A.).

8   See similar provisions in other corporate statutes. E.g., Ontario *Business Corporations Act*, R.S.O. 1990, c. B-16 [*OBCA*], s. 134(3), Alberta *Business Corporations Act*, R.S.A. 2000, c. B-9 [*ABCA*], s. 122(3); and *Companies Act*, R.S.B.C. 1996, c. 62 [*BCCA*], ss. 119, 135 & 136.

9   There is little case law on the issue of what weight to give to shareholder approval. The discussion in the text is based on an assessment of the prior case law in K.P. McGuiness, *The Law and Practice of Canadian Business Corporations* (Toronto: Butterworths, 1999) [McGuiness] at 944–946.

- the shareholder gives not less than fourteen days' notice to the directors of the corporation of her intention to apply for leave to bring an action if the directors do not;
- the shareholder is acting in good faith; and
- the action proposed to be initiated by the shareholder appears to be in the interests of the corporation (*CBCA*, s. 239).[10]

The requirement for notice does not mean that a shareholder must specify all the legal bases on which a claim might be made or the facts or evidence on which the shareholder relies. It is sufficient if the shareholder gives some general information disclosing the nature of the claim.[11] For example, a notice that refers to a sale of specific corporate assets at under value without specifying the legal basis of the claim is sufficient.[12]

An application for leave will be considered to meet the "good faith" requirement so long as no bad faith is shown. If the application is shown to be frivolous or vexatious, it will not be granted. In this regard, it has been held that a shareholder bringing an oppression action for an injury to him, based on the same facts as the derivative action, does not make the derivative action vexatious.[13] Where an applicant is motivated by a potential tactical advantage to be gained against directors in another proceeding, instead of the potential gain by the corporation, the applicant will be found not to be acting in good faith.[14]

The requirement that the action "appear to be in the interests of the corporation" represents a very low threshold of merit. This is justified, in part, because minority shareholders are not often in a position to obtain evidence to establish their case. The standard has been held to be less onerous than establishing a *prima facie* case (i.e., one that, in the absence of contradicting evidence, would be sufficient for the eventual lawsuit for breach of duty to be successful). Leave should be

---

10   This provision follows the *OBCA*, above note 8, s. 246. Under the *ABCA*, above note 8, reasonable notice is required. See also the similar rules in the *BCCA*, above note 8, s. 201(1)–(3).

11   *Marc-Jay Investments Inc.* v. *Levy* (1974), 5 O.R. (2d) 235 (H.C.J.) [*Marc-Jay*]; *Bellman* v. *Western Approaches Ltd.* (1981), 33 B.C.L.R. 45 (C.A.) [*Bellman*].

12   *Re Northwest Forest Products Ltd.*, [1975] 4 W.W.R. 724 (B.C.S.C.); *Bellman, ibid.* (failure to refer specifically to non-compliance with takeover-bid rules not fatal).

13   *Bellman, ibid.*

14   *Vedova* v. *Garden House Inn Ltd.* (1985), 29 B.L.R. 236 (Ont. H.C.J.). In *Roles* v. *Reimer* (1996), 146 Sask R. 213 (Q.B.), the applicant was found not to be acting in good faith where he was using the threat of litigation to force the corporation to buy his shares at an inflated price.

denied only if it appears that the action is bound to be unsuccessful.[15] Claims that a corporate asset has been sold at under value,[16] that the directors were subject to a conflict of interest in relation to a particular transaction they approved,[17] or that a mortgage should be found to be held in trust for the corporation[18] have all been held to be claims that appear to be in the interests of the corporation.

Several other aspects of the scheme governing derivative actions under the *CBCA* deserve mention.[19] First and most important, the *CBCA* expressly provides that evidence of shareholder approval, or the possibility of future shareholder approval, is not determinative of whether a derivative action may proceed (*CBCA*, s. 242(1)), thus eliminating the rule in *Foss v. Harbottle*.[20] As noted, shareholder approval may still be taken into account by a court, however, in deciding if leave to commence a derivative action should be given.

Second, once an application is made, it cannot be stayed, discontinued, or settled without approval of the court (*CBCA*, s. 242(2)). This rule was introduced to prevent corporations from settling so-called "strike suits" where a shareholder brings a frivolous suit to extort a financial settlement from the corporation. The inability of a corporation to settle without court approval should discourage such suits. It also may prevent corporations from buying off a shareholder who has obtained the leave of the court to commence an apparently meritorious action for the benefit of the corporation. The approach taken by the court will be to ask if the potential rewards of successful litigation, with its attendant risks and costs, are outweighed by the benefits of the proposed settlement.[21]

Third, contrary to the usual rules of civil procedure, a shareholder making an application for leave to commence a derivative action cannot be required to give security for the corporation's costs. Security for costs is often ordered against plaintiffs in ordinary civil suits on the basis of an application by the defendants. Under such an order, the plaintiff must post money or other security to cover any eventual award

---

15   *Marc-Jay*, above note 11.

16   Ibid.; *Bellman*, above note 11.

17   *Bellman*, ibid.

18   *Walter E. Heller Financial Corp. v. Powell River Town Centre Ltd.* (1983), 49 B.C.L.R. 145 (S.C.).

19   See similar provisions in other corporate statutes. E.g., *OBCA*, above note 8, s. 249, *ABCA*, above note 8, s. 243; and *BCCA*, above note 8, s. 201(4)–(7).

20   *Farnham v. Fingold*, [1973] 2 O.R. 132 (C.A.); *Pappas v. Acan Windows Inc.* (1991), 90 Nfld. & P.E.I.R. 126 (Nfld. S.C.T.D.) [*Pappas*].

21   *Sparling v. Southam Inc.* (1988), 66 O.R. (2d) 225 (H.C.J.) [*Sparling*].

of costs by the court in favour of the defendant. Such an award would usually be made if the defendant successfully defends against the plaintiff's claim. The availability of orders to provide security for costs is intended to discourage frivolous lawsuits. The exemption in the case of derivative actions is intended to assist an impecunious shareholder to take actions in the corporation's interest (*CBCA*, s. 242(3)). Since there is an opportunity for judicial scrutiny at the hearing on the leave application, security for costs is not necessary to prevent frivolous suits.

Finally, a court may award an impecunious shareholder interim costs to assist her to pay counsel to proceed with an action, though she may be required to repay them if she is unsuccessful (*CBCA*, s. 242(4)). There is some judicial authority to suggest that such costs in derivative actions will be routinely awarded.[22] Other courts have been reluctant to order interim costs where there has been some doubt regarding the merits of the complainant's claim.[23]

Although the people most likely to bring an application for leave to commence a derivative action are shareholders, the *CBCA* permits a much wider class of persons to do so. The *CBCA* permits applications for leave to be brought by a "complainant," which is defined to mean

- a current or former registered or beneficial holder of securities of the corporation or any affiliated corporation;
- a director or officer of the corporation or any of its affiliates;
- the Director appointed under the *CBCA*; and
- any other person whom a court determines is a proper person to make an application.

Notwithstanding the broad scope of the class of persons who, potentially, can bring a derivative action, it has been used primarily by shareholders.[24] None of the other identified kinds of complainants has made a successful application. In several cases, a creditor has sought a court order recognizing it as a complainant, but none has succeeded.[25] A complainant also defines the class of persons who may seek relief from

---

22 *Wilson v. Conley* (1990), 1 B.L.R. (2d) 220 (Ont. Gen. Div.) [*Wilson*].
23 *Intercontinental Precious Metals v. Cooke* (1993), 10 B.L.R. (2d) 203 (B.C.S.C.).
24 In *Oberkirsch v. Hanwell* (2001), 15 B.L.R. (3d) 237 (Sask. Q.B.), persons with a disputed claim to be shareholders were permitted to bring a derivative action. In *Richardson Greenshields of Canada Ltd. v. Kalmakoff* (1995) 22 O.R. (3d) 577 (C.A.), leave to appeal refused, [1995] S.C.C.A. xlo. No. 260 (QL), [*Richardson Greenshields v. Kalmakoff*], it was held that a person could buy shares in a corporation for the purpose of acquiring standing to bring a derivative action.
25 *Re Daon Development Corp.* (1984), 54 B.C.L.R. 235 (S.C.); *First Edmonton Place Ltd. v. 315888 Alberta Ltd.* (1989), 71 Alta. L.R. (2d) 61 (C.A.).

oppression. Unlike derivative action cases, there have been many oppression cases in which non-shareholder complainants, including the *CBCA* Director and creditors, have sought and obtained relief. Those who may seek relief from oppression are discussed in more detail in the next section.

C. OPPRESSION REMEDY

1) Introduction

Shortly after the oppression remedy was introduced as part of the new-*CBCA* in 1975,[26] Stanley Beck described it in the following terms: "... beyond question, the broadest, most comprehensive and most open-ended shareholder remedy in the common law world ... unprecedented in its scope."[27] Since the enactment of the *CBCA*, the accumulated judicial decisions addressing the oppression remedy have demonstrated the accuracy of Beck's appraisal. The oppression remedy has fundamentally changed not only what conduct by a corporation, its affiliates, and their respective directors gives rise to a claim for relief but also who may claim relief and what remedies may be sought. Traditional remedies such as the shareholder's derivative action for injuries to the corporation have been significantly displaced by the flexible and procedurally simple oppression action.

2) The Statutory Scheme

The key provisions of the *CBCA* governing the oppression remedy are sections 238, 241, and 242.[28] As noted above, section 238 defines

---

26   Now R.S.C. 1985, c. C-44, s. 241 [*CBCA*].

27   S.M. Beck, "Minority Shareholders' Rights in the 1980's" [1982] Spec. Lect. L.S.U.C. 311, at 312; cited in *Deluce Holdings Inc. v. Air Canada* (1992), 12 O.R. (3d) 131, at 150 (Gen. Div.) [*Deluce*]. See to similar effect, B. Welling, *Corporate Law in Canada: The Governing Principles*, 2d ed. (Butterworths: Toronto, 1991), at 563–64 [Welling].

28   The following Canadian corporate statutes provide for an oppression remedy on substantially these terms: *ABCA*, above note 8, s. 234; *BCCA*, above note 8, s. 200; *The Corporations Act*, R.S.M. 1987, c. C225 (Manitoba) [*MCA*], s. 234; *Business Corporations Act*, S.N.B. 1981, c. B-9.1 (New Brunswick) [*NBBCA*], s. 166; *Corporations Act*, R.S.N. 1990, c. C-36 (Newfoundland) [*NCA*], s. 371; *Companies Act*, S.N.S. 1990, c. 15 (Nova Scotia) [*NSCA*], s. 133(4)(k); *OBCA*, above note 8, s. 248; *The Business Corporations Act*, R.S.S. 1978, c. B-10

"complainant," the class of persons entitled to apply for relief from oppression, and section 242 deals with interim costs and other procedural issues. The substantive standard for oppression is established by section 241, set out in figure 9.1. For the sake of convenience, "oppression" will be used as a short-hand expression for the behaviour giving rise to remedy under section 241, unless expressly indicated otherwise.

Figure 9.1 Definition of Oppression in *CBCA*, s. 241

---

241. (1) A complainant may apply to a court for an order under this section.
  (2) If, on an application under subsection (1), the court is satisfied that in respect of a corporation or any of its affiliates
    (a) any act or omission of the corporation or any of its affiliates effects a result,
    (b) the business or affairs of the corporation or any of its affiliates are or have been carried on or conducted in a manner, or
    (c) the powers of the directors of the corporation or any of its affiliates are or have been exercised in a manner
    that is oppressive or unfairly prejudicial to or that unfairly disregards the interests of any security holder, creditor, director or officer, the court may make an order to rectify the matters complained of.

---

3) Interim Costs

As in derivative actions, a complainant seeking relief from oppression may apply for an award of interim costs. Section 242(4) of the *CBCA* provides that, in any application for relief from oppression,

> the court may at any time order the corporation or its subsidiary to pay to the complainant interim costs, including legal fees and disbursements, but the complainant may be held accountable for such interim costs on final disposition of the application or action.

In one of the first cases on interim costs, *Wilson v. Conley*,[29] the applicant was a minority shareholder of the respondent corporation.

(Saskatchewan) [*SBCA*], s. 234. There are some differences in wording. E.g., unlike the *CBCA*, above note 26, the *OBCA* specifically refers to threatened behaviour.

29 Above note 22.

She claimed to have been oppressed by the respondent shareholders as a result of excessive travel and similar expenses charged to the corporation by the respondents, excessive remuneration being paid to the respondents, and a complete discontinuance of the past practice of paying regular dividends despite a substantial increase in profits. Mr. Justice Rosenberg set out the following as the considerations applicable to the motion:

- the applicant is in financial difficulty;
- the financial difficulty arises out of the alleged oppressive actions of the respondents; and
- the applicant has made out a strong *prima facie* case.

Based on the material before him, consisting only of the application and the applicant's affidavit, which demonstrated the oppressive acts referred to above, Mr. Justice Rosenberg concluded that these requirements had been met. He directed the corporation to pay $20,000 in interim costs, even though the principal relief sought by the applicant was that the other shareholders buy her out and no relief was claimed against the corporation other than an order to cease making payments to the shareholder respondents.[30]

The interim costs provision was also considered in *Alles* v. *Maurice*.[31] In that case, the applicant was also a minority shareholder and complained of similar acts of oppression: certain other shareholders charging excessive bonuses and expenses to the corporation. Mr. Justice R.A. Blair considered the three requirements referred to in *Wilson v. Conley*. Regarding the first requirement, he found that the applicant was in financial difficulty, having depleted her savings to pay legal fees in connection with pursuing her claim and being unable to pay significant outstanding fees. Regarding the second, he expressed the view that, if Mr. Justice Rosenberg had meant that the applicant's financial situation must, in all cases, be caused directly by the alleged oppressive conduct, he disagreed. In his view it would be sufficient if the financial difficulties resulted from the "great drain on her resources"[32] due to her pursuit of the lawsuit: "There is nothing in the language of the statute

---

30   *Ibid.* Rosenberg J. also stated that he would have had some concern about ordering costs against the corporation except that there is "not the usual danger that such advance will not be repaid if later my order is found to be inappropriate," because the applicant's shares appeared to be worth "many hundreds of thousands of dollars" (at 223).

31   (1992), 5 B.L.R. (2d) 146 (Ont. Gen. Div.).

32   *Ibid.*, at 151.

or in its purpose which, to my mind, requires that the applicant demonstrate a cause and effect relationship between the conduct of the respondents and the need for funding."[33] Regarding the third requirement, Mr. Justice Blair was of the view similarly that showing a strong *prima facie* case, the test for an interlocutory injunction, was unduly onerous for the exercise of the discretion to award interim costs. Rather, he stated, the applicant need establish only that there is a case of sufficient merit to warrant pursuit.[34] He was satisfied that this requirement was met on the facts before him and ordered interim costs in the amount of $55,000 to be paid to the applicant by the corporation.

This approach has been followed in subsequent cases, though there is some uncertainty regarding the strength of the case that the complainant needs to show. In *Peretta* v. *Telecaribe*, the burden was described as an "arguable case with a reasonable chance of success."[35] It is clear that the financial difficulty of the complainant must be such that, but for an interim cost order, she would be unable to continue the litigation.[36]

4) Who May Claim Relief from Oppression: The Complainant

a) Introduction

Oppression is not just a "shareholder remedy." The courts have exploited the broad discretion contained in the *CBCA* and the statutes modelled after it to include creditors, employees, and even the corporation itself. Extending protection to creditors and others by giving them access to the oppression remedy was not contemplated by the Dickerson Committee, which was responsible for drafting the new federal legislation,[37] and, moreover, it challenges traditional corporate law notions about to whom corporate managers are responsible. To this extent, the oppression remedy represents an important enhancement in the position of creditors and other non-shareholder stakeholders seeking relief from corporate conduct.

---

33   *Ibid.*

34   *Ibid.*, at 152.

35   [1999] O.J. No. 4487 (Sup.Ct. J.).

36   *West* v. *Edson Packaging Ltd.* (1994), 46 A.C.W.S. (3d) 1262 (Ont. Gen. Div.). In *Strilec* v. *Alpha Pipe Fittings Inc.* (1995), 19 B.L.R. (2d) 316 (Ont. Gen. Div.), the court indicated that awards of interim costs should be made in exceptional circumstances only.

37   Dickerson, above note 2, at 158–63. The same observation was made by J.S. Ziegel, "Creditors as Corporate Stakeholders: The Quiet Revolution — An Anglo Canadian Perspective" (1993) 43 U.T.L.J. 511, at 527 [Ziegel].

Unfortunately, most of these cases provide little in the way of guidance about the circumstances in which creditors and others will be permitted to claim relief from oppression. Nor is there any effort to reconcile these decisions with traditional corporate theory or the intention of the drafters of the *CBCA*.

The *CBCA* definition of complainant is set out above.[38] Each of the categories of complainant will be examined in turn.

b) Statutory Complainants

i) *Security Holder, Section 238(a)*

The first statutory category of complainant is defined as "a registered holder or beneficial owner, and a former registered holder or beneficial owner, of a security of a corporation or any of its affiliates." Some of the terms used in the definition are themselves defined in section 1(1) of the *CBCA*. "[B]eneficial ownership" is defined broadly to include "ownership through any trustee, legal representative, agent or other intermediary." "[S]ecurity" means "a share of any class or series of shares or a debt obligation of a corporation and includes a certificate evidencing such a share or debt obligation." "[D]ebt obligation," in turn, is defined to mean "a bond, debenture, note or other evidence of indebtedness or guarantee of a corporation, whether secured or unsecured."

In drafting the *CBCA*, the Dickerson Committee did not set about to revolutionize corporate law by permitting creditors and others to seek relief from corporate behaviour. Their concern was to protect minority shareholders, and the broad language used in section 241(2) to describe the specific interests protected — those of "any security holder, creditor, director or officer" — was intended only to ensure that shareholders' interests were protected in whatever capacity they arose, acknowledging the complex multifaceted relationships that shareholders may have with the corporation, particularly where it is closely held.[39]

---

38 See above note 24 and accompanying text. Provincial statutes based on the *CBCA* model contain identical provisions defining "complainant: *ABCA*, above note 8, s. 231; *MCA*, above note 28, s. 239; *NCA*, above note 28, s. 368; *OBCA*, above note 8, s. 245; *SBCA*, above note 28, s. 231. Section 7(5) of the Third Schedule to the *NSCA*, above note 28, defines "complainant" in the same terms. Section 163 of the *NBBCA*, above note 28, also contains essentially the same definition of "complainant" except that "creditor" is expressly included. Section 200 of the *BCCA*, above note 8, permits "members" to apply for relief. Section 201(8) defines members for the purpose of section 200 to include "a beneficial owner of a share" and "any other person who, in the discretion of the court, is a proper person to make an application."

39 Dickerson, above note 2, at 163; Ziegel, above note 37, at 527.

As Jacob Ziegel has pointed out, "[i]t is obvious that the language of s. 241(2) does not remotely reflect this limited intention."[40] Nevertheless, many cases have expressed the view that the primary category of persons who should be entitled to seek relief from oppression are minority shareholders.[41] Most oppression cases have been commenced by minority shareholders and in these the courts have acknowledged, either expressly or implicitly, that minority shareholders have status as complainants under section 238(a) as security holders. The courts also have given effect to the express reference to "affiliates" in section 238(a), holding in *Moriarity* v. *Slater*[42] that a minority shareholder of an affiliate of the corporation in respect of which oppression was alleged may be a complainant. The courts have confirmed that former shareholders are complainants within the meaning of section 238(a).[43] It has been held as well that a person continues to have status as a complainant under section 238(a) even after the person has invoked her appraisal rights under section 190 of the *CBCA*, with the result that, by virtue of the operation of section 190(11) of the *CBCA*, the person loses all rights as a shareholder other than the right to be paid fair value for her shares.[44]

---

40   Ziegel, *ibid.*

41   See, for example, *Jacobs Farms Ltd.* v. *Jacobs*, [1992] O.J. No. 813 (QL) (Gen. Div.); *Royal Trust Corp. of Canada* v. *Hordo* (1993), 10 B.L.R. (2d) 86 (Ont. Gen. Div.) [*Hordo*].

42   (1989), 67 O.R. (2d) 758 (H.C.J.). In that case, a shareholder of a New York corporation, which wholly owned the Ontario corporation in respect of which the oppression was alleged, was permitted to commence an oppression action. The court expressed the view that, notwithstanding its holding regarding complainant status, it was not "crystal clear" that the shareholder was a "security holder" for the purposes of the substantive standard of protection against oppression. See also *PMSM Investments Ltd.* v. *Bureau* (1995), 25 O.R. (3d) 586 (Gen. Div.) [*PMSM*], discussed below under section D(5)(b)(v), "What Interests Are Protected?" An affiliate of a corporation is a corporation that is controlled by, controls, or is under common control with the first corporation (*CBCA*, above note 26, s. 2(2)).

43   *Private Equity Management Co.* v. *Vianet Technologies* (2000), 48 O.R. (3d) 294 (Sup. Ct. J.) and *Ontario (Securities Commission)* v. *McLaughlin* (1987), 11 O.S.C.B. 442 (H.C.J.) [*McLaughlin*]. See also *Michalak* v. *Biotech Electronics Ltd.*, (1986), 35 B.L.R. 1 (S.C.) [*Michalak*], where, although complainant status was acknowledged, relief was denied on the basis that the interests of the applicants were not being currently oppressed at the time of the application (at 9–11). In contrast, see *Richardson Greenshields of Canada Ltd.* v. *Kalmakoff*, above note 24, where it was held that there was no requirement that ownership be contemporaneous with acts of oppression.

44   *Brant Investments Ltd.* v. *KeepRite Inc.* (1987), 60 O.R. (2d) 737, (H.C.J.), additional reasons at (1987), 61 O.R. (2d) 469 (H.C.J.), aff'd (1991), 3 O.R. (3d) 289 (C.A.) [*Brant*]. Dissent and appraisal rights are discussed below in this chapter.

Several cases have addressed the issue of whether applicants claiming a right to become security holders are complainants. *Csak* v. *Aumon*[45] held that applicants with a contractual claim to be issued shares, a claim that was being denied by the controlling shareholder of the corporation, were beneficial owners of securities of the corporation for the purposes of section 238(a). In *Csak*, the court noted that the *CBCA* is remedial legislation and contemplates a "large and ... sweeping jurisdiction"[46] such that, in the absence of some reason inherent in the legislation or policy, the meaning of "beneficial owner" should be interpreted broadly. The court also cited the definition of "security" in the *CBCA* as indicating that ownership of a security means more than being the holder of a certificate, and the remedial provisions of the *CBCA* which contemplate, on a finding of oppression, "an order directing an issue ... of securities ..." (s. 241(3)(d)).[47]

Significantly, the court added that it is not a bar to complainant status that the applicant's claim to be a beneficial owner of shares is disputed. In the court's view:

> Parliament did not intend the absence of legal title to prevent the applicants here from bringing an application under ss. 238 and 241 until some other court had passed upon the validity of their claim to beneficial ownership. Their status is to be dealt with within the *CBCA* application and not as a condition precedent.[48]

The court also said that any issues of fact regarding the claim to be issued shares could be dealt with through a trial of an issue, and that requiring a party to establish its status in a separate proceeding before coming to court to seek relief from oppression would "multiply litigation to no good purpose."[49]

---

45   (1990), 69 D.L.R. (4th) 567 (Ont. H.C.J.) [*Csak*]. The court distinguished an earlier case, *Bernstein* v. *335861 (Alta.) Ltd.* (1986), 73 A.R. 188 (Q.B.).

46   *Csak, ibid.*, at 571.

47   *Ibid.*, at 572.

48   *Ibid.*

49   *Ibid.*, at 573. Persons with claims to be shareholders have been granted standing as complainants in several other cases. E.g., *Evans* v. *Facey*, [2000] O.J. No. 2276 (QL) (Sup. Ct. J.). In *Joncas* v. *Spruce Falls Power & Pulp Co.* (2000), 48 O.R. (3d) 179 (Sup. Ct. J.), it was held that certain employees who claimed to have a beneficial but not a legal right to be shareholders could not be complainants under s. 245(a) of the *OBCA*, above note 8. The court exercised its discretion to grant them standing under s. 245(c). The trial of an issue is a process by which the court orders a trial to deal with a issue of fact that is in dispute between the parties. The procedure is fixed by the court and may include many

A further related point was raised in *Csak*. It was alleged that, even if a person with a contractual claim to be issued a share was entitled to complainant status as a "beneficial owner" of a security under section 238(a), such a person did not have an interest protected under section 241(2), since that section refers only to "security holder," not beneficial owner. Mr. Justice Lane rejected this argument, holding, in effect, that if a person was entitled to complainant status under section 238(a), the person's interests were deserving of protection under section 241(2).

Even though the primary purpose of the oppression remedy envisioned by the drafters of the *CBCA* may have been the protection of minority shareholders, there is nothing in the section that expressly precludes a majority shareholder from commencing an oppression action as a complainant. Indeed, the availability of an oppression claim to a majority shareholder would appear to be consistent with the broad spectrum of situations where relief may be claimed. It seems quite possible that a majority shareholder could be oppressed by the acts of a corporation's directors.[50] The only question is whether, on the facts, the shareholder was oppressed. The availability of the oppression remedy to non-minority shareholders has been recognized in many cases.[51]

It is apparent in the statutory definition of "security" that some holders of debt obligations are also entitled to bring oppression actions, though no such actions have been brought successfully. At least one commentator has suggested that the reference to "registered

---

of the features of the regular civil litigation process, including production of documents, the examination of persons on discovery and examination and cross-examination of witnesses in court.

50   See, for example, *Hui v. Yamato Steak House Inc.*, [1988] O.J. No. 9 (QL) (Gen. Div.) [*Hui*], where the oppression alleged by the 90 percent shareholder was the directors' attempt to issue shares for the purpose of diluting the majority shareholder's interest to 10 percent.

51   *Gandalman Investments Inc. v. Fogle* (1985), 52 O.R. (2d) 614 (H.C.J.) (50 percent shareholder); *Tesari Holdings Ltd. v. Pizza Pizza Ltd.* (14 August 1987), (Ont. H.C.J.) [unreported] [summarized at 5 A.C.W.S. (3d) 430] [*Tesari*] (majority shareholder); *Cairney v. Golden Key Holdings Ltd.* (1987), 40 B.L.R. 263 (B.C.S.C.) (45 percent shareholder with effective control); *Hui, ibid.* (90 percent shareholder); *Jabaco Inc. v. Real Corporate Group Ltd.*, [1989] O.J. No. 68 (Gen. Div.) (QL) (60 percent of equity and 50 percent voting power); *Trnkoczy v. Shooting Chrony Inc.* (1991), 1 B.L.R. (2d) 202 (Ont. Gen. Div.) [*Trnkoczy*] (50 percent shareholder); *M. v. H.* (1993), 15 O.R. (3d) 721 (Gen. Div.) (50 percent shareholder). The same approach is followed in England. In *Parkinson v. Eurofinance Group Ltd.*, [2001] 1 B.C.L.C. 720 (Ch. D.), a majority shareholder successfully claimed relief from oppression.

holders" in section 238(a) suggests a legislative intention to limit claims by debt holders to those holding registered obligations or obligations that are susceptible of registration (such as some bonds and debentures), to the exclusion of other kinds of debts (such as trade debts), which are not registrable.[52] Given the expansive definition of debt obligation in the *CBCA*, it is not obvious that this is the correct interpretation.

Nevertheless, in the only reported decision to date to address directly the circumstances in which a debt holder may be a complainant for the purposes of section 238(a), it was held that only holders of registrable obligations have status. In *First Edmonton Place*, the court determined that an unpaid landlord was not a "security holder."[53] Some debt holders have been successful, however, in getting courts to exercise their discretion under section 238(d) to permit them to make an application as a complainant.[54] For more on this subject, see section C ("Discretionary Complainants"), below.

ii) Directors and Officers and the Director, Section 238 (b) and (c)
There have been few cases in which each of the other types of complainants expressly referred to in section 238 have sought relief from oppression. Several cases have addressed whether a claim by an officer or director that he was wrongfully dismissed may be the subject of an oppression proceeding. In these cases the courts have expressed their reluctance to consider wrongful-dismissal claims.[55] In *Naneff*[56] the applicant was an employee, director, officer, and shareholder of a corporation carrying on a family business. His family tried to exclude him from participating in the corporation in all his capacities, not for any legitimate reason connected with the business of the corporation, but

---

52   Welling, above note 27, at 521–23.
53   *First Edmonton Place Ltd. v. 315888 Alberta Ltd.* (1988), 40 B.L.R. 28, at 60–62 (Alta. Q.B.) [*First Edmonton*], rev'd on other grounds (1989), above note 25.
54   In *Metropolitan Toronto Police Widows and Orphans Fund v. Telus Communications Inc.*, [2003] O.J. No. 128 (QL) (Sup. Ct. J.) [*Metropolitan Police Widows and Ophans Fund*], bondholders were treated as complainants, though the issue of their status was not expressly addressed by the court. An additional point addressed by the courts in relation to who has standing as a complainant is whether the interests alleged to be oppressed must be those of the complainant. This is discussed below under 5(a)(vi) "What Interests Are Protected?"
55   See, for example, *Naneff v. Con-Crete Holdings Ltd.* (1993), 11 B.L.R. (2d) 218 (Ont. Gen. Div), rev'd in part (1994), 19 O.R. (3d) 691 (Div. Ct.), rev'd (1995), 23 O.R. (3d) 481 (C.A.) [*Naneff*].
56   *Ibid.*

because the family disapproved of his personal life. The trial court had held that, although "[in] normal circumstances, the wrongful dismissal of an employee would not of itself provide the basis or standing to make an 'oppression remedy' claim,"[57] in this case the dismissal was part of an "overall pattern of oppression"[58] such that the oppression of the applicant's interests as an employee was inextricably intertwined with the oppression of his interests in other capacities. This analysis was rejected by the Ontario Court of Appeal, which held that a court could protect the interests of a complainant only in his capacity as a shareholder, director, or officer.[59]

By contrast, in *Murphy* v. *Phillips*,[60] the general manager of a car dealership, who was not a shareholder,[61] was held to be an officer and thus a complainant who could pursue a wrongful-dismissal claim through the oppression remedy. Unfortunately, the court did not cite any authority in support of its conclusion, and the reasoning in *Naneff* is probably to be preferred.

Pursuant to section 238(c), the Director appointed under the *CBCA* has status as a complainant to commence oppression actions. The Director has used this status sparingly,[62] consistent with the expressed intention of the Dickerson Committee that the *CBCA* be largely "self-enforcing."[63]

---

57   *Ibid.*, at 250 (Ont. Gen. Div.).

58   *Ibid.*, at 254.

59   See also *West* v. *Edson Packaging Machinery Ltd.* (1993), 16 O.R. (3d) 24 (Gen. Div.); and *Deluce*, above note 27, in which the termination of an employee for the purpose of triggering a share-purchase option as part of a strategy by Air Canada to acquire 100 percent control of the corporation was held to be oppressive of the interests of the minority shareholder (a holding corporation controlled by the members of the employee's family). The court found that the shareholder had a reasonable expectation that, in the absence of the termination of the employee for reasons having to do with the interests of the corporation, it would continue as a shareholder.

60   (1993), 12 B.L.R. (2d) 58 (Ont. Gen. Div.).

61   The officer, with his wife, owned all the shares of a corporation that was a minority shareholder.

62   For example, *Sparling* v. *Javelin International Ltée.*, [1986] R.J.Q. 1073 (S.C.), aff'd (*sub nom. Doyle* v. *Sparling*), [1987] R.D.J. 307 (Que. C.A.) [*Javelin*]; *Sparling*, above note 21. Other Canadian corporate law regulators have been similarly reticent. The Ontario Securities Commission did commence an oppression action in *McLaughlin*, above note 43.

63   Dickerson, above note 2, at 160–62.

c) Discretionary Complainants, Section 238(d)

i) General

The class of complainant contemplated by section 238(d) of the *CBCA* is "any other person who, in the discretion of a court, is a proper person to make an application" for relief from oppression. Courts have been asked to exercise this discretion by creditors in a number of cases with varying success and, in a few cases, by the corporation itself.

ii) Creditors

The courts have been reluctant to exercise their discretion to permit an oppression action to be brought by a creditor, notwithstanding the express reference to the interests of creditors in section 241(2). This reluctance was expressed in *Royal Trust Corp. of Canada v. Hordo*[64]:

> The court may use its discretion to grant or deny a creditor status as a complainant under s. 238(d). It does not seem to me that debt actions should be routinely turned into oppression actions ... I do not think that the court's discretion should be used to give "complainant" status to a creditor where the creditor's interest in the affairs of a corporation is too remote or where the complaints of a creditor have nothing to do with the circumstances giving rise to the debt or if the creditor is not proceeding in good faith. Status as a complainant should also be refused where the creditor is not in a position analogous to that of the minority shareholder and has no "particular legitimate interest in the manner in which the affairs of the company are managed."[65] [Citations omitted.]

Though the passage quoted makes the court's reluctance clear, it is difficult to give operational content to most of the criteria articulated for refusing to grant complainant status to creditors: the creditor's interest in the affairs of the corporation is too remote; the creditor is not in a position analogous to that of a minority shareholder; or the creditor has no particular legitimate interest in the manner in which the affairs of the company are managed. The final criterion mentioned in *Royal Trust*, though also vague, does suggest a more workable standard: where the complaints of the creditor have nothing to do with the circumstances giving rise to the debt.

This standard was more fully elaborated in *First Edmonton Place*,[66] a case involving an oppression claim by an unpaid landlord. In a thor-

---

64   Above note 41.
65   *Ibid.*, at 92.
66   Above note 53, at 63 (Alta. Q.B.).

ough judgment, Mr. Justice McDonald made clear that to grant complainant status there must be some evidence of oppression. He identified two kinds of circumstances where this would occur, though he acknowledged that others were possible:

- an act of the directors or management of the corporation which constitutes using the corporation as a vehicle for committing fraud upon the applicant creditor; and
- an act or conduct of the directors or management of the corporation which constitutes a breach of the underlying expectations of the applicant arising from the circumstances in which the applicant's relationship with the corporation arose.[67]

As an example of the second circumstance, Mr. Justice McDonald suggested that there might be something in the circumstances in which the credit was granted which prevented the creditor from taking adequate steps to protect its interest against the occurrence of the conduct in respect of which it was now claiming oppression. In *First Edmonton*, no such impediment prevented an unpaid landlord of some office space from seeking some form of protection against non-payment in its contract with the tenant and the applicant was denied complainant status.

Most of the cases in which the courts have granted complainant status to creditors include no such principled analysis and appear to be based simply on the difficulty facing the creditor in enforcing its claim. In general, the courts have granted relief where there has been some action by the corporation, its directors, or officers, often intentional, which has had the effect of rendering the corporation unable to perform its obligations. In one of the first cases to grant complainant status to a creditor, *R. v. Sands Motor Hotel Ltd.*,[68] the Crown was given status as a complainant on the basis of being a creditor under the *Income Tax Act* where the ability of the Crown to recover income taxes owed by a corporation was impaired by dividends the corporation had paid to shareholders. The Crown sought and obtained an order setting aside the dividend payments. In *Canadian Opera Co. v. 670800 Ontario Inc.*,[69] the court granted complainant status to a creditor who had purchased a car, but not obtained possession, where the funds paid by the creditor had "gone south" from the corporation to an associate of the controlling shareholder. In another case, *Prime Computer of Canada Ltd.*

---

67 *Ibid.*, at 63–64.
68 *R. v. Sands Motor Hotel Ltd.* (1984), 36 Sask. R. 45 (Q.B.).
69 *Canadian Opera Co. v. 670800 Ontario Inc.* (1989), 69 O.R. (2d) 532 (H.C.J.).

v. *Jeffrey*,[70] a judgment creditor with no hope of recovery against a corporation because of excessive salary payments to the controlling shareholder was permitted to be a complainant. In both *Canadian Opera* and *Prime Computer*, on a finding of oppression, the complainant obtained an order directly against the controlling shareholder of the corporation.[71]

Some courts have held that a creditor must have been a creditor at the time the oppression occurred.[72] In *Devry* v. *Atwoods Furniture Showrooms Ltd.*,[73] it was held that it was not appropriate to give a judgment creditor standing as a complainant where the allegedly oppressive dividends were paid before the creditor became a judgment creditor. In other cases, however, it has been held that a creditor has a reasonable expectation that a corporation will not engage in conduct during as well as after the trial of a civil action which would render recovery impossible. Where the corporation does so, the creditor should be able to seek relief from oppression.[74]

These decisions appear to open up the oppression remedy as a flexible alternative to commencement of an ordinary civil action to pursue a creditor's claim as well as being an aid to enforcing a judgment. In most cases where complainant status has been granted, the creditor has already obtained a civil judgment, but this is not an absolute prerequisite.[75] For a creditor, there are two main advantages of an oppression action over an ordinary civil action. First because oppression actions may be commenced by way of application, without the pleadings and

---

70 (1991), 6 O.R. (3d) 733 (Gen. Div.). See also *Tropxe Investments Inc.* v. *Ursus Securities Corp.*, [1991] O.J. No. 2116 (QL) (Gen. Div.) [*Tropxe*], a case with essentially the same facts where the same relief was ordered. In *Royal Bank of Canada* v. *Amatilla Holdings Ltd.*, [1994] O.J. No. 198 (QL) (Gen. Div.), in similar circumstances, the shareholders were ordered to repay dividends to the corporation for the benefit of the creditor.

71 See also *Tavares* v. *Deskin*, (25 January 1993), (Ont. Gen. Div.) [unreported] [summarized at (1993), 38 A.C.W.S. (3d) 71], where an application to strike an oppression claim by a wrongfully dismissed employee was denied on the basis that the employee was entitled to complainant status where the corporation was stripping itself of assets in order to make itself judgment-proof. In *Sidaplex-Plastic Suppliers Inc.* v. *Etta Group Inc.* (1995), 131 D.L.R. (4th) 399 (Ont. Gen.Div.), varied on other grounds (1998) 40 O.R. (3d) 563 (C.A.), the court expressed the view that it is "well established" that a judgment creditor has status to bring an oppression application as a complainant (at 403).

72 *Trillium Computer Resources Inc.* v. *Taiwan Connection Inc.* (1992), 10 O.R. (3d) 249 (Gen. Div.).

73 (2000), 11 B.L.R. (3d) 227 (Ont. Sup. Ct.).

74 *Levy-Russell Ltd.* v. *Shieldings Ltd.* (1998), 41 O.R. (3d) 54 (Gen. Div.).

75 *Standal's Patents Ltd.* v. *160088 Canada Inc.*, [1991] R.J.Q. 1996 (Que. Sup. Ct.).

discovery required for a civil action, an oppression action can probably be brought to court faster than a civil action, provided that there are no significant factual issues in dispute. Where there is such issue, the court will direct a "trial of an issue," a process which may involve some of the same procedures and delays as a regular civil trial. Second, the discretionary powers granted to the court under the oppression remedy are much broader than those available in a civil action, expressly contemplating, for example, remedies against shareholders as granted in *Canadian Opera* and *Prime Computer*.

iii) The Corporation

Two Alberta decisions have held that the corporation itself may be a complainant.[76] The classes of persons identified in section 238 as entitled to bring an oppression application under section 238 make no reference to the corporation. Nevertheless, in *Kredl*,[77] the Alberta Court of Queen's Bench held that the corporation was a proper person to be a complainant where all the shareholders, other than the respondent who was alleged to have committed the oppression, were joined as plaintiffs in the action. The shareholders had only recently gained effective control of the corporation from the respondent and were seeking to recover funds on its behalf. This decision confirmed an earlier one in *Pocklington*,[78] in which Mr. Justice MacDonald had refused an application to strike out a statement of claim on the ground that the corporation was not a proper person to be a complainant. In *Pocklington*, the Crown had taken over control of the corporation and the complaint related to the acts of a director.

A contrary result was reached, in effect, in *Canada (A.G.) v. Standard Trust Co.*[79] In this case, Houlden J.A. (ad hoc) refused to grant leave to a trustee in bankruptcy to pursue an oppression claim on the basis that the trustee succeeded to the rights of the corporation and the transaction had been unanimously approved by the board of the corporation such that, in the view of the court, the corporation could not have

---

76   *Calmont Leasing Ltd. v. Kredl* (1993), 142 A.R. 81 at 105 (Q.B.), aff'd (1995), 165 A.R. 343 (C.A.) [*Kredl*], and *Gainers Inc. v. Pocklington* (1992), 132 A.R. 35 at 65–66 (Q.B.) [*Pocklington*].

77   *Kredl, ibid.*

78   Above note 76.

79   (1991), 5 O.R. (3d) 660 (Gen. Div.) [*Standard Trust Co.*]. A trustee was refused standing in *Canbrook Distribution Co. v. Borins* (1999), 45 O.R. (3d) 565 (Sup.Ct. J.). In *Dylex Ltd. (Trustee of) v. Anderson* (2003), 68 O.R. (3d) 662 (Sup. Ct. J.), Mr. Justice Lederman suggested that the approach in *Pocklington, ibid.*, was preferable and refused to strike out a claim by a trustee in a bankruptcy.

claimed oppression. The court expressly rejected an argument that the trustee should be given status as a complainant as a representative of the collective interests of creditors. *Standard Trust Co.* was distinguished in *Pocklington* on the basis that the claim related not to an oppression action by the corporation, but to an action by one of the directors.

Given the broad standard of fairness represented by the oppression remedy, granting the corporation status to claim oppression creates the risk that the oppression remedy will completely replace the fiduciary duty, a narrower standard and, by virtue of many years of judicial consideration, a more certain one. In this regard, it is important to note that, even if the corporation were not permitted to seek relief from oppression directly, the remedies expressly enumerated in section 241(3) include "an order compensating an aggrieved person," which would apparently include the corporation in any event.[80] So a shareholder could initiate an oppression action and seek relief both for themselves and for the corporation.

d) Summary

The intention of the Dickerson Committee in proposing the inclusion of the oppression remedy in the *CBCA* was the protection of minority shareholders in their capacities as shareholders, creditors, directors, and officers.[81] Enhanced protection for shareholders was needed because of the inadequacy of the existing corporate law, which was characterized by a high degree of judicial deference to management decision making and provided only very restricted access to limited kinds of remedies.[82] But, as the foregoing survey of cases makes clear, the categories of person who have standing as complainants to seek relief from oppression under section 238 of the *CBCA*, which uses the language recommended by the Dickerson Committee, are much broader. Section 238 expressly provides that all security holders, not just shareholders, as well as directors and officers and the Director appointed under the *CBCA* have standing; it also permits a court to grant standing to any other person it determines is a "proper person" to seek relief (*CBCA*, s. 238(d)). In *First Edmonton Place*, the court described this discretion as

---

80 This view is adopted by Welling, above note 27, at 561. It should be noted that approval by the directors does not relieve the directors from their duty to act in accordance with the *CBCA*, nor from liability for any breach of the Act (above note 26, s. 122(3)). The effect of this provision was apparently not argued before Houlden J.A. in *Standard Trust Co., ibid.*

81 Dickerson, above note 2, at 160–63.

82 *Ibid.*

"a grant to the Court of a broad power to do justice and equity in the circumstances of a particular case where a person who otherwise would not be a 'complainant' ought to be permitted to bring an action … to obtain compensation."[83] The primary category of person seeking to have the courts exercise this "power" has been creditors.

Though there are still too few cases to draw definitive conclusions, and although they have proceeded cautiously for the most part, the courts have been willing to grant complainant status to various groups that would not have had any status to seek relief under corporate law before the introduction of the oppression remedy: former shareholders, persons with contractual claims to be issued shares, creditors, and dismissed employees.[84] Potentially, this development represents a fundamental reordering of the responsibilities of corporate management under corporate law.

5) The Substantive Standard

a) Introduction
Any effort to describe what constitutes oppression without regard to the facts of a particular case is inherently problematic. As Mr. Justice Brooke said in one of the leading cases on oppression, *Ferguson v. Imax Systems Corp.*,[85] "… each case turns on its own facts. What is oppressive or unfairly prejudicial in one case may not necessarily be so in the slightly different setting of another." The section that follows will attempt to set out some of the overriding principles identified by the courts as governing the availability of the oppression remedy.

b) General Principles

i) General Approach to Interpretation
From the earliest cases following the enactment of the *CBCA*, the courts have uniformly expressed the view that the oppression remedy should be interpreted broadly to carry out its purpose: to reform the law applicable to business corporations with a view to improving the protection

---

83   Above note 53, at 62 (Alta. Q.B.).
84   Those with contractual claims to be issued shares, creditors, and dismissed employees did have and continue to have other legal means of seeking redress.
85   (1983), 43 O.R. (2d) 128, at 137 (C.A.) [*Ferguson*]. A similar result was reached on similar facts in *Soomal v. Sandhar & Soomal Developments Ltd.* (2001), 21 B.L.R. (3d) 142 (B.C.S.C.). The Court of Appeal confined its approach in *Themadel Foundation v. Third Canadian Trust Ltd.* (1998), 107 O.A.C. 188 [*Themadel*], at 192-3.

of minority shareholders.[86] In this regard, various courts have made it clear that the oppression remedy is intended to protect not just the strict legal rights of shareholders but also their interests.[87] Mr. Justice Farley explained this concept of shareholder interests in the following widely cited passage in *820099 Ontario Inc.* v. *Harold E. Ballard Ltd.*[88]:

> Shareholder interests would appear to be intertwined with shareholder expectations. It does not appear to me that the shareholder expectations which are to be considered are those that a shareholder has as his own individual "wish list." They must be expectations which could be said to have been (or ought to have been considered as) part of the compact of the shareholders. Expectations were discussed in B. Welling, *Corporate Law in Canada: The Governing Principles* (Toronto: Butterworths, 1984), pp. 533 and 535:
>
> > Thwarted shareholder expectation is what the oppression remedy is all about. Each shareholder buys his [or her] shares with certain expectations. Some of these are outlandish. But some of them, particularly in a small corporation with few shareholders, are quite reasonable expectations in the circumstances.

In *Westfair Foods Ltd.* v. *Watt*, the Alberta Court of Appeal endorsed this approach, adding that the reasonable expectations of shareholders relevant to a determination of oppression should not be limited to those existing when the relationship first arose.[89] They may change with the circumstances. Expectations may be based on public pronouncements by a corporation as well as on representations in investment agree-

---

86   Regarding the purpose of the *CBCA*, above note 26, in general see s. 4; and regarding the oppression remedy, in particular, see Dickerson, above note 2. The leading authority for a broad interpretation of the oppression provisions is *Ferguson*, *ibid.*, cited in *Deluce*, above note 27; and *Mason* v. *Intercity Properties Ltd.* (1987), 59 O.R. (2d) 631 at 635–36 (C.A.) [*Mason*]. See also *Stech* v. *Davies*, (1987), 80 A.R. 298 (Q.B.) [*Stech*]; and *First Edmonton*, above note 53, at 140 (Q.B.).

87   *Westfair Foods Ltd.* v. *Watt* (1991), 115 A.R. 34 (C.A.), leave to appeal refused, [1992] 1 W.W.R. lxv (note) (S.C.C.) [*Westfair*].

88   (1991), 3 B.L.R. (2d) 113, at 185–86 (Ont. Div. Ct.) [*820099*]; cited in *Deluce*, above note 27; *Beazer* v. *Hodgson Robertson Laing Ltd.* (1993), 12 B.L.R. (2d) 101 (Ont. Gen. Div.); *M.* v. *H.* above note 51; *Sexsmith* v. *Intek*, [1993] O.J. No. 711 (QL) (Gen. Div.) [*Sexsmith*]. This approach derives from the decision of the House of Lords in *Ebrahimi* v. *Westbourne Galleries Ltd.* (1972), [1973] A.C. 360 (H.L.) [*Ebrahimi*].

89   Above note 87. See similarly *Themadel*, above note 85, at 192.

ments and commitments in shareholder agreements.[90] In assessing reasonable expectations, however, a court should take into account not just circumstances unique to the relationship between the parties but also the legal rules that govern how directors and corporations are to operate, including, for example, majority rule and the grant of management power to the directors.[91]

ii) The Statutory Language

The oppression remedy is available on proof of an act or omission in respect of a corporation that is "oppressive or unfairly prejudicial to or that unfairly disregards the interests of any security holder, creditor, director or officer." Some courts have defined these three characterizations as establishing different standards.

The classic statement of the meaning of "oppression" comes from the decision of the House of Lords in *Scottish Co-operative Wholesale Society Ltd. v. Meyer*:

> [The society] had the majority power and . . . [it] exercised . . . [its] authority in a manner "burdensome, harsh and wrongful" — I take the dictionary meaning of the word. [Per Viscount Simonds.]

> Oppression under section 210 may take various forms. It suggests, to my mind . . . a lack of probity and fair dealing in the affairs of a company to the prejudice of some portion of its members. [Per Lord Keith of Avonholm.][92]

This construction, requiring a finding of bad faith, was adopted in numerous early Canadian decisions.[93] One commentator, however, has suggested that many courts have inferred bad faith from what was perceived as an unfair result.[94]

More recently, the courts have determined that "unfairly prejudicial" and "unfairly disregards" create a somewhat lesser standard. In

---

90 *Themadel, ibid.* (misrepresentation in management information circular regarding tax status of corporation); *C.I. Covington Fund Inc. v. White* (2000), 10 B.L.R. (3d) 173 (Ont. Sup. Ct. J.), affirmed (2001), 17 B.L.R. (3d) 277 (Div. Ct.) (misrepresentation by corporation that it owned patents on critical technology).

91 McGuiness, above note 9, at 966.

92 (1958), [1959] A.C. 324, at 342 & 363–64 (H.L.) [*Meyer*].

93 *Bank of Montreal v. Dome Petroleum Ltd.* (1987), 54 Alta. L.R. (2d) 289 (Q.B.) [*Dome*]; *Brant*, above note 44, at 303 (C.A.); *Tesari*, above note 51. On the meaning of bad faith, see, generally, J.G. MacIntosh, "Bad Faith and the Oppression Remedy: Uneasy Marriage or Amicable Divorce?" (1990) 69 Can. Bar. Rev. 276.

94 MacIntosh, *ibid.*, at 297.

particular, it is now clear, based on the Ontario Court of Appeal's decision in *Brant Investments Ltd.* v. *KeepRite Inc.*,[95] that a finding of bad faith is not required, though, of course, such a finding would be highly probative.[96] Indeed, the court in *Brant Investments Ltd.* v. *KeepRite Inc.* went so far as to say that "there will be few cases where there has not been some 'want of probity' on the part of the corporate actor where a remedy pursuant to s. 234 [now 241] will be appropriate." Nevertheless, it is sufficient if the conduct complained about had an effect contemplated in the statute, even if it was not caused intentionally.[97]

Several courts have expressed the view that, by referring to *unfairly* prejudicial and *unfairly* disregards, Parliament was expressing an intention to permit some prejudice or some disregarding.[98] Otherwise, however, the courts have given us only general statements about the meaning of these terms. For example, in *Stech* v. *Davies* the court offered the following: "… unjustly or without cause … pay no attention to, ignore or treat as of no importance …"[99]

In *Westfair Foods Ltd.* v. *Watt*,[100] the Alberta Court of Appeal rejected the idea that the different terms used to define the oppression standard could sensibly be given distinctive, operationally useful meanings, favouring instead a general fairness standard:

> I cannot put elastic adjectives like "unfair", "oppressive" or "prejudicial" into watertight compartments. In my view, this repetition of overlapping ideas is only an expression of anxiety by Parliament that one or the other might be given a restrictive meaning. … Recent changes adding words like "unfairly disregard" reflect just that concern … [I]n Peterson, *Shareholder Remedies in Canada*, (Butterworths, 1989), paragraph 18.60, the author contends that "unfairly disregards" implies that some "disregarding" is fair! I reject that kind of parsing. The original words, like the new additions, command the courts to exercise their duty "broadly and liberally" … the words charge the courts to impose the obligation of fairness on the parties. I must admit that the admonition offers little guidance to the public, and Parliament has left elucidation to us.

---

95 Above note 44.
96 *Ibid.*, at 311 (Ont. C.A.); *Tesari*, above note 51.
97 *WindRidge Farms Ltd.* v. *Quadra Group Investments Ltd.* (1999), 178 D.L.R. (4th) 603 (Sask. C.A) [*WindRidge*].
98 *Brant*, above note 44, at 761 (H.C.J.). See also cases cited by D.H. Peterson, *Shareholder Remedies in Canada* (Toronto: Butterworths, 1989) at para. 18.60.
99 Above note 86, at 302.
100 Above note 87, at 38.

Kerans J.A. went on to say that he did not understand that the delegation of this duty permits a judge to impose personal standards of fairness. The standard must be based on values that have gained wide acceptance as "principles adopted in precedent." Kerans J.A. identified the determination of fairness based on the reasonable expectations of the parties considering all their "words and deeds" as a principle running through all the cases on oppression.

The approach taken by Kerans J.A. would seem to be the most appropriate. While there may be some kinds of conduct where relief may be claimed because they are oppressive, all such conduct is likely to meet the standard of "unfairly prejudicial" or "unfairly disregards." This was the view of the drafters of the *CBCA*.[101] Accordingly, in every case one must consider the legal rights and reasonable expectations of the applicant for relief from oppression and the extent to which they have been affected. The following sections identify some of the other principles the courts have developed in considering claims for relief from oppression.

iii) Indicia of Oppressive Conduct

Although the highly fact-specific nature of the oppression remedy precludes anything like an exhaustive list of the factors suggesting oppression, Mr. Justice Austin in *Arthur v. Signum Communications Ltd.* set out the following helpful catalogue:

- lack of a valid corporate purpose for the transaction (e.g., paying excessive salaries, directors taking corporate assets);
- failure on the part of the corporation and its controlling shareholders to take reasonable steps to simulate an arm's-length transaction;
- lack of good faith on the part of the directors of the corporation;
- discrimination among shareholders, with the effect of benefiting the majority shareholder to the exclusion or the detriment of minority shareholders;
- lack of adequate and appropriate disclosure of material information to minority shareholders; and
- a plan or design to eliminate a minority shareholder.[102]

This listing has been cited with approval in several cases.[103]

---

101 Dickerson, above note 2, at 162–63.
102 (1991), 2 C.P.C. (3d) 74 (Ont. Gen. Div.), aff'd [1993] O.J. No. 1928 (QL) (Div. Ct.).
103 For example, *Millar v. McNally* (1991), 3 B.L.R. (2d) 102 (Ont. Gen. Div.) [*Millar*]; *M. v. H.*, above note 51.

iv) Actions of Directors

As noted above, actions of directors may constitute oppression. Nevertheless, the courts have made clear that the esssence of the oppression remedy is a claim about behaviour by the corporation.[104] Directors' actions are oppressive only when they are acting in their capacity as directors. Accordingly, claims that directors breached obligations owed personally to the complainant are not properly the subject of an oppression action.[105]

v) Personal and Derivative Claims

In *Farnham* v. *Fingold*,[106] the Ontario Court of Appeal expressed the traditional view that where an injury was an injury to the corporation, and any injury to the shareholder was only incidental to the corporate injury, such as where a breach of fiduciary duty was alleged, relief could be claimed only by the corporation itself or by a shareholder, with leave of the court, by way of a derivative action. In *Farnham*, the Court of Appeal dismissed the plaintiff's action to the extent that it was derivative in nature.

Subsequently, many courts have rejected arguments that claims for relief from oppression should be thrown out because the injury to the shareholder was incidental to the injury to the corporation, citing the broad scope of the statutory language creating the oppression standard.[107] One of these cases expressly distinguished *Farnham* on the basis that it was decided with regard to the Ontario corporate statute before the introduction of the oppression remedy.[108]

A contrary view was taken in *Pappas* v. *Acan Windows Inc.*[109] The court determined that where an applicant sought derivative and personal relief, including personal relief by way of the oppression remedy, and leave of the court had not been obtained to commence a derivative action,

---

104 *Budd* v. *Gentra Inc.* (1998), 43 B.L.R. (2d) 27 (Ont. C.A.).

105 *Ibid*. As a result, tort principles for individual liablity are not relevant.

106 [1973] 2 O.R. 132 (C.A.).

107 For example, *Deluce*, above note 27; *McLaughlin*, above note 43; *Javelin*, above note 62; *Jackman* v. *Jackets Enterprises Ltd.* (1977), 2 B.L.R. 335 (B.C.S.C.) [*Jackman*]; *Peterson* v. *Kanata Investments Ltd.* (1975), 60 D.L.R. (3d) 527 (B.C.S.C.) [*Kanata*]; *Diligenti* v. *RWMD Operations Kelowna Ltd.* (1976), 1 B.C.L.R. 36 (S.C.); *Thomson* v. *Quality Mechanical Service Inc.* (2001), 56 O.R. (3d) 234 (Sup. Ct. J.). In *Drove* v. *Mansvelt* (1999), 48 B.L.R. (2d) 72 (B.C.S.C.), the court held that an oppression action and a derivative action could be brought based on the same facts and the claims were heard together. See, generally, J.G. MacIntosh, "The Oppression Remedy: Personal or Derivative?" (1991) 70 Can. Bar Rev. 29.

108 *McLaughlin*, *ibid*.

109 Above note 20.

the court had to exercise a discretion whether to permit the claim for personal relief under the oppression remedy to proceed. The court stated that a claim for personal relief should not be permitted to proceed if the claim overall was "so saturated by derivative claims that it cannot be allowed to stand."[110] It examined each of the applicant's claims, permitting some to proceed but not others. In reaching its conclusion, the court engaged in an extensive case law analysis and concluded that oppression does not arise where the only injury to an applicant is incidental to an injury to the corporation. In the court's view, this conclusion was necessary if the other provisions of the corporate statute, including, in particular, the derivative action provisions, were to have any rationale.[111]

This case seems inconsistent with the clear weight of authority permitting shareholders to claim relief from oppression regardless of whether the conduct could be characterized as an injury to the corporation. It also seems inconsistent with the cases referred to above, holding that in some circumstances the corporation may be a proper person to be a complainant.[112] In most cases the courts ask only if the allegedly oppressive behaviour falls within the prohibition in the statute. If so, an application is permitted to proceed.

Are a director's fiduciary duty and other duties relevant at all to a finding of oppression? It has been held that the fiduciary standard may inform what constitutes oppression, but compliance with fiduciary duty's requirement for good faith does not mean that no oppression may be found.[113]

vi) What Interests Are Protected?

Section 241 identifies the interests that may not be oppressed as those of "any security holder, creditor, director or officer." A preliminary point addressed by the courts is whether the interests alleged to be oppressed must be those of the complainant. In *Re Abraham and Inter*

---

110 *Ibid.*, at 155.

111 *Ibid.* See also *Pak Mail Centers of America* v. *Flash Pack Ltd.*, [1993] O.J. No. 2367 (QL) (Gen. Div.), where it was held that a minority shareholder could not claim oppression based on an agreement transferring certain intellectual property rights from the corporation to a third party. The court indicated that, in its view, the oppression remedy was primarily designed to fight oppression by other shareholders. The court cited *Olympia & York Enterprises Ltd.* v. *Hiram Walker Resources Ltd.* (1986), 59 O.R. (2d) 254 (Div. Ct.) in support of this proposition.

112 See above, section D(4)(c)(iii).

113 *Deluce*, above note 27, at 310; *820099*, above note 88, at 178. In *Kredl*, above note 76, it was held that a breach of fiduciary duty constituted oppression (at 462).

Wide Investments Ltd.,[114] Mr. Justice Griffiths expressed the following view: "Essential to the right to relief is the requirement that the company or directors in carrying out the company's business or exercising the powers of the directors have been guilty of conduct oppressive or unfairly prejudicial or that unfairly disregards the interests of the *complainant*."[115] This requirement was satisfied on the facts before Mr. Justice Griffiths. Though one may be attracted by the requirement that a complainant have a personal stake in the oppression alleged, Welling has pointed out that such a requirement is not part of the statutory scheme.[116] This interpretation has been confirmed recently in *Themadel Foundation* v. *Third Canadian Trust Ltd.*[117]

A related point was raised in *Csak* v. *Aumon*,[118] in which it was alleged that even if a person with a contractual claim to be issued a share was entitled to complainant status as a "beneficial owner" of a security under section 238(a), such a person did not have an interest as a "security holder" which was protected under section 241(2), since that section refers only to "security holder," not "beneficial owner." Mr. Justice Lane rejected this argument, holding, in effect, that if a person was entitled to complainant status under section 238(a), her interests were deserving of protection under section 241.[119]

A further point of interpretation was addressed in *PMSM Investments Ltd.* v. *Bureau.*[120] In that case, the court held that although a shareholder of an affiliate of a corporation had status as a complainant, under section 238 (a), it could claim relief from oppression only if it had interest as a "security holder, creditor, director or officer" of the *corporation* that was oppressed. Its interest as a shareholder in the affiliate is not protected under section 241(2).

Various timing issues have arisen in oppression cases. Some cases have held that the interests of a security holder must be currently oppressed and that neither anticipated oppression nor past oppression

---

114 (1985), 51 O.R. (2d) 460, at 468 (H.C.J.).

115 Emphasis added. See also *Stone* v. *Stonehurst Enterprises Ltd.* (1987), 80 N.B.R. (2d) 290, at 305 (Q.B.).

116 Above note 27, at 555, n. 307.

117 *Themadel*, above note 85 (Gen. Div.). An appeal was granted on other grounds, and this issue was not addressed. See also *PMSM*, above note 42. McGuiness suggests that complainants should be able to complain only about oppression of their own interests (McGuiness, above note 9, at 970–971).

118 Above note 45.

119 See the discussion in the section "Who May Claim Relief from Oppression: The Complainant," above in this chapter.

120 The definition of "affiliate" is discussed above, note 42.

entitles relief under the *CBCA*.[121] Under the *CBCA*, the language of section 241(2) does not expressly contemplate future acts or omissions. Threatened behaviour can constitute oppression under some provincial statutes.[122]

A related timing issue is whether a person need have the standing of a complainant at the time of the alleged oppression. A claim by a person who bought his shares in a corporation after and with full knowledge of the alleged oppressive acts was thrown out in *Royal Trust v. Hordo* as frivolous, vexatious, and an abuse of the process of the court.[123] The statute itself does not help to resolve this interpretive uncertainty. As a policy matter, it would seem that if a person bought shares, the price of which had been reduced to reflect the oppression which had occurred, there would be no reason to allow the person to proceed with an oppression action. Apart from any question of interpretation, in these circumstances, what would be oppressive? By contrast, if a person bought shares and was unaware of the past oppression at the time of the purchase and the price was not discounted to reflect the oppression, such a person should be permitted to claim relief.

In cases involving creditors, it has been held that there is no oppression where the credit obligation did not exist at the time of the allegedly oppressive act. In *First Edmonton Place v. 315888 Alberta Ltd.*,[124] it was held that the interests of a lessor to whom no rent was owed at the time of the allegedly oppressive act could not be oppressed. In that case, the alleged oppressive act was the distribution by the corporation to its shareholders of a cash advance the landlord had made to the corporation. At the time of the distribution, no rent was owed to the landlord.[125]

vii) *Actions against Shareholders*

Because section 241 refers to oppressive acts by affiliates of the corporation, it apparently contemplates that relief may be obtained in relation

---

121 *Dome*, above note 93; *Michalak*, above note 43, at 9–11; *Goldbelt Mines (N.P.L.) v. New Beginnings Resources Inc.* (1984), 28 B.L.R. 130 (B.C.C.A.). A contrary view was expressed in *McLaughlin*, above note 43, at 449.

122 The *BCCA*, above note 8, s. 224, and the *OBCA*, above note 8, s. 248, expressly contemplate threatened behaviour.

123 Above note 41. A claim by a complainant in a similar situation was permitted to proceed in *Richardson Greenshields v. Kalmakoff*, above note 24. The claim in that case was for permission to commence a derivative action, and not for relief from oppression, but the analysis in *Royal Trust v. Hordo* was expressly not followed.

124 Above note 53.

125 See the discussion in the section "Who May Claim Relief from Oppression: The Complainant," above, in this chapter.

to the conduct of corporations that control, are controlled by, or are under common control with the corporation in which the shareholder has his interest.[126] The obvious implication is that oppression by non-corporate shareholders and corporate shareholders other than affiliates is not included. In at least one case, claims against non-affiliated shareholders have failed.[127] Nevertheless, in other cases courts have not been careful to distinguish between oppression inflicted by the corporation and that inflicted by the shareholders.[128] Ultimately, this conflict may be reduced to a matter of pleading in cases where the actions of the corporation or its directors or officers are somehow implicated in the action by the shareholder. Under section 241, it is clear that once there is a finding of oppression, an order may be made against a shareholder.

viii) Oppression and Shareholders' Agreements

A number of cases have considered whether actions under the provisions of shareholders' agreements may be oppressive. Several cases have held that a breach of a shareholders' agreement may be oppressive.[129] Compliance with the strict terms of a shareholders' agreement, however, does not guarantee that no oppression has taken place. In *Deluce Holdings Ltd.* v. *Air Canada*[130] it was held that even the exercise

---

126 See definitions of "affiliate" and "affiliated body corporate" in sections 2(1) and 2(2) of the *CBCA*, above note 26. In *Deluce*, above note 27, the actions of Air Canada as an affiliate of the corporation and the actions of its nominee directors were found to be oppressive. This case is discussed below, notes 129 to 135, and accompanying text.

127 *Ruffo* v. *IPCBC Contractors Canada Inc.* (1988), 33 B.C.L.R. (2d) 74 (S.C.), aff'd (1990), 44 B.C.L.R. (2d) 293 (C.A.).

128 For example, *Ferguson*, above note 85. This approach was also followed in *Meyer*, above note 92.

129 For example, *Lyall* v. *147250 Canada Ltd.* (1993), 106 D.L.R. (4th) 304 (B.C.C.A.). In *Fulmer* v. *Peter D. Fulmer Holdings Inc.* (1997), 36 B.L.R. (2d) 257 (Ont. Gen. Div.), failure to abide by the terms of a shareholders' agreement was held not to be oppressive.

130 Above note 27. A purported exercise of a right to sell subject to giving a minority shareholder a right of first refusal was held to be oppressive and the court ordered the majority shareholder not to sell its shares. The court took into acount that the transaction was part of a reverse takeover which would have resulted in the majority shareholder controlling a corporation holding the majority shareholder's shares and was not a sale to a *bona fide* third party offer as contemplated in the agreement (*Trudell Partnership Holdings* v. *Retirement Counsel of Canada Inc.* (2001), 20 B.L.R. (3d) 76 (Ont. Sup. Ct. J.). In *Metropolitan Police Widows and Orphans Fund*, above note 54, the exercise by a corporation of a right to redeem bonds under a trust indenture was held not to be inconsistent with the bondholders' reasonable expectations and therefore not oppressive.

of a share-purchase option in strict compliance with the terms of a shareholders' agreement might be oppressive where it was part of a larger strategy to get rid of a minority shareholder without regard to the best interests of the corporation. Nevertheless, the courts have generally been unwilling to find oppression where the alleged act of oppression is pursuant to a right accorded by the applicant to the alleged oppressor in a contract, such as the right to buy the applicant out.[131] At the very least, the mutual rights and obligations of the parties under the agreement would be found to inform the reasonable expectations of the parties.[132]

An interesting related issue that has arisen in some cases is whether it is appropriate to provide a remedy where the matter in dispute is governed by the terms of a shareholders' agreement. In *Beazer* v. *Hodgson Robertson Laing Ltd.*,[133] an application for an order directing the purchase of shares was denied on the ground that the parties had addressed share purchases, in the circumstances that had arisen, in their shareholders' agreement.[134]

In *Deluce Holdings Ltd.* v. *Air Canada*, mentioned above, Air Canada argued that an application for relief from oppression was precluded by the shareholders' agreement, which required arbitration if the parties could not agree on the valuation of the shares to be purchased. In accordance with the provisions of the *Arbitrations Act*,[135] an application relating to a matter the parties have agreed to submit to arbitration must be stayed. The court determined that the real subject matter of the oppression action was not the share valuation that the parties had agreed to submit to arbitration, but other acts of oppression, so the *Arbitrations Act* did not bar the application.

Interestingly, the court suggested that, if there had been a provision requiring a general resort to arbitration for all disputes, the result might have been different.[136] This suggestion would seem to indicate a planning opportunity for drafting shareholder agreements. It may be

---

131 For example, *Camroux* v. *Armstrong* (1990), 47 B.L.R. 302 (B.C.S.C.). In *obiter* the court suggested an alternative rationale for refusing to provide relief: even if the shareholders' agreement had been breached, "a breach of private arrangement outside the carrying on of the company's affairs cannot be oppressive conduct of the company's affairs" (at 308).

132 *Main* v. *Delcan Group Inc.* (1999), 47 B.L.R. (2d) 200 (Sup. Ct. J.) (breach of agreement held to be breach of reasonable expectations).

133 Above note 88.

134 See also *Korogonas* v. *Andrew (No. 1)* (1992), 128 A.R. 381, at 388 (Q.B.).

135 R.S.O. 1990, c. A.24, s. 7.

136 *Deluce*, above note 27, at 150–51.

possible to minimize the uncertainties associated with potential oppression applications by providing that all disputes between shareholders be submitted to arbitration.

It is unlikely that a court would permit parties to, in effect, contract out of their right to seek relief from oppression in all circumstances. Nevertheless, a very broad arbitration clause was upheld by the court in *Armstrong* v. *Northern Eyes Inc.* precluding access to the oppression remedy.[137] The applicant alleged that he had been excluded from the corporation and dismissed as vice-president of sales and marketing. Because the parties had agreed to submit all disputes between them to arbitration, the court refused to allow an application for relief from oppression to proceed, even though the court acknowledged that the arbitrator would not have the same freedom to grant a remedy that a court would.[138]

6) Remedies

a) Introduction

One of the most innovative features of the oppression remedy provisions is the unlimited flexibility granted to the court to fashion remedies. Under section 241(2) the court is generally empowered to make an order "to rectify the matters complained of." In section 241(3) the breadth of this grant of remedial power is confirmed: the court may make "any interim or final order it thinks fit." There follows a lengthy shopping list of orders a court may consider which overlap with virtually all the other remedial provisions in the *CBCA*,[139] as if to encourage courts to exercise their remedial powers creatively.[140]

It is clear from the cases that the courts have responded to this encouragement, using their broad remedial powers to tailor the remedy ordered to the particular nature of the oppressive act or omission

---

137 (2000), 48 O.R. (3d) 442 (Div. Ct.).

138 In *Kightley* v. *Beneteau*, [1999] O.J. No. 1892 (QL) (Ont. Sup. Ct. J.), a similar oppression claim was allowed to proceed where the clause required arbitration only with respect to matters related to the interpretation of the shareholders' agreement.

139 Above note 26. For example, compliance and restraining orders under section 247 are contemplated in section 241(3)(a); investigations under Part XIX are contemplated in section 241(3)(m); liquidation and dissolution, which are available under Part XVIII, are permitted under section 241(3)(l); the purchase by a corporation of a shareholder's shares, which is addressed in section 190, is contemplated in section 241(3)(f).

140 Welling characterizes these provisions as a "striking example of legislative overkill," above note 27, at 563.

found.[141] Given the fact-specific nature of oppression actions, it is difficult to articulate a principled basis for determining how remedies may be tailored to address precisely the seriousness of the oppression. Some examples of remedies employed, however, may be instructive.

b) Share Purchase

By far the most common remedy requested in oppression actions is the purchase by a corporation or a majority shareholder of the applicant's shares.[142] This remedy has been found to be appropriate where the parties have lost confidence in each other and their relationship has become unworkable.[143] A share purchase may not be appropriate if neither the corporation nor the controlling shareholders are in a financial position to purchase the applicant's shares. In such circumstances, where the parties' relationship has completely broken down, liquidation and dissolution of the corporation may be appropriate.[144] A share purchase was held not to be appropriate where the oppression consisted of only a failure to comply with various obligations under the BCCA, such as the requirements to appoint auditors and to hold annual meetings. The court determined that an order to comply with the BCCA would be sufficient.[145] Various valuation issues that arise in the context of such buy-outs have been the subject of extensive judicial consideration.[146]

c) Liquidation and Dissolution

As noted above, where the parties' relationship has completely broken down, liquidation and dissolution of the corporation may be the only remedy. In *Stel-Van Homes Ltd.* v. *Fortini*,[147] for example, winding up of

---

141 The need to tailor the remedy granted to the seriousness of the oppressive act was expressly recognized in *Jackman*, above note 107, as well as in *Tropxe*, above note 70.

142 For example, *Loveridge Holdings Ltd.* v. *King-Pin Ltd.* (1991), 5 B.L.R. (2d) 195 (Ont. Gen. Div.) [*Loveridge*]; *Millar*, above note 103; *Mason*, above note 86.

143 *Redekop* v. *Robco Construction Ltd.* (1978), 5 B.L.R. 58 (B.C.S.C.); *Liao* v. *Grittioen* (2001), 20 B.L.R. (3d) 61 (Ont. Sup. Ct. J.). In *West* v. *Blenchet*, [2001] B.C.L.C. 795 (Ch. D.), an English court that had to decide which shareholder would be allowed to buy out the other where the relationship had completely broken down determined that it was appropriate to consider the reasonableness of the offers made by each.

144 *Millar*, above note 103.

145 *Jackman*, above note 107.

146 *Brant*, above note 44, is one of the leading cases on the principles appropriate to valuation. Regarding valuation generally, see section G ("Corporate Purchase of Shares of Dissenting Shareholder") in this chapter.

147 (2001), 16 B.L.R. (3d) 103 (Ont. Sup. Ct. J.).

a family business was ordered where the partnership-like relationship of the parties had deteriorated to the point that one party had lost all confidence in the other. The courts have shown great reluctance to use this remedy, however.[148] Indeed, the courts have acknowledged that one of the reasons for introducing the flexible remedial regime in section 241 was to permit relief to be provided without winding up the corporation.[149] In one case, dissolution was ordered subject to a thirty-day stay to permit the parties to find a less disruptive solution.[150] Dissolution may also be sought by application under section 214 of the *CBCA*. Such applications are considered in section H ("Termination of the Corporation: Winding Up"), below.

d) Remedies against Shareholders

As indicated in section C.4(c) ("Discretionary Complainants"), above, the courts have been willing to grant remedies for oppression directly against shareholders at the instance of creditors where the shareholder has participated in rendering the corporation unable to satisfy the creditor's claim, though one judge called this a "drastic remedy."[151] Courts have also made orders against shareholders in oppression applications brought by other shareholders. Shareholders have been made to repay money to the corporation and even to pay creditors directly. Courts have ordered many other sorts of remedies against shareholders, including directing them to purchase the shares of the complainant.[152]

e) Compliance

In several cases, where there was a failure to prepare and distribute annual financial statements, hold annual meetings, or act in some other way required by the governing corporate statute, all of which effectively excluded a shareholder from a corporation, compliance with the statute was ordered.[153] Compliance orders may also be obtained by

---

148 For example, *Loveridge*, above note 142; *Rivers v. Denton* (1992), 5 B.L.R. (2d) 212 (Ont. Gen. Div.) [*Rivers*].

149 *Rivers*, *ibid.* at 203. See also *Mason*, above note 86.

150 *Rivers*, *ibid.*

151 *Tropxe*, above note 70.

152 *Loveridge*, above note 142; *Lajoie v. Lajoie Brothers Contracting Ltd.* (1989), 45 B.L.R. 113 (Ont. H.C.J.).

153 For example, *Millar*, above note 103; *Jackman*, above note 107. In *Sexsmith*, above note 88, however, the court refused to make an order under the oppression provisions to direct compliance with the *OBCA*, above note 8, where the irregularities were not accompanied by financial loss.

application under section 247 of the *CBCA*. Such applications are discussed in section D ("Compliance and Restraining Orders"), below.

f) Other

Courts have made a bewildering variety of other kinds of orders to address the particular acts or omission constituting oppression in individual cases, including orders directing the amendment of by-laws and the replacement of management,[154] the appointment of receivers,[155] the amendment of shareholder agreements,[156] and the creation of a pre-emptive right.[157]

7) Summary

The foregoing survey has attempted to sketch some of the evolving contours of the oppression remedy through a discussion of recent cases in which the courts have considered claims for relief from oppression. It is by no means exhaustive. It was not possible to catalogue fully the avalanche of cases decided since the introduction of the oppression remedy, nor to address all issues relating to the application of the oppression remedy. Nevertheless, this survey was intended to demonstrate two aspects of the revolutionary change being wrought by the application of the oppression remedy. First, the enactment of the oppression remedy has successfully convinced judges to shake off the restrictions imposed on the remedies available to minority shareholders under Canadian corporate law regimes before the *CBCA* and its provincial progeny. This was one of the express intentions of the Dickerson Committee in drafting the *CBCA*.[158] Indeed, because of the range of circumstances in which courts have provided relief and the enormous variety in remedies ordered, oppression is displacing other remedial routes, such as the derivative action, compliance, and liquidation and dissolution. This trend has implications for both corporate lawyers and litigators.

Second, the scope of the remedy is potentially exceedingly broad and, while the proliferation of cases is helping to clarify how the oppression remedy will work, there are still many issues remaining to be resolved. Many oppression cases are resolved without rigorous analysis regarding the precise nature of the legal standard, leading,

---

154 *Trnkoczy*, above note 51.
155 *Kanata*, above note 107.
156 *Tesari*, above note 51.
157 *Mazzotta v. Twin Gold Mines Ltd.* (1987), 37 B.L.R. 218 (Ont. H.C.J.).
158 Dickerson, above note 2, at 153.

inevitably, to inconsistent decisions on some issues. These issues, such as when relief can be claimed for injuries to the corporation and to creditors, are unlikely to be resolved until more oppression cases get to the courts of appeal.

D. COMPLIANCE AND RESTRAINING ORDERS

The *CBCA* and most other modern corporate statutes[159] allow a complainant as defined in section 238 or a creditor to apply for a court order requiring compliance with or restraining a breach of the Act, the regulations, the corporation's articles or by-laws, or a unanimous shareholders' agreement (*CBCA*, s. 247). Such an order may be made against the corporation itself as well as against any director, officer, employee, agent, auditor, trustee, receiver, receiver-manager, or liquidator of a corporation. Although, as noted above, a compliance order could be a remedy in an oppression action, the chief benefit of the compliance action is that it provides a summary procedure to deal with discrete problems of non-compliance. It has been used, for example, to require a corporation to act on the statutory rights of a dissenting shareholder to have his shares bought out.[160] The compliance remedy cannot be used, however, if making a finding of non-compliance requires a determination of complex issues of fact or law, such as a claim that there has been a breach of fiduciary duty.[161]

The compliance remedy is noteworthy in several respects. First, creditors have a right to make an application, unlike the derivative action and oppression remedies where they can make an application only with permission of the court. Also, the compliance remedy extends to a very wide range of people, much wider than any other remedy under the *CBCA*. Finally, as noted in Chapter 7, it is possible to use this remedy to enforce compliance with a unanimous shareholders' agreement.[162]

---

159 *ABCA*, above note 8, s. 240; *BCCA*, above note 8, s. 25; *MCA*, above note 28, s. 240; *NBBCA*, above note 28, s. 172; *NCA*, above note 28, s. 373; *OBCA*, above note 8, s. 253; *SBCA*, above note 28, s. 240.

160 *Skye Resources Ltd.* v. *Camskye Holdings Inc.* (1982), 38 O.R. (2d) 253 (H.C.J.). See also *Goldhar* v. *D'Aragon Mines Ltd.* (1977), 15 O.R. (2d) 80 (H.C.J.). These rights are discussed in section G ("Corporate Purchase of Shares of Dissenting Shareholders") in this chapter.

161 *Goldhar* v. *Quebec Manitou Mines Ltd.* (1975), 9 O.R. (2d) 740 (Div. Ct.).

162 *Duha Printers (Western) Ltd.* v. *R.* (1998), 1 S.C.R. 795.

E. RECTIFICATION OF CORPORATE RECORDS

Where a person's name has been wrongly entered or retained in the shareholder registers or other records of a corporation, a security holder or any other aggrieved person may apply to a court to have the register or record rectified (*CBCA*, s. 243).[163] Because the records of the corporation may be used to identify who should be given notice of meetings or receive dividends, the court may also restrain the calling or holding of any meeting or the payment of any dividend until the register or record is rectified to ensure that any wrongfully excluded shareholder may participate (*CBCA*, s. 243(3)).

In addition to ensuring that notices of meetings and dividends are sent to the correct persons, the right to obtain the rectification of records on an expeditious summary basis is important because corporate registers and other records are, in the absence of evidence to the contrary, proof of what they disclose (*CBCA*, s. 257).

F. INVESTIGATIONS

Part XIX of the *CBCA* sets out a comprehensive scheme under which investigations into the business and affairs of a corporation or any of its affiliates may be carried out. A court may order an investigation on the application of a security holder or the *CBCA* Director where it appears to the court that any of the following grounds has been made out:

- the business of the corporation or any of its affiliates is or has been carried on with intent to defraud any person;
- the business or affairs of the corporation or any of its affiliates are or have been carried on or conducted, or the powers of the directors are or have been exercised, in a manner that is oppressive or unfairly prejudicial to or that unfairly disregards the interests of a security holder;
- the corporation or any of its affiliates was formed for a fraudulent or unlawful purpose; or

---

163 *ABCA*, above note 8, s. 246; *BCCA*, above note 8, s. 68; *MCA*, above note 28, s. 236; *NBBCA*, above note 28, s. 168; *NCA*, above note 28, s. 349; *OBCA*, above note 8, s. 249; *SBCA*, above note 28, s. 236.

- persons concerned with the formation, business, or affairs of the corporation or any of its affiliates have in connection therewith acted fraudulently or dishonestly.[164]

The courts have held that they will not exercise their discretion to order an investigation to permit the applicant to obtain information that it could have obtained through the regular discovery process in a civil proceeding.[165] The *CBCA* sets out detailed provisions regarding the powers of inspectors, the procedures for hearings, and various procedural matters (*CBCA*, ss. 229–36). Courts also have broad jurisdiction to make rules for the conduct of an investigation (*CBCA*, s. 230). Normally, the corporation pays the costs of the investigation.[166]

G. CORPORATE PURCHASE OF SHARES OF DISSENTING SHAREHOLDERS

The *CBCA* and the statutes modelled after it provide that shareholders who dissent in relation to a shareholder vote on certain specified matters of fundamental importance to the corporation may require the corporation to buy their shares (*CBCA*, s. 190).[167] Shareholder votes on the following fundamental changes trigger this right, referred to as the shareholder's dissent and appraisal right:

- amendment to the corporation's articles to add, change, or remove any provision restricting or constraining the issue, transfer, or ownership of shares of the class held by the dissenter or to add, change, or remove any restriction on the business or businesses that the corporation may carry on;

---

164 Other statutes also provide investigation rights: *ABCA, ibid.*, s. 223; *BCCA, ibid.*, s. 233; *MCA, ibid.*, s. 222; *NBBCA, ibid.*, s. 155; *NCA, ibid.*, s. 354; *NSCA, ibid.*, s. 115; *OBCA, ibid.*, s. 160; *Quebec Companies Act*, R.S.Q. 1977, c. C-38, s. 110; *SBCA, ibid.*, s. 160.

165 *Budd* v. *Gentra*, above note 104; *Brown* v. *Maxim Restoration Ltd.* (1998), 42 B.L.R. (2d) 243 (Ont. Gen. Div.).

166 *Consolidated Enfield Corp.* v. *Blair* (1996), 28 O.R. (3d) 714 (Div. Ct.), leave to appeal to C.A. refused (1996) 63 A.C.W.S. (3d) 1271 (C.A.). An order that the corporation pay the costs of the investigation is listed as a possible order under *CBCA*, above note 26, s. 230(1)(l).

167 *ABCA*, above note 8, s. 184; *BCCA*, above note 8, s. 231; *MCA*, above note 28, s. 189; *SBCA*, above note 28, s. 184; *NBBCA*, above note 28, s. 131; *OBCA*, above note 8, s. 184; *NCA*, above note 28, ss. 300–1.

- amalgamation with other corporations;[168]
- continuation of the corporation under the laws of another jurisdiction, with the result that the corporation becomes governed under a corporate statute other than the *CBCA*;
- the sale, lease, or exchange of all or substantially all of the corporation's property other than in the ordinary course of business; or
- a going-private transaction or a squeeze-out transaction (*CBCA*, s. 190(1)).[169]

Also, the holder of any shares entitled to vote separately as a class on any amendment to the articles in accordance with section 176 has dissent and appraisal rights in relation to that vote (*CBCA*, ss. 176 & 190(2)). In general terms, class votes are required where amendments of articles affect a class in some way that is different from other classes and potentially prejudicial. Class votes were discussed in Chapter 6. The list of fundamental changes which trigger dissent and appraisal rights is different under some provincial statutes.

All these triggering events are fundamental changes to the nature of a shareholder's investment. Since they will affect significantly the risk and return characteristics of the shares, the shareholder is given an exit right if he does not agree with the change. At the same time, the majority is not prevented from changing the corporation to respond to changing circumstances. The existence of the right, however, also indirectly gives minority shareholders enhanced power to determine whether the corporation goes ahead with one of these fundamental changes. If many shareholders will dissent, the resulting purchase obligation may require a substantial expenditure for the corporation. With this in mind, management may decide not to put a fundamental change to a shareholder vote, even in circumstances where it knows there will be sufficient votes to pass the special resolution approving it. Alternatively, if permitted in the resolution itself, management may decide not to implement the change after it is approved. As a result, minority shareholders may have more leverage to prevent fundamental changes than their votes would indicate. Dissent and appraisal right must be disclosed in the notice of the shareholder meeting at which a fundamental change will be voted on.

---

168 So-called "short form" amalgamations between corporations under common ownership do not give rise to the dissent and appraisal right. These transactions are discussed in Chapter 10.

169 These are transactions in which a shareholder's interest in the securities of the corporation is effectively terminated. They are discussed in Chapter 10, section F.

Although some issues arise in connection with the rather cumbersome procedure for the exercise of dissent and appraisal rights provided for in the corporate legislation, the issue most frequently before the courts has been the price at which the corporation must buy the dissenting shareholders' shares. The corporation's obligation is to purchase the shares of dissenting shareholders for "fair value." Upon the exercise of dissent and appraisal rights, the corporation must make an offer of a price at which it will buy the dissenters out. The shareholder may object to the price and request the court to determine fair value. Alternatively, the corporation can apply to the court to determine what is fair value. Although it is beyond the scope of this book to present a complete analysis of the determinants of fair value, some general comments may be made.[170]

The basic approach to calculating fair value is to determine the value of all the shares of the corporation, then allocate to the dissenting shareholder her *pro rata* share of that value. The significance of this approach is that it values minority shareholder interests on the same basis as majority holdings. Because of the operation of shareholder democracy, in the open market it is usually possible to obtain a higher price per share for a block of shares that represents control of the corporation, whether this is defined as the power to elect the majority of the board of directors or otherwise. The higher incremental value of a control block is referred to as a "premium for control," and the corresponding reduction in value attributed to minority holdings is called a "minority discount." In some early cases it had been held that a minority discount should be applied to determine the fair value of dissenters' shares. In *Brant Investments Ltd.* v. *KeepRite Inc.*,[171] the Ontario Court of Appeal authoritatively determined that this was not the correct approach, at least in Ontario.

In the same case, the Court of Appeal identified four widely accepted methods for valuing all the shares of the corporation:

- *Market Value*: The value determined by reference to the price at which shares trade on some market — for example, the Toronto Stock Exchange.
- *Asset Value*: The value of the assets of the corporation, either on a going-concern basis or as though the corporation's assets were being sold as part of a liquidation.

---

170 See V. Krishna, "Determining the 'Fair Value' of Corporate Shares" (1988) 13 Can. Bus. L.J. 132.

171 Above note 44 (Ont. C.A.).

- *Earnings Value*: Some sustainable level of earnings is established (such as the average over the last five years) and the value of the corporation is calculated as the value today of those earnings received by the corporation in an indefinite number of future years.
- *Combination Method*: The fourth method is simply to determine value based on the consideration of the value generated by the other three methods. A common way of doing so is to assign a weight to the value generated by each method and to calculate the average.

The Canadian courts have used each of these methods and have stated that no rigid rule can be adopted about which method is appropriate. In each case, the choice of method will depend on the facts, including, in particular, the nature of the corporation's business and its share holdings. For example, where a corporation's shares are widely held and actively traded, the best method may be to take the market value.[172] On the other hand, the market-value approach will not be appropriate where the trading is thin and dominated by a controlling shareholder.[173] Where a corporation has sold most of its assets and ceases to carry on an operating business, the value of the corporation may be best determined by the value of its remaining assets as if they were sold on a liquidation.[174] If the business will continue to be carried on, it may be more appropriate to value the assets on a going-concern basis or to use the earnings value. Where a corporation's sole asset is a large landholding with little income flow, it will not be appropriate to determine fair value based on earnings.[175] Finally, in a high-technology business which is just getting started, there may be no assets or revenues and only an idea. In such cases, some other basis for valuation will be necessary.

There are some additional general rules about valuation. Valuations must be conducted as of a particular date with reference only to the facts as they were known at that time.[176] The valuation date for fair-value determinations is as of the close of business on the day before the resolution from which the shareholder dissents is adopted (*CBCA*, s. 190(3)). The purpose of this provision is to try to ensure that the effect of the change dissented from is not taken into account in determining

---

172 *Montgomery v. Shell Canada Ltd.* (1980), 3 Sask. R. 19 (Q.B.). Note that market prices incorporate an inherent minority discount, since the market price is the price at which minority interests trade in the market.

173 *Manning v. Harris Steel Group Inc.* (1986), 7 B.C.L.R. (2d) 69 (S.C.).

174 *Kelvin Energy Ltd. v. Bahan* (1987), 79 A.R. 259 (Q.B.).

175 *LoCicero v. B.A.C.M. Industries Ltd.*, [1988] 1 S.C.R. 399 [*LoCicero*].

176 *New Quebec Raglan Mines Ltd. v. Blok-Andersen* (1991), 4 B.L.R. (2d) 71 (Ont. Gen. Div.).

fair value. The courts have made clear that any benefit resulting from the transaction dissented from is not to be taken into account.[177]

Also, dissenting shareholders are not entitled to a special premium just because they are dissenting.[178] Some early cases had held that dissenters were in a position similar to that of people whose property is expropriated and so should receive additional compensation because of the involuntary nature of the sale of their shares.[179] The Ontario Court of Appeal in *Brant Investments Ltd.* v. *KeepRite Inc.* held that no such premium should be paid to dissenters as an element of fair value.[180]

H. TERMINATION OF THE CORPORATION: WINDING UP AND DISSOLUTION

One of the remedies that a court may grant on an application for relief from oppression is to terminate the corporation's existence, after "winding up" the corporation. This involves selling off or liquidating all the assets of the corporation, using the proceeds to pay off all the corporation's liabilities, and paying out any surplus to the corporation's shareholders in accordance with the scheme for the distribution of assets on dissolution set out in the corporation's articles. The holders of any shares with a preference on dissolution will be paid first, and any remaining surplus will be paid to the holders of shares with a claim to the residual assets of the corporation on dissolution — typically, the common shares. After this is completed, the corporation is dissolved, meaning that its legal existence is terminated.

In addition to permitting a winding-up and dissolution order in an oppression action, the *CBCA* separately provides for an application for a winding up and dissolution (*CBCA*, ss. 213 & 214). The process for obtaining a court order to wind up and dissolve a corporation under these provisions is described in Chapter 10, section G ("Termination of

---

177 *LoCicero*, above note 175; *Neonex International Ltd.* v. *Kolasa* (1978), 84 D.L.R. (3d) 446 (B.C.S.C.).

178 *Brant*, above note 44.

179 For example, *Domglas Inc.* v. *Jarislowsky, Fraser & Co.* (1982), 138 D.L.R. (3d) 521 (Que. C.A.).

180 *Ibid.* A premium may be appropriate where shareholders are forced to sell as a result of a going-private transaction or the exercise of the statutory compulsory acquisition rights described in Chapter 11. See *Investissements Mont-Soleil Inc.* v. *National Drug Ltd.*, [1982] C.S. 716 (Que. S.C.) (premium ordered on amalgamation squeeze-out).

the Corporation's Existence"). In this chapter, we briefly discuss the grounds for such an order.[181]

The separate provisions relating to winding up restate, in a somewhat duplicative way, that winding up and dissolution may be obtained if oppression is found. For this purpose, oppression is defined in the same way as in section 241. Since winding up and dissolution is the most extreme form of shareholder relief, it will not be granted in all cases of oppression. Consistent with the general approach developing in the courts of seeking to balance the remedy granted with the specific problem creating the oppression, a court will order winding up and dissolution only where the oppression is very serious. When winding up will be ordered in the context of a claim for relief from oppression was discussed above.

Winding up and dissolution may be ordered also where the court is satisfied that a unanimous shareholders' agreement entitles the complaining shareholder to demand liquidation and dissolution. The other general ground on which a court may order winding up is when "it is just and equitable that the corporation should be liquidated and dissolved" (*CBCA*, s. 214(b)(ii)). This was the primary ground on which the courts would order winding up and dissolution prior to the creation of the oppression remedy. The courts have made it clear that the circumstances in which this requirement may be satisfied may not be defined exhaustively; each case must be judged based on its own facts. Nevertheless, several categories of cases may be identified.

First, courts have been willing to order winding up and dissolution where it is no longer possible for the corporation to carry on the business for which it was created.[182] Second, winding up and dissolution has been ordered where the shareholder seeking relief has a "justifiable lack of confidence" in the conduct of the management of the corporation.[183] Such a lack of confidence cannot consist only of a disagreement about the policies of the management. Rather, there must be some serious misbehaviour on the part of management. This would include not only fraud but also deliberate violations of corporate policy, such as failing to hold annual meetings and attempting to prevent shareholders from exercising their rights to participate in the corporation. Third,

---

181 The winding up, or liquidation and dissolution, of a corporation under the corporate statutes is only permitted if the corporation is solvent. If the corporation is insolvent, winding up must be accomplished in accordance with the *Bankruptcy and Insolvency Act*, R.S.C. 1985, c. B-3.

182 *Piggot v. Zubovits* (1995), 58 A.C.W.S. (3d) 52 (Ont. Div. Ct.), affirming (1995) 56 A.C.W.S. (3d) 506 (Gen. Div.).

183 *Loch v. John Blackwood Ltd.*, [1924] A.C. 783, at 788 (P.C.).

courts have ordered winding up and dissolution where the corporation is, in effect, a partnership between two or more persons with more or less equal power in the corporation who have come to disagree fundamentally on how the business should be operated.[184] The courts have been particularly sympathetic where, because of the decision-making structure in place in the corporation, the disagreement has made it impossible for the corporation to act.[185] This situation is referred to in the cases as a "deadlock."

The purpose of the drafters of the *CBCA* in including the oppression ground in the winding up and dissolution section was to try to ensure that the courts would grant winding up in more liberal circumstances than they had under the "just and equitable" rule.[186] In some respects, however, precisely the opposite has occurred. Because of the flexibility under the oppression remedy to fashion remedies to address the oppressive behaviour, courts have been willing to order a winding up and dissolution only as a last resort.[187] Many of the cases in which winding up and dissolution has been ordered in oppression cases have been in one of the three categories mentioned above, where a less intrusive order will not work.[188]

I. CHAPTER SUMMARY

In this chapter, we looked at the various ways in which shareholders may seek relief from actions by the corporation, management (including the directors), and other shareholders. Historically, the ability of

---

184 *Ebrahimi*, above note 88.

185 For example, *Re Yenidje Tobacco Co. Ltd.*, [1916] 2 Ch. 426 (C.A.).

186 Dickerson, above note 2, at 158–63.

187 In *Hunemaayer v. Freure* (1999), 2 B.L.R. (3d) 269 (Ont. Sup. Ct. J) at 319, winding up was described as a drastic measure warranted only in extreme circumstances.

188 For example, *Re Cravo Equipment* (1982), 44 C.B.R. (N.S.) 208 (Ont. H.C.J.) (partnership-like relationship broken down, lack of confidence based on absence of good faith and improper conduct); *Re Alf's Roofing & Contracting Ltd.* (1985), 61 A.R. 16 (Q.B.) (irreconcilable differences between two equal shareholders); *Di Giacomo v. Di Giacomo Canada Inc.* (1989), 28 C.P.R. (3d) 77 (Ont. H.C.J.), additional reasons at (1990), 28 C.P.R. (3d) 447 (Ont. H.C.J.) (corporation had ceased operations and licence to use confidential trade secrets terminated). Other Canadian statutes also have winding-up remedies: *ABCA*, above note 8, s. 207; *BCCA*, above note 8, s. 224; *MCA*, above note 28, s. 207; *NBBCA*, above note 28, s. 143–45; *NCA*, above note 28, ss. 339 & 341; *OBCA*, above note 8, s. 206; *SBCA*, above note 28, s. 207.

shareholders to obtain relief in such circumstances was limited, but now a variety of effective options are available.

In addition to attempting to sue personally where an individual shareholder right has been infringed, shareholders may seek leave of the court to sue for relief from injuries caused to the corporation resulting from the breach of duties owed by directors and officers to the corporation or any other cause. Leave will be granted so long as the action appears to be in the interests of the corporation, the shareholder has given notice to the directors to permit them to decide whether they should cause the corporation to take action, and the shareholder is acting in good faith.

The most significant enhancement in shareholder remedies is the oppression remedy. Shareholders may now claim relief in a wide range of circumstances where their interests have been oppressed or unfairly disregarded or prejudiced. The courts have interpreted their mandate to provide relief broadly and have sought to tailor remedies to the precise problem arising in each case. Though the case law is still developing, the oppression remedy seems to be changing corporate law in several significant ways. First, as courts grant complainant status to creditors of various kinds, the courts are changing the categories of stakeholders to whom management is directly responsible. As discussed in Chapters 8 and 12, the courts have generally considered management's obligations to flow only to the corporation and, for the purpose of defining what the corporation's interests are, they have refused to consider interests of stakeholders other than shareholders. Nevertheless, under the oppression remedy, creditors, former shareholders, and others have been able to obtain relief. Second, it seems that, by beginning to impose remedies on shareholders, the courts are developing a kind of duty owed by shareholders to each other.

The *CBCA* and other modern corporate statutes provide various other remedies, including compliance orders, orders to rectify corporate records, investigations, dissent and appraisal remedies on the occurrence of fundamental changes to the corporation, and winding up and dissolution of the corporation.

FURTHER READINGS

BECK, S.M., "Minority Shareholders' Rights in the 1980s" [1982] Spec. Lect. L.S.U.C. 311

BECK, S.M., "The Shareholders' Derivative Action" (1974) 52 Can. Bar Rev. 159

BUCKLEY, F., M. GILLEN, & R. YALDEN, *Corporations: Principles and Policies*, 3d ed. (Toronto: Emond Montgomery, 1995) at 700–796

CAMPION, J.A. *et al.*, "The Oppression remedy: reasonable expectations of shareholders" (1995) Spec. Lect. L.S.U.C. 229-253

CHEFFINS, B.A., "An Economic Analysis of the Oppression Remedy: Working Toward a More Coherent Picture of Corporate Law" (1990) 40 U.T. L. J. 775

KRISHNA, V., "Determining the 'Fair Value' of Corporate Shares" (1988) 13 Can. Bus. L.J. 132

MCGUINESS, K.P., *The Law and Practice of Canadian Business Corporations* (Toronto: Butterworths, 1999) c. 9

MACINTOSH, J.G., "Bad Faith and the Oppression Remedy: Uneasy Marriage or Amicable Divorce?" (1990) 69 Can. Bar Rev. 276

MACINTOSH, J.G., "Minority Shareholder Rights in Canada and England, 1860–1987" (1988) 27 Osgoode Hall L.J. 1

MACINTOSH, J.G., "The Oppression Remedy: Personal or Derivative?" (1991) 70 Can. Bar Rev. 29

MACINTOSH, J.G., "The Shareholders' Appraisal Right in Canada: A Critical Reappraisal" (1986) 24 Osgoode Hall L.J. 201

MACINTOSH, J.G., J. HOLMES, & S. THOMPSON, "The Puzzle of Shareholder Fiduciary Duties" (1991) 19 Can. Bus. L.J. 86

PETERSON, D.H., *Shareholder Remedies in Canada* (Toronto: Carswell, 1989) (looseleaf)

VANDUZER, J.A., "Who May Claim Relief from Oppression: The Complainant in Canadian Corporate Law" (1993) 25 Ottawa L. Rev. 463

WALDRON, M.A., "Corporate Theory and the Oppression Remedy" (1982) 6 Can. Bus. L.J. 129

ZIEGEL, J.S., *et al.*, *Cases and Materials on Partnerships and Canadian Business Corporations*, 3d ed. (Toronto: Carswell, 1994) c. 12

CHANGES TO CORPORATE ORGANIZATIONS

A. CHANGES IN CORPORATE CHARACTERISTICS

1) Introduction

After a corporation is incorporated, it may be necessary to change its characteristics for a variety of reasons. Perhaps a new class of shares must be created to meet the needs of a new investor, or the number of directors needs to be increased. Changing these characteristics involves amending the articles of the corporation, and in this chapter we discuss how this may be done. This chapter also sets out what is required to effect various other corporate changes under the *CBCA*, including adjustments to a corporation's stated capital, continuing the corporation under the laws of another jurisdiction, amalgamating the corporation with other corporations, selling substantially all the corporation's assets, and terminating the corporation's existence.

2) Amendment of Articles

The articles of the corporation must be amended to add, change, or remove any provision contained in the articles (*CBCA*, ss. 173–79).[1] Specifically, amendment is required to do any of the following:

---

1   Each province with a statute based on the *Canada Business Corporations Act*, R.S.C. 1985, c. C-44 [*CBCA*], has a scheme for amending articles. E.g., the

- change the corporate name;
- change the province of the corporation's registered office;
- add, change, or remove provisions relating to the classes of shares of the corporation;
- add, change, or remove any restriction on the issue, transfer, or ownership of shares;
- change the number or the minimum or maximum number of directors;
- add, change, or remove any restriction on the business the corporation may carry on or on the powers the corporation may exercise; or
- add any provision that might have been set out in articles or by-laws at the time of incorporation but was not.

Subject to the exceptions described below, amendment of the articles requires approval by special resolution. This is a resolution passed at a meeting of shareholders by a majority of not less than two-thirds of the votes cast at the meeting or consented to in writing by all shareholders. A level of approval higher than two-thirds may be specified in a shareholders' agreement or in the corporation's articles. As with all shareholder meetings, notice of a meeting to consider a resolution to amend the articles must be sent to shareholders. The notice must state the nature of the proposed amendment in sufficient detail to permit shareholders to form a reasoned decision about whether to vote for or against the amendment and must include the text of the special resolution on which the shareholders will be asked to vote (*CBCA*, s. 135(6)). In addition, if the corporation has more than fifty shareholders, the management must send shareholders a form of proxy and a management proxy circular that provide further information (*CBCA*, s. 149(1)).[2] Shareholders may initiate amendments to articles themselves by making a shareholder proposal (*CBCA*, s. 175(1)). Proposals and the proxy solicitation process were discussed in Chapter 7.

At the meeting, only those shareholders who would otherwise be entitled to vote are permitted to do so. Any class or series of shares that is affected by the amendment in a manner set out in section 176 of the

---

Ontario *Business Corporations Act*, R.S.O. 1990, c. B.16 [*OBCA*], ss. 168–172, 273(3); and the Alberta *Business Corporations Act*, R.S.A. 2000, c. B-9 [*ABCA*], ss. 173-179. British Columbia's scheme for amending the memorandum and articles of association is set out in the *Companies Act*, R.S.C. 1996, c. 62 [*BCCA*], ss. 204, 217, 219 221, 223–226, 229–232.

2 Under the *OBCA*, *ibid.*, this obligation applies only to offering corporations (*OBCA*, s. 11). Under the *ABCA*, *ibid.*, this obligation applies to all corporations with more than fifteen shareholders (s. 149).

CBCA are entitled to vote separately as a class. Section 176 lists exhaustively the specific circumstances when such a separate vote is required. Essentially, a class or series is entitled to a separate vote whenever it will be more prejudicially affected by the adoption of the amendment than other classes or series. This might occur, for example, where an amendment would create a new class that would be entitled to receive dividends before any dividends were paid to holders of shares of an existing class.[3] A separate vote is required even if the class or series of shares would not otherwise have the right to vote (*CBCA*, s. 176(5)). If a separate vote is required, the amendment is not passed unless it is approved by a special resolution of the class or series entitled to vote separately, in addition to any other required approval (*CBCA*, s. 176(6)). In effect, the class entitled to a class vote has a veto over the proposed amendment.

If an amendment is approved by special resolution in circumstances where a class or series was entitled to vote separately, the shareholders of that class or series who voted against the amendment are entitled to have the corporation buy them out for fair value. This so-called "dissent and appraisal right" is also available to all shareholders who vote against an amendment approved by the requisite special resolution to add, change, or remove any provision restricting the issue, transfer, or ownership of shares of the class held by them or restricting the business the corporation is permitted to carry on (*CBCA*, s. 190).[4] The dissent and appraisal right was discussed in Chapter 9.

Once the amendment is approved, the directors must file articles of amendment with the relevant corporate authority. Under the *CBCA*, this is the Director appointed under the Act. On receipt of the articles of amendment, the Director issues a certificate of amendment. The amendment is effective from the date of the certificate. The resolution authorizing the amendment may provide that the directors may revoke

---

3   Section 176(1) contemplates that the articles may exclude the right to a class vote for amendments identified in s. 176(1)(a), (b) and (e). With respect to a particular class, these are amendments to (i) increase or decrease any maximum number of authorized shares of such class, or increase any maximum number of authorized shares of a class having rights and privileges equal or superior to the shares of such class; (ii) effect an exchange, reclassification or cancellation of all or part of the shares of such class; and (iii) create a new class of shares equal or superior to the shares of such class.

4   In order to exercise the dissent and appraisal right, a shareholder must satisfy the procedural requirements of the *CBCA*, above note 1, s. 190, including giving notice to the corporation of her intention to dissent before the meeting at which the vote will take place.

the resolution before they file articles of amendment without further authorization from the shareholders (*CBCA*, s. 173(2)). Such a provision might be useful to include in a resolution amending the articles if the directors wanted to see how many dissenters would have to be bought out by the corporation if the resolution passed. If the number of dissenters was significant and the cost of buying them out was too high as a result, the directors would be able to decide not to go ahead with the amendment.

One amendment may be made without the approval of shareholders. A corporation that received only a number for a name when it incorporated (such as 123456 Canada Inc.) may adopt a new name without shareholder authorization (*CBCA*, s. 173(3)). Finally, as noted in Chapter 6, fixing the rights, privileges, conditions, and restrictions of a series of shares within a class may be done by the directors alone if authorized in the articles (*CBCA*, s. 27). In each case, the directors must file articles of amendment reflecting the change.

3) Changes to Stated Capital

As outlined in Chapter 6, a stated capital account must be maintained for each class and series of shares which records the full amount of any consideration received by the corporation in return for issuing shares of the class or series. The stated capital account must be reduced when the corporation acquires its own shares and in some other circumstances (*CBCA*, s. 38). In addition, the corporation may want to reduce its stated capital for a variety of reasons. A reduction might be desirable in connection with a dividend that is to constitute a repayment of capital to shareholders. In general, such capital dividends may be received by shareholders tax free. The reduction in stated capital would reflect the fact that some of what had been contributed by shareholders was being returned. As well, a reduction in stated capital may be desirable where there has been a decline in the value of a corporation's assets to the point at which the realizable value of the corporation's assets exceeds the aggregate of its liabilities plus the stated capital of all classes of shares, and a reduction in stated capital may be necessary to permit the corporation to do certain other things which are prohibited where this financial test is not met, such as paying dividends. This financial test is discussed in Chapter 6.

If a corporation's stated capital is set out in its articles, then a reduction can be accomplished only by articles of amendment (*CBCA*, s. 173(1)(f)). In practice, this is rarely done. In all other circumstances, a reduction in stated capital must be approved by a special resolution of the shareholders (*CBCA*, s. 38(1)). A corporation cannot reduce its stated capital if it is insolvent, or, where a dividend to shareholders will be paid out of capital, if there are reasonable grounds for believing that the realizable value of the corporation's assets will be less than its liabilities after the dividend is paid (*CBCA*, s. 38(3)). This constraint is intended to protect creditors.

Where shares are redeemed or purchased, the stated capital account for the class or series of shares redeemed or acquired must be reduced accordingly (*CBCA*, s. 39). The amount that must be deducted is determined as follows: the stated capital for the class is multiplied by the number of shares redeemed or purchased and the product obtained is divided by the total number of issued shares in the class prior to the redemption or purchase. No shareholders' resolution is required. All that is needed is for the directors to pass a resolution authorizing the redemption or purchase. The requirements to be satisfied before a redemption or acquisition is permitted are discussed in Chapter 6.

A corporation must increase its stated capital account for a class or series of shares if it pays a stock dividend on shares of the class or series. The declared amount of the dividend in money must be added to the stated capital account for the class or series (*CBCA*, s. 43(2)). Stated capital accounts may have to be adjusted in certain other circumstances, including amendment of articles, amalgamations and arrangements, discussed later in this chapter, as well as the conversion of shares from one class into another (*CBCA*, s. 39(4)).[5]

4) By-laws

The directors may make, amend, or repeal by-laws. Their action is effective as soon as the directors' resolution is passed, but the directors must submit their action to the shareholders at their next meeting. The shareholders may confirm, reject, or amend the directors' action. If the directors' action is rejected by the shareholders or if the directors fail to submit it to the shareholders, the action ceases to have effect on the date of rejection or on the date of the meeting when it should have been submitted. In such a case, no subsequent resolution of directors to make, amend, or repeal a by-law having substantially the same purpose or effect is effective until it is confirmed by shareholders (*CBCA*, s. 103).

---

5   Statutes modelled on the *CBCA*, above note 1, contain similar provisions. E.g., *OBCA*, above note 1, ss. 34 & 35; and *ABCA*, above note 1, ss. 39(4) & 44. The *BCCA*, above note 1, has no concept of stated capital but has similar provisions regarding changes in capital (ss. 233 & 234).

New by-laws, as well as changes to and the repeal of by-laws, can also be initiated by shareholders in a shareholder proposal (*CBCA*, s. 103(5)). Such an action becomes effective as soon as it is approved by the shareholders. No action from the directors is needed. Proposals are discussed in Chapter 7.

Regardless of who initiates a new by-law or the amendment or repeal of a by-law, shareholder approval need be by ordinary resolution only (*CBCA*, s. 103(2)). If some greater majority is considered desirable, it can be specified in the corporation's articles. Alternatively, a higher approval level may be specified in a unanimous shareholders' agreement.[6]

B. CONTINUANCE

1) Introduction

The corporate law of most jurisdictions in Canada permits corporations governed by its laws to leave the jurisdiction (the "exporting jurisdiction") and to be continued under and governed by the corporate laws of another jurisdiction (the "importing jurisdiction") (*CBCA*, ss. 187 & 88).[7] The basic requirement for doing so is the permission of the exporting jurisdiction and, in the case of export from the *CBCA* and other Canadian jurisdictions, shareholder approval. A continuance may be desirable to take advantage of some particular provision of the corporate law of the importing jurisdiction, though this has little relevance in the Canadian context in most cases because of the substantial similarity of Canadian corporate laws.[8] The most common reason to continue is to permit an amalgamation. In order to effect this statutory procedure, discussed below, all the corporations must be governed under the same corporate law.

---

6   Similar rules are set out in the *OBCA*, *ibid.*, s. 116; and *ABCA*, *ibid.*, s. 102. The *BCCA*, *ibid.*, has a similar provision relating to articles of association (s. 219).

7   Similar rules are set out in the *OBCA*, *ibid.*, ss. 180 & 181; *ABCA*, *ibid.* ss. 188 & 189; and *BCCA*, *ibid.*, ss. 36–38.

8   There are, however, differences, particularly between *CBCA* model and non-*CBCA* model jurisdictions, which may be extremely important in particular circumstances. For an example of a continuance to take advantage of a difference between the corporate law of Nova Scotia and the *CBCA*, see *Jacobsen v. United Canso Oil & Gas Ltd.* (1980), 40 N.S.R. (2d) 692 (S.C.T.D.), discussed in Chapter 6.

2) Import

If a corporation wanted to become governed by the *CBCA*, it must make an application to the Director in the form of articles of continuance (*CBCA*, Form 11), which require information similar to that required in articles of incorporation (*CBCA*, s. 187). The articles of continuance become the articles of incorporation on continuance. Articles of continuance require some additional information as well: any previous name of the corporation, the name of the exporting jurisdiction, and the date of incorporation. In the articles of continuance, it is also necessary to make any changes needed to conform the characteristics of the corporation to the *CBCA*. Any other amendments that are desired may also be made to the corporation's characteristics so long as the same shareholder approval as would be required under the *CBCA* for such a change is given to the continuance (*CBCA*, s. 187(2)).

In addition to the articles of continuance, it is necessary to file a letter of satisfaction or some other document issued by the exporting jurisdiction indicating that the corporation is authorized to apply for continuance under the *CBCA*, a Notice of Directors, a Notice of Registered Office, a list of the provinces in which the corporation is registered as an extra-provincial corporation, the required fee of $200, and a name-search report. Unless the corporation is incorporated under the laws of Alberta, British Columbia, Manitoba, Saskatchewan, New Brunswick, Newfoundland, Prince Edward Island, Northwest Territories, Yukon Territory, or Ontario, it is also necessary to file a legal opinion that the laws of the exporting jurisdiction allow the corporation to apply for continuance under the *CBCA*, and any authorization required under such law has been obtained. The *CBCA* Director then refers the question of whether the continuance is properly authorized and meets the requirements of the *CBCA* to the Department of Justice.[9] If a favourable opinion is received by the Director, the continuance will be allowed to proceed.

3) Export

Under the *CBCA*, the export of a corporation must be authorized by special resolution of the shareholders (*CBCA*, s. 188(5)). The resolution should contain authority for the directors to do the following:

---

9   *Canada Business Corporations Act* Continuance (Import) Kit (Corporations Directorate, Industry Canada, 29 January 1999).

- to apply for continuance under laws of the importing jurisdiction;
- to apply to the Director under the *CBCA* to authorize the continuance; and
- to make all necessary amendments to conform to the laws of the importing jurisdiction.

All shareholders have the right to vote on a resolution authorizing a continuance, even if they do not otherwise have the right to vote (*CBCA*, s. 188(4)).[10] Shareholders also have the right to have their shares bought by the corporation for fair value if they vote against the continuance, but it is nevertheless adopted (*CBCA*, s. 190(1)(d)). The notice of meeting must refer to this right to dissent and to be bought out (*CBCA*, s. 188(3)).

The resolution authorizing continuance may permit the directors to abandon the continuance. As with amendments to the articles, this may be desirable to guard against the risk that so many shareholders exercise their dissent rights that the continuance becomes too expensive for the corporation.

Once the shareholders have approved the continuance, the directors must file an application for permission to continue. Under the *CBCA*, there is no prescribed form for this purpose, so a letter to the Director is sufficient.[11] The Director recognizes that the laws of British Columbia, Alberta, Saskatchewan, Manitoba, Ontario, Nova Scotia, New Brunswick, Newfoundland, and Yukon Territory have suitable import provisions. For all other jurisdictions, a legal opinion must be provided that the laws of the importing jurisdiction meet certain requirements specified in section 188(10) of the *CBCA*. As well, a copy of the law of the importing jurisdiction must be filed along with an affidavit that the shareholders and creditors of the corporation will not be adversely affected and that the shareholders have approved the continuance after full disclosure regarding the transaction. Essentially, these requirements are intended to ensure that both the rights and the obligations of the corporation will continue, so that no one is prejudiced by the continuance. The Director will not approve the continuance

---

10   This special voting right does not exist under the *OBCA*, above note 1.

11   Under the *OBCA*, *ibid.*, Form 7 must be used. In Ontario, several other items must be filed to get permission to leave Ontario: filings under the *Corporations Information Act*, R.S.O. 1990, c. C.39, must be up to date; consent must be obtained from the Ontario Corporations Tax Branch; and, if the corporation was offering its securities to the public, a consent must be obtained from the Ontario Securities Commission.

unless he is satisfied that it will not adversely affect shareholders and creditors.[12] A fee of $200 must also be paid.

Once these requirements have been satisfied, the Director issues a document to that effect called a letter of satisfaction. This document is submitted to the importing jurisdiction. If not submitted, it ceases to have effect ninety days after it is issued. Once the importing jurisdiction has given effect to the continuance, the corporation must file a notice of the continuance with the Director. Then the Director issues a certificate of discontinuance (Form 14), dated retroactively to the date of the continuance in the importing jurisdiction. The *CBCA* ceases to apply to the corporation on the date shown in the certificate of discontinuance (*CBCA*, s. 188(9)).[13]

C. AMALGAMATION

1) Introduction

Amalgamation is a procedure provided for under corporate statutes by which two or more corporations (the "amalgamating corporations") are combined into one corporation (the "amalgamated corporation") (*CBCA*, ss. 181–86).[14] Amalgamations may be motivated by a variety of business and tax reasons. One common tax reason is to combine a corporation earning taxable income with one that has tax losses, so as to permit the losses to be deducted against the income.[15] The effect of an amalgamation is that the amalgamated corporation is subject to all the liabilities, owns all the property, and has all the rights of each amalgamating corporation.

As noted in the previous section, to carry out an amalgamation all the amalgamating corporations must be governed by the same corporate law. Where the amalgamating corporations have different share-

---

12 Regarding the criteria that the Director uses to assess whether the shareholders and creditors will be adversely affected and guidelines regarding the procedures, see *Policy of the Director as to "Export" Transactions under the CBCA* (Corporations Directorate, Industry Canada, 30 March 1998).

13 Similar rules are set out in the *OBCA*, above note 1, s. 181; *ABCA*, above note 1, s. 189; and *BCCA*, above note 1, s. 37.

14 Similar rules are set out in the *OBCA*, *ibid.*, s. 174–179; and *ABCA*, *ibid.*, ss. 181–186. The *BCCA*, *ibid.*, has rules relating to amalgamations: ss. 247, 248, 250 & 251.

15 Various requirements under the *Income Tax Act*, R.S.C. 1985 (5th Supp.), c. 1, must be satisified for losses to be deducted in this situation.

holders, a "long-form" amalgamation is required, as discussed below. Where amalgamating corporations are affiliated,[16] a simpler "short-form" amalgamation is permitted in some circumstances. A short-form *vertical* amalgamation may be effected between a corporation and one or more subsidiaries which are either wholly owned by the corporation or where the only shares not held by the corporation are owned by one or more of the other amalgamating subsidiaries. Similarly, a short-form *horizontal* amalgamation may be effected between subsidiaries which are either wholly owned by a parent corporation or where any shares not held by the parent corporation are held by one of the other amalgamating subsidiaries.

2) Long Form

To complete a long-form amalgamation, the amalgamating corporations need to enter into an amalgamation agreement setting out the terms of the amalgamation. Although this agreement takes the form of a contract between the amalgamating corporations, some of the items that must be addressed are stipulated in the statute (*CBCA*, s. 182). The agreement must set out the provisions of the articles of the amalgamated corporation, including all the same elements as the articles of incorporation, as well as the names and addresses of the directors of the amalgamated corporation. In addition, the agreement must set out the basis on which the holders of shares in the amalgamating corporations will receive money or securities in the amalgamated corporation in exchange for their shares. Often, in an amalgamation, the shareholders of each amalgamating corporation receive similar shares of equivalent value in the amalgamated corporation, but shareholders may receive shares with different characteristics or cash in lieu of some or all of their shares. The amalgamation agreement must provide what shares will be issued and what cash, if any, will be paid. Where the amalgamating corporations cannot agree on the values to be attributed to their own shares or those of the other amalgamating corporations, it may be necessary to obtain independent valuations. If valuations cannot be completed by the date contemplated for the amalgamation, adjustments may have to be made after the amalgamation is completed. Consistent with the rule that a corporation may not hold shares in itself,

---

16   Under the *CBCA*, above note 1, corporations are affiliated with each other if one of them is a subsidiary of the other or they are controlled by the same person or corporation (s. 2(2) to (5)).

any shares of one of the amalgamating corporations which are held by another must be cancelled upon the amalgamation (*CBCA*, s. 182(2)).

There is one other matter that must be addressed in the amalgamation agreement. The amalgamating corporations will have to set out some arrangements for the management and operation of the amalgamated corporation, including whether the by-laws of the amalgamated corporations will be those of one of the amalgamating corporations or whether new by-laws will be needed (*CBCA*, s. 182(1)(f) & (g)). In the latter case, the proposed new by-laws must be set out in the agreement.

If the shareholders in the amalgamating corporations are not closely related, then each amalgamating corporation may insist on the other making representations and warranties regarding their assets, liabilities, and business. What these representations and warranties consist of will depend on the nature of the transaction and the businesses being carried on by the amalgamating corporations. For example, an amalgamation is one way of giving effect to the combination of two or more businesses in a form of joint venture. In this case, the parties will want to know what each is bringing into the joint venture through the amalgamating corporation. Each party will make representations in the amalgamation agreement regarding its business and assets.

An amalgamation may also be used to give effect to an acquisition of a business. For example, if Jane owns all the shares of Jane Inc. and Tom owns all the shares of Tom Inc., an amalgamation of Tom Inc. with Jane Inc. is one way that Jane could acquire the business of Tom Inc. In the amalgamation, Jane could be given all the shares in the amalgamated corporation. Tom could receive cash. When this amalgamation is complete, the result will be functionally similar to Jane buying all of Tom's shares in Tom Inc. and amalgamating Tom Inc. and Jane Inc. or Jane Inc. acquiring all the assets of Tom Inc., in the sense that Jane has acquired control of the business of Tom Inc. There are certain tax, liability, and other differences that would have to be taken into account in determining which form of acquisition is desirable. In any such transaction, the representations and warranties that Tom and Jane would make regarding their businesses and assets would be like those one would find in any agreement to purchase a business.

In order to proceed with an amalgamation, the board of each amalgamating corporation must approve the amalgamation on the terms of the amalgamation agreement, then submit the agreement to the shareholders for approval by special resolution (*CBCA*, s. 183(1)). There must be a separate class vote only if the amalgamation agreement contains a provision that, if it was in articles of amendment, would require a class vote under section 176 of the *CBCA* (*CBCA*, s. 183(4)). All shareholders have the right to vote on the resolution to approve the amalgamation, even if they do not otherwise have the right to vote (*CBCA*, s. 183(3)).[17] The notice of the shareholders' meeting must include a copy of the amalgamation agreement or a summary of it (*CBCA*, s. 183(2)(a)).

All shareholders have dissent and appraisal rights if they vote against an amalgamation but the amalgamation is nevertheless approved (*CBCA*, s. 190(1)(c)). The availability of the dissent and appraisal right must be stated in the notice of the meeting (*CBCA*, s. 183(2)(b)).

As discussed below, to complete the amalgamation, articles of amalgamation must be filed with the Director. These contain whatever was provided for in the amalgamation agreement.

3) Short Form

a) Introduction
Amalgamations may be done on a so-called "short-form" basis between certain corporations that are affiliated without the approval of their shareholders. For a short-form amalgamation, approval is required from the directors only and no amalgamation agreement is necessary (*CBCA*, ss. 184(1)(a) & (2)(a)). Short-form amalgamations do not trigger dissent and appraisal rights.

b) Vertical
A vertical short-form amalgamation may be used if the proposed amalgamation is between a corporation (the "parent corporation") and one or more wholly-owned subsidiaries. A vertical short-form amalgamation may also be used if the subsidiaries are not wholly-owned, so long as all the shares of each amalgamating subsidiary are held by either the parent or one of the other amalgamating subsidiaries. In such an amalgamation, the shares of each amalgamating subsidiary are cancelled without any repayment of capital to the shareholders. No securities are issued and no assets are distributed by the amalgamating corporations. Also, the stated capital of the amalgamated corporation remains the same as that of the parent corporation (*CBCA*, s. 184(1)).

The articles of amalgamation of the amalgamated corporation must be the same as the articles of the parent corporation (*CBCA*, s. 184(1)(b)(ii)). So, if the intention of the parties is for the articles to be different from the parent's, a short-form amalgamation alone cannot be used. In such a case, it would be necessary to amend the articles of the

---

17   No such special right is provided for in the *OBCA*, above note 1.

parent corporation before the amalgamation, amend the articles of the amalgamated corporation after the amalgamation, or use a long-form amalgamation. The vertical short-form amalgamation is a simple way to reorganize a corporate group to eliminate unnecessary subsidiaries.

c) Horizontal

A horizontal short-form amalgamation may be used if the proposed amalgamation is between two or more wholly-owned subsidiaries of one corporation. In such an amalgamation, the shares of all but one of the subsidiaries are cancelled without repayment of capital to the shareholders. The stated capital of the shares of the amalgamating subsidiaries whose shares are cancelled must be added to the stated capital of the subsidiary whose shares are not cancelled (*CBCA*, s. 184(2)).

The articles of the amalgamated corporation are the same as the articles of incorporation of the amalgamating subsidiary whose shares are not cancelled (*CBCA*, s. 184(2)(b)(ii)). Accordingly, if different articles are needed, some additional or alternative procedures like those described above in relation to vertical short-form amalgamations will be necessary.

4) Procedure after Approval of Long- and Short-Form Amalgamations

Under the *CBCA*, after approval by the shareholders of a long-form amalgamation or approval by the directors of a short-form amalgamation, articles of amalgamation (*CBCA*, Form 9) must be prepared and filed with the Director, along with the required fee of $200, a Notice of Directors, and a Notice of Registered Office (*CBCA*, s. 185(1)). A name-search report must also be filed if the name of the amalgamated corporation is not the same as the name of one of the amalgamating corporations. The required name-search is identical to that required on incorporation. Name searches filed on incorporation are discussed in Chapter 4.

The articles of amalgamation must have attached to them a statutory declaration by an officer or director of each amalgamating corporation establishing to the satisfaction of the Director that there are reasonable grounds for believing that

- each amalgamating corporation is and the amalgamated corporation will be solvent, and
- the realizable value of the amalgamated corporation's assets will be greater than its liabilities and the stated capital of its shares.

Also, the declarations must address the risk of prejudice to creditors. Each declaration must state either that (i) there are reasonable grounds for believing that no creditor will be prejudiced by the amalgamation or (ii) that adequate notice has been given to all known creditors of the amalgamating corporations and no creditor objects, except on grounds that are frivolous or vexatious (*CBCA*, s. 185(2)). There is no case on what constitutes prejudice. One could argue that the creditors of the financially stronger amalgamating corporation will always be prejudiced as a result of amalgamating with a financially weaker corporation. This, however, would make it impossible to amalgamate under the statute without notice to creditors except in the rare case where all amalgamating corporations are financially equal. It would seem more sensible to adopt the view that no prejudice occurs so long as it is reasonable to believe that all creditors will be paid on the same terms and conditions to which they were entitled prior to the amalgamation.

The *CBCA* spells out what will be considered adequate notice. The statute requires that

- notice be given to each creditor with a claim exceeding $1000;
- notice be published once in a newspaper published or distributed in the place where the corporation has its registered office; and
- each notice names the corporations with which the corporation intends to amalgamate, and indicates that a creditor may object to the amalgamation within thirty days from the date of the notice (*CBCA*, s. 185(3)).[18]

Under the *OBCA*, in order for notice to creditors to be adequate, it must state as well that a creditor has the status of complainant for the purpose of seeking relief from oppression (*OBCA*, s. 178(2)(d)(ii)).

Once these documents are filed, the *CBCA* Director will issue a certificate of amalgamation. The amalgamated corporation will then have to be organized in much the same way as a newly incorporated corporation must be. Post-incorporation organization is discussed in Chapter 4. There are some additional issues to be considered. New by-laws may be required. A certificate recording the amalgamation should be filed in any land registry office where any land held by the corporation is registered. Some agreements provide that certain things must be done on amalgamation, such as giving notice to the other parties. For example, a software licence to a corporation may provide that the licensor must be given notice of an amalgamation. Notices should be

---

18   See, generally, *Canada Business Corporations Act* Amalgamation Kit (Corporations Directorate, Industry Canada, 1 April 2001).

given to governmental authorities, including the Employment Insurance Commission and the Canada Pension Plan. And it will be necessary to file final tax returns for the amalgamating corporations. Under the *Income Tax Act*,[19] a year end is deemed to occur for tax purposes on the date the amalgamation becomes effective.

D. ARRANGEMENTS

An arrangement under the *CBCA* is a procedure used to effect certain fundamental changes to the corporation where it is not practicable to follow the procedure contemplated in the Act for some reason. One example is a reorganization of share capital of two corporations where some share interests in one corporation are exchanged for share interests in another. Another example is the transfer of all the property of a corporation in circumstances where it is impossible to obtain the necessary approval by special resolution, but the transaction is in the interests of the corporation (*CBCA*, s. 192). Complex reorganizations may be effected through arrangements where there would be simply too many corporate steps to complete the reorganization in the manner contemplated in the *CBCA* in a timely way.[20]

The requirement that it be not "practicable" to follow the procedure comtemplated in the Act does not mean that it must be impossible. It is sufficient if following the usual procedure would be inconvenient or less advantageous for the corporation.

To implement an arrangement, it is necessary to obtain court approval. In connection with the approval, the court may make any order it thinks fit, including requiring that the arrangement be approved by shareholders or that shareholders be granted dissent and appraisal rights (*CBCA*, s. 192(4)). Under the *OBCA*, subject to court order, an arrangement must be approved by a special resolution of shareholders (*OBCA*, s. 182). Also, each separate class is entitled to a class vote if the arrangement contains anything that, if it was in the articles of amendment, would require a class vote under section 170 of the *OBCA*.

---

19 R.S.C. 1985 (5th Supp.), c. 1. See Interpretation Bulletin IT-474R, "Amalgamations of Canadian Corporations" (14 March 1986).

20 Under the *OBCA*, above note 1, it is not necessary to show that the other procedures in the Act are not practicable.

Under the *CBCA*, after the requirements of any court order have been satisfied, articles of arrangement (*CBCA*, Form 14.1) must be prepared and filed with the Director, along with the required fee of $200 and a notice of change of registered office and notice of change of directors, if relevant.

Arrangements have become increasingly common but are still relatively rare. This is due, in part, to the extraordinary nature of the circumstances in which an arrangement is needed. As well, in many cases in which an arrangement might otherwise be a useful procedure, the corporation is in financial difficulty. Where a corporation is insolvent, an arrangement is not permitted (*CBCA*, s. 192(2)). For the purposes of an arrangement, a corporation is insolvent when it cannot meet its liabilities as they become due, or the realizable value of its assets is less than the aggregate of its liabilities and stated capital. Then, it is necessary to proceed under the *Bankruptcy and Insolvency Act*[21] or the *Companies' Creditors Arrangement Act*.[22] In some circumstances, arrangements have been permitted where the applicant is solvent but other corporations involved in the arrangement are not.[23]

The test employed by the courts to determine if an arrangement should be approved is whether an intelligent and honest business person acting in her own best interests would approve the plan. In applying this test the courts have looked at various factors, including the level of shareholder approval,[24] compliance with statutory requirements, and whether the arrangement is fair and reasonable.[25] A practice has emerged of getting an opinion from an investment adviser on the fairness of the terms.

Notice to the *CBCA* Director must be given when a corporation makes an application for approval of an arrangement. The Director may appear in court to oppose the proposed arrangement (*CBCA*, s. 192(5)). The Policy of the Director Concerning Arrangements Under Section 192 of the *Canada Business Corporations Act*, sets out guidelines to be followed with respect to a proposed arrangement.[26] While not binding, the Director is unlikely to intervene if the guidelines are satisfied. The Policy recognizes that the arrangement provisions are intended to be facilitative of corporate reorganizations.

---

21 R.S.C. 1985, c. B-3 [*BIA*].
22 R.S.C. 1985, c. C-36.
23 *Savage v. Amoco Acquisition Co.* (1988), 61 Alta. L.R. (2d) 279 (C.A.).
24 *Re Renaissance Energy Ltd.*, [2000] A.J. No. 1030 (QL) (Q.B.).
25 *Re T. Eaton Co.* (1999), 15 C.B.R. (4th) 311 (Ont. Sup. Ct. J.).
26 Corporations Directorate, Industry Canada, 17 April 1998.

E. SALE OF ALL OR SUBSTANTIALLY ALL OF THE CORPORATION'S ASSETS

The "sale, lease or exchange of all or substantially all the property of a corporation other than in the ordinary course of business of the corporation" is a fundamental change affecting shareholders' investments and cannot be completed without the approval of the shareholders by special resolution (*CBCA*, ss. 189(3)–(9)).[27]

The notice of the shareholders' meeting must include a copy or summary of the agreement giving effect to the transaction and a statement that shareholders are entitled to dissent from the resolution approving the transaction and to require the corporation to buy their shares for fair value. At the meeting, the shareholders may authorize the transaction and may fix, or authorize the directors to fix, any of the terms and conditions of the transaction. The shareholders may authorize the directors to abandon the transaction without any further approval of the shareholders.

On a resolution, each share has the right to vote whether or not it otherwise has the right to vote, and any class or series of shares is entitled to a class vote if it is affected differently from another class or series.

F. GOING-PRIVATE TRANSACTIONS

1) Introduction

The *OBCA* has special provisions to deal with certain transactions called "going-private transactions," meaning transactions that result in the extinguishing of a shareholder's interest in an offering corporation (s. 190). Special procedures, including enhanced levels of shareholder approval, must be followed to give effect to such a transaction. Similar, but more detailed, procedures must be observed by all corporations subject to the *Securities Act* (Ontario),[28] as provided in the Ontario Securities Commission Rule 61-501.

Under the *OBCA* scheme, a going-private transaction is defined as any amalgamation, arrangement, amendment of articles, or other transaction carried out under that Act which would cause the interest

---

27   Virtually identical words are set out in the *OBCA*, above note 1, ss. 184(3)–(9) (though shareholders are not entitled to a special vote); and *ABCA*, above note 1, ss. 189(3)–(9). The *BCCA*, above note 1, has a similar provision (s. 126).

28   R.S.C. 1990, c. S.5.

of a holder of a "participating security" to be terminated without the consent of the holder and without the substitution of an interest of equivalent value in another participating security. A participating security usually means one that has a right to participate in earnings that is not fixed or limited in amount, such as common shares that carry a right to receive dividends when declared by the directors, and a right to receive the remaining property of the corporation on dissolution (*OBCA*, s. 190).[29]

Prior to the *2001 Amendments*, the *CBCA* did not deal specifically with going-private transactions. The *2001 Amendments* provide that such transactions involving *CBCA* corporations must meet the requirements of applicable provincial securities laws (*CBCA*, s. 193).[30] The *2001 Amendments* also include a provision dealing with "squeeze-out transactions," which are, essentially, going-private transactions involving non-distributing corporations (*CBCA*, ss. 2(1) (definition of "squeeze-out transaction") & 194). In most cases, these transactions are not subject to provincial securities laws. The *CBCA* establishes a special approval process for such transactions.[31]

Two examples of going-private transactions are set out in figure 10.1.

Figure 10.1 Examples of Going-Private Transactions

Amalgamation Squeeze-Out of Minority Shareholder

Corporation A has one shareholder who holds seventy-five shares and a minority shareholder who holds the remaining twenty-five. The controlling shareholder of Corporation A incorporates Corporation B and transfers to it all shares he owns in Corporation A. He then causes Corporation A to amalgamate with Corporation B. The amalgamation agreement provides that the controlling shareholder gets common shares in the amalgamated corporation, and the minority shareholder gets cash or redeemable shares, which are subsequently redeemed, thus terminating the minority shareholder's interest in Corporation A.

---

29   Going-private transactions are defined in a similar way in the *Canada Business Corporations Regulations, 2001*, SOR/2001-512, s. 3.

30   Prior to the *2001 Amendments* to the *CBCA*, above note 1, S.C. 2001, c. 14, the Director had issued a policy statement to the same effect (Notice of Revised Policy on Going-Private Transactions (9 January 1997)).

31   Under the *CBCA Going Private Transactions Policy*, *ibid.*, no specific approval process was referred to. The Director had indicated simply that, because a minority shareholder may seek relief though the oppression remedy, usually the Director would not take any action in relation to a going-private transaction. The oppression remedy is discussed in Chapter 9.

Consolidation at High Ratio

Assume the facts from the previous example. Instead of an amalgamation, the controlling shareholder approves articles of amendment which consolidate all issued shares on the basis of seventy-five shares for one and provides that any outstanding fractional shares are to be repurchased by the corporation. This arrangement leaves the minority shareholder with only one-third of a share. The corporation buys back the fractional share, and the minority shareholder's interest in the corporation is terminated.

2) Approval Process

In order to implement a going-private transaction under the *OBCA*, it is necessary to obtain an independent valuation of the securities affected indicating the value or a range of values per security (*OBCA*, s. 190(2)). If the transaction contemplates giving securities in exchange for those extinguished, a valuation is required to show whether the value of these securities, combined with any cash to be received by the person whose interest will be extinguished is greater or lesser than that of the affected security (*OBCA*, s. 190(2)(c)).

Each class of affected securities must approve the transaction. The most complex rules governing going-private transactions relate to the level of shareholder approval required to give effect to the transaction (*OBCA*, s. 190(4)). In addition to any other approval that may be required, approval need only be by ordinary resolution of each class of affected securities unless non-cash consideration is being offered to shareholders whose interests are being extinguished or the price being offered is less than the amount of the valuation of the affected securities, in which case a special resolution is required. For the purpose of the shareholder vote, the votes of certain security holders with an interest in the transaction are not counted. The most common type of going-private transaction results in the controlling shareholder owning 100 percent of the issued shares of a corporation and the minority shareholders being bought out for cash. Such a transaction must be approved without counting the votes of the controlling shareholder.[32] Approval will require a resolution to be passed by a majority of the minority shareholders. For this reason, the going-private transaction-approval requirement is often referred to as the "majority of the minority" test, where the minority means the sharehold-

---

32   Another kind of interested party is any person who receives a consideration per security greater than that available to other security holders of the same class.

ers other than the controlling shareholder. Affiliates of the corporation and any shareholder who would receive greater consideration or superior rights compared to other shareholders in the class as a result of the transaction are not entitled to vote either (*OBCA*, s. 190(4)).

Management must send notice of the meeting at which the going-private transaction will be voted on and a management information circular to shareholders not less than forty days before the meeting. The circular must contain the following information:

- a summary of the valuation;
- a statement that the valuation may be inspected at the registered office of the corporation and that a shareholder may obtain a copy;
- a certificate that no material fact relevant to the valuation was not disclosed to the valuer;
- what shareholder approval is required;
- what securities are affected; and
- what votes will not be taken into account for the purposes of the shareholder approval (*OBCA*, s. 190(3)).

The Ontario Securities Commission may grant an exemption from the application of this procedure (*OBCA*, s. 190(6)). If a going-private transaction is approved by shareholders, any dissenting shareholder may exercise a right to have her shares bought by the corporation for fair value (*OBCA*, s. 190(7)). Also, notwithstanding that the corporation may have complied with the approval procedure described above, a shareholder is not precluded from claiming that the transaction is oppressive (*OBCA*, s. 248). Both the right to be bought out, called the dissent and appraisal remedy, and the oppression remedy are described in Chapter 9.

The approval process contemplated for squeeze-out transactions under the *CBCA* is simpler. All such transactions must be approved by a simple majority of each class of shares affected by the transaction voting separately as a class, regardless of whether such shares otherwise have the right to vote. The *CBCA* rules regarding who is entitled to vote are similar to those in the *OBCA* (*CBCA*, s. 194).

This approval is in addition to any other approval required under the Act. Since the definition of squeeze-out transactions limits them to transactions requiring amendment of the articles, approval by a special resolution of all shareholders entitled to vote will be required as well (*CBCA*, s. 2(1)(definition of "squeeze-out transaction")). A shareholder who votes against a squeeze-out transaction is entitled to dissent and have her shares bought for fair value (*CBCA*, s. 190(1)(f)). Nothing prevents a squeezed-out shareholder from seeking relief under the oppression remedy (*CBCA*, s. 241).

F. TERMINATION OF THE CORPORATION'S EXISTENCE

1) Introduction

There are a variety of circumstances in which it may be desirable to terminate the existence of a corporation. Perhaps its business has ceased or been sold, the corporation was being used for a tax-planning purpose that is no longer relevant, or the shareholder/managers can no longer agree on how to carry on business together and have decided to go their separate ways. The *CBCA* and other Canadian corporate statutes provide several methods by which a corporation may be terminated. Which one is most appropriate will depend on whether the corporation has many assets to dispose of, whether the directors will supervise the termination or an outside professional is needed, whether the shareholders all agree that termination is desirable, and various other factors. If the reason termination is necessary is that the corporation is insolvent, however, the corporate law procedures may not be used (*CBCA*, s. 208). In such a case the corporation may be terminated only under the *Bankruptcy and Insolvency Act*[33] or the *Winding Up Act*.[34] In some cases where the corporation is inactive or is in default of some requirement under its governing statute or some other legislation, the corporation's existence may be terminated by the corporate regulators. The following sections outline the termination options available under the *CBCA*.[35]

2) Voluntary Dissolution

Voluntary dissolution is the simplest and most common form of termination. It is handled by corporate management or by another person appointed for that purpose.

If the corporation has never issued any shares, it may be dissolved at any time by its directors (*CBCA*, s. 210(1)). A corporation that has issued shares but has no property and no liabilities may be dissolved by special resolution of the shareholders or, if the corporation has more than one class of shares, by special resolutions of the shareholders of

---

33   Above note 21.

34   R.S.C. 1985, c. W-11.

35   Other corporate statutes also have complex schemes dealing with dissolution. E.g., *OBCA*, above note 1, ss. 191-244; *ABCA*, above note 1, ss. 211-229; and *BCCA*, above note 1, ss. 256-296.

each class, whether they are otherwise entitled to vote or not (*CBCA*, s. 210(2)). If the corporation has assets or liabilities or both, it may be dissolved with the same level of approval so long as the shareholders also authorize the directors to discharge all the liabilities and distribute any remaining assets (*CBCA*, s. 210(3)). In any of these three cases, once the appropriate approval has been obtained and, in the last case, the liabilities of the corporation have been discharged and the assets distributed, articles of dissolution (Form 17) may be sent to the *CBCA* Director, who will issue a certificate of dissolution dissolving the corporation (*CBCA*, s. 210(4)–(6)).

Where the assets and liabilities cannot be dealt with easily, which will often be the case if the corporation carried on any substantial business, the *CBCA* provides a more complex procedure (*CBCA*, s. 211). On the proposal of any director or shareholder entitled to vote at an annual meeting of shareholders, a special meeting of shareholders must be held to consider liquidating the corporation's assets and dissolving the corporation. If liquidation and dissolution is approved by a special resolution or, if the corporation has issued more than one class of shares, a special resolution of the holders of shares of each class, whether or not they are otherwise entitled to vote, the corporation must send a statement of intent to dissolve (Form 19) to the *CBCA* Director. The Director must then issue a certificate of intent to dissolve. From the date of the certificate, the corporation may not carry on business except to the extent necessary to complete the liquidation and dissolution.

After the issuance of the certificate, the corporation must do the following:

- send a notice to each known creditor;
- take reasonable steps to give public notice in each province in which the corporation does business;
- liquidate the business by collecting all the corporation's property, discharging its liabilities, and selling off any assets not to be distributed in kind to the shareholders; and,
- after completing the foregoing, distribute the remaining assets to the shareholders.

Any interested party may apply to have the liquidation supervised by the court (*CBCA*, ss. 211(8) & 215).

Once these steps have been completed, the corporation may prepare and file articles of dissolution with the *CBCA* Director. No fee is required to be filed with the articles of dissolution. On receipt of articles of dissolution, the Director issues a certificate of dissolution.

Although it is not required by the *CBCA*, it is advisable to obtain the consent of the Canada Customs and Revenue Agency to the dissolution. If no consent is obtained, directors will be personally liable for any unpaid corporate tax or any other amount owed to the Canada Customs and Revenue Agency up to the amount distributed to shareholders on dissolution. It is also useful to obtain consents from provincial taxation authorities in provinces where the corporation carried on business.

3) Involuntary Dissolution

a) By Court Order

Any shareholder, the *CBCA* Director, or any other interested person, such as a creditor, may apply to have a corporation liquidated and dissolved on a variety of grounds set out in the *CBCA* (ss. 213 & 214). Such a court-supervised process is sometimes referred to as "winding up" the corporation. The grounds include failing to comply with certain provisions of the Act, the occurrence of an event that entitles a complaining shareholder to demand dissolution in accordance with a unanimous shareholders' agreement, and circumstances in which it is just and equitable to dissolve the corporation. The *CBCA* also expressly provides that a court may order dissolution in the same circumstances as relief for oppression may be granted under section 241. Consistently, liquidation and dissolution may be ordered if oppression is found in an application under the oppression section (*CBCA*, s. 241(3)(l)). These grounds for winding up are discussed in Chapter 9, section H ("Termination of the Corporation: Winding Up and Dissolution").

The court may make any order it thinks fit in connection with the liquidation or the dissolution of a corporation, including appointing a liquidator and directing that notice be given or payments be made to identified parties (*CBCA*, s. 217). Any liquidator appointed by the court has certain statutory powers to assist with the liquidation as well as certain duties, such as giving notice to creditors (*CBCA*, ss. 221 & 222). Once the liquidation process is complete, the liquidator has submitted its final accounts, and the court has approved these accounts, the court must order that articles of dissolution be filed (*CBCA*, s. 223(5)). The liquidator then prepares and files the articles, and the *CBCA* Director issues a certificate of dissolution (*CBCA*, ss. 223(6) & (8)).

b) Dissolution by the Director

Under the *CBCA*, there are three grounds on which the Director can issue a certificate of dissolution on her own initiative and dissolve a corporation:

- the corporation has not carried on business for three years,
- the corporation is in default in filing any document required to be filed under the Act for one year, or
- the corporation has no directors (s. 212).

Before dissolving the corporation, the Director must give at least 120 days' notice to the corporation and include the notice in the bulletin published under her authority (*CBCA*, s. 212(2)).

4) Effect of Dissolution

If, as a result of any of the procedures described above, a certificate of dissolution is issued by the *CBCA* Director, the corporation ceases to exist on the date of the certificate. Nevertheless, legal proceedings existing at the date of dissolution may be continued and new proceedings may be commenced within two years. Each shareholder remains liable for property received on the dissolution (*CBCA*, s. 226). Any property not disposed of at the time of dissolution vests in the Crown.

Under the corporate laws of most Canadian jurisdictions, there is a procedure by which corporations may be revived in some circumstances on the application of any interested person (e.g., *CBCA*, s. 209).[36] Under the *CBCA*, the Director can impose conditions for issuing a certificate of revival and retains a discretion as to whether to issue a certificate or not. Where a corporation is revived, any assets vesting in the Crown on dissolution are returned to it or, if the property has been disposed of, a payment of money equal to the value at the date of dissolution is made (*CBCA*, s. 228(2)). Otherwise, the revived corporation is returned to the legal position it had prior to dissolution, with all the same rights and liabilities as if it had never been dissolved (*CBCA*, s. 209(4)).

H. CHAPTER SUMMARY

In this chapter, we discussed the various ways in which a corporation may change after it is incorporated, and the procedures required to be followed to effect such changes.

It is possible to change any of a corporation's characteristics set out in its articles by articles of amendment approved by the shareholders

---

36   Other corporate statutes also have revival provisions. E.g., *OBCA*, *ibid.*, s. 241(5)–(7); *ABCA*, *ibid.*, ss. 208–210; and *BCCA*, *ibid.*, ss. 252–265. Some of these provisions operate differently from the *CBCA*, above note 1.

by special resolution. By-laws may be made, amended, or repealed by directors or shareholders, though in the former case, for a new by-law or a change to a by-law to continue to be effective, the shareholders must approve it by an ordinary resolution. A corporation's stated capital account must be adjusted in certain circumstances, such as the redemption by the corporation of shares, and may be changed by special resolution in some circumstances. A corporation might want to reduce its stated capital where there has been a decline in the realizable value of its assets, such that it is no longer capable of performing certain acts, like paying dividends.

The laws of most Canadian jurisdictions permit corporations to migrate in and out of the jurisdiction. Such a migration is called a "continuance." We discussed the process by which a corporation governed by the *CBCA* can cease to be so governed by continuing under the laws of another jurisdiction. We also discussed how a corporation governed under the laws of another jurisdiction can become continued and therefore governed under the *CBCA*.

One reason to continue a corporation under the laws of a particular jurisdiction is to merge with another corporation governed under the same jurisdiction through a statutory procedure called "amalgamation." The corporations who are to be the parties to the amalgamation must enter into a detailed amalgamation agreement setting out the terms of the transaction, and the amalgamation must be approved by a special resolution of shareholders. Certain affiliated corporations can use a "short-form" amalgamation, which requires the approval of the directors only and does not require an amalgamation agreement.

We also discussed restructuring transactions that are impracticable to complete in accordance with the requirements of the relevant corporate legislation because there is no other provision for the kind of transaction desired under the corporate statute, or because the particular requirements of the statute are difficult or impossible to meet for some reason. An arrangement may be used to implement such a transaction. The corporation may complete an arrangement with the approval of the court on any terms ordered by the court.

Sometimes, usually at the instigation of a controlling shareholder, corporations will engage in an amalgamation or some other transaction that results in the interest of one or more shareholders being extinguished. Because of the potential for such going-private transactions to be inconsistent with minority shareholders' interests, the *OBCA* imposes strict requirements on them regardless of the form they take. The most significant is that the transaction must be approved by a majority of shareholders other than the controlling shareholder and any shareholders who receive consideration of higher value than other shareholders of the same class. Provincial securities laws impose similar, but more detailed, requirements on corporations subject to their jurisdiction. Under the *CBCA*, compliance with applicable provincial securities rules is sufficient for distributing corporations. For non-distributing corporations, the *CBCA* imposes approval requirements which are similar but more straightforward than those discussed above.

Finally, we discussed the various ways in which a corporation's existence may be terminated. Where a corporation has no assets to sell off and no liabilities to pay, this may be done by a special resolution of shareholders. If the corporation has assets and liabilities, the process will be more complex, possibly involving, in addition to shareholder approval, the appointment of a liquidator, notices to creditors, sale of all the corporation's assets, payment of all its liabilities, and distribution of any remaining assets to the shareholders — sometimes under court supervision. Termination may also occur involuntarily by court order on the application of any interested party, including a creditor, or by the *CBCA* Director. If the corporation has been inactive for three years, has no directors, or is in default of certain filing requirements the Director may terminate the corporation's existence herself.

FURTHER READINGS

BUCKLEY, F.H., M. GILLEN, & R. YALDEN, *Corporations: Principles and Policies*, 3d ed. (Toronto: Emond Montgomery, 1995) c. 11

Canadian Corporations Law Reporter (Toronto: CCH Canadian, 1997) (looseleaf)

GILLEN, M.R., *et al.*, *Corporations and Partnerships: Canada* (Boston: Kluwer, 1994)

GRAY, W.D., *The Annotated Canada Business Corporations Act*, 2d ed. (Toronto: Carswell, 2002)

KINGSTON, R.A., & W. GROVER, *Canada Corporation Manual* (Toronto: Carswell, 1996) (looseleaf)

LAW SOCIETY OF UPPER CANADA, *Bar Admission Course Reference Materials: Business Law* (Toronto: Law Society of Upper Canada, 2003) c. 9

McGuiness, K.P., *The Law and Practice of Canadian Business Corporations* (Toronto: Butterworths, 1999) c. 10 & 11

VanDuzer, J.A., "Shareholder Approval of Asset Sales: The 'All or Substantially All' Threshold" (1991) 4 Can. Corp. L.R. C145

CHAPTER 11

THE PUBLIC CORPORATION

A. INTRODUCTION

Often in this book, we have referred to the special rules that apply only to corporations which offer their shares to the public. We have also discussed the differing ways in which corporate law rules that apply to such corporations operate as compared to smaller, closely held corporations. In this chapter, we expand on some areas of particular relevance when one is dealing with a public corporation, focusing on provincial securities laws.

Securities law is complex and a thorough discussion of securities law is far beyond the scope of this book.[1] Securities legislation in each province seeks to regulate both the issuance of securities by businesses and the marketplace in which securities are traded once securities are issued. We will look briefly at the basic scheme of securities regulation, based on the Ontario legislation. The *CBCA* contains a few provisions that parallel some of the provisions of provincial securities laws. These provisions are enacted under the federal government's jurisdiction over corporate law and apply only to corporations gov-

---

1   For a more comprehensive discussion, see M.R. Gillen, *Securities Regulation in Canada*, 2d ed. (Toronto: Carswell, 1998) [*Gillen*]; J.G. MacIntosh and C.C. Nicholls, *Securities Law*, (Toronto: Irwin Law, 2002) [MacIntosh & Nicholls]; and D. Johnston & K.D. Rockwell, *Canadian Securities Regulation*, 3d ed. (Toronto: Butterworths, 2002).

erned under the *CBCA*.[2] If a *CBCA*-incorporated corporation offers its shares for sale in a province, both the *CBCA* and the provincial securities laws will apply.

Our discussion focuses on four aspects of securities regulation. First, we will discuss the way that professional participants in the securities markets, such as investment advisers and securities dealers, are regulated. Next we will look at the manner in which securities legislation seeks to protect investors by requiring public disclosure regarding the business of issuers of securities and the securities they are offering. We will look also at securities trading by directors, officers, significant shareholders, and other insiders of corporations. Because of the special knowledge such people have about the corporations they are associated with, their trading of securities is closely regulated under provincial securities laws.

Finally, we will consider the regulation of efforts to take over a corporation by acquiring its shares. In closely held corporations, the selling of shares is a negotiated transaction between the buyer and the seller or sellers. Because of the large number of shareholders in a widely held public corporation, such negotiation is not possible. A takeover bid may be made through communication of a "take it or leave it offer" to shareholders. Such takeover bids are regulated under provincial securities laws to ensure that shareholders have a meaningful opportunity to participate in any bid that is made and are fairly treated.[3]

B. SECURITIES REGULATION

1) Introduction

Securities[4] are issued by business organizations to investors in order to raise the money they need to carry on their businesses. The funds contributed by investors in exchange for securities constitute the capital of a business and may be used to buy production equipment, inventory, and other assets needed to start a new business or to expand an existing business.

---

2   See Chapter 3 for a discussion of federal jurisdiction in this regard.

3   Some of the corporate law aspects are discussed in Chapters 7 (effect of market for corporate control) and 8 (requirements of fiduciary duty of directors of target corporations).

4   Securities are shares or debt obligations, like bonds, or other claims on a corporation or other business organization. See the definition in section 1(1) of the Ontario *Securities Act*, R.S.O. 1990, c. S.5 [*OSA*], discussed below in the section "What is a Security?"

Each province has a law concerned with regulating the market-place for the trading of securities, with a view to protecting investors from unfair, improper, and fraudulent practices, ensuring that securities markets function fairly and efficiently so that investors will have confidence in their operation (*OSA*, s. 1.1).

The basic approach taken in securities laws to accomplish these objectives has four main aspects. The first is the regulation of securities market participants. Securities dealers, such as BMO Nesbitt Burns, ScotiaMcleod, and others who make a business of being involved in or advising regarding securities transactions, are subject to registration requirements and are regulated to ensure that they meet high standards of competence and responsibility. Provincial regulators also oversee the activities of certain so-called self-regulating organizations (SROs) that regulate the operations and practice standards of their members, and, in doing so, play an important role in securities regulation (*OSA*, Part VIII). SROs in Ontario include the Investment Dealers Association (IDA), the Mutual Fund Dealers Association (MFDA), and The Toronto Stock Exchange (*OSA*, ss. 1.1 (definition of SRO) & 21.7). Securities dealers and brokers must be members of the IDA (OSC Rule 31-507 SRO Membership — Securities Dealers and Brokers), and mutual fund dealers must be members of the MFDA (OSC Rule 31-506 SRO Membership — Mutual Fund Dealers). Securities regulators have the authority to review directions, decisions, orders, and rulings of SROs. The second aspect of securities regulation is to require businesses offering securities to the public to disclose timely and accurate information about the securities and their business when the securities are first offered for sale, and thereafter on a regular basis, as well as whenever something happens that is likely to affect the value of the securities. The third and fourth aspects are the regulation of insider trading and of takeover bids.

The administration and enforcement of the securities laws of each province is the responsibility of some specialized agency of the government of that province. In Ontario, it is the Ontario Securities Commission (the OSC). The OSC uses a range of enforcement powers to achieve the objectives of securities regulation referred to above. The OSC prosecutes offences under the *OSA*, may make court applications for a declaration that there has been non-compliance with the Act or other orders and, most significantly, has a very wide discretion to make orders itself relating to market place activities where it determines that some action is in the public interest (*OSA*, ss. 122, 127 & 128). Under its public interest jurisdiction the OSC may order that

• a person's registration as a securities market participant be terminated;

- trading cease in the shares of a particular corporation or by a particular person; or
- a person resign as a director or officer of a corporation and that the person be prohibited from becoming a director or officer of a public corporation in Ontario in the future (OSA, s. 127(1)).

Because the nature of behaviour in securities markets is constantly changing, ensuring that they have the right rules to discharge their responsibilities effectively is a significant challenge for securities regulators. In recent years, for example, securities regulators have had to grapple with how to ensure effective corporate governance in response to the disclosure of widespread fraud and malfeasance by some public corporations.[5] To be responsive to changes in the marketplace, securities regulators have augmented provincial legislation and regulations with policy statements that can be more quickly modified to address new conditions. National Policy Statements are issued by the Canadian Securities Administrators (CSA), an unofficial body to which all provincial and territorial regulators belong. These statements represent an effort by securities regulators to coordinate their activities and to promote uniformity and predictablity in securities market regulation across Canada. Individual securities administrators also issue policies indicating the way they interpret the legislation they administer.

In the early 1990s, the authority of the OSC to enforce its policy statements was successfully challenged in the courts.[6] In response, in 1994, the Ontario government gave the OSC power to make binding rules.[7] OSC Rules have the same legal effect as regulations (OSA, s. 143(13). Indeed, regulations themselves can be amended or revoked by an OSC Rule, subject to the approval of the Ontario Minister of Finance. Rule making is subject to certain procedures to ensure that the OSC is accountable. Before they can be enacted, Rules must be published in the OSC Bulletin and interested persons must be given a reasonable opportunity to comment within at least ninety days of publication. As well, the Minister of Finance has a residual power to reject Rules proposed by

---

5   The most prominent example was the alleged fraud at Enron Corp., ultimately resulting in its bankruptcy in December 2001 and the prosecution of some of its senior officers. Some of recent initiatives in this area by the OSC and others are discussed in Chapter 7.

6   *Ainsley Financial Corp. v. Ontario (Securities Commission)* (1994), 21 O.R. 3d 104 (C.A.), aff'g (1993), 14 O.R. (3d) 280 (Gen. Div.).

7   *An Act to Amend the Securities Act*, S.O. 1994, c. 33, implementing the recommendations of a task force struck to consider the issue (Ontario, *Final Report of the Ontario Task Force on Securities Regulation: Responsibility and Responsiveness* (Toronto: Queen's Printer, 1994)).

the OSC (*OSA*, ss. 143.2 & 143.3). Not all provincial regulators have rule-making power.

Recently, the CSA has begun to issue National Instruments which can be adopted by provincial jurisdictions either as rules or regulations having legal effect. National Instruments in effect in some but not all provinces are called Multilateral Instruments. Anyone engaged in securities practice must be familiar with all these sources of law and policy.

2) The Relationship Between Corporate Law and Securities Law

A number of distinctions can be made between corporate laws, discussed in the rest of this book, and securities laws.

- *Scope of Application*: Corporate and securities law differ in their scope of application. The corporate laws of a jurisdiction are concerned only with corporations incorporated in that jurisdiction. The corporate laws of its jurisdiction of incorporation apply to the corporation and its shareholders whether or not the corporation operates in that jurisdiction or the shareholders are resident there. The securities laws of a jurisdiction, by contrast, are concerned with all business organizations, not just corporations, selling or offering to sell securities to investors within that jurisdiction regardless of the jurisdiction under which the business organization was created. Because securities laws are directed to the operation of markets, they are concerned with prospective investors as much as current shareholders, whereas, for the most part, corporate law affects only current shareholders.
- *Enforcement*: Under many provincial securities regimes, securities regulators, such as the OSC, have broad discretionary powers to ensure that participants in the securities markets are acting in the public interest (*OSA* s. 127). In some provinces, especially Ontario, the securities commission actively uses its administrative and quasi-judicial powers to regulate corporate activity, particularly by public corporations. Although corporate statutes provide that the government officials responsible for corporations may play a role in enforcing the law,[8] in practice they rarely do. The enforcement of corporate law rules is generally left to the parties affected.

---

8   See, for example, *Canada Business Corporations Act*, R.S.C. 1985, c. C-44 [*CBCA*], s. 239, which allows the Director appointed to administer the *CBCA* to commence oppression actions. Under the Ontario *Business Corporations Act*, R.S.O. 1990, c. B.5 [*OBCA*], the Ontario Securities Commission is charged with the enforcement of the Act.

• *Substantive Law*: Corporate law addresses a significant number of areas not dealt with in securities laws. The nature of the corporation, the detailed enabling rules for the incorporation and operation of corporations, and the rules regarding the nature of shares are not addressed at all by securities law. Securities laws deal with a number of areas not covered in corporate statutes: the regulation of professional securities-market participants and requiring disclosure regarding the securities that are to be issued. In the interests of investor protection, however, securities laws have evolved to overlap with corporate law in important ways. For example, both securities and corporate law govern the disclosure that must be made to shareholders in connection with meetings, and both are concerned with ensuring that corporate decisions are made in ways that are fair to minority shareholder interests. Because of differences in the scope of application and overlaps in the substantive requirements in corporate and securities laws and provincial differences in securites laws, many corporations, especially those with shareholders in more than one province, are subject to multiple, sometimes different, requirements. Within each province the requirements of that province's corporate and securities laws are consistent. If a corporation is federally incorporated, however, there is the possibility of different, even inconsistent, rules applying. A federal corporation must comply with the *CBCA* and the securities law requirements in each jurisdiction in which its securities holders are resident or in which it offers its securities which relate to, for example, proxy solicitation and the contents of proxy circulars. Similarly, provincially incorporated corporations must comply with the requirements of their jurisdiction of incorporation as well as the securities laws of each jurisdiction in which their securities are held or offered. This complexity has caused corporations and securities market participants to lobby for a single set of requirements or, at least, acceptance of the requirements of one jurisdiction as meeting those of the other jurisdictions.[9]

In June 1996 the federal government and the governments of all provinces except Quebec and British Columbia announced an agreement in principle to establish a national securities regulator to replace regulators in each province.[10] If it had been implemented, this agree-

---

9   Securities regulators are continually engaged in a process of harmonizing their requirements throught the efforts of the Canadian Securities Administrators.

10   B. McKenna & A. Freeman, "Eight Premiers Endorse National Securities Commission: Quebec, B.C. Want No Part of Federal Agency" *The Globe and Mail* (22 June 1996), at B1. Perhaps the first recommendation for a single securities reg-

ment would have greatly simplified compliance with securities requirements in Canada. The proposal was discussed on and off in the succeeding years, but no consensus evolved on moving forward with the proposal.[11] A single national securities regulator was recently strongly endorsed by a Committee charged with reviewing the *OSA*.[12]

In addition to proposals to create a single regulator, a considerable amount of work has been done and continues to be done to reduce the burden of securities regulation. Though the CSA, Canadian securities regulators are continuing to work toward harmonizing provincial and territorial requirements.[13] The CSA has also implemented the mutual reliance review system (MRRS) under which, since 1999, the analysis and actions of one securities regulator are accepted by regulators in other provinces. So a corporation seeking to issue shares across the country can deal with a single lead regulator in one province. Each province retains the right to opt out of MRRS at any time.[14] Other examples of cooperation are the System for Electronic Document Analysis and Retrieval (SEDAR), a web based database of materials filed with securities regulators, and the System for Electronic Disclosure by Insiders (SEDI), a centralized system for insider trade reporting discussed below.[15]

Various initiatives are underway to further reduce the burden of securities regulation by multiple jurisdictions. For example, in October 2002 Finance Minister John Manley appointed Howard Mackay to report on how to ensure that Canada has a "modern and efficient securities regulatory system that inspires investor confidence and supports innovation, competitiveness and growth." In November 2002 Mackay presented his report to the finance minister. The report concluded that something needed to be done to unify the fragmented structure of securities regulation in Canada and recommended the formation of a "Wise Persons" committee to make specific recommendations regarding what should be

---

ulator was made by the Royal Commission on Banking and Finance in 1964 (Ottawa: Queens Printer, 1964).

11   D. Carlson, "Merger of Securities Commissions – Hot Topic," Law Times, 30 April, 2001, at 9.

12   *Five Year Review Committee Final Report: Reviewing the Securities Act (Ontario)* , 2003 (available at www.osc.gov.on.ca) [*Five Year Review Committee Final Report*].

13   See CSA notice 11-303, The Uniform Securities Legislation Project (8 March, 2002).

14   Memorandum of Understanding – Mutual Reliance Review System (1999), 22 O.S.C.B. 6813.

15   See below section C(2)(c) ("Reporting Obligations").

done.[16] At the time of writing, the Minister of Finance had appointed the members of the committee. The British Columbia Securities Commission is promoting its own model of simplified securities regulation.[17] The Ministers of Finance from Ontario, Alberta, British Columbia, and Quebec are also engaged in a review of securities regulation.

3) What Is a Security?

In general, in order for securities legislation to have any application to a transaction, the transaction must involve a "security."[18] In recognition of the wide and continually expanding ways in which businesses raise money, "security" is defined broadly to ensure that the protection for investors provided by securities legislation is not avoided (OSA, s.1(1)). Securities are not restricted to shares and debt obligations, such as bonds, which are traded in public markets at prices reported in the business pages of any newspaper. Securities include, for example, options to purchase shares and units in limited partnerships and mutual funds. In general, a security is any "evidence of title to or interest in the capital, assets, property, profits, earnings or royalties of any person or company."[19] The Ontario Securities Act (OSA) definition then goes on to provide a non-exhaustive list of sixteen examples of securities including an "investment contract," which is a catch-all. An investment contract exists whenever the following criteria are met: an investment of money is made in a common enterprise with an expectation of profit solely from the efforts of others.[20] The "common enterprise" requirement means that the return to the investor is related to the ability and skill of

---

16   Letter to Minister of Finance, John Manley, from Harold Mackay, dated 15 November 2002, available at <http://www.fin.gc.ca/news02/data/02-094_1e.html> (date accessed 27 January 2003).

17   British Columbia Securities Commission Notice BC 2003/12 (available at www.bcsc.bc.ca).

18   The Ontario Securities Commission has asserted a jurisdiction to regulate in some circumstances, even where the regulatory intervention does not relate to securities, if it feels that the public interest requires it. See Re Albino (1991), 14 O.S.C.B. 365, a case involving stock appreciation rights which were not securities. In Committee for Equal Treatment of Asbestos Minority Shareholders v. Ontario Securities Commission, [2001] 2 S.C.R. 132, the Supreme Court of Canada endorsed the view that the public interest ground could be invoked so long as a prejudicial effect on Ontario securities holders could be identified.

19   OSA, above note 4, s. 1(1).

20   Pacific Coast Coin Exchange of Canada v. Ontario (Securities Commission) (1975), 7 O.R. (2d) 395 (Div. Ct.), aff'd (1975), 8 O.R. (2d) 257 (C.A.), aff'd [1978] 2 S.C.R. 112 applying S.E.C. v. W.J. Harvey Co., 328 U.S. 293 (1946).

the person to whom the investor entrusts his funds. A pooling of funds for a common purpose indicates a common enterprise.

Pacific Coast Coin Exchange of Canada v. *Ontario (Securities Commission)*[21] illustrates the breadth of this definition. The issue in that case was whether contracts for the purchase of silver on particular terms should be considered securities. Pacific Coin offered prospective purchasers the following deal. A purchaser could contract to purchase a specific quantity of silver for a particular price. The purchaser paid 35 percent of the purchase price at the time of contracting and was entitled to demand delivery of the silver on forty-eight hours' notice in which case the purchaser would have to pay the balance of the purchase price. Purchasers could also resell the silver at any time to Pacific Coin and receive the difference between the contract price and the going market price at the time of the sale. Most purchasers chose the second alternative. When the contracts were closed out, Pacific Coin received interest on the 65 percent of the purchase price that it effectively financed, a commission, and storage charges. Even though the gains for a purchaser depended to a significant extent on the price of silver set in international commodity markets, it was held that the purchase contract was nevertheless a security. The nature of the business created signficant risk for Pacific Coin. Pacific Coin maintained only a small inventory of silver, not enough to satisfy all purchasers. If the price of silver increased substantially above the prices at which it had agreed to deliver the silver to its purchasers, Pacific Coin might not be able to meet its obligations to them. Pacific Coin engaged in various strategies to manage this risk. The Supreme Court of Canada concluded that, because the returns to the purchasers depended on these managerial strategies working successfully and Pacific Coin remaining solvent, the purchase contracts were investment contracts and therefore fell within the definition of security.

Although the scope of the definition of security is very wide, the effective application of many of the obligations under securities legislation is cut back by the many exemptions from the obligations that are available. These exemptions are discussed below.[22]

4) Regulation of Securities Dealers and Other Professional Participants in the Market

As noted above, one way in which securities law attempts to ensure that securities markets function effectively is to regulate those profes-

---

21 *Ibid.*
22 The definition of security is discussed extensively in MacIntosh & Nicholls, above note 1, at 23–55.

sionals who participate in buying and selling securities. In general terms, professional securities-market participants assist in bringing together those with money to invest and businesses seeking to raise funds. They are regulated by the SROs to which they belong, as well as through requirements in the *OSA* that they be registered. The main categories of securities-market professionals are as follows:

- *Underwriters*: Underwriters are market intermediaries that assist businesses in selling their securities in two main ways. An underwriter may undertake to buy the entire issue of securities from a business seeking to raise money and then try to resell the securities to its clients and others in return for a commission. This is called a "firm commitment underwriting." For example, when a corporation wants to issue shares to the public, it will enter into a contract with an underwriter, such as ScotiaMcleod, who agrees to buy all the shares that a corporation wants to issue and then tries to resell the shares to the public through its network of account executives. Underwriters bear the risk that purchasers for the securities will not be found.[23] Alternatively, the underwriter may commit only to marketing the securities on behalf of the issuer. In this so-called "best efforts underwriting," the underwriter has no responsibility for any securities that it cannot find a buyer for.[24] In either case, the underwriter provides the issuer with advice regarding the pricing of the securities to be offered and the condition of the markets.
- *Brokers*: Brokers are in the business of acting on behalf of others in buying and selling securities. They do not buy or sell shares as principals but only as agents for others. Brokers and dealers are sometimes referred to as traders.
- *Dealers*: Dealers trade in securities for themselves, as principals.
- *Advisers*: Advisers are in the business of advising people regarding the purchase or sale of securities.

Large securities firms like BMO Nesbitt Burns perform all of these functions. There are also smaller, more specialized firms in the market that provide some subset of these services for their clients.

---

23 Even in firm-commitment underwritings, however, it is common for the underwriter to negotiate certain kinds of protections. Typically an underwriting agreement will provide that the underwriter will not be obliged to purchase the securities if it reasonably determines that the conditions in securities markets are such that the securities cannot be sold profitably ("market out clause") or some significant event, like the terrorist attacks of 11 September 2001, has negatively affected the market or the issuer's business ("disaster out clause").

24 The distribution of securities is discussed in detail in Gillen, above note 1, at 20–24.

As noted, the primary method of regulating securities-market participants is to require them to register as a condition of their participation in securities markets (*OSA*, s. 25).[25] Registration is required for all persons who trade in securities or act as an adviser or underwriter of securities (*OSA*, s. 25(1)). To obtain registration, a participant must meet certain standards of integrity, competence, and financial solvency (*OSA Regulation*, ss. 96, 107, OSC Rules 31-502 & 31-505).[26] To ensure continuing compliance with the last requirement, registrants must provide financial reports to the OSC on a regular basis and maintain a minimum level of capital. In addition, registrants must comply with certain requirements for record keeping and most must participate in an investor-compensation fund (*OSA Regulation*, s. 110). In Ontario, the OSC has a broad discretion to suspend, cancel, restrict, and impose terms and conditions on the registration of participants where it determines that it is in the public interest to do so (*OSA*, ss. 25, 26, 127).

Certain categories of people benefit from limited exemptions from these requirements. Lawyers and accountants, for example, do not need to register as advisers so long as any investment advice provided by them is solely incidental to their principal business or occupation (*OSA*, s. 34(b)). The *OSA* also contains exemptions for isolated trades involving people who are not in the securities business, such as banks taking securities which had been pledged as collateral for a loan (*OSA*, s. 35(1)). Further exemptions are available for certain kinds of securities (*OSA*, s. 35(2)). If a debt security is being issued by the federal government, no registration is necessary since there is no risk of default on such a security.[27]

It is also possible to apply to securities regulators for an exemption from registration if the security or the purchaser does not otherwise qualify for an exemption. In Ontario, the OSC has the power to grant an exemption from the registration requirements if to do so would not be prejudicial to the public interest (*OSA*, s. 74).

---

25   *OSA* registration categories are set out in General Regulation made under the *Securities Act*, R.R.O. 1990, Reg. 1015, s. 100 [*OSA Regulation*], and discussed in MacIntosh & Nicholls, above note 1, at 95.

26   For example, in most circumstances, registered dealers and advisers as well as anyone registered as a salesperson, officer or partner of a registered dealer or adviser is obliged to make enquiries to establish the identity and creditworthiness of their client. If there is any reason to doubt regarding the reputation of the client, enquiries must be made to establish the client's good reputation. As well, enquiries must be made to ensure that a proposed purchase or sale of a security for a client is suitable for that client, given the client's investment needs and objectives (OSC Rule 31-505).

27   Trades that are exempt from the prospectus filing requirements discussed below in this chapter have corresponding exemptions from the registration requirements for those engaged in such trades.

5) Regulation of the Distribution of Securities

a) Introduction

A business that is going to sell its securities to investors has several options regarding how to proceed. The simplest way is for the management of the business to negotiate the sale of securities with investors directly. When a new business is being started, the entrepreneur may seek to sell securities to her friends and family as well as investing in the business herself. As the business grows and more capital is required, the entrepreneur may seek out sophisticated investors who are in the business of investing. These may be high net-worth individuals or, in the case of businesses with significant growth potential, venture capitalists. All these kinds of transactions are negotiated directly between the issuer of the securities and the investor.

When a business and its financial needs have reached a certain scale, it may seek to sell its securities directly to a small number of institutional investors, like banks, trust companies, insurance companies, and pension funds. These kinds of investment transactions are often facilitated by a securities broker.[28] The broker may provide advice regarding the appropriate characteristics of the securities, such as the interest rate on bonds, and use its contacts to find institutional investors interested in buying the securities.

Where larger amounts of capital are needed and the issuer[29] decides to sell securities to the general public, the issuer will engage the services of an underwriter, both for advice and for marketing. Issuers rely on the underwriter's expertise in setting the terms of the securities to be issued as well as regarding changes to the management or organization of the issuer that will make the issue more attractive to investors.

All of these types of sales of securities are regulated under securities law. In order to issue securities, an issuer must provide substantial disclosure about both its business and about the securities to be issued in a document called a "prospectus." The purpose of the prospectus requirements is to ensure that people considering investing in securities have enough information to make an informed decision. Securities law also provides a variety of important exemptions from the prospectus requirements for transactions in which the purchaser does not need the protection of such mandatory disclosure, perhaps because she is a

---

28 "Brokers" are discussed in the previous section.

29 An issuer is any business organization that has outstanding issues or proposes to issue securities, including a corporation, a trust, and a limited partnership offering units of the limited partnership (*OSA*, above note 4, s. 1(1)).

sophisticated investor, or the burdens of preparing a prospectus would be too onerous.[30] Such exempt trades are often referred to as "private placements." If no prospectus was filed to qualify the securities to be freely traded at the time they were issued, and the securities were issued under an exemption they can only be resold under another exemption.[31] The securities regime is called a "closed system" because either a prospectus must be filed in relation to the securities of an issuer or a specific exemption must be found in order for the securities to be issued. The basic operation of securities rules relating to the distribution of securities is discussed below.

b) Prospectus Requirements

Under the *OSA*, a prospectus must be prepared and filed in relation to a security before a person can trade in the security if the trade constitutes a "distribution" and no exemption is available (*OSA*, s. 53). Each of the following kinds of trade is a distribution:

- an issue of previously unissued securities;
- a disposition of any securities by a control person (that is, in general, any person who owns more than 20 percent of the voting securities of the issuer); and
- a trade in previously issued securities that were acquired under an exemption from the prospectus requirements (*OSA*, s. 1(1)).

As noted, under a "closed system" either a prospectus must be filed in relation to the securities of the issuer or a specific exemption must be found in order for the securities to be issued. Once the prospectus requirements have been met and securities are issued, they may be resold, subject to certain limitations.[32] If no prospectus had been filed, and the securities were issued under an exemption, they may be resold only pursuant to another exemption. The only exception to the requirement for an exemption is if the issuer of the securities has become subject to the public disclosure obligations under the *OSA* (meaning it has

---

30   The various rationales for exemptions from the prospectus requirements are discussed in the *Five Year Review Committee Final Report*, above note 12.

31   As discussed below, where securities were sold under an exemption, in some circumstances they may become freely tradeable upon compliance with certain resale restrictions.

32   Sales by a control person of securities bought on the market can be made only under a prospectus or pursuant to an exemption (see *OSA*, above note 4, s. 72(7)). Such a sale is called a "secondary offering" and most of the same requirements apply to such an offering as to an initial issuance of securities. The discussion in this chapter deals only with initial issuances of securities. See OSC Rule 45-501, s. 2.8.

become a "reporting issuer"[33]) and specified time periods have expired. These resale restrictions are discussed below in more detail.

To fulfil the prospectus requirements, it is necessary to prepare and file a prospectus with the securities regulators in each provincial and territorial jurisdiction in which it is intended to offer the securities for sale. Each securities regulator must issue a receipt for the prospectus. The prospectus is a long, detailed document that must provide "full, true and plain disclosure of all material facts" about the securities offered (*OSA*, s. 56). In addition to a description of the business of the issuer and the characteristics of the securities to be offered, the prospectus must specifically identify the risks associated with an investment in the securities, include complete audited financial statements, and address various other specific disclosure items (see *OSA Regulation*, ss. 53–62, OSC Rules 41-101, 41-501). The prospectus must include certificates stating that the required level of disclosure has been satisfied from the chief executive officer, the chief financial officer, two directors on behalf of the board, and any person who has acted as a promoter[34] of the issuer (*OSA*, s. 58(1)). The underwriter must also provide a certificate but is required to certify only that the prospectus provides the required level of disclosure to the best of its "knowledge, information and belief" (*OSA*, s. 59(1)).

The preparation of a prospectus is expensive and time-consuming. Lawyers and accountants and, in some cases, other experts must be hired to prepare the prospectus and to ensure that it meets the disclosure requirements. Translation is required if the securities are to be offered in Quebec and printing must be paid for. As well, underwriters must be paid a commission to compensate them for their work in selling the securities[35] and there may be additional fees associated with listing the shares on a stock exchange. Avoiding these costs is the main reason that businesses typically rely on an exemption unless a substantial amount of money is to be raised from the securities issue.

The *OSA* imposes civil liability on the issuing corporation, the underwriter, the directors, and any officer who signed the prospectus

---

33   A "reporting issuer" is defined in s. 1(1) of the *OSA*, *ibid.*, as a business organization that has, among other things, filed a prospectus with respect to any of its securities.

34   A "promoter" is defined in s. 1(1) of the *OSA*, *ibid.*, as someone who "takes the initiative in founding, organizing or substantially reorganizing an issuer."

35   Commissions average between 4 and 7 percent of the issue price of the offering (MacIntosh & Nicholls, above note 1, at 140).

for any misrepresentation in the prospectus (*OSA*, s. 130).[36] As well, experts who gave consent to the use of their opinions in the prospectus are liable for any misrepresentation in their opinion. Where a prospectus contains a misrepresentation, a purchaser may claim rescission[37] or damages against the underwriter who sold her the securities[38] and damages against the other possible defendants. A defence is available for persons, other than the issuer, if they made adequate inquiries such that they had reasonable grounds to believe that there was no misrepresentation (*OSA*, ss. 130(5), 131 & 132). This is referred to as a "due diligence" defence.[39] The issuer can escape liability only if it can show that the investor knew of the misrepresentation at the time of the investment (*OSA*, s. 130(2)). This defence is similarly available to all possible defendants. The risk of liability encourages all those engaged in the process of preparing the prospectus to conduct an intensive investigation to ensure that all material information is properly disclosed.

Once the prospectus is drafted, it is filed with the securities regulators, who issue a receipt for it. At this stage, the prospectus is called a "preliminary prospectus." While it must contain substantially all the information that will be in the final prospectus, it may omit certain information which can be determined only near the time of issue based on the market conditions at that time, such as the price of the securities (*OSA*, s. 54). The securities regulators will review the preliminary prospectus to ensure that the disclosure is adequate. While it used to be that all prospectuses were thoroughly reviewed by regulators, this is no longer the case. Now review is selective. The OSC staff must decide whether to subject the prospectus to a full review, a review limited to certain issues, or no review. Initial public offerings are usually subject to a full review.[40] On the basis of the review, comment letters will be sent

---

36   A selling security holder is subject to this liability where the prospectus relates to shares to be sold by the security holder in what is referred to as a "secondary offering". See above note 32. Misrepresentation is defined as "(a) an untrue statement of a material fact, or (b) an omission to state a material fact that is required to be stated or that is necessary to make a statement not misleading in the light of the circumstances in which it was made" (*OSA*, s. 1(1)).

37   Persons entitled to rescission may return the securities to the issuer and receive their money back.

38   *Kerr v. Danier Leather Inc.* (2001), 13 B.L.R. (3d) 3248 (Ont. S.C.J.) held that rescission was available against an underwriter from whom the securities were bought but not the issuer of the securities, who sold them to the underwriter in a bought deal underwriting.

39   Certain other defences are available (*OSA*, above note 4, s. 130(3)(a)–(e), & (6)). Damage claims are subject to certain limits (*OSA*, s. 130(6), & (7)).

40   (1994) O.S.C.B. 4386.

to the issuer indicating the areas in the preliminary prospectus where more or better disclosure is required. Once the deficiencies have been addressed, which often involves some discussions between the issuer's lawyers and the regulator, a final prospectus is prepared and any missing information is inserted. When the final prospectus has been filed and a receipt has been issued by the regulator, the securities can be sold. As noted above, under the MRRS, a corporation seeking to issue shares across the country must file its prospectus with the securities regulator in each jurisdiction but will deal with a single lead regulator in one province with respect to deficiencies in the preliminary prospectus.

After the preliminary prospectus has been filed, but before the receipt is issued for the final prospectus, the issuer and anyone acting on its behalf, such as the underwriter, can solicit expressions of interest from prospective purchasers based only on the preliminary prospectus.[41] The preliminary prospectus must have a warning printed on it in red ink indicating that it is a preliminary prospectus and the information may not be complete. A copy of the final prospectus must be sent to each purchaser. A purchaser who does not receive a copy of the final prospectus has a right to rescind her agreement to purchase (*OSA*, s. 133). As well, a purchaser has two days to withdraw from any commitment made to purchase securities after receiving the final prospectus (*OSA*, s. 71(2)).

It is important to note that the primary purpose of securities regulators is not to review the terms on which securities are offered to ensure that the price is appropriate or that the terms are otherwise fair. Rather, their main concern is to ensure that the disclosure is adequate, so that investors may make an informed choice. Securities laws in most jurisdictions do, however, provide some scope for regulators to review the merits of the transaction (e.g., *OSA*, s. 61(2)). Despite the role played by securities regulators, it remains the responsibility of the issuer to ensure that full, true, and plain disclosure is made in the prospectus.[42]

c) Exemptions from Prospectus Requirements

Securities laws provide various exemptions from the requirement to provide prospectus disclosure. These exemptions are a critical part of the scheme of securities regulation because, in the absence of the exemptions, the prospectus requirements would make it impractical for small- and medium-sized businesses to raise money other than by bor-

---

41 See OSC Staff Notices 47-701, 47-703.
42 *Peterson v. Ontario (Securities Commission)*, [2001] O.J. No. 1495 (QL) (S.C.J.).

rowing from a financial institution.[43] Any new issuance of shares would be a distribution requiring prospectus disclosure, no matter how few investors were involved or how little capital was being raised. Compliance with the prospectus is too time-consuming and expensive unless a substantial amount of money is to be raised by the issue of securities.

Many of the prospectus exemptions for distributions have the same rationale as the exemptions from registration. So, for example, an exemption is available where securities involve little risk to the investor, such as Canada Savings Bonds (*OSA*, s. 73(1)(a)). An exemption is also available if the purchaser does not need the protection of the securities legislation, perhaps because it is a registered securities dealer, a financial institution, or the government. These sorts of purchasers are "accredited investors" under the *OSA* (s. 72(1)(a), OSC Rule 45-501, s. 1.1, para. (a)–(j)). They are deemed to be sufficiently sophisticated to protect their own interests and do not need the protection of mandatory disclosure obligations. They can negotiate for the level of disclosure that they determine they need. For the same reason, the accredited-investor exemption extends to purchasers who, together with their spouses, beneficially own net financial assets exceeding $1,000,000 or have net individual before tax income of at least $200,000 in each of the last two years or, combined with their spouses, have net before tax income of at least $300,000 (*OSA*, s. 1.1; OSC Rule 45-501, s. 1.1, para. (m), (n)).[44] Accredited investors also include persons in a close relationship with the issuer such as controlling shareholders, affiliated corporations, and relatives of officers and directors. Purchases by officers and directors themselves are exempt under another provision (OSC Rule 45-504).

There is also an exemption from registration in connection with trades in securities of a "closely held issuer,"[45] defined as an issuer meeting the following criteria after the trade:

---

43   Many of the exemptions under the *OSA*, above note 4, were amended substantially in 2001 to conform to the exemptions in British Columbia and Alberta. On the financing problems faced by such businesses, see J.G. MacIntosh, *Legal and Institutional Barriers to Financing Innovative Enterprise in Canada* (Kingston: Queen's University, Policy Studies, 1994).

44   For investors who are not individuals, accredited investor status requires net financial assets of at least $5,000,000 (OSC Rule 45-501(t)).

45   This replaces the exemption for securities of a "private company," meaning a corporation whose articles provide that the number of shareholders shall not exceed fifty, exclusive of employees and former employees, share transfer is restricted and any invitation to the public to subscribe for its securities is prohibited. Private company exemption continues to exist under the laws of some other provinces. See Chapter 4.

- Shares of the issuer are subject to a restriction on transfer, requiring approval of either the board of directors or the shareholders of the issuer;
- Outstanding securities of the issuer are beneficially owned by not more than thirty-five investors, other than
  - accredited investors, and
  - current or former directors, officers, or employees of the issuer or an affiliate of the issuer, or current or former consultants to the issuer provided that they own only securities issued as compensation or under an incentive plan;[46]
- Aggregate proceeds received by the issuer in reliance on this exemption are not more than $3,000,000; and
- No selling or promotional expenses are paid in connection with the trade, except for services performed by a registered securities dealer (OSC Rule 45-501, s. 2.1).[47]

An issuer of securities under this exemption must provide the purchaser with an information statement in prescribed form at least four days before the trade indicating the risk of investing in securities of a small business (OSC Rule 45-501, s. 2.1(2)).

Finally, it is possible to apply to the OSC for an exemption from the prospectus requirements if a trade does not fit within any of the specific exemptions (*OSA*, s. 74).[48]

Even though a prospectus may not be required, an issuer may want to provide information to prospective investors. This is done in a document referred to as an "offering memorandum." There is no obligation to deliver such a memorandum, nor any prescribed content, but, in practice, the level of disclosure is similar to that of a prospectus. If an issuer does provide an offering memorandum and is relying on certain exemptions, including the accredited investor and the closely held issuer exemption, investors have a contractual right of action that entitles them to claim rescision or damages if there is a misrepresentation in the offering memorandum. This right must be described in the offering memorandum (*OSA*, s. 130.1). As a matter of practice, an offering

---

46 The OSC has indicated that the requirement that directors and officers must hold securities as compensation or under an incentive plan is a drafting error (MacIntosh & Nicholls, above note 1, at 189).
47 Certain other criteria apply as well.
48 Other exemptions are discussed in MacIntosh & Nicholls, above note 1, at 179–192.

memorandum is prepared and delivered to prospective investors in most situations where these exemptions are relied upon.[49]

d) Resale Restrictions

If securities are sold under an exemption, the purchaser cannot resell them freely. Under the closed system securities acquired under an exemption may be sold only

- under an exemption,
- by filing a prospectus in relation to the securities, or
- after the issuer has been a "reporting issuer" for a minimum period of time (called the *seasoning period*) and, in some cases, after a specified time period (called a *restricted period*) has expired.

Restrictions on resale are necessary since exactly the same considerations apply to the resale of securities sold under an exemption as to the initial issuance of securities. Purchasers often need the protection of prospectus disclosure. In order for the seasoning and restricted periods to begin running, a corporation must become a "reporting issuer." In most cases, a corporation becomes a reporting issuer by preparing and filing a prospectus. The seasoning period and restricted period requirements are intended to ensure that, before securities are sold, a certain amount of information regarding the issuer and the securities has been publicly available for at least a minimum period of time. In addition to a prospectus, a reporting issuer has obligations to provide continuous and timely disclosure, as discussed in the next section of this chapter.

In general under the resale rules, securities may be resold freely, so long as

- the issuing corporation has been a reporting issuer for at least a seasoning period of either four months, if the issuer is a "qualifying issuer,"[50] or twelve months for all other issuers, and
- a restricted period beginning at the date of the initial exempt trade or the date that the issuer became a reporting issuer, whichever is later, has expired.

Restricted periods are four months for qualifying issuers and twelve months for all other issuers. For securities acquired under some

---

49 An offering memorandum must be delivered when the issuer is relying on the exemption for trades in government securities which give certain tax advantages (OSC Rule 45-501, s. 2.13).

50 Qualifying issuers are defined in OSC Rule 45-102 as reporting issuers that, among other things, have securities listed on certain Canadian or foreign stock exchanges.

exemptions, such as the closely held issuer exemption, there is no restricted period and resales may occur immediately upon the expiry of the seasoning period and so long as certain other conditions are met (*OSA*, s. 72(1), (4), (5), & (6), OSC Rules 45-102 & 45-501).

e) Continuous and Timely Disclosure

Once a corporation has become a reporting issuer, it has certain mandatory "continuous" disclosure obligations which are designed to ensure that buyers and sellers in the market have sufficient up-to-date information to make informed decisions. Continuous disclosure requires issuers to distribute to security holders certain financial information as well as certain information in connection with annual and special meetings of securities holders. These requirements are similar to those imposed under the *CBCA* which were described in Chapter 7.

Within 140 days of the end of each financial year, the corporation must file with the OSC and distribute to securities holders audited financial statements showing the results of that year and comparative information for the previous year (*OSA*, ss. 78 & 79, OSC Rule 52-501, s. 2.1).[51] Usually these statements are included in a more or less glossy annual report in which management describes the firm's business and its expectations for the future. Reporting issuers must also file and distribute to security holders unaudited interim financial statements showing the results for each three-month period within sixty days of the end of the period (*OSA*, ss. 77 & 78; OSC Rule 52-501, s. 2.2).

Reporting issuers exceeding the financial thresholds set out below have additional obligations. They must prepare a "management's discussion and analysis of financial condition and results" (OSC Rule 14-501, Form 44-101 F1 & F2). In this so-called "MD&A," management provides a supplemental explanation of the issuer's financial statements, as well as the issuer's future prospects, a matter not addressed in the financial statements. The MD&A must be filed with the OSC with its annual statements and sent to shareholders. Typically, the MD&A is included in the issuer's annual report. Issuers must file and deliver an updated MD&A with their quarterly financial statements.

Issuers are obliged to comply with these obligations regarding the MD&A only if either of the following financial thresholds is exceeded:

- shareholder's equity (the amount left when liabilities are deducted from assets) or revenue exceeds $10,000,000, or

---

51   These statements must include a balance sheet, income statement, statement of retained earnings, and cash flow statement.

- market capitalization (the value of all outstanding shares determined by market price) exceeds $75,000,000.

If these requirements are met, an issuer must also file an Annual Information Form (AIF) within 140 days of its financial year end (Form 44-101 F1). The information required to be disclosed is similar to that required in a prospectus relating to the issuer.[52]

In addition to these continuous disclosure obligations, securities law imposes "timely" disclosure obligations that arise each time a material change occurs in the affairs of a reporting issuer. In each case, the issuer must issue a press release disclosing the nature and substance of the change and file a material change report with the OSC (*OSA*, s. 75, *OSA Regulation*, s. 3(1)(a), Form 27).

Material changes are those that relate to the business, operations, or capital of the issuer and have a significant effect on the market price or value of the issuer's securities. They include decisions to implement such changes (*OSA*, s. 1(1)). It has proven to be extremely difficult to determine when a material change has occurred in practice. Some clarification is provided by National Policy 51-201. For changes initiated by the issuer, disclosure must be made as soon as a decision is taken to implement the change. This may occur prior to board approval where approval is probable. The National Policy also provides an extensive but not exhaustive list of material changes, including

- various kinds of changes in corporate structure (such as major corporate reorganizations),
- changes in share capital (such as changes in dividend policies),
- changes in financial results,
- changes in business or operations,
- acquisitions and dispositions, and
- changes in credit arrangements.[53]

---

52 Under the *OSA*, a reporting issuer must also send out an information circular to shareholders in connection with shareholder meetings which must include certain prescribed informations (*OSA*, above note 4, ss. 84–86, *OSA Regulation*, above note 25, s. 177). Section 88 of the *OSA* relieves an issuer from these obligations if it complies with substantially similar corporate law rules such as those discussed in Chapter 7.

53 National Policy 51-201 replaces National Policy 40, which somewhat confusingly suggested that issuers had to disclose material facts as well as material changes. This issue is discussed in MacIntosh & Nicholls, above note 1, at 274–275. National Policy 51-201 also deals with selective disclosure to some persons but not the general public and other disclosure practices by issuers.

Failing to comply with the timely disclosure requirements or a misrepresentation in a required disclosure document can result in a penal sanction (*OSA*, s. 122(1)(b) & (c)). The OSC may seek a compliance order from a court, or order that trading in an issuer's shares be ceased (*OSA*, ss. 127(1), (2) & (5), 128(3)).[54] In December 2002 the Ontario legislature passed Bill 198, to amend the continuous disclosure rules to impose civil liability for damages on issuers, directors, certain officers, and others caused by misrepresentations in disclosure and failure to make timely disclosure. At the time of writing, these amendments were not in force.[55]

C. INSIDER TRADING

1) Introduction

As discussed in Chapter 7, market prices for securities are established by the buying and selling activity of people trading their shares in the market. In each case, traders' decisions are based on the information that they have. The continuous and timely disclosure obligations discussed in the preceding section are intended to ensure that that anyone participating in the market has access to basic information regarding issuers of securities. We noted in Chapter 7 that all public information is rapidly impounded into the prices of publicly traded securities.

Not all information is public, however. Some information may be known only to senior management, the directors, or others closely associated with the issuer. If the public disclosure of such "inside information" would have an effect on the price of an issuer's securities, anyone in possession of such information will have an advantage over other traders; they will be able make decisions to buy or sell securities knowing that the price will fall or rise when the information is eventually disclosed. The perceived unfairness of this inequality of information in the market has led to securities laws regulating what is referred to as "insider trading."

At common law, there was no prohibition on insider trading; corporate insiders had no duty to disclose any inside information in their possession to people they bought from or sold to.[56] The genesis of

---

54   Stock exchanges on which securities of a corporation are listed also impose disclosure obligations.

55   *Keeping the Promise for a Strong Economy Act (Budget Measures), 2002*, S.O. 2002, c. 22. Part XXVI.

56   *Percival v. Wright*, [1902] 2 Ch. 421.

statutory regulation of insider trading was the Kimber Report, completed for the Ontario government in 1965.[57] The Report recommended that regulation of trading by insiders was necessary to prevent them from making profits from their inside information and to ensure public confidence in the securities markets.[58] As will be discussed below, there are many commentators who have challenged the way in which insider trading is regulated and even the basis for such regulation, but, before discussing these criticisms of the statutory scheme, the scheme itself is outlined below.

2) The Statutory Scheme

a) Overview

Statutory schemes governing insider trading are extraordinarily complex; the following is only an outline. In most provincial jurisdictions the scheme has the following elements:

- an obligation on insiders to report their trades;
- with respect to insiders and certain others in a special relationship with the issuer,
  - a prohibition on trading with undisclosed information,
  - liability to the issuer for profits made by persons from trading with undisclosed information,
  - liability to other traders in the marketplace for damages suffered as a result of trading with persons with undisclosed information,
  - quasi-criminal liability imposed on persons trading with undisclosed information, including fines and imprisonment, and
  - administrative sanctions on persons trading with undisclosed information, such as being banned from trading securities.

Depending on the jurisdiction, insider trading rules may be found in corporate statutes, in securities statutes, or in both. Securities legislation in each jurisdiction regulates insider trading involving securities of business entities that have distributed securities in that jurisdiction. Trading by insiders of non-offering corporations incorporated in Ontario is dealt with in the *OBCA* (Part X). The *CBCA* formerly provided a complete scheme for the regulation of insider trading which applied only to insiders of corporations incorporated under the *CBCA*

---

57   Ontario, *Report of the Attorney General's Committee on Securities Legislation in Ontario* (Toronto: Queen's Printer, 1965) (Chair: J.R. Kimber) [Kimber Report].

58   *Ibid.*, at para. 2.02.

(Part XI). Since the *2001 Amendments*, the *CBCA* only imposes a prohibition on trading with insider information and only in certain circumstances. These various schemes for the regulation of insider trading often overlap. Insiders in some corporations will be subject to regulation in the jurisdiction of incorporation as well as in the other provinces in which they are doing business. Insiders of federally incorporated corporations will be subject to the *CBCA* as well as provincial rules in each province where they offer securities. The following discussion is based on the Ontario Securities Act and the *CBCA*.

b) Definition of Insider

The first and perhaps the most complex element of the statutory schemes regulating insider trading is the definition of those to whom the scheme applies. The starting point for the application of insider trading rules is the following group of persons, all of whom are defined to be insiders under the *OSA*:

- the corporation issuing the securities,
- directors and senior officers of the corporation,
- directors and senior officers of subsidiary corporations and corporations that are themselves insiders, and
- persons who own more than 10 percent of the shares of the corporation or who exercise control over more than 10 percent of the votes attached to shares of the corporation (*OSA*, s. 1(1)).[59]

The scope of this definition is extremely wide and may result in a heavy burden on businesses. It is possible to obtain an exemption from the reporting obligations, though not from civil liability, as will be discussed below in this section (*OSA*, s. 121(2)).[60]

c) Reporting Obligations

Except in the circumstances described below, insiders are free to buy and sell securities in the corporations with respect to which they are insiders. Insiders must, however, report all trades they make (*OSA*, s. 107). Under the *OSA*, reporting obligations apply only to insiders of reporting issuers.[61] For simplicity, the balance of the discussion of

---

59 See also the *OBCA*, above note 8, s. 138(1). The *OBCA* definition includes all officers and employees of the corporation, all persons retained by the corporation, and all affiliated corporations, not just subsidiaries. As discussed below, the *CBCA*, above note 8, has a broader definition of insider.

60 Certain exemptions are provided for in OSC Rule 55-101.

61 Reporting issuers were discussed in the previous section.

insider trading will refer only to reporting issuers. In Ontario, reports must be filed with the OSC within ten days of the date on which a trade is made by an insider or by which a person became an insider (*OSA*, ss. 107(1) & (2)). The purpose of disclosure is to provide information on the trading activity of insiders. Failure to file when required is an offence (*OSA*, ss. 122(1)–(3)).

Reports must be filed in each jurisdiction in which a reporting issuer has security holders. Securities regulators have agreed on a common form and a system has been created to permit filings to be made electronically once in satisfaction of the requirements of all jurisdictions. This system called the System for Electronic Disclosure by Insiders and known by its acronym SEDI should not only facilitate and encourage the filing of insider trading reports, but also permit the rapid dissemination of information regarding insider trades contributing to the efficiency of the operation of the Canadian capital market.[62] This system became operational in June 2003.

Prior to the *2001 Amendments*, the *CBCA* imposed a separate reporting regime on insiders of *CBCA*-incorporated corporations. This regime has now been repealed.

d) Regulation of Trading with Inside Information

i) *Scope of Application*
The *OSA* prohibits insiders and certain other persons in a special relationship with a reporting issuer from

- trading with information regarding a material change or a material fact that has not been generally disclosed (sometimes referred to as "insider information"), and
- disclosing insider information to someone else (a "tippee") who may profit by trading with such information (*OSA*, s. 76).[63]

Breach of this prohibition can lead to fines, imprisonment, administrative sanctions from the OSC, and civil liability. For the purpose of this prohibition, the definition of who is liable is much broader than for the reporting requirements discussed above. Liability attaches to any person or corporation in a "special relationship" with a reporting issuer.

---

62 Insider reporting obligations are subject to certain exemptions (OSC Rule 55-101 and Companion Policy 55-101).
63 The *OBCA* imposes civil liability in such circumstances in relation to non-offering corporations (*OBCA*, above note 8, s. 138(5)).

Such a special relationship may arise in a wide variety of circumstances, including the following:

- a person is an insider (as defined above), an affiliate, or an associate[64] of
  - the reporting issuer,
  - a person who is proposing to make a takeover bid[65] for the securities of the reporting issuer (a "takeover bidder"), or
  - a person who is proposing to become a party to a reorganization, amalgamation, merger or arrangement, or similar business combination with the reporting issuer or to acquire a substantial amount of its property (a "party to a reorganization");[66]
- a person is engaged in or proposes to engage in any business or professional activity with or on behalf of the reporting issuer, a takeover bidder, or a party to a reorganization, such as a lawyer (a "business associate");
- a person is a director, officer or an employee of the reporting issuer, a takeover bidder, a party to a reorganization, or a business associate;
- a person learned of a material fact or a material change with respect to the reporting issuer while any of the above; and
- a person (defined above as a tippee) who learns of a material fact or a material change with respect to the issuer from an insider or any other person referred to above, including a person who receives such information from a tippee and knows or ought reasonably to know that the other person is a person in a special relationship (*OSA*, ss. 76(5) & 134(7)).

Under the *CBCA*, all these persons are defined as insiders (*CBCA*, s. 131(1), (3) & (3.1), *CBCA Regulations*, ss. 39, 40, 41). The *CBCA* scheme of regulation is more limited than that in the *OSA*, as discussed below.

ii) Prohibition on Trading with Inside Information
Every person in such a special relationship with a reporting issuer, as defined, may not purchase or sell the issuer's securities with knowledge

---

64 "[A]ssociate" is defined in section 1(1) of the *OSA*, above note 4, and includes relatives and entities in which the person has a significant interest; "affiliated companies" is defined in sections 1(2), (3), & (4) of the OSA and includes corporations that control each other and corporations under common control.

65 Takeover bids were discussed in Chapters 7 and 8 and are the subject of the next section in this chapter.

66 These forms of corporate changes were discussed in Chapter 10. A reorganization includes an amalgamation, merger, or similar business arrangement (*OSA*, above note 4, s. 76(5)(a)(ii)).

of a material fact or of a material change concerning the issuer that has not been generally disclosed. Any person in a special relationship who trades with such insider information or gives a tip is guilty of an offence under the *OSA* (ss. 76 & 122). Note that any tippee who trades with the information or passes it along to someone else before it is generally disclosed is also liable.

Liability may be avoided if the person in the special relationship can prove that she reasonably believed that

- the material fact or change had been generally disclosed, or
- the material fact or change was known or ought reasonably to have been known to the seller or purchaser (*OSA*, s. 76(4), *OSA Regulation*, s. 175(5)).

Reasonable mistake of fact is also a defence that has been established in the case law. So, for example, if a person were to trade in shares with certain undisclosed knowledge that was material, in fact, which she reasonably but mistakenly believed would not affect the share price, she would not be liable.[67] A tippee can also avoid liability if she reasonably believed that the person from whom she received the information was not in a special relationship with the issuer (*OSA*, s. 76(5)(e)).

Under the *OSA*, a person who contravenes the prohibition on trading with inside information is liable to imprisonment for two years (*OSA*, s. 122(1)). The violator is also liable to a fine of not less than the profit made or the loss avoided by the person. Fines cannot be more than the greater of three times the profit made or loss avoided and $5,000,000 (*OSA*, s. 122(4)). Enforcement has been relatively rare.[68]

The OSC can also impose administrative sanctions.[69] If the person who breached the insider trading prohibition is a professional securities-market participant, such as an investment dealer or adviser, the OSC can suspend, restrict, or terminate the person's registration (*OSA*, s. 27). The OSC can ban all violators from trading securities in Ontario or prohibit them from acting as a director of a reporting issuer (*OSA*, s. 127).

---

67 See MacIntosh & Nicholls, above note 1, at 242. Certain other defences and exemptions are available under the *OSA Regulation*, above note 25, s. 175.

68 Enforcement does occur, however. In *R. v. Harper*, [2000] O. J. No. 3664 (QL) (Sup. Ct. J.), the accused was sentenced to one year's imprisonment on each of two counts of insider trading and approximately $4 million in fines. On appeal, the prison term was reduced to six months and the fine to $2 million ([2002] O. J. No. 8 (QL) (C.A.)).

69 The OSC's compliance policy is set out in OSC Policy 33-601.

The *CBCA* has a much narrower offence provision. As noted, the *CBCA* defines insider to include, in effect, all persons in a special relationship within the meaning of the *OSA*. Under the federal statute, it is an offence for an insider to "short sell" securities of the corporation in which he is an insider or any of its affiliates. The situation contemplated in the legislation is an insider selling shares that he does not own at one price with the expectation that the price of the shares will go down so that he can satisfy his eventual obligation to deliver the shares to the purchaser by buying cheaper shares after the price falls. Insiders may not "bet against the stock" in this way (*CBCA*, s. 130(1)).[70] The policy objective of this provision is to prevent insiders who are charged with maximizing shareholder value, like directors and officers, or who have a close relationship with such people from profiting from a decline in share price. An insider who contravenes this prohibition is liable for a fine not exceeding the greater of $1,000,000 or three times the profit made by the insider or for a prison term not exceeding six months or both (*CBCA*, s. 130(4)).[71]

iii) Civil Liability
Under both the *OSA* and the *CBCA*, an insider or other person in a special relationship, including a tippee, who trades with insider information is liable to compensate the seller or the purchaser, as the case may be, for damages resulting from the trade (*OSA*, s. 134(1); *CBCA*, s. 131(4)). Liability may be avoided if

---

70 The *CBCA*, above note 8, also prohibits an insider, defined under the *CBCA* to include all those persons in a special relationship with the issuer, from selling a call (an obligation to sell securities at a specified price) or buying a put (a right to buy securities at a specified price) on the securities of the issuer (s. 130(2)). Under the *OSA*, above note 4, the insider trading rules prohibit all persons in a special relationship from engaging in insider trading with respect to a wider variety of derivative instruments (*OSA*, s. 76(6)). These provisions are intended to prevent insiders from benefiting from any insider knowledge, regardless of the form of security.

71 On June 12, 2003, the federal government introduced Bill C-46, *An Act to amend the Criminal Code (capital markets fraud and evidence gathering)* which creates new criminal offences related to insider trading and tipping, supplementing the offences created under the *CBCA* and provincial securities laws. While it is not clear that the new prohibited conduct would not already be covered by other laws, the new law, if passed, represents a single national standard and provides for imprisonment for up to ten years.

- the person in the special relationship can prove that she reasonably believed that the material fact or change had been generally disclosed, or
- the material fact or change was known or ought reasonably to have been known to the seller or purchaser (*OSA*, ss. 134(1); *CBCA*, s. 131(4)).

Similar rules govern the liabililty of an insider or other person in a special relationship who gives a tip. When such a person informs another person of a material fact or change that has not been generally disclosed, she is liable to compensate any person who thereafter sells securities of the reporting issuer to or buys such securities from the tippee. The same defences mentioned above are available (*OSA*, s. 134(2); *CBCA*, s. 131(6)). The tipper may also avoid liability if the information was given in the necessary course of business (*OSA*, s. 134(2)(f) & (g); *CBCA*, s. 131(6)(c)).

In addition to this liability to sellers and purchasers of securities from persons with insider information, an insider or an affiliate or associate of a reporting issuer who trades with insider information or gives a tip is accountable to the corporation for any advantage received as a result of the purchase, sale, or tip, unless the person reasonably believed that the inside information had been generally disclosed or, in the case of tipping, the information was given in the necessary course of business (*OSA*, s. 134(4); *CBCA*, ss. 131(5), (7)). It is not clear whether the advantage is reduced to the extent of any compensation the insider is required to pay under the *OSA* or the *CBCA* to a person with whom the insider, associate, or affiliate dealt. Note that, under the *OSA*, this liability to the corporation does not extend to everyone in a special relationship with the corporation but only to insiders, affiliates, and associates. Under the *CBCA*, liability extends to insiders as defined in that act, who include, in effect, all those in a special relationship within the meaning of the *OSA*.

Where an insider trade or a tip has occurred and no action is being taken by the reporting issuer to seek relief, the OSC or any security holder of the issuer at the time of the trade or the tip may apply to the court for an order directing the OSC or any other person to initiate an action on behalf of the reporting issuer (*OSA*, s. 135(1)). Under the *CBCA*, such an action could be taken in accordance with the procedure for commencing a derivative action discussed in Chapter 9 (*CBCA*, s. 239). For an illustration of how insider trading rules operate, see figure 11.1 below.

Figure 11.1 An Example of Insider Trading Rules in Operation

Assume that the shares of Corporation A are listed on the Toronto Stock Exchange and have been trading at an average price of $10 per share for the last month. The directors have been advised that someone will make a takeover bid for all the shares of a corporation at a price of $15 per share. On obtaining this information, one director buys 1000 shares for $10. The bid is made a few days later and the market price jumps to $15 per share and the director sells his shares for a profit of $5 per share. The director will be accountable to the corporation for the $5 profit per share and liable to those who sold him the 1000 shares for the same amount. If, instead of buying the shares himself, he told his dentist that the takeover bid was imminent and it was the dentist who bought 1000 shares at $10 and sold them for $15, the director would have the same liability to the seller of the shares, but he may have no liability to the corporation because he received no benefit from the tip. The tippee, the dentist, would also be liable to the seller. As well, each would be liable to a fine, imprisonment, and administrative sanctions. Liability of the director and the tippee would be subject to the defences mentioned.

3) Some Observations on Insider Trading Regulation

The approach to the regulation of insider trading recommended by the Kimber Commission and adopted in Canadian legislation has intuitive appeal in that it seeks to prevent insiders from taking advantage of information denied to others in the marketplace. All market players should be on a level playing field. If insider trading were permitted, investors' confidence in the securities markets could be undermined and, to that extent, it would become more difficult for a business to attract investment.[72]

Nevertheless, there is a substantial academic literature claiming various benefits from insider trading and arguing for less onerous regulation.[73] All this literature is based on certain assumptions about the way securities markets work, which may be summarized as follows.

---

72 This concern was expressed in the Kimber Report, above note 57, and reiterated by an OSC panel in a recent insider trading case (*M.C.J.C. Holdings Inc., (Re)*, (2002), 25 O.S.C.B. 1133, at 1143).

73 For the purposes of the discussion in this section, "insider" refers to all those whose behaviour is subject to the insider trading regime (i.e., defined insiders and those in a special relationship with the issuer). For a discussion of this literature, see MacIntosh & Nicholls, above note 1, at 224–231.

Investors buy securities to receive returns in the form of dividends and the increase in the value of the securities over time. The price investors are willing to pay is a function of these returns and the risk associated with these returns — meaning how likely it is that they will be received. An assessment of both these variables is based on all available information about the corporation and its business. An investor's buying and selling decisions are based on whether the price in the market is above or below what she calculates is the value of the shares or, more practically, the price she is prepared to pay. To oversimplify, if her calculated price of a share is more than the market price, she will buy (or hold the share if she already owns it); if it is less than the market price, she will not buy (or sell the share if she already owns it). Transactions in the marketplace between investors, each of whom is making these calculations, are what determine the price in the market. Based on these assumptions, the price should change only when new information causes investors to redo their calculations of risk and return and make different buy, sell, or hold decisions.

Assume, for example, that the shares of a gold mining corporation trade on the Toronto Stock Exchange. Investors will buy the shares up to the point at which, in their calculations, the price represents a fair approximation of the present-value of the future returns on the share, taking into account the risk associated with those returns. The price should stay at this equilibrium level until some new information, good or bad, is disclosed which will cause investors to do their present-value calculations differently. So, if it was disclosed that the corporation had made an enormous gold find, investors would increase their assessment of their expected returns from the shares and be prepared to pay more for the shares. Their purchases would push up the price of the shares. By contrast, if certain claims in which the corporation had expected to find gold turned out not to have any deposits that were commercially feasible to extract, the disclosure of this news would cause investors to reduce the price they would be willing to pay for the shares. Investors holding the shares would try to sell them. These sales, in turn, should cause the price to decline. Needless to say, this process of re-evaluating share price based on new information is going on constantly. It is because of the importance of information to the working of the market that the continuous and timely disclosure obligations described above were imposed.

It is also because of this link between information and securities price that insider trading is regulated. Insiders are not permitted to trade with information that is not disclosed generally, and, if they do, they must pay compensation to those with whom they trade. This regime seeks to ensure that trading in markets is fair, in the sense that no one is making a buying or selling decision without access to information that the other person involved in the transaction has.

The claim that insider trading needs to be regulated in the interests of equal access to information can readily be challenged, however, since it is obvious that not all participants have equal access even to publicly available information. The full-time professional investment adviser will have access to information and, more important, analysis that will not be shared with the investor who reads only the financial pages of the local newspaper. In this context, it is possible to ask why insider information may not be used when other information not universally shared may be.[74] Also, if securities markets function efficiently, there is no obvious reason to suppose that, if insider trading were permitted, prices would not adjust to reflect any risk associated with such trading. Nevertheless, the unfairness of insiders' access to undisclosed information is the main basis on which insider trading regulation is justified.[75]

Insider trading regulation is sometimes defended on the ground that the inside information is the property of the corporation which cannot be appropriated by the insider for her own benefit. This is why insiders must compensate the corporation for any advantage received by them from insider trading or tipping. This position suffers from some obvious conceptual weaknesses. It can justify compensation only to the corporation, not to people who trade with insiders. As well, it would be consistent with this position to permit a corporation to issue and purchase its own shares based on insider information, which, as discussed, is prohibited. The inside information is not a source of value to the corporation.

Even if the regulation of insider trading were justifiable in principle, it is possible to criticize the current scheme of civil liability for insider trading regulation on the basis of the arbitrary way it operates in modern securities markets. The scheme gives a claim only to the person who actually traded with the insider, even though it is com-

---

74 Recently, securities regulators have become concerned about another situation in which there is inequality of access to information. For some time, it had been the practice of large corporations to meet with financial analysts and give them information related to future earnings which was not generally disclosed to the public. Securities regulators in Canada and the U.S. have begun to take steps to address such disclosures (e.g., National Policy 51-201 & Regulation FD (financial disclosure) Securities Exchange Act Release No. 34-43154 (15 August 2000)).

75 See *Green v. Charterhouse Group Canada Ltd.*, [1973] 2 O.R. 677 (H.C.J.), at 741, aff'd (1976), 12 O.R. (2d) 280 (C.A.).

pletely arbitrary whose buy or sell order is matched with the insider's in the marketplace. All sellers and buyers in the marketplace arguably suffer a loss when an insider trades. For example, assume that a shipment of a corporation's gold has been stolen and that the price of the corporation's shares will fall when this information reaches the market. Assume further that the corporation's president sold 1000 shares of the corporation before the information was disclosed to avoid a personal loss. The person who bought the president's shares would suffer a loss when the news was disclosed and the price dropped to $5, but so would anyone else buying after the theft but before its disclosure.[76] The penal and administrative sanctions under securities laws do not suffer from this arbitrariness.

In addition to attacking the conceptual underpinnings and the practical operation of current insider trading regulation, commentators have attributed some benefits to insider trading. The main benefit claimed is that insider trading facilitates the operation of securities markets by tending to push securities prices towards fair prices. Because insiders trade on information not generally available, their buying and selling decisions will be better informed and more accurately reflect the true price of the security. Where the volume of securities traded by insiders is relatively small, the direct effect on supply and demand is correspondingly limited. Yet, insider trading may still have a significant effect on price because the insider trading itself is information that other participants in the market will respond to. So, for example, when the president in the example above sells her shares, this sale signals to other participants in the marketplace that, based on her inside information, she expects share price to fall. It should encourage other traders to sell as well, driving down the price towards where it should be, given the change in the corporation's circumstances, even before the change is disclosed to the public. In this way, it is said that insider trading speeds the transition from one equilibrium price to another.

Accurate pricing of securities encourages investor confidence in the securities markets, facilitating the raising of capital and liquidity in securities markets. The policy implication of this analysis is that insider trading should not give rise to criminal or civil liability. The magnitude of the benefits of insider trading has been questioned, however, on

---

76 While one option might appear to be imposing liability to compensate all such traders, it would be impractical to administer. Under such a regime, an insider trading even one share would thereby potentially be subject to almost unlimited liability.

the basis that, given continuous and timely disclosure requirements, insider information should be disclosed and impounded into share price relatively quickly in any event.

In conclusion, finding the optimal scheme for the regulation of insider trading is problematic. There appear to be benefits and costs associated with insider trading in principle. Greater accuracy in securities pricing must be balanced against a concern about fairness in securities markets if markets are to work most efficiently. Also, even acknowledging that some regulation is desirable, defining the class of persons who should be eligible for compensation is both conceptually and practically difficult.

D. TAKEOVER BIDS

1) Introduction

A "takeover" occurs when control over management of a corporation or another issuer changes. A shareholder may solicit the votes of other shareholders with a view to changing the board of directors and having a new management team put into place. If successful, this change in management would be a takeover. A takeover could also be accomplished through various kinds of consensual transactions, such as an amalgamation of two corporations or an acquisition by one corporation of the assets and business of another.[77] In this section, we will discuss yet another method of taking over a corporation, the "takeover bid." A takeover bid occurs when someone (the *bidder*) makes an offer to some or all shareholders of a public corporation (the *target*) to acquire their shares with the objective of gaining control of the target. The bidder's offer may consist of cash or securities or some combination of both and is made on a "take-it-or-leave-it" basis. There is no negotiation with shareholders. A takeover bid may be "friendly," meaning that it has the support of the management and directors of the target, or "hostile," meaning that it is opposed by management and the directors.

One of the most written about situations involving public corporations is the hostile takeover bid. Some of the reasons for management

---

77 The rules regarding the solicitation of the votes of shareholders are discussed in Chapter 7. Amalgamations are discussed in Chapter 10. Takeovers may also be accomplished by various other forms of transactions, including, in particular, arrangements, which are discussed in Chapter 10.

opposition to takeover bids were discussed in Chapter 7. In that chapter, we also described how the operation of the market for corporate control is one of the non-legal mechanisms that tends to reduce the incentives for directors and officers to engage in behaviour to benefit themselves at the expense of the corporation. Takeover bids and, perhaps more important, the threat of them reduce agency costs in this way. In Chapter 8, we discussed requirements of directors' fiduciary duty when a hostile bid is made.

In this section, we briefly discuss the framework for the regulation of takeover bids and the ways it seeks to ensure that bids are conducted in a manner that is fair to all shareholders. The main ways in which takeover-bid regulation seeks to meet this objective are by imposing requirements for disclosure and minimum time periods for shareholders of target corporations to decide what to do and by seeking to ensure that shareholders are treated equally.[78]

2) The Statutory Framework

a) The Basic Scheme of Takeover-Bid Regulation

Provincial securities laws require disclosure regarding takeover bids, establish a procedure that bids must follow, impose rules to ensure that all security holders are treated equally, and provide exemptions from these obligations. Prior to the *2001 Amendments*, takeover bids were also regulated under the *CBCA*. Where a bid was made for a *CBCA*-incorporated corporation, it had to satisfy the requirements of the *CBCA* and the securities legislation in any province where persons holding securities subject to the bid resided. Because the laws were not the same, this overlap imposed different and sometimes conflicting requirements. With the *2001 Amendments*, the federal government no longer regulates takeover bids. The following discussion describes the scheme of takeover-bid regulation in Ontario under the *OSA*.

Takeover-bid requirements apply only when there is a "takeover bid" as defined in the relevant legislation. Under the *OSA* scheme, a takeover bid occurs when an "offer to acquire" outstanding voting or equity[79] securities of a class is made and the acquisition would result in the bidder ending up with more than 20 percent of the outstanding

---

78   A much more comprehensive discussion of takeover bids and their regulation is provided by MacIntosh & Nicholls, above note 1, at 295–330.

79   An equity security is defined as any security with a residual right to participate in the earnings of the issuer and, on liquidation or dissolution, in its assets (*OSA*, above note 4, s. 89(1)). Common shares are equity securities. See Chapter 6.

securities of that class (*OSA*, s. 89(1)).[80] For a public corporation, the shares of which are widely held, control over 20 percent of the votes may be sufficient for a person to have control in fact.[81] This is because large numbers of other shareholders will not vote their shares. An "offer to acquire" is made not only where the bidder makes an offer to purchase shares but includes a solicitation of an offer and an acceptance of an offer to sell shares (*OSA*, s. 89(1)). Where a person already owns 20 percent or more of the outstanding securities of any class, each additional purchase is a takeover bid. An offer by a corporation to acquire its own securities is also a takeover bid, usually referred to as an "issuer bid."[82]

In order to make a takeover bid, the bidder must prepare a disclosure document called a takeover bid circular and send it to all securities holders to whom the bid is made, the target corporation whose shares are the subject of the bid, and the securities authorities in each jurisdiction in which there are persons holding securities subject to the bid (*OSA*, ss. 98 & 100; *OSA Regulation*, s. 170, Form 32).

Alternatively, the bidder may make a public announcement in a major daily newspaper and send a copy of the announcement to the office of the target, along with a copy of the takeover bid and the takeover bid circular (*OSA*, ss. 98(1), 100(7)). All this material must be filed with the OSC as well. On or before the date of the announcement, the bidder must have requested a list of shareholders from the target. The bidder must then mail the takeover bid and the circular to the shareholders of the target within two days of the bidder receiving a list of securities holders of the target (*OSA*, s. 100(7)).[83] Fixing the date that the bid is made is important because the bid must remain open for acceptance for a minmum number of days from that date, as discussed

---

80 The *OSA*, *ibid.*, contains various exemptions that are discussed in the next section. Also the *OSA* contains a number of provisions designed to ensure that transactions that are takeover bids do not fall outside this definition (e.g., *OSA*, ss. 89(3), 90 & 92).

81 The 20 percent threshold is essentially arbitrary. It was originally adopted following the recommendations in the Kimber Report, above note 57, released in 1965. The definition in the *CBCA*, above note 8, is different (s. 206(1)).

82 The balance of the discussion of takeover bids will refer to bids other than issuer bids. In general terms, the same standards apply to issuer bids. See *OSA*, *ibid.*, ss. 93(3), & 95–98.

83 Under most provincial rules, the target has up to ten days to deliver the list of shareholders. Commencing a bid by public announcement has been permitted in Ontario only since 31 March 2001 (*More Tax Cuts for Jobs, Growth and Prosperity Act*, S.O. 1999, c. 9). This alternative has not yet been frequently used.

below. Since the bidder cannot mail the bid and the circular to all securities holders until provided with a list from the management of the target, commencing the bid by public announcement allows the bidder to get the period during which the bid must remain open running sooner. However the bid is commenced, under the *OSA*, the bidder must make its offer to all holders of securities of the class of securities subject to the bid resident in Ontario (*OSA*, s. 95(1)).

The bidder, its directors, and anyone else who signs the takeover bid circular are civilly liable for any misrepresentation in the circular (*OSA*, s. 131). Civil liability is imposed also on any expert whose opinion is in the circular with respect to any misrepresentation in the opinion. Persons, other than the offeror, have a defence if they can show that on the basis of a reasonable investigation, they had reasonable grounds for believing that there was no misrepresentation.[84] The bidder's only defence is that the security holder of the target knew of the misrepresentation (*OSA*, s. 131(4)). This defence is also available to others.

The directors of the target must send all offeree security holders a director's circular within fifteen days of the bid being made. In their circular, the directors must recommend acceptance or rejection of the bid or state that they make no recommendation. Whatever their recommendation, they must provide their reasons (*OSA*, s. 99; *OSA Regulation*, ss. 172 & 173, Forms 34 & 35). Offeree securities holders have a civil right of action for a misrepresentation in a directors' circular (*OSA*, s. 131).

Once the bid is made, it must remain open for acceptance by the offeree securities holders for at least thirty-five days (*OSA*, s. 95(2)). If a variation is made in the terms of the bid, the bid must remain open for at least ten days from the date of notice of the variation (*OSA*, s. 98(5)). These time periods are to ensure that securities holders have a reasonable opportunity to consider the bid, to allow directors to consider whether to defend against it, and to allow for the emergence of a competing bid. The bidder may not take up and pay for securities deposited under the bid during these minimum periods. Also, where a bid is made for less than all the securities of a particular class, the bidder cannot simply accept the first securities that are tendered. If this were permitted, shareholders might feel stampeded into tendering their securities as soon as possible to ensure that they will be able to sell to the bidder. Where a bid is made for less than all the securities of a class (called a "partial bid") and more securities are tendered than the bidder sought, the bidder must acquire securities on a *pro rata* basis

---

84   Other defences are also available.

from each securities holder who tendered up to the maximum amount sought (*OSA*, s. 95(7)).

Sometimes competing takeover bids will be made for a target corporation. For offeree securities holders, such competition is highly desirable since it typically will result in better terms being offered to them. In order to facilitate the competitive process, securities holders who tender their securities under one bid retain the right to withdraw them and tender them to another bidder any time up to the expiry of the thirty-five day period, or prior to the securities being taken up (*OSA*, ss. 95(4)–(6)). Withdrawal rights also allow securities holders to change their minds. If the terms of the bid are varied by the bidder, the withdrawal rights period does not expire until at least ten days after notice of the variation is delivered to all persons who were sent the takeover bid circular (*OSA*, s. 95(4)). If only cash is being offered to the offerees and the change is either a waiver of a condition imposed by the bidder, such as the tendering of a minimum percentage of securities in a class, or an increase in the consideration being offered, no such increase in the withdrawal rights period is required (*OSA*, ss. 95(4), (5), & 98(6)). The rationale is that neither of these changes can have any prejudicial effect on a shareholder who has deposited securities. Securities tendered under a takeover bid must be taken up by the bidder within ten days of the expiry of the bid and must be paid for within three days thereafter (*OSA*, ss. 95(9) & (10)). If securities are not paid for within the three days, securities holders are entitled to withdraw them (*OSA*, s. 95(4)).

Takeover bid rules are designed to ensure that shareholders are treated equally by bidders, although this objective is not stated explicitly in the *OSA*. There are several concerns in this regard. One concern is that shareholders holding a controlling interest will be offered a better price than other shareholders. A block of shares representing the power to elect directors and determine the outcome of shareholder decisions would normally command a premium over shares that do not have this power. Another concern is that shareholders who have tendered their securities in response to a bid at a particular price should not be prejudiced if the same bidder makes a better offer. To address these concerns, all shareholders must be offered identical consideration (*OSA*, ss. 97(1) & (2)). If the consideration to be paid to shareholders is increased after the bid is made, the increased consideration must be paid to all shareholders, including those who had already tendered their securities before the increase (*OSA*, s. 97(3)).

Also, the bidder's ability to purchase securities on the open market outside the bid is restricted during the period of the bid. If the bidder intends to make such purchases, it must announce its intention to do so in the takeover bid circular and cannot start to do so until at least three days after the commencement of the bid. The purchases must be made through the facilities of a stock exchange and the total number of securities purchased cannot exceed 5 percent of the total of outstanding securities. The bidder must issue a press release at the close of business of the exchange on each day that it makes purchases (*OSA*, s. 94(2), (3), & (4)). Finally, while a bid is open, the bidder cannot tender securities into another bid or otherwise sell securities subject to the bid (*OSA*, s. 94(8)).[85]

b) Exemptions

A variety of transactions that would otherwise be takeover bids are not subject to the requirements described above. The general objective here is to exempt certain transactions where the burden of complying with the complex scheme of takeover bid regulation is likely to exceed the benefits to investors. Some of the exemptions most commonly relied on are described in this section.

Perhaps the most commonly relied on exemption is for the acquisition of securities of a closely held corporation. Securities laws generally exempt a bid to acquire securities where there are fewer than fifty holders of securities of that class, excluding present and former employees of the issuer and its affiliates, the target is not a reporting issuer,[86] and there is no published market for the securities (*OSA*, s. 93(1)(d)).

An exemption is also available for the acquisition of a controlling block of securities from up to five shareholders so long as the offer price does not exceed the market price by more than 15 percent (*OSA*, s. 93(1)(c)). Another important exemption is for what are referred to as "normal course purchases." Any acquisition of securities by a person with 20 percent of the securities of a particular class falls within the definition of takeover bid and so would be subject to the full requirements described above. Since, for small purchases, this would serve no useful purpose, securities laws exempt purchases of up to 5 percent of the securities of a class within any twelve-month period at the market price (*OSA*, s. 93(1)(b)).

---

85 Some other rules designed to ensure that target corporation shareholders are treated equally are discussed in MacIntosh & Nicholls, above note 1, at 318–319.

86 In Ontario, a reporting issuer is a corporation or other form of business organization that has issued its securities to the public under a prospectus or is otherwise an offering corporation under the *OBCA*, above note 8 (*OSA*, above note 4, s. 1(1)).

An exemption is also available where only a relatively small number of holders of securities subject of a bid are in Ontario and the bid is regulated elsewhere. This is referred to as the *de minimus* exemption. A bid is exempt if

- the number of security holders in Ontario is less than fifty;
- the securities held by Ontario security holders constitute less than 2 percent, in the aggregate, of all outstanding securities of the class subject to the bid;
- the bid is made in compliance with the laws of a jurisdiction that is recognized for the purposes of this exemption by the OSC; and
- all material sent by the bidder to security holders of the target class is also sent to security holders in Ontario and filed with the OSC (*OSA*, s. 93(1)(d)).

Bids made through a recognized stock exchange, such as the Toronto Stock Exchange, are exempt, though stock exchanges have their own requirements that are more or less similar to those under securities legislation (*OSA*, s. 93(1)(a); e.g., *Toronto Stock Exchange By-law*, ss. 23.01–23.15).[87] Finally, in all jurisdictions it is possible to make an application to the relevant authority for an exemption for a bid that does not fit within any of the available exemptions (*OSA*, s 104(2)(c)).

c) Compulsory Acquisitions

In some jurisdictions, where a takeover bidder has successfully acquired the overwhelming majority of the shares of the class subject to the bid, the bidder has a right to acquire the remaining securities it does not own. Under the *CBCA* and the *OBCA*, if a bidder has acquired 90 percent of the securities of a class subject to a takeover bid, not counting those held by the bidder when the bid was made, within 120 days of making the bid the bidder is entitled to put the holders of shares not tendered to an election: the shareholders must either transfer their shares to the bidder on the terms of the bid or notify the bidder that they demand to be paid fair value for their shares (*CBCA*, s. 206; *OBCA*, s. 188).[88] "Fair value" is discussed in Chapter 9, section G

---

87 E.g., Part 6 of the *Rules of the Toronto Stock Exchange*, Appendix F to the *Toronto Stock Exchange Company Manual*; Toronto Stock Exchange Policy on Stock Exchange Takeover Bids and Issuer Bids. Various other exemptions are provided for in the *OSA*, *ibid.*, s. 93.

88 Under the *CBCA*, above note 8, these rules only apply if the target is a distributing corporation and the bid is for all of the shares of a class of the target (s. 206). Under the *OBCA*, above note 8, these rules apply only if the target is an offering corporation and the bid is for voting securities (s. 187). The definition of takeover bid is different from that under the *OSA*, *ibid.*

("Corporate Purchase of Shares of Dissenting Shareholders"). It may be more or less than the amount offered by the bidder under the bid. At the request of either the bidder or the shareholder whose shares are being acquired, a court will determine fair value. The rationale for this provision is to permit a bidder who has been substantially successful to cause the target to cease to be a reporting issuer and thus to avoid the burden of the related disclosure obligations where only a small number of public shareholders remain.[89]

In addition, where a bidder has acquired 90 percent of a class of shares, any shareholder who has not tendered her shares is entitled to force the target corporation to acquire her shares. Under the *OBCA*, where the 90 percent threshold has been exceeded, the corporation must send all security holders so entitled a notice informing them of this right and offering a price that the corporation is willing to pay (*OBCA*, s. 189). If the security holder is not satisfied with the price, he may require the corporation to apply to a court to have the fair value of the securities fixed. A new provision added to the *CBCA* by the *2001 Amendments* provides a more limited right. Where a shareholder in a *CBCA* corporation has not received an offer to buy out her shares following a takeover bid meeting the requirements described above for compulsory acquisitions, she may require the bidder to buy her shares at the price offered in the bid (*CBCA*, s. 206.1).

E. CHAPTER SUMMARY

The focus of this chapter is a cluster of subjects of particular concern to corporations whose shares are publicly traded:

- the regulation of professional participants in securities markets;
- the requirements of the closed system under which securities cannot be distributed by an issuer unless the issuer either files a prospectus or relies on an exemption;
- insider trading regulation; and
- takeover-bid regulation.

---

89   Once a bidder acquires all or almost all of the publicly traded shares of a corporation, it may cause the corporation to apply to cease being a reporting issuer (*OSA*, above note 4, s. 83). These transactions are exempted from the going-private transaction rules described in Chapter 10 (OSC Rule 61-501, s. 1.1(3), *OBCA*, *ibid.*, s. 190(1)). The *CBCA*, *ibid.*, says simply that compliance with provincial securities laws is sufficient to carry out a going-private transaction under that act (s. 193).

These subjects are dealt with under securities laws in each provincial and territorial jurisdiction in which an issuer's securities are offered for sale or traded and, in the case of insider trading and takeover bids to a very limited extent, for federally incorporated corporations under the *CBCA*. The general purpose of such regulation is to ensure that participants in the market act honestly and competently and that buyers and sellers have sufficient information to make decisions regarding the purchase and sale of securities with a view to maintaining investors' confidence in the integrity of securities markets.

The general threshold requirement for the application of securities laws in relation to some activity is that the activity involve a "security." This requirement is easily met in most cases because the definition of security is extremely broad and open-ended. It extends far beyond shares of corporations.

One of the ways in which securities laws seek to ensure that securities markets function effectively is to require securities dealers, investment advisers, underwriters, and others who make a business of participating in securities markets to meet certain standards of honesty, competency, and financial solvency. This is done by requiring such persons to register as a condition of their being eligible to participate. Certain exemptions from registration are available. Securities regulators also oversee the activities of certain SROs that regulate the operations and practice standards of their members, such as the TSX and the IDA, and, in doing so, play an important role in securities regulation.

Securities laws also regulate the distribution of securities by requiring that a corporation desiring to issue securities to prepare and distribute to prospective investors a prospectus which contains detailed disclosure about the corporation's business as well as the securities to be issued. Complying with the prospectus requirements is time-consuming and expensive. Civil liability attaches to any misrepresentation in the prospectus, subject to limited defences.

The only way securities may be issued without complying with the prospectus requirements is if the trade qualifies for one of the exemptions provided under securities laws. The general purpose of these exemptions is to waive the prospectus requirements where the nature of the purchaser or the security is such that prospectus disclosure is not required. Securities traded under an exemption can be sold only pursuant to another exemption unless the issuing corporation has become a reporting issuer (usually by filing a prospectus) and certain other requirements, including the expiry of certain time periods, are satisfied.

Once a corporation has issued its securities under a prospectus, it becomes a reporting issuer and must comply with certain continuous and timely disclosure obligations; these include sending financial statements to shareholders on a regular basis and disclosing any material change that may affect the price of the corporation's shares.

An additional aspect of disclosure in relation to reporting issuers is that insiders of the corporation, including directors, senior officers, and significant shareholders, must report their trades in the corporation's securities. If an insider, or anyone in a broadly defined group of people in a special relationship with the corporation, including anyone who receives insider information from any such person (known as a tippee), trades with information that has not been generally disclosed to the public, that person has committed an offence and may be liable to a fine or imprisonment or both. Securities regulators may also impose administrative sanctions.

A person in a special relationship, including a tippee, may be civilly liable to everyone with whom she traded for any loss they incur. In addition to this liability, an insider or an affiliate or associate of a reporting issuer who trades with insider information or gives a tip[90] is accountable to the corporation for any advantage received as a result of the purchase, sale, or tip.

The regulation of insider trading is intended to ensure that people who have information denied to others are not permitted to profit from it by trading in securities markets. The regulation of insider trading has, however, been criticized on several bases. First, inside information is just one example of the information inequalities that characterize securities markets. Second, insiders should be encouraged to trade, since such trading reflects the best information available about a corporation and so leads to more accurate pricing of securities. Third, current liability schemes operate in an arbitrary way because they compensate only the person who actually traded with the insider or the person in a special relationship, while the persons injured by insider trading include anyone who trades before the disclosure of the insider information.

Finally, we discussed the regulation of takeover bids. Securities laws impose detailed requirements for how bids may be conducted to ensure that the bid is fair to all shareholders. Regulation sets minimum standards for disclosure and the length of time the bid must be left open and seeks to ensure that all shareholders be treated in the same way.

---

90   This is a narrower set of persons than all persons in a special relationship. Under the *CBCA, ibid.*, the definition of insider extends, in effect, to all persons in a special relationship within the meaning of the *OSA, ibid.*

FURTHER READINGS

ALBOINI, V.P., *Securities Law and Practice*, 11 vols., (Toronto: Carswell, 1984) (looseleaf)

ANAND, A., D. JOHNSTON, & G. PETERSON, *Securities Regulation: Cases, Notes, and Materials* (Markham: Butterworths, 1999)

ANISMAN, P., J.L. HOWARD, & W. GROVER, *Proposals for a Securities Market Law for Canada*, 2 vols. (Ottawa: Consumer & Corporate Affairs, 1979)

BUCKLEY, F.H., M. GILLEN, & R. YALDEN, *Corporations: Principles and Policies*, 3d ed. (Toronto: Emond Montgomery, 1995), cc. 5, 8, and 11

Five Year Review Committee Final Report: Reviewing the Securities Act (Ontario), 2003 (available at www.osc.gov.on.ca)

GILLEN, M.R., "Sanctions against Insider Trading: A Proposal for Reform" (1991) 70 Can. Bar Rev. 215

GILLEN, M.R., *Securities Regulation in Canada*, 2d ed. (Toronto: Carswell, 1998)

JOHNSTON, D. & K.D. ROCKWELL, *Canadian Securities Regulation*, 3d ed. (Toronto: Butterworths, 2002)

MACINTOSH, J.G. & C.C. NICHOLLS, *Securities Law* (Toronto: Irwin Law, 2002)

MACINTOSH, J.G., *Legal and Institutional Barriers to Financing Innovative Enterprise in Canada* (Kingston: Queen's University, Policy Studies, 1994)

MANNE, H.G., *Insider Trading and the Stock Market* (New York: Free Press, 1966)

ONTARIO, *Report of the Attorney General's Committee on Securities Legislation in Ontario* (Toronto: Queen's Printer, 1965)

ZIEGEL, J.S., *et al.*, *Cases and Materials on Partnerships and Canadian Business Corporations*, 3d ed. (Toronto: Carswell, 1994) at 643–739

CHAPTER 12

CORPORATE SOCIAL
RESPONSIBILITY

A. INTRODUCTION

In Chapter 1 we described a business organization as the intersection or locus of the claims of stakeholders, including owners, managers, creditors, customers, the public, government, tort victims, and others. All these groups are stakeholders because they have a stake in business decision making. In this context, both partnership law and corporate law represent an intervention into the marketplace which, to a greater or lesser extent, pre-empts bargaining between these groups and puts in place a regime that allocates, among the stakeholders, the risks associated with business activities carried on through corporations and partnerships. As we have seen, in many respects the law of corporations favours the interests of shareholders over those of other stakeholders by allocating the risks associated with a business to other stakeholders, as a way of encouraging shareholders to invest in businesses. As discussed in Chapter 8, one of the ways that it does so is through the fiduciary duty, which requires management decision making to be directed to maximizing the value of shareholders' investment in the corporation.

Most of the previous chapters focused on the relationship between management and shareholders in corporations incorporated under the *CBCA* and other Canadian corporate statutes. We discussed the allocation of responsibilities under the *CBCA* among shareholders, directors, and officers, in the legislation and in practice, for both large and small corporations, as well as the mechanisms in place for shareholders to ensure that management is accountable to them.

In this chapter, we revisit and expand on this previous discussion from the perspective of the interests of non-shareholder stakeholders by looking at the extent to which corporate law permits management to take their interests into account in making decisions about the business. This is a critically important issue because of the conflicts between the interests of shareholders and those of other stakeholders which arise in some situations. Once we have sketched out the existing law and the general nature of the interests of non-shareholder stakeholders, we will look at the policy arguments regarding the appropriateness of obliging management to maximize only the value of shareholders' investment in the corporation. At the end of the chapter, we will discuss some possible changes to corporate law rules to enhance management sensitivity to the broader social consequences of their actions while maintaining in place the basic obligation to put shareholders' interests first.

B. THE INTERESTS OF NON-SHAREHOLDER STAKEHOLDERS IN THE CORPORATION[1]

It is a trite observation that corporations have an enormous and multi-dimensional impact on Canadian society. Decisions taken by management on a day-to-day basis affect the profitability of the corporation and the value of shareholder investments as well as the security of the stakes of others with financial claims against the corporation, including employees, creditors, customers and suppliers, and the community in which the corporation operates. The interests of all these stakeholders often coincide: all have a general interest in the financial health of the corporation. In general, maximizing shareholder value will have the effect of increasing the security of any fixed claim that a stakeholder has against the corporation, including those of creditors, employees, suppliers, and customers.[2] Maximizing shareholder value means maximizing the surplus over what is required to pay fixed

---

1   Much of this chapter is a revised and updated version of J.A. VanDuzer, "To Whom Should Corporations Be Responsible? Some Ideas for Improving Corporate Governance" in *Governance in the 21st Century: Transactions of the Royal Society of Canada* (Series VI, Vol. X, 1999) (Toronto: U of T Press, 2000), with permission.

2   R. Romano, "Comment: What is the value of other constituency statutes to shareholders?" (1993) 43 U. of T. L. J. 533 [Romano].

claims. In most situations, maximizing this surplus makes it more likely that fixed claims will be paid.[3] There is also increasing evidence that behaviour by corporations which is sensitive to a broad range of stakeholder interests is often profitable.[4]

Sometimes, however, the value of the shareholders' investment in the business of the corporation may be maximized only at the expense of other stakeholder interests. Shutting down a money-losing plant to preserve corporate profitability is one example. The workers laid off and the community in which they live and work may suffer greatly from such a decision designed to safeguard shareholders' financial interests. Seeking to maximize profits by scrimping on pollution-control technology is another example of management imposing a cost on society for the benefit of shareholders.

We seek to prevent some of these sorts of adverse social effects by direct regulation. It is also commonplace, however, to hear claims that corporations should be responsible for the effects of their actions on society, even in the absence of direct legislative intervention.[5] Assertions by corporate managers confirm that they view themselves as accountable to a wide range of societal interests.[6] Recently, we have witnessed greater concern about the social impact of corporate action on two other fronts. First, both individual and institutional shareholders have shown increasing concern about interests apart from their own financial gain. The growing role of ethical investment funds and the adoption by some

---

3   As discussed below (see note 17 and accompanying text), where the corporation is on the brink of insolvency, high-risk strategies to create some value for shareholders may prejudice fixed-claim holders.

4   C. Forcese, *Owning Up: The Case for Making Corporate Managers More Responsive to Shareholder Values* (Ottawa: Democracy Watch, 1997) [Forcese], at 7; E. Reguly, "Winning in Industry Doesn't Have to Mean Wasting the Environment," *The Globe and Mail*, 5 March 2002. See J. Andriof, S. Waddock, B. Husted, & E. Sutherland Rahman, *Unfolding Stakeholder Thinking: Theory, Responsibility and Engagement* (Sheffield: Greenleaf, 2002), for an extensive study of the link between good corporate citizenship and financial success.

5   J. Richard Findlay, "Too Many Boards Still Fail to Grasp Public's Expectations: Corporations Must Consider Society's Needs As Well As Shareholders," *The Globe and Mail*, 19 January 2000, B13.

6   E.g., more than a decade ago, a vice-president of the Royal Bank was quoted as saying that contrary to the old belief that the shareholder is king, today's corporation is responsible to a wide variety of groups beyond shareholders — customers, employees, suppliers, and even the general public ("Shareholder Activists Out of Line: Banker Says," *The Globe and Mail*, 8 December 1990 at B-3). The increasing currency of such views in the 1990s was described in L. E. Hebb, "Consider the Other Stakeholders," *The Globe and Mail*, 2 July 1996, B2.

institutional investors of investment policies based, in part, on ethical and other non-financial considerations indicates a broadening of the dimensions of societal interests for which management will be held accountable by shareholders.[7] Second, consumer preferences regarding the corporations they buy from are increasingly influenced by their views regarding the sensitivity of corporate management to social issues and the impact of a corporation's conduct on society.[8]

In light of the significant social impact of corporate conduct, the increasing concerns of shareholders and consumers, and the self-professed sense of obligation expressed by some corporate managers, it may seem odd that the general standards of behaviour established for directors and officers in Canadian corporate law do not impose responsibility for social consequences in some way. As discussed in Chapter 8, however, the obligation of management is to serve the interests of the corporation, which, with few exceptions, has been treated as coextensive with the financial interests of shareholders.[9] In 1998, the Canadian Centre for Corporate Ethics and Social Responsibility made a proposal to amend the federal corporate statute to permit but not require management to take into account non-shareholder interests in determining

---

7   The Ontario Municipal Employees Retirement System, one of the largest pension funds in Canada, has a policy of supporting "Proposals Calling for Reasonable Information and Disclosure on Environmental, Employment and Human Rights Issues of Substantial Consequence" (*OMERS Proxy Voting Guidelines*, at 31). There are also an increasing number of market participants applying some form of ethical screen to their investment decisions. See, for example, "Animal-Friendly Mutual Fund Launched," *The National Post*, 12 August 1999 D-2 (reporting on the creation of a new U.S. mutual fund committed to investing only in businesses friendly to animals) and "Calpers Wears a Party or Union Label," *The New York Times*, 13 October 2002, (reporting on the social activist agenda of the board of the California Public Employees Retirement System, a pension fund administering $136 billion (U.S.)).

8   Forcese, above note 4.

9   Daniels has stated that the debate over to whom corporate managers are responsible has largely been won by those who assert that shareholders should be the exclusive beneficiaries (R.J. Daniels, "Must Boards Go Overboard? An Economic Analysis of the Effects of Burgeoning Statutory Liability on the Role of Directors in Corporate Governance" (1994) 24 Can. Bus. L.J. 229 [Daniels, "Boards"], at 231). Chapman describes this as an overstatement (B. Chapman, "Corporate Stakeholders, Choice Procedures and Committees" (1995-6) 26 Can. Bus. L. J. 211). The issue was raised in a discussion paper circulated by Industry Canada in connection with its efforts to reform the *Canada Business Corporations Act* (R.S.C. 1985 c. C-34) [*CBCA*]. No change to the rules regarding the basic responsibilities of directors and officers was made when the *CBCA* was overhauled in 2001.

the best interests of the corporation. No such change in the law regarding management duties was made in the *2001 Amendments* to the *CBCA*.

In contrast to the seeming acceptance in Canada of the view that shareholder interests are entitled to be the exclusive beneficiaries of management responsibilities, there has been a vigorous debate on this issue in other jurisdictions, notably the United States, for a long time.[10] Recently, American scholars using arguments based on economic theory have argued strongly that shareholder-wealth maximization should be the only goal of corporate management.[11] Other scholars, however, have argued for a model of corporate law which permits consideration of the interests of other stakeholders.[12] Corporate statutes in more than half of the American states have been amended expressly to permit management to do so. In European countries, the conception of the corporation has always been a broader one in which the interests of all stakeholders, not just shareholders, are to be considered in corporate decision making.[13]

In the following sections of this chapter, we canvass the arguments in favour of the shareholder-primacy norm, concluding that the case

---

10   The exchange between M. Dodd, in "For Whom Are Corporate Managers Trustees?" (1932) Harvard L. Rev. 1145, and A. Berle, in "For Whom Corporate Managers Are Trustees: A Note" (1932) Harvard. L. Rev. 1365, for example, is often referred to as the starting point of the modern debate.

11   Milton Freedman stated this position with great clarity in "A Friedman Doctrine — The Social Responsibility of a Corporation is to Increase its Profits," *The New York Times*, 13 September 1970 (Magazine), at 32. The following are some of the many examples of recent scholarship: O. Hart, "An Economist's View of Fiduciary Duty" (1993) 43 U. of T. L. J. 299 [Hart]; J. R. Macey "Fiduciary Duties as Residual Claims: Obligations to Non-shareholder Stakeholder Constituencies from a Theory of the Firm Perspective" (1999) 84 Cornell L. Rev. 1265; J.R. Macey & G. P. Miller, "Corporate Stakeholders: A Contractual Perspective" (1993) 43 U. of T. L. J. 410 [Macey & Miller]; R. Romano, "Metapolitics and Corporate Law Reform" (1984) 36 Stan. L. Rev. 923 at 955.

12   J. W. Singer, "Jobs and Justice: Rethinking the Stakeholder Debate" (1993) 43 U. of T. L. J. 475. Some scholars have made this argument using the same tools of micro-economic analysis used by advocates of shareholder primacy. See, for example, W.S.W. Leung, "The Inadequacy of Shareholder Primacy: A Proposed Corporate Regime that Recognizes Non-Shareholder Interests" (1997) 30 Columbia J. of L. and Social Problems 587 [Leung].

13   In some cases, this commitment is reflected in the structural requirements of corporate law, such as the requirement for labour representation on supervisory boards in Germany (see L.A. Cunningham, "Commonalities and Prescriptions in the Vertical Dimension of Global Corporate Governance" (1999) 84 Cornell L. Rev. 1133, at 1139–1142). Others describe a broad conception of the stakeholders to whom management is responsible as part of the ethical/cultural milieu (P. Nobel, "Social Responsibility of Corporations" (1999) 84 Cornell L. Rev. 1255, at 1260).

for making shareholders the exclusive beneficiary of managements' legal responsibilities is not convincing. Despite this conclusion, however, imposing a requirement on management to base its decisions on its own assessment of the relative importance of the interests of all stakeholders may not be desirable. Requiring management to be responsible to all stakeholders would impose an impossible standard which managers are ill-equipped to meet and could result in their being accountable to no one but themselves. In any case, the existing shareholder-primacy norm in Canada as elsewhere already permits a high degree of management discretion, allowing managers to take other stakeholder interests into account though not permitting them to abandon their primary goal of promoting shareholder interests. At the end of the chapter, some possible changes to corporate law rules designed to promote management accountability are considered.

C. THE LAW AND ECONOMICS OF CORPORATE SOCIAL RESPONSIBILITY

1) Introduction

As discussed in Chapter 3, the purpose of corporate law is to facilitate economic activity by encouraging entrepreneurs to engage in business. Shareholders invest capital, which is used by managers in their businesses to generate profits for their benefit. In carrying on the business, the corporation becomes the focus of a web of relationships with other stakeholders. Employees work in the business, creditors lend money or supply other inputs for the business activity, and the corporation has important relationships with customers, government, and the community. Through these relationships, social benefits in terms of employment, production and consumption of products, payment of taxes, and so on result from the economic activities of corporations.

Several analytical models may be applied to the problem of ascertaining to whom corporations should be responsible within this web of relationships but the most powerful analytical approach and the one that has come to dominate corporate law discourse is microeconomics.[14]

---

14 Bainbridge asserts that the debate over the proper analytical approach is over, noting that even the critics of many of the prescriptions of law and economics analysis use the same tools in their critique (S. M. Bainbridge, "Community and Statism: A Conservative Contractarian Critique of Progressive Corporate Law Scholarship" (1997) 82 Cornell L. Rev. 856, at 859–860).

Under this approach, the corporation is considered a "nexus of contracts" and the rights and obligations of each stakeholder are determined by their voluntary bargains with the others. Since rational people will not enter into bargains unless each party is made better off as a result, in general parties' bargains should be enforced. The state should not intervene to impose rules except where there are systematic impediments to the bargaining process in the form of high transactions costs or information asymmetries between the parties.[15]

2) Arguments in Favour of Shareholders Being the Exclusive Beneficiaries of Management Duties

At first glance, in this conception of the corporation as a nexus of contracts, the position of shareholders appears to be no different from that of other stakeholders. The nexus of contracts model of the corporation does not acknowledge the rhetorically powerful depiction of shareholders as the owners of the corporation, which has often been used to justify giving shareholders special protection. From a nexus-of-contracts perspective, however, what distinguishes shareholder interests from other interests is that the value of their claims is determined uniquely by the residual value of the corporation after all other claims are satisfied. Shareholders invest in the corporation in return for shares, which represent a claim to receive what is left after all claims of other stakeholders have been paid. While the claims of most other stakeholders, such as employees and creditors, are fixed, the shareholder's claim varies with the success of the business in generating profits in excess of the fixed claims of other stakeholders.[16]

This residual character of shareholder claims suggests that managers should be exclusively committed to maximizing shareholder welfare for two main reasons. First, only shareholders have a positive interest in maximizing the success of the firm. Other stakeholders are indifferent to the value of the firm so long as sufficient profits are generated to satisfy their fixed claims. Second, shareholders cannot easily negotiate protection for their interests because of the positive nature of their claims. It is not possible for shareholders to specify fully what management must do for the business to be successful, whereas it is

---

15   H.N. Butler & F.S. McChesney, "Why they give at the office: Shareholder Welfare and Corporate Philanthropy in the Contractual Theory of the Firm" (1999) 84 Cornell L. Rev. 1195, at 1197 *et seq.*

16   The residual nature of shareholders' claims against the corporation is discussed in Chapters 3 and 6.

relatively easier for fixed-claim stakeholders to negotiate restrictions on management which prevent management from engaging in specific conduct that will jeopardize the payment of their fixed claims, such as prohibiting management from stripping assets out of the firm to the prejudice of creditors or reducing employee benefits.

However, this analysis may be criticized on several grounds. First, distinguishing shareholder claims from those of other stakeholders on the basis that only shareholders have a positive interest in how well the corporation is managed is tenuous, at least in some circumstances. Second, all stakeholders, not just shareholders, face impediments to bargaining which may prevent them from negotiating adequate protection for their interests. Finally, shareholders have the benefit of additional legal and market mechanisms to help ensure that management is responsive to their interests. Each critique is discussed in turn in the next section.

3) Arguments Against Shareholders Being the Exclusive Beneficiaries of Management Duties

a) Other Stakeholders have a Positive Stake in Corporate Performance

There are some situations in which other stakeholders have what amounts to a positive stake in management decision making, just like shareholders. Consider the following examples. Management that is responsive only to shareholder interests may be encouraged to manage the corporation in a way that reduces the value of the firm to the prejudice of all fixed claimants, including employees and creditors, when the firm is on the verge of insolvency. In this situation, shareholders have nothing to lose since the value of their residual claim is nil. Managers may seek to obtain some return for shareholders by investing the corporation's resources in highly risky projects, which provide the possibility of sufficiently high returns to generate some benefit to shareholders even if the likelihood that such returns will be received is remote. If, as is expected, the return is not realized, shareholders are no worse off. The holders of fixed claims, however, will be prejudiced by such a strategy.[17] Consequently, fixed-claim holders, just like share-

---

17 This well-known example is discussed in Hart, above note 11, at 305. Macey & Miller, above note 11, also refer to this situation and argue that the U.S. courts have acknowledged the requirement for creditor interests to be taken into account in complying with the fiduciary duty in such circumstances (at 413). Jacob Ziegel suggests that, unlike other commonwealth jurisdictions, the duty of

holders, have a significant stake in day-to-day management decisions of the firm, at least in this situation.

Employees may be considered to have a positive interest in the management of the firm in another sense. Employees make substantial firm-specific investments in their corporate employers. Their employer is the source of some, if not all, of their income and, through their work, they invest in the development of their knowledge and skills.[18] This kind of investment may not be easily recoverable if employees lose their jobs. Their knowledge and skills may not be transferable and the job market may not provide ready alternative employment. Consequently, employees have a substantial interest in particular management decisions that are likely to have an impact on the security of their jobs. These include not only decisions that are directly related to employment, such as decisions about layoffs, but also a wide range of management decisions which will affect job security by virtue of their impact on the success of the firm. In this sense, employees have a strong interest in the firm being managed effectively. This interest may not be identical to shareholders', but it has the same essential character: it is a positive interest in how well the firm is managed.

Finally, the community in which a corporation operates has no fixed claim against the corporation. It does, however, have a positive interest in good management by the corporation to the extent that such management leads to secure and expanding local employment and tax revenues, provides effective environmental stewardship, and so on.

b) Non-Shareholder Stakeholders Face Impediments to Bargaining to Protect Their Interests

A second problem with the argument for shareholder primacy is that non-shareholder stakeholders face inherent impediments to contractual bargaining, just like shareholders. The nature and effect of such

---

corporate directors in Canada has not evolved to take into account creditor interests, though the remedy for relief from oppression under Canadian corporate statutes modelled on the *CBCA*, above note 9 s. 241, is increasingly being used to protect creditors leading to a similar functional result (J.S. Ziegel, "Creditors as Corporate Stakeholders: The Quiet Revolution — An Anglo Canadian Perspective" (1993) 43 U. of T. L. J. 511). The oppression remedy is discussed in Chapter 9. Some recent Canadian cases discussed in Chapter 8 have suggested that directors and officers may have a duty to creditors of the corporation on the brink of insolvency, though there is no consensus in this regard.

18 Employees may also have other forms of investment in their employers — where, for example, they receive some of their compensation in the form of securities of their employer.

impediments varies depending on the stakeholder group being considered. Nevertheless, the important general point is that the case for the primacy of shareholder-wealth maximization depends upon there being few impediments, which is manifestly not the case in the real world. Real-world bargaining is characterized by gaps in information that make it impossible for stakeholders to reach accurate assessments of the full implications of their bargain. There are also transaction costs, which preclude negotiating agreements that address all the risks to which stakeholders are subject.[19]

Financial creditors, like banks, would seem to face the fewest impediments to bargaining. Creditors often have large investments in corporations, giving them significant incentives to collect and analyse information regarding their corporate customers and spend time negotiating to protect their investments. Typically, financial creditors negotiate detailed contracts designed to protect them against management defaults, contracts that often contain strict controls on certain kinds of activities backed up by rigorous reporting requirements. For some debt instruments, like bonds issued by public corporations, with respect to which creditors cannot individually negotiate for protective provisions, prices are determined in markets and are rated by credit-rating agencies such that the likelihood that creditors will unknowingly end up bearing uncompensated risk is relatively small. Finally, any concern about creditors' ability to protect their interests by contract will be mit-

---

19   Leung, above note 12, at 594–595. Some have suggested that the nexus-of-contracts framework may be reimagined as including not just explicit contracts, but also implicit bargains. From this perspective, the nature of the relationship between stakeholders and the corporation is not simply what they have reflected in their express contracts, but also what is contained in their implicit understandings and expectations regarding the behaviour of the other party. For example, employees may have an implicit understanding that they will accept lower wages in the present in exchange for a promise by management that they will receive additional compensation in the future if they remain with the firm. In theory, implicit contracts provide a basis for arguing in favour of a limited set of commitments of management to non-shareholder stakeholders. See J. Coffee, "Shareholders versus Managers: The Strain in the Corporate Web" (1986) 85 Mich. L. Rev. 1; "The Uncertain Case for Takeover Reform: An Essay on Stockholders, Stakeholders and Bust-Ups" (1988) Wisconsin L. Rev. 435; "Unstable Coalitions: Corporate Governance as a Multiplayer Game" (1990) 78 Georgetown L. J. 1495. This position is criticized in R. J. Daniels, "Stakeholders and Takeovers: Can Contractarianism be Compassionate?" (1993) 43 U. of T. L. J. 315 [Daniels, *Contractarianism*] at 331–340. Daniels argues that it is extremely difficult to be confident regarding the operational content to be given to such implicit contracts and to determine to what extent they should be enforced.

igated where creditors can reduce their risks on particular investments by diversifying their holdings.[20]

Employees also make substantial investments in the firms for which they work, but, unlike creditors, they have a limited ability to reduce their risk through diversification. As well, it is not clear from the available empirical evidence that even employees who are unionized are able to obtain adequate information to allow them to predict accurately the likelihood of major risks to their investment, such as plant closings and other major corporate restructurings, perhaps following on from takeover bids.[21] For employees who are not unionized, these problems are even more substantial.[22] In general, employees do face impediments to bargaining effectively to protect their interests.

Suppliers who are largely or exclusively dependent upon one corporate customer may be in a similar position to employees. They may have made large investments in anticipation of a continuing long-term relationship, which would not be recoverable if the customer was to change suppliers. This would occur, for example, where the supplier produced a specialized input for the corporate customer's operations which no one else would buy. In the auto parts industry, a parts supplier may produce a small number of customized parts for a single car manufacturer. Just like employees, such suppliers may be substantially at risk where they cannot foresee the need to negotiate contractual protection against changes in the buyer's commitment to purchase its products or lack sufficient bargaining power to negotiate such protection. As suppliers become more diversified in terms of the customers they sell to, their risk is reduced.

Customers may also be at risk from unanticipated corporate decisions that are adverse to their interests, such as terminating a product

---

20 The nature of creditors' contractual relationship is discussed in Daniels, *Contractarianism, ibid.*, at 344–345; Macey & Miller, above note 11, at 417–419. Portfolio theory provides that holding a large diversified portfolio of investments results in much of the business-specific risk of poor returns on individual investments being offset by higher returns on other investments in the portfolio. Typically, most creditors will be owed obligations by a number of debtors. See, generally, P. Halpern, J.F. Weston, & E.F. Brigham, *Canadian Managerial Finance*, 4th ed. (Toronto: Holt, Rinehart & Winston, 1994).

21 Daniels, *Contractarianism, ibid.*, at 345–349; Stone provides a comprehensive critique of the nexus-of-contracts model as used to limit protection of employees to the terms of their bargains (K.V.W. Stone, "Policing Employment Contracts Within the Nexus of Contracts Firm" (1993) 43 U. of T. L. J. 353). See Daniels, *Contractarianism, ibid.*, at 321–322.

22 Macey & Miller, above note 11, at 417, argue that workers *can* protect themselves by contracting though they may not in practice.

line that would make their investment in the terminated product less valuable. The scope for bargaining for protection by individual customers is likely to be small and the prospects for collective bargaining remote. Nevertheless, customers would appear to be less at risk than employees and suppliers. Their level of investment is likely to be much smaller. More fundamentally, no corporation can embark on a strategy that is indifferent to its effect on customers.

The community, defined broadly to include all people affected by corporate behaviour who do not have a defined relationship with the corporation, would appear to have the least scope for negotiating contractual protection against conduct by the corporation adverse to its interests. Unlike other stakeholders, the community does not, typically, engage in contractual bargaining with the corporation. There is no ready context in which protections may be negotiated, nor, often, any specific input that the corporation requires from the community for which it must negotiate. As well, the individuals who make up the community suffer from serious collective-action problems in relation to the corporation. The benefits to any individual of gathering information about any particular corporate decision, analysing it, and organizing the community to seek to have the corporation address community concerns are small in relation to the costs involved. Individual members of the community will have little incentive to initiate a challenge to corporate decision making or seek protection from corporate action. Each member will hope to benefit, at no cost to themselves, from the efforts of other members of the community.[23]

If one expands the notion of community beyond those living in the vicinity of the corporation's business premises, and their immediate concerns with such matters as local air pollution and layoffs, to encompass the ethical norms of our broader Canadian community regarding, for example, labour, human rights, and environmental standards, which might be affected by corporate conduct in Canada and elsewhere, the prospects for the negotiation of contractual protection is even more remote. The capacity of concerned citizens to identify the kinds of issues and organize collectively to bargain with a corporation regarding their resolution will be negligible in most circumstances. Typically, resort to the political process will be the only option.[24]

---

23 These are examples of collective-action and "free-rider" problems. These kinds of problems are discussed in Chapter 7.

24 Even advocates of the shareholder-primacy norm acknowledge that the prospects for communities negotiating adequate protection is remote (e.g., Macey & Miller, above note 11, at 419–420). They suggest that direct government intervention may be preferable.

c) Other Legal and Market Mechanisms Ensure Management Accountability to Shareholders

i) Introduction

A third concern regarding the argument in favour of a legal requirement to give primacy to shareholder interests is that other legal and market mechanisms may ensure that management will act in the interests of shareholders. To the extent that this is true, it may be unnecessary have in place general legal norms of management behaviour designed to achieve the same objective. Both types of mechanisms are discussed below.

ii) Legal Mechanisms

As discussed in Chapter 7, Canadian corporate statutes provide three main types of protection for shareholder interests: (i) the right to vote for the election of directors; (ii) access to information rights; and (iii) shareholder remedies where management has failed to fulfil its obligations.[25] Of these, perhaps the most direct shareholder-protection mechanism is shareholders' power to vote. If management is not maximizing shareholder returns, the shareholders acting collectively can either replace the board of directors or refuse to elect them at the next annual meeting. In practice, however, the ability of shareholders to ensure that directors are accountable to act in the corporation's interests through these legal mechanisms may be impaired for a variety of reasons.

One reason is that access to information rights is limited. Once a year, shareholders are entitled to receive audited financial statements. Corporations subject to continuous disclosure obligations under provincial securities laws must also disclose quarterly results and, in some cases, management's analysis of financial results. Material changes to the corporation's business must be disclosed to the public on a timely basis.[26] Despite these and some additional access to information rights, however, shareholders often lack sufficient information to understand and evaluate management's performance. While adequate information and analysis may be obtainable with sufficient effort, they will not make such an effort because they have a small financial stake relative to the cost of obtaining adequate information. Considering that effective evaluation will often require paying for professional advice, they have little incentive to invest in information gathering and analysis. Because the benefits associated with an investment in infor-

---

25 These types of protection are discussed in Chapter 7. The critique of the legal model for corporate governance is developed in more detail in Chapter 7.

26 These obligations are discussed in Chapter 11.

mation gathering will accrue to all shareholders regardless of their individual contributions, it may seem to make sense to let others spend their money on doing it.

Even if shareholders did gather sufficient information and analyse it, mobilizing the large number of geographically and otherwise disparate shareholders who would be needed to defeat a management proposal or to elect a new board of directors will be difficult and costly. Again, the relatively small financial stake of individual shareholders discourages collective activity.

Concerns about collective-action problems of this kind have dominated the academic discourse on corporate law in the United States. In Canada, however, the marketplace is somewhat different. Seven out of ten public corporations have a controlling shareholder. In these corporations, the majority shareholder has strong incentives to hold management accountable and suffers from none of the collective-action problems described above.[27] Nevertheless, accountability concerns do not vanish completely. Instead, they shift to focus on the risk of the controlling shareholder and management acting together in ways that are detrimental to the interests of the corporation, such as by cooking up sweetheart deals which disproportionately benefit the controlling shareholder at the expense of the corporation.[28]

The growing involvement in the securities markets of institutional investors, such as pension funds and mutual funds, may result in more effective monitoring of opportunistic behaviour by management and collusion between management and controlling shareholders.[29] However, a number of commentators have suggested that, while the presence of institutional investors may reduce collective-action problems, such problems are likely to persist. As well, other impediments operate

---

27   R.K. Morck, "On the Economics of Concentrated Ownership" (1996) 26 Can. Bus. L. J. 63 [Morck], at 69. This high level of concentration is declining for various reasons (see R.J. Daniels & P. Halpern, "Too Close for Comfort: The Role of the Closely Held Public Corporation in the Canadian Economy and the Implications for Public Policy" (1996) 26 Can. Bus. L. J. 11 [Daniels & Halpern], at 46–56).

28   R.J. Daniels & J.G. MacIntosh, "Toward a Distinctive Canadian Corporate Law Regime" (1991) 29 Osgoode Hall L. J. 863 [Daniels & MacIntosh], at 885. Morck and Daniels & Halpern both provide evidence that the existence of a controlling shareholder is negatively correlated with corporate performance (Morck, *ibid.*, at 75–80, and Daniels & Halpern, *ibid.*, at 14–28).

29   R. J. Daniels & E. J. Waitzer, "Challenges to the Citadel: A Brief Overview of Recent Trends in Corporate Governance" (1994) 23 Can. Bus. L.J. 23; J. G. MacIntosh, "The Role of Institutional and Retail Shareholders in Canadian Capital Markets" (1993) 31 Osgoode Hall L. J. 371 [MacIntosh, "Shareholders"].

to discourage the exercise by institutional shareholders of their shareholder rights.[30]

Shareholders face other barriers to exercising their legal rights. For example, under Canadian corporate statutes, for the most part, the directors determine what goes on the agenda for meetings, how it is described, and what information goes to shareholders.[31] This tends to constrain the ability of shareholders to use their rights to address their concerns. Again, the presence of a controlling shareholder and large institutional investors may mitigate this concern for particular corporations.

Shareholder litigation to seek the enhanced shareholder remedies provided for in modern Canadian corporate statutes and discussed in Chapter 9[32] also faces certain challenges. Most important, litigation is an expensive, time-consuming, and uncertain exercise. Despite improvements made recently in some jurisdictions, such as Ontario, to facilitate class actions by shareholders, the impediments to shareholders acting collectively to vote apply also to shareholder litigation. Consequently, as a mechanism for holding management accountable to shareholders, shareholder litigation suffers from significant weaknesses.

iii) Market Mechanisms

As discussed in Chapter 7, corporate law rules comprise only one set of accountability mechanisms. Where shares are traded in a marketplace, the dynamic of the marketplace itself will impose a certain discipline on management to act in shareholders' interests. People decide to buy or sell shares based on their assessment of the value of the shares, taking into account all the information they have. Empirical evidence has demonstrated that prices in markets for securities tend to reflect accurately all publicly available information.[33] This characteristic, called market efficiency, means that all public information about

---

30   J.G. MacIntosh, "Institutional Investors and Corporate Governance" (1996) 26 Can. Bus. L. J. 145; [MacIntosh, "Institutional Investors"] J.G. MacIntosh, "Shareholders," *ibid*. MacIntosh refers to investment restrictions, limited monitoring capabilities, fiduciary conflicts of interest, a culture of passivity and other factors as discouraging institutional investor activism. Impediments are also discussed in R. Crête & S. Rousseau, "De la passivité à l'activisme des investisseurs institutionnel au sein des corporations: le reflet de la diversité des facteurs d'influence" (1997) 42 McGill L.J. 3.

31   E.g., *CBCA*, above note 8, ss. 137(4), 149, 150.

32   Such as a shareholder's right to seek relief where the corporation or the directors have acted in a manner that oppresses, unfairly disregards, or unfairly prejudices the interests of the shareholder under s. 241 of the *CBCA*, *ibid*. The oppression remedy is discussed in Chapter 9.

33   This evidence is reviewed in Daniels & MacIntosh, above note 27, at 872–74.

the risks of management not being sufficiently attentive to shareholder interests should be factored into the price. Consequently, a prospective investor can rely on the fact that the price of the shares will already be reduced to reflect these agency costs[34] at the time she bought them.

There are, however, still risks associated with opportunistic behaviour by management. For example, not all risks of such behaviour are foreseeable and so may not be factored into share price. Studies of stock markets suggest that prices do not reflect non-public or insider information known only to officers and directors of the corporation.[35] Risks, known only to insiders, will not be factored into share price. Despite this important caveat, to the extent that agency costs are reflected in share price, corporate law mechanisms designed to monitor and control agency costs become less important.

What is sometimes called the market for corporate control also reduces concerns about agency costs. A corporation that is not being managed in the interests of maximizing the value of shareholders' investment represents an opportunity. Anyone who acquires sufficient shares to gain control of the corporation could replace the board of directors and, through the new board, senior management. By implementing improvements to management, the new management could enhance the value of the shares acquired. As discussed in Chapters 7 and 11, such a change in control may be accomplished by a takeover bid. The bidder offers to buy some or all of the shares held by existing shareholders, typically at a price in excess of the current market price, in order to acquire enough shares to replace the board of directors. The threat of a takeover bid which, if successful, will result in the board and the officers losing their positions should encourage management to

---

34 We discussed "agency costs" in Chapter 7. Where there is a separation between those who own the shares of the corporation and those who manage it, there is an incentive for managers to engage in opportunistic behaviour, favouring their own interests over those of shareholders. If managers are shareholders at all, the size of their interest, typically, is very small relative to the aggregate of all shareholder interests and so the proportion of benefit to them associated with acting in ways that further the corporation's interests rather than their own is correspondingly small. Consequently, they may appropriate corporate assets to their own benefit or shirk their responsibilities, thereby imposing a loss on shareholders. Any loss they suffer as shareholders is a small fraction of the benefit they receive in their capacity as managers. The costs associated with this kind of behaviour and related costs incurred as a consequence of devoting resources to monitoring management to ensure that such behaviour does not occur are referred to as "agency costs."

35 J. Gordon & L. Kornhauser, "Efficient Markets, Costly Information and Securities Research" (1985) 60 N.Y. Univ. L. R. 761.

manage so as to maximize shareholder value. Doing so would avoid making their corporation the target of a takeover bid. Various commentators have suggested that the discipline on management provided by the market for corporate control is so important that management's ability to defend against a hostile takeover bid should be severely limited.[36]

Several other market mechanisms that encourage management to maximize the value of shareholders' investment may be identified. One is the market for managers' services. A manager will be discouraged from engaging in self-interested behaviour at the expense of shareholders by the adverse effect such behaviour may have on her reputation and consequent prospects for promotion and future employment.[37] Also, product markets will provide some discipline on management behaviour. The success of a firm in today's intensely competitive marketplace requires management to produce at the lowest possible cost an attractive product and sell it for a reasonable price if it is to survive, much less prosper. This discipline will tend to rebound to shareholders' interest by ensuring that the firm is well managed, with the result that the value of shareholders' investments is maximized.[38]

The existence of these market mechanisms to address agency problems has led some corporate law scholars to assert that legal rules can be justified only to the extent that the market can be shown not to operate effectively. Some such scholars view markets as working well, leaving a narrow sphere of operation for corporate law.[39] Others have suggested that the capital and corporate control markets do not work efficiently, so a substantial role must be played by mandatory corporate law rules.[40]

---

36   F. Easterbrook & D. Fischel, "The Proper Role of a Target's Management in Responding to a Tender Offer" (1982) 94 Harvard L. Rev. 1161. Other commentators, however, suggest that hostile takeovers suffer from high transactions costs and may be misdirected, as a consequence of which directors need to be able to take defensive measures in some circumstances (e.g., Morck, above note 27, at 65). This issue of whether management should be permitted to take defensive measures is discussed in Chapter 8.

37   B.R. Cheffins, *Company Law: Theory, Structure and Operation* (Oxford: Clarendon, 1997), at 117–118; E. Fama, "Agency Problems and the Theory of the Firm" (1980) 88 J. of Pol. Econ. 288.

38   Cheffins, *ibid.*, at 118. The requirement for firms to seek funds in capital markets with the attendant disclosure regarding corporate operations and the opportunities for scrutiny by investors, will also tend to ensure that management focuses on maximizing shareholder value.

39   E.g., F. Easterbrook & D. Fischel, "Corporate Control Transactions" (1982) 91 Yale L.J. 698, at 700–73.

40   E.g., V. Brudney, "Corporate Governance, Agency Costs, and the Rhetoric of Contract" (1985) 85 Columbia L. Rev. 1403, at 1410–1411.

While there may be disagreement regarding the effectiveness of this array of legal procedures and market mechanisms which help to ensure that management's behaviour is consistent with the interests of shareholders, considering them altogether, the case for making shareholders the exclusive beneficiary of management's duty seems weak. This conclusion is confirmed by the various kinds of barriers faced by non-shareholder stakeholders, which impair their ability to fully negotiate contractual protection. Consequently, it is hard to justify the Canadian rule that corporate managers are exclusively responsible to shareholders as the optimal one.

3) Should Managers be Responsible to Non-shareholder Stakeholders?

a) Introduction
If the case for singling out shareholders as the exclusive beneficiary of management duties is not convincing, the next question is the extent to which this argues for changing the existing shareholder-primacy norm. Should we be requiring managers to be responsible for the interests of all stakeholders? Would doing so improve corporate governance in Canada by making managers more attuned to social concerns? As discussed below, some serious problems would arise if the shareholder primacy-rule were abandoned.

b) Effect on Management Accountability
If corporate management were obliged to take into account the interests of all corporate stakeholders, the result would be a standard of accountability that would be impossible to enforce in practice. Management would be required to assess and balance such a diverse array of interests that almost any decision could be justified on the basis that it would promote some stakeholder interest. Costly litigation to sort out what the duty requires in particular cases would be frequent.[41] Indeed, management accountability to all stakeholders may result in a complete absence of accountability in practice. The risk that management would engage in self-serving behaviour would be substantial because often managers would be able to find some stakeholder inter-

---

41 J.G. MacIntosh, "Designing an Efficient Fiduciary Law" (1993) 43 U. of T. L. J. 425, at 456 [MacIntosh, "Fiduciary"]. For a demonstration of this point based on a theory of organizational economics, see E. Neave, "Organizational Economics and Directors' Control" (1996) 27 Can. Bus. L. J. 106 [Neave].

est that would be served by decisions that benefited themselves.[42] Where the directors are empowered to take into account the interests of non-shareholder stakeholders but are not required to, the risk of self-serving behaviour would remain. No one could complain that their interests had been ignored so long as some other interest is benefited.[43]

Many commentators have attributed the movement in the United States to corporate law rules that expressly permit managers to take into account non-shareholder interests, at least in some circumstances, to management's selfish interest in being relieved of its accountability to shareholders.[44] It has been suggested, for example, that some of the U.S. state stakeholder statutes were enacted for the singular purpose of permitting a large business incorporated in the state to take action to fend off unwanted takeover bids which, if successful, would have resulted in layoffs of local employees and cost current managers their jobs. While shareholder interests might have favoured a bid being made, the ability to put other interests, such as those of employees, ahead of shareholders would allow managers to take steps to discourage or block such a bid and thus protect their own positions. Management could justify its opposition to a bid on the basis that it was protecting the jobs of the employees who would be laid off under the takeover bidder's restructuring plans.[45]

c) Managers' Competence to Respond to Non-shareholder Interests

Opponents of management duties to stakeholders emphasize that management does not have the expertise or the information to make assessments regarding the appropriate course of action based on a consideration of all the conflicting interests which may be affected.[46] They argue that the accommodation of a wide range of interests is better addressed through the political process. These proponents of the

---

42   Daniels, "Boards," above note 9. Several commentators have pointed out that, even if management duties ran exclusively to shareholders, the standard of accountability is not straightforward. This is obviously the case when the corporation has different classes of shares with different characteristics but it arises in all situations where the interests of shareholders are not uniform (e.g., Macey & Miller, above note 11, at 416). MacIntosh suggests that it is more likely that shareholders will agree on their goals than other stakeholders (MacIntosh, "Fiduciary," *ibid.*, at 455).

43   Macey & Miller, *ibid.*, at 412–413.

44   J. R. Macey, "Transcript: Corporate Social Responsibility: Paradigm or Paradox" (1999) 84 Cornell L. Rev. 1282, at 1348.

45   *Ibid.*

46   E.g., MacIntosh, "Fiduciary," above note 41, at 433–435 & 442–444; Macey & Miller, above note 11, at 420.

shareholder-primacy norm suggest that, for making such assessments, the state has a comparative advantage over the corporation in terms of access to more policy-relevant information. Politicians are elected and have a mandate to govern in accordance with their electoral platform, allowing them to make the hard distributional choices about whose interests should be protected in a particular situation. Politicians are accountable to the public for these choices at the next election. Business people, by contrast, are both ill-equipped to make these kinds of decisions and not accountable to the public for their consequences.

The claim that business people are not well positioned to make decisions taking into account stakeholder interests is most convincing in relation to the interests of the community in which a corporation operates. In relation to employees, creditors, suppliers, and customers, management must continually engage in an arithmetic which assesses the nature of these interests and their relation to the corporation's business, if the business is to thrive and the value of shareholders' investment maximized. Thus, it is not clear to what extent permitting management to take into account other interests would result in behaviour that is significantly different from that engaged in currently. In relation to broader community interests, however, this claim is more telling. In a broad sense, the interests of the community include compliance with its ethical norms in terms of, for example, human rights and environmental protection as well as more parochial concerns such as local employment. Such interests are likely to be more abstract and much more difficult for management to assess compared to the interests of the other stakeholders.

The availability of political action is not a complete solution to the protection of community interests, however. As discussed above, individual members of a community are likely to suffer serious collective-action problems in making their case to their elected representatives, even where corporate activities directly affect them, such as by emitting noxious fumes into the local environment. Corporations, by contrast, may be well positioned to mount a focused and coherent defence to any such efforts. Where the issue is the consistency of corporate behaviour with community ethical norms relating to human rights and similar issues rather than a specific significant injury to an identifiable group, the likelihood of a political solution becomes even more remote.

d) The Ability of the Shareholder-Primacy Norm to Accommodate Interests of Other Stakeholders

The rule that management must work to maximize shareholders' investment does not preclude management from taking into account the effect of a particular action on other stakeholders. Management may seek to promote the interests of other stakeholders to the extent that doing so is reasonably incidental to carrying on the corporation's business for profit. How much room this leaves to take into account the interests of other stakeholders depends on how broadly one is willing to interpret "reasonably incidental." It is impossible to articulate the appropriate interpretation in the abstract, but it is possible to identify some of the factors upon which an assessment of reasonableness will depend in particular circumstances. These include how far into the future the benefits may arise and how indirect the benefits may be. If one is prepared to include in the category of "reasonably incidental" actions that have no direct or immediate benefit for shareholders in terms of profits but may produce benefits in the longer term, many actions primarily intended for the benefit of non-shareholder stakeholders may be upheld. For example, enhancing employee benefits may reduce short-term profits but may have benefits in terms of improved employee relations and fewer days lost to strikes as well as a better public image, all of which may increase future profits. Although some statements by Canadian courts have suggested a broad view of what may be considered reasonably incidental in reviewing decisions of management challenged by shareholders,[47] the rhetoric typically used by courts suggests a relatively narrow conception.[48] At the same time, however, as discussed in Chapter 8, the courts tend to be highly deferential to management in matters of business judgment.[49] The end

---

47   *Teck Corporation Limited* v. *Millar* (1972), 33 D.L.R. (3d) 288 (B.C.S.C.) at 314. A classical theory that once was unchallengeable must yield to the facts of modern life. In fact, of course, it has. If today directors of a company were to consider the interests of its employees no one would argue that in doing so they were not acting *bona fide* in the interests of the company itself. Similarly, if the directors were to consider the consequences to the community of any policy that the company intended to pursue, and were deflected in their commitment to that policy as a result, it could not be said that they had not considered *bona fide* the interests of the shareholders. See, to similar effect, *Miles* v. *Sydney Meat-Preserving Co. Ltd.* (1913), 16 C.L.R. 50 (H.C. Aust.), at 64, aff'd (1914) 17 C.L.R. (P.C.) 639.

48   E.g., *Dodge* v. *Ford Motor Company*, 170 N.W. 668 (1919); and *Report of the Industrial Inquiry Commission on Canadian National Railways "Run-Throughs"* (Ottawa: Queen's Printer, 1965).

49   As noted in Chapter 8, the so-called business judgment rule was formally adopted in Ontario in *CW Holdings Inc.* v. *WIC International Communications Inc.*, [1998] O.J. No. 1886 (QL) (Sup. Ct. J.). Under this rule, courts will not substitute their business judgment for that of the corporation's managers so long as the managers' decision was made honestly and in a reasonable manner.

result is that, despite the courts' rhetoric, in practice, management has a broad discretion to determine the extent to which accommodating non-shareholder stakeholder interests is consistent with maximizing the value of shareholder interests in particular situations.

Examples of how such discretion permits management to take into account the interests of non-shareholder stakeholders may be readily identified. A desire to head off more intrusive direct regulation may encourage management to adopt a broad conception of shareholder interest which takes other interests into account. Where firms can get out ahead of direct regulation by setting standards in the areas of employee health and safety or environmental protection that exceed what is currently required, they may be able to avoid such regulation altogether, or at least be able to time the move to higher standards in accordance with their own priorities as opposed to the state's. Such firms may advocate a regulatory regime consistent with the improvements already implemented by them. While this may be costly to shareholders in the short run and appear to elevate other interests above their own, it may be justifiable in the long run on the basis of reduced compliance costs and the public-relations benefits associated with being seen to be an industry leader.

Similarly, management may be inclined to grant concessions to employees and live up to any expectations employees may have regarding job security or increases in benefits because its failure to do so would reduce the security of all informal, implicit bargains with stakeholders. The resulting low levels of mutual trust would impair the efficiency with which the corporation may operate, in part because it would mean greater reliance on costly explicit contract negotiation in its relations with employees.[50] Management may be inclined to live up to its informal commitments to suppliers and customers for the same reason.

These are just two examples of the wide range of management decisions in which the interests of shareholders and many other stakeholders may be congruent in the longer run. They illustrate the extent to which the shareholder-primacy norm is compatible with taking into account the interests of other stakeholders.

---

50 MacIntosh, "Fiduciary Duty," above note 41, at 471; B. Chapman, "Trust, Economic Rationality and Corporate Governance" (1993) 43 U. of T. L. J. 547; Romano, above note 2, at 533.

D. SOME OTHER LEGAL REFORMS TO IMPROVE CORPORATE SOCIAL RESPONSIBILITY

1) Introduction

If the shareholder-primacy norm cannot be unequivocally accepted but abandoning it would create serious problems, as discussed above, is there no alternative to maintaining a second-best rule? Various possible approaches to this problem have been suggested. The remainder of this chapter discusses two ways in which community concerns about social responsibility issues may be addressed within the framework of existing corporate law. The two policy options discussed are facilitating shareholder proposals and mandatory disclosure by corporations of their record on social responsibility.

2) Shareholder Proposals

Usually, the agenda for shareholder meetings in large corporations where shareholders are remote from management is set by management. As discussed in Chapter 7, however, the corporate statutes in a majority of Canadian jurisdictions do provide a limited right for shareholders to add items to the agenda including the amendment of by-laws and articles.[51] Under the *CBCA* and most other Canadian corporate statutes, any shareholder entitled to vote may submit to the corporation a "proposal" giving notice of any matter the shareholder would like to discuss (*CBCA*, s. 137). For corporations required to solicit proxies,[52] the proposal, along with a brief supporting statement from the proposing shareholder, must be included with the notice of meeting and other supporting material sent to shareholders in connection with the meeting. Essentially, the proposal mechanism is intended to facilitate communication between shareholders at the expense of the corporation. It has significant potential to raise issues of corporate

---

51   E.g., *CBCA*, above note 9, ss. 137, 103(5) (to make or amend by-laws), 175(1) (to amend articles). The corporate statutes in Quebec, Nova Scotia, and Prince Edward Island do not permit shareholder proposals. British Columbia's *New Company Act* (S.B.C. 1999, c. 27) has the most shareholder-friendly proposal rules in Canada (Division 7). These provisions are not yet in force.

52   As discussed in Chapter 7, all distributing corporations and all corporations with more than fifty shareholders are required to solicit proxies under the *CBCA, ibid.*

social responsibility that are of concern to shareholders, thereby both encouraging management to be more socially responsible and ensuring that any bottom-line benefits associated with socially responsible behaviour are realized.[53]

Shareholder proposals can be a source of innovative thinking about social responsibility. For example, in 1990 a shareholder of Noranda Inc. proposed that the corporation provide a public report on its environmental policies. Although the proposal was supported only by 8 percent of shareholder votes, Noranda ultimately implemented such a reporting scheme. At the time, few other firms were providing this level of disclosure. Today, in part because of Noranda's leadership, such reporting is an industry standard.[54]

A proposal made to Placer Dome Inc. in 1988 is another example of how shareholder proposals may anticipate future issues. A shareholder proposed an independent assessment of the environmental and socio-economic impact of the corporation's Marcopper Mine in the Philippines. The proposal was not passed and no assessment was undertaken. Within eight years, the mine was closed and criminal charges had been laid against some of the corporation's employees in connection with the corporation's environmental practices.[55] If management had acted on the proposal, perhaps these serious adverse effects on the corporation and the local community could have been avoided. The Placer Dome example also shows how shareholder proposals may address areas where direct regulation is not feasible because the concerns relate to international operations out of reach of Canadian regulators.[56]

---

53 The proposal mechanism was introduced into Canadian law with the *Canada Business Corporations Act* (S.C. 1974-5, c. 33; now R.S.C. 1985, c. c-44). The study on which the new act was based describes the purpose of the shareholder proposal as to "provide shareholders with machinery that enables them to communicate with co-owners on matters of common concern relating to the affairs of the corporation" (R. Dickerson, J. Howard & L. Getz, *Proposals for a New Business Corporations Law in Canada*, volume 1 (Ottawa: Information Canada, 1971), at 95).

54 The Noranda proposal is described by C. McCall in "Update on Shareholder Proposals in Canada" (1997) 9 Corporate Governance Rev. 5, at 7. McCall indicates that there are now awards for such reporting. See, generally, Neave on the need for a continuing source of fresh ideas to management (above note 41, at 106).

55 The Placer Dome proposal is described by M.C. Jantzi in "Canadian Shareholder Proposals: A Tool for Change" (1997) 9 Corporate Governance Rev. 1 [Jantzi], at 1.

56 For example, in 1986, a proposal was made to Alcan requesting the corporation to divest its interests in South Africa. One week before the annual meeting, the corporation sold its interests and the proposal was withdrawn. The Alcan proposal is described by B. Davis in "Canada's Successful Activists, the Churches" (1994) 6 Corporate Governance Rev. 1, at 2. An earlier proposal was made at

There are only a small number of proposals each year in Canada and few of these deal with social responsibility issues,[57] but the small numbers may not fully reflect the use and significance of proposals. Canadian observers have noted that many proposals are withdrawn before meetings on the basis of discussions with management.[58] Nevertheless, the proposal mechanism appears to be used much less frequently in Canada than in the United States. Annually, as many as nine hundred shareholder proposals are made in the United States and many of these relate to social issues.[59] Why the difference?

Restrictions in Canadian corporate statutes may be partly to blame for the low use of the proposal process in Canada. Under Canadian law, there are certain limits on the content of a proposal designed to prevent use of this process that is either frivolous or aimed at raising issues not connected with the business of the corporation. Some of these limitations have been interpreted broadly by the courts in Canada to allow corporations to exclude proposals relating to social responsibility issues.[60] Many of the early cases limiting the use of proposals were based on an exclusion in the *CBCA*, which allowed management to refuse to distribute a proposal where it was "primarily for the purpose of promoting general economic, political, racial, religious, social or similar causes." The *2001 Amendments* to the *CBCA* eliminated this exclusion. Now the *CBCA* permits corporations to refuse to circulate a proposal if it "does not relate in a significant way to the business or affairs of the corporation" (*CBCA*, s. 137(5)(b.1)).[61] Whether this provision will be interpreted in a manner which is more accommodating to proposals relating to corporate social responsibility is uncertain.

Alcan's 1982 annual meeting requesting the corporation to establish a committee of the board to report to shareholders on the relationship between the corporation and the military in South Africa. It received 8.8 percent of the vote.

57 One study found that in 1998 there were eight shareholder proposals made by shareholders in 264 of the 294 corporations listed on the Toronto Stock Exchange 300 that were subject of the study and none related to social issues (D.S. Gauris, "1998 Proxy Season Review" (1998) 10 Corporate Governance Rev. 6).

58 Kazanjian gives several examples (J. Kazanjian, "Canadian Shareholder Proposals" (1997) 9 Corporate Governance Rev. 1 [Kazanjian] at 3).

59 In 1991, for example, 300 U.S. shareholder proposals related to social issues, while in the same year in Canada there were none (C. McCall & R. Wilson, "Shareholder Proposals: Why Not in Canada?" (1993) 5 Corporate Governance Rev. 12, at 12, citing the Investor Responsibility Research Center) [McCall & Wilson].

60 Some of the case law is discussed in Chapter 7.

61 This language follows that used in the Ontario *Business Corporations Act*, R.S.O. 1990, c. B.5, s. 99(5) [*OBCA*]. The social cause exclusion still exists in some corporate statutes (e.g., *Alberta Business Corporations Act*, R.S.A. 2000, c. B. 9).

Some recent cases dealing with proposals relating to corporate governance issues suggest that the attitude of the courts may be shifting slightly in favour of shareholder participation through the proposal mechanism. In its 1996 decision in *Verdun* v. *Toronto-Dominion Bank*,[62] the Supreme Court of Canada stated that it was evident that the shareholder-proposal provisions "constitute an effort by the legislature to promote shareholder participation in the management of companies."[63] In 1997 the Superior Court of Quebec upheld the right of a shareholder of one of the banks to make proposals raising a range of corporate governance issues which the bank had sought to exclude.[64] Among other things, the proposals dealt with increasing managerial accountability and limits on executive pay.

In contrast to the Canadian system, U.S. corporations are permitted to exclude shareholder proposals based on their content only in very limited circumstances. While the Rules of the Securities and Exchange Commission (SEC) once contained a broad exclusionary provision applying to social responsibility proposals, this is no longer the case.[65] The SEC's interpretation of the other exceptions under U.S. law has varied over the years,[66] but it has not prevented substantial numbers of proposals on social policy issues.[67] In 1998 the Commission issued a revised rule suggesting a greater openness to proposals

---

62 [1996] S.C.R. 550.

63 *Ibid.* The Court, nevertheless, held that the shareholder could not make the proposals because he was not a registered shareholder. Under the amendments to the *CBCA*, above note 8, (S.C. 2001, c. 15) [*2001 Amendments*], being a registered shareholder is no longer a requirement for making a proposal under the *CBCA*.

64 *Michaud* v. *Banque Nationale du Canada*, [1997] R.J.Q. 547 (S.C.).

65 17 CFR (Code of Federal Regulations) § 240.14a-8 (1999). See, generally, M. Curzan & M. Pelesh, "Revitalizing Corporate Democracy: Control of Investment Managers' Voting on Social Responsibility Proxy Issues" (1980) 93 Harvard L. Rev. 670, at 675.

66 The SEC exceptions are discussed in B.R. Cheffins, "*Michaud* v. *National Bank of Canada* and Canadian Corporate Governance: A Victory for Shareholder Rights?" (1998) 30 Can. Bus. L. J. 20 [Cheffins], at 40; K.W. Waite, "The Ordinary Business Operations Exception to the Shareholder Proposal Rule: A Return to Predictability" (1995) 64 Fordham L. Rev. 1253, at 1268-1270; and C.L. Ayotte, "Reevaluating the Shareholder Proposal Rule in the Wake of *Crackerbarrel* and the Era of Institutional Investors" (1999) 48 Catholic Univ. L. Rev. 510 [Ayotte]. For a thorough discussion of the differences between the Canadian and U.S. systems, see R. Crête, *The Proxy System in Canadian Corporations — A Critical Analysis* (Montréal: Wilson & Lafleur, Martel, 1986), at 187 *et seq.*

67 A line of judicial decisions requiring corporations to circulate proposals relating to social responsibility, sometimes even contrary to SEC rulings, is discussed in Forcese, above note 4, at 34–38.

dealing with social policy issues relating to employment, such as affirmative action.[68]

The Canadian rules respecting shareholder proposals are more restrictive that U.S. rules in other ways as well. For example, they put the onus on shareholders to take action to deal with the refusal of management to circulate a proposal. If management refuses, a shareholder can only challenge the refusal in court, a time-consuming and expensive process (*CBCA*, s. 137(8)). By contrast, the U.S. system puts the onus on the corporation that is refusing to circulate a proposal. If management wants to exclude a proposal, it must submit the proposal to the SEC for its consideration. The shareholder may submit a statement in support of the proposal. The corporation must demonstrate that it is entitled to exclude the proposal. If the SEC staff agrees with the corporation, a "no action" letter is issued in which the staff advise that it will not recommend to the Commission that enforcement action be taken. If the SEC staff determines that the corporation is not permitted to exclude the proposal, it will issue an "action letter" indicating that it will recommend action by the Commission to require the proposal to be included. In most cases, the decision of the staff is determinative of the issue of whether the corporation includes the proposal.[69]

Another difficulty under the Canadian rules is that, if a shareholder making a proposal seeks to speak to another shareholder about it or communicates in writing, there is a risk that it would become obliged to prepare and send to all shareholders a dissident's proxy circular which includes extensive disclosure regarding the person making the proposal and other information.[70] Industry Canada has suggested that "solicitation" may consist of "almost any expression of views, including, for example, an informal discussion among shareholders or a personal letter from one associate to another criticizing the quality of a company's management."[71] On this view, most communications between shareholders relating to a proposal may result in an obligation to incur the effort and expense of preparing and distributing a circular. Failure to comply may lead to a fine not exceeding $5000 or a prison term of up to six months or both. With the *2001 Amendments*, two

---

68 Amendments to Rules on Shareholder Proposals, Exchange Act Release No. 40,018, 63 Fed. Reg. 29106 (1998), now codified at 17 C.F.R. § 240.14a-8 (1999). The amendment is discussed in Ayotte, above note 66, at 551–553.

69 This process is described in Cheffins, above note 66, at 38–41.

70 E.g., *CBCA*, above note 9, ss. 147, 150. These provisions are discussed in Chapter 7.

71 Industry Canada, *Canada Business Corporations Act Discussion Paper: Shareholder Communications and Proxy Solicitation* (Ottawa: Industry Canada, 1995) at 69.

exclusions from the requirement to prepare and distribute a dissident proxy circular were created which will facilitate shareholder communication. Now the *CBCA* allows targeted solicitations to less than sixteen shareholders and solicitations by public broadcast, speech, or publication in prescribed circumstances.[72]

Again, despite these changes, U.S. law remains more accommodating to shareholder proposals. The obligation to distribute a circular is not triggered by any oral communication.[73] As well, it exempts all other communications except those by "any person who, because of a substantial interest in the subject matter of the solicitation, is likely to receive a benefit from a successful solicitation that will not be shared pro rata by all other shareholders of the same class of securities."[74] This exemption would be available in connection with most proposals relating to issues of social responsibility.

Some commentators have expressed the concern that relaxing the rules regarding the circulation of shareholder proposals to follow the U.S. example would risk creating excessive demands upon the corporations.[75] Evidence from the U.S. experience, however, would seem to provide no basis for such concerns.[76]

Shareholder proposals, potentially, are an important mechanism by which management may be made aware of shareholder expectations,

---

72 *CBCA*, above note 9, ss. 150(1.1) & (1.2), *Canada Business Corporations Regulations*, SOR/2001-512 [*CBCA Regulations*], ss. 67–69. These provisions are discussed in Chapter 7.

73 McCall & Wilson, above note 59, at 14.

74 SEC Rule 14a-29(b)(1). Under the *CBCA Regulations*, above note 72, the prescribed exemptions from the requirement to circulate a dissident proxy circular, referred to above, do not apply in these circumstances (s. 68(2)). Another issue is the extent to which proposals may be excluded on the ground that a similar proposal was made previously. With the *2001 Amendments*, above note 63, the *CBCA* rules have been brought into line with U.S. law. Now, under the *CBCA*, a proposal that is substantially the same as one submitted within the past five years may be excluded if certain levels of approval were not received (3 percent for the first submission, 6 percent for the second and 10 percent for any subsequent submission (*CBCA Regulations*, ibid., s. 51)). The rules under many provincial statutes provide that any proposal substantially similar to a previous proposal, which was presented and defeated within two years, may be excluded (e.g., *OBCA*, above note 61, s. 99(5)).

75 Kazanjian raises the prospect of unrestrained shareholder proposals undermining the existing system of management control and responsibility by creating "some form of sporadic 'town hall' democracy" (Kazanjian, above note 58, at 3).

76 Jantzi, above note 55, at 4. Cheffins, above note 66, suggests various reasons for a likely lack of interest by institutional shareholders in initiating or supporting shareholder proposals (at 47–61).

insights, and concerns. The examples given suggest that shareholder proposals may provide innovative ideas and be useful to initiate debate on social responsibility issues. Management is obliged to act in the interests of shareholders and the proposal mechanism provides a way for management to reach a better assessment of how to do so. The proposal is not a device for substituting shareholder judgment for management's on how shareholder interests should be served. Its purpose is rather hortatory and educative; as one commentator has put it, shareholder proposals can have a "sunlight effect."[77] In light of this function, there would seem to be no compelling need to change the existing system to render proposals binding, as some advocates have suggested.[78] Instead, it would be sufficient to remove the existing impediments to making shareholder proposals an effective instrument. In this regard, the American system appears to provide a ready model.[79]

3) Corporate Disclosure Regarding Social Responsibility

One of the goals of shareholder proposals, as illustrated by the examples discussed above, may be simply improved corporate disclosure regarding the social consequences of the corporation's activities. An innovative approach to corporate disclosure on corporate governance issues was adopted by the Toronto Stock Exchange (TSX), which provides a possible model for corporate disclosure regarding social responsibility.

As discussed in Chapter 7, in 1995 the TSX amended its rules applicable to listed companies in an effort to enhance the effectiveness of corporate governance. The amended rules set out some benchmarks for best practices in corporate governance. TSX-listed corporations are not required to meet the benchmarks; rather, they are required to disclose their governance practices in relation to these benchmarks and to discuss the extent to which they do not meet each one.[80]

---

77 McCall & Wilson, above note 59, at 13.
78 Some commentators have recommended that proposals have binding effect (e.g., Forcese, "Owning Up," above note 4, at 38). Under the *OBCA*, above note 60, proposals to amend by-laws are binding (s. 116(5)).
79 Recent amendments to the British Columbia *Companies Act* will put in place a regime for shareholder proposals that allows proposals in a broader range of circumstances than the U.S. regime (S.B.C. 1999, c. 94, Division 7, not yet in force).
80 Listing Rules 472 to 475 and TSX by-law s. 19.17 were changed. The impetus for the changes was the recommendations contained in *Where Were the Directors* (Toronto: The Toronto Stock Exchange, 1994) [the Dey Report]. These recommendations drew from the earlier *Report of the Committee on Corporate Governance* (London: Gee, 1992) [the Cadbury Report].

This approach could be readily adapted for use in the social responsibility context. While the development of benchmarks or best-practices goals in relation to social responsibility would be complex and require research, substantial work has already been done. Many large corporations and industry associations have voluntarily adopted codes of conduct that address some social responsibility issues. Significantly, the Conference Board of Canada released a major study in 1999 which included a Corporate Social Responsibility Assessment Tool. This could serve as a useful starting point for the development of mandatory disclosure rules.[81]

While it is far beyond the scope of this chapter to suggest the content of such a mandatory disclosure regime, it is possible to suggest some of the benefits of such an approach. First, it would permit ready comparability of social responsibility across corporations, though, admittedly, consistency in the questions to be answered may not necessarily lead to consistency in the comprehensiveness of the information provided in response.[82] Second, mandatory disclosure would give corporations substantial flexibility in determining whether and how to conform to the benchmarks and how to address concerns raised by its disclosures. This is particularly important given the differing scale and scope of operations of corporations in Canada.[83] The thrust of a mandatory disclosure regime would be to educate regarding best practices and focus management attention on social responsibility issues. Management would remain able to develop an approach to social responsibility issues which is appropriate for its business. The alternative of mandating specific practices would inevitably require setting the standard at some relatively low level attainable by all corporations. Third, and most important, the disclosure regime would rely on the marketplace to assess the significance of management's behaviour for the corporation.[84]

---

81   G. Khoury, J. Rostami, and P.L. Turnbull, *Corporate Social Responsibility: Turning Words into Action* (Ottawa: Conference Board of Canada, 1999).

82   This has been a problem with respect to the reporting under the TSX rules (D.W. Binet, "TSX Corporate Governance Rules: One Year Later" (Federated Press) paper presented at the 2nd Annual Corporate Summit, Toronto, 3–5 December 1996). See below note 85.

83   One of the significant concerns expressed regarding the new TSX rules was their applicability to smaller public corporations (C. Hansell "Corporate Governance Disclosure in Canada: Background and Compliance" in L. Sarna, ed., *Corporate Structure, Finance and Operations: Essays on the Law and Business Practice*, vol. 9 (Scarborough: Carswell, 1996) 29, at 49–50 [Hansell]).

84   Adrian Cadbury described the initiatives in the Cadbury Report, above note 80, which adopt an approach similar to the TSX rules as "relying primarily on what can best be described as market regulation to bring about compliance" (from an

The available evidence suggests that disclosure called for under the TSX rules has resulted in pressure to comply with the benchmarks established and some progress towards meeting them.[85]

A proposal for mandatory disclosure along the lines of the TSX rules on corporate governance would have critics. Inevitably, there would be costs associated with understanding the obligations, considering their relevance, and preparing the disclosure statements. Empirical work has not demonstrated clear benefits associated with mandatory disclosure rules imposed by securities regulators.[86] Nevertheless, there is evidence that Canadian corporations lag significantly behind U.S. corporations in the adoption of voluntary codes of conduct for dealing with social responsibility.[87] In this context, enhanced disclosure rules may have some value.

E. CHAPTER SUMMARY

The case usually made in favour of the existing legal rule requiring corporate managers to act exclusively to maximize the value of shareholders' investment is not compelling. Other stakeholders, at least in some situations, will have a stake in corporate decision making which is like

---

address to the Association of Certified Accountants, as quoted by Alice Belcher in "Regulation by the Market: the Case of the Cadbury Code and Compliance Statement" (1995) J. of Business L. 321, and cited in Hansell, *ibid.*, at 50).

85   Anecdotal evidence is referred to in Cheffins, above note 66, at 62, and Hansell, *ibid.* A report on the effect of the TSX Rules, *Report on Governance: Five Years to the Dey* (Toronto: Institute of Corporate Directors and The Toronto Stock Exchange, 1999), found varying degrees of compliance with the benchmarks but suggested that progress was being made. A more recent study found significant non-compliance with the reporting obligations (Patrick O'Callaghan & Associates, *Corporate Board Governance and Director Compensation in Canada* (2003), cited in J. McFarland, "Companies don't respect governance rules: study," *The Globe and Mail*, 20 January 2003 at B-1)

86   Mark Gillen reviews the literature on this issue and concludes that empirical evidence has not resolved the question of whether mandatory disclosure is beneficial and argues that further research is needed (M. Gillen, *Securities Regulation in Canada*, 2nd ed. (Toronto: Carswell, 1998), at 308–321).

87   Forcese, above note 4, cites research showing that roughly 75–80 percent of large public corporations in the U.S. have some type of corporate code but a 1992 survey of 461 Canadian firms in the *Financial Post* 500 revealed that of the 225 responding, only seventy-five considered themselves to have a "fairly well-developed codes of ethics." A more recent study reported in *Maclean's* found that roughly 50 percent of the forty-three Canadian public companies surveyed had implemented corporate codes ("Misbehaving Abroad" *Maclean's*, 26 May 1997).

that of shareholders: they, too, have a positive interest in the success of the firm, one that cannot be protected adequately by contract. Non-shareholder stakeholders also face impediments to bargaining successfully to protect their interests. As well, unlike other stakeholders, shareholders have legal procedural protections which they may use to control management, though there may be practical impediments to their doing so. In any case, the stock market, the market for corporate control, the market for management services, and product markets should all help to ensure that management is responsive to shareholder interests.

Even if the shareholder-primacy norm cannot be justified in a straightforward way, however, moving to a regime in which management is accountable to all stakeholder interests, or may balance shareholder interests with other stakeholder interests, is fraught with uncertainty and risks relieving management of any accountability at all. As well, under the present rules, the shareholder-primacy norm does not have to be rejected in order to permit management to act in a socially responsible way. Management has significant flexibility to decide how to maximize shareholder value in a manner consistent with the interests of other stakeholders.

The structures of accountability for Canadian corporations may be modified to improve corporate social responsibility without changing the basic requirement for management accountability to shareholders. One possible way to achieve improved corporate social responsibility would be to relax the rules that limit the ability of shareholders to bring issues before meetings of shareholders, along the lines of the approach followed in the United States. As well, requirements for managers to disclose the social and ethical effects of their decision making would better enable shareholders to hold them accountable.

FURTHER READINGS

BAINBRIDGE, S.M., "Community and Statism: A Conservative Contractarian Critique of Progressive Corporate Law Scholarship" (1997) 82 Cornell L. Rev. 856

BERLE, A., "For Whom Corporate Managers Are Trustees: A Note" (1932) Harvard. L. Rev. 1365

BUTLER, H.N. & F.S. McCHESNY, "Why they give at the office: Shareholder Welfare and Corporate Philanthropy in the Contractual Theory of the Firm" (1999) Cornell L. Rev. 1195

CANADIAN DEMOCRACY & CORPORATE ACCOUNTABILITY COMMISSION, *Canadian Democracy & Corporate Accountability: An Overview of the Issues* (2001)

CHAPMAN, B., "Corporate Stakeholders, Choice Procedures and Committees" (1995-6) 26 Can. Bus. L. J. 211

CHEFFINS, B.R., "*Michaud* v. *National Bank of Canada* and Canadian Corporate Governance: A Victory for Shareholder Rights?" (1998) 30 Can. Bus. L. J. 20

CUNNINGHAM, L.A., "Commonalities and Prescriptions in the Vertical Dimension of Global Corporate Governance" (1999) 84 Cornell L. Rev. 1133

DODD, M., "For Whom Are Corporate Managers Trustees?" (1932) Harvard L. Rev. 1145

FORCESE, C., *Owning Up: The Case for Making Corporate Managers More Responsive to Shareholder Values* (Ottawa: Democracy Watch, 1997)

FORCESE, C., *Putting Conscience into Commerce?* (Montreal: Int'l Centre for Human Rights and Democratic Development, 1997).

INDUSTRY CANADA, *Canada Business Corporations Act Discussion Paper: Shareholder Communications and Proxy Solicitation* (Ottawa: Industry Canada, 1995)

JANTZI, M.C., "Canadian Shareholder Proposals: A Tool for Change" (1997) 9 Corporate Governance Rev. 1

KHOURY, G., J. ROSTAMI & P.L. TURNBULL, *Corporate Social Responsibility: Turning Words into Action* (Ottawa: Conference Board of Canada, 1999)

LEUNG, W.S.W., "The Inadequacy of Shareholder Primacy: A Proposed Corporate Regime that Recognizes Non-Shareholder Interests" (1997) 30 Columbia J. of L. and Social Problems 587

MACEY, J.R., "Transcript: Corporate Social Responsibility: Paradigm or Paradox" (1999) 84 Cornell L. Rev. 1282

MACEY, J.R., "Fiduciary Duties as Residual Claims: Obligations to Non-shareholder Stakeholder Constituencies from a Theory of the Firm Perspective" (1999) 84 Cornell L. Rev. 1265

MACEY, J.R. & G.P. MILLER, "Corporate Stakeholders: A Contractual Perspective" (1993) 43 U. of T. L. J. 410

NOBEL, P., "The Social Responsibility of the Corporation" (1999) 84 Cornell L. Rev. 1255

SINGER, J.W., "Jobs and Justice: Rethinking the Stakeholder Debate" (1993) 43 U. of T. L.J. 475.

ZIEGEL, J.S., "Creditors as Corporate Stakeholders: The Quiet Revolution — An Anglo Canadian Perspective" (1993) 43 U. of T. L. J. 511

GLOSSARY

Affiliated corporations: corporations where one is the subsidiary of the other, both are subsidiaries of the same corporation, or both are controlled by the same person. One corporation is the subsidiary of another if it is controlled by the other. These are the basic and most common types of affiliated corporations. If two corporations are affilated with the same corporation, they are deemed to be affiliated. "Control" for the purpose of the definition of "affiliate" is legal control: holding voting securities of the corporation which carry more than 50 percent of the votes that may be cast for the election of directors, where such votes are sufficient to elect a majority of the board of directors. *See CBCA*, ss. 2(2)–(5), and Chapter 9.

Agency costs: costs arising as a result of someone other than the shareholders being responsible for managing the corporation's business. They include the direct costs associated with directors and officers acting to further their personal interests, in an opportunistic way, at the expense of the corporation, and the related costs that shareholders must incur to monitor their agents, the directors and officers, for the purpose of guarding against such opportunistic behaviour and to hold them accountable. *See* Chapter 7.

Amalgamation: a statutory procedure by which two or more corporations are combined into one. The rights and liabilities of the amalgamating corporations continue as rights and obligations of the amalgamated corporation. *See* Short-form amalgamation, and Chapter 10.

Annual meetings: meetings of shareholders that must be held at least every fifteen months or six months after the end of the corporation's financial year. Annual meetings are identified and defined by the happening of three items of business:

- election of directors;
- receipt of annual financial statements and the report of the auditor on such statements; and
- appointment of an auditor (unless dispensed with by unanimous agreement of shareholders in certain circumstances).

All other meetings are called "special meetings." To the extent any business other than the three items above is carried on at an annual meeting, it is called an "annual and special meeting." *See CBCA*, s. 133, and Chapter 7.

Articles or Articles of Incorporation: the document filed with the Director appointed under the *CBCA* and the statutes modelled after it to create a corporation. They must be filed in the form established by the Director (Form 1), along with a notice of registered office (Form 3) and a notice of directors (Form 6). They set out the fundamental characteristics of the corporation — for example, the class and number of shares authorized to be issued, any restrictions on transferring shares, and any restrictions on the business the corporation may carry on. Once the Director issues a certificate to which the articles are attached, a corporation with the characteristics set out in the articles comes into existence. *See* Chapters 3 & 4.

Auditor: the chartered accountant or firm of chartered accountants appointed by the shareholders at each annual meeting to audit the financial statements of the corporation. An auditor must examine and report to shareholders on the financial statements. *See CBCA*, ss. 161–71, and Chapter 7.

Authorized capital: the classes and number of shares of each class a corporation is permitted to issue as stated in its articles. The articles also set out the rights, privileges, restrictions, and conditions attaching to each class of shares (e.g., Class A preferred shares that are entitled to an annual dividend of $5 per share). The *CBCA* and the other corporate statutes contain certain default provisions that apply if the articles are silent. *See CBCA*, s. 24, and Chapters 4 & 6.

By-laws: one way in which a corporation establishes rules for its governance. They may be initiated either by shareholder proposal or by the directors. If a by-law is initiated and approved by the directors, it takes effect immediately, but must be approved by ordinary resolution at the next meeting of shareholders. The main purpose for which by-laws are used in practice is to set out the rules for conducting director and shareholder meetings and to designate and assign responsibilities of officers of the corporation. *See CBCA*, s. 103, and Chapters 4, 7, & 10.

Capital: generally refers to amounts contributed to a business organization which gives the contributors a claim to the residual value of the organization after all other claims have been paid. In relation to a corporation, capital refers to contributions by shareholders. In relation to a partnership, it refers to amounts contributed by partners. Sometimes, however, capital may be used to refer to amounts lent to a business organization as well. *See* Chapters 2 & 3.

Capital Cost Allowance: Under the *Income Tax Act*, a person carrying on a business may deduct from income from the business capital cost allowance (CCA). Notionally, this deduction reflects the decline in the remaining useful life of certain kinds of property used in the business, like equipment, which has occurred over the year. It is similar, in this respect, to the accounting concept of depreciation. In practice, the *Income Tax Act* sets specific percentages of the acquisition or capital cost of property which may be deducted for a number of broad categories of property. These annual percentage deductions may or may not reflect the decline in the remaining useful life of property over a year. As well, the government may increase or accelerate permitted CCA deductions for certain kinds of property to encourage investment in targeted industries which use these kinds of property. *See* Chapter 2.

Capital impairment test: a test appearing in several places in the *CBCA* which requires that the realizable value of the corporation's assets is not less than its liabilities and the stated capital of all classes before certain actions, such as declaring dividends, may be taken. *See CBCA*, ss. 34 & 42, and Chapter 6.

Class of shares: a category of shares designated and given certain rights, privileges, restrictions, and conditions in a corporation's articles, such as dividend entitlements and voting rights. *See* Chapter 6.

Closely held corporation: a corporation that has a small number of shareholders. *See* Chapter 4.

Co-ownership: a relationship between persons under which they hold title to some property, usually real property, together — for example, as tenants in common. The principal feature of this relationship which distinguishes it from partnership is that the parties' property interests remain separate; each co-owner is free to dispose of her interest as she chooses. *See* Chapter 2.

Common Law: the law in areas not governed by statute consisting of the accumulation of rules made in judicial decisions. Once a rule is applied in a particular case, it becomes a precedent: all courts lower in the judicial hierarchy are bound to decide all subsequent cases in a manner consistent with this rule. The application of the rule from the precedent case to different facts in subsequent cases clarifies and refines the rule. As a result of this binding character of precedent cases, it is often said that common law is made by judges. *See* Chapter 2.

Company: was the traditional English term to refer to the entity created under English registration model statutes, and it is still used in the U.K. *Companies Act*. Following the English practice, "company" was used in early Canadian legislation and is still the proper term in three provinces: British Columbia, Nova Scotia, and Prince Edward Island. "Company" is also the appropriate term to describe charities or other non-profit organizations incorporated under the Ontario *Corporations Act* (R.S.O. 1990, c. C.38). Under the *CBCA* and in the provinces and territories with corporate legislation modelled after it, "corporation" is the proper term. Nevertheless, even in reference to entities incorporated in these jurisdictions, "company" is still used colloquially. "Company" is also used colloquially to refer to a collection of people engaged in any common activity.

Corporation: the entity created by incorporation under the *CBCA* or any of the provincial or territorial statutes modelled after it. It was adopted from American usage. The term "company" was the traditional English term. *See* Company.

Debenture: sometimes refers to a document evidencing a debt obligation (e.g., *Salomon* v. *Salomon & Co.*, [1897] A.C. 22 (H.L.), discussed in Chapter 3), but when it is used by bankers it may mean the document evidencing the security for repayment of a debt as well as the document evidencing the debt. When the term is used by accountants it means an unsecured debt obligation. The term has no precise meaning.

Directors: the persons responsible under corporate statutes for managing or supervising the management of the business and affairs of the corporation (e.g., *CBCA*, s. 102(1)). The directors are elected by the shareholders, and there may be one or more (see Chapter 7). If there are more than one, they must act collectively. The "Director" is the person appointed under section 260 of the *CBCA* to carry out the duties and exercise the powers of the Director to administer the Act. *See* Chapter 7.

Directors' resolutions: the means by which directors act. When directors make decisions, they pass resolutions either by voting on them at a meeting or by signing a document expressing the resolution. *See CBCA*, ss. 114 & 117, and Chapter 7.

Dissent and appraisal right: the right of a shareholder to have the corporation buy her shares for fair value which arises when she dissents from a shareholder vote approving certain fundamental changes prescribed by statute. *See CBCA*, s. 190, and Chapter 9.

Dissident proxy circular: the document that must be sent to all shareholders by any shareholder who solicits the votes of shareholders against management, subject to certain exceptions. The form of the circular is prescribed by regulation. *See CBCA*, s. 150, *CBCA Regulations*, ss. 60–65, and Chapter 7.

Distributing Corporation: a corporation incorporated under the *CBCA* that is a "reporting issuer" under provincial securities laws, has filed a prospectus or similar document to permit its shares to be publicly traded in Canada or any foreign jurisdiction, or the shares of which are listed on a stock exchange inside or outside Canada. Distributing corporations are subject to a higher level of obligation under the Act. *See CBCA*, s. 2(1), and *CBCA Regulation*, s. 2(1), and Chapters 4, 7, & 11.

Dividends: payments by a corporation to its shareholders authorized by the directors of the corporation. Dividend entitlements may be provided for in the corporation's articles, but whether dividends are paid is always a matter in the discretion of the directors. *See* Chapter 6.

Fiduciary duty: in relation to a corporation, the duty of directors and officers to act honestly and in good faith with a view to the best interests of the corporation. It is provided for in section 122(1)(a) of the *CBCA* and the common law. *See* Chapter 8. Partners also owe each other a fiduciary duty. *See* Chapter 2.

Fractional Share: less than one whole share. Various events can create fractions of shares issued by a corporation. If a corporation consolidates its shares on some basis, shareholders may end up with less than a whole share. For example, if all common shares of a corporation were consolidated on a ten for one basis, a holder of five shares would end up holding just one-half of a share. Fractional shares can also arise on certain kinds of corporate reorganizations, such as amalgamations, where existing shares of each amalgamating corporation are exchanged for shares of the corporation that results from the amalgamation. Under the *CBCA*, corporations may purchase fractional shares for cancellation so long as certain financial tests are met (s. 34). *See* Chapters 6 & 10.

Franchise: a purely contractual relationship under which the franchisor gives the franchisee the right to operate its "system" in return for a set of fees. The parties typically provide in their agreement that their relationship does not constitute a partnership or joint venture. The basic terms of the relationship consist of a licence from the franchisor giving the franchisee the right to use its trade-marks and promises to provide certain assistance in running the franchised business, including training. In return, the franchisee agrees to operate the franchised business in accordance with the standards of the franchisor and to pay certain fees based, in part, on the sales of the business. *See* Chapter 1.

Fully paid and non-assessable shares: shares with respect to which the consideration has been paid in full before they may be issued, and no further amounts can be assessed after they are issued. Under the *CBCA*, all shares must be issued as fully paid and non-assessable. *See CBCA*, s. 25(2), and Chapter 6.

General partnership or partnership: a relationship that exists when two or more persons carry on a business in common with a view to a profit. A partnership is not a legal entity separate from the partners who make it up, and each partner is fully responsible for all the obligations of the business. *See* Chapter 2.

Goodwill: the value associated with a business in excess of the value of its assets. It may exist by virtue of the reputation of operators of the business, the quality of its products, or for some other reason. *See* Chapter 3.

Indemnification and indemnity: A promise by one person to compensate another person for an obligation incurred or payment made by the second person. Usually, an indemnity is given for obligations or payments imposed on the second person caused by something that the first person did. One partner, for example, may agree to indemnify the other partners for payments that the other partners are forced to make under obligations the first partner imposes on the partnership in breach of the partnership agreement. Corporate statutes provide that corporations must indemnify officers, directors and certain other persons for expenses incurred in connection with performing duties for or at the request of the corporation, but only if certain requirements are satisfied (e.g., *CBCA*, s. 124). Corporations have a discretion to indemnify in a broader range of circumstances. *See* Chapters 2 & 7.

Issued capital: the shares of the corporation which have been issued by the directors to the shareholders. *See* Chapter 6.

Joint venture: a term used loosely to refer to a wide variety of legal arrangements in which one or more parties combine their resources for some limited purpose, for a limited time, or both. It is not a distinct form of business organization, nor a relationship that has any precise legal meaning. A joint venture may be established, for example, by a contract in which the joint venturers agree that they will do certain things to carry out their common purpose; by two people carrying on business together, in which case the joint venture is a partnership; or by two people forming a corporation to carry out their common purpose. While the legal consequences of a joint venture that is a corporation or a partnership are clear, the legal consequences of a joint venture relationship that is not a partnership or a corporation are not. *See* Chapter 2.

Licence: a purely contractual relationship under which one party, the licensor, agrees to permit the other, the licensee, to use something (usually some form of intellectual property such as a patent, trade-mark, or copyright) in return for compensation (usually in the form of a payment based on sales revenues, referred to as a royalty). *See* Chapter 1.

Limited partnership: a partnership where at least one of the partners, the general partner, has unlimited liability and at least one other, called a limited partner, has limited liability. The liability of the limited partner is limited, typically, to the amount he has contributed to the limited partnership. In general partnerships, all partners are general partners in the sense that they all have unlimited personal liability. Limited partnerships come into existence only upon a filing being made with the appropriate government authority under provincial limited partnership legislation. Limited partners cannot take part in the management of the business of the partnership without losing their limited liability status. *See* General partnership, and Chapter 2.

Management proxy circular: the document that management of a distributing corporation or a corporation with more than fifty shareholders incorporated under the *CBCA* must send to shareholders in connection with shareholder meetings. Its form is prescribed by regulation and includes general disclosure about the corporation as well as specific disclosure about the items of business to be dealt with at the meeting. Some corporations incorporated in other jurisdictions, including all public companies, are required to distribute management proxy circulars as well. *See* Distributing corporation, Public Company, Solicitation of proxies, *CBCA*, s. 150, *CBCA Regulations*, s. 57, and Chapters 6 & 7.

Memorandum and articles of association: the constitution of a corporation under English registration model corporate statutes, such as is in force in British Columbia. The memorandum is similar to the articles under a *CBCA* model statute. The articles are similar to a general by-law under a *CBCA* model statute. The memorandum and articles constitute a contract between the corporation and the members. *See* Chapter 3.

Minute book: a book in which the records of the corporation are kept. Corporate law requires that certain records be kept, including the articles and by-laws (including any amendments), any unanimous shareholders' agreement, minutes of meetings and resolutions of shareholders, and a securities register (*CBCA*, s. 20(1)). It is usual to include minutes of meetings and resolutions of directors as well though shareholders have no right to access to such records. *See* Securities Register, *CBCA*, s. 20, and Chapter 4.

Obiter **and** *obiter dicta*: statements made by a judge in the course of giving his or her reasons for a decision in a particular case which are not necessary elements of the reasons for decision. That is, the judge could have reached the decision without making the statements. Under the common law, *obiter dicta* are not binding on courts in subsequent cases.

Officer: a person appointed by the directors and certain other persons in a corporation to whom certain responsibilities to manage the business and affairs of the corporation are delegated. The *2001 Amendments* to the *CBCA*, introduced a definition of officer on the following terms:

> "officer" means an individual appointed as an officer under section 121, the chairperson of the board of directors, the president, a vice-president, the secretary, the treasurer, the comptroller, the general counsel, the general manager, a managing director, of a corporation, or any other individual who performs functions for a corporation similar to those normally performed by an individual occupying any of those offices;

There are few requirements for officers. In most corporations, the offices are designated in a by-law, and the directors appoint people to fill them by resolution. *See CBCA*, ss. 2(1) and 121, and Chapter 7.

Ordinary resolution: a resolution of shareholders passed by a majority of the votes cast by the shareholders who voted in respect of the resolution. *See* Chapter 7.

Par value: a provision in a corporation's articles which was intended to represent the issue price of the shares. In many circumstances, however, shares were issued at prices above the par value. Par value has been abolished under the *CBCA* and statutes modelled after it. *See CBCA*, s. 24(2), and Chapter 6.

Parent corporation: a corporation that controls another corporation. The controlled corporation is a "subsidiary corporation."

Partner: a person who carries on business with another person in a relationship that is a partnership. *See* General partnership, and Chapter 2.

Partnership: *see* General partnership.

Pre-emptive rights: rights of the existing shareholders of a corporation to have any shares the directors propose to issue offered first to them, on some basis, usually in proportion to their exising holdings of shares. Such rights may be set out in the articles or in a shareholders' agreement. *See CBCA*, s. 28, and Chapters 4 & 6.

Private company: a term are used colloquially and in many places in this book, along with "private corporation," to refer to any corporation that has a small number of shareholders, and the shares of which do not trade in a public market. *See* Chapters 4 & 7.

Profits: what is left after all expenses incurred to earn revenue, including operating expenses such as the cost of materials and labour, as well as other expenses such as interest on debt and taxes, are deducted from all amounts a business has earned. *See* Chapter 2.

Proxy: a document by which a shareholder designates another person to exercise her votes at a meeting of shareholders. The term is sometimes used to refer also to the person who is designated in such a document. Such a person, who is also sometimes referred to as a proxy holder, must act in accordance with the instructions of the shareholder. Until such a document is executed by the shareholder, it is called a form of proxy. *See CBCA*, ss. 147 & 148, and Chapters 6 & 7.

Public company: a corporation that is not a private company (or corporation). "Public company" and "public corporation" are used colloquially and in many places in this book to refer to corporations whose shares trade on public markets such as the Toronto Stock Exchange. *See* Private company, and Chapters 4, 7, & 11.

Rateably: If something must be divided rateably, it must be allocated equally among all members of the class of persons entitled to share in the distribution. So, if a dividend in the amount of $1,000,000 were declared and there were ten shares outstanding, it would be distributed rateably if each share entitled the holder to be paid an equal proportion of the total dividend amount, in the example, $100,000. This is how dividends must be paid in the absence of some special entitlement for a particular class of shares set out in the corporation's articles. *See* Chapter 6.

Record date: the date for determining who the shareholders are for the purposes of giving notice of a shareholder meeting, paying dividends, or for any other purpose. The directors may set the date. In relation to notice of meetings and voting rights, if the directors do not set a date, the record date is deemed to be the close of business on the day before the day the notice is sent. In all other cases, if the directors do not set a date, the record date is the day the directors pass the resolution in relation to which it is necessary to determine who the shareholders are. *See CBCA*, s. 134, and Chapter 6.

Redemption: the acquisition by a corporation of its own shares pursuant to a provision of the corporation's articles permitting the acquisition. Depending on the provision, redemption may be at the option of the corporation or the shareholder or either. *See* Chapter 6.

Repurchase: the acquisition by a corporation of its own shares pursuant to an agreement negotiated between the selling shareholder and the corporation. *See* Chapter 6.

Securities: shares or debt obligations, such as bonds, or other claims on a corporation or other business organization. *See* the definition in *CBCA*, s. 1(1), and s. 1(1) of the Ontario *Securities Act*, R.S.O. 1990, c. S.5, and Chapter 11.

Securities register: a record of the securities issued by a corporation in registered form showing the names and latest known address of each person who is a security holder, the number of securities held by each security holder, and the date and particulars of the issue and transfer of each security. *See CBCA*, s. 50(1), and Chapter 4.

Series of shares: a division of a class of shares. If a corporation's articles permit shares of a class to be issued in one or more series, the directors may designate and assign characteristics to a series of shares which, subject to some limitations, may be different from shares of the same class in other series. Series characteristics may also be set in the articles. In the absence of the creation of a separate series within a class of shares, all shares of a class are equal in all respects. *See CBCA*, ss. 24(3) & 27, and Chapter 6.

Share: a claim against the corporation issued by the directors in exchange for money, property, or past services, the characteristics of which are defined by the provisions in the corporation's articles creating the class of shares. There are also certain mandatory rules in corporate law about shares, such as the rule that all shares of a class must be treated equally. *See CBCA*, s. 25, and Chapter 6.

Shareholder: the holder of a share. For most purposes — for example, giving notice of meetings and paying dividends — the *CBCA* is concerned only with the holder who is registered in the securities register of the corporation, not the beneficial holder of shares. Beneficial holders of shares are entitled to limited protection under the *CBCA* (e.g., they are entitled to claim relief from oppression under section 241). *See* Chapters 6 & 7.

Shareholders' resolutions: the means by which shareholders act. Resolutions may be passed by a vote at a meeting or signed by all shareholders. *See* Ordinary resolution, Special resolution, *CBCA*, s. 142, and Chapter 7.

Short-form amalgamation: an amalgamation between certain affiliated corporations which requires only the approval of the directors. A short-form vertical amalgamation may be effected between a corporation and one or more subsidiaries that are either wholly owned by the corporation or where the only shares not held by the corporation are owned by one or more of the other amalgamating subsidiaries. Similarly, a short-form horizontal amalgamation may be effected between subsidiaries that are either wholly owned or where any shares not held by the parent corporation are held by one of the other amalgamating subsidiaries. *See* Affiliate, and Chapter 10.

Sole proprietorship: a person carrying on business for his own account without adopting some other form of business organization, such as a corporation. *See* Chapter 1.

Solicitation of proxies: seeking the votes of shareholders in favour of a resolution or the election of directors at a meeting of shareholders. Under the *CBCA*, management of a distributing corporation or a corporation with more than fifty shareholders must solicit proxies. Management is required to send to shareholders a "management proxy circular" in a form prescribed by regulation and a form of proxy so that shareholders can exercise their vote without attending the meeting. Any other person seeking to influence shareholder voting must also send out a circular in prescribed form subject to certain exceptions. *See* Dissident's proxy circular, Distributing corporation, Management proxy circular, Proxy, *CBCA*, s. 143, and Chapter 7.

Special meeting: a meeting of shareholders other than an annual meeting. *See* Annual meeting, and Chapter 7.

Special resolution: a resolution passed by a majority of not less than two-thirds of the votes cast by shareholders who voted in respect of that resolution, or signed by all the shareholders entitled to vote on that resolution. *See CBCA*, s. 2(1).

Stated capital: the historical total of the value of all the money, property, and past services that have been contributed to the corporation in return for shares it has issued. Each corporation must keep a record of the stated capital for each class and series of shares. *See* Class of shares, Series of shares, *CBCA*, s. 26, and Chapter 6.

Strategic alliance: a term that has no precise legal meaning used to refer to a wide variety of relationships involving more or less legal formality and greater and lesser degrees of working together among the alliance partners. A joint venture or partnership may be referred to as a strategic alliance. The term may also be used to describe, for example, an agreement to do research and development together, to market products jointly, or simply to share information. *See* Chapter 1.

Subsidiary corporation: a corporation that is controlled, directly or indirectly, by another corporation. "Control" for the purpose of the definition of "subsidiary" is legal control: holding voting securities of the corporation which carry more than 50 percent of the votes that may be cast for the election of directors, where such votes are sufficient to elect a majority of the board of directors. *See CBCA*, ss. 2(3)–(5), and Chapter 9.

Thin capitalization: the situation in a corporation in which shareholders have invested a very small amount in return for shares. Even though most Canadian corporate statutes do not require any minimum capitalization, thin capitalization has been argued to be a ground on which the separate legal personality of the corporation should be disregarded. *See* Chapter 3.

Tort: an act or omission giving rise to civil liability. The most important tort is negligence. If a person can prove that the act or omission of another meets the legal standard for negligence, that person will be entitled to compensation from such other person for losses suffered as a result. *See* Chapter 1.

Trade-name: a name used by a business, whether it is the name of a corporation, trust, partnership, sole proprietorship, or an individual. It includes any name used by a corporation other than its corporate name. *See* Chapter 4.

Trade-mark: a mark used to distinguish goods or services as defined in the *Trade-marks Act* (R.S.C. 1985, c. T-13). Trade-marks may be incorporated into trade-names, but need not be. *See* Trade-name, and Chapter 4.

Unanimous shareholders' agreement: an agreement among all shareholders of a corporation that restricts, in whole or in part, the powers of the directors to manage the business and affairs of the corporation and includes a declaration to the same effect by a sole shareholder. The powers and liabilities of the directors are transferred to the shareholders to the extent of the restriction. *See CBCA*, ss. 1(1) & 146(2), and Chapters 7 & 12.

Widely held corporation: a term that refers to a corporation that has many shareholders. Usually the shares of a widely held corporation are traded on some form of public market, such as the Toronto Stock Exchange. *See* Chapter 4.

Winding up a corporation: the process of gathering in the assets of the corporation, converting them to cash, using the cash to discharge any liabilities of the corporation, and paying out any excess to shareholders before terminating the corporation's existence. Usually, "winding up" refers to this process being carried out under the supervision of a court rather than by agreement of all shareholders. *See* Chapters 9 & 10.

TABLE OF CASES

INDEX

ABOUT THE AUTHOR

J. Anthony VanDuzer, B.A., LL.B., LL.M., is an Associate Professor in the Faculty of Law, Common Law Section, at the University of Ottawa where he teaches courses in business organizations, advanced business law, major business transactions and international business transactions. He has also taught in the University of Ottawa's Executive MBA program. Professor VanDuzer has served as an adviser on corporate law to the Department of Industry and as a consultant to the Competition Bureau, the Department of Foreign Affairs and International Trade, and the NAFTA Secretariat. He has written extensively on corporate law, competition law, taxation, international trade, and intellectual property law and worked with international development agencies delivering technical assistance on business and trade law in Russia, China, Ukraine, Georgia, Bulgaria, Bosnia, Vietnam, Kyrgyz Republic and the countries of the Caribbean Community.